ADVANCES IN REINFORCEMENT LEARNING

Edited by **Abdelhamid Mellouk**

Advances in Reinforcement Learning
Edited by Abdelhamid Mellouk

Published by InTech
Janeza Trdine 9, 51000 Rijeka, Croatia

Publishing Process Manager Jelena Marusic

Technical Editor Teodora Smiljanic

Cover Designer InTech Design Team

Additional hard copies can be obtained from orders@intechopen.com

Advances in Reinforcement Learning, Edited by Abdelhamid Mellouk
p. cm.
ISBN 978-953-307-369-9

For EU product safety concerns:
IN TECH d.o.o., Prolaz Marije Krucifikse Kozulić 3, 51000 Rijeka, Croatia,
info@intechopen.com or visit our website at intechopen.com.

Meet the editor

Full Professor of Networks and Telecommunications Department (IUT C/V) at the University of Paris-Est (UPEC), Abdelhamid Mellouk is currently the Technical Program Chair of the IEEE Technical Committee on Communications Software in Communications Society and IEEE Senior Member. Founder of TINC (Transport Infrastructure and Network Control) research activity, his general area is in high-speed new generation wired/wireless networking, end to end quality of service and quality of experience. Currently, he is working on routing and switching optimization in dynamic traffic networks; human and bio-inspired artificial intelligence approaches. He investigates particularly the use of artificial neuronal intelligence together with biologically inspired techniques such as reinforcement learning, to control network decision in real-time.

Contents

Preface

Reinforcement Learning (RL) is often referred to as a branch of artificial intelligence and has been one of the central topics in a broad range of scientific fields for the last two decades. Understanding of RL is expected to provide a systematic understanding of adaptive behaviors, including simple classical and operant conditioning of animals as well as all complex social and economical human behaviors that are designed to maximize benefits; and is also useful in machine learning and robotics. RL aims to find an appropriate mapping from situations to actions in which a certain reward is maximized. It can be defined as a class of problem solving approaches in which the learner (agent) learns through a series of trial-and-error searches and delayed rewards. The purpose is to maximize not just the immediate reward, but also the cumulative reward in the long run, such that the agent can learn to approximate an optimal behavioral strategy by continuously interacting with the environment. This allows the agent to work in a previously unknown environment by learning about it gradually. Hence, it is closely related to various scientific domains as Optimization, Vision, Robotic and Control, Theoretical Computer Science, etc.

This book brings together many different aspects of the current research on several fields associated to Reinforcement Learning. Based on 24 Chapters, it covers a very broad variety of topics in Reinforcement Learning and their application in autonomous systems. A set of chapters in this book provide a general overview of RL while other chapters focus mostly on the applications of RL paradigms: Game Theory, Multi-Agent Theory, Robotic, Networking Technologies, Vehicular Navigation, Medicine and Industrial Logistic. Much of this work has been published in refereed journals and conference proceedings and these papers have been modified and edited for content and style.

This book shows that RL is a very dynamic area in terms of theory and application. The field of RL has been growing rapidly, producing a wide variety of learning algorithms for different applications. There is also a very extensive literature on RL, and to give a complete bibliography and a historical account of the research that led to the present form would have been impossible. It is thus inevitable that some topics have been treated in less detail than others.

I would like to thank all contributors to this book for their research and effort. I hope you will enjoy reading this book and get many helpful ideas and overviews for your own study.

Abdelhamid Mellouk
Network &Telecom Dept and LiSSi Laboratory
University Paris-Est Creteil (UPEC), IUT Creteil/Vitry,
France

1

Wireless Networks Inductive Routing Based on Reinforcement Learning Paradigms

Abdelhamid Mellouk
Network &Telecom Dept and LiSSi Laboratory
University Paris-Est Creteil (UPEC), IUT Creteil/Vitry,
France

1. Introduction

Wireless networks, especially Sensor ones (WSN), are a promising technology to monitor and collect specific measures in any environment. Several applications have already been envisioned, in a wide range of areas such as military, commercial, emergency, biology and health care applications. A sensor is a physical component able to accomplish three tasks: identify a physical quantity, treat any such information, and transmit this information to a sink (Kumar et al., 2008; Buford et al., 2009; Olfati-Saber et al., 2007).
Needs for QoS to guarantee the quality of real time services must take into account not only the static network parameters but also the dynamic ones. Therefore, QoS measures should be introduced to the network so that quality of real time services can be guaranteed. The most popular formulation of the optimal distributed routing problem in a data network is based on a multicommodity flow optimization whereby a separate objective function is minimized with respect to the types of flow subjected to multicommodity flow constraints. Given the complexity of this problem, due to the diversity of the QoS constraints, we focus our attention in this paper on bio-inspired QoS routing policies based on the Reinforcement Learning paradigm applied to Wireless Sensor Networks.
Many research works focus on the optimization of the energy consumption in sensor networks, as it directly affects the network lifetime. Routing protocols were proposed to minimize energy consumption while providing the necessary coverage and connectivity for the nodes to send data to the sink. Other routing protocols have also been proposed in WSN to improve other QoS constraints such as delay.
The problem here is that the complexity of routing protocols increases dramatically with the integration of more than one QoS parameter. Indeed, determining a QoS route that satisfies two or more **non-correlated constraints (for example, delay and bandwidth)** is an NP-complete problem (Mellouk et al., 2007), because the Multi-Constrained Optimal path problem cannot be solved in polynomial time. Therefore, research focus has shifted to the development of pseudopolynomial time algorithms, heuristics, and approximation algorithms for multi-constrained QoS paths.
In this chapter, we present an accurate description of the current state-of-the-art and give an overview of our work in the use of reinforcement learning concepts focused on Wireless Sensor Networks. We focus our attention by developing systems based on this paradigm called AMDR and EDAR. Basically, these inductive approaches selects routes based on flow

QoS requirements and network resource availability. After developing in section 2 the concept of routing in wireless sensor networks, we present in section 3 the family of inductive approaches. After, we present in two sections our works based on reinforcement learning approaches. Last section concludes and gives some perspectives of this work.

2. Routing problem in Wireless Sensor Networks

Goal aspects that are identified as more suitable to optimize in WSNs are QoS metrics. Sensor nodes essentially move small amounts of data (bits) from one place to another. Therefore, equilibrium should be defined in QoS and energy consumption, to obtain meaningful information of data transmitted. Energy efficiency is an evident optimization metric in WSNs. More generally, several routing protocols in WSNs are influenced by several factors:

Minimum life of the system: In some cases, no human intervention is possible. Batteries of sensors can not be changed; the lifetime of the network must be maximized.

Fault tolerance: Sensor network should be tolerant to nodes failures so as the network routes information through other nodes.

Delay: Delay metric must be taken into account for real-time applications to ensure that data arrives on time.

Scalability: Routing protocols must be extendable, even with several thousand nodes.

Coverage: In WSN, each sensor node obtains a certain view of the environment. This latter is limited both in range and in accuracy (fig. 1); it can only cover a limited physical area of the environment. Hence, area coverage is also an important design parameter in WSNs. Each node receives a local view of its environment, limited by its scope and accuracy. The coverage of a large area is composed by the union of several smaller coverages.

Connectivity: Most WSNs have high density of sensors, thus precluding isolation of nodes. However, deployment, mobility and failures vary the topology of the network, so connectivity is not always assured (Tran et al., 2008).

Quality of Service: In some applications, data should be delivered within certain period of time from the moment it is sensed; otherwise the data will be useless. Therefore bounded latency for data delivery is another condition for time-constrained applications. However, in many applications, energy saving -which is directly related to the network's lifetime- is considered relatively more important than the quality of the transmitted data. As the energy gets depleted, the network may be required to reduce the quality of the results in order to reduce energy dissipation in nodes and hence lengthen network lifetime. Hence, energy-aware routing protocols are required to capture this requirement.

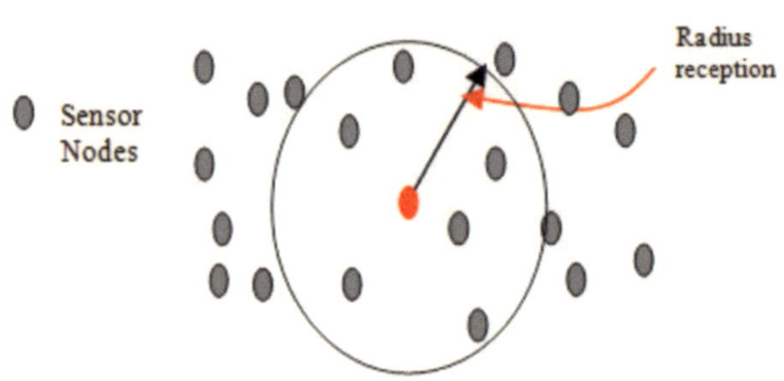

Fig. 1. Radius of reception of a sensor node.

To ensure these aspects, one can find two methods to routing information from a sensor network to a sink:

Reactive (*requested*): If one wants to have the network status at a time *t*, the sink broadcasts a request throughout the network so that sensors send their latest information back to the sink. The information is then forwarded in multi-hop manner to the sink (Shearer, 2008).

Proactive (*periodical*): The network is monitored to detect any changes, sending broadcasts periodically to the sink, following an event in the network such as a sudden change in temperature and movement. Sensors near the event then back the information recorded and route it to the sink (Lu & Sheu, 2007).

Otherwise, depending on the network structure, routing can be divided into flat-based routing, hierarchical-based routing, and location-based routing. All these protocols can be classified into multi-path based, query-based, negotiation-based, QoS-based, or coherent-based routing techniques depending on the protocol operation.

Below, we present some QoS routing protocols:

QoS_AODV (Perkins et al., 2000): The link cost used in this protocol is formulated as a function which takes into account node's energy consumed and error rate. Based on an extended version of Dijkstra's algorithm, the protocol establishes a list of paths with minimal cost. Then, the one with the best cost is selected [10],[13]. This protocol uses hierarchical routing; it divides the network into clusters. Each cluster consists of sensor nodes and one cluster head. The cluster head retrieves data from the cluster and sends it to the sink. QoS routing is done locally in each cluster.

Sequential Assignment Routing (SAR) (Ok et al., 2009): SAR manages multi-paths in a routing table which attempts to achieve energy efficiency and fault tolerance. SAR considers trees of QoS criteria during the exploration of routing paths, the energy resource on each path and the priority level of each packet. By using these trees, multiple paths of the sensors are well trained. One of these paths is chosen depending on energy resources and QoS of path. SAR maintains multiple paths from nodes to sink [9]. High overhead is generated to maintain tables and states at each sensor.

Energy Aware Routing (EAR) (Shah & Rabaey, 2002): EAR is a reactive routing protocol designed to increase the lifetime of sensor networks. Like EDAR, the sink searches and maintains multiple paths to the destinations, and assigns a probability to each of these paths. The probability of a node is set to be inversely proportional to its cost in terms of energy. When a node routes a packet, it chooses one of the available paths according to their probabilities. Therefore, packets can be routed along different paths and the nodes' energy will be fairly consumed among the different nodes. This technique keeps a node from being over-utilized, which would quickly lead to energy starvation.

SPEED (Ok et al., 2009): This protocol provides a time limit beyond which the information is not taken into account. It introduces the concept of "real time" in wireless sensor networks. Its purpose is to ensure a certain speed for each packet in the network. Each application considers the end-to-end delay of packets by dividing the distance from the sink by the speed of packet before deciding to accept or reject a packet. Here, each node maintains information of its neighbors and uses geographic information to find the paths. SPEED can avoid congestion under heavy network load.

3. State dependent routing approaches

Modern communication networks is becoming a large complex distributed system composed by higher interoperating complex sub-systems based on several dynamic parameters. The drivers of this growth have included changes in technology and changes in regulation. In this context, the famous methodology approach that allows us to formulate this problem is dynamic programming which, however, is very complex to be solved exactly. The most popular formulation of the optimal distributed routing problem in a data network is based on a multicommodity flow optimization whereby a separable objective function is minimized with respect to the types of flow subject to multicommodity flow constraints (Gallager, 1977; Ozdaglar & Bertsekas, 2003). In order to design adaptive algorithms for dynamic networks routing problems, many of works are largely oriented and based on the Reinforcement Learning (RL) notion (Sutton & Barto, 1997). The salient feature of RL algorithms is the nature of their routing table entries which are probabilistic. In such algorithms, to improve the routing decision quality, a router tries out different links to see if they produce good routes. This mode of operation is called exploration. Information learnt during this exploration phase is used to take future decisions. This mode of operation is called exploitation. Both exploration and exploitation phases are necessary for effective routing and the choice of the outgoing interface is the action taken by the router. In RL algorithms, those learning and evaluation modes are assumed to happen continually. Note that, the RL algorithms assigns credit to actions based on reinforcement from the environment (Fig 2).

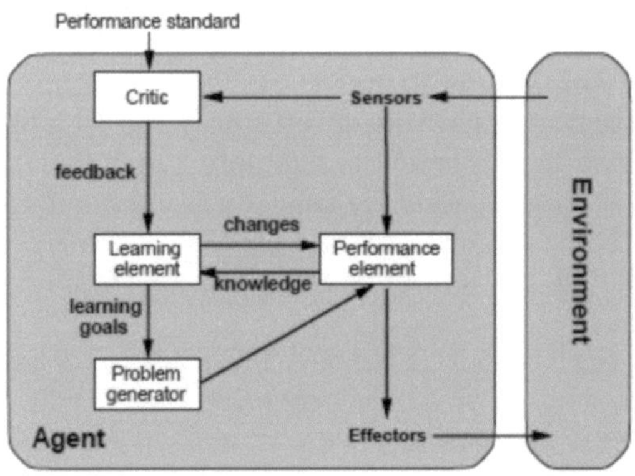

Fig. 2. Agent's learning from the environment.

In the case where such credit assignment is conducted systematically over large number of routing decisions, so that all actions have been sufficiently explored, RL algorithms converge to solve stochastic shortest path routing problems. Finally, algorithms for RL are distributed algorithms that take into account the dynamics of the network where initially no model of the network dynamics is assumed to be given. Then, the RL algorithm has to sample, estimate and build the model of pertinent aspects of the environment.

Many of works has done to investigate the use of inductive approaches based on artificial neuronal intelligence together with biologically inspired techniques such as reinforcement learning and genetic algorithms, to control network behavior in real-time so as to provide users with the QoS that they request, and to improve network provide robustness and resilience.

For example, we can note the following approaches based on RL paradigm:

Q-Routing approach- In this technique (Boyan & Littman, 1994), each node makes its routing decision based on the local routing information, represented as a table of Q values which estimate the quality of the alternative routes. These values are updated each time the node sends a packet to one of its neighbors. However, when a Q value is not updated for a long time, it does not necessarily reflect the current state of the network and hence a routing decision based on such an unreliable Q value will not be accurate. The update rule in Q-Routing does not take into account the reliability of the estimated or updated Q value because it depends on the traffic pattern, and load levels. In fact, most of the Q values in the network are unreliable. For this purpose, other algorithms have been proposed like Confidence based Q-Routing (CQ-Routing) or Confidence based Dual Reinforcement Q-Routing (DRQ-Routing).

Cognitive Packet Networks (CPN)- CPNs (Gelenbe et al., 2002) are based on random neural networks. These are store-and-forward packet networks in which intelligence is constructed into the packets, rather than at the routers or in the high-level protocols. CPN is then a reliable packet network infrastructure, which incorporates packet loss and delays directly into user QoS criteria and use these criteria to conduct routing. Cognitive packet networks carry three major types of packets: smart packets, dumb packets and acknowledgments (ACK). Smart or cognitive packets route themselves, they learn to avoid link and node failures and congestion and to avoid being lost. They learn from their own observations about the network and/or from the experience of other packets. They rely minimally on routers. The major drawback of algorithms based on cognitive packet networks is the convergence time, which is very important when the network is heavily loaded.

Swarm Ant Colony Optimization (AntNet)- Ants routing algorithms (Dorigo & Stüzle, 2004) are inspired by dynamics of how ant colonies learn the shortest route to food source using very little state and computation. Instead of having fixed next-hop value, the routing table will have multiple next-hop choices for a destination, with each candidate associated with a possibility, which indicates the goodness of choosing this hop as the next hop in favor to form the shortest path. Given a specified source node and destination node, the source node will send out some kind of ant packets based on the possibility entries on its own routing table. Those ants will explore the routes in the network. They can memory the hops they have passed. When an ant packet reaches the destination node, the ant packet will return to the source node along the same route. Along the way back to the destination node, the ant packet will change the routing table for every node it passes by. The rules of updating the routing tables are: increase the possibility of the hop it comes from while decrease the possibilities of other candidates. Ants approach is immune to the sub-optimal route problem since it explores, at all times, all paths of the network. Although, the traffic generated by ant algorithms is more important than the traffic of the concurrent approaches.

AntHocNet (Di Caro et al., 2005) is an algorithm for routing in mobile ad hoc networks. It is a hybrid algorithm, which combines reactive route setup with proactive route probing, maintenance and improvement. It does not maintain routes to all possible destinations at all times but only sets up paths when they are needed at the start of a data session. This is done in a reactive route setup phase, where ant agents called reactive forward ants are launched by the source in order to find multiple paths to the destination, and backward ants return to the source to set up the paths in the form of pheromone tables indicating their respective quality. After the route setup, data packets are routed stochastically over the different paths following these pheromone tables. While the data session is going on, the paths are monitored, maintained and improved proactively using different agents, called proactive forward ants.

BeeAdHoc (Wedde et al., 2005) is a new routing algorithm for energy efficient routing in mobile ad hoc networks. This algorithm is inspired by the foraging principles of honey bees. The algorithm utilizes Essentialy two types of agents, scouts and foragers, for doing routing in mobile ad hoc networks. BeeAdHoc is a reactive source routing algorithm and it consumes less energy as compared to existing state-of-theart routing algorithms because it utilizes less control packets to do routing.
KOQRA (Mellouk et al., 2008; Mellouk et al., 2009) is an adaptive routing algorithm that improves the Quality of Service in terms of cost link path and end-to-end delay. This algorithm is based on a Dijkstra multipath routing approach combined with the Q-routing reinforcement learning. The learning algorithm is based on founding K best paths in terms of cumulative link cost and the optimization of the average delivery time on these paths. A load balancing policy depending on a dynamical traffic path probability distribution function is also introduced.

4. AMDR protocol: Adaptive Mean Delay Routing protocol

Our first proposal, called "AMDR" (Adaptive Mean Delay Routing), is based on an adaptive approach using mean delay estimated proactively by each node. AMDR is built around two modules: Delay Estimation Module (DEM) and Adaptive Routing Module (ARM). In order to optimize delay in mobile ad hoc networks, it's necessary to be able to evaluate delay in accurate way. We consider in DEM, the IEEE 802.11 protocol, which is considered to be the most popular MAC protocol in MANET.
DEM calculates proactively mean delay at each node without any packets exchange. The ARM will then exploit mean delay value. It uses two exploration agents to discover best available routes between a given pair of nodes (s, d). Exploration agents gather mean delay information available at each visited node and calculate the overall delay between source and destination. According to delay value gathered, a reinforcement signal is calculated and probabilistic routing tables are updated at each intermediate node using an appropriate reinforcement signal.
ARM ensures an adaptive routing based on estimated mean delay. It combines, on demand approach used at starting phase of exploration process (generation of the first exploration packet for the destination) with proactive approach in order to continue the exploration process even a route is already available for the destination. Proactive exploration keeps AMDR more reactive by having more recent information about network state.

4.1 Delay Estimation Model (DEM)

In order to optimize delay in mobile ad hoc networks, it's necessary to be able to evaluate delay in an accurate way. We propose in this section to estimate one-hop delay in ad hoc networks. It's well known that node delay depends greatly on MAC layer protocol. We consider in our study, the particular case of IEEE 802.11 protocol.
Our Delay Estimation Model (DEM) is based on *Little's theorem* (Little, 1961). Each mobile node, in DEM, is considered as a buffer. Packets arrive to the buffer in *Poisson* distribution with parameter λ. Each mobile node has a single server performing channel access.
Thus, a mobile node is seen as a discrete time M/G/1 queue (Saaty, 1961). According to *Little's* theorem, node delay corresponds to mean response delay defined as fellow:

$$W = \frac{\lambda M_2}{2(1-\sigma)} + b \qquad (1)$$

- λ: arriving rate of data packets to the buffer
- b: represents mean service time needed to transmit a data packet with success including retransmission delays
- σ: represents server's rate occupation, it's equal to λb
- M_2: is the second moment of service time distribution.

The generator function of delay service defined in (Meraihi, 2005) is noted $B(z, L, p, k)$, (L : packet size, p : collision rate and k: backoff stage). This generator function can be defined in recursive manner as fellow:

$$B(z,L,p,k) = T_x(z,k,L)\left(1 - p + p * B(z,L,p,2k)\right) \qquad (2)$$

$T_x(z,k,L)$ is a transmission delay of a data packet (packet size: L). $B(z, L, p, 2k)$ function is invoked in case of collision with a probability p. In order to differentiate link's delays, we know that collision rate p is different from one neighbor to another. Thus, collision rate becomes a very important parameter for mean delay estimation.

4.2 Adaptive Routing Module (ARM)

AMDR uses two kinds of agents: Forward Exploration Packets (FEP) and Backward Exploration Packets (BEP). Routing in AMDR is determined by simple interactions between forward and backward exploration agents. Forward agents report network delay conditions to the backward ones. ARM consists of three parts:

4.2.1 Neighborhood discovery

Each mobile node has to detect the neighbor nodes with which it has a direct link. For this, each node broadcasts periodically *Hello messages*, containing the list of known neighbors and their link status. The link status can be either symmetric (if communication is possible in both directions) or asymmetric (if communication is possible only in one direction). Thus, *Hello messages* enable each node to detect its one-hop neighbors, as well as its two-hop neighbors (the neighbors of its neighbors). The *Hello messages* are received by all one-hop neighbors, but are forwarded only by a set of nodes calculated by an appropriate optimization-flooding algorithm.

4.2.2 Exploration process

So, FEP agents do not perform any updates of routing tables. They only gather the useful information that will be used to generate backward agents. BEP agents update routing tables of intermediate nodes using new available mean delay information. New probabilities are calculated according to a reinforcement-learning signal.

Forward agent explores the paths of the network, for the first time in reactive manner, but it continues exploration process proactively.

FEP agents create a probability distribution entry at each node for all its delay-MPR neighbours. Backward agents are sent to propagate the information collected by forward agents through the network, and to adjust the routing table entries. Probabilistic routing tables are used in AMDR. Each routing table entry has the following form (Fig. 3):

Dest	($Next_1$, p_1)	($Next_2$, p_2)	.....	($Next_n$, p_n)

Fig. 3. AMDR's routing table entry.

When a new traffic arrives at source node *s*, periodically this node generates a Forward Exploration Packet called FEP. The FEP packet is then sent to the destination in broadcast manner. Each forward agent packet contains the following informations: *Source node address, Destination node address, Next hop address, Stack of visiting nodes, Total_Delay.*
If the entry of the current destination does not exist when the forward agent is created, then a routing table entry is immediately created. The stack field contains the addresses of nodes traversed by forward agent packet and their mean delay. The FEP sending algorithm is the following:

Algorithm (Send FEP)
    At Each T_interval_seconds ***Do***
      Begin
        Generate a FEP
       If *any entry for this destination* ***Then***
         Create an entry with uniform probabilities.
      End If
    Broadcast the FEP
    End
End (Send FEP)

When a FEP arrives to a node *i*, it checks if the address of the node *i* is not equal to the destination address contained in the FEP agent then the FEP packet will be forwarded. FEP packets are forwarded according to the following algorithm:

Algorithm (Receive FEP)
    If *any entry for this destination* ***Then***
      Create an entry with uniform probabilities
    Else If *my_adress ≠ dest_adress* ***Then***
      If *FEP not already received* ***Then***
        Store address of the current node,
        Recover the available mean delay,
        Broadcast FEP,
      Else
        Send BEP
      End If
    End If
End (forward FEP)

Backward Exploration Packet
As soon as a forward agent FEP reaches its destination, a backward agent called BEP is generated and the forward agent FEP is destroyed. BEP inherits then the stack and the total delay information contained in the forward agent. We define five options for our algorithm in order to reply to a FEP agent. The algorithm of sending a BEP packet depends on the chosen option. The five options considered in our protocol are:

Reply to All: for each reception of a FEP packet, the destination node generates a BEP packet which retraces the inverse path of the FEP packet. In this case, the delay information is not used and the overhead generated is very important.
Reply to First: Only one BEP agent is generated for a FEP packet. It's the case of instantaneous delay because the first FEP arriving to destination has the best instantaneous delay. The mean delay module is not exploited. It's the same approach used in the AntNet. The overhead is reduced but any guarantee to have the best delay paths.
Reply to N: We define an integer *N*, stored at each node, while *N* is positive the destination reply by generating a BEP. It is an intermediate solution between *Reply to all* and *Reply to First* (N=1). The variable *N* is decremented when a BEP is sent. The overhead is more important than *The Reply to First* option.
Reply to the Best: We save at each node the information of the best delay called *Node.Total_delay*. When the first FEP arrives to the destination, *Node.Total_delay* takes the value of total delay of the FEP packet. When another FEP arrives, we compare its *FEP.Total_delay* with the *Node.Total_delay*, and we reply only if the FEP has a delay better or equal to the *Node.Total_delay*. In such manner, we are sure that we adjust routing tables according to the best delay. We have a guarantee of the best delay with reduced overhead.
If the *FEP_Total_delay* is equal or less than a fixed value *D*, the BEP is generated and sent to the source of the FEP. The algorithm of sending a BEP is the following:

```
Algorithm (send BEP)
    Select Case Option
    Case: Reply to All
      Genarate BEP
      BEP.Total_Delay=0,
      BEP.dest = FEP.src,
      Send BEP
    Case: Reply to first
    If (First (FEP) ) Then
      Genarate BEP
      BEP.Total_Delay=0,
      BEP.dest = FEP.src,
       Send BEP
    endIf
    Case: Reply to N
    If (N>0) Then
      Genarate BEP
      BEP.Total_Delay=0,
      BEP.dest = FEP.src,
      Send BEP,
      N=N-1
    endIf
    Case: Reply to Best
    If (FEP.Total_Delay <= Node.Total_Delay) Then
      Genarate BEP
      BEP.Total_Delay=0,
      BEP.dest = FEP.src,
```

Send BEP,
Node.Total_Delay= FEP.Total_Delay,
endIf
***Case**: Reply to Delay Constraint (D)*
If** (FEP.Total_Delayl <= D) **Then
Genarate BEP
BEP.Total_Delay=0,
BEP.dest = FEP.src,
Send BEP,
***End** If*
End (Send BEP)

Backward Exploration Packet retraces the inverse path traversed by the FEP packet. In other words, unlike FEP packets, a BEP packet is sent in a unicast manner because it must take the same path of its FEP generator. During its trip, the BEP agent calculates the total mean delay of its route and uses this new delay to adjust the probabilistic routing table of each intermediate node. The algorithm of forwarding BEP agent is the following:

Algorithm (Receive BEP)
If (my_address = BEP.dest) Then
Update probabilistic routing table
Else
Update probabilistic routing table
Forward BEP
End If
End (forward BEP)

4.3 Reinforcement updating routing tables

Routing tables are updated when a BEP agent is received. This phase can take many forms, and we have chosen updating rules based on (Baras & Mehta, 2003). Since routing table is calculated, data packets are then routed according to the highest probabilities in the routing tables.

Unlike on demand routing protocols, there is no guarantee to route all packets on the same route due to the proactive exploration. A positive reinforcement r^+ will be allotted to node f visited by the BEP agent, when a negative reinforcement r- will be allotted to the all remaining neighbours called n. Let:

- p_{fd}, the last probability that node f choose node d as next neighbour.
- p_{nd}, the last probabilities allotted to the other neighbours (n≠f).
- r, the reinforcement signal which is computed dynamically according to the delay information gathered by the BEP agent.

We assume that D is the delay and μ it's mean (first moment). The value of r indicates the delay quality and is computed according to the following rules:

$$r = \begin{cases} 1/\alpha\left(D/\mu\right) & \text{if } D < \alpha\mu \\ 1, \text{else} & \end{cases} \tag{3}$$

α is a parameter of delay quality defining the interval of delays to be considered as good ones. We apply a correction strategy on r in order to take into account the reliability of D. For example, in the case where α=2, we tend to reinforce more a link when r is less than 0.5, by reducing the r value. In the other case (r> 0.5), the link is penalized by increasing the r value.
The value reinforcement signal r^+ is a positive reinforcement applied to the current node and the punished r^- is a negative reinforcement applied to the remaining MPR neighbours.

$$\begin{aligned} r^+ &= (1-r)*(1-p_{fd}) \\ r^- &= -(1-r)*p_{nd} \end{aligned} \quad (4)$$

BEP makes changes to the probability values at the intermediate and final node according to the following update rules:

$$\begin{aligned} p_{fd} &\leftarrow p_{fd} + r^+ \\ p_{nd} &\leftarrow p_{nd} - r^- \end{aligned} \quad (5)$$

4.4 Flooding Optimization Algorithm

To improve AMDR performance, we introduce a new Flooding Optimization Algorithm (FOA), in order to reduce the overhead generated by the broadcast process. FOA is a delay oriented MPR selection algorithm. Using FOA, we guarantee a reduced overhead generated by exploration agents because FEP agents are forwarded, only, by delay-MPR neighbours selected by FOA.
FOA takes into account the mean delay available at each node. The delay-MPR selection is inspired by bandwidth-MPR algorithm proposed in [9]. Unlike bandwidth-MPR algorithm, FOA defines only one kind of MPRs called delay-MPR. Delay-MPR selection algorithm is composed of the following steps:

1. A node N_i selects, first, all its neighbours that are the only neighbours of a two hop node from N_i.
2. Sort the remaining one-hop delay neighbours in increasing order of mean delay.
3. Consider each one-hop neighbour in that order: this neighbour is selected as MPR if it covers at least one two-hop neighbour that has not yet been covered by the previous MPR.
4. Mark all the selected node neighbours as covered and repeat step 3 until all two-hop neighbours are covered.

4.5 Performance evaluation

We use NS-2 simulator to implement and test AMDR protocol. DEM implementation is based on three informations: collision probability τ, channel capacity C and traffic rate λ. Collision probability is calculated using sequence number of 'Hello' messages.
We present in the rest of this section three scenarios of simulation. In the first scenario, we define a static topology of 8 nodes. In order to compare AMDR's performances to both reactive and proactive protocols, we used DOLSR [1] and have extended AODV implementation available on NS-2 in order to be delay oriented routing protocol, noted here QAODV. We have chosen AMDR *Reply to Best* option for comparisons.

Fixed Scenario

The following table summarizes the simulation environment:

Routing	QAODV, AMDR, DOLSR
MAC Layer	802.11
Bandwidth	11Mb/s
TERRAIN	1000m,1000m
Nodes	8
Simulation time	1000 sec
Data traffic	Exponential

Table 1. Simulation settings fixed scenario

At first, in scenario 1, we generate a traffic between nodes '0' and '5'. Few times later, we add a new traffic between node '2' and node '3'.

In a second scenario, we keep the same configuration and we inject simultaneously a third set of traffic between nodes '4' and '1', as showed in figure 4. We compare for each simulation the trace files for each routing protocol.

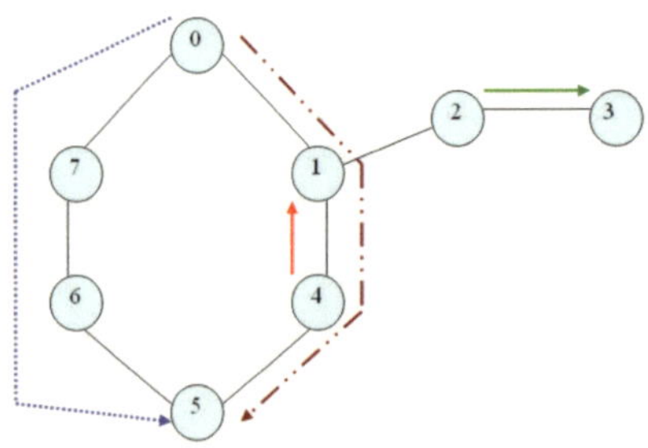

Fig. 4. Topology of fixed scenarios

The comparison of the end-to-end delay realized by QAODV, AMDR and DOLSR protocols is shown on figure 5. We can observe that, at first DOLSR realizes best delays when AMDR and QAODV show a large initial delay, which is necessary for routes to be set up. After initialisation stage, AMDR shows more adaptation to changes in the network load. It realizes the best end-to-end delay followed by QAODV and at last DOLSR.

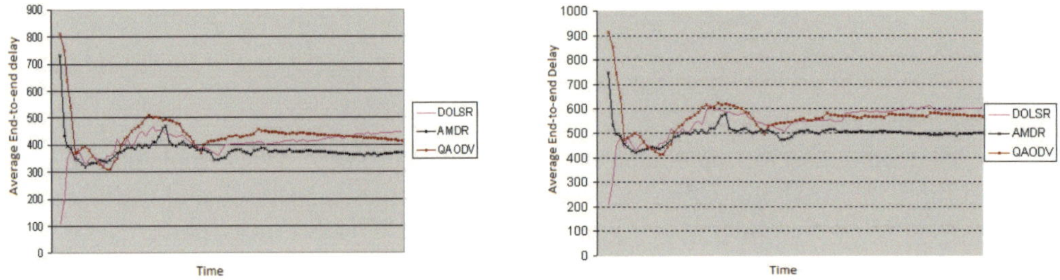

Fig. 5. Packets delay comparison in fixed scenarios (scenario1 & 2)

On the other hand, comparing loss rate performances of the three protocols shows in figure 6, that DOLSR realizes the best performances followed by AMDR and then QAODV.

AMDR performance is justified by keeping alternative paths used when the actual path is broken. Any additional delay is need to route waiting traffics and deliverance ratio is well improved than QAODV. In term of generated overhead, DOLSR was the most important followed by AMDR and QAODV. We explain this by the proactive exploration process used by AMDR, even a route is already established. The difference between overhead of AMDR and QAODV is not very important due to the flooding optimization mechanism used in AMDR.

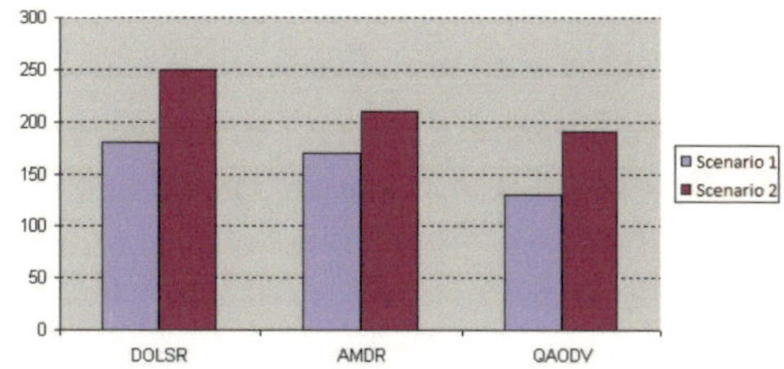

Fig. 6. Loss rate comparison in fixed scenario

Mobility scenario

We study now mobility impact on AMDR and compare its performances with DOLSR and QAODV. We define a random topology of 50 nodes. Table 2 summarizes the simulation setting parameters. We started with a low traffic rate and increase it periodically. After each simulation, we calculate the end-to-end delay realized by each protocol.

Traffic model	Exponential
Surface of simulation	1000m,1000m
Packets size	512 byte
Bandwidth	1Mbs
Mobility rate	5m /s , 10m/s
Number of connections	5, 10, 15, 20, 25
Packets rate	5 packets/s
Simulation duration	500 s

Table 2. Simulation settings scenario 2

Figure 7 summarizes our comparison. We can observe that in low load conditions, there is no difference in end-to-end delays. However, more the network is loaded more AMDR is better in term of delay. Such performance is justified by the easier adaptation of AMDR to changes in the network load.

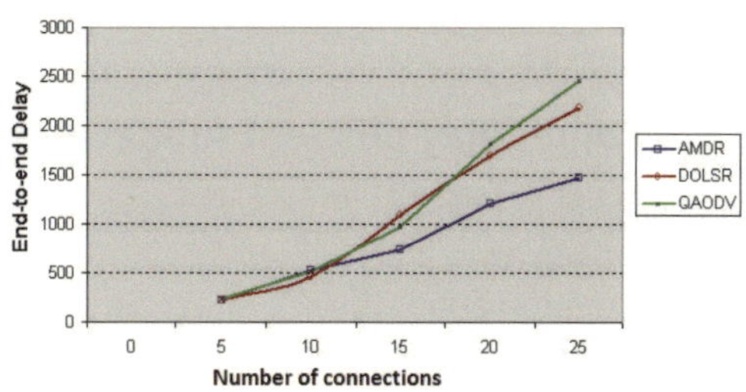

Fig. 7.a Packets delay comparison for low mobility scenario

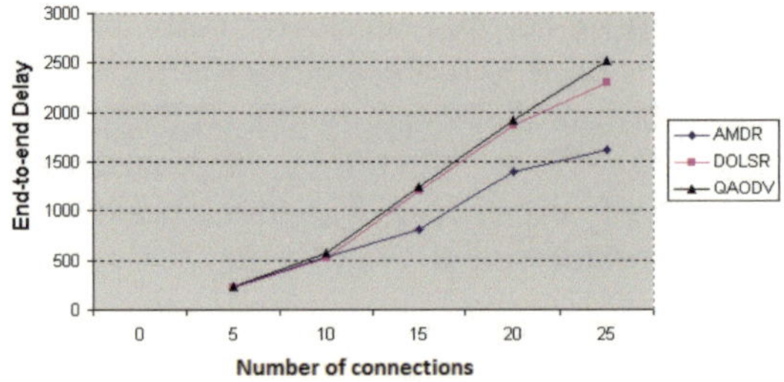

Fig. 7.b Packets delay comparison for high mobility scenario

Comparing loss rate performance between QAODV, AMDR and DOLSR, shows in figure 8 that both AMDR and DOLSR have, in a low loaded network, the same performance when QAODV realises the best performance.

However, in a high loaded network (case of 20 or 25 connections), QAODV becomes less good than AMDR and DOLSR. We justify such results by the adaptation of AMDR to load changes when AODV needs more route request function. We can also observe from mobility scenarios that in high mobility rate conditions, AMDR becomes more interesting than DOLSR and QAODV.

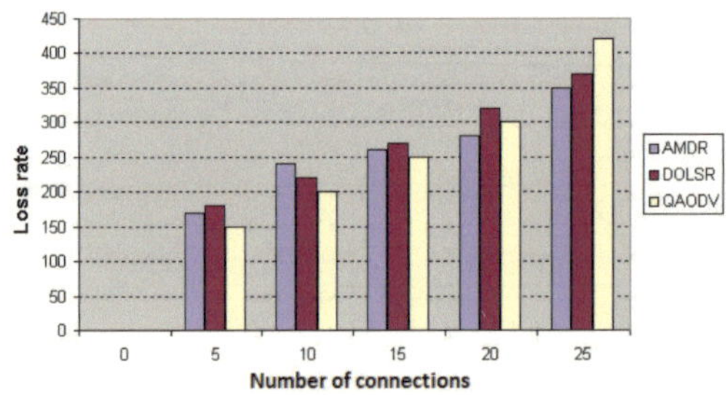

Fig. 8.a Loss rate comparison for low mobility scenario

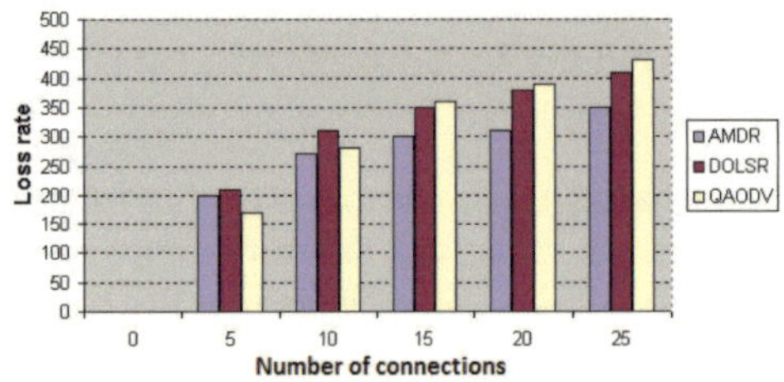

Fig. 8.b Loss rate comparison for high mobility scenario

5. EDAR protocol : Energy and Delay efficient Adaptive Routing protocol

EDAR is our second proposal in this chapter. EDAR is based on adaptive approaches; its objective is to find the best path in terms of energy consumed and end-to-end delay. It assumes that at each node, information about the residual energy, the energy consumed and the average delay links are available even before the route is requested. We assume that these estimates are made during the discovery of neighbors by an external mechanism independent of routing process.

Our proposal is also considered as a hybrid protocol; it combines the concept of on-demand route search, and the proactive exploration concept. This joint mechanism in the exploration phase allows to EDAR to find alternative routes missed in the first phase. For this, EDAR is based on two explorer agents: *Int-E-Route* (Interest Exploration Route) and *Resp-E-Route* (Response Exploration Route). The first one, generated at the sink when this one demands a request, is available in the network to find routes to the source node. To limit overhead generated by route discovery, we use an optimized distribution mechanism based on *Multi Point Relay* (MPR) OLSR protocol (Nguyen & Minet, 2007).

Of these two explorer agents, one is sent by the sink to a node, and the other is sent by the node in response to the first one. The arrival of an *Int-E-Route* agent to the source node initiates the creation of the second agent, *Resp-E-Route*. This latter takes the reverse path followed by the first *Int-E-Route* agent.

5.1 EDAR's agents

5.1.1 Int-E-Route agent

We use the mechanism of periodic "Hello" messages to discover neighbors. Each node broadcasts Hello messages, containing a list of its neighbors and the links state with its symmetrical neighbors, asymmetrical or lost. "Hello" messages are received by its one-hop neighbors and will not be relayed; each node is able to know its one- and two-hop neighbors. A message is sent in broadcast and will not be relayed (the distribution is local). This latter is composed by: (1) a list of addresses of its symmetrical neighbors, and (2) a list of addresses of its asymmetrical neighbors. There is a neighbor table in each node of the network. Fig. 9 describes the content of this table.

Symbol	Definition
N-ID	ID of its one-hop neighbors.
N-states	link state with its one hop neighbors (symmetric or asymmetric).
N-2 ID	ID of its two-hop neighbors
E_r	Residual energy of node
E_c	Energy consumed on each link by one-hop neighbors
D_{link}	Link delay
QE_c	Cost energy consumed on the link
QD_{link}	Cost delay of the link

Fig. 9. EDAR's Neighbors table.

When a "Hello" message is received by a neighbor, if a node finds its own address in the asymmetrical list, then it declares that this link is valid. A node is considered as a neighbor if and only if the collision rate of "Hello" packets sent to it, is below a certain threshold fixed initially.

Whenever *Int-E-Route* gets through an intermediate node, it retrieves its address and the information of its residual energy, energy consumed on the link and the average delay. *Int-*

E-Route packets are sent periodically as the route to this node is requested. This period is defined by the exploration interval which is calculated by simulation (for our scenarios, this value started with 10 seconds). Thus, at each iteration, a new packet *Int-E-Route* with a new sequence number is created and sent in the same manner as the first *Int-E-route*.
This agent is sent in broadcast to all one-hop neighbors nodes. To reduce the overhead generated by route exploration, only MPRE nodes will be allowed to relay this packet.
Int-E-Route recovers energy consumed and delay with its neighbors and stores it in its memory. The sequence number of the packet does not change. This process continues until *Int-E-Route* arrives to the source node.
The cost of the path from the source to sink is calculated as follows.
Let the minimal residual energy of each node be a parameter fixed beforehand (it corresponds to the energy required to send a fixed volume of information):

$$E_r \geq \varepsilon \tag{6}$$

where E_r represents the residual energy and the threshold of minimum energy for all active nodes before sending all data.
The cost of a node i for a link between nodes i and j is computed as:

$$\text{Cost of node}_i^j = \text{Cost of link}_i^j = \gamma QE_{C_i}^j + \theta QD_i^j \tag{7}$$

where:

$$f_{\text{cost}} = \sum_{j=1}^{K} h_j C_j \tag{8}$$

- QE_c is the cost of energy consumed on link (i, j),
- QD represents the cost of mean delay on link (i, j),
- γ and θ are tuneable parameters, with $\gamma \succ \theta$ to give more importance to the energy metric.

The cost function can be completed as the cost of path as follows:
C is a scalable vector for QoS metrics, and K represents the number of QoS criteria considered in the routing process.
The cost of the whole path constructed with N nodes between the source node and the sink is:

$$\text{Cost of path} = \gamma \sum_{i=1}^{N-1} QE_{C_i} + \theta \sum_{i=1}^{N-1} QD_i \tag{9}$$

5.1.2 EDAR's exploration mechanism

In our EDAR proposal, we used the same mechanism as OLSR (Nguyen & Minet, 2007by replacing the cost function by the energy cost stored in the neighbors table (fig. 9). So, the choice of MPRE for each node will be based on the links that offer the best cost estimated locally. The algorithm for selecting MPRE should be summarized as follows:

- Each node N_i of the network as MPRE chooses among its neighbors for one-hop, all the nodes up to a neighbor with two-hops.

- Each node selects as MPRE node that has the best link cost. In the case of equality between two nodes, the one that covers more than two-hop neighbors is chosen. This step is repeated until all neighbors at two hops are covered.

5.1.3 EDAR's Resp-E-Route agent

Agent *Resp-E-Route* updates routing tables based on information in the neighbors tables over all nodes crossed. This update consists of readjustment of link costs associated with each entry in routing table and generated by source node upon reception of *Int-E-Route* packet. It retrieves all information gathered by the packet *Int-E-Route* at the sink. The Packet *Resp-E-Route* is sent in unicast mode and takes the opposite route borrowed by the packet *Int-E-Route*. The source node generates packets *Resp-E-Route* on the basis of information on total cost of path followed by the packets *Int-E-Route*. When the arrival of the first packet *Int-E-Route* to source node is happen, the variable *"best cost path"* is used to store the cost of the path. At each arrival *Int-E-Route* packet to the source node, the cost of path calculated for this route is compared with the lowest cost path saved in the variable "best cost route". If there is a better path, the traffic will switch to this one. Each *Resp-E-Route* packet retraces exactly the same path taken by the *Int-E-route* packet which is at the origin of the path. At each passage trough the intermediate node, it compares its address with the destination address of sink *Resp-E-Route* packet to verify if it reaches the destination.

5.1.4 EDAR's updating and calculating routing table

Routing process consist to find the path with minimum cost in order to minimize simultaneously node energy consumed on all paths and the end-to-end delay between sink and source node. The fundamental problem is to update the link cost; the algorithm that we propose is adaptive and is based on routing tables maintained at each node. When a route is requested, the node controls its routing table if there is an entry that corresponds to requested node. If no entry appears for that node, the node creates an entry and initializes the cost of links; evenly distributed over all its neighbors MPRE.

These costs are updated during transition from the agent *Resp-E-Route* based on information of links cost retrieved by visiting all nodes on the route. The link costs are updated as follows:

$$Cost\ of\ node_i^j = Cost\ of\ link_i^j = \gamma QE_c + \theta QD \tag{10}$$

The new costs at $(t+\delta t)$ in the node i on the link (i, j) is:

$$QE_{c_i}^j(t+1) = \frac{E_{c_i}^j(t)}{E_{c_i}^j(t+\delta t)} * QE_{c_i}^j(t) \tag{11}$$

and

$$QD_{c_i}^j(t+1) = \frac{D_{c_i}^j(t)}{D_{c_i}^j(t+\delta t)} * QD_{c_i}^j(t) \tag{12}$$

Where:

$E_{c_i}^j(t)$: Energy consumption in the node i on the link (i, j) at a time t.

$D_{c_i}^{j}(t)$: Link delay in the node *i* on the link *(i, j)* at a time t.

We refresh then the new cost of the path based on equation (4) and continues iteratively the update process.
Finally, the variable "Best cost route" is updated as follow:

$$\text{Best cost route} = \text{Max}\left(\gamma \sum_{i=1}^{N-1} QE_{c_i} + \theta \sum_{i=1}^{N-1} QD_i\right) \tag{13}$$

5.2 Performance evaluation

This section first describes our simulation setup and the metrics we used to evaluate EDAR. Then, it presents the results obtained under three scenarios designed to compare EDAR with three other protocols (section 2): QoS_AODV, SAR and EAR. In the case of QoS_AODV, we have modified the original algorithm in order to use the energy metric for the choice of the paths. Our extension takes into account the end-to-end delay and replaces the bandwidth metric with the energy consumed along the path.

5.2.1 Simulation setup and metrics

We use NS-2 for our simulations. We randomly distribute 100 nodes on a 200x200m area. The nodes send 35 bytes messages at a maximum of 200 kbps. The initial energy for each node is 5J. For each scenario, we run 10 simulations with a topology chosen at random. Each run lasts 300 seconds. Finally, we set γ to 0.75 and θ to 0.25, to give more importance to the energy metric.
For the evaluation, we stress the four protocols (QoS_AODV, SAR and EAR and EDAR) by varying mobility network conditions. Varying each network parameter allows to study a different feature of the routing algorithms. Highly mobile nodes will test the algorithm's ability to quickly detect route failures and establish new ones. For each mobility scenario, we increase one of these network parameters to force network congestion and energy starvation. We expect that the different protocols will react and behave differently to protect the network's lifetime, while guaranteeing a good QoS.
To this end, we are interested in three metrics to evaluate EDAR and compare it to the other protocols. These metrics were carefully chosen in order to give a broad idea of the improvements achieved by our protocol:

- The *Energy consumption* represents the energy (in mJ) spent by the nodes to route the packets to the sink. It includes both data packets and signalling packet. Energy consumption has a direct impact on the lifetime of a sensor network.
- The *End-to-end delay* is the time for a packet to reach the sink. It includes the time spent to discover the routes, as well as the time spent in the nodes queues and in the air. This metric represents the global response time of the network, and depends on the protocol efficiency is terms of the number of congested nodes and stability.
- The *Delivery rate* is the number of lost packets divided by the number of packets sent. This metric represents the reliability of the protocol in terms of packet delivery.

5.2.2 Results

Our study concerns the evaluation of the protocols for an increasing mobility of the deployed sensors. The first case shows the protocol's behaviour when nodes are completely static (0 m/s), and we consider extreme cases where nodes move at up to 30 m/s.

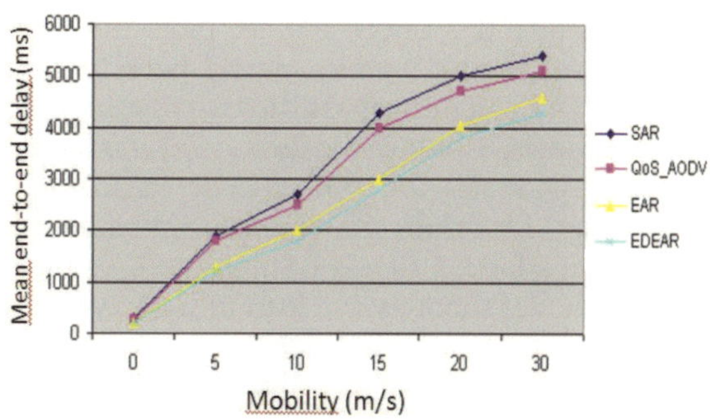

Fig. 9. Mean delay for various mobility patterns

Fig. 9 plots the mean end-to-end delay achieved by all four protocols under various speeds of the nodes. In the case of a static topology, the results for all protocols are quite similar. However, increasing the mobility reveals a clear difference in the protocols' efficiency. The plot indicates that, for speeds above 5 m/s, the performances of Qos_AODV and SAR degrade quickly (the delay increases from 2000 to 5000 ms), while EAR and EDAR keep delivering packets on a reasonable delay, for a speed up to 10 ms/s. Still, our protocol resists better to increasingly harder conditions.

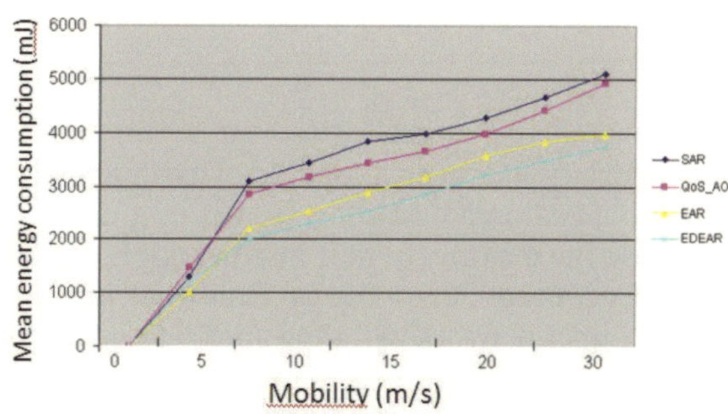

Fig. 10. Mean energy consumption for various mobility patterns

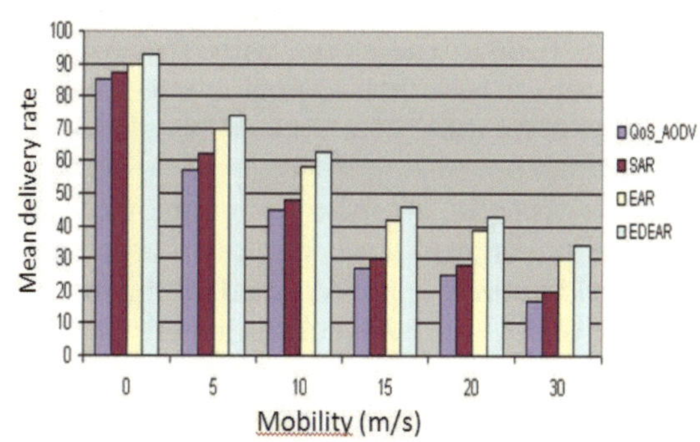

Fig. 11. Mean delivery rate for various mobility patterns

When nodes are mobile, topology changes are frequent. These changes cause a frequent loss of the currently selected best paths, therefore triggering route discovery phases more frequently. Discovery phases generate additional control traffic, consuming more energy and bandwidth. As a result, resources for data traffic are reduced, and the nodes quickly consume their energy. To study this effect, Fig. 10 plots the energy consumption when nodes move at various speeds. The dynamics clearly have less impact on EDAR, which takes advantage of its improved reactive capabilities when compared to the other protocols. Indeed, the choice of both energy-saving and low delay nodes dramatically reduces the energy consumption. Routing tables are probabilistic in EDAR; several paths may be selected to reach a destination. Therefore, if a node's neighbours change, the mechanism of adjusting probabilities can be adapted almost instantly to degradation performance on the selected path. Furthermore, nodes mobility can lead to the creation of new routes involving nodes with a high residual energy. EDAR quickly detects and selects these high quality nodes, thus allowing it to resist more efficiently to frequent route changes.

Finally, Fig.11 considers the mean delivery rate achieved when the mobility increases. Under a static scenario, all protocols achieve a very good delivery rate, EDAR being the only one higher than 90%. As expected, the delivery rate dramatically decreases with an increasing mobility, but the decrease is less significant for adaptive protocols, especially for EDAR. For a speed of 10 m/s, EDAR still achieves a delivery rate greater than 60%, while SAR and Qos_AODV are well below 50%. Packet losses occur more frequently as the network dynamicity increases, because routing protocols have to face the problem of recomputing new routes all the time. During this phase, no routes are known to reach the destination, and the nodes have no choice but dropping the packets. However, thanks to EDAR's exploration process and its probabilistic nature, it is able to quickly reallocate a new route, thus decreasing the time when no route is available.

6. Conclusion

QoS management in networking has been a topic of extensive research in a last decade. As the Internet network is managed on a best effort packet routing, QoS assurance has always been an open issue. Because the majority of past Internet applications (email, web browsing, etc.) do not used strong QoS needs, this issue is somewhat made less urgent in the past. Today, with the development of network real-time application and the convergence of voice and data over heterogeneous networks, it is necessary to develop a high quality control mechanism to check the network traffic load and ensure QoS requirements. Constraints imposed by QoS requirements, such as bandwidth, delay, or loss, are referred to as QoS constraints, and the associated routing is referred to as QoS routing which is a part of Constrained-Based Routing (CBR). Therefore, with the wide emergence of real time applications in mobile and sensor networks, QoS guarantees become increasingly required. Therefore, protocols designed for MANETs and WSNs should be involved in satisfying application requirements while optimizing network resources use. A considerable amount of research has been done recently in order to ensure QoS routing in mobile ad hoc networks. Several multi-hop routing protocols have been developed. In addition to proactive, reactive and hybrid approaches, often used by the most known routing protocols, adaptive routing protocols which are by nature oriented QoS have already proved their success in wired networks. They are based on reinforcement learning mechanisms and mainly built around exploration agents having for task to discover routes and gather information about the state of visited links. However, for a network node to be able to make an optimal routing decision, according to relevant performance criteria, it requires not only up-to-date and complete knowledge of the state of the entire network but also an accurate prediction of the network dynamics during propagation of the message through the network. This problem is naturally formulated as a dynamic programming problem, which, however, is too complex to be solved exactly. Reinforcement learning (RL) is used to approximate the value function of dynamic programming. In these algorithms, the environment is modeled as stochastic, so routing algorithms can take into account the dynamics of the network. However no model of dynamics is assumed to be given.

In this chapter, we have focused in first part our attention in some special kind of Constrained Based Routing in mobile networks which we called QoS self-optimization Routing. It is shown from simulation results that combining proactive exploration agents with the on-demand route discovery mechanism, our AMDR routing protocol would give reduced end-to-end delay and route discovery latency with high connectivity. This is ensured due to the availability of alternative routes in our algorithm. The alone case where our approach can provide more important delay is the first connection where any route is yet established. On the other hand, the use of delay-MPR mechanism, guarantees that the overhead generated will be reduced. From simulation results we can estimate that AMDR realizes best performance than adaptive routing protocols based on swarm intelligence using instantaneous delay.

Secondary, we study the use of reinforcement leaning in EDAR protocol in the case of Wireless Sensor Networks. We presented a new way to make adaptive routing with quality of service in order to improve the end-to-end delay and increase the lifetime of a delay tolerant network. Our protocol, called EDAR, explores the network and chooses the best path routing in terms of energy and delay to route information based on reinforcement learning paradigm. For that, an explorer agent is used and learns from past experiences to choose the next path; data is always sent over the best path. Our approach offers advantages compared with other classical approaches. In particular, it reduces much better the energy consumed required for information sent, updates routing and network exploration more reactively. The proposed algorithm takes into account the network state in a better way than the classical approaches do. Also, our protocol is well-suited for a dynamic mobile environment., especially in Delay Tolerant Networks.

Finally, extensions of the framework for using these techniques across hybrid networks to achieve end-to-end QoS needs to be investigated, in particular on large scalable networks. Another challenging area concerns the composite metric used in routing packets (especially residual bandwidth) which is so complex and the conditioning of different models in order to take into account other parameters like the information type of each flow packet (real-time, VBR, ...).

In Final, we show in this chapter that an adaptive algorithm based on RL that simultaneously processes an observation and learns to perform better is a good way to consider time evolving networks. Such adaptive algorithms are very useful in tracking a phenomenon that evolves over time.

7. Acknowledgments

The work presented here is a part of UPEC-LISSI research activities team, especially in the scope of the supervising Nesrine Ouferhat, Saida Ziane PhD's thesis and discussions with Dr. Brice Augustin and Dr. Said Hoceini. I would like to thank them for their support and their suggestions.

8. References

Baras, J.S., Mehta, H. (2003). A Probabilistic Emergent Routing Algorithm (PERA) for Mobile Ad Hoc Networks, *Proceedings of WiOpt '03: Modeling and Optimization in Mobile, AdHoc and Wireless Networks*, Sophia-Antipolis, France.

Boyan, J. A., Littman, M. L., (1994). Packet routing in dynamically changing networks: A reinforcement learning approach, *Advances in Neural Information Processing Systems 6*, Morgan Kaufmann, San Francisco, CA, pp. 671-678.

Di Caro G., Ducatelle F., Gambardella M., (2005). "AntHocNet: An Adaptive Nature-Inspired Algorithm for Routing in Mobile Ad Hoc Networks". *European Transactions on Telecommunications (ETT), Special Issue on Self Organization in Mobile Networking*, Volume 16, Number 5, Pages 443-455.

Dorigo, M., Stüzle, T., (2004). *Ant Colony Optimization*, MIT Press, Cambridge, MA.

Gallager, R.G. (1977). A minimum delay routing algorithm using distributed computations. *IEEE Transactions on Communications*, 25(1), 73-85.

Gelenbe, E., Lent, L., Xu, Z, (2002). Networking with Cognitive Packets, Proc. ICANN 2002, Madrid, Spain, pp. 27-30.

Little, J.DC. (1961). *A proof of the Queueing Formula L=λW*, Operations Research.

Lu Y.J., Sheu T.L., (2007). "An efficient routing scheme with optimal power control in wireless multi-hop sensor networks", *Computer Communications*, vol. 30, no. 14-15, pp. 2735-2743.

Mellouk, A., Lorenz, P., Boukerche, A., Lee, M.H., (2007). Impact of Adaptive Quality of Service Based Routing Algorithms in the next generation heterogeneous networks, *IEEE Communication Magazine*, IEEE Press, vol. 45, n°2, pp. 65-66.

Mellouk, A., Hoceini, S., Cheurfa, M., (2008). Reinforcing Probabilistic Selective Quality of service Routes in Dynamic Heterogeneous Networks, *Computer Communication Journal*, Elsevier Ed., Vol. 31, n°11, pp. 2706-2715.

Mellouk, A., S. Hoceini, S. Zeadally, (2009). Design and performance analysis of an inductive QoS routing algorithm, *Computer Communications Journal*, Elsevier Ed., Volume: 32 n°12, pp. 1371-1376, Elsevier, 2009.

Naimi Meraihi A., (2005). *802.11 AdHoc Networks Delay and Routing*, PhD Thesis, INRIA Rocquencourt, France.

Nguyen D-Q., Minet P., (2007). "Analysis of MPR selection in the OLSR protocol". *Proc. Of PAEWN*, Niagara Falls, Ontario, Canada.

Ok C., Lee S., Mitra P., Kumara S., (2009). "Distributed energy balanced routing for wireless sensor networks", *Computers & Industrial Engineering*, vol. 57, no. 1, pp. 125-135.

Ozdaglar, A.E., Bertsekas, D.P. (2003). Optimal Solution of Integer Multicommodity Flow Problem with Application in Optical Networks. *Proc. Of Symposium on Global Optimisation*, June, 411-435.

Perkins C.E., Royer. S, Das R., (2000). "Quality of Service for Ad hoc On-Demand Distance Vector Routing", *IETF Internet Draft*.

Saaty T.L., (1961). *Elements of Queueing Theory and its applications*, Mac Graw-Hill Ed.

Shah R.C., Rabaey J.M., (2002). "Energy aware routing for low energy ad hoc sensor networks". *Proceeding of IEEE Wireless Communications and Networking Conference* (WCNC), Orlando, FL, USA.

Shearer F., (2008). "System-Level Approach to Energy Conservation", *Power Management in Mobile Devices*, pp. 217-259.

Sutton, R.S., Barto, A.G. (1997). *Reinforcement Learning*. Ed. MIT Press.

Wedde H.F., Farooq M., Pannenbaecker T., Vogel B., Mueller C., Meth J., Jeruschkat R., (2005). "BeeAdHoc: an energy efficient routing algorithm for mobile ad hoc networks inspired by bee behavior", In *Genetic And Evolutionary Computation Conference Proceedings*, pp 153-160.

2

Cooperative Agent Learning Model in Multi-cluster Grid

Qingkui Chen, Songlin Zhuang and He Jia, XiaoDong Ding
School of Computer Engineering,
University of Shanghai for Science and Technology
China

1. Introduction

With the rapid development of the information techniques and Internet, and their popular application, the research results based on CSCW became the key techniques to build the enterprise information infrastructure (Raybourn & Newman, 2002).The computer based on cooperative work environments is playing the more and more important role in the business behavior of the enterprise today. Especially, the CSCW contains a lot of computation-intensive tasks and they need to be processed in some high performance computes. On the other hand, Intranet is more and more extended and a great number of cheap personal computers are distributed everywhere, but the utilization rate of their resources is very low. The researches of papers (Markatos & Dramitions, 1996) (Acharya&Setia, 1998) point out that many resources are idle in most network environments at a certain time. Even it is the busiest time of a day, still one third of their workstations aren't used completely. So, the paper (Chen & Na, 2006) proposed a framework which is how to collect and use the idle computing resources of CSCW environment that composed of multi-clusters connected by Intranet. It uses the idle computing resources in CSCW environment to construct a Visual Computational System (VCE). VCE can support two kinds of migration computations: (1) the Serial Task based on Migration (STM); (2) the Task based on Data Parallel Computation (TDPC). For adapting these heterogeneous and dynamic environments, we use the Grid (Foster & Kesselman, 1999) techniques and multi-agent (Osawa, 1993) (Wooldridge, 2002) techniques, and collect the idle resources of CSCW environment to construct multi-cluster grid (MCG). Because the migration of computing task and the dynamic changes of the idle resources in MCG, the intelligence of computing agents for raising the utilization rate of idle resource becomes very important. So, the effective learning model of agents is the key technique in multi-cluster grid. There are a lot of researches about agent learning (Kaelbling et al., 1996)(Sutton, 1988)(Watkins & Dayan,1992)(Rummery&Niranjan, 1994)(Horiuchi&Katai, 1999) nowadays. It includes two aspects: passive learning and active learning. The main theory of active learning is the reinforcement learning. At the same time, the agent organization learning (Zambonelli et al., 2000) (Zambonelli et al., 2001) model become another focus. The problem of distributed and cooperative multi-agent learning is studied through complex fuzzy theory in the paper (Berenji&Vengerov,

2000). But all these methods can't satisfy the need of dynamic multi-cluster grid. Especially, owing to the migration of the cooperative computing team, which is a group of cooperative computing agent to support data parallel computing, and the dynamic changes of grid idle resources, the cooperative learning model is very important for cooperative computing.

This chapter proposed a cooperative learning model of agents in multi-cluster grid that is composed of many computer-clusters connected by Intranet. By using the idle resource state of computer and the cooperative idle resource state, the state space is constructed; by using the sub-actions, the action space is built; through the state space and the action space, we construct dynamic rule space; through the reinforcement learning, the dynamic rule is revised. This model can support the grid computing and pervasive computing based on task-migratory mechanism, and it can fit the heterogeneous and dynamic network Environment. The experimental results show that this model can increase the percentage of the resources utilization in CSCW environment.

2. VCE

We collect and use the idle computing resources of CSCW environment to construct a Visual Computational System (VCE).There are two kinds of migration computations in VCE. The first is STM (Serial Task based on Migration). This kind of the task is the traditional serial task, and its description is based on the task packet. By delivering the task packet in CSCW environment, the task is executed by the computational service agents running on many idle computers in CSCW. The computational process is that the task packet is migrated for executing. The second is TDPC (the Task based on Data Parallel Computation). Making use of the overlapped size of segments of idle time of some computers in CSCW networks, we cluster these computers to become some Logical Computer Clusters (LCC), and each LCC is composed of the computers whose segments of the idle time are homology. So TDPC is the task running on LCC of CSCW environment.

In order to support the migration computations of VCE, a Grid Computation Environment was designed and implemented. It includes six parts and the architecture is presented as Figure 1.

CSCW is the traditional cooperative design system. Grid Computation Environment only concerns the Role Space (RS) and the Work Flow Space (WFS) of CSCW. **PCE** (Physical Computational Environment) is the physical computational environment of CSCW, and it is composed of many computer clusters connected by Internet or Intranet. PCE is the physical basis of CSCW, SDS, VCE and MAS. The single computational node (SC) and logical computer cluster (LCC) compose **VCE** which support STM and TDPC, and SC and LCC are called computational component (CC). The core of Grid Computation Environment is **MAS** (Multi-Agent System) which is composed of multi-Agents system.MAS can manage the Grid resources, do match works between the two kinds of the migration computations and computational component of VCE and execute computation. As we can see from Figure 1, MAS include four sub-systems, which are TAS (Task Agent System), SAS (Service Agent System), RAS (Resource Agent System) and MCAS (Matching Agent System). The four agent sub-systems of MAS communicate with each other by four shared data tables, and these tables are the task table (TT), the Service Table (ST), the Resource Management Table (RMT), and the Running Service Table (RST).TT is the set of all computing tasks whose state is *"Committed"*. ST is the set of all computational services. RMT is the set of all computational components of VCE. RST is the set of all binding elements, and a binding element is a binding relation among the computing tasks, the computational services and the computational components.TAS receives the computing tasks from the users of RS and commits them to the table TT, and then monitors their states. When the computing tasks were "Completed", TAS delivers their results to the original user or WFS.SAS receives the computational services from the users of RS, then SAS checks up their legitimacy and register them to ST, and saves their service code to **SDS**. SDS can store the data of Grid Computation Environment and all computational classes. The MCAS, whose function is the match work between the migration computations and the computational components, runs on the Master of Grid Computation Environment.The main functions of RAS are the computational resources management, VCE monitor and the task scheduler. **Master** is a special computer, and it controls Grid Computation Environment.

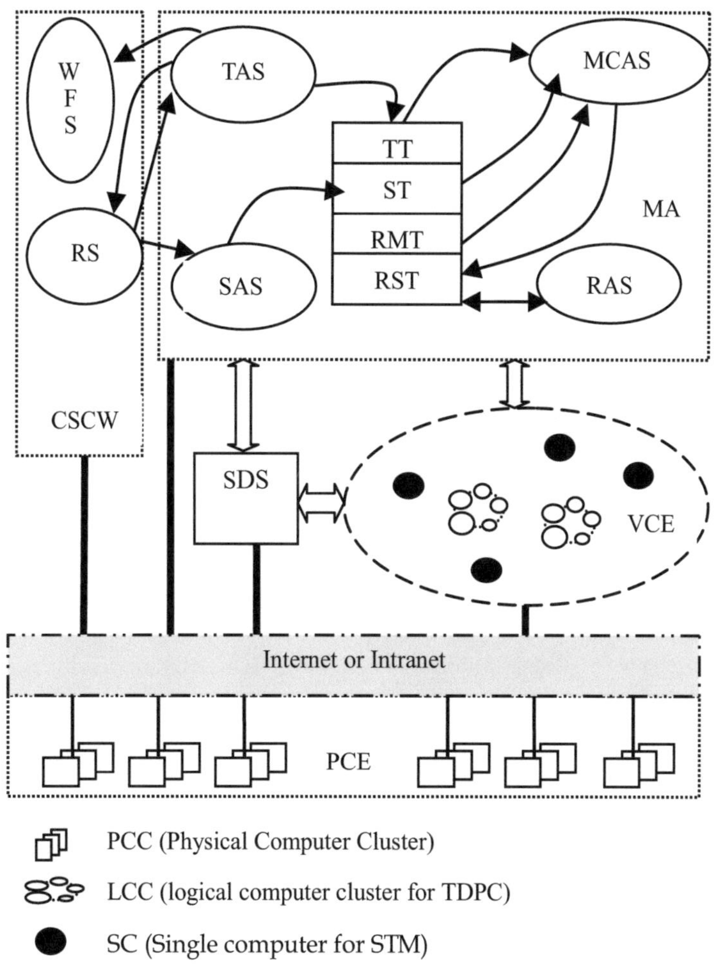

Fig. 1. Architecture of Grid Computation Environment

3. Architecture of MCG

In order to simplify the problem, we construct MCG (Multi-cluster grid) which is the simplification of Grid Computation Environment. MCG is composed of the idle computing resources of CSCW environment and support the computation-intensive tasks of CSCW. The Computation-Intensive Task needs very long time to run, and also needs high performance computer to support, such as the finite element analysis. For the description of learning model, we introduce some definitions:

Computing Node (CN) is defined as *CN* (*id, CT, Am, AS*), where *id* denotes the identifier of *CN*; *CT* denotes the type of computing node; *Am* denotes the main control agent of *CN*; *AS* is the set of agents running on *CN*.

Computer cluster (CC) is defined as *CC* (*Ma, CS*), where *Ma* denotes the main computer of *CC*; *CS*= {*CN1, CN2…CNp*} denotes the set of all computing nodes which *CC* includes;

Computing Agent (CA) is defined as *CA* (*id, PRG, BDI, KS, CE*), where *id* denotes the identifier of *CA*; *PRG* denotes the executable program set of *CA*; *BDI* is the description of its BDI; *KS* is its knowledge set; *CE* is its configuration environment.

CA is the basic element of executing computation task and support STM. If *CA* could complete the task independently, we call it the **independent computing agent** (*ICA*). If *CA* couldn't complete the task independently, and it must cooperate with others, we call it the **cooperative computing agent** (*CCA*).

Cooperation Computing Team (CCT) is defined as *CCT* (*id, Am, CAS, BDI, CKS, CCE*), where *id* denotes the identifier of *CCT*; *Am* denotes the main control agent of *CCT*; *CAS* denotes the set of all cooperative computing agents which *CCT* includes; *BDI* is the description of its BDI; *CKS* is its knowledge set. *CCE* is its configuration environment. *CCT* can support the TDPC in the logical computer cluster.

Global Computing Group (GCG) is defined as *GCG* (*id, Am, ICAS, CCTS, GKS, GCE*), where *id* denotes the identifier of *GCG*; *Am* denotes the main control agent of *GCG*; *ICAS* denotes the set of *ICA* which *GCG* includes; *CCTS* denotes the set of *CCT* which *GCG* includes; *GKS* is its knowledge set. *GCE* is its configuration environment.

Multi-cluster grid (MCG) is defined as *MCG* (*Ma, CCS, N,R, GCG*), where *Ma* denotes the main computer of *MCG*; *CCS* denotes the set of all computer clusters which *MCG* includes; *N* is the connection network set of *MCG*; *R* is the rules of connections; *GCG* is the global computing group.

Many tasks are executed together in *GCG* during the same time, and the tasks are calculated by a lot of *ICA*s or *CCT*s.

4. Rule descriptions

For the description of learning model, we introduce some definitions at first, and then described the organization method for the multi-agent rules.

A basic Rule (*br*) is defined as *br* (*id, rul, MRS*), where *id* denotes its identifier; *rul* denotes the formalization description of *br*; *MRS* denotes the meta-rule set for revising *br*.

Basic Rule Set (BRS) is the set of all the basic rules which *GCG* includes.

The state information in *MCG* can be decided by the scale of its idle computing resource, the computing task information, and the shared resource information. The state conception is described as follows:

A state (*st*) is defined as *st* (*id, sort, CSET*), where *id* denotes the state identifier; *sort* denotes the sort of this state; *CSET*= $(c_1,c_2 \ldots c_k)$ denotes its condition vector. The number of the condition elements which condition vector includes is k, and all states of the same sort have the same value of *k*. If the condition vector of a state only includes single computing node information, this state can be called *the independent state*; if the condition vector of a state includes the complex information about many computing nodes, shared network, etc., this state can be called *the cooperative state*. All states in *MCG* formed *the state space* (*SSP*).

An action (Ac) is defined as *ac* (*id*, μ, *AcDes*, *Revis*), where *id* denotes the action identifier; *AcDes* denotes the formalization description for this action. *Revis* is the set of revised strategies.

A sub-Action of *ac* can be defined as *ac* (*id*, μ, *AcDes*(μ), *Revis*), where *id* denotes the action identifier; μ is a decimal and $0<\mu<1$, *and* μ denotes the sub-action factor; *AcDes*(μ) denotes the formalization description for this sub-action. *Revis* is the set of revised strategies that make *AcDes* become stronger or weaker through the factor μ, and the revised result is *AcDes*(μ). So, a sub-action can be generated based on its father action *ac* and can be presented as *ac* (μ). All actions and their all sub-actions in *MCG* formed *the action space* (*ASP*).

Dynamic Rule (*dr*) is defined as *dr*(*id* ,*st*, *ac*, *br*, *w*, *sta*, *life*), where *id* denotes the rule identifier; $st \in SSP$, $ac \in ASP$, $br \in BRS$; *sta* is the state of *dr*, and $sta \in$ {*"Naive"*, *"Trainable"*, *"Stable"*}; *"Naive"* denotes that the *dr* is a new rule; *"Trainable"* denotes that the *dr* is revised rule; *"Stable"* denotes that the *dr* is a mature rule; *w* denotes the weight value of *dr*; *life* denotes the value of its life. The *dr* means that if the state is *st* then do sub-action *ac* (μ).If the state of *dr* is independent state, the *dr* is called *the independent rule*; if the state of *dr* is cooperative state, the *dr* is called *the cooperative rule*. The formed process of the dynamic rule and the relations between *st*, *ac* and *dr* are presented in Figure 2. All the rules in *MCG* formed *the rule space* (*RSP*). *RSP*, *ASP* and *SSP* formed GKS of *GCG*.

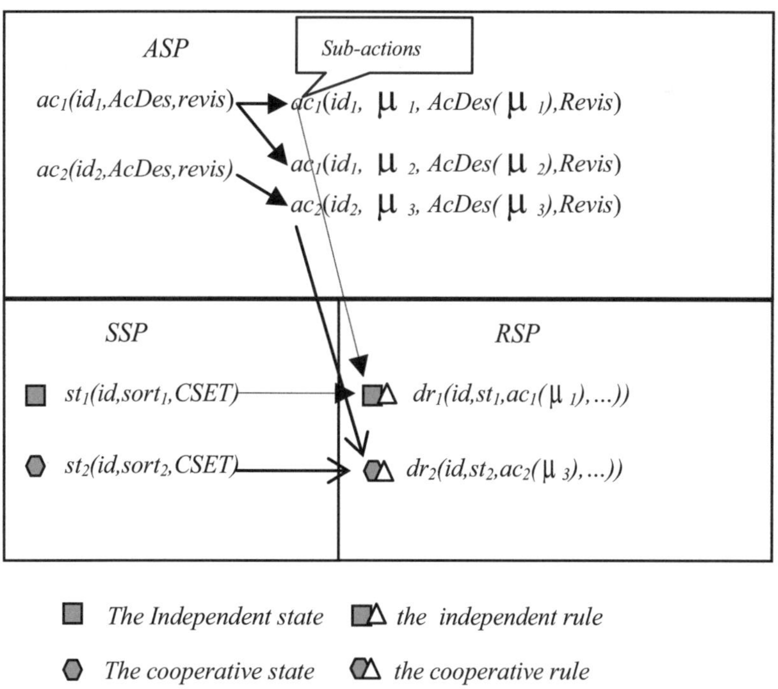

Fig. 2. The relations between *st*, *ac* and *dr*

If *dr* is a dynamic rule and *dr.w>MaxWeight*, and *MaxWeight* is a constant in *MCG*, we call *dr* the static rule (*sr*). Its state is *"Static"*.
If *dr* is a dynamic rule and *dr.w<MinWeight*, and *MinWeight* is a constant in *MCG*, we call *dr* the castoff rule (*cr*). Its state is *"Castoff"*.
The state graph of rules is presented in Figure 3.
The dynamic knowledge is the set of all the dynamic rules in *MCG*. The static knowledge is the set of all the static rules in *MCG*. The basic knowledge can be formed by passive learning. For adjusting the dynamic knowledge established by the basic knowledge, we can revise them through the reinforcement learning and the multi-agent cooperation during the computing process.
Task (TSK) *is* defined as *TSK* (*id, DAT, AS*), where *id* denotes the identifier of *TSK*; *DAT* denotes the data set; *AS* is the set of agents which execute *TSK*.

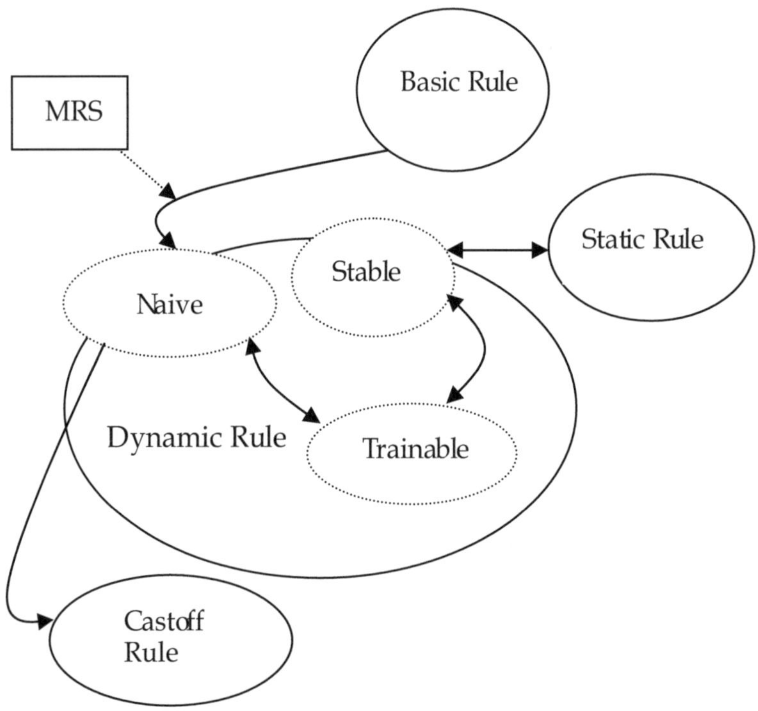

Fig. 3. State graph of rules

5. Description of learning model

5.1 Initialization of knowledge

Algorithm1 (Initialization of basic rules)
(1)The users construct the *BRS* through *MRS* and initialize the state space *SSP*;
(2)Construct the initialization action space *ASP*:
    Decide the action set *TMP* by users;
    Set *ASP*=φ;
    While *TMP*≠φ Do

Get an action *ac* from *TMP*;
Set μ=1;
Construct the *AcDes* and *Revis* for *ac* by users;
Set *AcDes*(μ) =*AcDes*;
Construct the sub-action *ac* (μ);
ASP=ASP+ {ac (μ)};
TMP=TMP-{ac};
End while;
(3)Construct the initialization rule space *RSP*:
TMP=*SSP*;
RSP=φ;
While *TMP*≠φ Do
Get a state *st* from *TMP*;
Choose a sub-action *ac* (μ) from *RSP* through the *st.sort* by users;
Construct a new dynamic rule *dr*:
{*dr.st*=*st*;
dr.ac=*ac* (μ);
dr.w=0;
dr.sta="*Naive*";
dr.life=0;
}
Add the *dr* to *RSP*;
TMP=TMP-{*st*};
End while;
(4)Output *RSP*, *ASP* and *SSP*;
(5)End.

For fitting the variety of computing device resources, the dynamic rules must be generated and the process is described as follows:

Algorithm2 (Generation of dynamic rules)
Input: a new state *st* (*id*, *sort*, *CSET*), *RSP*, *ASP* and *SSP*;
Output: the new *RSP*, *SSP* and *ASP*;
(1)Get the sort of *st* and save it to *TmpSort*;
(2)Get all states with the same sort of *TmpSort* from *SSP*, and form the state set *SubSSP*;
(3)Construct condition relation matrix:
Suppose that *TmpSort* sort state has *k* conditions, and the number of the elements in *SubSSP* is *m*; these condition vectors are $(c_{11}, c_{12}\ldots c_{1k})$, $(c_{21},c_{22}\ldots c_{2k})\ldots$ $(c_{m1},c_{m2}\ldots c_{mk})$ and the condition vector of *st* is $(c_{m+1,1},c_{m+1,2}\ldots c_{m+1,k})$; All $c_{ij}(1\le i\le m+1,\ 1\le j\le k)$ are integer and can be defined by real applications;
Construct a $(m+1)$ xk matrix $CM=\{c_{ij} \mid (1\le i\le m+1,\ 1\le j\le k)\}$ by using all condition vectors of states in *SubSSP*;
(4)Construct the fuzzy matrix $FM=\{f_{ij} \mid (1\le i\le m+1,\ 1\le j\le m+1)\}$, where
$f_{ii}=1$;
$f_{ij}=1-\beta\,(w_1 | r_{i1}-r_{j1} | +w_2 | r_{i2}-r_{j2} | +\ldots+w_k | r_{ik}-r_{jk} |)$,
when $i\ne j$, $0<\beta<1$, $w_1+w_2+\ldots+w_k=1$, and $w_l>0$ $(1\le l\le k)$;
(5)Construct the fuzzy equivalence matrix (please refer the document (Zadeh, 1975)):

Repeat do
  FT=FM ⊙ *FM*; // ⊙ is the operation theorem to take the maximum and minimum.
  If *FT=FM*, then go to (4);
  FM=FT;
End repeat;

(6)Calculate the *th*-cut matrix *FMth* according to the threshold *th* , and *th* ∈ [0, *Z1*] or *th* ∈ [*Z1*, *Z2*] or *th* ∈ [*Z2*, *Z3*] or *th* ∈ [*Z3*,1],0≤*Z1*≤*Z2*≤*Z3*≤1,where *Z3* is the minimum of the *effective threshold*, *Z2* is the minimum of the *average threshold*, *Z1* is the minimum of the *artificial threshold*; (Refer to step (9))

(7)Divide the *FM* into several equivalent classes *SFM1* ∪ *SFM2* ∪ …*SFMe* according to *FMth*; The element number of every equivalent class must be greater than 1, and it can decrease the value of *th*;

(8)Choose the equivalent class *SFM* that includes the condition of *st*;
  Form the candidate rule set *CRSET* from *RSP* through *SFM*;

(9)/*effective threshold*/
{
If *th* ∈ [Z3,1], then
  {Get the dynamic rule *dr* which has the maximum weight in *CRSET*;
  Construct a new dynamic rule *ndr* through *st* and *dr*;
  RSP=RSP+ {*ndr*};
  SSP=SSP+ {*st*}
  };
    /**average threshold**/
If *th* ∈ [*Z2*, *Z3*), then
  {Calculate the *avm*=average (*dr.μ* | *dr* ∈ *CRSET*);
  Search a dynamic rule *sdr* which satisfies |*avm-sdr.μ*| ≤ε (*sdr* ∈ *CRSET and* 0≤ε≤1);
  If *sdr* existed, then
    Construct a new dynamic rule *ndr* according to *st* and *sdr*;
    Else
    {Build a new sub-action *nac(μ)*according to *ac*, *avm* and *Revis*, Where *μ=avm*;
    Construct a new dynamic rule *ndr* according to *st* and *nac(μ)*;
    }
  RSP=RSP+ {*ndr*};
  SSP=SSP+ {*st*};
  ASP=ASP+ {*nac* (*μ*)}
  };
    /**artificial threshold**/
If *th* ∈ [*Z1*, *Z2*) or *th* ∈ [0, *Z1*), then
  {Calculate the *avm*=average (*dr.μ* | *dr* ∈ *CRSET*);
  Build a new sub-action *nac(μ)* through *ac* and *avm* by *users*, Where *μ=avm*;
  Construct a new dynamic rule *ndr* through *st* and *nac(μ)*;
  };
RSP=RSP+ {*ndr*};
SSP=SSP+ {*st*};
ASP=ASP+ {*nac(μ)*};
}.

5.2 Life and weight of dynamic rule

According to the algorithm2, the dynamic rule is constructed, and it must be adjusted when the *TSK* is calculated. The adjusting mechanism can adopt the reinforcement learning, and the resources utilization rate of *TSK* can be considered as the reinforcement function.

Algorithm3 (Adjusting weight and life for rules)

Suppose that *Y1* is the *castoff threshold,* and *Y2* is the *mature threshold; Q(urt)* is the *reinforcement function* and *Q(urt)*>0, and *urt* is the resources utilization rate; *MaxWeight* is the maximum of the rule weight, and *MinWeight* is the minimum of the rule weight, and let $MinWeight<Y1<Y2<MaxWeight$; *MaxLife* is the maximum of life value.

(1)Suppose that a computing agent *CA* adopted a dynamic rule *dr* of *CA.KS;*
dr.life+ +; /* increase the value of life */
Wait for the *urt* from the computing system;
(2)If *urt*>0, then
dr.w=dr.w+ *Q(urt)*; /*increase weight*/
If *urt*<0, then
    dr.w=dr.w-Q(urt); /*decrease weight*/
(3)If *dr.w>MaxWeight*, then
dr.w=MaxWeight;
If *dr.w*<*MinWeight,* then
    dr.w=MinWeight;
(4)If $dr.w<Y_1$ and dr.life>MaxLife, then
    dr.sta= "*Castoff*"; /*Castoff rule */
(5)If $Y_2<dr.w<$MaxWeight, then
    dr.sta="*Stable*"; /*Stable rule */
(6)If *dr.w*>= MaxWeight, then
    dr.sta= "*Static*"; /*Static rule */
(7)If $Y_1<dr.w<Y_2$, then
    dr.sta= "*Trainable*"; /*Trainable rule */
(8)If $MinWeight<dr.w<Y_1$, then
    dr.sta="*Naive*"; /*Naive rule */
(9)End.

When the learning and executing process runs for a long time, the dynamic knowledge is excessive and it will reduce the searching efficiency. So, it needs the artificial adjustment for dynamic knowledge to reduce the number of the rules. The process is omitted.

The dynamic cooperation knowledge of *CCT* usually uses shared resources, such as the network bandwidth, so the value of *urt* is the average resources utilization rate of *CCT.*

5.3 Learning in migration process

In order to persist and improve the global knowledge in *MCG* , the main control agents *Am* in *CN, CCT* and *GCG* get the shared organization knowledge through the organization learning (Zambonelli et al., 2000)(Zambonelli et al., 2001). Owing to the agent migration in *MCG,* the running environments of *ICA* and *CCT* are in the dynamic change. For fitting the change, the migration learning of the organization is very important.

Algorithm4 (Migration learning of *ICA*)

An *ICA* running on the computing node *CNi* must be migrated to the computing node *CNj,* so the migration learning process is presented as follows:

(1)*ICA* commits its *KS* to *Am* in *CNi,* and *Am* saves the *KS;*
(2)*ICA* asks for a new computing node *CNj* from *MCG* and consults with *Am* of *CNj,* and migrates into *CNj;*
(3)*ICA* gets the current state set *CSS* in *CNj* and searches the corresponding dynamic rule form *RSP* according to *CSS,* then refreshes it's *KS*:

    TMP=CSS;
    OTHER=φ;
    While TMP≠φ Do
      Get a state st from TMP;
      Search a dynamic rule dr from RSP by st;
      If dr≠φ, then /* successful*/
        Add dr to ICA.KS;
        TMP=TMP-{st};
      Else
        TMP=TMP-{st};
        OTHER=OTHER+{st};
      End if;
    End while

(4)If *OTHER*≠φ, then

    While OTHER≠φ Do
      Get a state st from OTHER;
      Start the algorithm2 to generate a new dynamic rule ndr above st;
      Add ndr to ICA.KS;
      OTHER=OTHER-{st};
    End while;
    End if;

(5)*CNi* and *CNj* report their *KS* and *CE* to *RSP, ASP and SSP* in *GCG;*
(6)*ICA* continues executing and learning on *CNj;*

Algorithm5 (Migration learning of CCT)
Suppose that *CCT*(*id, Am, CAS, BDI, CKS, CCE*) is a cooperation computing team running on the computer cluster *CCi*, *CAS=MIG*∪*NMIG*, where *MIG* is the set of the computing agents that will be migrated; *NIMG* is the set of the non-migration computing agents. The migration learning process is as follows:
(1)All the computing agents of *MIG* migrate to their new computing nodes respectively and learn the new knowledge according to the algorithm4;
(2)All *CA*∈*MIG*∪*NMIG* commit their state information to *Am*; *Am* calculates the new cooperative state information set *CISET;*
(3)If *CISET*≠φ then

    Am generates a new dynamic set NRSET according to CISET, and the process is similar to the step (3) (4) in aglorithm4.
    Am refreshes CCT.CKS;
    End if;

(4)*CCT* start the calculation work in a new environment;
(5)End.

5.4 Learning process of GCG

Algorithm6 (GCG learning process)

(1)*GCG* calls the algorithm1 to do initialization work;
(2)*GCG* receives a task *TSK;*
(3)*GCG* allots a computing device *PE* (that is a *CN* or a *CC*) for *TSK,* and starts the computing agents for *TSK;*
(4)While *TSK* is not finished Do
    All computing agents cooperative calculate the *TSK;*
    If *TSK* must be migrated, then
        Start the migration learning algorithm (4 and 5);
        Calculate the resource utilization rate *urt;*
        Start the algorithm3 to adjust the weight and life of dynamic rules;
        Refresh ASP, SSP, and RSP;
    End if;
  End while;
(5)End.

6. Experiments

We construct a *MCG* that is composed of 12 computers and 3 computer-clusters that connected by Intranet. The independent state of the computer can be decided by its idle CPU resource, idle memory resource, idle disk resource and idle net adapter resource, so, the condition vector of the state is (*CPU, memory, disk, net adapter*). The cooperative state of *CCT* can be decided by the *CCT* scale, the bandwidth of *CCT,* the total idle CPU of *CCT,* the total idle memory, the total idle disk of *CCT* and the total net adapter power. The *ASP* is the strategy set, such as the buffer size, the size of basic communication unit and the synchronous time, etc. The computing tasks provided by *MCG* are the matrix operations and the linear programming. The *CCT* algorithms (Parallel algorithms based on computer cluster) for the matrix operations and the linear programming are given. The Intranet clock is synchronous by GTS protocol. The initial basic rules include 24 rules for *ICA* and 7 rules for *CCT* and the parameter values are as follows: *MaxLife*=43200(s), *Y1*=15, *Y2*=80, *Y3*=0.3 ,*Z1* =0, *Z2*=0.6,*Z3*=0.9, *MaxWeight*=100 and *MinWeight*=0. The experiment includes seven times and each time has 12 hours, and the total time is 84 hours. The tests adopt a random function to choose some tasks (the matrix operation, the linear programming and their parallel edition) in each time. In order to make the tasks migrate as far as possible in the *MCG,* We make use of the random migration function *RandMigration()* and form the migration strategy during the test processes. Through the average values of the test information, we observe the learning results of this model. The experiment results are as follows:

The changes of the average resource utilization rate of *MCG* along with the learning process have been tested. The thick solid line means the utilization rate distribution in the figure 4(a). This test result shows that this model can raise the resource utilization rate of *MCG.*

The changes of the number of new dynamic rules which are generated during the learning process have been tested. The solid line means the distribution of the dynamic rules whose state is always the *"Naive"* during their life period in the figure 4(a). The dotted line means

the distribution of the *"Trainable"* dynamic rules whose state has become the *"Stable"* during their life period. The test results show that the learning efficiency of this model increases gradually along with the learning process.
The number of the artificial adjustment has been counted. The solid line means the distribution of the number during the tests in the figure 4(b). This test result shows that the number of artificial adjustments decreases gradually along with learning process.

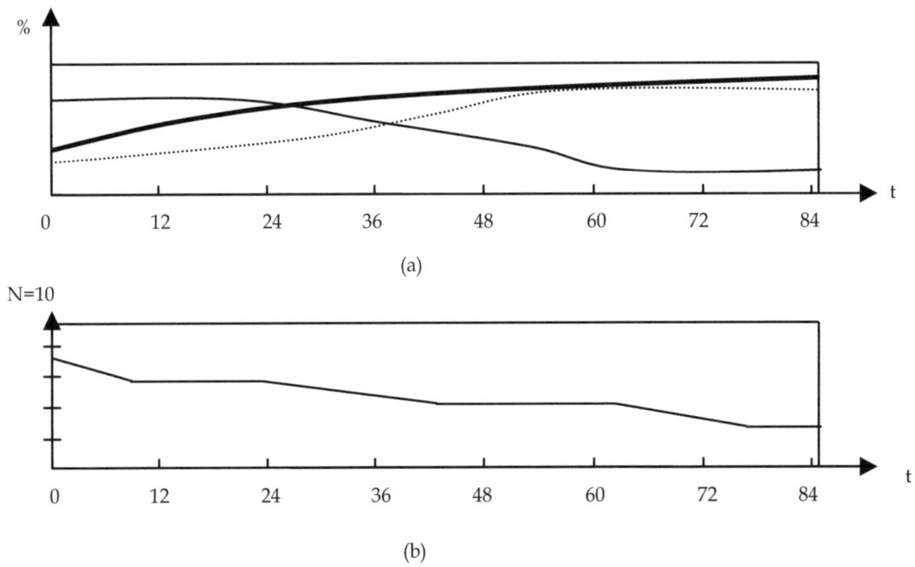

Fig. 4. The results of tests

7. Conclusions

In order to support the computation-intensive tasks, we collect the idle computational resources of CSCW environment to construct the multi-cluster grid. Because of the heterogeneous resources, the state of the idle computing resources changes in the process of the computing and the task migration. For fitting the state changes, the dynamic rule mechanisms of agents are proposed. According to the Grid techniques, Computing Agent, Cooperation Computing Team, the state space, the action space, the dynamic rule space, the reinforcement learning and so on, a cooperative learning model of agent was designed and implemented in this chapter. In the multi-cluster environment, using resources effectively is very difficult for the grid computing, however, a good learning model can improve the intelligence of multi-agent and also can raise the resources utilization rate. We do the experiment and the results prove that the cooperative learning model of agent which is introduced in this chapter can not only improve the intelligence of multi-agent, but also increase the utilization rate of idle resources in CSCW.

8. References

Acharya,A.&Setia,S.(1998).UsingIdle Memory for Data-Intensive Computations, *Proceedings of the 1998 ACM SIGMETRICS Conference on Measurement and Modeling of Computer*

Systems, pp.278-279, ISBN :0163-5999,Madison, Wisconsin, USA, 1998.6, ACM New York, NY, USA.

Berenji,H.R.&Vengerov,D.(2000). Advantages of Cooperation Between Reinforcement Learning Agents in Difficult Stochastic Problems. *Proceedings of theNinth IEEE IntConf on Fuzzy System*, pp. 871-876, ISBN: 0-7803-5877-5, San Antonio, TX, 2000.5, IEEE press.

Chen, Q.K.&Na,L.C.(2006).Grid Cooperation Computational System for CSCW, *Proceedings of the 10th IEEE International Conference on Computer Supported Cooperative Work in Design (CSCWD2006)* , ISBN: 1-4244-0963-2, Nanjing, China,2006.5, IEEE Press, New York,USA.

Foster,I.&Kesselman,C.(1999).The Grid: Blueprint for a New Future Computing Infrastructure, Morgan Kaufmann Publishers, ISBN: 1558609334,San Francisco, USA.

Horiuchi,T.&Katai, O. (1999).Q-PSP learning: An exploitation-oriented Q-learning algorithm and its applications, Transactions of the Society of Instrument and Control Engineer, VOL.35, NO.5 (1999), pp.645-653, ISSN: 0453-4654.

Kaelbling, L.P.; Littman, M.L. &Moore, A.W.(1996). Reinforcement learning: A survey, Journal of Artificial Intelligence Research, Volume 4,pp.237-285, ISSN: 1076-9757.

Markatos,E.P.&Dramitions, G. (1996). Implementation of Reliable Remote Memory Pager, *Proceedings of the 1996 annual conference on USENIX Annual Technical Conference*, pp.177-190 , San Diego, CA, 1996.1, USENIX Association , Berkeley, CA, USA.

Osawa,E.(1993).A Scheme for Agent Collaboration in Open MultiAgentEnvironment *.Proceedings of the 13th international joint conference on Artificial intelligence - Volume 1*,pp.352-358, Chambéry, France,1993.8, Morgan Kaufmann Publishers Inc, San Francisco, CA, USA.

Rummery, G. Niranjan, M.(1994).On-line Q-learning using connectionist systems. Technical Report CUED/F-INFENG/TR 166, Cambridge University Engineering Department.

Raybourn, E.M.& Newman, J. (2002).WETICE 2002 Evaluating Collaborative Enterprises Workshop Report, *Proceeding of the Eleventh IEEE international Workshops on enabling technologies: Infrastructure for Collaborative Enterprises*, pp.11-17 , ISBN : 0-7695-1748-X, Pittsburgh, Pennsylvania, USA, 2002.6, IEEE Computer Society ,Washington, DC, USA.

Sutton,R.S. (1988).Learning to predict by the methods of temporal differences, Machine Learning, pp.9-44, ISSN: 0885-6125 (Print) 1573-0565 (Online).

Watkins, C.J.C.H. & Dayan, P.(1992).Q-learning, Machine Learning, pp.279-292, ISSN: 0885-6125 (Print) 1573-0565 (Online).

Wooldridge, M.(2002).An Introduction to MultiAgent Systems, John Wiley & Sons (Chichester, England). ISBN: 0 47149691X.

Zadeh,L.A. (1975).The concept of a linguistic variable and its application to approximate reason-ing, *Information Sciences*, Vol. 8, No. 3. (1975), pp. 199-249.

Zambonelli, F.; Jennings, N.R. &Wooldridge, M. (2000).Organizational abstractions for the analysis and design of multi-agent systems, *Proceedings of the1st International*

Workshop on Agent-Oriented Software Engineering, pp.127-141, ISBN: 3-540-41594-7, Limerick, Ireland, 2000, Springer-Verlag New York, Inc. Secaucus, NJ, USA.

Zambonelli, F.; Jennings, N.R.&Wooldridge,M.(2001).Organizational rules as an abstraction for the analysis and design of multi-agent systems. International Journal of Software Engineering and Knowledge Engineering, pp.303-328, ISSN: 0302-9743 (Print) 1611-3349 (Online)

3

A Reinforcement Learning Approach to Intelligent Goal Coordination of Two-Level Large-Scale Control Systems

Nasser Sadati[1,2] and Guy A. Dumont[1]
[1]*Electrical and Computer Engineering Department*
The University of British Columbia, Vancouver
[2]*Electrical Engineering Department, Sharif University of Technology,*
[1]*BC, Canada*
[2]*Iran*

1. Introduction

Two principles for coordination of large-scale systems, namely Interaction Prediction Principle and Interaction Balance Principle were postulated by Mesarovic et al. [1], [2] to provide guidance in synthesizing structures for multi-level or hierarchical control of large-scale systems and obtain the optimal solution. Hierarchical structures are feasible structures which reduce the complexity of large-scale control systems and improve the solution through decomposition, coordination and parallel processing [3]-[6]. In two-level hierarchical approaches, the overall system is first decomposed into several interactive sub-systems, at the first level, where the optimization problem is redefined for each one of them. The interactions between these sub-systems, at the first level, and the coordinator, at the second level, called the coordination parameters, are used so that the overall solution is obtained. In compare to centralized approaches, where the whole problem is considered for the solution at once, the computational efforts in hierarchical approaches are based on sub-problems, having smaller order, requiring less computational time, in addition to the coordination strategy.

The Goal Coordination based on Interaction Balance Principle approach of Mesarovic et al. has already been applied to large-scale systems and the results are reported in [3]- [5]. In applying the Interaction Balance Principle, the supremal controller modifies the infimal (i.e. first-level) performance functions, compares the interface inputs (interactions) demanded by the infimal controllers and those which actually occur, then provides new performance modifications whenever the error is observed as being outside the acceptable bounds. A brief description of the Goal Coordination and Interaction Balance Principle is presented in the following section. Although a more detailed discussion of this principle can be found in [1] ,[2] and also, voluminous literature on large-scale systems theories and applications including survey articles, textbooks and monographs can be found in [6]-[12].

Based on Interaction Balance Principle, a new goal coordination scheme, as a foundation for intelligent coordination of large-scale systems is postulated in this chapter. The approach is formulated in an intelligent manner such that it provides the update of the coordination parameters so to reduce the coordination errors directly and improve the convergence rate of the solution. The proposed scheme is a neuro-fuzzy based reinforcement learning approach which can be used to synthesize a new supervisory coordination strategy for the overall two-level large-scale systems, in which the sub-systems, at the first level of hierarchy, and also the overall process control objectives are considered as optimization problems. So with the aim of optimization, the control problem is first decomposed into m sub-problems at the first level, where each sub-problem can be solved using a neuro-regulator. The neural networks which are capable of learning and reconstructing non-linear mappings could also be used for modeling each corresponding sub-system. By using the new methodology which is based on a Fuzzy Goal Coordination System and Reinforcement Learning; using TSK model, a critic vector and the gradient of the interaction errors (difference between the actual interactions and the optimum calculated interaction values) and also their rate of changes, appropriate change of coordination parameters are generated at the second level and the coordination of the overall large-scale system is done. The proposed scheme results in faster reduction of the interaction errors, which finally vanish to zero.

This chapter is organized into several sections. In Section 2, the problem formulation and control problems are defined. Also a brief review of the classical Goal Coordination and Interaction Balance Principle is presented. In Section 3, decomposition of the overall large-scale system into m sub-problems and modelling each corresponding subsystem is done. In Section 4, the first level sub-problems are solved with neuro-regulators, and in Section 5, the new Fuzzy Goal Coordination System based Reinforcement Learning is presented to generate the appropriate change of coordination parameters. In Section 6, the efficacy and advantages of the proposed approach is demonstrated in an open-loop power system consisting of a synchronous machine connected to an infinite bus bar through a transformer and a transmission line. It is shown how the convergence of the interaction errors exceeds substantially those obtained using the classical goal coordination method. Finally, Section 7 contains some concluding remarks.

2. Statement of the problem

As it was mentioned in the Introduction, two cases arise as how the coordination might be effected and the infimal control problems can be defined. In this chapter, a new approach for coordination of large-scale systems based on Interaction Balance Principle, which is more convergent than the previously suggested classical methods, has been presented.

2.1 Goal coordination and Interaction Balance Principle

Let $\boldsymbol{B}$ be a given set such that each β in **B** specifies, for each $i=1,\ldots, m$, a performance function $G_{i\beta}:\boldsymbol{U}_i \times \boldsymbol{Z}_i \times \boldsymbol{X}_i \rightarrow \mathbf{V}$ which is a modification of the original G_i. Let the mapping $g_{i\beta}$ be defined on $\boldsymbol{U}_i \times \boldsymbol{Z}_i$ in terms of P_i and G_{iB}. For each β in $\boldsymbol{B}$, the infimal control problems is to find a pair $(\hat{U}_i, \hat{Z}_{pi})$ in $\boldsymbol{U}_i \times \boldsymbol{Z}_i$ such that

$$g_{i\beta}(\hat{U}_i, \hat{Z}_{pi}) = \min_{\boldsymbol{U}_i \times \boldsymbol{Z}_i} g_{i\beta}(U_i, Z_i), \tag{1}$$

where minimization is over both sets $\boldsymbol{U}_i$ and $\boldsymbol{Z}_i$; the interface inputs are treated as free variables. Let β in $\boldsymbol{B}$ be given; let $\hat{Z}_1(\beta), \ldots, \hat{Z}_m(\beta)$ be the interface inputs required by the infimal controllers to achieve local optimum; let $Z_1(\beta),\ldots, Z_m(\beta)$ be the interface inputs that occur if the control $\hat{U}(\beta)=[\hat{U}_1(\beta),\ldots,\hat{U}_m(\beta)]$ is implemented, then the overall optimum is achieved if the actual interface inputs are precisely those required by local optimization

$$\hat{Z}_i(\beta)=Z_i(\beta) \tag{2}$$

for each $i = 1, \ldots, m$ (Interaction Balance Principle). If the Interaction Balance principle applies, the supremal control problem is to find β in B such that $e_i=\hat{Z}_i(B)-Z_i(B)=0$, for each $i = 1, \ldots, m$. The application of the Interaction Balance Principle is shown in Fig. 1.

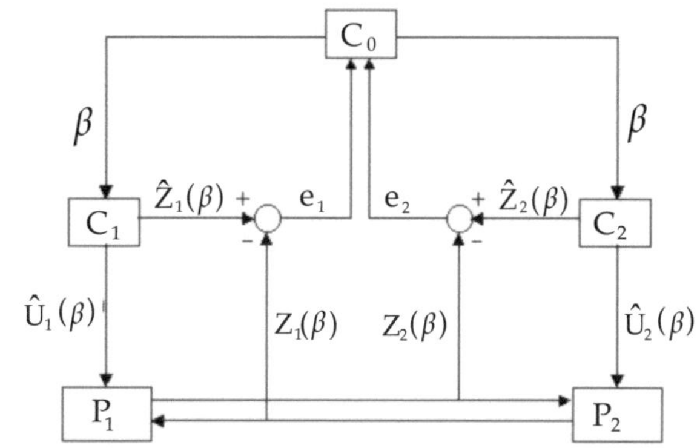

Fig. 1. Application of Interaction Balance Principle for coordination of two sub-problems.

Now, let us suppose that we have a general non-linear dynamic system described by the following state space equation

$$\underline{X}[k+1]=F\left(\underline{X}[k],\underline{U}[k]\right) \tag{3a}$$

$$\underline{X}[0]=\underline{X}_o \tag{3b}$$

where $\underline{X}$ is the state vector, $\underline{U}$ is the control vector and F is a continuously double differentiable analytical vector function which is going to be replaced by 2m neural models to describe the actual dynamics of m sub-systems and their interactions. The initial state $\underline{X}_o$ is also assumed to be known.
Now, the problem is to find $\underline{U}$ which minimizes the cost function given by

$$J=G_{n+1}\left(\underline{X}[n+1]\right)+\sum_{k=0}^{n}G_k\left(\underline{X}[k],\underline{U}[k]\right) \tag{4}$$

where G_k is in general, a scalar non-linear function of its arguments.

3. Decomposition of the overall problem into m sub-problems

Let us assume that the overall system comprises of m interconnected sub-systems. We assume that the sub-systems themselves can be described by non-linear state space equations of the following form

$$X_i[k+1] = F_i(X_i[k], U_i[k], Z_i[k]) \tag{5a}$$

$$X_i[0] = X_{i0} \tag{5b}$$

where X_i is the state, U_i is the control and Z_i is the interaction input of the ith sub-system that is assumed to be a non-linear function of the states of the m sub-systems

$$Z_i[k] = H_i(\underline{X}[k]) = H_i(X_1[k], \ldots, X_m[k]) \tag{6}$$

In Goal Coordination method, it is necessary for non-linear functions H_i to be separable. So the interaction variables Z_i must be defined in such a way that H_i functions to be separable, i.e.

$$Z_i[k] = H_i(X_1[k], \ldots, X_m[k]) = \sum_{j=1}^{m} H_{ij}(X_j[k]) \tag{7}$$

The interaction relations which can be expressed as $Z[k] = H(\underline{X}[k])$ are considered to be the optimization constraints. So the Lagrangian can be defined as

$$L = G_{n+1}\left(\underline{X}[n+1]\right) + \sum_{k=0}^{n} G_k\left(\underline{X}[k], \underline{U}[k]\right) + \sum_{k=0}^{n+1} \beta[k]^T \left(\underline{Z}[k] - H(\underline{X}[k])\right) \tag{8}$$

where $\beta[k]$'s are the Lagrange multipliers that we refer to them as the coordination parameters. Now, since the interaction function $H(\underline{X}[k])$ is separable, the Lagrangian can be decomposed as

$$L = \sum_{i=1}^{m} L_i \tag{9a}$$

where

$$L_i = G_{i_{n+1}}\left(X_i[n+1], Z_i[n+1]\right) + \sum_{k=0}^{n} G_{ik}(X_i[k], U_i[k], Z_i[k]) + \sum_{k=0}^{n+1}\left(\beta_i[k] Z_i[k] - \sum_{j=1}^{m} \beta_j[k] H_{ji}(X_i[k])\right) \tag{9b}$$

So the overall problem can be decomposed into m first level sub-problems of the following form

$$\begin{aligned} \min_{X_i, U_i, Z_i} \ L_i = {} & G_{i_{n+1}}\left(X_i[n+1], Z_i[n+1]\right) + \sum_{k=0}^{n} G_{ik}(X_i[k], U_i[k], Z_i[k]) \\ & + \sum_{k=0}^{n+1}\left(\beta_i[k] Z_i[k] - \sum_{j=1}^{m} \beta_j[k] H_{ji}(X_i[k])\right) \end{aligned} \tag{9b}$$

$$s.t. \quad X_i[k+1] = F_i(X_i[k], U_i[k], Z_i[k])$$

$$X_i[0] = X_{i0} \tag{10}$$

and also one second level problem expressed as:

Updating the coordination parameters $\beta_i[k]$ such that the interaction errors; $Z_i[k] - H_i\,(X_i[k]\,, \ldots, X_m[k])$, become zero (Interaction Balance Principle).
Remark. In general, H(.) can be considered as a function of X[k] and U[k].

3.1 Modeling the corresponding sub-systems with neural networks

It should be noted that the dynamics of each sub-system and its interactions which are denoted by F_i and H_{ij}, respectively, could also be replaced by neural network models. So in this case, they can be denoted by NF_i and NH_{ij}, respectively.

$$X_i[k+1] = F_i(X_i[k], U_i[k], Z_i[k]) \underline{\underline{\Delta}}\; NF_i(X_i[k], U_i[k], Z_i[k]) \tag{11}$$

$$Z_i[k] = H_i(\underline{X}[k]) \underline{\underline{\Delta}}\; NH_i(X_1[k], \ldots, X_m[k]) = \sum_{j=1}^{m} NH_{ij}(X_j[k]) \tag{12}$$

The first step in identification of the sub-systems is to provide the training data using the actual system. To generate the training data, random inputs are applied to the actual system and the resulting state values, in addition to the input data are used for training the neural models.

4. Optimizing the first level sub-problems with neuro-regulators

In this approach, the first level sub-problems could be optimized with neuro-regulators [13]. The optimal control and interaction of each sub-system will be generated by non-linear feedback functions of the following forms

$$U_i[k] = NR_{Ui}(X_i[k], W_{Ui})\,;\;\; k = 0, 1, \ldots, n \tag{13}$$

$$Z_i[k] = NR_{Zi}(X[k], W_{Zi})\,;\;\; k = 0, 1, \ldots, n+1 \tag{14}$$

where NR_{Ui} and NR_{Zi} could be considered as multilayer perceptron (MLP) neural networks, and W_{Ui} and W_{Zi} are their parameters including weights and biases, respectively.
Now, the new Lagrangian L_i can be defined as follows

$$\begin{aligned}
L_i = {} & G_{i_{n+1}}(X_i[n+1], Z_i[n+1]) + \sum_{k=0}^{n} G_{ik}(X_i[k], U_i[k], Z_i[k]) \\
& + \sum_{k=0}^{n+1}\left(\beta_i[k]Z_i[k] - \sum_{j=1}^{m}\beta_j[k]H_{ji}(X_i[k])\right) \\
& + \sum_{k=0}^{n}\lambda_i[k](X_i[k+1] - F_i(X_i[k], U_i[k], Z_i[k])) \\
& + \sum_{k=0}^{n}\mu_{Ui}[k](U_i[k] - NR_{Ui}(X_i[k]; W_{Ui})) \\
& + \sum_{k=0}^{n+1}\mu_{Zi}[k](Z_i[k] - NR_{Zi}(X_i[k]; W_{Zi}))
\end{aligned} \tag{15}$$

where $\lambda_i[k]$, $\mu_{Ui}[k]$ and $\mu_{Zi}[k]$ are the Lagrange multipliers.

Thus, the necessary conditions for optimality become

$$\frac{\partial L_i}{\partial U_i[k]} = \frac{\partial G_{ik}}{\partial U_i[k]} - \frac{\partial F_{ik}}{\partial U_i[k]}\lambda_i[k] + \mu_{Ui}[k] = 0\,; \quad k = 0,1,\ldots,n \tag{16}$$

$$\frac{\partial L_i}{\partial Z_i[n+1]} = \frac{\partial G_{i_{n+1}}}{\partial Z_i[n+1]} + \mu_{Zi}[n+1] = 0 \tag{17}$$

$$\frac{\partial L_i}{\partial Z_i[k]} = \frac{\partial G_{ik}}{\partial Z_i[k]} - \frac{\partial F_{ik}}{\partial Z_i[k]}\lambda_i[k] + \mu_{Zi}[k] = 0\,; \quad k = 0,1,\ldots,n \tag{18}$$

$$\frac{\partial L_i}{\partial X_i[n+1]} = \frac{\partial G_{i_{n+1}}}{\partial X_i[n+1]} + \lambda_i[n] - \frac{\partial NR_{Zn+1}}{\partial X_i[n+1]}\mu_{Zi}[n+1] = 0 \tag{19}$$

$$\frac{\partial L_i}{\partial X_i[k]} = \frac{\partial G_{ik}}{\partial X_i[k]} + \lambda_i[k-1] - \frac{\partial F_{ik}}{\partial X_i[k]}\lambda_i[k] - \frac{\partial NR_{Uk}}{\partial X_i[k]}\mu_{Ui}[k] - \frac{\partial NR_{Zk}}{\partial X_i[k]}\mu_{Zi}[k] = 0\,; \quad k = 1,2,\ldots,n \tag{20}$$

where

$$G_{ik} = G_i(X_i[k], U_i[k], Z_{pi}[k]) \tag{21}$$

$$F_{ik} = F_i(X_i[k], U_i[k], Z_{pi}[k]) \tag{22}$$

$$NR_{Uk} = NR_{Uk}(X_i[k]; W_{Ui}) \tag{23}$$

$$NR_{Zk} = NR_{Zk}(X_i[k]; W_{Zi}) \tag{24}$$

Now to train the neuro-regulators; NR_{Ui} and NR_{Zi}, based on preceding optimality conditions, the following algorithm can be suggested

1. Choose initial small values for neuro-regulator parameters, namely W_{Ui} and W_{Zi}.
2. Using initial state X_{i0} and equations (3), (13) and (14), find the values of $X_i[1], X_i[2], \ldots, X_i[n+1]$, $U_i[0], U_i[2], \ldots, U_i[n]$, and $Z_i[0], \ldots, Z_i[n+1]$.
3. Calculate $\lambda_i[k]$, $\mu_{Ui}[k]$, $\mu_{Zi}[k]$ for $k = n, n-1, \ldots, 0$, by using the following necessary conditions, backward in time;

$$\mu_{Zi}[n+1] = -\frac{\partial G_{i_{n+1}}}{\partial Z_i[n+1]} \tag{25}$$

$$\lambda_i[n] = -\frac{\partial G_{i_{n+1}}}{\partial X_i[n+1]} + \frac{\partial NR_{Zn+1}}{\partial X_i[n+1]}\mu_{Zi}[n+1] \tag{26}$$

$$\mu_{Ui}[k] = \frac{\partial F_{ik}}{\partial U_i[k]}\lambda_i[k] - \frac{\partial G_{ik}}{\partial U_i[k]}\,; \quad k = n, n-1, \ldots, 0 \tag{27}$$

$$\mu_{Zi}[k] = \frac{\partial F_{ik}}{\partial Z_i[k]} \lambda_i[k] - \frac{\partial G_{ik}}{\partial Z_i[k]} ; \quad k = n, n-1, \ldots, 0 \tag{28}$$

$$\lambda_i[k-1] = \frac{\partial F_{ik}}{\partial X_i[k]} \lambda_i[k] + \frac{\partial NR_{Uk}}{\partial X_i[k]} \mu_{Ui}[k] + \frac{\partial NR_{Zk}}{\partial X_i[k]} \mu_{Zi}[k] - \frac{\partial G_{ik}}{\partial X_i[k]} ; \; k = n, n-1, \ldots, 1 \tag{29}$$

4. Calculate $\frac{\partial L_i}{\partial W_{Ui}}$ and $\frac{\partial L_i}{\partial W_{Zi}}$ for $k = n, n-1, \ldots, 0$, using $\mu_{Ui}[k]$ and $\mu_{Zi}[k]$

$$\frac{\partial L_i}{\partial W_{Ui}} = \sum_{k=0}^{n} \frac{\partial NR_{Uk}}{\partial W_{Ui}} \mu_{Ui}[k] \tag{30}$$

$$\frac{\partial L_i}{\partial W_{Zi}} = \sum_{k=0}^{n} \frac{\partial NR_{Zk}}{\partial W_{Zi}} \mu_{Zi}[k] \tag{31}$$

5. Update W_{Ui} and W_{Zi}, by adding $\Delta W_{Ui} = -\eta_U \frac{\partial L_i}{\partial W_{Ui}}$ and $\Delta W_{Zi} = -\eta_Z \frac{\partial L_i}{\partial W_{Zi}}$ to the prior values of W_{Ui} and W_{Zi}.
6. If $\left\| \frac{\partial L_i}{\partial W_{Ui}} + \frac{\partial L_i}{\partial W_{Zi}} \right\| < \varepsilon$ stop the algorithm, else go to step (2).

Remark. We should indicate that, in case the use of neural networks and neuro-regulators are not of interest, then the modelling and optimization process at the first level, can be easily done using the same approach as explained in Ref. [14]-[16].

5. Reinforcement Learning

To evaluate the operation of the fuzzy goal coordination system, with the use of reinforcement learning, we define a critic vector [17] and develop a method to train the new coordination strategy. The training is based on minimizing the energy of the critic vector. In this approach, we use both the errors and the rate of errors to increase the speed of convergence of the coordination algorithm.

5.1 Designing the critic vector

The critic vector includes m critic signals, where each of them evaluates the operation of the corresponding sub-system. The value of each critic signal is in the range of [-1 , 1] and is expressed by a fuzzy system of the following form

$$r_i[k] = \tilde{R}_i(e_i[k], d_i[k]) ; \quad i = 1, 2, \ldots, m \tag{32}$$

where $\tilde{R}_i$ is the fuzzy system, $e_i[k]$ is the interaction error and $d_i[k]$ is the rate of error, defined by

$$e_i[k] = Z_i[k] - Z_i^*[k] \tag{33a}$$

$$d_i[k] \triangleq d_i[k]^{(l)} = e_i[k]^{(l)} - e_i[k]^{(l-1)} \tag{33b}$$

also l is the iteration index.

The fuzzy system $\tilde{R}_i$ can now be defined by the fuzzy sets and rules as follows;

$$\underline{r = \tilde{R}(e,d)}$$

$$\begin{array}{l} \text{if } e \text{ is } \tilde{E}_1 \text{ and } d \text{ is } \tilde{D}_1 \text{ then } r = R_1 \\ \quad\vdots \\ \text{if } e \text{ is } \tilde{E}_M \text{ and } d \text{ is } \tilde{D}_M \text{ then } r = R_M \end{array} \tag{34}$$

where R_j is a real value in the range of

$$-1 \le R_j \le 1 \ ; \ j = 1,2,\dots,M \tag{35}$$

The relation of r with e and d can also be given by the following fuzzy inference system

$$r = \tilde{R}(e,d) = \frac{\sum_{j=1}^{M} \mu E_j(e) \cdot \mu D_j(d) R_j}{\sum_{j=1}^{M} \mu E_j(e) \cdot \mu D_j(d)} \tag{36}$$

where μE_j and μD_j are the membership functions of E_j and D_j, respectively.

5.2 Updating the coordination parameters

To update the coordination parameters, we use a fuzzy system that calculates the variation of the coordination parameters as follows

$$\Delta \underline{\beta}[k] = S(\underline{e}[k], \underline{d}[k]) \tag{37}$$

where S is a fuzzy system based on Takagi-Sugeno-Kang (TSK) model [18], [19] and in this case, is defined by the fuzzy sets and rules as follows;

$$\underline{\underline{s} = S(\underline{e},\underline{d})}$$

$$\begin{array}{l} \text{if } \underline{e} \text{ is } A_1 \text{ and } \underline{d} \text{ is } B_1 \text{ then } \underline{s} = a_1 \underline{e} + b_1 \underline{d} + c_1 \underline{v} \\ \quad\vdots \\ \text{if } \underline{e} \text{ is } A_N \text{ and } \underline{d} \text{ is } B_N \text{ then } \underline{s} = a_N \underline{e} + b_N \underline{d} + c_N \underline{v} \end{array} \tag{38}$$

where

$$\underline{v} = [\ \overbrace{1\,1\,....\,1}^{m}\ ]^T . \tag{39}$$

Also A_j and B_j are the m dimensional fuzzy sets, expressed as

$$A_j = A_{j1} \times A_{j2} \times ... \times A_{jm} \tag{40}$$

$$B_j = B_{j1} \times B_{j2} \times ... \times B_{jm} \tag{41}$$

where their membership functions are given by

$$\mu A_j(\underline{e}) = \mu A_{j1}(e_1) \cdot \mu A_{j2}(e_2) \cdot \cdots \cdot \mu A_{jm}(e_m) \tag{42}$$

$$\mu B_j(\underline{d}) = \mu B_{j1}(d_1) \cdot \mu B_{j2}(d_2) \cdot \cdots \cdot \mu B_{jm}(d_m) \tag{43}$$

also

$$\underline{e} = [e_1, e_2, ..., e_m]^T \tag{44}$$

$$\underline{d} = [d_1, d_2, ..., d_m]^T , \tag{45}$$

where μA_{jk} and μB_{jk} are the membership functions of A_{jk} and B_{jk}, respectively. Moreover, a_j , b_j and c_j are real constant parameters.
To summarize, the relation of $\underline{s}$ with $\underline{e}$ and $\underline{d}$ is given by the following fuzzy inference system;

$$\underline{s} = S(\underline{e}, \underline{d}) = \frac{\sum_{j=1}^{N} \mu A_j(\underline{e}) \cdot \mu B_j(\underline{d}).\ (a_j \underline{e} + b_j \underline{d} + c_j \underline{v})}{\sum_{j=1}^{N} \mu A_j(\underline{e}) \cdot \mu B_j(\underline{d})} \tag{46}$$

5.3 Training the fuzzy goal coordination system

The aim of training is to minimize the energy of the critic vector related to the system parameters; a_j , b_j and c_j , where

$$E = \frac{1}{2} \sum_{k=0}^{n+1} \underline{r}[k]^T \underline{r}[k] \tag{47}$$

also

$$\underline{r}[k] = [\ r_1[k], r_2[k], ..., r_m[k]\ ]^T \tag{48}$$

Now to update the fuzzy system parameters, we use the following updating rule

$$\Delta W = -\eta \frac{\partial E}{\partial W} = -\eta \sum_{k=0}^{n+1} \frac{\partial \underline{r}[k]}{\partial W}^{T} . \underline{r}[k] \tag{49}$$

where η is the training rate coefficient, and W can be considered as each of the fuzzy system parameters, given by

$$W = a_j, b_j, c_j \quad ; \quad j = 1,2,\ldots,N \tag{50}$$

Now, using the chain rule, we can write

$$\frac{\partial \underline{r}[k]}{\partial W} = \frac{\partial \underline{r}[k]}{\partial \underline{e}[k]} \cdot \frac{\partial \underline{e}[k]}{\partial W} + \frac{\partial \underline{r}[k]}{\partial \underline{d}[k]} \cdot \frac{\partial \underline{d}[k]}{\partial W} \tag{51}$$

So to calculate the right side of this equation, we need to calculate $\frac{\partial \underline{r}[k]}{\partial \underline{e}[k]}, \frac{\partial \underline{e}[k]}{\partial W}, \frac{\partial \underline{r}[k]}{\partial \underline{d}[k]}$ and $\frac{\partial \underline{d}[k]}{\partial W}$, where

$$r_i[k] = \tilde{R}(e_i[k], d_i[k]) = \frac{\sum_{j=1}^{M} \mu E_j(e_i[k]).\mu D_j(d_i[k]) R_j}{\sum_{j=1}^{M} \mu E_j(e_i[k]).\mu D_j(d_i[k])} \triangleq \frac{NUM_i}{DEN_i} . \tag{52}$$

Hence, we have

$$\frac{\partial\, r_i[k]}{\partial\, e_i[k]} = \frac{\sum_{j=1}^{M} \mu E_j'(e_i[k]).\mu D_j(d_i[k]) R_j}{DEN_i} - \frac{NUM_i \sum_{j=1}^{M} \mu E_j'(e_i[k]) \mu D_j(d_i[k])}{DEN_i^2} \tag{53}$$

and

$$\frac{\partial\, r_i[k]}{\partial\, d_i[k]} = \frac{\sum_{j=1}^{M} \mu E_j(e_i[k]) \mu D_j'(d_i[k]) R_j}{DEN_i} - \frac{NUM_i \sum_{j=1}^{M} \mu E_j(e_i[k]).\mu D_j'(d_i[k])}{DEN_i^2} \tag{54}$$

where $\mu E_j'(.)$ and $\mu D_j'(.)$ denote the derivatives of the corresponding membership functions, respectively. Therefore

$$\frac{\partial \underline{r}[k]}{\partial \underline{e}[k]} = \begin{bmatrix} \frac{\partial r_1[k]}{\partial e_1[k]} & & & 0 \\ & \frac{\partial r_2[k]}{\partial e_2[k]} & & \\ & & \ddots & \\ 0 & & & \frac{\partial r_m[k]}{\partial e_m[k]} \end{bmatrix} \tag{55}$$

and

$$\frac{\partial \underline{r}[k]}{\partial \underline{d}[k]} = \begin{bmatrix} \frac{\partial r_1[k]}{\partial d_1[k]} & & & 0 \\ & \frac{\partial r_2[k]}{\partial d_2[k]} & & \\ & & \ddots & \\ 0 & & & \frac{\partial r_m[k]}{\partial d_m[k]} \end{bmatrix} \tag{56}$$

The gradient of the interaction errors related to the system parameters is also given by

$$\frac{\partial \underline{e}[k]}{\partial W} = \frac{\partial \underline{e}[k]}{\partial \underline{\beta}[k]} \cdot \frac{\partial \underline{\beta}[k]}{\partial W} = D[k] \frac{\partial \Delta \underline{\beta}[k]}{\partial W} \underline{\underline{\Delta}} \, T[k] \tag{57}$$

where $D[k] \triangleq \frac{\partial \underline{e}[k]}{\partial \underline{\beta}[k]}$, as given in Appendix.

Now in order to calculate $\frac{\partial \Delta \underline{\beta}[k]}{\partial W}$, since we have

$$\Delta \underline{\beta}[k] = S(\underline{e}[k], \underline{d}[k]) \underline{\underline{\Delta}} \frac{NUM}{DEN} = \frac{\sum_{j=1}^{N} \mu A_j(\underline{e}[k]) \mu B_j(\underline{d}[k])(a_j \underline{e}[k] + b_j \underline{d}[k] + c_j \underline{v})}{\sum_{j=1}^{N} \mu A_j(\underline{e}[k]) \mu B_j(\underline{d}[k])} \tag{58}$$

Thus we get

$$\frac{\partial \Delta \underline{\beta}[k]}{\partial a_j} = \frac{\mu A_j(\underline{e}[k]).\mu B_j(\underline{d}[k]) \underline{e}[k]}{DEN} \tag{59}$$

$$\frac{\partial \Delta \underline{\beta}[k]}{\partial b_j} = \frac{\mu A_j(\underline{e}[k]).\mu B_j(\underline{d}[k]) \underline{d}[k]}{DEN} \tag{60}$$

$$\frac{\partial \Delta \underline{\beta}[k]}{\partial c_j} = \frac{\mu A_j(\underline{e}[k]).\mu B_j(\underline{d}[k]) \underline{v}}{DEN} , \tag{61}$$

where $\underline{e}[k]$ and $\underline{d}[k]$ are the values in the previous iteration i.e., $\underline{e}[k]^{(l-1)}$ and $\underline{d}[k]^{(l-1)}$.

Now to calculate $\frac{\partial \underline{d}[k]}{\partial W}$, since we have

$$\underline{d}[k]^{(l)} = \underline{e}[k]^{(l)} - \underline{e}[k]^{(l-1)} , \tag{62a}$$

according to the definition of $T[k]$, we get

$$\frac{\partial \underline{d}[k]}{\partial W} = T[k]^{(l)} - T[k]^{(l-1)} \tag{62b}$$

So we can calculate $\frac{\partial E}{\partial W}$.

The fuzzy system parameters can now be updated using the following updating rule

$$\Delta W = -\eta \frac{\partial E}{\partial W} = -\eta \sum_{k=0}^{n+1} \frac{\partial \underline{r}[k]}{\partial W}^{T} \underline{r}[k] \tag{63a}$$

where

$$W = a_j, b_j, c_j \quad ; \quad j = 1,2,\ldots,N. \tag{63b}$$

Now, considering W as the fuzzy system parameters, we can update the coordination parameters with the following rule

$$\Delta\underline{\beta}[k] = S(\underline{e}[k], \underline{d}[k]; W) \tag{64}$$

where W is the updated value, given by

$$W^{(l+1)} = W^{(l)} + \Delta W^{(l+1)} \tag{65}$$

Thus, we can write

$$\begin{aligned}\underline{\beta}[k]^{(l+1)} &= \underline{\beta}[k]^{(l)} + \Delta\underline{\beta}[k]^{(l+1)} \\ &= \underline{\beta}[k]^{(l)} + S(\underline{e}[k]^{(l)}, \underline{d}[k]^{(l)}; W^{(l+1)})\end{aligned} \tag{66}$$

The various steps of the new coordination algorithm based on Interaction Balance Principle using Fuzzy Goal Coordination System based Reinforcement Learning, can now be summarized as follows:

1. Choose initial values for $\underline{\beta}$ and W.
2. Solve the first level sub-problems using neuro-regulators (or the gradient technique, as described in [14], [15]).
3. Calculate the gradient matrices $\frac{\partial \underline{e}}{\partial \underline{\beta}}$ and $D[k]$. Then update W and consequently update the coordination parameters $\underline{\beta}$, using the Fuzzy Goal Coordination System.
4. Calculate the sum-squared error. If it is smaller than a small constant stop the algorithm, else go to step (2).

The new goal coordination strategy based on Fuzzy Goal Coordination System, Neural Modeling, Neuro-Regulators and Reinforcement Learning is shown in Fig. 2.

6. Simulation results

The application of this approach is demonstrated on an open-loop power system, consisting of a synchronous machine connected to an infinite bus bar through a transformer and a transmission line. For this system, Iyer and Cory [20], [4] have derived a sixth order non-linear dynamical model. The optimization problem is to minimize a cost function of the following form

$$J = \frac{T}{2}\sum_{k=0}^{K_f-1}\left[\left\|(\underline{X}[k]-\underline{X}_f)\right\|_Q^2 + \left\|(\underline{U}[k]-\underline{U}_f)\right\|_R^2\right] \tag{67}$$

where Q and R are the weighting matrices, with appropriate dimensions and definiteness. Now, the system can be decomposed into two sub-systems of orders 4 and 2, respectively, using the following sate vectors

$$\underline{X}_1[k] = [X_1[k] \quad X_2[k] \quad X_3[k] \quad X_4[k]]^T \tag{68}$$

$$\underline{X}_2[k] = [X_5[k] \quad X_6[k]]^T, \tag{69}$$

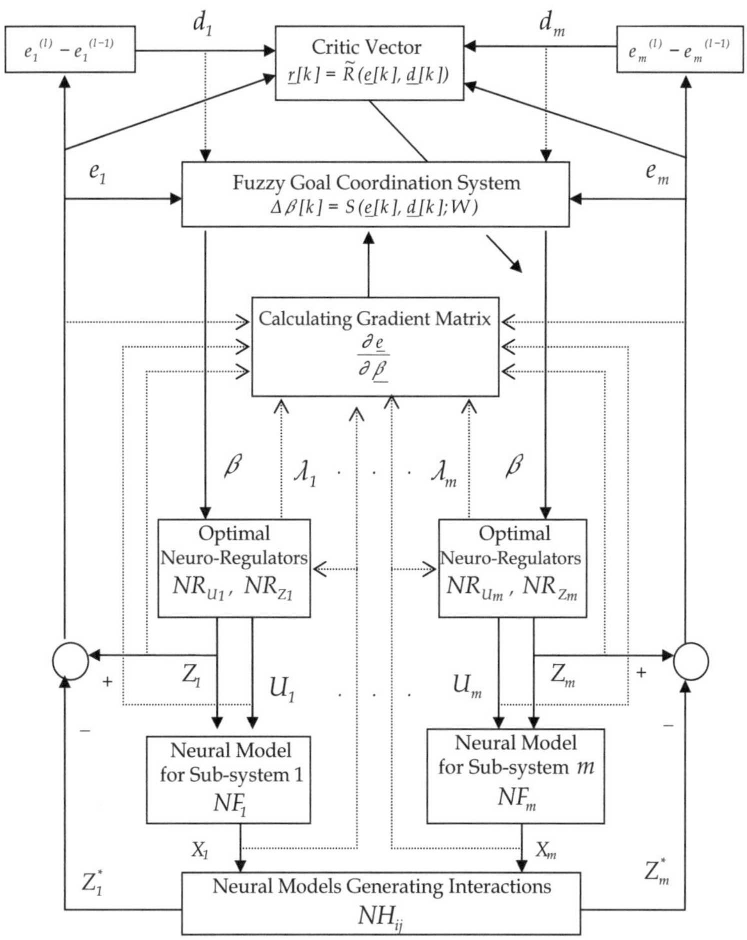

Fig. 2. Intelligent goal coordination strategy based on fuzzy goal coordination system and reinforcement learning.

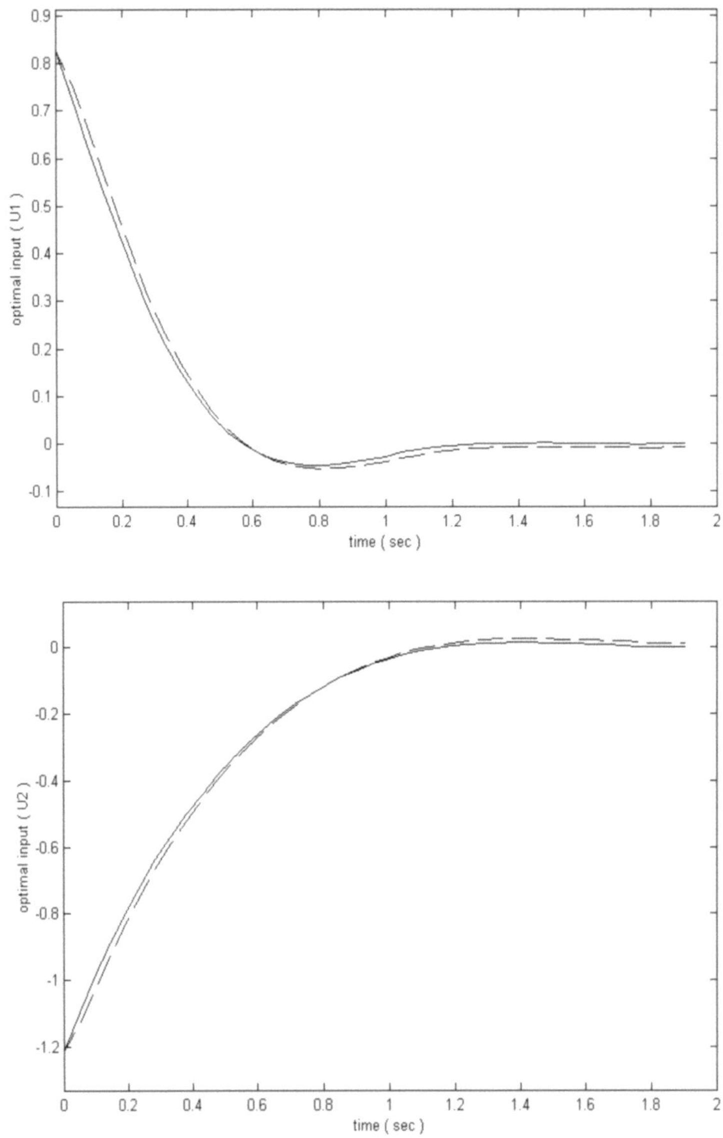

Fig. 3. Optimal control actions of sub-systems 1 and 2. Solid: The new goal coordination approach; Dot: classical method.

and four neural networks, as represented below, to model these two sub-systems and their interaction generators

$$\underline{X}_1[k+1] \underline{\underline{\Delta}} NF_1(\underline{X}_1[k], U_1[k], \underline{Z}_1[k], W_{F_1}) \tag{70}$$

$$\underline{X}_2[k+1] \underline{\underline{\Delta}} NF_2(\underline{X}_2[k], U_2[k], \underline{Z}_2[k], W_{F_2}) \tag{71}$$

$$\underline{Z}_1[k] \underline{\underline{\Delta}} NH_1(\underline{X}_1[k], \underline{X}_2[k], W_{H_1}) \tag{72}$$

$$\underline{Z}_2[k] \underline{\underline{\Delta}} NH_2(\underline{X}_1[k], \underline{X}_2[k], W_{H_2}) \tag{73}$$

In this example, for describing the fuzzy system $\tilde{R}_i$ defined in (34) and also the Fuzzy Goal Coordination System defined in (38), triangular membership functions are used for fuzzy sets E_j and D_j, and also Gaussian membership functions are used for fuzzy sets A_j and B_j, respectively.

The resulting optimum control actions, state trajectories and the plot of the norm of the interaction errors, using the proposed approach and the classical goal coordination method are all shown in Figs. 3-5.

The results of using the goal coordination approach based on the proposed intelligent coordination strategy shows that the interaction errors vanish rapidly. The advantage of this method is its faster convergence rate in compare to the classical method. This is mainly because of using the new strategy which the update of the coordination parameters directly causes the reduction of the coordination error with the fuzzy goal coordination system based reinforcement learning.

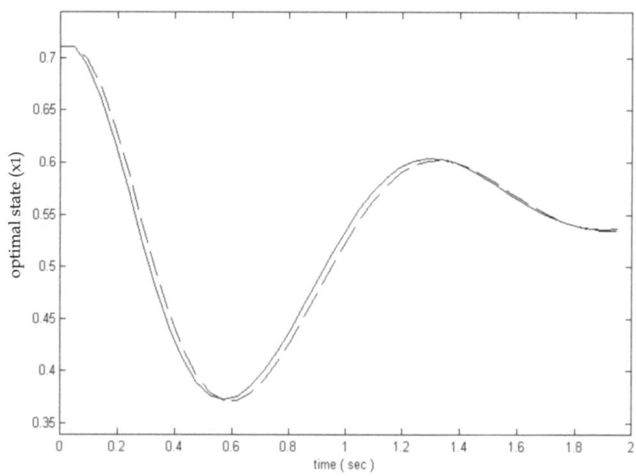

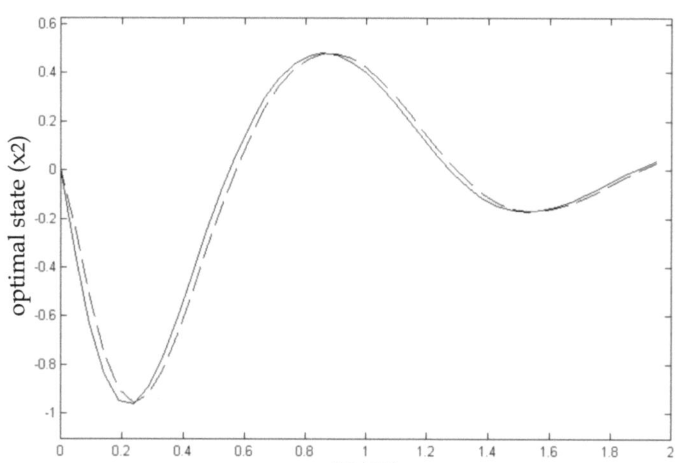

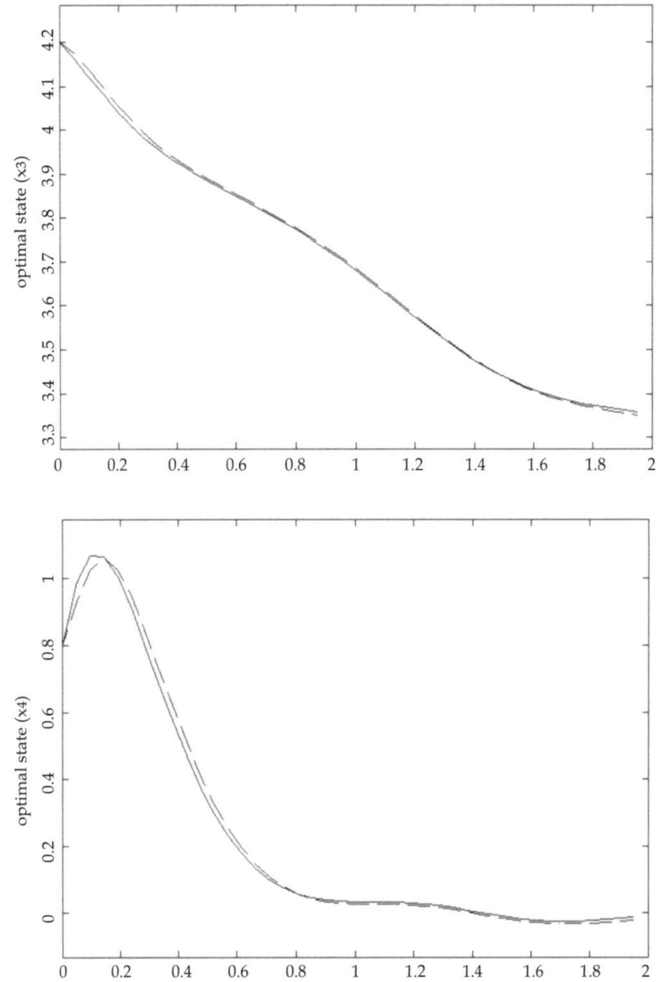

Fig. 4. Optimal state trajectories of sub-system 1. Solid: The new goal coordination approach; Dot: classical method.

7. Conclusion

In this chapter, a new intelligent approach for goal coordination of two-level large-scale control systems is presented. At the first level, sub-systems are modelled using neural networks, while the corresponding sub-problems are solved using neuro-regulators. Fuzzy Goal Coordination System based Reinforcement Learning is also used at the second level, to coordinate the overall large-scale control system. The fuzzy goal coordination system learns its dynamics through minimization of an energy function defined by a critic vector. The minimization process is done using the gradient of interaction errors, while in addition, both the critic vector and fuzzy goal coordination system use the variation of errors (rate of errors) to update their parameters.

As it can be seen, the proposed goal coordination approach, in compare to the classical one, results in much faster reduction of the interaction prediction errors.

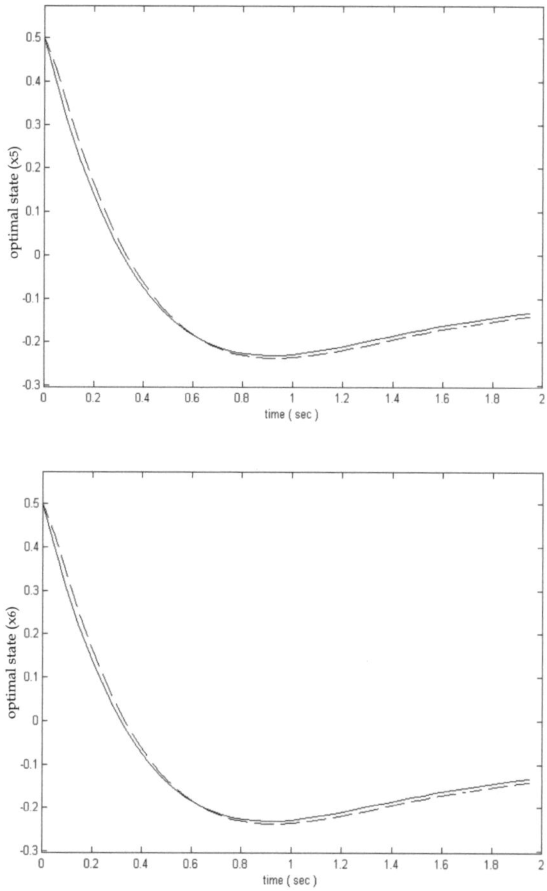

Fig. 5. Optimal state trajectories of sub-system 2. Solid: The new goal coordination approach; Dot: classical method.

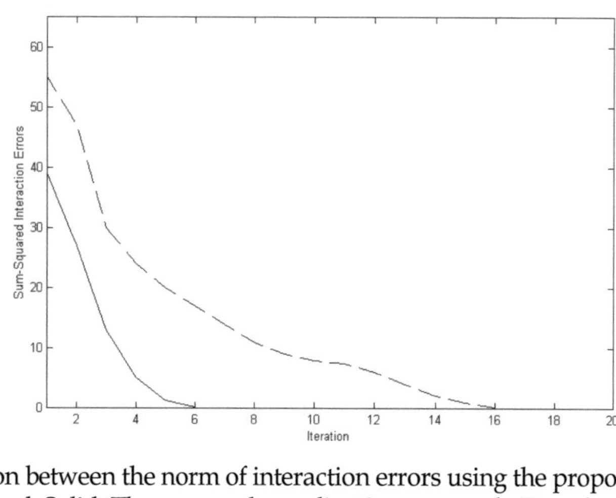

Fig. 6. Comparison between the norm of interaction errors using the proposed approach and the classical method. Solid: The new goal coordination approach; Dot: classical method.

With an extended version of the model coordination approach presented in [21], and the proposed goal coordination strategy of this chapter, the interaction prediction approach (mixed method) [22], [23], can also be extended to a new intelligent interaction prediction strategy.

8. Appendix

In the sequel, the elements of the matrix $D \triangleq \frac{\partial \underline{e}}{\partial \underline{\beta}}$ will be calculated

$$\frac{\partial \underline{e}}{\partial \underline{\beta}} = \frac{\partial \underline{Z}}{\partial \underline{\beta}} - \frac{\partial \underline{Z}^*}{\partial \underline{\beta}} \tag{74}$$

where,

$$\underline{e} = \begin{bmatrix} \underline{e}_1 \\ \underline{e}_2 \\ \vdots \\ \underline{e}_m \end{bmatrix}, \quad \underline{\beta} = \begin{bmatrix} \underline{\beta}_1 \\ \underline{\beta}_2 \\ \vdots \\ \underline{\beta}_m \end{bmatrix}, \quad \underline{Z} = \begin{bmatrix} \underline{Z}_1 \\ \underline{Z}_2 \\ \vdots \\ \underline{Z}_m \end{bmatrix}, \quad \underline{Z}^* = \begin{bmatrix} \underline{Z}_1^* \\ \underline{Z}_2^* \\ \vdots \\ \underline{Z}_m^* \end{bmatrix} \tag{75}$$

and

$$\underline{e}_i = \begin{bmatrix} \underline{e}_i[0] \\ \underline{e}_i[1] \\ \vdots \\ \underline{e}_i[n+1] \end{bmatrix}, \quad \underline{Z}_i = \begin{bmatrix} \underline{Z}_i[0] \\ \underline{Z}_i[1] \\ \vdots \\ \underline{Z}_i[n+1] \end{bmatrix}, \quad \underline{Z}_i^* = \begin{bmatrix} \underline{Z}_i^*[0] \\ \underline{Z}_i^*[1] \\ \vdots \\ \underline{Z}_i^*[n+1] \end{bmatrix}, \quad \underline{\beta}_i = \begin{bmatrix} \underline{\beta}_i[0] \\ \underline{\beta}_i[1] \\ \vdots \\ \underline{\beta}_i[n+1] \end{bmatrix} \tag{76}$$

$$\underline{X}_i = \begin{bmatrix} \underline{X}_i[1] \\ \underline{X}_i[2] \\ \vdots \\ \underline{X}_i[n+1] \end{bmatrix}, \quad \underline{U}_i = \begin{bmatrix} \underline{U}_i[0] \\ \underline{U}_i[1] \\ \vdots \\ \underline{U}_i[n] \end{bmatrix}, \quad \underline{\lambda}_i = \begin{bmatrix} \underline{\lambda}_i[0] \\ \underline{\lambda}_i[1] \\ \vdots \\ \underline{\lambda}_i[n] \end{bmatrix} \tag{77}$$

Now using the optimization of the first level, we have

$$\underline{L}_i^x = \frac{\partial \underline{L}_i}{\partial \underline{X}_i} = 0, \quad \underline{L}_i^u = \frac{\partial \underline{L}_i}{\partial \underline{U}_i} = 0, \quad \underline{L}_i^\lambda = \frac{\partial \underline{L}_i}{\partial \underline{\lambda}_i} = 0, \quad \underline{L}_i^z = \frac{\partial \underline{L}_i}{\partial \underline{Z}_i} = 0 \tag{78}$$

where the corresponding variations can also be written as

$$\begin{cases} \frac{\partial \underline{L}_i^x}{\partial \underline{X}_i} \delta \underline{X}_i + \frac{\partial \underline{L}_i^x}{\partial \underline{U}_i} \delta \underline{U}_i + \frac{\partial \underline{L}_i^x}{\partial \underline{\lambda}_i} \delta \underline{\lambda}_i + \frac{\partial \underline{L}_i^x}{\partial \underline{Z}_i} \delta \underline{Z}_i + \frac{\partial \underline{L}_i^x}{\partial \underline{\beta}} \delta \underline{\beta} = 0 \\ \frac{\partial \underline{L}_i^u}{\partial \underline{X}_i} \delta \underline{X}_i + \frac{\partial \underline{L}_i^u}{\partial \underline{U}_i} \delta \underline{U}_i + \frac{\partial \underline{L}_i^u}{\partial \underline{\lambda}_i} \delta \underline{\lambda}_i + \frac{\partial \underline{L}_i^u}{\partial \underline{Z}_i} \delta \underline{Z}_i + \frac{\partial \underline{L}_i^u}{\partial \underline{\beta}} \delta \underline{\beta} = 0 \\ \frac{\partial \underline{L}_i^\lambda}{\partial \underline{X}_i} \delta \underline{X}_i + \frac{\partial \underline{L}_i^\lambda}{\partial \underline{U}_i} \delta \underline{U}_i + \frac{\partial \underline{L}_i^\lambda}{\partial \underline{\lambda}_i} \delta \underline{\lambda}_i + \frac{\partial \underline{L}_i^\lambda}{\partial \underline{Z}_i} \delta \underline{Z}_i + \frac{\partial \underline{L}_i^\lambda}{\partial \underline{\beta}} \delta \underline{\beta} = 0 \\ \frac{\partial \underline{L}_i^z}{\partial \underline{X}_i} \delta \underline{X}_i + \frac{\partial \underline{L}_i^z}{\partial \underline{U}_i} \delta \underline{U}_i + \frac{\partial \underline{L}_i^z}{\partial \underline{\lambda}_i} \delta \underline{\lambda}_i + \frac{\partial \underline{L}_i^z}{\partial \underline{Z}_i} \delta \underline{Z}_i + \frac{\partial \underline{L}_i^z}{\partial \underline{\beta}} \delta \underline{\beta} = 0 \end{cases} \tag{79}$$

or equivalently,

$$\begin{cases} \underline{L}_i^{xx}\delta\underline{X}_i + \underline{L}_i^{xu}\delta\underline{U}_i + \underline{L}_i^{x\lambda}\delta\underline{\lambda}_i + \underline{L}_i^{xz}\delta\underline{Z}_i + \underline{L}_i^{x\beta}\delta\underline{\beta} = 0 \\ \underline{L}_i^{ux}\delta\underline{X}_i + \underline{L}_i^{uu}\delta\underline{U}_i + \underline{L}_i^{u\lambda}\delta\underline{\lambda}_i + \underline{L}_i^{uz}\delta\underline{Z}_i + \underline{L}_i^{u\beta}\delta\underline{\beta} = 0 \\ \underline{L}_i^{\lambda x}\delta\underline{X}_i + \underline{L}_i^{\lambda u}\delta\underline{U}_i + \underline{L}_i^{\lambda\lambda}\delta\underline{\lambda}_i + \underline{L}_i^{\lambda z}\delta\underline{Z}_i + \underline{L}_i^{\lambda\beta}\delta\underline{\beta} = 0 \\ \underline{L}_i^{zx}\delta\underline{X}_i + \underline{L}_i^{zu}\delta\underline{U}_i + \underline{L}_i^{z\lambda}\delta\underline{\lambda}_i + \underline{L}_i^{zz}\delta\underline{Z}_i + \underline{L}_i^{z\beta}\delta\underline{\beta} = 0 \end{cases} \tag{80}$$

which can be summarized as

$$\begin{bmatrix} \underline{L}_i^{xx} & \underline{L}_i^{xu} & \underline{L}_i^{x\lambda} & \underline{L}_i^{xz} \\ \underline{L}_i^{ux} & \underline{L}_i^{uu} & \underline{L}_i^{u\lambda} & \underline{L}_i^{uz} \\ \underline{L}_i^{\lambda x} & \underline{L}_i^{\lambda u} & \underline{L}_i^{\lambda\lambda} & \underline{L}_i^{\lambda z} \\ \underline{L}_i^{zx} & \underline{L}_i^{zu} & \underline{L}_i^{z\lambda} & \underline{L}_i^{zz} \end{bmatrix} \begin{bmatrix} \delta\underline{X}_i \\ \delta\underline{U}_i \\ \delta\underline{\lambda}_i \\ \delta\underline{Z}_i \end{bmatrix} = -\begin{bmatrix} \underline{L}_i^{x\beta} \\ \underline{L}_i^{u\beta} \\ \underline{L}_i^{\lambda\beta} \\ \underline{L}_i^{z\beta} \end{bmatrix} \delta\underline{\beta} \tag{81}$$

where

$$\begin{cases} \underline{L}_i^{x\beta} = \begin{bmatrix} -\underline{H}_{1i}^{xT} & \cdots & -\underline{H}_{mi}^{xT} \end{bmatrix} \ , \ \underline{L}_i^{u\beta} = \begin{bmatrix} -\underline{H}_{1i}^{uT} & \cdots & -\underline{H}_{mi}^{uT} \end{bmatrix} \\ \underline{L}_i^{\lambda\beta} = 0 \ , \ \underline{L}_i^{z\beta} = \begin{bmatrix} \underline{L}_{i1}^{z\beta} & \cdots & \underline{L}_{im}^{z\beta} \end{bmatrix} \ , \ \underline{L}_{ij}^{z\beta} = \begin{cases} I & ; \ i = j \\ 0 & ; \ i \neq j \end{cases} \end{cases} \tag{82}$$

and

$$\begin{cases} \underline{L}_i^{xx} = M_{i31} \\ \underline{L}_i^{uu} = M_{i22} \\ \underline{L}_i^{\lambda\lambda} = 0 \\ \underline{L}_i^{zz} = -D_{Zi} \\ \underline{H}_{ji}^{x} = T_{\beta i2j}{}^{T} \\ \underline{H}_{ji}^{u} = T_{\beta i3j}{}^{T} \end{cases} , \quad \begin{cases} \underline{L}_i^{\lambda x} = \underline{L}_i^{x\lambda T} = M_{i11} \\ \underline{L}_i^{ux} = \underline{L}_i^{xuT} = M_{i21} \\ \underline{L}_i^{\lambda u} = \underline{L}_i^{u\lambda T} = M_{i12} \\ \underline{L}_i^{\lambda z} = \underline{L}_i^{z\lambda T} = -T_{Zi11} \\ \underline{L}_i^{uz} = \underline{L}_i^{zuT} = -T_{Zi21} \\ \underline{L}_i^{xz} = \underline{L}_i^{zxT} = -T_{Zi31} \end{cases} \tag{83}$$

In (83), the matrices M_{i11}, M_{i12}, M_{i21}, M_{i22}, M_{i31}, T_{Zi11}, T_{Zi21}, T_{Zi31}, $T_{\beta i2j}$, $T_{\beta i3j}$ and D_{Zi} can be find in Appendix of [22].
Now using (7), we can write

$$\delta\underline{Z}_i^* = \sum_{j=1}^{m} \begin{bmatrix} \underline{H}_{ij}^{x} & \underline{H}_{ij}^{u} & 0 & 0 \end{bmatrix} \begin{bmatrix} \delta\underline{X}_j \\ \delta\underline{U}_j \\ \delta\underline{\lambda}_j \\ \delta\underline{Z}_j \end{bmatrix} \tag{84}$$

also $\delta\underline{Z}_i$ can be written as

$$\delta\underline{Z}_i = \begin{bmatrix} 0 & 0 & 0 & I \end{bmatrix} \begin{bmatrix} \delta\underline{X}_i \\ \delta\underline{U}_i \\ \delta\underline{\lambda}_i \\ \delta\underline{Z}_i \end{bmatrix} \tag{85}$$

Therefore, by using the following definitions

$$\underline{V} \triangleq \begin{bmatrix} \underline{V}_1 \\ \underline{V}_2 \\ \vdots \\ \underline{V}_m \end{bmatrix}, \quad \underline{V}_i \triangleq \begin{bmatrix} \underline{X}_i \\ \underline{U}_i \\ \underline{\lambda}_i \\ \underline{Z}_i \end{bmatrix} \tag{86}$$

$$\begin{cases} \underline{L}_i^{vv} \triangleq \begin{bmatrix} \underline{L}_i^{xx} & \underline{L}_i^{xu} & \underline{L}_i^{x\lambda} & \underline{L}_i^{xz} \\ \underline{L}_i^{ux} & \underline{L}_i^{uu} & \underline{L}_i^{u\lambda} & \underline{L}_i^{uz} \\ \underline{L}_i^{\lambda x} & \underline{L}_i^{\lambda u} & \underline{L}_i^{\lambda\lambda} & \underline{L}_i^{\lambda z} \\ \underline{L}_i^{zx} & \underline{L}_i^{zu} & \underline{L}_i^{z\lambda} & \underline{L}_i^{zz} \end{bmatrix}, \quad \underline{L}_i^{v\beta} \triangleq \begin{bmatrix} \underline{L}_i^{x\beta} \\ \underline{L}_i^{u\beta} \\ \underline{L}_i^{\lambda\beta} \\ \underline{L}_i^{z\beta} \end{bmatrix} \\ \underline{H}_{ij}^{v} \triangleq \begin{bmatrix} \underline{H}_{ij}^{x} & \underline{H}_{ij}^{u} & 0 & 0 \end{bmatrix}, \quad \underline{H}_{i}^{v} \triangleq \begin{bmatrix} \underline{H}_{i1}^{v} & \cdots & \underline{H}_{im}^{v} \end{bmatrix}, \quad \underline{I}_i^{v} \triangleq \begin{bmatrix} 0 & 0 & 0 & I \end{bmatrix} \end{cases} \tag{87}$$

and using (81), (84) and (85), for each subsystem, we obtain

$$\begin{cases} \underline{L}_i^{vv}\delta\underline{V}_i = -L_i^{v\beta}\delta\underline{\beta} \\ \delta\underline{Z}_i^{*} = \sum_{j=1}^{m} \underline{H}_{ij}^{v}\delta\underline{V}_j = \begin{bmatrix} \underline{H}_{i1}^{v} & \cdots & \underline{H}_{im}^{v} \end{bmatrix}\delta\underline{V} = \underline{H}_i^{v}\delta\underline{V} \\ \delta\underline{Z}_i = \underline{I}_i^{v}\delta\underline{V}_i \end{cases} \tag{88}$$

Now, for the overall system we have

$$\begin{cases} \underline{L}^{vv}\delta\underline{V} = -L^{v\beta}\delta\underline{\beta} \\ \delta\underline{Z}^{*} = \underline{H}^{v}\delta\underline{V} \\ \delta\underline{Z} = \underline{I}^{v}\delta\underline{V} \end{cases} \tag{89}$$

where

$$\begin{cases} \underline{L}^{vv} \triangleq \begin{bmatrix} \underline{L}_1^{vv} & 0 & 0 \\ 0 & \ddots & 0 \\ 0 & 0 & \underline{L}_m^{vv} \end{bmatrix}, \quad L^{v\beta} \triangleq \begin{bmatrix} L_1^{v\beta} \\ \vdots \\ L_m^{v\beta} \end{bmatrix} \\ \underline{I}^{v} \triangleq \begin{bmatrix} \underline{I}_1^{v} & 0 & 0 \\ 0 & \ddots & 0 \\ 0 & 0 & \underline{I}_m^{v} \end{bmatrix}, \quad \underline{H}^{v} \triangleq \begin{bmatrix} \underline{H}_1^{v} \\ \vdots \\ \underline{H}_m^{v} \end{bmatrix} \end{cases} \tag{90}$$

and using (89), it can be concluded that

$$\delta \underline{V} = -\left(\underline{L}^{vv}\right)^{-1} L^{v\beta} \delta \underline{\beta} \tag{91}$$

Therefore, by substituting (91) in (89), we obtain

$$\begin{cases} \delta \underline{Z}^{*} = -\underline{H}^{v}\left(\underline{L}^{vv}\right)^{-1} L^{v\beta} \delta \underline{\beta} \\ \delta \underline{Z} = -\underline{I}^{v}\left(\underline{L}^{vv}\right)^{-1} L^{v\beta} \delta \underline{\beta} \end{cases} \tag{92}$$

and as a result

$$\delta \underline{e} = \delta \underline{Z} - \delta \underline{Z}^{*} = -\left(\underline{I}^{v} - \underline{H}^{v}\right)\left(\underline{L}^{vv}\right)^{-1} L^{v\beta} \delta \underline{\beta} \tag{93}$$

Finally,

$$\frac{\partial \underline{e}}{\partial \underline{\beta}} = -\left(\underline{I}^{v} - \underline{H}^{v}\right)\left(\underline{L}^{vv}\right)^{-1} L^{v\beta} \tag{94}$$

9. References

[1] M. D. Mesarovic, D. Macko and Y.Takahara, "*Two coordination principles and their application in large-scale systems control,*" Pergamon Press, New York, March 1970.

[2] M. D. Mesarovic, D. Macko and Y.Takahara, *Theory of Hierarchical Multilevel Systems.* Academic Press, New York, 1970.

[3] J. D. Pearson, *Dynamic decomposition techniques,* in Wismer, D. A., ed., *Optimization Methods for Large- Scale Systems.* McGraw-Hill, New York, 1971.

[4] M. G. Singh and A.Titly, *Systems: Decomposition, Optimisation and Control.* Pergamon Press, Oxford, 1978.

[5] M. G. Singh, *Dynamical Hierarchical Control.* rev. ed., North Holland, Amsterdam, 1980.

[6] M. Jamshidi, *Large-Scale Systems–Modeling and Control.* North Holland, New York, 1983.

[7] M. F. Hassan and M. G. Singh, "*The optimisation of non-linear systems using a new two-level method,*" Automatica, 12: 359-363, 1976.

[8] M. F. Hassan and M. G. Singh,"*A two-level costate prediction algorithm for non-linear systems,*" Cambridge University, Engineering Dept., Report No. CUEDF-CAMS/TR (124), 1976.

[9] M. S. Mahmoud, "*Multilevel systems control and applications: A survey,*" IEEE Trans. Sys. Man. and Cyb., SMC-7:125-143, 1977.

[10] S. M. Mahmoud, M. F. Hassan, M. G. Darwish , *Large-Scale Control Systems: Theories and Techniques.* Marcel Dekker, New York, 1985.

[11] D. C. Siljak, *Large-Scale Dynamic Systems : Stability and Structure.* North-Holland, Amesterdam, 1978.

[12] E. J. Bauman, "*Multi-level optimization techniques with application to trajectory decomposition,*" in C. T. Leondes, ed., Advances in Control Systems. Pp. 160-222, 1986.

[13] Y. M. Park, M. S. Choi and K. Y. Lee, *"An optimal tracking neuro-controller for non-linear dynamic systems,"* IEEE Trans. Neural Networks, vol.7, no.5, Sept. 1996.

[14] N. Sadati , *"A novel approach to coordination of large-scale systems; Part I* - interaction prediction principle," IEEE Int. Conf. on Industrial Technology, pp. 641-647, 2005.

[15] N. Sadati, *"A novel approach to coordination of large-scale systems; Part II* - interaction balance principle," IEEE Int. Conf. on Industrial Technology, pp. 648-654, 2005.

[16] N. Sadati, A. Babazadeh, *"Optimal control of robot manipulators with a new two-level gradient based approach,"* Journal of Electrical Engineering, Springer, 88, pp. 383-393, 2006.

[17] C.T. Lin and C.S.G. Lee, "Reinforcement structure/ parameter learning for neural network-based fuzzy logic control systems," IEEE Trans. on Fuzzy Systems, vol. 2, no. 1, Feb. 1994.

[18] T. Takagi, M. Sugeno, *"Fuzzy identification of systems and its applications to modelling and control,"* IEEE Trans. on Syst. Man and Cyber., vol. 15, 116-132, 1985.

[19] M. Sugeno and G.T. Kang, "Structure identification of fuzzy *model,"* Fuzzy Sets and Syst., vol. 28, pp. 15-33, 1988.

[20] S. N. Iyer and B. J. Cory, *"Optimization of turbo–generator transient performance by differential dynamic programming ,"* IEEE Trans. Power Appar. Syst., PAS- 90: 2149-2157, 1971.

[21] N. Sadati, M. M. Emamzadeh, *"A novel fuzzy reinforcement learning approach in two-level control of 3-DOF robot manipulators,"* IEEE Symposium on Approximate Dynamic Programming and Reinforcement Learning, Honolulu, Hawaii, April 2007.

[22] N. Sadati, M. H. Ramezani, *"Optimization of large-scale systems using gradient type interaction prediction approach,"* Journal of Electrical Engineering, Springer, vol. 91, Dec. 2009.

[23] N. Sadati, M. H. Ramezani, *"Novel interaction prediction approach to hierarchical control of large-scale systems,"* IET Control Theory Application, vol. 4, issue 2, pp. 228-243, March 2010.

4

Reinforcement Learning of User Preferences for a Ubiquitous Personal Assistant

Sofia Zaidenberg and Patrick Reignier
Prima, Grenoble Informatics Laboratory (LIG) / INRIA
France

1. Introduction

New technologies bring a multiplicity of new possibilities for users to work with computers. Not only are spaces more and more equipped with stationary computers or notebooks, but more and more users carry mobile devices with them (smart-phones, personal digital assistants, etc.). Ubiquitous computing aims at creating smart environments where devices are dynamically linked in order to provide new services to users and new human-machine interaction possibilities. *The most profound technologies are those that disappear. They weave themselves into the fabric of everyday life until they are indistinguishable from it* (Weiser, 1991). This network of devices must perceive the context in order to understand and anticipate the user's needs. Devices should be able to execute actions that help the user to fulfill his goal or that simply accommodate him. Actions depend on the user's context and, in particular, on the situation within the context. The context is represented by a graph of situations (Crowley et al., 2002). This graph and the associated actions reflect the user's work habits. Therefore it should be specified by the user him-self. However, this is a complex and fastidious task.
The objective of this work is to construct automatically a context model by applying reinforcement learning techniques. Rewards are given by the user when expressing his degree of satisfaction towards actions proposed by the system. A default context model is used from the beginning in order to have a consistent initial behavior. This model is then adapted to each particular user in a way that maximizes the user's satisfaction towards the system's actions. The ambient intelligence application domain imposes constraints that we had to consider for the selected reinforcement learning approach.
We will first introduce the Ambient Intelligence application domain and the associated constraints. We will then present a qualitative user study conducted to validate our hypothesis. We will motivate our reinforcement learning algorithm selection and present the way we have modified it to fulfill our particular constraints. We will then present experimental results.

2. Pro-active ambient intelligence

Our research domain is Pro-active Ambient Intelligence applications development. We have decided to use reinforcement learning as a paradigm to let the end user adapt the application's behavior to his own needs. In this section, we will briefly present the Ambient Intelligence domain to motivate this choice and to introduce the particular constraints we have to manage.

2.1 Ubiquitous computing: Weiser's vision

In the late 1980s and early 1990s, Xerox PARC researcher Mark Weiser developed the concept of ubiquitous computing presented in his seminal paper: The Computer for the 21st Century (Weiser, 1991). He characterized the computer evolution in three main eras:

1. mainframes: a central processing unit shared by a group of users,
2. personal computers: one central unit per user,
3. mobility: several processing units per user, following his movements.

The integration of computing devices into everyday environments has been one of the predominant trends over the last decade. Cell phones, PDAs and laptop computers as well as WLAN networks have become part of almost every household. This trend enables computer-everywhere environments. The objective is to make computers not only user-friendly but also invisible to the user. Interaction with them should be possible in forms that people are naturally comfortable with:

> *"The most profound technologies are those that disappear. They weave themselves into the fabric of everyday life until they are indistinguishable from it."*

Some of the first ubiquitous applications were the *tabs*, *pads* and *boards* developed by Xerox PARC between 1988 and 1994 (Adams et al., 1993). Other examples can be found from the *Things That Think*[1] consortium of the MIT Media Lab. This group is inventing tomorrow's artifacts by embedding computers in everyday life objects.

In 1995, Weiser has introduced the new notion of calm computing. Calm computing is an approach that engages both the center and the periphery of our attention. Our attention can move from one to another. When we drive a car, our center of attention is on the road and the noise of the engine is on the periphery. If this noise is unusual, our attention will instantly move from the center to the periphery. Periphery can inform without overwhelming, center allows to get control.

The multiplication of computing devices goes also with a proliferation of interconnected sensors. These sensors can measure physical parameters (temperature, humidity, light, etc.). They can also be software probes as for instance the next appointment in his diary, the arrival of a new email. Ambient Intelligence (or AmI) is the conjunction of ubiquitous computing and artificial intelligence. The goal is to exploit the perception capacities of all these sensors to analyze the environment, users and activities and allow the system to react to the *current context*. Ambient Intelligence concept has been first defined in 1998 by Philips in their reflection on the future of consumer electronic equipments. Among the very first applications, we can cite the Coen Intelligent Room (Coen, 1998), the Abowd eClass Project (Abowd et al., 1996) or the Mozer Adaptive House (Michaël, 1998).

In the rest of this chapter, we will consider *pro-active* Ambient Intelligence applications, as defined by Salovaara and Oulasvirta (Salovaara & Oulasvirta, 2004):

> *"...the concept proactive refers to two critical features of a system: 1) that the system is working on behalf of (or pro) the user, and 2) is taking initiative autonomously, without user's explicit command."*

[1] `http://ttt.media.mit.edu`

2.2 Where are we now?

Since 2000, the number of computer devices in our personal and professional life has exploded: personal computers, smart-phones, PDAs, video game consoles connected to the Internet etc. Weiser's vision of ubiquitous computing has been partly achieved (the multiplication of CPUs around us). But pro-active Ambient Intelligence applications are still in the laboratories and did not reach everyday life. What are the difficulties?

There are many. Some of them are directly inherited from "classical" Artificial Intelligence, as for instance the *frame problem*: how should we model the environment (context model) and how shall we update this model based on the sensors' values (Lueg, 2002)? In this chapter, we will focus on the important problem of the user's confidence in his proactive applications.

User's confidence in an automated system is a common problem that is not limited to Ambient Intelligence. In particular, Muir and Morray have shown in the field of process automation that the user's trust in an automatic system is directly related to the user's perception of the skill of that system (Muir & Moray, 1996). The end user should not underestimate or overestimate the capabilities of that system to optimally use it (calibration of trust).

One way to establish this trust relation is to let the system expose its internal behavior to the end user. This is what Bellotti and Edwards named the *intelligibility* (Bellotti & Edwards, 2001):

> *"Context-aware systems that seek to act upon what they infer about the context must be able to represent to their users what they know, how they know it, and what they are doing about it."*

Cheverst (Cheverst et al., 2005) talked about *comprehensibility* to suggest that the user should be able to look inside the device (like a glass box) to examine its inner working. In particular, comprehensibility reduces the fear of having a system doing something "in our back" (Abowd & Mynatt, 2000). Comprehensibility is also associated to *scrutability*, which refers to the ability for a user to interrogate his user model to understand the system's behavior. As stated by Kay (Kay et al., 2003), scrutability is contradictory with the invisible computer concept as defined by Weiser, but it seems to be necessary to gain the user's acceptance.

Based on scrutability and on the level of system control versus user control (pro-activity), Cheverst is categorizing the various Ambient Intelligence applications. In figure 1 adapted from his article, the gray circle characterizes the kind of applications we want to develop.

Developing a pro-active Ambient Intelligence application is a complex task. It cannot be supported only by the developer or the end user. Pattie Maes argued that to gain trust, the end user must be involved in the specification of the system's behavior, but he usually cannot directly program it (Maes, 1994). User's habits are also evolving through time (Byun & Cheverst, 2001), implying repeated modifications of the application. Machine learning has been proposed as a possible solution for those problems. In particular, Remagnino (Remagnino & Foresti, 2005) thinks that the future of Ambient Intelligence is correlated to machine learning researches because associations between sensory outputs and intelligent behavior are too complex to be hand-coded.

We have presented in this section a brief introduction on Ambient Computing. We have focused on particular characteristics that those applications must exhibit to gain user's acceptance. This gives us some constraints that must be considered for building our assistant. To validate those constraints, we have first conducted a user study that we will present in the next section.

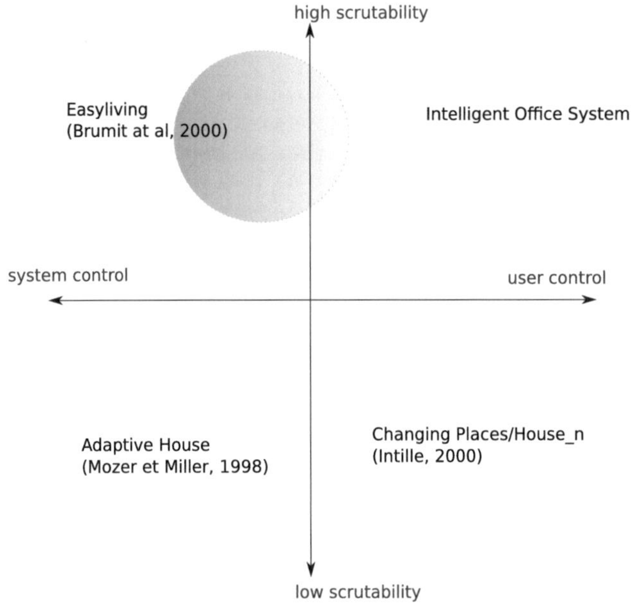

Fig. 1. Two-dimensional design space spanning control and scrutability dimensions, adapted from (Cheverst et al., 2005): the gray circle characterizes the applications we are considering.

3. User study

The goal of this user study was to measure the expectations and needs of users with regard to an ambient personal assistant. Subjects were 26 active persons, 12 women and 14 men, distributed in age categories as follows: 9 subjects between 18 and 25, 7 between 26 and 40, 7 between 40 and 60, and 3 over 60. None of the subjects had advanced knowledge in computer science.

3.1 Description

The study was based on ~1 hour interviews with every subject. The interviewer followed a predefined script. The script started with a few open questions about information and communication technologies to evaluate the subject's general knowledge, but also his perception and his uses of such technologies. Then, the interviewer presented our ubiquitous system using a model (an interactive power point presentation: some of the slides are shown figure 2). This interacting powerpoint was exposing a simple scenario about the user's laptop. The scenario starts in the morning and the user is at home, browsing for movies and restaurants (figure 2(a)). When he arrives at work, the laptop automatically switches to the user's "work" setting (figure 2(b)). Then, the assistant turns the user's cellphone to vibrate and displays a message about this action. The user can ask for an explanation about this action and choose to undo it or select another action for this situation (figure 2(c)). At the end of the day, the system switched back to the "home" setting. The interviewer explained also orally other examples of services that could be offered by the assistant.

After the presentation, the subject was asked for his opinion about such a system. He could freely express the advantages and drawbacks of what he saw and the situations in which he thought the assistant was particularly useful or interesting. This gave him the opportunity to talk about ubiquitous assistants in general and about what their usage implies for his

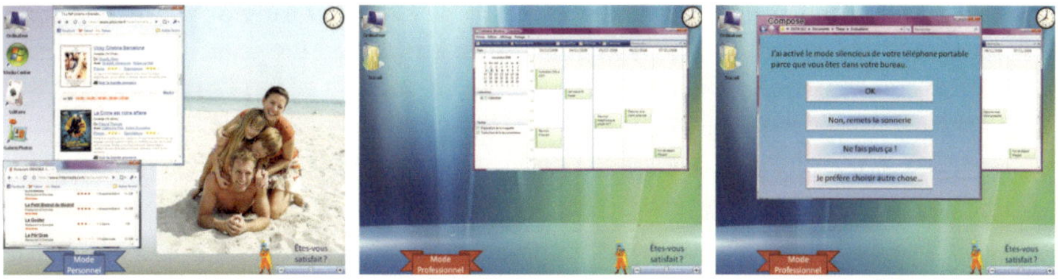

(a) Slide 1 (b) Slide 2 (c) Slide 5

Fig. 2. A few slides from the model used to present our system to the subjects.

everyday life. Another goal of the conversation was to determine the acceptability of the system. The interviewer asked the following questions:

- "If the assistant learns badly, if it offers you wrong services at wrong times, what would be your reaction?"
- "If the assistant makes mistakes, but you know that he is learning to adapt to your behavior, would you give him a chance?"
- "Would you accept to spend some time to answer questions to make the assistant learn more quickly?"
- "What would you gain from getting an explanation about the assistant's decisions?"

We were also interested in finding out if the subjects would feel observed and fear that their privacy was in jeopardy. If they would not bring the subject up themselves, we would ask questions about this.

3.2 Results

After analyzing all the interviews, it appeared that 44% of subjects were interested in our assistant, and 13% were conquered. Interested persons share the same profile: they are very active, very busy in their professional as well as personal lives, they suffer from cognitive overload and would appreciate some help to organize their schedule. Other noticeable observations standing out from the interviews are the following:

- Having a *learning* assistant is considered as a plus by users. In fact, subjects felt a learning system would be more reliable since it would respond to their own training.
- Users prefer a gradual training versus a heavy configuration at the beginning.
- This training must indeed be simple and pleasant ("one click").
- The initial learning phase must be short (one to three weeks).
- It is absolutely necessary for the assistant to be able to explain its decisions. This aspect was particularly discussed by (Bellotti & Edwards, 2001).
- The amount of interactions wanted between the user and the assistant varies from one subject to another. Some accept only to give one-click rewards while others would be happy to give more inputs to the system. This confirms that people are interested in *engaging* systems, as stated by (Rogers, 2006). For those users, we could add an optional debriefing phase where the assistant goes through the learned behavior and the user corrects or approves it.

- Mistakes made by the system are accepted to some extent as long as the user knows that the system is learning and as the system is useful enough to the user. But errors must not have critical consequences. Users always want to remain in control, to have the last word over the system and even have a "red button" to stop the whole system at any time.
- Some subjects pointed out that the assistant could even reveal to them their own automatic and subconscious customs.
- A recurrent worry expressed by interviewees is the fear of becoming dependant of a system that cares for them and becoming unable of living without it (what if the system is broken-down?).

This user study justifies our ubiquitous assistant since a sizeable part of interviewed subjects were prone to using it. Points listed above give us constraints to respect in our system. They will be listed in the next paragraph.

3.3 Our constraints

Based on the Ambient Intelligence presentation (section 2) and this user study, we will now present the constraints we have considered for our approach.
We want to build a personal assistant whose behavior is learned from user inputs. We have to respect several constraints:

(a) The system must not be a black box. As detailed in (Bellotti & Edwards, 2001), a context-aware system can not pretend to understand all of the user's context, thus it must be responsible about its limitations. It must be able to explain to the user what it knows, how it knows it, and what it is doing about it. The user will trust the assistant (even if it fails) if he can understand its internal functioning.

(b) The training is going to be performed by the user thus it must be simple, non intrusive and it must not put a burden on the user.

(c) The learning should be *Life-Long* learning to continuously track the user's changes of preferences.

(d) The training period must be short, unless the user changes preferences.

(e) The system must have an initial behavior that is not incoherent.

We have been exploring in a previous work a supervised learning approach for situation $\leftrightarrow$ action association (Brdiczka, 2007) for a virtual assistant. Another example is the *a CAPpella* system (Dey et al., 2004). Even if they produce some promising results, both approaches are based on an off-line annotation of recorded data. This annotation process can be quite painful for the end user and because of the off-line nature of the process, it is performed "out of context". To overcome these limitations, we have been considering Reinforcement Learning as a solution for getting "in context" qualitative (not too intrusive) feedback from the user.

4. Reinforcement learning: a quick overview

4.1 Definition

Reinforcement learning (Sutton, 1988; Sutton & Barto, 1998) is an approach where an agent acts in an environment and learns from its previous experiences to maximize the sum of rewards received from its action selection. The reward is classically a continuous function between -1 and 1. 1 corresponds to satisfaction, -1 disapproval and 0 means no opinion.

In reinforcement learning approaches, the environment is typically modeled as a Markov Decision Process (or MDP). A Markov Decision Process is defined by $\langle \mathcal{S}, \mathcal{A}, \mathcal{R}, \mathcal{P} \rangle$:

- $\mathcal{S}$ is the set of all possible states of the environment.
- $\mathcal{A}$ is the list of possible actions.
- $\mathcal{R} : \mathcal{S} \times \mathcal{A} \times \mathcal{S} \rightarrow [-1; 1]$ is the reward function. $\mathcal{R}(s,a,s')$ indicates the opportunity to choose action a in situation s.
- $\mathcal{P} : \mathcal{S} \times \mathcal{A} \times \mathcal{S} \rightarrow [0; 1]$ is the transition function modeling the environment. $\mathcal{P}(s,a,s')$ gives the probability of being in situation s' when applying action a in situation s. The Markov property specifies that the next situation depends *only* on the current situation and action and is not based on previous situations.

With Markov Decision Processes (and so, with classical reinforcement learning approaches), the current state must be completely known. The environment's evolution may be stochastic (hence the probabilistic transition function), but it must be *stationary*: the probabilistic law must not change over time.
An agent has a policy function $\pi : \mathcal{S} \rightarrow \mathcal{A}$, proposing an action for every situation: the agent's behavior. This policy function can be evaluated using a *value function* $V^{\pi}(s)$. This value function computes the expected discounted future rewards received by the agent being currently in state s and applying its policy π. This value function is expressed by the following equation:

$$V^{\pi}(s) = E\left\{ \sum_{k=0}^{\infty} \gamma^k r_{t+k+1} | s_t = s \right\} \text{ with } 0 < \gamma < 1 \tag{1}$$

The goal is to build an optimal policy π^* maximizing the corresponding value function V^{π^*}. This optimal value function is the solution of the recursive Bellman's equation (equation 3):

$$V^{\pi^*}(s) = max_a \left(E\left\{ \sum_{k=0}^{\infty} \gamma^k r_{t+k+1} | s_t = s \right\} \right) \tag{2}$$

$$= max_a \left(\sum_{s'} \mathcal{P}(s,a,s')(\mathcal{R}(s,a,s') + \gamma V^{\pi^*}(s')) \right) \tag{3}$$

Once the optimal value function is determined, the optimal policy is directly calculated with:

$$\pi^*(s) = argmax_a \left(\sum_{s'} \mathcal{P}(s,a,s')(\mathcal{R}(s,a,s') + \gamma V^*(s')) \right) \tag{4}$$

If we have a model of the environment (the $\mathcal{P}$ and $\mathcal{R}$ functions of the corresponding Markov Decision Process), the Bellman equation is fully determined. The optimal strategy can be found using dynamic programming. It is an off-line optimization problem.
If the environment model is unknown, there are two main categories of approaches:

Model-Free : no explicit model of the environment is constructed. The optimal strategy is built as a result of the agent's interactions with its environment. Some examples of Model-Free approaches are: Q-Learning (Watkins & Dayan, 1992), SARSA (Rummery & Niranjan, 1994), Actor-Critic etc.

Model-Based : a model of the environment is constructed (learning phase) and then exploited (planning phase) to build the optimal strategy. This is for instance the Dyna approach (Sutton, 1991) that we will present in subsection 4.4.

4.2 Examples

Reinforcement learning application domain covers a lot of ground, from robotics to industrial manufacturing or combinatorial search problems such as computer game playing. We will present some examples involving pro-active agents interacting with an end-user.

Robyn Kozierok and Pattie Maes (Kozierok & Maes, 1993) have proposed in 1993 an agent helping the user to schedule meetings (agenda assistant). One of the very interesting aspects of this approach is the smooth control transfer from the end user to the agent. This smooth transition allows a progressive trust relation establishment, an important step for the system acceptance. The agent's learning is a combination of memory based and reinforcement learning. The agent is first observing the end user, recording every *situation* $\leftrightarrow$ *action* association. When a new situation is detected, the agent extracts from its database the closest previously observed situation and the associated action. If the proposed action is incorrect, reinforcement learning is used to try to correct it. This approach combines two important properties: establishing a trust relationship with the user based on a smooth control transfer and consolidating this relationship with an intelligible model. If the agent is choosing a wrong action, the system tells the user the reasons for its choice and the user can explain why this is incorrect. One of its main drawbacks is the simplicity of the situation model (well suited for the agenda problem).

Another example is Walker's application of reinforcement learning to dialog selection in a spoken dialog system for emails (Walker, 2000). The agent must learn to optimally vocally interact with the end user to quickly provide him the right information. The difficulty of this application is the complexity of the state space: 13 discrete variables that can take between 2 and 4 different values each. The authors recommend to reduce the state space to significantly improve the system's performances. This state space reduction is done by searching for irrelevant variables in the learning process.

4.3 The Markovian hypothesis

Our learning agent perceives the environment's state. This environment is both "physical" (user entering a room, ...) and "computer based" (new email arriving, agenda alarm, ...).

In our problem, the agent is not the only acting entity modifying the environment. The environment is modified by external elements, out of the agent's control. The end user is one of those elements: for instance, he enters or leaves his office, triggering localization events, sends emails, etc. All those actions modify the environment. They are motivated by the user's internal state. The agent would need to access this internal state to fully understand and predict the environment's evolution. As this is not possible, the agent has only a *partial* perception of the environment.

4.3.1 Partial environment perception

An agent in a Markov Decision Problem that has only a partial perception of its environment breaks the Markov hypothesis. Let us consider for instance the classical maze problem. If the robot has an exact perception of its state in the environment (position and nearest obstacles), it might be able to correctly decide its next action to reach the goal (see top part of figure 3). If it has a partial perception (the nearest obstacles for instance), there is an ambiguity on its real position: it cannot decide anymore what to do based on the current perceived state (see bottom part of figure 3). The Markov hypothesis is no more true: it needs to remember previous states and actions to disambiguate its current position. The action selection is no more based solely on the current state.

(a) The robot has a complete perception of its state

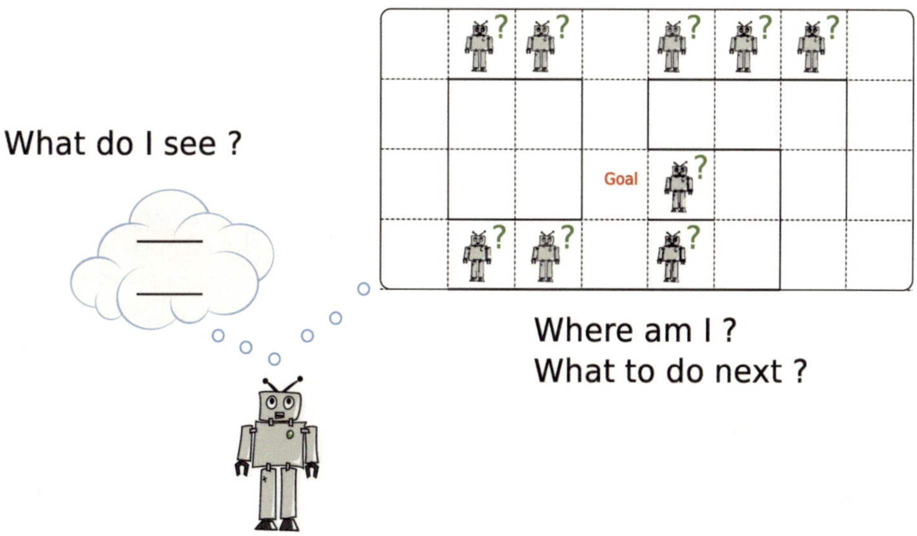

(b) The robot perceives only surrounding obstacles

Fig. 3. Consequences of having a complete or partial state observation

When an agent has only a partial access to the current state, Markov Decision Processes are then replaced by Partially Observable Markov Decision Processes[2] (Aström, 1965). In a Partially Observable Markov Decision Process approach, the agent does not know its real state s but it only has access to an observation o. It then acts based on an estimated state b (belief state) defined by a probability distribution on S (all states). A Partially Observable Markov Decision Process is a non-Markovian process which can be reduced to a Markovian process on a continuous state space: the belief space. The belief space is the space which, from the probability of being in each state and an action, gives the new probability of being in each state (for a quick introduction, see for example (*POMDPs for Dummies: Page 5*, 1999)).
Partially Observable Markov Decision Processes are used in particular for multi-agent problems. In a multi-agent system, each agent has access to its internal state, to the external environment state but has no perception of the other agents' internal state: each agent has

[2]POMDP

a partial view of the global system's state (Littman, 1994). If each agent is governed by a Partially Observable Markov Decision Process, we talk of Decentralized Partially Observable Markov Decision Process or DEC-POMDP.
Solving a Partially Observable Markov Decision Process problem is *p-space hard* (Papadimitriou & Tsitsiklis, 1987). There are some approximate solutions: (Pineau et al., 2003), (Spaan & Vlassis, 2005) or (Smith & Simmons, 2005) for instance. But it remains very difficult, especially with convergence speed constraints imposed by the end user being in the loop.

4.3.2 Non Markovian stationary or Markovian non stationary?

Considering the end-user as part of the environment, our learning agent problem can be naturally modeled as a Partially Observable Markov Decision Process. The agent cannot perceive the end-user's internal state, responsible for the user's actions and part of the environment evolution. As stated by Buffet in his PhD (Buffet, 2003), our system is non Markovian and stationary. It is stationary because:

- the environment without the user can be considered as stationary (the rules of evolution are not changing);
- the end user might introduce a non stationary aspect (his behavior is evolving through time) but this non stationary part is embedded in the non observable part.

We could also consider that the end-user is not part of the agent's environment. The agent has a full perception of the state: the problem is now Markovian but it is no more stationary. The end user is a "disruptive" element, causing non deterministic environment state changes. As we have seen in subsection 4.1, a non deterministic evolution of the environment is compatible with a Markov Decision Process as long as the probabilistic evolution law is not changing (stationary). In our case, the non stationary part corresponds to the end-user's behavior evolution. We can consider that this behavior evolution is slow and that our problem is locally stationary. If the agent's learning speed is much faster that the user behavior's evolution, then the agent can track user evolutions and constantly adapt to them.
As we have explained in the previous section, Partially Observable Markov Decision Process approaches are difficult. We have preferred to use a more classical Markov Decision Process approach, selecting the second solution: the end user is seen as a "disruptive" element, outside of the agent's environment.

4.4 Reducing user's burden: indirect reinforcement learning

Reinforcement learning approaches need a lot of steps to converge. For instance, the backgammon agent had to play 1.5 million games to learn (Kaelbling, 2004). In a reinforcement learning approach, the agent is building its policy through interaction with its environment. If this environment is virtual (like for the Backgammon game), the convergence time (due to a high number of learning steps) can be partly reduced by parallelizing the algorithm for instance or by using faster processors. But in a real environment, especially if the end-user is part of the learning step giving for instance the rewards, the bottleneck is not the processor speed but the end-user himself who can quickly get bored.
To limit end-user's interactions, indirect reinforcement learns a real world model that can be used by the agent as a "virtual playground" to produce as many off-line experiments as necessary. The world model allows *imaginary* experiments as defined by Craik (Craik, 1943).
The world model is a transformation $S \times A \rightarrow S$. Building a world model is a life-long learning process. The agent is repeatedly updating its world model based on new available

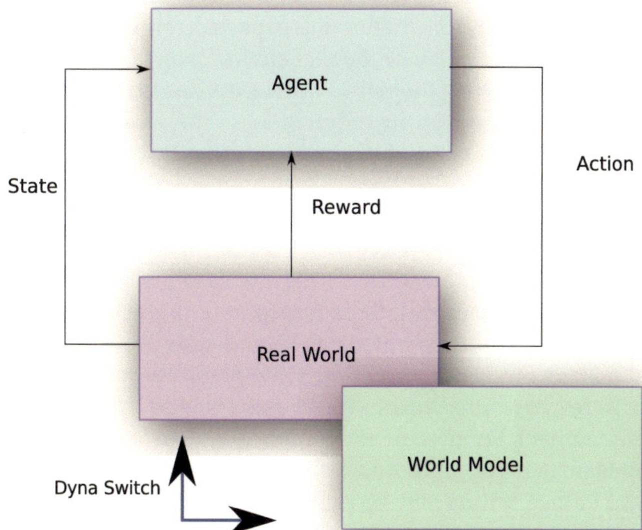

Fig. 4. The Dyna architecture: the agent is learning either on the real world or the world model

observations (s, a, s') coming from the real environment (supervised learning). Because it is a life long process, the world model can track evolutions of the real environment. Building an optimal policy (planning phase) is a quick process, exploiting the current world model.
Indirect reinforcement learning approaches have been introduced by Sutton with the Dyna architecture (Sutton, 1991). The Dyna system is composed of three *asynchronous* tasks:

1. learn a world model
2. build a policy from this world model
3. build a policy from the real world interactions (not using the world model).

The first task is executed in parallel with the two others. The agent is acting and learning either in the real world or in the world model (Dyna switch) as illustrated in figure 4.

5. Our approach

5.1 Indirect reinforcement learning adaptation

As stated in section 3.3, learning the user preferences must not be a burden on the end-user. The system has to learn quickly and without over-soliciting the user. Indirect reinforcement learning, presented section 4.4, proposes a solution by using a world models. Applying Dyna implies describing two parts: interactions with the user in the real environment and the non-interactive learning part using world models.
In the interactive part, the system perceives events from the environment through its sensors. The internal representation of the environment's state is updated accordingly (see section 5.2 for further details on state representation). As a reaction to the state change (caused by the detected event), the system selects an action to be executed through its actuators.
The non-interactive part consists in running episodes of Q-Learning in the world model (composed of a transition function and a reward function). Instead of sending actions to the

real environment, we query the transition function for the next state given the last action and state. Similarly, the reward function returns us the expected reward for action a in state s. Those functions have to be representative of the real environment's dynamics, which are not fixed but evolving over time. Acquiring them through supervised learning seems appropriate. This learning will be a life-long process in order to keep the models up-to-date with the environment. The learning of the transition function is described section 5.3.1 and the learning of the reward function is the concern of section 5.3.2.

5.2 Internal state representation

One of our constraints defined section 3.3 concerns the intelligibility of the agent (constraint a). The internal functioning of the system should be transparent to the user for him to trust the agent. The modelling choice of environment states should take this constraint into account. We chose to represent a state as a set of *predicates*. Each predicate represents a relevant part of the environment. Zero-order predicates would not provide a sufficiently informative description of the environment because of its complexity. We use first-order predicates, defined with arguments which can take any value or no value. A state is a particular assignment of argument values, which may be null. These predicates are described below.

alarm(title, hour, minute) A reminder fired by the user's agenda.

xActivity(machine, isActive) The activity of the X server of a machine.

inOffice(user, office) Indicates the office that a user is in, if known, null otherwise.

absent(user) States that a user is currently absent from his office.

hasUnreadMail(from, to, subject, body) The latest new email received by the user.

entrance(isAlone, friendlyName, btAddress) Expresses that a bluetooth device just entered the user's office. *isAlone* tells if the user was alone or not before the event.

exit(isAlone, friendlyName, btAddress) Someone just left the user's office.

task(taskName) The task that the user is currently working on.

user(login), userOffice(office, login), userMachine(machine, login) The main user of the assistant, his office and main personal computer (not meant to be modified).

computerState(machine, isScreenLocked, isMusicPaused) Describes the state of the user's computer regarding the screen saver and the music.

An example would be the state:

```
alarm(minute=<null>, title=<null>, hour=<null>);
xActivity(isActive=<null>, machine=<null>);
inOffice(office=<null>, user=<null>);
absent(user=<null>);
hasUnreadMail(from=<null>, to=<null>, body=<null>,
     subject=<null>);
entrance(isAlone=<null>, friendlyName=<null>,
     btAddress=<null>);
exit(isAlone=false, friendlyName=Sonia,
     btAddress=00:12:47:C9:F2:AC);
task(taskName=<null>);
screenLocked(machine=<null>, isLocked=<null>);
musicPaused(isPaused=<null>, machine=<null>);
user(login=zaidenbe);
userOffice(office=E214, login=zaidenbe);
userMachine(login=zaidenbe, machine=hyperion);
```

In this example, the main user is `zaidenbe` and a bluetooth device just left the office.

Each predicate is endowed with a timestamp accounting for the number of steps since the last value change. Among other things, this is used to maintain integrity of states, *e.g.* the predicate `alarm` can keep a value only for one step and only one of `inOffice` and `absent` can have non-null values.
Our states contain free values. Therefore, our state space is very large. This exact information is not always relevant for choosing an action. The user might wish for the music to stop when anyone enters the office, but to be informed of emails only from his boss. As soon as we observe the state "Bob entered the office", we have an estimated behavior for the state "someone entered the office", which is more satisfying for the user. We generalize states in the behavior definition by replacing values with wildcards: "<+>" means any value but "`<null>`" and "<*>" means any value.
In this manner, an action is associated to a "super-state" encompassing numerous actual states. A generalized state may be split when it is relevant to distinguish between encompassed, more particular, states. This splitting can be done offline, by analyzing the history of rewards and detecting persistent inconsistencies of user rewards for a state. This aspect has not been further studied yet.

5.3 World model

The world model is intended to replace the real world in part of the actions executed for exploration, as shown figure 4. In classical reinforcement learning, the world model takes as input an action executed by the agent and the state that the world was in at the time the action was chosen. The output of the model is the state of the environment after the action and the expected reward (see section 4.4).
In our case, as explained section 4.3.2, the environment state is modified by actions from the agent as well as by exterior events generated by the user. Our world model takes as input the current state and an action *or* an event.
The world model is composed of the transition and reward functions $\mathcal{P}$ and $\mathcal{R}$. We modify slightly the classical definition given section 4.1 by the following definition of the transition function: $\mathcal{P} : \mathcal{S} \times \mathcal{O} \times \mathcal{S} \to [0; 1]$, where $\mathcal{O} = \mathcal{A} \cup \mathcal{E}$ represents the set of occurrences, an occurrence being an action or an event ($\mathcal{E}$ is the set of events), as illustrated figures 5(a) and 5(b).
The world model is automatically acquired using supervised learning based on real interactions examples. The system *records every state, event and reward and action*, and uses these examples for supervised learning as described in sections 5.3.1 and 5.3.2.

(a) The classical world model (b) Our world model

Fig. 5. World model definition

Algorithm 1: The supervised learning of the transition function.

Input: A set of examples $\{s, o, s'\}$
Output: $\mathcal{P}$
foreach *example* $\{s, o, s'\}$ **do**
  if *a transformation t that obtains s′ from s with the occurrence o, can be found* **then**
    Increase the probability of t;
  else
    Create a transformation starting with s, having the action a or a generic event created from e and ending in s', with a low probability;
    Decrease the probability of any other transformation t' that matches the starting state s and the occurrence o but whose ending state is different from s';

5.3.1 Supervised learning of the transition function

In our case, the transition function $\mathcal{P}(s,o,s')$ gives the probability of being in situation s' when applying action a, or perceiving event e (where o is an occurrence a or e), in situation s. We modeled our transition function as a set of transformations. Each transformation includes a starting state s^t, an occurrence o^t, a probability p^t and the modifications that will be applied on the observed starting state to compute the next state $M^t = \{m_i^t, i \in [1;n]\}$.
A modification operates on an predicate's argument. It can erase the argument's value, set a given value, copy the value of one of predicate's `a` argument into one of predicate's `b` argument. The transformation can also be to reset the timestamp. We denote a transformation by $t(s^t, o^t, p^t, M^t)$.
In the same way as we factorize states for the behavior definition (see section 5.2), we use generic transformations in order to reduce the size of the transition function. The starting state s^t is a generalized state, defined with wildcards (for instance, "some entered the office", no matter what the other argument values are).
The transition function is initialized using common sense, and it is enriched by the supervised learning algorithm 1. For instance, consider: $s^t = <*>$, which matches any state, $a^t =$ `lockScreen`, the action of activating the screen saver. The transformation would be to set to `true` argument `isScreenLocked` of predicate `computerState`, indicating that the screen is locked in the next state. When new examples confirm knowledge already included in the model, they strengthen the corresponding transformation. If an example contradicts the existing model, we decrease slowly the probability of the concerned transformation. As a consequence, if this example is an outlier, it will not disturb the model too much. If it is a sign of an actual change, then it will be observed again and will slowly change the model.
This model has a generalization ability since we create new transformations with generic starting states. This accelerated the learning of preferences because we make most use of each example. Having seen one example with the starting state "Bob entered the office", we have a transformation for all states where someone enters the office. This transformation can efficiently be used during offline reinforcement learning.

5.3.2 Supervised learning of the reward function

The reward function $\mathcal{R}(s,a,s')$ indicates the opportunity of choosing action a in situation s. Similarly to the model for the transition function, the model for the reward function is a set of entries, each entry being defined by a starting state s^e, an action a^e and a numerical reward r^e.

Algorithm 2: The supervised learning of the reward function.

Input: A set of examples $\{s, a, r\}$
Output: $\mathcal{R}$
foreach *example* $\{s, a, r\}$ **do**
  if *an entry* $e = \{s_e, a_e, r_e\}$ *such as s matches* s_e *and* $a = a_e$, *can be found* **then**
    Update e, set $r_e = mix(r, r_e)$, where mix is a merging function;
  else
    Add a new entry $e = \{s, a, r\}$ to the reward model;

The given reward usually depends only on a subset of the predicates defining a state. For example if in the starting state the user was typing on his computer and the action is to lock the screen, the reward should be quite negative and does not depend on the presence of other people or on the state of the music player. The starting state s^e may be a generalized state, indicating only relevant filtering constraints. Though, during learning we cannot determine automatically which predicate is relevant for a given reward, since the reward depends on the internal state of the user. The reward model, as well as the transition model, is initialized using common sense. Only these initial entries have generalized starting states. New entries are created with the exact perceived state, without generalization. The model is then learned with the supervised learning algorithm 2. The merging function used in algorithm 2 amalgamates a newly received reward with the one present in the model for the entry corresponding to the current example. As for the transition function, we want the reward model to evolve smoothly and to be stable. We define $mix(r, r_e) = 0.3r + 0.7r_e$. If the user changes his reward because he changes his preferences, the model will slowly follow the change. If a given reward is inconsistent for another reason, the model will not undergo an unwanted change.
Having numerous user rewards makes the reward model more reliable, but users do not always give rewards. To increase the number of examples, it is possible to infer indirect rewards. For instance, if the user immediately refuses a service proposed by the assistant, for example by closing the mail client opened automatically, we deduce a negative reward. The magnitude of values for indirect rewards is limited to take into account their uncertainty.

5.4 Offline reinforcement learning

The behavior learning is done completely offline, in a non interactive manner. We use a classical algorithm for reinforcement learning: the Q-Learning algorithm (Watkins & Dayan, 1992), and we modify it slightly to match our pattern "event-action" (see algorithm 3). Unlike classical Dyna (section 4.4), we use only the world model for learning the behavior. The user acts in the real world and interaction histories are stored for learning the world model. In this way, we can completely separate the learned behavior from the used behavior at a given point in time. The user, who is confronted with the behavior of the assistant, implicity learns his own internal model of the assistant, as he does with every system he uses. If this behavior is constantly updated, the user might get destabilized and lose trust (see constraint a section 3.3). If the learned behavior is not the same as the one used for interactions, it becomes possible to warn the user before replacing the online behavior by the newly updated one.
In algorithm 3, k is the number of iterations of an episode. Each episode starts in an initial state which can be either an empty state (all arguments are `<null>`) or a randomly generated state, or a state randomly chosen from history. The two latter options enable a better exploration

of the state space than the first option. Starting from a random state that has never been observed makes sense only because our transition model has a generalization ability. It can estimate a transition from a state never seen during learning (section 5.3.1). Starting from a state encountered during interaction allows to make most use of observed experience. During episodes, events cause state transitions. Likewise, events can be randomly generated or selected from history. Generating unseen events enables better exploration whereas using observed events strengthens past experience.

The world model is initialized using common sense. Before activating the assistant, we run initial episodes of Q-Learning (algorithm 3) to "convert" the initial world model into an initial behavior, to respect constraint e defined section 3.3.

6. Experimental results

6.1 Learning an initial behavior

As mentioned section 5.4, before starting to act, the assistant learns an initial behavior from a given initial world model. For these initial episodes of Q-Learning (algorithm 3) there are four parameters introduced section 5.4 to fix: the number of episodes, the number of iterations of each episode (k), the choice of the initial state and the choice of events during episodes. We ran initial episodes with different options. First, we found that it was more efficient to select both initial states and events randomly from history. Then, we ran 100 episodes of 10, 25, 50 and 100 iterations each and computed a grade for every behavior obtained after an episode. The results are shown figure 6.

The grade of a behavior is for the most part its correspondence to what the user wants. The experimenter who gave the initial rewards is presented with the best action in each state and indicates whether this actions is the one he expected. In a much smaller proportion, the grade takes into account the number of states where the system has an estimation of the action to select. It allows to keep behaviors that have performed enough states explorations (that is, the selected action will not be random in more states).

Algorithm 3: An episode of Q-Learning run during the planing stage by the assistant.

Input: $\mathcal{P}, \mathcal{R}$

Select an initial state s;

for i *from* 1 *to* k **do**

- Choose an event e;
- Send the current state s and the event e to the world model and receive an estimation of the next state s':
- $s' \leftarrow max_{s' \in \mathcal{S}} \mathcal{P}(s'|s,e)$;
- Select an action $a = \pi(s')$;
- Send s' and a to the world model and receive estimations of the next state s'' and the reward r:
- $s'' \leftarrow max_{s'' \in \mathcal{S}} \mathcal{P}(s''|s',a), r \leftarrow \mathcal{R}(s',a)$;
- Apply a reinforcement learning method on the hypothetical experience $\langle s', s'', a, r \rangle$:
- $Q(s',a) \leftarrow Q(s',a) + \alpha(r + \gamma \max_{a'} Q(s'',a') - Q(s',a))$;
- $s \leftarrow s''$;
- $i \leftarrow i + 1$;

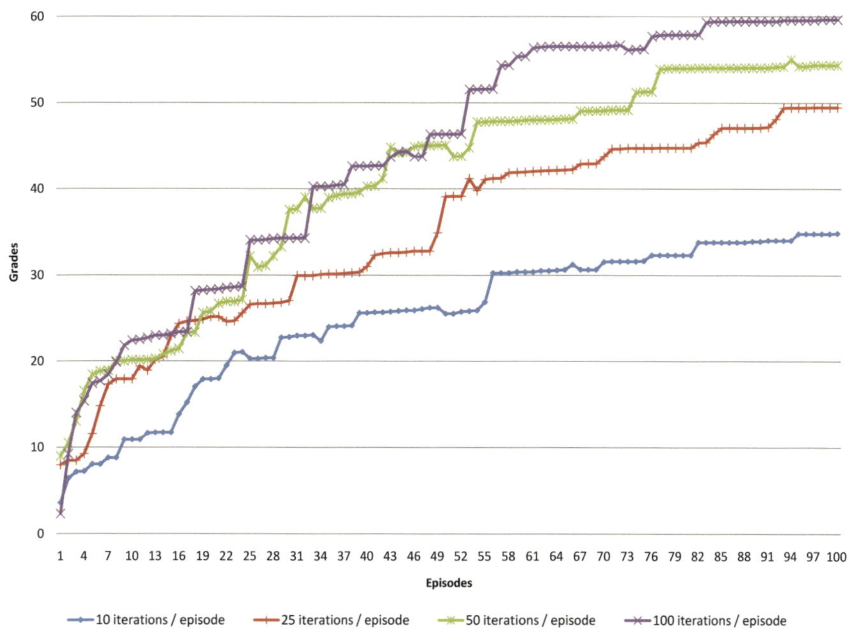

Fig. 6. Initial episodes with events and initial states randomly selected from history.

The curves figure 6 show that the more episodes we run, and the longer the episodes, the better the behavior. But this figure does not show the computation time needed for each point in the curves. Episodes with 100 iterations take twice as long as episodes with 50 iterations whereas the grade is only approximately 1.1 times higher in the end. Hence, we choose to keep $k = 50$ iterations per episode. The same principle applies to the number of episodes. During the first 50 episodes, the grade raises notably. The last 50 episodes take, again, twice as long and result in a grade only 1.2 times higher. Therefore, the assistant can start acting after 50 episodes of 50 iterations, its behavior will be acceptably good. Anyway, after this initial learning, episodes are run regularly and the behavior continues enhancing. This result is presented section 6.2.

6.2 Learning user preferences during interactions

Once an initial behavior was acquired, we performed an experience to measure the efficiency of learning during the "normal" life of the assistant with its user. The role of the user was taken by a human experimenter and consisted in "generating" real life events, such as leaving and entering the office, receiving emails and reminders, having other people coming in and out of the office, playing or pausing the music and starting and stopping the screensaver. To send these events to the assistant, the experimenter used a graphical interface, facilitating him the experience. He was also in charge of giving rewards to the assistant. For that, the

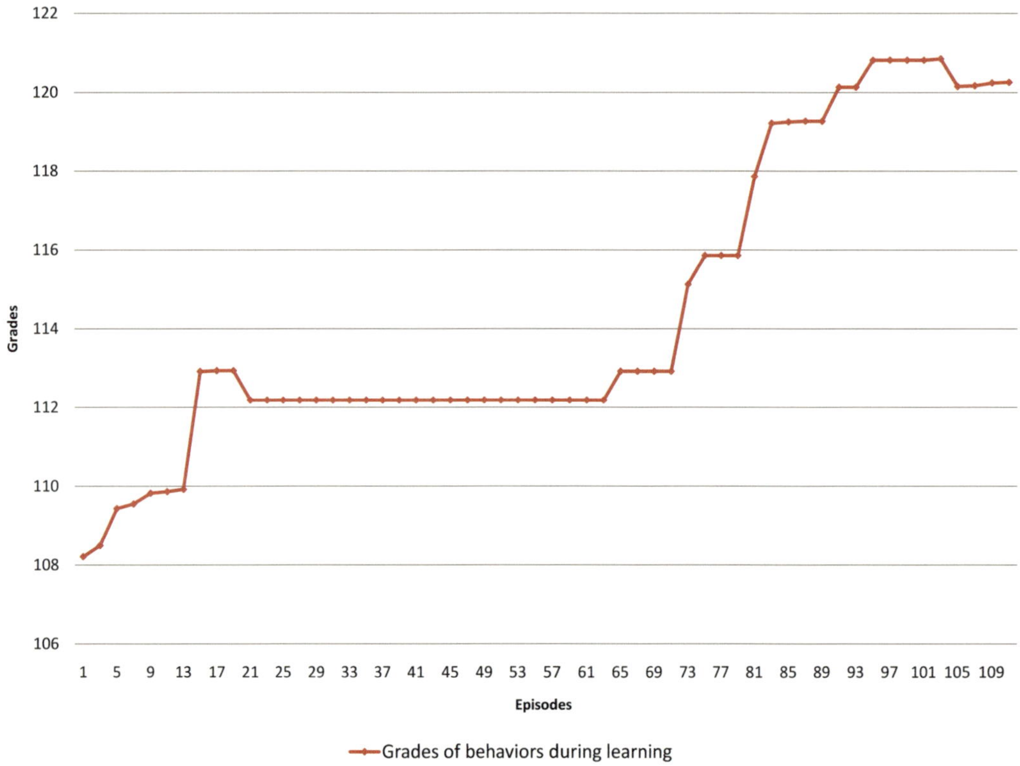

Fig. 7. Grades of behaviors produced by the reinforcement learning algorithm.

experimenter had a goal behavior in mind and gave rewards mostly consistent with this goal. Like a normal user, the experimenter did not give rewards for all actions. During these interactions, at regular time intervals, reinforcement learning episodes were executed and the resulting behavior was evaluated by the experimenter. As previously, he was interviewed about the best action in every state and answered whether this action was the one he had in mind or not. The resulting grades are shown figure 7.

The periods in figure 7 where the curve is rising correspond to periods where user events were new to the assistant (they were not included in the initial world model). The curve is flat when the learned behavior is optimal for the time being.

Figure 8 shows an example where the experimenter changed his mind on a part of the expected behavior. The grade drops and then the system adapts to the new reinforcements.

7. Conclusion

The aim of this research is to investigate Ambient Intelligence systems and their acceptability by users. We exploit a ubiquitous system to provide personalized, context-aware services to users. The personalization of the system is achieved by learning user preferences during interactions. We proposed a reinforcement learning method corresponding to the pattern "event-action" existing in ubiquitous systems. The classical reinforcement learning or indirect

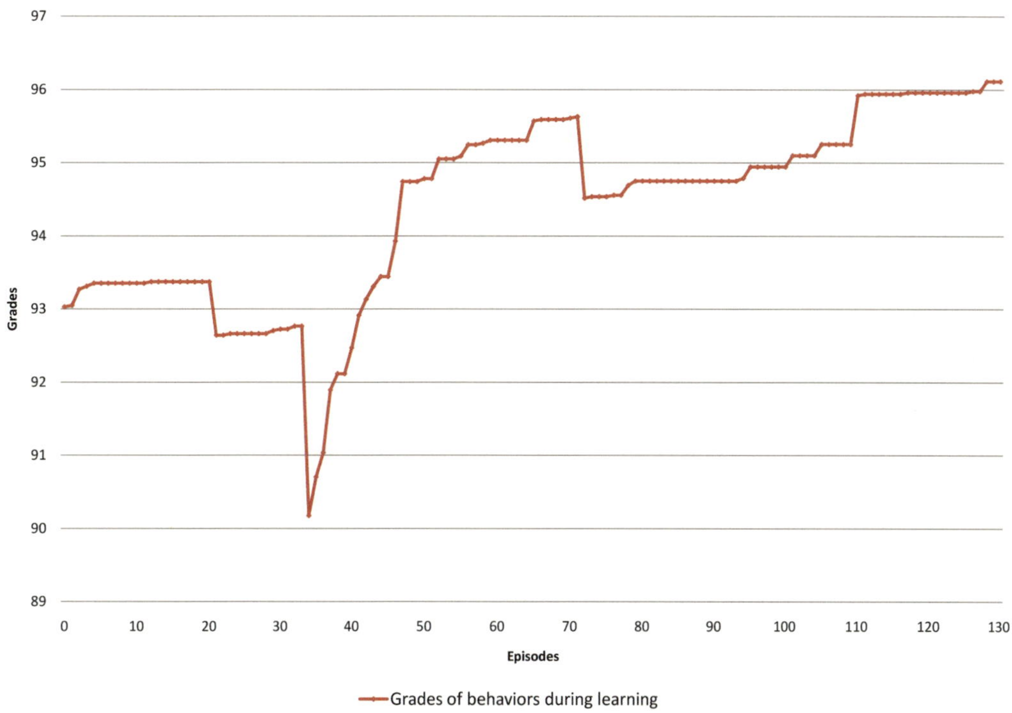

Fig. 8. Grades of behaviors produced by the reinforcement learning algorithm. Example of preference change.

reinforcement learning is not adapted directly to real world applications where the user is in the loop. We conducted a user study in order to validate the relevance of such an application and reveal constraints for the acceptability of such a system. We adapted existing methods to those requirements and developed a prototype showing the correct functioning of our ubiquitous assistant.

8. References

Abowd, G. D., Atkeson, C. G., Feinstein, A., Hmelo, C., Kooper, R., Long, S., Sawhney, N. & Tani, M. (1996). Teaching and learning as multimedia authoring: the classroom 2000 project, *Proceedings of the fourth ACM international conference on Multimedia*, ACM, Boston, Massachusetts, United States, pp. 187–198. *URL:http://portal.acm.org/citation.cfm?doid=244130.244191*

Abowd, G. D. & Mynatt, E. D. (2000). Charting past, present, and future research in ubiquitous computing, *ACM Trans. Comput.-Hum. Interact.* 7(1): 29–58. *URL:http://portal.acm.org/citation.cfm?id=344988*

Adams, N., Gold, R., Schilit, B. N., Tso, M. & Want, R. (1993). An infrared network for mobile computers, *Proceedings USENIX Symposium on Mobile & Location-independent Computing*, p. 41–52.

Aström, K. J. (1965). Optimal control of markov decision processes with incomplete state estimation, *Journal of Mathematical Analysis and Applications* 10: 174–205.

Bellotti, V. & Edwards, K. (2001). Intelligibility and accountability: human considerations in context-aware systems, *Hum.-Comput. Interact.* 16(2): 193–212. *URL:http://portal.acm.org/citation.cfm?id=1463108.1463113*

Brdiczka, O. (2007). *Learning Situation Models for Providing Context-Aware Services*, PhD thesis, Institut National Polytechnique de Grenoble (INPG). *URL:http://www-prima.inrialpes.fr/prima/pub/Publications/2007/Brd07/*

Brumitt, B., Meyers, B., Krumm, J., Kern, A. & Shafer, S. (2000). EasyLiving: technologies for intelligent environments, *Handheld and Ubiquitous Computing*, pp. 97–119. *URL:http://dx.doi.org/10.1007/3-540-39959-3_2*

Buffet, O. (2003). *Une double approche modulaire de l'apprentissage par renforcement pour des agents intelligents adaptatifs*, PhD thesis, Université Henri Poincaré, Nancy 1. Laboratoire Lorrain de recherche en informatique et ses applications (LORIA).

Byun, H. E. & Cheverst, K. (2001). Exploiting user models and Context-Awareness to support personal daily activities, *PERSONAL DAILY ACTIVITIES, WORKSHOP IN UM2001 ON USER MODELLING FOR CONTEXT-AWARE APPLICATIONS* pp. 13—16. *URL:http://citeseerx.ist.psu.edu/viewdoc/summary?doi=10.1.1.106.4677*

Cheverst, K., Byun, H., Fitton, D., Sas, C., Kray, C. & Villar, N. (2005). Exploring issues of user model transparency and proactive behaviour in an office environment control system, *User Modeling and User-Adapted Interaction* 15(3): 235–273. *URL:http://dx.doi.org/10.1007/s11257-005-1269-8*

Coen, M. H. (1998). Design principles for intelligent environments, *Proceedings of the fifteenth national/tenth conference on Artificial intelligence/Innovative applications of artificial intelligence*, American Association for Artificial Intelligence, Madison, Wisconsin, United States, pp. 547–554. *URL:http://portal.acm.org/citation.cfm?id=295733*

Craik, K. (1943). *The Nature of Exploration*, Cambridge University Press, Cambridge, England.

Crowley, J., Coutaz, J., Rey, G. & Reignier, P. (2002). Perceptual components for context aware computing, *UbiComp 2002: Ubiquitous Computing*, pp. 117–134. *URL:http://dx.doi.org/10.1007/3-540-45809-3_9*

Dey, A. K., Hamid, R., Beckmann, C., Li, I. & Hsu, D. (2004). a CAPpella: programming by demonstration of context-aware applications, ACM, Vienna, Austria, pp. 33–40. *URL:http://portal.acm.org/citation.cfm?id=985692.985697*

Intille, S. S. (2002). Designing a home of the future, *IEEE Pervasive Computing* 1(2): 76–82.

Kaelbling, L. P. (2004). Life-Sized learning. Published: Lecture at CSE Colloquia. *URL:http://www.uwtv.org/programs/displayevent.aspx?rID=3566*

Kay, J., Kummerfeld, B. & Lauder, P. (2003). Managing private user models and shared personas, *UM03 Workshop on User Modeling for Ubiquitous Computing*, p. 1–11.

Kozierok, R. & Maes, P. (1993). A learning interface agent for scheduling meetings, *IUI '93: Proceedings of the 1st international conference on Intelligent user interfaces*, ACM Press, New York, NY, USA, p. 81–88. *URL:http://portal.acm.org/citation.cfm?id=169908*

Littman, M. L. (1994). Markov games as a framework for Multi-Agent reinforcement learning, *IN PROCEEDINGS OF THE ELEVENTH INTERNATIONAL CONFERENCE ON MACHINE LEARNING*, pp. 157—163. *URL:http://citeseerx.ist.psu.edu/viewdoc/summary?doi=10.1.1.48.8623*

Lueg, C. (2002). Looking under the rug: On Context-Aware artifacts and socially adept technologies, *Proceedings of Workshop "The Philosophy and Design of Socially Adept Technologies", ACM SIGCHI Conference on Human Factors in Computing Systems.*

Maes, P. (1994). Agents that reduce work and information overload, *Com. ACM* 37(7): 30–40. *URL:http://portal.acm.org/citation.cfm?id=176792*

Michaël, M. (1998). The neural network house : An environment that adapts to its inhabitants, *Proceedings of the American Association for Artificial Intelligence Spring Symposium on Intelligent Environments*, AAAI Press, Menlo Park, CA, pp. 110–114.

Muir, B. M. & Moray, N. (1996). Trust in automation. part II. experimental studies of trust and human intervention in a process control simulation, *Ergonomics* 39(3): 429. *URL:http://www.informaworld.com/10.1080/00140139608964474*

Papadimitriou, C. H. & Tsitsiklis, J. N. (1987). The complexity of markov decision processes, *Mathematics of Operations Research* 12(3): 441–450. *URL:http://www.mit.edu/ jnt/publ.html*

Pineau, J., Gordon, G. & Thrun, S. (2003). Point-based value iteration: An anytime algorithm for pomdps, *International Joint Conference on Artificial Intelligence (IJCAI)*, pp. 1025–1032. *URL:http://www-old.ri.cmu.edu/pubs/pub_4826.html#text_ref*

POMDPs for Dummies: Page 5 (1999). *URL:http://www.cs.brown.edu/research/ai/pomdp/tutorial/pomdp-solving.html*

Remagnino, P. & Foresti, G. (2005). Ambient intelligence: A new multidisciplinary paradigm, *Systems, Man and Cybernetics, Part A: Systems and Humans, IEEE Transactions on* 35(1): 1–6.

Rogers, Y. (2006). Moving on from weiser's vision of calm computing: Engaging UbiComp experiences, *UbiComp 2006: Ubiquitous Computing*, pp. 404–421. *URL:http://dx.doi.org/10.1007/11853565_24*

Rummery, G. A. & Niranjan, M. (1994). On-line q-learning using connectionist systems, *Technical report*, Cambridge University Engineering Department.

Salovaara, A. & Oulasvirta, A. (2004). Six modes of proactive resource management: a user-centric typology for proactive behaviors, *Proceedings of the third Nordic conference on Human-computer interaction*, ACM, Tampere, Finland, pp. 57–60. *URL:http://portal.acm.org/citation.cfm?id=1028014.1028022*

Smith, T. & Simmons, R. G. (2005). Point-based POMDP algorithms: Improved analysis and implementation, *Proc. Int. Conf. on Uncertainty in Artificial Intelligence (UAI)*. *URL:http://www.cs.cmu.edu/ trey/pubs/b2hd-smith05hsvi.html*

Spaan, M. T. J. & Vlassis, N. (2005). Perseus: Randomized point-based value iteration for pomdps, *Journal of Artificial Intelligence Research* 24: 195–220. *URL:http://citeseerx.ist.psu.edu/viewdoc/summary?doi=10.1.1.72.9217*

Sutton, R. (1988). Learning to Predict by the Methods of Temporal Differences, *Machine Learning* 3: 9–44.

Sutton, R. S. (1991). Dyna, an integrated architecture for learning, planning, and reacting, *SIGART Bull.* 2(4): 160–163. *URL:http://portal.acm.org/citation.cfm?id=122377*

Sutton, R. S. & Barto, A. G. (1998). *Reinforcement Learning: An Introduction (Adaptive Computation and Machine Learning)*, The MIT Press.

Walker, M. A. (2000). An application of reinforcement learning to dialogue strategy selection in a spoken dialogue system for email. *URL:http://citeseerx.ist.psu.edu/viewdoc/summary?doi=10.1.1.43.1121*

Watkins, C. & Dayan, P. (1992). Q-Learning, 8(3-4): 279–292. ISSN 0885-6125.
Weiser, M. (1991). The computer for the 21st century, *Scientific American* . *URL:http://www.ubiq.com/hypertext/weiser/SciAmDraft3.html*

5

Cooperative Behavior Rule Acquisition for Multi-Agent Systems by Machine Learning

Mengchun Xie
Wakayama National College of Technology
Japan

1. Introduction

Multi-agent systems are the systems in which several interacting, intelligent agents pursue some set of goals or perform some set of tasks (Wooldridge, 2000). In multi-agents systems, each agent must behave independently according to its states and environments, and, if necessary, must cooperate with other agents in order to perform a given task. Multi-agent systems have more robustness and flexibility than conventional centralized management one. However, it is difficult to beforehand predict the action of the agent and give the action rule for the multi-agent systems, because the interaction between agents is complicated.
The acquisition of an autonomous agent's intellectual action rule is a very interesting topic. Recently, extensive research has been done on models such as Robocap (Stone & eloso, 1996, Matsubara et al., 1998). Studying computation models of cooperative structure to accomplish a given task is known to be a difficult problem (Jeong & Lee, 1997).In the field of self-learning reactive systems, it is not even desirable to have a clear idea of a computational model. Thus, being adaptable, autonomous agents imply minimally pre-programmed systems. Numerous studies regarding autonomous agents in the multi-agent systems have been conducted. Nolfi and Foreano (Nolfi & Floreano, 1998) simulated a pursuit system with two agents (predator and prey) in real environments. They evolved both agents reciprocally using a genetic algorithm. Jim and Lee (Jim & Lee, 2000) evolved the autonomous agents with a genetic algorithm. Zhou (Zhou, 2002) used both a fuzzy controller and a genetic algorithm. The fuzzy function displayed the position of the agent, and the genetic algorithm was used for learning. Fujita and Matsuo (Fujita & Matsuo, 2005) learned the autonomous agent using reinforcement learning. The reinforcement learning method involves developing an agent's behavior by means of the interrelationship with the environment and resulting reinforcement signals. The reinforcement learning method can guarantee learning and adaptability without precise pre-knowledge about the environment.
In this chapter, we focused on the problem of "trash collection", in which multiple agents collect all trash as quickly as possible. The goal is for multiple agents to learn to accomplish a task by interacting with the environment and acquiring cooperative behavior rules. Therefore, for a multi-agent system, we discuss how to acquire the rules of cooperative action to solve problems effectively.
First we used a genetic algorithm as a method of acquiring the rules for an agent. Individual coding (definition of the rule) methods are performed, and the learning efficiency is evaluated.

Second, we construct the learning agent using the Q-learning which is a representative technique of reinforcement learning. Q-learning is a method to let an agent learn from delayed reward and punishment. It is designed to find a policy that maximizes for all states. The decision policy is represented by a function. The action vale function is shares among agents.
The third, we concentrate on an application of Multi-agent systems to disaster relief using Q-learning. We constructed a simplified disaster relief multi-agent system and acquired action rules by Q-learning. We then observe how the autonomous agents obtain their action rules and examined the influence of the learning situations on the system. Moreover, we discuss how the system was influenced by learning situation and the view information of the agent.

2. Cooperative action of multi-agent

2.1 Cooperative action of agents

When multiple autonomous agents exist, the environment changes from static to dynamic, compared to the case of an individual agent. An agent engaged in cooperative action decides its actions by referring to not only its own information and purpose, but to those of other agents as well (Jennings et al., 1998).
Multi-agent systems enable problems to be solved more efficiently. In addition, multi-agent systems can solve problems that may be impossible for individual agents to solve, because multi-agents have one common aim and can adjust to their environment and perform cooperative actions. Occasionally, in order to proceed with a task in a changing environment, multi-agents must judge precise situations in order to make adaptive moves. In order to realize cooperative action, it is necessary to perform actions based on the rule that working as a group takes priority over the actions of the individual. Generally speaking, individual action is natural, whereas group action is acquired by learning to accomplish goals through cooperative actions.
Multi-agents are not always advantageous. For example, if multiple agents in the same environment act independently, then the situation that each agent has to deal with becomes more complex because each agent has to consider the other agents movements before performing an action. If an agent tries to perform an autonomously decided action, the agent may not be able to perform the action as planned because of disturbances caused by the other agents. Changes to the environment caused by the actions of other agents may make understanding the environment difficult for the agents.

2.2 Establishment of the problems environment

This chapter considers the "trash collection" problem, in which trash is placed on a field of fixed size and agents must collect the trash as fast as possible.
As in Figure 1, the field is divided into $N \times N$ lattice. Agents are denoted by • symbols, and trash is denoted by the ■ symbols.
In the trash collection problem, the actions of agents are defined as follows:

i. The action of an agent is determined once per unit time.
ii. An agent can move to an adjoining lattice, where up-and-down and right-and-left are connected per unit time.
iii. An agent collects the trash when the agent has the same position as the trash.

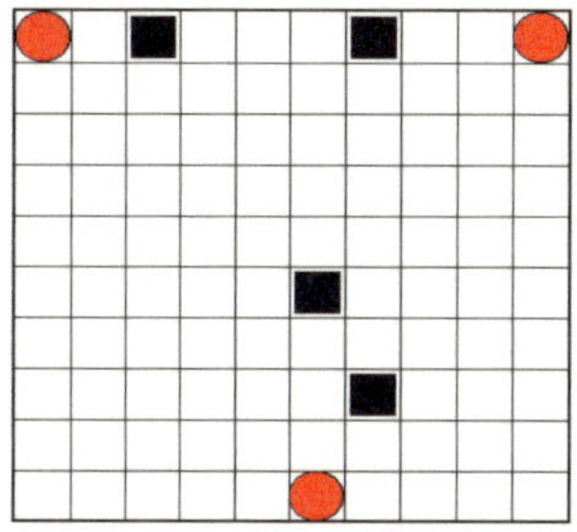

Fig. 1. An example of the problem environment

For the trash collection problem, an example of agent actions is shown in Figure 2 for cooperative behavior and non-cooperative behavior. If the priority of each agent is to act to increase individual profit, by collecting as much trash as possible, then the agents are expected to act as shown in Figure 2(a). However, if each agent has a complete understanding of the entire situation and has the priority of collecting all of the trash as fast as possible, then agents are efficient and act as shown in Figure 2(b). In this case, the priority action of an agent is called cooperative action. The goal of the present study is to have agents acquire, through learning, the rules that are necessary to take cooperative action.

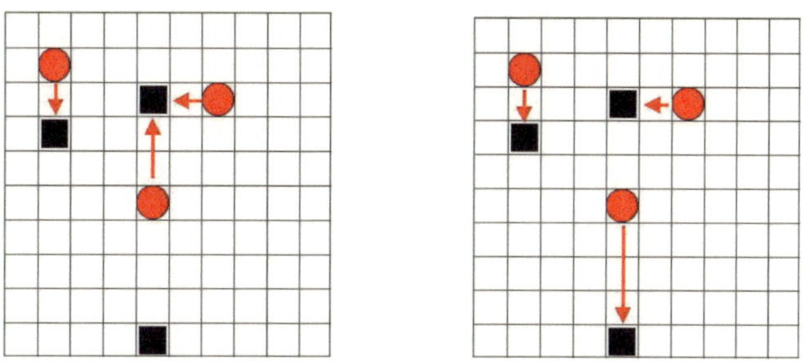

(a) Non-cooperative action (b) Cooperative action

Fig. 2. Example of agent action

3. Acquisition of cooperative rule using GA

In this section, we use a genetic algorithm (GA) to acquire the cooperative action rule (Goldberg, 1989, Holland, 1975). The number of steps taken to collect all of the trash is used to evaluate the rule. We used a GA, which agents use to decide actions, to evolve and acquire the cooperative rules needed.

3.1 Structure of the system

The system to acquire the cooperative rules is described by the action rules of agents. An agent realizes the state from the field's information, compares the state with the internal rules, and then decides on its next action. The renewal of the rules is carried by GA. The structure of the system is as follows:

1. Development of the field - arrange the decided number of pieces of trash and agents on the established field.
2. Each agent determines its next move - each agent decides the direction of its next move based on the situation of the field, the internal rules and knowledge.

3. Movement of agents - all agents move simultaneously. A piece of trash is collected if an agent occupies the same position.
4. Repeat Items (2) ~ (3) until all of the trash is collected. Repetition of Items (2) ~ (3) is considered as one step.
5. When collection is completed, evaluate the actions of the agents based on the number of steps required to complete the action. Agents also learn on the basis of this evaluation.
6. The experiment is continued by returning to Item (1), and agents continue to learn.

3.2 Acquisition of cooperative rule by GA

The behavior of each agent is governed by a rule. A rule is a condition-action rule of the form. The condition part of the rule represents the situation of the field (the arrangement of agents and trash). The action part of the rule indicates the piece of trash toward which the agent moves at the next time step.
An agent compares the present state of the field with the action part of the rules and decides a rule that is closest to the present state of the field. An agent executes the decided action.
Because multiple agents are present in a dynamic environment, it is necessary for each agent to have the ability to learn from the environment in order to develop cooperative action. In this section, the acquisition of cooperative rules is performed using a GA. We propose two methods of individual representation are as follows:

Representation Method 1: one rule for one individual

This representation method takes one rule as a single individual, as shown in Table 1.

Distance from Agent A					Next Movement:
Agent1	Agent2		Trash1	Trash2	
Distance from Agent B					The No. Trash
Agent1	Agent2		Trash1	Trash2	watch
Distance from Agent C					etc.
Agent1	Agent2		Trash1	Trash2	

Table 1. Structure of the individual by Representation Method 1

The condition part of the rule represents the assumed field state at a distance. That is to say, each agent identifies the positions of agents to a central agent. The action part is the hamming distance from the central agent to each trash and to others agents rearranged in order of ascending proximity. The action part represents the piece of trash toward which the agent will move next.

Representation Method 2: Multiple rules for one individual

The form of a rule is as described in Method 1; however, one individual consists of a group of rules (Table 2).

Evaluation of the individual

Representation Method 1 takes one rule as a single individual for GA. An agent chooses a rule from the population consisting of such individuals and decides its next move. For the population of individuals, genetic operations, such as crossover, mutation and selection, are performed. The evaluation of each individual agent is based on that next move and the time required to finish collecting one piece of trash. The evaluation value of the individual agent is given a constant value when an agent applies the rule and collects one piece of trash. Once

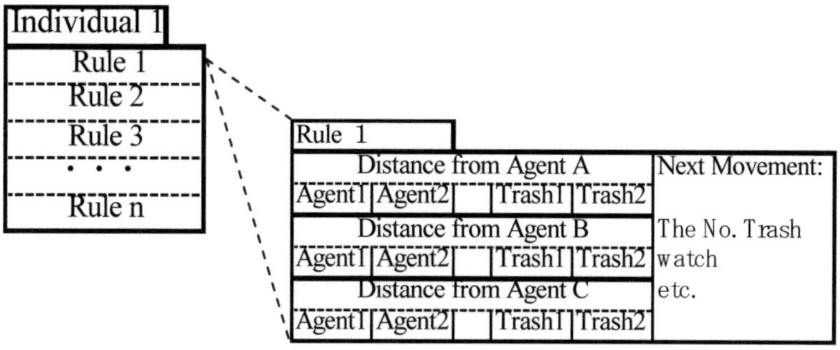

Table 2. Structure of the individual by Representation Method 2

collection is completed, the result is compared to the previous collection and the required number of steps is evaluated. The fewer the steps, the better the result.

For Representation Method 2, an agent has some individual (group of rules). Evaluation of individuals is performed based in the decrease in the number of steps required for collection compared to the previous collection by giving in proportion to the degree. Trash collection is performed once by one individual, and each individual is evaluated by changing the individual used for the trash collection. After finishing the evaluation of all individuals, a GA is selected based on the above evaluation.

3.3 Results and discussion

Using the representation method of the proposed individual, the acquisition of the cooperative action of the multi-agent system was attempted using a GA. In the experiment, the size of the field was 15 × 15. There were 15 pieces of trash and three agents. The average results for 20 repetitions until all of the trash was collected by the agents for the same initial distribution are shown below.

An example experimental result

An experimental result is shown in Figure 3. In this result, the agents are denoted by ● and pieces of trash are denoted by ■, and the lines indicate the tracks of agents.

When the cooperative action is learned using the Representation Method 1, each agent had 50 rules. In other words, the population size of the GA is 50. The number of steps required in order to collect all trash differs in every generation, but fluctuates in the range from 20 to 60 steps. That is because there are different rules taken for every generation by the GA. The shortest step of 20 was obtained by trial-and-error. As a result of the learning using the GA, this elite individual could be obtained in approximately 30 generations (Xie, 2006).

In Representation Methods 2, each agent has 10 rule groups. In short, the population size of the GA is 10. One rule group consists of 50 rules. That is, the results for the number of steps required for 10 individuals fluctuate in the range from 20 to 50 steps, which is fewer than that for Representation Method 1.

4. Cooperative behavior acquisition using Q-learning

In this section, we discuss the cooperative behavior acquisition of agents using the Q-learning which is a representative technique of reinforcement learning. Q-learning is a method to let an agent learn from delayed reward and punishment. It is designed to find a policy that maximizes for all states.

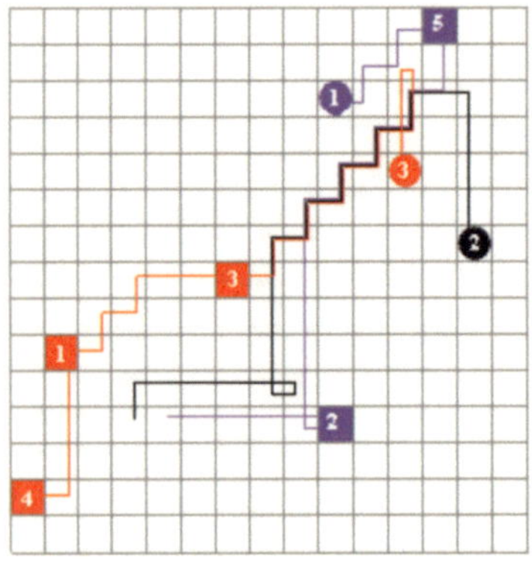

Fig. 3. An example experimental result

4.1 Agent and environment

The agent decides the action based on the condition of perceived environment, and some changes are caused environment by the action. Therefore, agent and environment are relationships of the interaction.

An accessible environment is one in which the agent can obtain complete, accurate, up-to-date information about the environment's state. Most moderately complex environments are inaccessible. The more accessible can environment is, the simpler it is to build agent to operate in it (Alex et al., 2005). In the meantime, when the environments are inaccessible, the information which can be perceived from the environment is limited, and it is inaccurate, and it entails delay.

When there is only one the agent, the environment is static. However, it is not always static for the environment, when other agent exists. Because, the condition of the environment may be due to be changed by other agent.

4.2 The composition of agents

In this section, the composition and each function of the agent are described. The structure of an agent is shown in Figure 4. The figure has shown each component of the agent, and the transmission of information has been expressed in the arrow. First, the agent perceives the condition of the environment in the detector. Next, the rule is compared with the condition that it was perceived by the acting decider, and the action is decided. Finally, the action is carried out in effector.

The detector of the agent can't always perceive the condition of the environment completely. It is similar to there being a limit at the human visual acuity. Therefore, an agent can perceive only a part of condition of the environment or the state just in the neighborhood.

The whole environment and the environment which an agent perceived are respectively shown in Figure 5 and Figure 6. Figure 5 shows whole of the arranged field of agents. The round sign is an agent, and the number is the label of the agent in Figure 6. The frame which each agent is enclosed with is the range that an agent can perceive, and it is the range that it has been limited. Figure 6 is the environment which each agent perceived. The symbol X is an agent itself, and the number is other agents.

The conditions (position) of all the agents are included in the whole environment as like Figure 5. An agent 1 and an agent 2 perceive the respectively different environment.

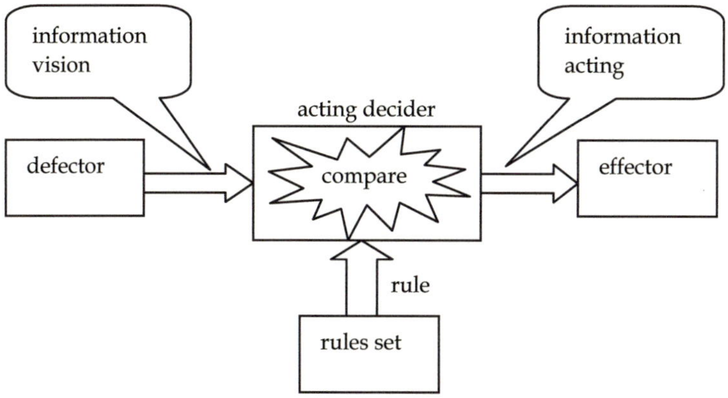

Fig. 4. Composition of an agent

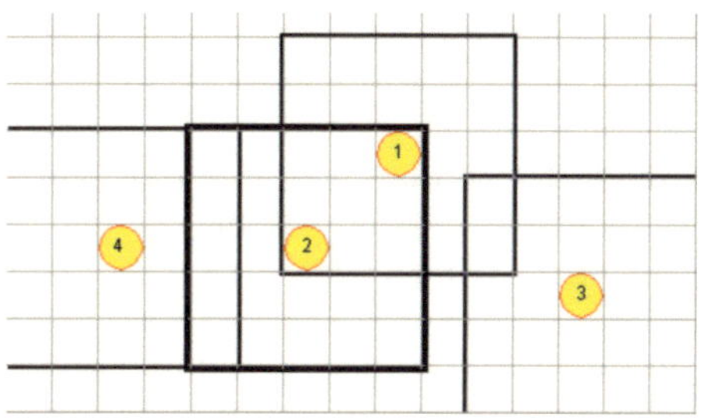

Fig. 5. The whole environment

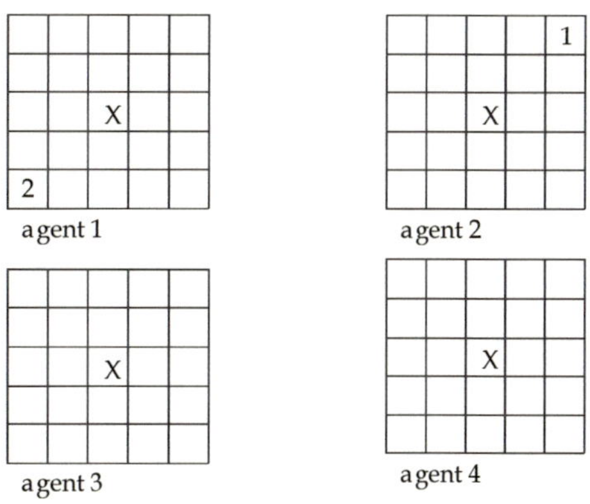

Fig. 6. The environment which each agent perceives

However, though each agent is located in the different environment, an agent 3 and an agent 4 perceive it as a condition of the same environment. This problem is called the imperfect perception problem, and it becomes one of the important problems in the agent design. It is considered that the visual field range of the agent is increased in order to avoid this problem.

The behavior of each agent is governed. A rule is a condition-action rule of form. The condition part of the rule represents the situation of the environment which the defector perceives. The action part of the rule indicates the action of the agent. When the number of patterns of the condition of an environment which the defector perceives increases, the number of rules increases. An example of the condition-action rules is shown in Table 3.

Situation of environment	action
200000000000X000000010020	up
002000010000X000000020000	down
000000000000X000000002000	left
002000000000X000000001000	right
000000000000X000002000000	down

Table 3. An example of rules

The effector decides the action by the rule. For example, if the condition of the environment was perceived with "000000000000X000002000000", the action to the "down" is chosen on the action of the agent in Table 3 rules.

4.3 Q-Learning

A prominent algorithm in reinforcement learning is the Q-Learning. In an environment of finite Markov decision process (MDP), the goal is to find the optimal policy in each state visited to maximize the value of a performance metric, e.g , long-run discounted reward using Q-Learning (Schleiffer, 2005).

A policy defines the action in every state visited. Let A denote the set of actions allowed and let S denote the set of states. We will assume that both A and S are finite. Let r_{t+1} denote the immediate reward earned in going from state s_t to state s_{t+1}, when action $a_t \in A$ is selected in state s_t, and let γ denote the discounting factor. Then with s_t as the starting state, for the policy π, the total discounted reward - generally referred to as discounted reward - is defined as (Bradtkes & Duff, 1994, Parr & Russell, 1998):

$$R_t^{\pi} = r_{t+1} + \gamma r_{t+2} + \gamma^2 r_{t+3} + \cdots + \gamma^{T-1} r_T = \sum_{k=1}^{T-t} r^{k-1} r_{t+k} \tag{1}$$

where T denotes the finished time of the system. If the Markov chain associated with the policy π is irreducible and a periodic, the discounted reward, R_t^{π} , is independent of the starting state s_t.

In Q-Learning, which can be implemented in simulators or in real time, the algorithm iterates are the so-called Q-factors. $Q(s,a)$ will denote the Q-factor for state $s \in S$ and $a \in A$. The updating in Q-Learning is asynchronous. One iteration of the algorithm is associated with each state transition in the simulator. In one transition, only one Q-factor is updated. Let $Q(s,a)$ denote the Q-factor for state s and action a. When the system transitions from state s_t to state s_{t+1} and a_t denotes the action chosen in state s_t, then the Q-factor for state s_t and action a_t is updated as follows:

$$Q(s_t, a_t) \leftarrow Q(s_t, a_t) + \alpha \left[r_{t+1} + \gamma \max_a Q(s_{t+1}, a) - Q(s_t, a_t) \right] \tag{2}$$

where $0 \leq \alpha \leq 1$, which denotes a step-size parameter in the iteration, must satisfy some standard stochastic-approximation conditions, and all other Q-factors are kept unchanged.

Theoretically, the algorithm is allowed to run for infinitely many iterations until the *Q*-factors converge.

4.4 Action acquisition by Q-learning

The action-value function is renewed in which the agent acts. When an agent pick up a trash, the reward which affects the renewal of the action value is given for the agent. And, the field is initializes, when all trashes on the field are picked up. But, action-value function and agent learning number of step would not be initialized. It is repeated to learning number of step decided.

The flow of the trash collection agent learning is as follows.

```
Initialize Q(s, a) arbitrarily
 Initialize state of field
          (Arrange initial position of agents and trash)
Loop (until decided step){
    Decide randomly action a, then act
    IF ( pick up a trash )
         r=M (M is any positive number)
    ELSE
         r=0 (don't pick up)
    Acquire present state s
    Acquire next state s'
    Acquire max Q(s', a') in the next state
    Renew Q-factor
         Q(s,a) ← (1 − α)Q(s,a) + α(r + γ max Q(s',a'))
  IF ( All trashes on the field are picked up )
         Initialize state of field
}
```

The trash collection carries out the action based on action-value function. Action rule of trash collection agent is shown as Table 4. Action part is replaced with the action-value function.

The action of the agent is decided by the value of action-value function moved to the each direction. For example, the action is decided by the each value of *Q(B, up)*, *Q(B, down)*, *Q(B, left)* and *Q(B, right)* when the state of the environment is B. As a method for deciding the action from these four values, there are two techniques are as follows (Watkins, 1989, Bridle, 1990):

1. ε-greedy policies

It is a method that most of time they choose an action that has maximal estimated action value, but with probability ε they instead select at random. That is, all nongreedy action are given the minimal probability of selection, and the remaining bulk of the probability is given to the greedy action.

Although ε-greedy action selection is an effective and popular means of balancing exploration and exploitation in reinforcement learning, one drawback is that when it explores it chooses equally among all action. This means that it is as likely to choose the worst-appearing action as it is to choose the next-to-best action.

2. Softmax policies

It is a method to vary the action probabilities as a graded function of estimated value. The greedy action is still given the highest selection probability, but all the others are ranked and weighted according to their value estimates.

state	action-value function			
	up	down	left	right
A	Q(A, up)	Q(A,	Q(A, left)	Q(A, right)
B	Q(B, up)	Q(B,	Q(B, left)	Q(B, right)
Z	Q(Z, up)	Q(Z,	Q(Z, left)	Q(Z, right)

Table 4. Environment 's state and action-value

4.5 Experiment results and discussion

Using the system as has been mentioned in 4.2, the experiment on the learning of the agent was carried out. The size of the field was 15×15. There were 10 pieces of trash and five agents. An agent moves to the one square of relative position in 1 step. And, each agent has the ability of perceiving the condition of the environment of the circumference of 2 squares. It is called a task that the trash is picked up. The reward is given, when each agent picked up the trash. And, action-value function Q is shared between each agents.

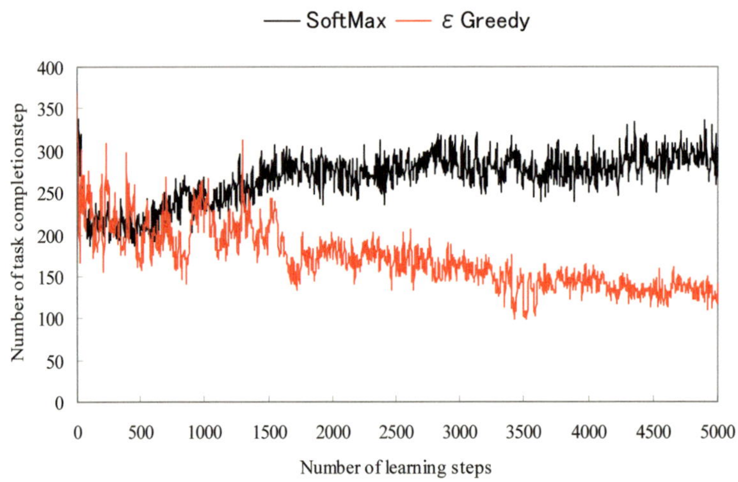

Fig. 7. Comparison policies

The effect of ε-greedy policies and softmax policies on the learning of the agent is shown in the Figure 7. The task completion step decreases with the increase of the learning step, when ε-greedy policies were used. However, it reversely increases on the task completion step, when the softmax policies were used. This is because the action value to each direction is equalized with the increase of the learning step, and the difference of the probability moved to the each direction decreased using the softmax policies.

The effects of step-size parameter, reward size and discount-rate parameter in update Q-factor were examined.

The step-size parameter shows which degree is renewed when the learning-value function is updated. It is a small positive fraction which influences the rate of learning. The range of the step-size is from 0.1 to 1. Learning results of different step-size α = 0.1, 0.4 and 0.7 were shown in Figure 8. In Figure 8, when step-size α is 0.4, there are smaller tasks completion steps than α is 0.1. However, in Figure 8, the learning has not been very much stabilized in the time of step-size 0.7. From this fact, it was proven that it can not skillfully learn when the step-size too is greatly set.

The reward size is a value given when the agent picked up a trash. It is shown in Figure 9 as a result of the learning as the reward size is set to 10, 100 and 1000. In this Figure, it was proven that the reward size does not affect the learning. Then in this chapter, we use the same reward size value for all experiments. It seems to be important to give the reward than its value.

The discount rate shows the degree of reference of Q-factor in next state. The learning results are shown in Figure 10 as the discount rate was set from 0.1 to 0.9. It was proven that it could not learn skillfully, when the discount rate is too small.

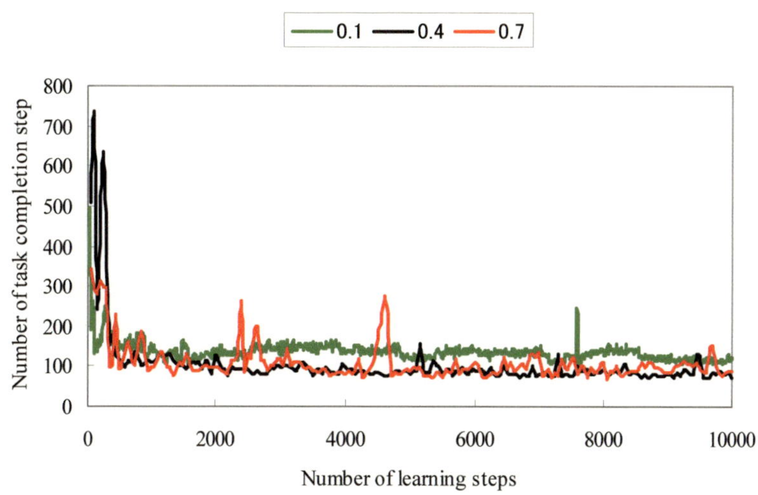

Fig. 8. Step-size comparison

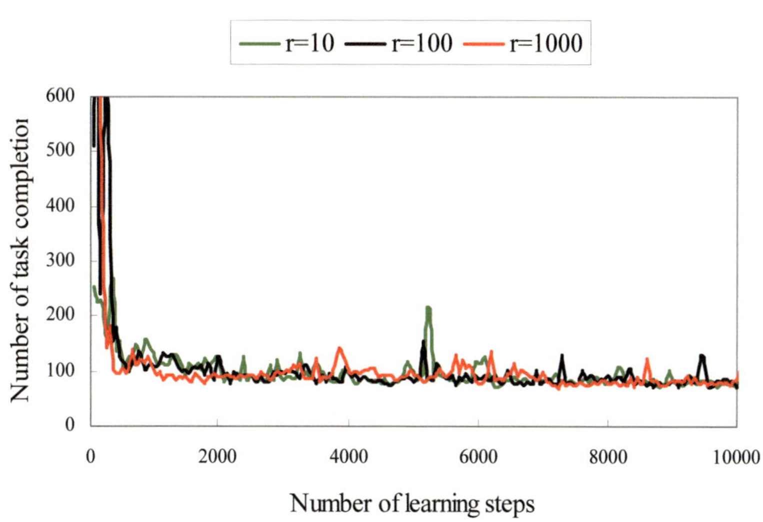

Fig. 9. Comparison of reward size

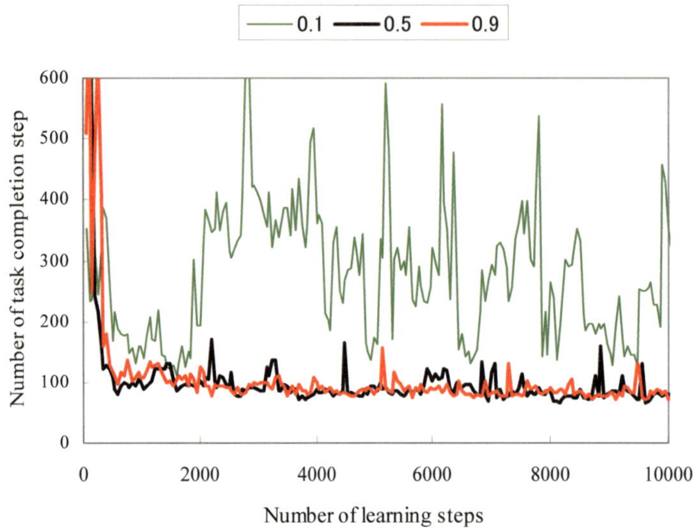

Fig. 10. Comparison of discount rate

5. Disaster relief multi-agent systems using Q-learning

In this section, we concentrate on an application of Multi-agent systems to disaster relief using Q-learning. We constructed a simplified disaster relief multi-agent system and acquired action rules by Q-learning. We then observe how the autonomous agents obtain their action rules and examined the influence of the learning situations on the system. Moreover, we discuss how the system was influenced by learning situation and the view information of the agent.

5.1 Disaster relief multi-agent systems

We consider the "disaster relief" problem, in which the injured are placed on a field of fixed size and agents must rescue the injured persons as fast as possible. It aims to rescue the injured person efficiently as the whole system when the agent is achieving own target. This can be considered as a multi-agent system (Xie & Okazaki, 2008).

5.2 Representation of the perceived environment

An agent has constant view in the disaster relief multi-agent system. The agent can perceive the surrounding environment and can recognize other agents and injured individuals within its range of vision. When an agent has a visual field N, it is assumed that the agent can move N steps.

An example within the range of vision is shown in Figure 11 Agent 1's visual field is 2, and Agent 1 can recognize two injured individuals within its visual field.

In the disaster relief multi-agent system, in order to handle visual field information that the agent receives from the environment by reinforcement learning, it is necessary that pattern is provided of visual field information by replacing with the numerical value. The agent expresses the information of other agents and injured individuals within its visual field range numerically and arranges this information in a fixed order. This string is called the visual field pattern.

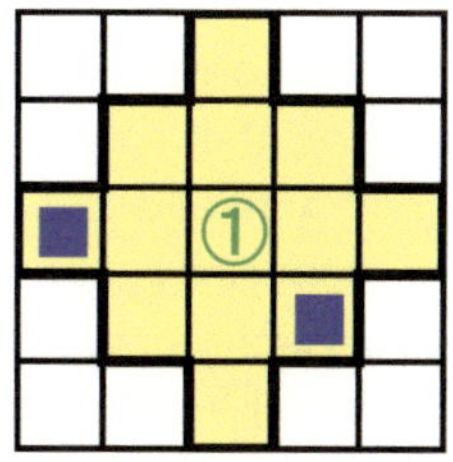

Fig. 11. Range of vision of an agent

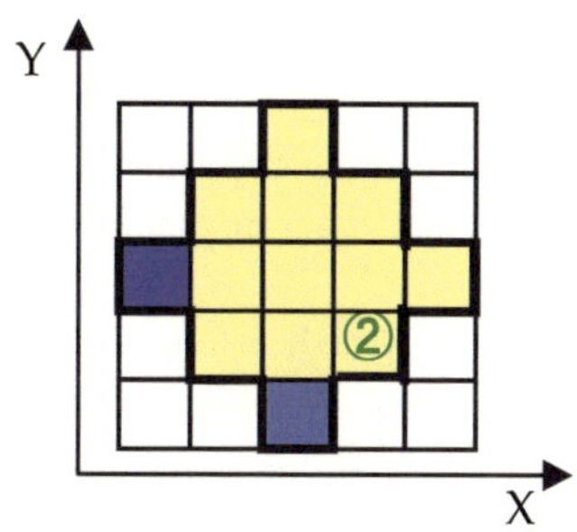

position of agent 1 is centered at (0,0)

coordinate (-2, 0) P (injured)
coordinate (0, -2) P (injured)
coordinate (1, -1) A (agent 2)

visual filed pattern: -20P0-2P1-1A

Fig. 12. Creation of visual field information pattern

The technique for creating the pattern of the visual field information is shown in Figure 12. First, Agent 1 perceives the relative position of the other agents and injured individuals in a fixed order, and the coordinates of Agent 1 are assumed to be (0, 0). In this example, the relative positions and patterns are as follows:

at (-2,0) an injured person (P) >> -20P

at (0,-2) an injured person (P) >>0-2P

at (+1,-1) other agent 2 (A) >>1-1A

The string -20P0-2P1-1A is the visual field pattern in proportion to recognized visual field information that there are some injured individuals and other agents. Here, the visual field range is limited to 9. Compared to the case in which the information of all masses in the visual field range is acquired, there is the merit in which the string of the visual field pattern shortens on this technique.

In reinforcement learning, the wider the range of the vision pattern, the more information can be recognized. However, reinforcement learning has some disadvantages in that the number of states of the visual field pattern increase and the learning speed is decreased.

5.3 Experiment and discussion

In the disaster relief multi-agent system constructed using Q-learning, experiment and consideration are carried out by changing the learning conditions. One movement of the agent is set to correspond to one step, and all agents are assumed to move simultaneously. The action value functions are shared between agents. In all of the experiments, the field size is 10×10, the number of rescue agents is three, the step size α is 0.1, the discount rate γ is 0.9, the probability ε is 0.1, and the number of iterations is 100.

5.3.1 Effect of number of learning iterations

The relationship between the number of steps, which depended on the rescue, and the number of injured individuals that are rescued varied with the number of learning iterations of the agent, as shown in Figure 13. Figure 13 shows the learning results for 10, 100, 1,000, and 10,000 learning iterations. There were 10 injured individuals and three agents. In one step, each agent moves one square to an adjacent position, namely, up, down, right, or left. The visual field of each agent is 2.

The horizontal axis shows the number of individuals rescued, and the vertical axis shows the number of steps, which depends on the specific conditions of the rescue. As the number of learning iterations increases, the number of steps required in order to effect a rescue decreases. This is an effect by the learning of agents. Moreover, the number of steps required to effect rescue increased rapidly, when the number of injured individuals exceeded eight. Since there is no information that agent is obtained and agents choose the random action, when the injured were in visual field outside of all agents.

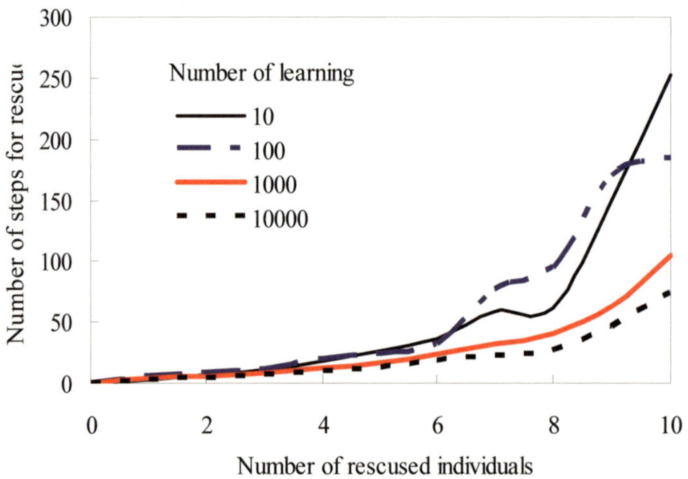

Fig. 13. Effect of number of learning iterations

5.3.2 Density of the injured

The relationship between number of steps required for rescue and the rescue rate of injured individuals is shown in Figure 14, where the injured of the different density were arranged. The number of learning iterations is 10,000, the visual field is 3, and number of injured individuals is 5, 10, and 20.

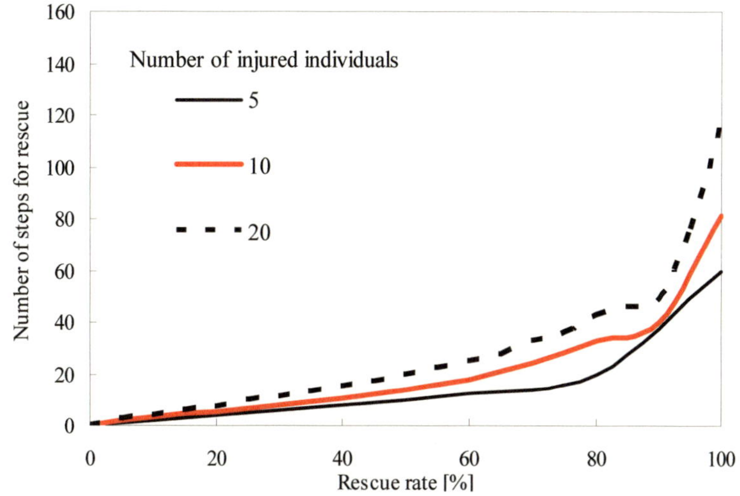

Fig. 14. Effect of density of injured

In Figure 14, the horizontal axis shows the rescue rate, i.e., the ratio of the number of individuals rescued to the total number of injured individuals in the entire field. The experimental results revealed that the number of steps necessary to effect a rescue increased as the number of injured individuals increased. The frequency with which the rescue agent moves on the field is considered to have increased as the number of injured individuals increased.

5.3.3 Visual field range

When the visual field range of the agent is changed, the relationship between the number of individuals rescued and the number of steps required for rescue is shown in Figure 15. The experimental conditions assume that the number of iterations if 10,000, the number of injured is 10, and the visual field range is varied as 2, 3, and 4.

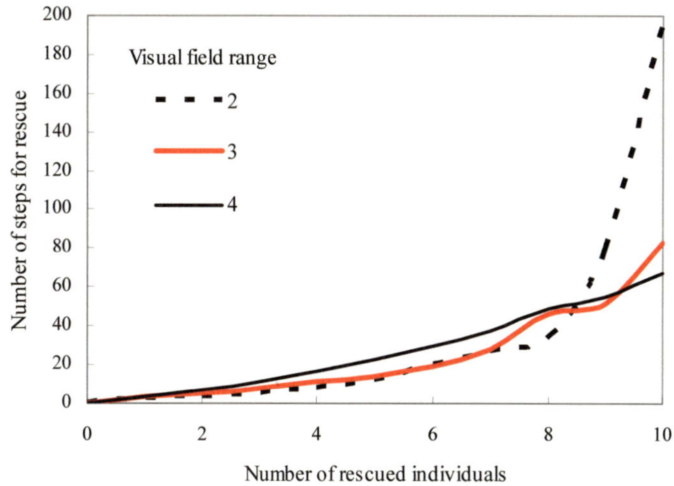

Fig. 15. Effect of visual field range

This figure shows that the fewest steps in which all injured individuals could be rescued occurred when the visual field range was 4. This is because the visual field range of the rescue agent is wide, and the situation in which injured individuals are located outside the visual fields of all rescue agents rarely occurs. However, in some cases, a visual field range of 2 allowed the quickest rescue when the number of injured individuals was small. The reason for this is that the visual field pattern number decreased, because the visual field range is narrow, and a more accurate action value function could be obtained. Moreover, it became a result of combining both characteristics of visual field range 2, 4 in visual field range of 3.

5.3.4 Acquisition of the cooperation action rule

It is possible that the agent efficiently rescued after it carried out Q-learning because the cooperation action was accurately carried out between agents. To confirm the cooperative behavior of agents, a number of action rules acquired from the action value function were examined after 10,000 learning iterations (Figure 16).

In this Figure, agents are denoted by • symbols, and the injured individuals are denoted by ■ symbols. In rule 1, for Agent 1, the probability of moving to the left, where nearest injured individual 1 is located, increased most. However, in rule 2, the probabilities of moving toward the bottom and the right, where an injured individual 2 is located, were highest, because another agent, Agent 2, is positioned near the other injured individual 1. As a result, Agent 1 performed a cooperation action.

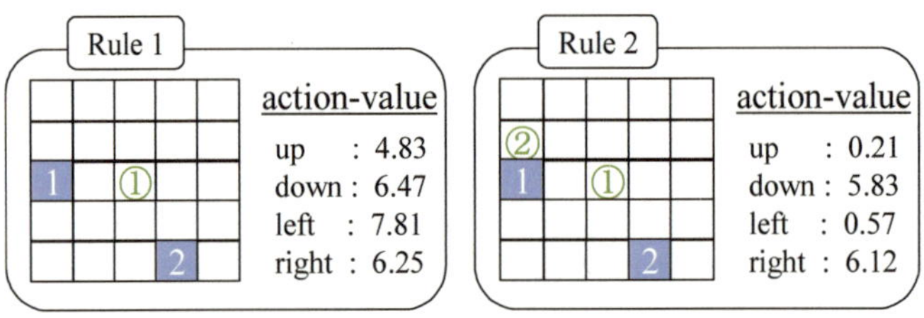

Fig. 16. Example of an action rule

6. Conclusions

In this chapter, we attempted to acquire a cooperative action rule for agents through the use of a GA and Q-Learning, and carried out an application of Multi-agent system to disaster relief by Q-Learning.

We used two representation methods to describe individual agents and to learn cooperative action through a GA. We used the GA based on the fact that each agent acts cooperatively by learning to finish trash collection as fast as possible without any indication. However, further research on the individual evaluation of GA and crossover methods is required. The rule and individual of the present study are intended to learn the most efficient action in response the arrangement of the field by repeating tasks using the same arrangement. However, this makes the learned rules less efficient if the arrangement of the field is different than that used in training. At this stage, we were not able to determine clearly whether agents engaged in cooperative action.

We use the Q-Learning based on the fact that the action-value is high when agents will act cooperatively, and each agent acts cooperatively by learning to finish trash collection as fast as possible without any indication. The task completion step decreases with the increase of the learning step, when ε-greedy policies were used. However, it reversely increases on the task completion step, when the softmax policies were used. This is because the action value to each direction is equalized with the increase of the learning step, and the difference of the probability moved to the each direction decreased using the softmax policies. In present, the number of states is very large because all the environments where the agent appeared under learning are used. In future research, we intend to improve the representation methods of action rule to solve that problem.

In the disaster relief multi-agent system, the number of steps required to effect the rescue of an injured individual decreased with the increase in the number of learning iterations. This is considered to be the effect of the learning of agents. However, the number of steps, which depends on the rescue situation, increased rapidly when the number of injured individuals in the field decreased. When the injured individuals are outside the visual field of all rescue agents, there is no information available to the agents, and so the agents perform random actions. The effect of density and visual field range of the injured individuals on the system was also examined. The number of environment patterns becomes large because, at present, all of the environments that the agent considers during learning are considered. In the future, the number of environment patterns should be decreased.

7. References

Wooldridge, M. (2000). Intelligent Agent, in: *Multiagent Systems,* Gernard Weiss, 27-73, The MIT Press, 0262731312, Cambridge, Massachusetts

Stone, P. & eloso, M. (1996). Using Machine learning in the Soccer Server, *Proc. of IROS-96 Workshop on Robocup*

Matsubara, H.; Frank, I. & Tanaka, K. (1998). Automatic Soccer Commentary and RoboCup, *The 2nd Proceedings of RoboCap Workshop*

Jeong, K. & Lee, J. (1997). Evolving cooperative mobile robots using a modified genetic algorithm, *Robotics and Autonomous Systems,* Vol. 21, 197-205

Nolfi, S. & Floreano, D. (1998). Co-evolving predator and prey robts: do 'arm races' arise in artificial evolution? *Artificial Life 4 (4)* , 311-335

Jim, K.C. & Lee, C. (2000). Talkin helps: evolving communicating robots for the predator-prey pursuit problem, *Artificial Life,* No.6, 237-254

Zhou, C. (2002). Robot learning with GA-based Fuzzy reinforcement learning agents, *Information Science,* Vol. 145, 45-68

Fujita, K. & Matsuo, H. (2005). Multi-Agent Reinforcement Learning with the Partly High-Dimensional State Space, *The transactions of the institute of electronics, information and communication engineers,* Vol. J88-D-I No.4, 864-872

Jennings, N.R.; Sycara, K. & Wooldridge, M. (1998). A roadmap of agent research and development, *Autonomous Agent and Multi-Agent Systems,* 1:7-38

Goldberg, D.E. (1989). *Genetic Algorithms in Search, Optimization, and Machine Learning,* 0201157675, Addison-Wesley Longman Publishing Co., Inc. Boston, MA, USA

Holland, J.H. (1975). *Adaptation in Natural and Artificial Systems,* Univ. of Michigan Press

Xie, M.C. (2006). Cooperative Behavior Rule Acquisition for Multi-Agent systems Using a Genetic Algorithm, *Proceedings of the IASTED International Conference on Advances in Computer Science and Technology,* pp.124-128

Alex, V.; Conradie, E. & Aldrich, C. (2005). Development of neurocontrollers with evolutionary reinforcement learning, Computers & Chemical Engineering Vol.30, 1-17

Schleiffer, R. (2005). An intelligent agent model, *European Journal of Operational Research*, Vol.166, No.1, pp.666-693

Bradtkes, S. J. & Duff, M. O. (1994). Reinforcement Learning Method for Continuous- Time Markov Decision Problems, *Advances in Neural Information Processing Systems 7*, pp.393-400

Parr, R. & Russell, S. (1998). Reinforcement Learning with Hierarchies of Machines, *Advances in Neural Information Processing Systems 10*, pp.1043-1049

Watkins, C. H. (1989). Learning from Delayed Rewards, *Ph.D. thesis*, Cambridge University

Bridle, J. S. (1990). Training stochastic model recognition algorithms as networks can lead to maximum mutual information estimates of parameters, Advances in Neural Information Processing Systems: *Proceedings of the 1989 Conference*, pp.211-217

Xie, M.C.& Okazaki, K. (2008). Application of Multi-Agent Systems to Disaster Relief Using Q-Learnin, *Proceedings of the IASTED International Conference on Software Engineering and Applications* ,pp.143–147

6

Emergence of Intelligence Through Reinforcement Learning with a Neural Network

Katsunari Shibata
Oita University
Japan

1. Introduction

"There exist many robots who faithfully execute given programs describing the way of image recognition, action planning, control and so forth. Can we call them intelligent robots?" In this chapter, the author who has had the above skepticism describes **the possibility of the emergence of intelligence or higher functions by the combination of Reinforcement Learning (RL) and a Neural Network (NN)**, reviewing his works up to now.

2. What is necessary in emergence of intelligence(1)(2)

If one student solves a very difficult problem without any difficulties facing a blackboard in a classroom, he/she looks very intelligent. However, if the student wrote the solution just as his/her mother had directed to him/her, the student cannot answer questions about the solution process, and cannot solve even similar or easier problems. Further interaction shows up less flexibility in his/her knowledge. When we see a humanoid robot is walking fast and smoothly, or when we see a communication robot responds appropriately to our talking, the robot looks an existence with intelligence. However, until now, the author has never met a robot who looks intelligent even after a long interaction with it. Why can't we provide enough knowledge for a robot to be really intelligent like humans?

When we compare the processing system between humans and robots, a big difference can be noticed easily. Our brain is massively parallel and cohesively flexible, while the robot process is usually modularized, sequential and not so flexible as shown in Fig. 1. As mentioned later, the massive parallelism and cohesive flexibility seem the origin of our very flexible behaviors considering many factors simultaneously without suffering from the "Frame Problem"(3)(4). The keys to figuring out the cause of the big difference are "modularization" and "consciousness", the author thinks.

When we survey the brain research and robotics research, we notice that the common fundamental strategy "functional modularization" lies in both. In the brain research, identification of the role of each area or region seems to be its destination. While, in the robotics research, the process is divided into some functional modules, such as recognition and control, and by sophisticating each functional module, high-functionality is realized in total.

At present, each developed function does not seem so flexible. Furthermore, as for the higher functions, unlike recognition that is located close to sensors, and unlike control that is located close to actuators, they are not located close to sensors or actuators. Therefore, either "what

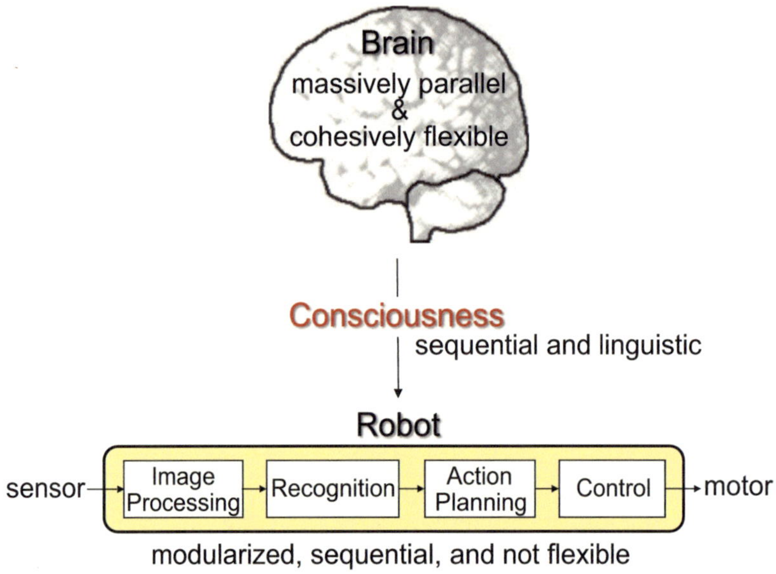

Fig. 1. Comparison of processing between humans and robots. The robot process is developed based on the understanding of the brain function through consciousness.

are the inputs" or "what are the outputs" is not predefined, and the both have to be designed by humans. However, since in higher functions such as language acquisition and formation of novel concept, very flexible function acquisition is required, it is difficult to decide even what are the inputs or what are the outputs in advance. Then the flexibility is deeply impaired when some definition of inputs and outputs are given. Accordingly, it is very difficult to develop a flexible higher function separately. The fundamental problem seems to lie in the isolation of each function from the system according to the "functional modularization" approach.

Why do we manage to modularize the entire process? It seems natural that researchers think the brain is too big to understand or develop. The fact that the brain seems to be divided into some areas by some major sulci probably promotes the modularization especially in the brain research. However, the author focuses on another more fundamental reason. That is the gap between the "brain" and "consciousness". It is said that the brain is a massively parallel system consisted of tens of billions or a hundred billion of neurons. We can see many reports showing that the flexibility of the brain is beyond expectation(5). Among them, a recent report is very impressive that the neuronal circuit remodeling for recovery after stroke spreads to the contralateral cortical hemisphere(6). On the other hand, our "consciousness" that is generated in the "brain" is sequential and its representation seems linguistic. So, it is difficult to represent and understand the function of the brain exactly as a massively parallel and very flexible system. Then by seeing the brain or brain functions through the frame of functional module, we reduce the amount of information, and try to understand it roughly by representing it linguistically. Thus, in the robot process that is designed in our conscious world, the functional modules are usually arranged in series as shown in Fig. 1.

Accordingly, it is thought to be impossible to understand the brain completely as long as through consciousness. However, since we do not notice the subconscious massively parallel processing directly, but notice only what we can see through consciousness, we cannot help but consider what we understand through the consciousness is all the processes that the brain is doing. We assume that since the brain is "doing", the brain must be able to "understand" what the brain is doing. Then we expect that the brain will be understood by understanding each module individually, and also expect that human-like robots will be developed by building-block of sophisticated functional modules.

The existence of subconscious processes is undisputed even from the fact that the response of each "orientation selectivity cell" cannot be perceived. The phenomena such as "optical illusion" or "choice blindness"(7) can be considered as a result of the gap between "brain" and "consciousness". When we walk up non-moving escalator stairs, although we understand that the escalator is not moving, we feel very strange as if we are pushed forward. This suggests the existence of subconscious compensation for the influence of escalator motion that occurs only when we are on an escalator. When we type a keyboard, many types of mistypings surprise us: neighbor key typing, character-order confusing, similar-pronunciation typing, similar-meaning word confusion and so forth. That suggests that our brain processing is more parallel than we think though we assume it difficult for our brain to consider many things in parallel because our consciousness is not parallel but sequential.

Even though imaging and electrical recording of brain activities might provide us sufficient information to understand the exact brain function, we would not be able to understand it by our sequential consciousness. The same output as our brain produces may be reproduced from the information, but complete reconstruction including flexibility is difficult to be realized, and without "understanding", "transfer" to robots must be impossible.

From the above discussion, **in the research of intelligence or higher-functions, it is essential to notice that understanding the brain exactly or developing human-like robots based on the biased understanding is impossible. We have to drastically change the direction of research.** That is the first point of this chapter. Furthermore, to realize the comprehensive human-like process including the subconscious one, **it is required to introduce a massively parallel and very flexible learning system that can learn in harmony as a whole**. This is the second point.

Unlike the conventional sequential systems, Brooks advocated to introduce a parallel architecture and "Subsumption architecture" has been proposed(8). The agile and flexible motion produced by the architecture has made a certain role to avoid the "Frame Problem"(3)(4). However, he claimed the importance of understanding of complicated systems by the decomposition of them into parts. He suggests that functional modules called "layer" are arranged in parallel, and interfaces between layers are designed. However, as he mentioned by himself, the difficulties in interface design and scalability towards complicated systems are standing against us as a big wall.

Thinking again what a robot process should be, it should generate appropriate actuator outputs for achieving some purpose referring to its sensor signals; that is "optimization" of the process from sensors to actuators under some criterion. If, as mentioned, the understanding through "consciousness" is limited actually, by prioritizing human understanding, it constrains robot's functions and diminishes its flexibility unexpectedly.

For example, in action planning of robots or in explaining human arm movement(9), the term "desired trajectory" appears very often. The author thinks that the concept of "desired trajectory" emerges for human understanding. As the above example of the virtual force perceived on non-moving escalators, even for motion control, subconscious parallel and flexible processing must be performed in our human brain. In the case of human arm movement, commands for muscle fibers are the final output. So the entire process to move an arm is the process from sensors to muscle fibers. The inputs include not only the signals from muscle spindles, but also visual signals and so on, and the final commands should be produced by considering many factors in parallel. Our brain is so intelligent that the concept of "desired trajectory" is yielded to understand the motion control easily through "consciousness", and the method of feedback control to achieve the desired trajectory has been developed. The author believes that the direct learning of the final actuator commands using a parallel learning system with many sensor inputs leads to acquisition of more flexible control from the viewpoint of the degrees of freedom. The author knows that the approach of giving a desired trajectory to each servo motor makes the design of biped robot walking easy, and actually, the author has not yet realized that a biped robot learns appropriate final motor commands for walking using non-servo motors. Nevertheless, the author conjectures that to realize flexible and agile motion control, a parallel learning system that learns appropriate final actuator commands is required. The feedback control does not need the desired trajectories, but needs the utilization of sensor signals to generate appropriate motions. That should be included in the parallel processing that is acquired or modified through learning.

Unless humans develop a robot's process manually, "optimization" of the process should be put before "understandability" for humans. To generate better behaviors under given sensor signals, appropriate recognition from these sensor signals and memorization of necessary information also should be required. Accordingly, the optimization is not just "optimization of parameters", but as a result, it has a possibility that a variety of functions emerge as necessary. If the optimization is the purpose of the system, avoiding the freedom and flexibility being spoiled by human interference, harmonious "optimization" of the whole system under a uniform criterion is preferable.

However, if the optimized system works only for the past experienced situations and does not work for future unknown situations, learning has no meaning. We will never receive exactly the same sensor signals as those we receive now. Nevertheless, in many cases, by making use of our past experiences, we can behave appropriately. This is our very superior ability, and it is essential to realize the ability to develop a robot with human-like intelligence. For that, the key issue is "abstraction" and "generalization" on the abstract space.

It is difficult to define the "abstraction" exactly, but it can be taken as extraction of important information and compression by cutting out unnecessary information. By ignoring trivial differences, the acquired knowledge becomes valid for other similar situations. Brooks has stated that "abstraction" is the essence of intelligence and the hard part of the problems being solved(8). For example, when we let a robot learn to hit back a tennis ball, first we may provide the position and size of the ball in the camera image to the robot. It is an essence of intelligence to discover that such information is important, but we usually provide it to the robot peremptorily. Suppose that to return the serve exactly as the robot intends, it is important to consider a subtle movement of the opponent's racket in his/her serve motion. It is difficult to discover the fact through learning from a huge amount of sensor signals. However, if the images are preprocessed and only the ball position and size in the image are extracted and given, there is no way left for the robot to discover the importance of opponent movement by itself. As an alternative, if all pieces of information are given, it is inevitable to introduce a parallel and flexible system in which learning enables to extract meaningful information from huge amount of input signals. That has a possibility to solve the "Frame Problem" fundamentally, even though the problem remains; how to discover important information effectively.

A big problem in "abstraction" is how the criterion for "what is important information" is decided. "The degree of reproduction" of the original information from the compressed one can be considered easily. Concretely, the introduction of a sandglass(bottleneck)-type neural network(10)(11), and utilization of principal component analysis can be considered. A non-linear method(12), and the way of considering temporal relation(13)(14)(15) have been also proposed. However, it may not match the purpose of the system, and drastic reduction of information quantity through abstraction process cannot be expected because the huge amount of sensor signals has to be reproduced. Back to basics, it is desirable that the criterion for "abstraction" matches the criterion of "optimization" of the system. In other words, the way of "abstraction" should be acquired in the "optimization" of the system.

From the discussions, the third point in this chapter is **to put "optimization" of the system before the "understandability" for humans, and to optimize the whole of the massively parallel and cohesively flexible system under one uniform criterion**. Furthermore, **to eliminate too much interference by humans and to leave the intelligence development to the "optimization" by themselves** are included in the third point.

3. Marriage of reinforcement learning (RL) and neural network (NN)

The author has proposed the system that is consisted of one neural network (NN) from sensors to actuators, and is trained by the training signals generated based on reinforcement learning (RL). The NN is a parallel and flexible system. The NN requires training signals for learning, but if the training signals are given by humans, they become a constraint on the system optimization, and the NN cannot learn functions beyond what humans provides. RL can generate the training signals autonomously, and the NN can optimize the entire system flexibly and purposively based on the signals. Therefore, the system is optimized in total to generate appropriate motions for getting more reward and less punishment and also to evaluate states or actions appropriately. Sometimes it acquires unexpected abilities because of being free from the constraints that are unwillingly produced by its designer.

On the other hand, RL is usually taken as a learning for actions that appropriately generates the mapping from a sensor space to an action space. By introducing a NN, not only non-linear function approximation, but also acquisition of various function, including recognition and control, through learning to generate better actions are expected. When introducing a

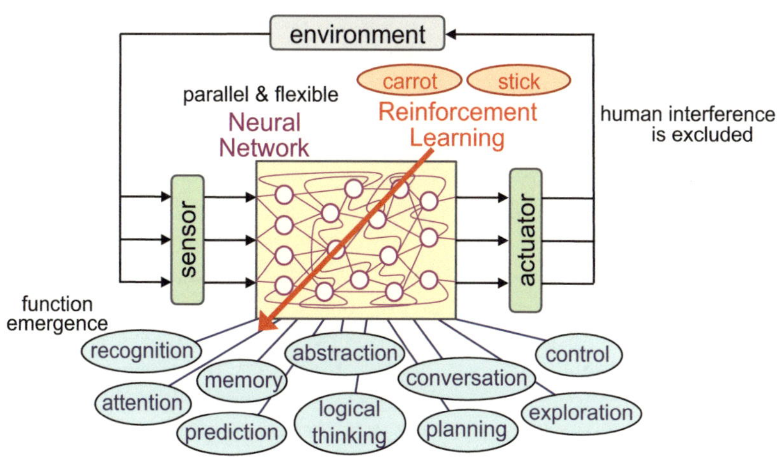

Fig. 2. The proposed learning system that is consisted of one neural network (NN) from sensors to actuators, and that is trained based on reinforcement learning (RL). Emergence of necessary functions based on the parallel and cohesively flexible learning is expected.

recurrent NN, functions that need memory or dynamics are expected to emerge. Thanking to its parallel and flexible learning system, flexible response to the real world considering various things in parallel is expected.

Comparing with the subsumption architecture that requires prior design of interactions among modules, flexibility, parallelism and harmony are stronger in the proposed system. The entire system changes flexibly, purposively and in harmony, and the interactions between neurons are formed autonomously. That is expected to solve the "Frame Problem" fundamentally. It is also expected that in the hidden neurons, meaningful information is extracted among a huge amount of inputs, and the abstraction is consistent with the system optimization. Furthermore, from the viewpoint of higher functions, since the inside of the NN changes very flexibly, it is possible that necessary functions emerge without prior definition of "what higher function should be developed", "what signals are inputs" or "what signals are outputs" of the higher function.

It is considered that "symbol emergence" and "logical thinking" is the most typical higher functions of humans. Symbol processing has been separately considered from pattern processing, linking to the difference of function between right and left hemispheres of the brain(16). NNs have been considered as a system for pattern processing. The idea has disturbed the investigation of symbol processing with a NN. Until now, it is not clear how these functions emerge, or which kind of necessity drives the emergence of these functions. However, if symbol processing emerges in an artificial NN with sensory signal inputs, it is expected that the clear boundary between symbols and patterns disappears, and the "Symbol Grounding Problem"(17) is solved. It might be no doubt that the human brain, which is consisted of a natural NN, realizes our logical thinking. Even though it is said that the function of the right hemisphere is different from that of the left one, one hemisphere looks very similar to the other.

At present, in RL, a NN is positioned mainly as a nonlinear function approximator to avoid the "curse of dimensionality" problem(18), and the expectation towards purposive and flexible function emergence based on parallel processing has not been seen. A NN was used in an inverted pendulum task(19) and Backgammon game(20), but since the instability in RL was pointed in 1995(21), function approximators with local representation units such as NGnet (Normalized Gaussian network)(22) are used in many cases(23). In the famous book as a sort of bible of RL(18), little space is devoted for the NN.

However, the very autonomous and flexible learning of the NN is surprising. Even though each neuron performs output computation and learning (weight modification) in a uniform way, the autonomous division of roles among hidden neurons through learning and purposive acquisition of necessary internal representation to realize required input-output relations make us feel the possibility of not only function approximation, but also function emergence and "intelligence".

As mentioned, it is said that the combination of RL and a NN destabilizes the learning(21). In RBF network(24) including NGnet(22) or tile coding (CMAC)(25)(26), since a continuous space is divided softly into local states, learning is performed only in one of the local states and that makes learning stable. However, on the other hand, they have no way to represent more global states that integrate the local states. The sigmoid-based regular NN has an ability to reconstruct a useful state space by integrating input signals each of which represents local information, and through the generalization on the internal state space, the knowledge acquired in past experiences can be utilized in other situations(27)(28).

The author shows that when each input signal represents local information, learning becomes

stable even using a regular sigmoid-type NN(29). Sensor signals such as visual signals originally represent local information, and so learning is stable when sensor signals are the inputs of the NN. On the contrary, when the sensor signals are put into a NN after converting them to a global representation, learning sometimes became unstable. If the input signals represent local information, a new state space that is good for computing the outputs is reconstructed in the hidden layer flexibly and purposively by integrating the input signals. Therefore, both learning stability and flexible acquisition of internal representation can be realized. For the case that input signals represent global information, Gauss-Sigmoid NN has been proposed where the input signals are passed to the sigmoid-type regular NN after localization by a Gaussian layer(30).
On the other hand, in the recent researches of learning-based intelligence, "prediction" of a future state from the past and present states and actions has been focused on because it can be learned autonomously by using the actual future state as the training signals (13)(31)(32)(14)(33). However, it is difficult and also seems meaningless to predict all of the huge amount of sensor signals. Then it becomes a big problem how to decide "what information at what timing should be predicted". This is similar to the previous discussion about "abstraction". A way to discover the prediction target from the aspect of linear independence has been proposed(34). However, same as the discussion about "abstraction", thinking about the purposive property and consistency with the system purpose, "prediction" should be considered in RL. The author's group shows that through learning a prediction-required task using a recurrent NN, the function of "prediction" emerges(35) as described later.
Next, how to learn a NN based on RL is described. In the case of actor-critic(36), one critic output unit and the same number of actor output units as the actuators are prepared. Actuators are operated actually according to the sum of the actor outputs $\mathbf{O}a(\mathbf{S}_t)$ for the sensor signal inputs $\mathbf{S}_t$ and random numbers $\mathbf{rnd}_t$ as trial and error factors. Then the training signals for critic output Tc_t and for actor outputs $\mathbf{T}a_t$ are computed using the reward r_{t+1} obtained by the motion and critic output $Oc(\mathbf{S}_{t+1})$ for the new sensor signals $\mathbf{S}_{t+1}$ as

$$
\begin{aligned}
Tc_t &= Oc(\mathbf{S}_t) + \hat{r}_t = r_{t+1} + \gamma Oc(\mathbf{S}_{t+1}) && (1)\\
\mathbf{T}a_t &= \mathbf{O}a(\mathbf{S}_t) + \alpha \hat{r}_t \mathbf{rnd}_t && (2)\\
\hat{r}_t &= r_{t+1} + \gamma Oc(\mathbf{S}_{t+1}) - Oc(\mathbf{S}_t) && (3)
\end{aligned}
$$

where $\hat{r}$ indicates TD-error, γ indicates a discount factor and α indicates a constant. After that, the sensor signals $\mathbf{S}_t$ at the time t are provided as inputs again, and the NN is trained by the BP (Error Back Propagation) learning(10) using the training signals as above. If the neural network is recurrent-type, BPTT(Back Propagation Through Time)(10) can be used.
On the other hand, in the case of Q-learning(37), the same number of output units as the actions are prepared in the NN, and each output $O_a(\mathbf{S}_t)$ is used as the Q-value for the corresponding action a. Using the maximum Q-value for the new sensor signals $\mathbf{S}_{t+1}$ perceived after the selected action a_t, the training signal for the output for the action a_t at the time t as

$$T_{a_t,t} = r_{t+1} + \gamma(\max_a O_a(\mathbf{S}_{t+1})). \quad (4)$$

Then, after input of the sensor signals $\mathbf{S}_t$ and forward computation, only the output for the selected action a_t is trained. When the value range of critic, actor or Q-values is different from

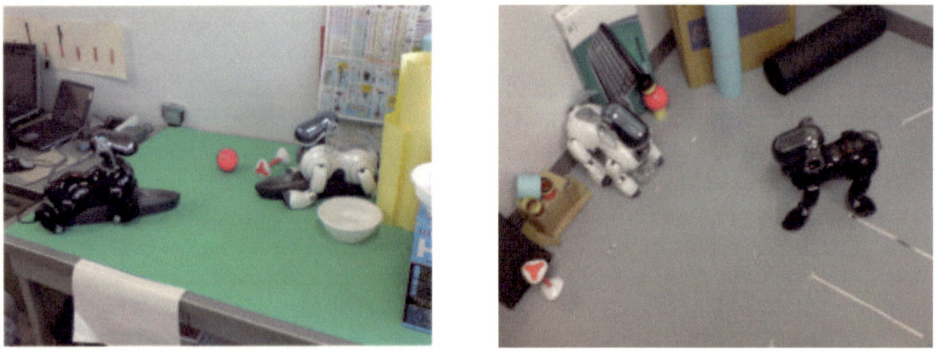

(a) head rotation task (b) walkling task

Fig. 3. Two learning tasks using two AIBO robots.

the value range of the NN output, linear transformation can be applied. The learning is very simple and general, and can be widely applied to various tasks.

4. Some examples of learning

In this section, some examples are introduced in each of which emergence of recognition in a real-world-like environment, memory, prediction, abstraction or communication is aimed. To purely see the abilities and limitations of function emergence, the author has intentionally insisted in "learning from scratch". Therefore, the required functions are still very simple, but it is confirmed that various functions except for logical thinking emerge in a NN through RL almost from scratch. It must be the honest impression for the readers who read this chapter up here that only by connecting from sensors to actuators by a flat NN and training it very simply and generally only from a scalar reinforcement signal, it is just too much for a robot or agent to solve a difficult task or to acquire higher functions from scratch. The author are pleased if the readers feel a new tide that is different from the previous approach in robotics research, and the possibility of function emergence by the couple of RL and a NN. In order to see them from the viewpoint of function emergence, the readers are asked to focus on the ratio of acquired function versus prior knowledge and also the flexibility of the function. The feasibility of the proposed approach and method will be discussed in the next section. The details of the following examples can be referred to the reference for each.

4.1 Learning of flexible recognition in a real-world-like environment

We executed two experiments using two AIBO robots as shown in Fig.3. In one of them(2) that is named "head rotation task", two AIBOs were put face-to-face as shown in Fig.3(a). The head can be one of 9 discrete states with the interval of 5 degree. The AIBO can take one of the three actions: "rotate right", "rotate left" and "bark". When it barks capturing the other AIBO at the center of the image, a reward is given, on the other hand, when it barks in the other 8 states, a penalty is given. In the second task(38) named "walking task", the AIBO is put randomly at each trial, and walks as shown in Fig.3(b). When it kisses the other AIBO, a reward is given, and on the other hand, when it loses the other AIBO, a penalty is given. The action can be one of the three actions: "go forward", "turn right", and "turn left". In this task, state space is continuous, and the orientation and size of the other AIBO in the image are varied.

As shown in Fig. 4 that is for the case of walking task, the 52×40 pixel color image that is captured by the camera mounted at the nose of the AIBO are the input of the NN in both tasks. A total of 6240 signals are given as inputs without any information about the pixel location. The NN has 5 layers, and the numbers of neurons are 6240-600-150-40-3 from the input layer to the output layer. The network is trained by the training signals generated based on Q-learning. The lighting condition and background are changed during learning. Figure 5 shows some sample images in the second task. Since no information about the task is given and no knowledge to recognize the AIBO is given, it is expected for the readers to understand that the learning is not so easy.
The success rate reached more than 90% in the first task after 20,000 episodes of learning, and around 80 or 90% in the second task after 4,000 episodes of learning with additional learning using the experienced episode. Of course, that is far inferior than when a human do the same task, but it is interesting that without giving any knowledge about the task or image recognition, image recognition of the AIBO can be acquired to some extent through the learning with only reward and punishment. What are even more interesting can be found in the analysis of the internal representation of the NN.
At first, the 6240 connection weights from the input neurons to each of the 600 lowest hidden neurons were observed as a color image with 52×40 pixels. When the weights are normalized to a value from 0 to 255, the image looks almost random because of the random initial weights. Then the weight change during learning is normalized to a value from 0 to 255. For example, when the connection weight from the red signal of a pixel increases through learning, the corresponding pixel looks redder, and when it decreases, the pixel looks less red. Figure 6 (a) shows some images each of which represents the change of the connection weights to one of the 600 lowest hidden neurons in the head rotation task. In the head rotation task, one or more AIBO's figures can be found in the image although there are two ways of the

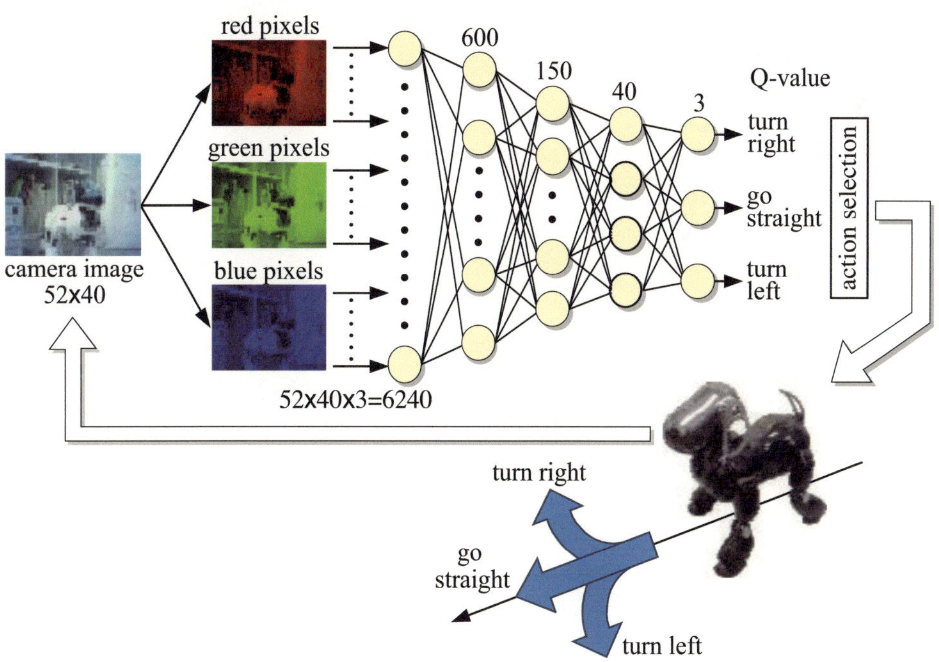

Fig. 4. The learning system and flow of the signals in the AIBO walking task.

(a) (b) (c)

Fig. 5. Variety of images whose pixel values are directly put into a NN as input signals (2).

view of AIBO; positive one and negative one. Because the AIBO is located at only one of the 9 locations, it seems natural that AIBO figures can be found in the image, but the place where the AIBO figure appears is different among the hidden neurons. In (a-1), the neuron seems to detect the AIBO at the left of the image, and in (a-5), the neuron seems to contribute to make a contrast whether the AIBO is located at the center or not. It is interesting that autonomous division of roles among hidden neurons emerged just through RL. It is possible that the contrast by simultaneous existence of positive and negative figures contributes to eliminating the influence of lighting condition.

Figure 6 (b) shows the weight change from the view of a middle hidden neuron. The image is the average of the images of 600 lowest hidden neurons weighted by the connection weights from the lowest hidden neurons to the middle hidden neuron. In many of the images of middle hidden neurons, AIBO figure looks fatter. It is possible that that absorbs the inaccurate head control of AIBO due to the use of a real robot.

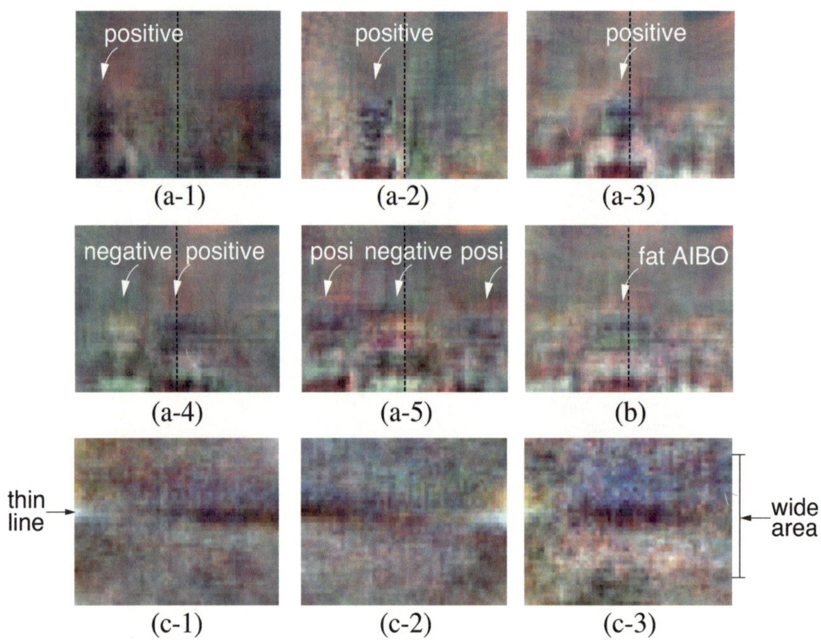

Fig. 6. Images to represent weight change in some hidden neurons during RL. (a) weight change in 5 lowest hidden neurons during the head rotation task, (b) weight change in a middle hidden neuron during the head rotation task, (c) weight change in 3 middle hidden neurons during the walking task.

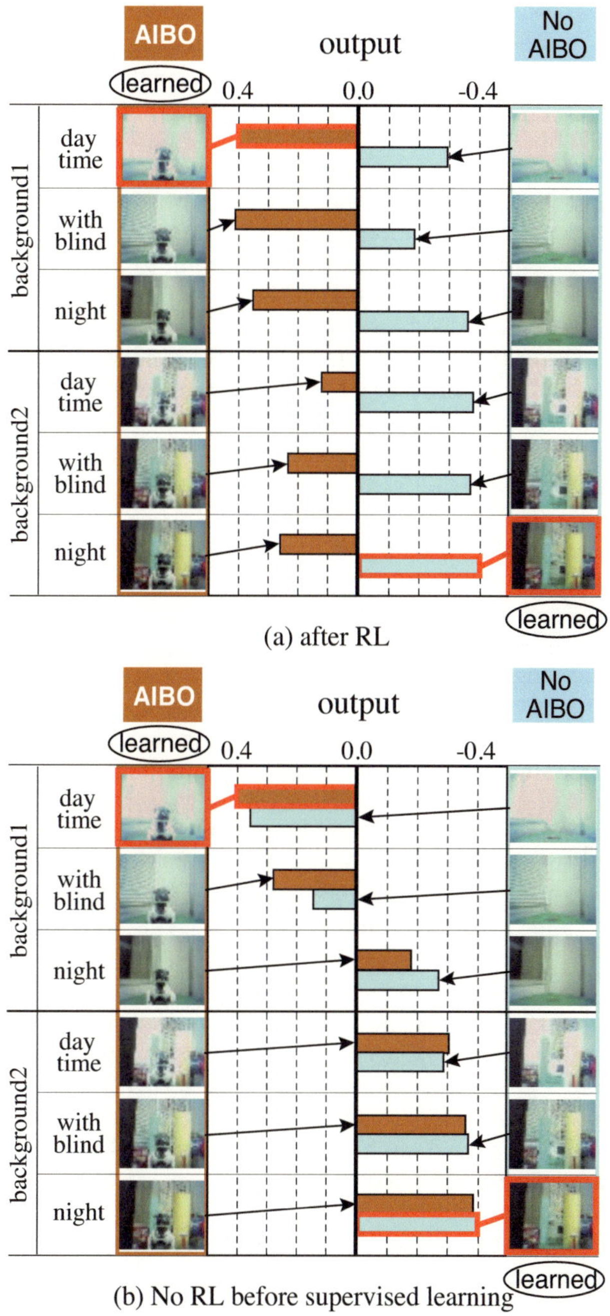

Fig. 7. To see the change of internal representation through RL in the head rotation task, after supervised learning of 2 learning patterns, which are surrounded by a red frame in this figure, the output for 10 test patterns are compared between the NN after RL and that before RL. After RL, the output depends deeply on whether the AIBO exists or not, while before RL, the output depends on the brightness and background.

In the case of walking task, most of the weight images for the lowest hidden neurons are very vague, and in some of them, various vague AIBO figure can be found. Figure 6 (c) shows weight images for 3 middle hidden neurons. Unlike the case of head-rotation task, black and white thin line arranged one above the other can be seen in many images. In this task, since the location and orientation of the target AIBO are not limited, the walking AIBO seems to learn to recognize the target AIBO more effectively by focusing the black area of its face and the white area around its chin or of its body. The neurons as shown in Fig. (c-1)(c-2) seem to contribute to detecting lateral location of AIBO. While the neuron as shown in Fig. (c-3), which has a wide dark-blue area and wide white area, seems to contribute to detecting that the AIBO is closely located, because when the AIBO is close to the other AIBO, the face occupies a wide area of the camera image as shown in Figure 5(c).
It is interesting that the acquired way to recognize the AIBO is different between the two tasks. In the head rotation task, the recognition seems based on pattern matching, while in the walking task, it seems based on feature extraction.
One more analysis about the internal representation is reported. Here, the acquisition of internal representation of AIBO recognition not depending on the light condition or background is shown in the head rotation task. After RL, one output neuron is added with all the connection weights from the highest hidden neurons being 0.0. As shown in Fig. 7, 12 images are prepared. In the supervised learning phase, 2 images are presented alternately, and the network is trained by supervised learning with the training signal 0.4 for one image and -0.4 for the other. The output function of each hidden and output neuron is a sigmoid function whose value ranges from -0.5 to 0.5. One of the images is taken in daytime and bright, and the other is taken at night under fluorescent light and dark, and the background is also different. In the bright image, the AIBO exists in the center, and in the dark one, there is no AIBO. In 6 images, there is the AIBO at the center, and in the other 6 images there is no AIBO. Each of the 6 images with AIBO has a corresponding image in the other 6 images. The corresponding images are captured with the same lighting condition and background, and only the difference is whether the AIBO exists or not. In the 6 images, each 3 images have the same background, but different lighting condition. 3 lighting conditions are "daytime", "daytime with blind" and "night". The output of the NN is observed when each of 12 images is given as inputs. For comparison, the output is also observed when using the NN before RL. Figure 7 shows the output for the 12 images. After RL, the output changes mainly according to whether the AIBO exists or not, while before RL, the outputs is not influenced so much by the existence of the AIBO but is influenced by the lighting conditions and background. When the lighting condition or background is different between two images, the distance between them becomes larger than when the existence of AIBO is different. This result suggests that through RL, the NN acquired the internal representation of AIBO recognition not depending on the lighting conditions and backgrounds.

4.2 Learning of memory with a recurrent neural network (RNN)(39)

Next, learning of a memory-required task using a recurrent neural network (RNN) is reported. In this task, a wheel-type robot can get a reward when it goes to the correct one of two possible goals. One switch and two goals are located randomly, and the robot can perceive two flag signals only on the switch. When the flag1 is one, the correct goal is goal1, and on the other hand, when the flag2 is one, the correct goal is goal2. The inputs of the NN are the signals representing angle and distance to each of the switch and goals, distance to the wall, and also two flag signals. For the continuous motion, actor-critic is employed, and for the necessity of

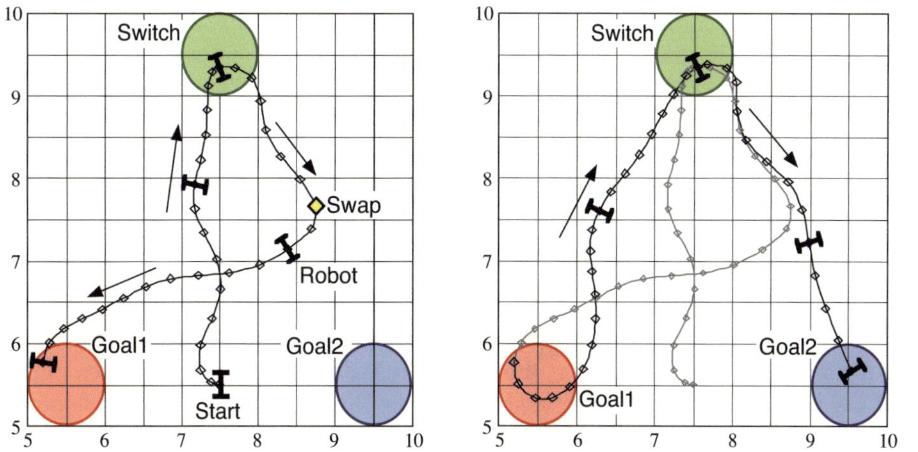

(a) Former Behavior (b) Latter Behavior

Fig. 8. An interesting memory-based behavior acquired through RL. The robot gets a reward when it goes to the correct goal that can be known from the flag signals perceived only on the switch. In this episode, on the way to the goal2, the outputs of all the hidden neurons are swapped to the previously stored ones.

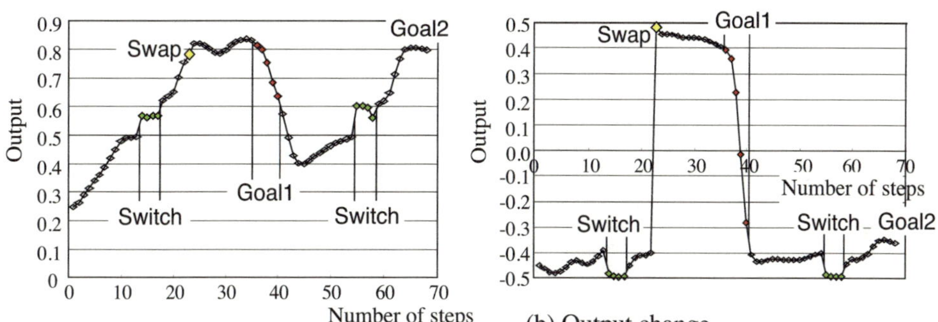

(a) Change of critic output (b) Output change of a type 1 hidden neuron

Fig. 9. The change of the outputs of critic and a type 1 hidden neuron during the episode as shown in Fig. 8.

keeping the flag signals, a RNN is used. When it collides with the wall, when the robot comes to the goal without going to the switch, and also when it comes to the incorrect goal, a penalty is given to the robot.
After learning, the robot went to the switch at first, and then went to the correct goal that was known from the flag signals on the switch. When the output of each hidden neuron was observed, three types of hidden neurons that contribute to memory of necessary information could be found. Type1 neurons kept the flag1 signal, type2 neurons kept the flag2 signal, and type3 neurons kept either of the flag1 or flag2 signal is one. After the robot perceived that the flag1 was one on the switch, the output of one of the type1 neurons was reset to the initial value on the way to the goal1. Then the output soon returned to the value representing that the flag1 signal was one. That represents that a fixed-point attractor was formed through learning; in other words, associative memory function emerged through learning.

When some outputs of hidden neurons were manipulated, the robot showed interesting behaviors as shown in Fig. 8. The outputs of all the hidden neurons after perceiving flag1 being one were stored on the way to the goal1. At the next episode, the robot began to move from the same location with the same arrangement of switch and goals as the previous episode, but in this episode, the flag2 was on. After perceiving the flag signals on the switch, the robot approached the goal2. On the way to the goal2, the outputs of the hidden neurons were swapped by the ones stored on the way to the goal1 at the previous episode. Then the robot changed its traveling direction suddenly to the goal1. However, in this case, the goal1 was not the real goal, the robot could not get a reward and the episode did not terminate even though the robot reached the goal1. Surprisingly, the robot then went to the switch again, and finally went to the goal2 after perceiving the flag signals again. The NN during the behavior was investigated. As shown in Fig. 9 (a), the critic output decreased suddenly when the robot arrived at the goal1 as if the robot understood the goal1 is not the real goal. As shown in Fig. 9(b), a type 1 neuron kept a high value after the value swapping, but when it reaches the goal1, the value decreased suddenly. It is interesting to remind us the person who returns to check something again when they get worried.

4.3 Learning of prediction(35)

The next example shows the emergence of prediction and memory of continuous information through RL. In this task, as shown in Fig. 10, an object starts from the left end ($x = 0$) of the area, and its velocity and angle to go are decided randomly at each episode. The object can be seen until it reaches $x = 3$, but it often becomes invisible at $x > 3$ or a part of $x > 3$. The velocity of the object is decreased when it reflects at a wall. The agent moves along the line of $x = 6$, and decides the timing to catch the object. As input, the agent can receive the signals representing the object or the agent location locally. When the object cannot be seen, the signals for the object location are all 0.0. The agent can choose one of four possible actions; those are "go up", "go down", "stay" and "catch the object". If the agent can catch the object at the place close to the object, the agent can get a reward. The reward is larger when the object is closer to the agent. When it selects catch action away from the object, or does not select catch action before the object reaches the right end of the area, a small penalty is imposed to the agent. In this case, a RNN and Q-learning are used.

After learning, the agent became to catch the object appropriately even though the average reward was a little bit less than the ideal value. It is thought that the complete mechanism of prediction and memory cannot be understood easily, but a possible mechanism was found.

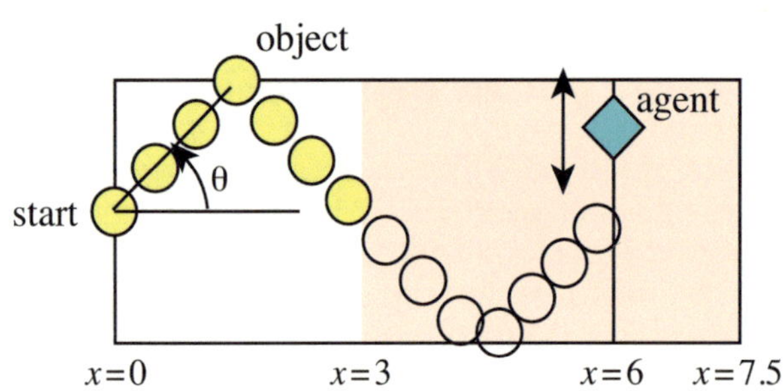

Fig. 10. Prediction task. The object velocity and traveling direction are randomly chosen at each episode, and the object becomes invisible in the range of $x > 3$ or a part of the range. The agent has to predict the object motion to catch it at an appropriate place and timing.

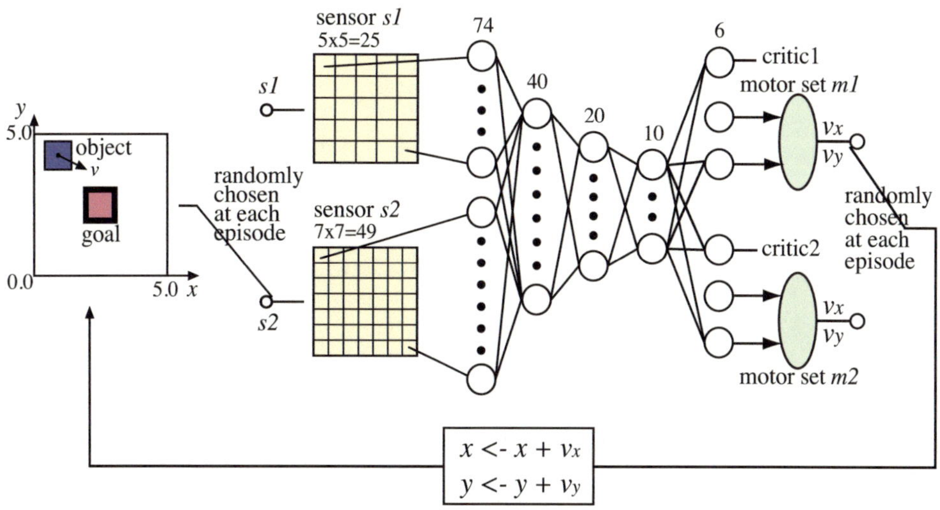

Fig. 11. Abstraction task. One of the two sensors and one of the two motor sets are randomly chosen at each episode. Learning is done for 3 of 4 combinations and the performance of s2-m2 combination is observed.

The agent detected the velocity in the x-direction from the period of staying specific area just before $x = 3$. The predicted value that should be memorized until the agent catches the object is not binary. If the memorized information is binary, the RNN can learn to memorize it by forming a bistable dynamics. However, in this case, it was observed that hidden neurons represent non-binary information for a while, and then relay it to the other neurons until the memorized information is utilized. Similar memory function also emerged in the learning of deterministic exploration task(40).

4.4 Learning of abstraction and knowledge transfer(41)

As mentioned before, one of the human's superior functions is abstraction and knowledge transfer. In our life, completely the same situation or sensor signals at present will never appear in the future. Nevertheless, we can behave appropriately in many cases utilizing our past experiences.

Then a simple task as shown in Fig. 11 is introduced to show the purposive abstraction clearly. An agent has two sensors s1 and s2, and two motor sets m1 and m2. Either sensor can perceive the positional relation of the object from the goal though the way of perception is different between the two sensors. In the same way, either motor set can control the object location though the way of control is different between the two motor sets. At each episode, one sensor and one motor set are selected randomly. The sensor signals from the non-selected sensor are all 0.0. From the view of NN, even though the positional relation of the object and goal is completely the same, the sensor signals from the two sensors are completely different. When the object reaches the goal area, the agent can get a reward.

Three of four sensor-motor combinations are used alternately in learning. The other combination s2-m2 is not used in learning, but just the performance is observed. Figure 12 shows the learning curve. The performance of s2-m2 combination is getting better even though no learning is done for the combination. When two of the four combinations were used in learning, the performance of either of the non-trained combinations did not get better. Through the learning for s1-m1 and s2-m1 combinations, the common representation not

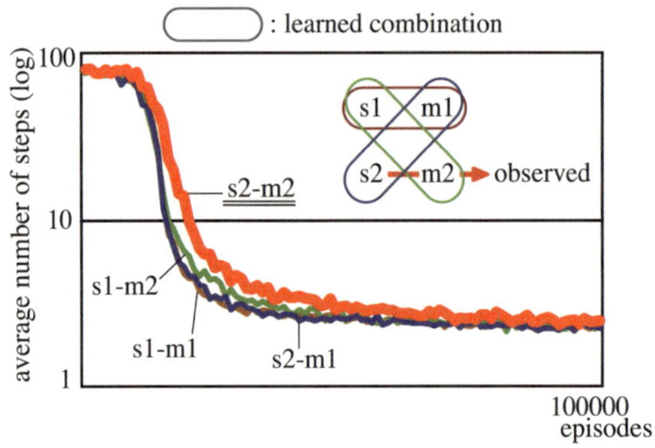

Fig. 12. Learning curve for 4 sensor-motor combinations. The performance is getting better for the s2-m2 combination for which no learning is done.

depending on the used sensor can be obtained in the hidden layer because when the desired output is similar, the hidden representation becomes similar after learning even though input signals are different(27)(28). Furthermore, through the learning for s1-m2 combination, the mapping from the common representation to the motor set m2 can be acquired. Since the conventional abstraction methods(10)-(15) abstract input signals by watching only the input signals or the time series of them as mentioned, this purposive abstraction obtained by the proposed method cannot be acquired by the conventional ones.

4.5 Learning of communication and binarization of signals(42)

Last report is concerning about one of the typical higher functions: communication. As shown in Fig. 13, one of two agents can transmit two continuous-valued signals sequentially based on the perceived location of the other agent, but cannot move by itself. The other agent can receive the transmitted signals and move, but it cannot see the other agent. When they meet, that means the receiver agent reaches close to the transmitter agent, they can both get a reward. They are in one-dimensional space, and the receiver agent can reach the transmitter in one step from anywhere when it takes an appropriate motion. As shown in Fig. 14, each of them has a RNN, and the network works to generate two sequential signals or to generate appropriate motion from the two sequential signals received. Furthermore, some noise is added to the communication signals. If the noise level is large, the information of the original signals is lost when the signal has an analog representation.

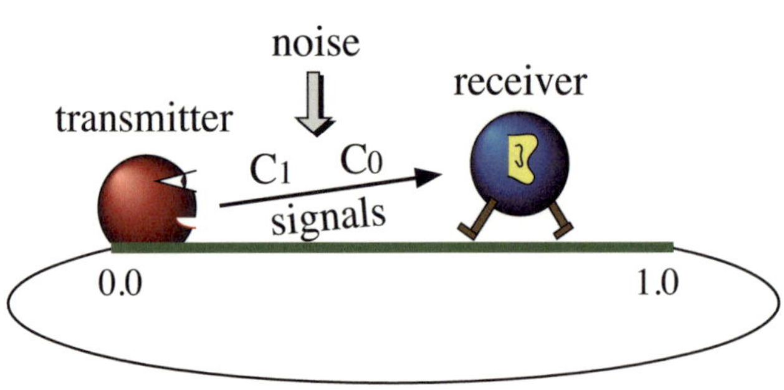

Fig. 13. Communication learning task. Two signals are transmitted sequentially, and the receiver moves according to the signals. Random noise is added to the signals.

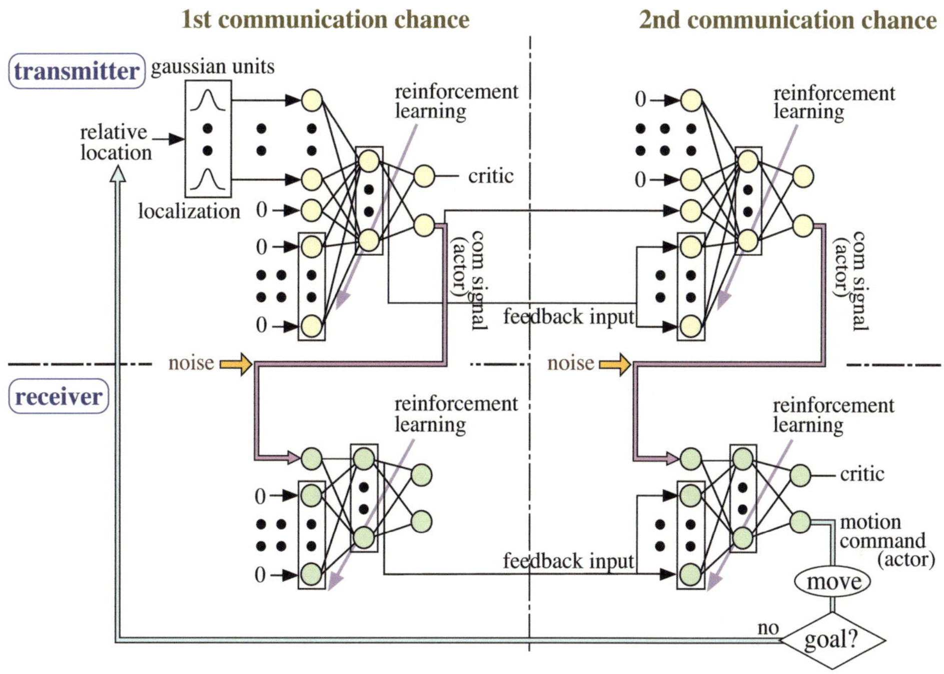

Fig. 14. The architecture and signal flow in the communication learning. Each agent has a recurrent neural network.

After learning, they could meet in one step in almost all cases. Figure 15 shows two communication signals generated by the transmitter as a function of the receiver's location in two cases when no noise is added and when a large level of noise is added. It is interesting that when the agents learned in the noisy environment, the signals get to have an almost binary representation even though no one told them to binarize the signals. If the representation is binary, the original signal before adding the noise can be restored. In this task, division of the receiver's location into 4 states is enough to generate a motion to reach the goal in

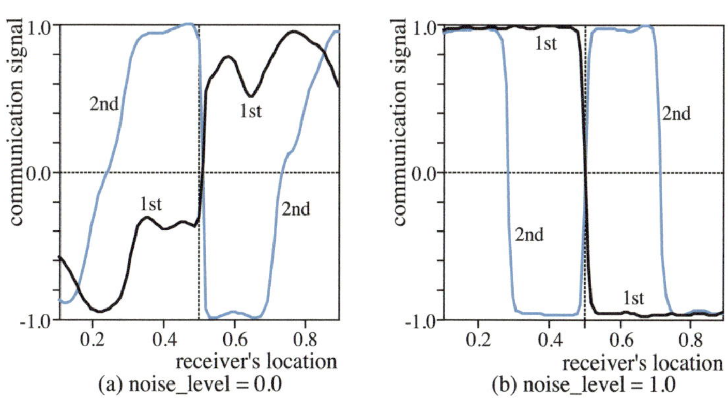

Fig. 15. Communication signals acquired through learning. In the case of large noise level(b), the signals have almost binary representation. That means that 2bit serial communication was established through RL.

one step. The sequential two signals represent different information, and the 4 states are represented by the combination of two binary communication signals. The receiver also generates appropriate motions according to the received sequential two signals. It can be said that 2bit serial communication emerged by RL of communication in a noisy environment.

5. Discussions, conclusions and future works

In this chapter, the author has advocated the introduction of parallel and flexible learning system and also the priority on optimization rather than understanding. As a concrete framework, it has been proposed that a neural network (NN) connects from sensors to actuators, and reinforcement learning (RL) trains the NN. The author hopes that through the above examples, the readers have felt a difference from the general approaches in conventional robotics research. From the viewpoint of the ratio of acquired functions vs. the prior knowledge, it is more than expected that even though only a scalar signal as reward and punishment is given except for sensor signals, various functions emerge flexibly, purposively and in harmony by the marriage of RL and a NN. Especially, in the communication-learning task, the gap between the reward for meeting and the establishment of two-bit serial communication is very interesting.

On the other hand, it is also true that the acquired abilities of robots or agents in the above examples have not yet reached the level to compare to human abilities and are insufficient from what the author claimed magnificently in the former part of this chapter. When we, humans, solve some difficult problem, we try to solve it by thinking logically, and a good idea often comes up suddenly. To realize such kind of intelligent and effective processing, an additional breakthrough may have to be waited for. However, the author still believes the proposed approach, which are introduction of parallel and flexible learning system and priority on optimization rather than understanding, is not wrong as a fundamental base to realize higher functions avoiding "Frame Problem" or "Symbol Grounding Problem".

The tallest wall that the author can see towards the higher functions is "symbol emergence" and "logical thinking". If it is assumed that symbols are equal to discrete representations, as shown in the communication-learning example(42), noise tolerance can be the necessity for the symbol emergence especially when communication is considered. The result that the two sequential signals are used to represent a piece of information makes the author feel the extensibility to the emergence of word or language. It is not impossible to consider that logical thinking is internalized communication, in other words, the communication from oneself to oneself, and logical thinking may not emerge before the communication with others is learned. If so, the noise tolerance can be the origin of symbol emergence.

Logical thinking has an important role; that is problem solving on a very high-level abstraction space. But, the author cannot imagine that from the necessity of such problem solving, logical thinking emerges. However, it is possible that forming of fixed-point attractors or chaos dynamics promotes symbol emergence. The dynamics makes only small number of isolated internal representations more stable, and on the contrary, makes the other most representations less stable. The author has suggested that fixed-point attractors are formed adaptively and purposively in a recurrent neural network (RNN) through learning(43). Tani's group has shown some pioneering works in which dynamics of RNN is introduced in robotics research(44).

By introducing a RNN, the function of memory and state evaluation considering past state can be dealt with. However, the author feels the necessity to think more about the time axis in RL. For example, stochastic motion or action selection is usually done for exploration at each step in RL, but exploration should be designed considering the time axis. Temporal abstraction(45), improvement of the learning ability of RNN, and more flexible operation of time axis also should be considered more. One idea the author think now is that the state is not periodically sampled, but more event-based framework is introduced.

Recently, many works suggest that even newborn baby has much talent(46)(47), and it is a well-known fact that a horse can stand up soon after its birth. Furthermore, nowadays, the author has felt the limitation of the "learning from scratch" approach to develop higher functions. At least, our brain does not have a flat structure, but is structured, and the artificial neuron model used here is far simpler than our biological real neuron. The requirement of some modularized structure may be suggested to achieve coexistence of multiple dynamics such as talking while walking. Probably, initial knowledge should be introduced considering that it harms the flexibility as little as possible. The initial knowledge includes initial structure and connection weights, and also constraint of learning process.

Next, let us discuss the biological aspect. It is often said that RL is employed in the basal ganglia(48) and it is also said that the basal ganglia contributes action selection or decision making. Along the idea of function emergence by the couple of RL and a NN, author thinks that RL is highly possible to work in wider area including the frontal lobe, though the coexistence with another learning is not denied. Functions in the brain should be purposive, and RL can realize purposive function emergence. As for the NNs, the difference between artificial NN and biological NN was as mentioned. The author knows there are many negative opinions to Error Back Propagation (BP) learning when it is considered whether our brain employs BP or not. However, effective and harmonious learning and the autonomous and purposive division of roles in the network deeply thank to BP, in the authors' works. Furthermore, the author thinks that the studies of neurotrophic factors such as NGF(49) suggest us the existence of some backward signal flow for learning in our brain.

In the use of NN in RL, a difficulty has been pointed out(50), but the author does not think it so difficult if you prepare input signals in a local representation. However, when a RNN is used, it is a little bit difficult to adjust learning rate and bias to each neuron. Usually, learning rate should be small for feedback connections, and the bias should be 0 for the neurons in a loop. Setting self-feedback connection weights to be 4.0 often makes learning of memory easy and stable when a sigmoid function whose value range is from -0.5 to 0.5 or 0.0 to 1.0 is used as the output function. The symmetrical value range such as from -0.5 to 0.5 is good for stable learning. BPTT and RTRL are popular learning algorithms for RNNs, but are not practical from the viewpoint of computational cost and required memory capacity even though it is implemented in a parallel hardware. More practical learning algorithm with $O(n^2)$ computational cost and $O(n^2)$ required memory capacity is waited for(51)(52).

The author also thinks that towards realization of higher functions, "growing and developing from a simple form to a complicated one" should be the basic approach on behalf of "functional modularization". NNs are very flexible and very suitable for the approach. There is also a possibility that a NN structure flexibly and purposively changes according to learning(53)(54). However, it must be a difficult problem to design the growth and development. Introduction of evolutionary process may be inevitable.

Finally, the author would like to propose the necessity of supervision and discussion about this kind of research, considering the possibility of the emergence of out-of-control robots or systems(55).

6. Acknowledgement

At first, the author deeply thanks to all the students who tackled or are tackling to this impenetrable opponent. The AIBO task was done by Mr. Tomohiko Kawano, the memory task was done by Mr. Hiroki Utsunomiya, and the prediction task and exploration task are done by Mr. Kenta Goto. The author would like to express his gratitude to Prof. Yosuke Ito and Mr. Hironori Kakiuchi in Naruto University of Education for permitting us to use their AIBO walking software. The author also would like to express his appreciation to Prof. Yoich Okabe, Prof. Koji Ito, and Prof. Richard S. Sutton for giving him a chance to do a part of the above works and fruitful discussion. The author will never forget the exciting discussions with Prof. Sutton or Prof. Juergen Schmidhuber. This research has been supported for more than 10 years by MITI or JSPS Grant-in-Aid for Scientific Research and Research for the Future Program. Sorry for introducing only the most recent one, that is Grant-in-Aid for Scientific Research #19300070.

7. References

[1] Shibata, K. (2009). Emergence of Intelligence by Reinforcement Learning and a Neural Network, *Journal of SICE (Keisoku to Seigyo)*, Vol. 48, No. 1, pp. 106-111 (In Japanese)

[2] Shibata, K. & Kawano, T. (2009). Acquisition of Flexible Image Recognition by Coupling of Reinforcement Learning and a Neural Network, *SICE Journal of Control, Measurement, and System Integration (JCMSI)*, Vol. 2, No. 2, pp. 122-129

[3] McCarthy, J. & Hayes, P. J. (1969). Some philosophical problems from the standpoint of artificial intelligence, *Machine Intelligence*, Vol. 4, pp. 463-502

[4] Dennett, D. (1984). Cognitive Wheels: The Frame Problem of AI, *The Philosophy of Artificial Intelligence*, Margaret A. Boden, Oxford University Press, pp. 147-170

[5] Tsumoto, T. (1986). *Brain and Development*, Asakura Publishing Co. Ltd. (in Japanese)

[6] Takatsuru, Y. et al. (2009). Neuronal Circuit Remodeling in the Contralateral Cortical Hemisphere during Functional Recovery from Cerebral Infraction, *J. Neuroscience*, Vol. 29, No. 30, pp. 10081-10086

[7] Johansson, P., Hall, L., Sikstrom, S. & Olsson, A. (2005). Failure to Detect Mismatches Between Intention and Outcome in a Simple Decision Task, *Science*, Vol. 310, pp. 116-119

[8] Brooks, R. A. (1991). Intelligence Without Representation. *Artificial Intelligence*, Vol. 47, pp.139-159

[9] Kawato, M. (1999). Internal Models for Motor Control and Trajectory Planning, *Current Opinion in Neurobiology*, Vol. 9, pp. 718-727

[10] Rumelhart, D. E. et al. (1986). Learning Internal Representation by Error Propagation, *Parallel Distributed Processing*, MIT Press, Vol. 1, pp. 318-364

[11] Irie, B. & Kawato, M. (1991). Acquisition of Internal Representation by Multilayered Perceptrons, *Electronics and Communications in Japan*, Vol. 74, pp. 112-118

[12] Saul, L. & Roweis, S. (2003). Think globally, fit locally: Unsupervised learning of nonlinear manifolds, *Journal of Machine Learning Research*, Vol. 4, pp. 119-155

[13] Littman, M.L., Sutton, R.S. & Singh, S. (2002). Predictive Representations of State, *In Advances in Neural Information Processing Systems*, Vol. 14, MIT Press, pp. 1555-1561

[14] Sutton, R. S., Rafols, E. J. & Koop, A. (2006). Temporal abstraction in temporal-difference networks, *Advances in Neural Information Processing Systems*, Vol. 18, pp. 1313-1320

[15] Bowling, M., Ghodsi, A. & Wilkinson, D. (2005). Action respecting embedding *Proc. of the 22nd Int'l Conf. on Machine Learning*, pp. 65-72

[16] Sperry, R.W. (1968). Hemisphere Deconnection and Unity in Conscious Awareness, *American Psy- chologist*, Vol. 23, pp. 723-733

[17] Harnad, S. (1990). Symbol Grounding Problem, Phisica D, Vol. 42, pp. 335-346

[18] Sutton, R. S. & Barto, A. G. (1998). *Reinforcement Learning: An Introduction*, A Bradford Book, The MIT Press

[19] Anderson, C. W. (1987). Strategy learning with multilayer connectionist representations, *Proc. of the 4th Int'l Workshop on Machine Learning*, pp. 103-114

[20] Tesauro, G. J. (1992). TD-Gammon, a self-teaching backgammon program, achieves master-level play, *Neural Computation*, Vol. 6, No. 2, pp. 215-219

[21] Boyan, J. A. & Moore, A. W. (1995). Generalization in Reinforcement Learning, *Advances in Neural Information Processing Systems*, Vol. 7, The MIT Press, pp. 370-376

[22] Moody, J. & Darken, C. J. (1989). Fast Learning in Networks of Locally-tuned Processing Units, *Neural Computation*, Vol. 1, pp. 281-294

[23] Morimoto, J. & Doya, K. (2001). Acquisition of stand-up behavior by a real robot using hierarchical reinforcement learning, *Robotics and Autonomous Systems*, Vol. 36, No. 1, pp. 37-51

[24] Possio, T. & Girosi, F. (1990). Networks for Approximation and Learning, *Proc. of the IEEE*, Vol. 78, No. 9, pp. 1481-1497

[25] Albus, J. S. (1981). *Brain, Behavior, and Robotics*, Byte Books, Chapter 6, pp. 139-179

[26] Sutton, R. S. (1996). Generalization in reinforcement learning: Successful examples using sparse coarse coding, *Advances in Neural Information Processing Systems*, Vol. 8, MIT Press, pp. 1038-1044

[27] Shibata, K. & Ito, K. (2007). Adaptive Space Reconstruction on Hidden Layer and Knowledge Transfer based on Hidden-level Generalization in Layered Neural Networks, *Trans. SICE*, Vol. 43, No.1, pp. 54-63 (in Japanese).

[28] Shibata, K. & Ito, K. (1998). Reconstruction of Visual Sensory Space on the Hidden Layer in a Layered Neural Networks, *Proc. ICONIP '98*, Vol. 1, pp. 405-408

[29] Shibata, K., Sugisaka, M. & Ito, K. (2001). Fast and Stable Learning in Direct-Vision-Based Reinforcement Learning, *Proc. of AROB (Int'l Sympo. on Artificial Life and Robotics) 6th*, Vol. 1, pp. 200-203

[30] Shibata, K. and Ito, K. (1999). Gauss-Sigmoid Neural Network, *Proc. of IJCNN (Int'l Joint Conf. on Neural Networks) '99*, #747

[31] Schmidhuber, J. (2002). Exploring the Predictable, *Advances in Evolutionary Computing*, Springer, pp. 579-612

[32] Tani, J. (2003). Learning to Generate Articulated Behavior Through the Bottom-up and the Top-down Interaction Processes, *Neural Networks*, Vol. 16, No. 1, pp. 11-23

[33] Oudeyer, P. -Y., Kaplan, F. & Hafner, V. V. (2007). Intrinsic Motivation Systems for Autonomous Mental Development, *IEEE Trans. on Evolutionary Computation*, Vol. 11, No. 1, pp. 265-286

[34] McCracken, P. & Bowling, M. (2006). Online Discovery and Learning of Predictive State Representations, *Advances in Neural Information Processing Systems*, Vol. 18 , pp. 875-882

[35] Goto, K. & Shibata, K. (2010). Emergence of Prediction by Reinforcement Learning Using a Recurrent Neural Network, *J. of Robotics*, Vol. 2010, Article ID 437654

[36] Barto, A. G. et al. (1983). Neuronlike adaptive elements can solve difficult learning control problems, *IEEE Trans. on Systems, Man, and Cybernetics*, Vol. 13, No. 5, pp. 834-846

[37] Watkins, C. J. C. H. (1989). Learning from Delayed Rewards, *PhD thesis*, Cambridge University, Cambridge, England

[38] Shibata, K. & Kawano, T. (2009). Learning of Action Generation from Raw Camera Images in a Real-World-like Environment by Simple Coupling of Reinforcement Learning and a Neural Network, *Advances in Neuro-Information Processing*, LNCS, Vol. 5506, pp. 755-762
[39] Utsunomiya, H. & Shibata, K. (2009). Contextual Behavior and Internal Representations Acquired by Reinforcement Learning with a Recurrent Neural Network in a Continuous State and Action Space Task, *Advances in Neuro-Information Processing*, LNCS, Vol. 5506, pp. 755-762
[40] Goto, K. & Shibata, K. (2010). Acquisition of Deterministic Exploration and Purposive Memory through Reinforcement Learning with a Recurrent Neural Network, *Proc. of SICE Annual Conf. 2010*
[41] Shibata, K. (2006). Spatial Abstraction and Knowledge Transfer in Reinforcement Learning Using a Multi-Layer Neural Network, *Proc. of Fifth Int'l Conf. on Development and Learning*
[42] Shibata, K. (2005). Discretization of Series of Communication Signals in Noisy Environment by Reinforcement Learning, *Adaptive and Natural Computing Algorithms, Proc. of ICANNGA'05*, pp. 486-489
[43] Shibata, K. & Sugisaka, M. (2002). Dynamics of a Recurrent Neural Network Acquired through the Learning of a Context-based Attention Task, *Proc. of AROB (Int'l Sympo. on Artificial Life and Robotics) 7th*, pp. 152-155
[44] Yamashita, Y. & Tanni, J. (2008). Emergence of Functional Hierarchy in a Multiple Timescale Neural Network Model: a Humanoid Robot Experiment, *PLoS Comupt. Biol.*, Vol. 4, No. 11, e1000220
[45] Shibata, K. (2006). Learning of Deterministic Exploration and Temporal Abstraction in Reinforcement Learning, *Proc. of SICE-ICCAS (SICE-ICASE Int'l Joint Conf.)*, pp. 4569-4574
[46] Bremner, J. G. (1994). *Infancy*, Blackwell Publishers limited
[47] Meltzoff, A. N. & Moore, M. K. (1994). Imitation, memory, and the representation of persons, *Infant Behavior and Development*, Vol. 17, pp. 83-99
[48] Schultz, W. et al. (1992). Neuronal Activity in Monkey Ventral Striatum Related to the Expectation of Reward, *J. of Neuroscience*, Vol. 12, No. 12, pp.4595-4610
[49] Brunso-Bechtold, J.K. and Hamburger, V. (1979). Retrograde transport of nerve growth factor in chicken embryo, *Proc. Natl. Acad. Sci. USA.*, No.76, pp. 1494-1496
[50] Sutton, R. S. (2004). Reinforcement Learning FAQ, http://webdocs.cs.ualberta.ca/ sutton/RL-FAQ.html
[51] Shibata, K., Ito, K. & Okabe, Y. (1985). Simple Learning Algorithm for Recurrent Networks to Realize Short-Term Memories, *Proc. of IJCNN (Int'l Joint Conf. on Neural Networks) '98*, pp. 2367-2372
[52] Samsudin, M. F. B., Hirose, T. and Shibata, K. (2007). Practical Recurrent Learning (PRL) in the Discrete Time Domain, *Neural Information Processing of Lecture Notes in Computer Science*, Vol. 4984, pp. 228-237
[53] Kurino, R., Sugisaka, M. & Shibata, K. (2003). Growing Neural Network for Acuqisition of 2-layer Structure, *Proc. of IJCNN (Int'l Joint Conf. on Neural Networks) '03*, pp. 2512-2518
[54] Kurino, K., Sugisaka, M. & Shibata, K. (2004). Growing Neural Network with Hidden Neurons, *Proc. of The 9th AROB (Int'l Sympo. on Artificial Life and Robotics)*, Vol. 1, pp. 144-147
[55] Joy, B. (2000). Why the Future doesn't Need Us, *WIRED*, Issue 8.04

7

Reinforcement Learning using Kohonen Feature Map Probabilistic Associative Memory based on Weights Distribution

Yuko Osana
Tokyo University of Technology
Japan

1. Introduction

The reinforcement learning is a sub-area of machine learning concerned with how an agent ought to take actions in an environment so as to maximize some notion of long-term reward(Sutton & Barto, 1998). Reinforcement learning algorithms attempt to find a policy that maps states of the world to the actions the agent ought to take in those states.
Temporal Difference (TD) learning is one of the reinforcement learning algorithm. The TD learning is a combination of Monte Carlo ideas and dynamic programming (DP) ideas. TD resembles a Monte Carlo method because it learns by sampling the environment according to some policy. TD is related to dynamic programming techniques because it approximates its current estimate based on previously learned estimates. The actor-critic method(Witten, 1977) is the method based on the TD learning, and consists of two parts; (1) actor which selects the action and (2) critic which evaluate the action and the state.
On the other hand, neural networks are drawing much attention as a method to realize flexible information processing. Neural networks consider neuron groups of the brain in the creature, and imitate these neurons technologically. Neural networks have some features, especially one of the important features is that the networks can learn to acquire the ability of information processing. The flexible information processing ability of the neural network and the adaptive learning ability of the reinforcement learning are combined, some reinforcement learning method using neural networks are proposed(Shibata et al., 2001; Ishii et al., 2005; Shimizu and Osana, 2008).
In this research, we propose the reinforcement learning method using Kohonen Feature Map Probabilistic Associative Memory based on Weights Distribution (KFMPAM-WD)(Osana, 2009). The proposed method is based on the actor-critic method, and the actor is realized by the KFMPAM-WD. The KFMPAM-WD is based on the self-organizing feature map(Kohonen, 1994), and it can realize successive learning and one-to-many associations. The proposed method makes use of this property in order to realize the learning during the practice of task.

2. Kohonen feature map probabilistic associative memory based on weights distribution

Here, we explain the Kohonen Feature Map Probabilistic Associative Memory based on Weights Distribution (KFMPAM-WD)(Koike and Osana, 2010) which is used in the proposed

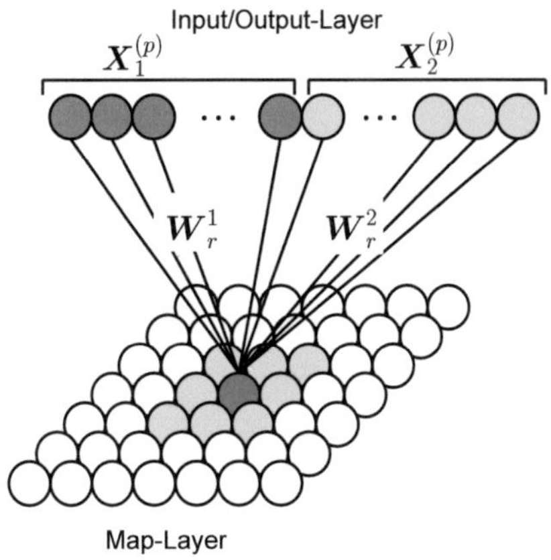

Fig. 1. Structure of KFMPAM-WD.

method.

2.1 Structure

Figure 1 shows the structure of the KFMPAM-WD. As shown in Fig.1, the KFMPAM-WD has two layers; (1) Input/Output(I/O)-Layer and (2) Map-Layer, and the I/O-Layer is divided into some parts.

2.2 Learning process

In the learning algorithm of the KFMPAM-WD, the connection weights are learned as follows:

(1) The initial values of weights are chosen randomly.

(2) The Euclidean distance between the learning vector $X^{(p)}$ and the connection weights vector W_i, $d(X^{(p)}, W_i)$ is calculated.

$$d(X^{(p)}, W_i) = \sqrt{\sum_{k=1}^{M} (X_k^{(p)} - W_{ik})^2} \tag{1}$$

(3) If $d(X^{(p)}, W_i) > \theta^t$ is satisfied for all neurons, the input pattern $X^{(p)}$ is regarded as an unknown pattern. If the input pattern is regarded as a known pattern, go to (8).

(4) The neuron which is the center of the learning area r is determined as follows:

$$r = \operatorname*{argmin}_{\substack{i:\, D_{iz}+D_{zi}<d_{iz} \\ (\text{for } \forall z \in F)}} d(X^{(p)}, W_i) \tag{2}$$

where F is the set of the neurons whose connection weights are fixed. d_{iz} is the distance between the neuron i and the neuron z whose connection weights are fixed. In the KFMPAM-WD, the Map-Layer is treated as torus, so the distance between the neurons i and j d_{ij} is given by

$$d_{ij} = \sqrt{(d_{ij}^x)^2 + (d_{ij}^y)^2} \tag{3}$$

$$d^x_{ij} = \begin{cases} x_j - x_i, & (|x_j - x_i| \leq x_{max}/2) \\ -\text{sgn}(x_j - x_i)\,(x_{max} - |x_j - x_i|), & \text{(otherwise)} \end{cases} \tag{4}$$

$$d^y_{ij} = \begin{cases} y_j - y_i, & (|y_j - y_i| \leq y_{max}/2) \\ -\text{sgn}(y_j - y_i)\,(y_{max} - |y_j - y_i|), & \text{(otherwise)} \end{cases} \tag{5}$$

where x_i and y_i are the coordinates of the neuron i in the Map-Layer, x_j and y_j are the coordinates of the neuron j in the Map-Layer, and x_{max} and y_{max} are width and height of the Map-Layer. In Eq.(2), D_{ij} is the radius of the ellipse area whose center is the neuron i for the direction to the neuron j, and is given by

$$D_{ij} = \begin{cases} \sqrt{\dfrac{a_i{}^2 b_i{}^2}{b_i{}^2 + m_{ij}{}^2 a_i{}^2}(m_{ij}{}^2 + 1)}, & (d^x_{ij} \neq 0 \text{ and } d^y_{ij} \neq 0) \\ a_i, & (d^y_{ij} = 0) \\ b_i, & (d^x_{ij} = 0) \end{cases} \tag{6}$$

where a_i is the long radius of the ellipse area whose center is the neuron i and b_i is the short radius of the ellipse area whose center is the neuron i. In the KFMPAM-WD, a_i and b_i can be set for each training pattern. m_{ij} is the slope of the line through the neurons i and j, and is given by

$$m_{ij} = \frac{d^y_{ij}}{d^x_{ij}} \qquad (d^x_{ij} \neq 0). \tag{7}$$

In Eq.(2), the neuron whose Euclidean distance between its connection weights and the learning vector is minimum in the neurons which can be take areas without overlaps to the areas corresponding to the patterns which are already trained. In Eq.(2), the size of the area for the learning vector are used as a_i and b_i.

(5) If $d(X^{(p)}, W_r) > \theta^t$ is satisfied, the connection weights of the neurons in the ellipse whose center is the neuron r are updated as follows:

$$W_i(t+1) = \begin{cases} W_i(t) + \alpha(t)(X^{(p)} - W_i(t)), & (d_{ri} \leq D_{ri}) \\ W_i(t), & \text{(otherwise)} \end{cases} \tag{8}$$

where $\alpha(t)$ is the learning rate and is given by

$$\alpha(t) = \frac{-\alpha_0(t-T)}{T}. \tag{9}$$

α_0 is the initial value of $\alpha(t)$ and T is the upper limit of the learning iterations.

(6) (5) is iterated until $d(X^{(p)}, W_r) \leq \theta^t$ is satisfied.

(7) The connection weights of the neuron r W_r are fixed.

(8) (2)∼(7) are iterated when a new pattern set is given.

2.3 Recall process

In the recall process of the KFMPAM-WD, when the pattern X is given to the I/O-Layer, the output of the neuron i in the Map-Layer, x_i^{map} is calculated by

$$x_i^{map} = \begin{cases} 1, & (i = r) \\ 0, & (\text{otherwise}) \end{cases} \tag{10}$$

where r is selected randomly from the neurons which satisfy

$$\frac{1}{N^{in}} \sum_{k \in C} g(X_k - W_{ik}) > \theta^{map} \tag{11}$$

where θ^{map} is the threshold of the neuron in the Map-Layer, and $g(\cdot)$ is given by

$$g(b) = \begin{cases} 1, & (|b| < \theta^d) \\ 0, & (\text{otherwise}). \end{cases} \tag{12}$$

In the KFMPAM-WD, one of the neurons whose connection weights are similar to the input pattern are selected randomly as the winner neuron. So, the probabilistic association can be realized based on the weights distribution. For example, if the training patterns including the common term such as $\{X, Y_1\}$, $\{X, Y_2\}$ are memorized, and the number of the neurons whose connection weights are similar to the pattern pair $\{X, Y_1\}$ is larger than the number of the neurons whose connection weights are similar to the pattern pair $\{X, Y_2\}$, then the probability that the pattern pair $\{X, Y_1\}$ is recalled is higher than the probability that the pattern pair $\{X, Y_2\}$ is recalled.

When the binary pattern X is given to the I/O-Layer, the output of the neuron k in the I/O-Layer x_k^{io} is given by

$$x_k^{io} = \begin{cases} 1, & (W_{rk} \geq \theta_b^{io}) \\ 0, & (\text{otherwise}) \end{cases} \tag{13}$$

where θ_b^{io} is the threshold of the neurons in the I/O-Layer.

When the analog pattern X is given to the I/O-Layer, the output of the neuron k in the I/O-Layer x_k^{io} is given by

$$x_k^{io} = W_{rk}. \tag{14}$$

3. Reinforcement learning using Kohonen feature map probabilistic associative memory based on weights distribution

Here, we explain the proposed reinforcement learning method using Kohonen Feature Map Probabilistic Associative Memory based on Weights Distribution (KFMPAM-WD)(Osana, 2009).

3.1 Outline

In the proposed method, the actor in the Actor-Critic(Witten, 1977) is realized by the KFMPAM-WD. In this research, the I/O-Layer in the KFMPAM-WD is divided into two parts corresponding to the state s and the action a, and the actions for the states are memorized.

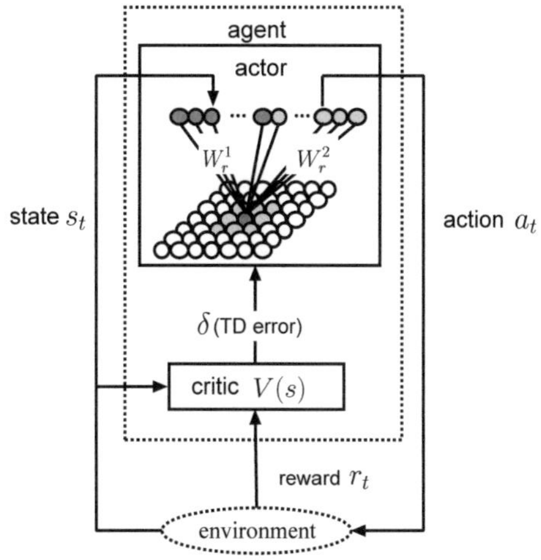

Fig. 2. Flow of Proposed Method.

In this method, the critic receives the states which are obtained from the environment, the state is estimated and the value function is updated. Moreover, the critic outputs Temporal Difference (TD) error to the actor. The KFMPAM-WD which behaves as the actor (we call this "actor network") is trained based on the TD error, and selects the action from the state of environment. Figure 2 shows the flow of the proposed method.

3.2 Actor network

In the proposed method, the actor in the Actor-Critic(Witten, 1977) is realized by the KFMPAM-WD.

3.2.1 Dynamics

In the actor network, when the state s is given to the I/O-Layer, the corresponding action a is recalled. In the proposed method, the other action is also selected randomly (random selection), and the more desirable action from the recalled action and the action selected in the random selection is chosen as the action finally.

When the pattern X is given to the network, the output of the neuron i in the Map-Layer at the time t $x_i^{map}(t)$ is given by Eq.(10), and the output of the neuron k in the I/O-Layer at the time t $x_k^{io}(t)$ is given by Eq.(13) or Eq.(14). In the actor network, only the state information is given, so the input pattern is given by

$$X = (s(t), 0)^T \tag{15}$$

where $s(t)$ is the state at the time t.

3.2.2 Learning

The actor network is trained based on the TD error from the critic.

The learning vector at the time t $X^{(t)}$ is given by the state $s(t)$ and the corresponding action $a(t)$ as follows.

$$X^{(t)} = (s(t), a(t))^T \tag{16}$$

(1) When action is recalled by actor network

When the pair of the state and the selected action are memorized in the actor network, the area size corresponding to the pair is updated. If the TD error is larger than 0, the area is expanded. If the TD error is smaller than 0, the area is reduced.

(1-1) When state and action are stored

(a) When TD error is larger than 0

When the TD error is larger than 0, the area including the fired neuron whose center is the neuron z is expanded.

$$a_z^{(new)} \leftarrow \begin{cases} a_z^{(old)} + \Delta a^+, & (a_z^{(old)} + \Delta a^+ \leq a^{max}) \\ a_z^{(old)}, & \text{(otherwise)} \end{cases} \tag{17}$$

$$b_z^{(new)} \leftarrow \begin{cases} b_z^{(old)} + \Delta b^+, & (b_z^{(old)} + \Delta b^+ \leq b^{max}) \\ b_z^{(old)}, & \text{(otherwise)} \end{cases} \tag{18}$$

where $\Delta a^+, \Delta b^+$ are the increment of a_z and b_z, and a^{max}, b^{max} are the maximum of a_z and b_z. The connection weights are updated as follows.

$$W_i(t+1) = \begin{cases} W_i(t) + \alpha(t)(X^{(tr)}(t) - W_i(t)), & (d_{zi} < D_{zi}) \\ W_i(t), & \text{(otherwise)} \end{cases} \tag{19}$$

where d_{zi} is the distance between the neuron i and the neuron z, and D_{zi} is the radius of the ellipse area whose center is the neuron z for the direction to the neuron i.

(b) When TD error is smaller than 0

When the TD error is smaller than 0, the area including the fired neuron whose center is the neuron z is reduced.

$$a_z^{(new)} \leftarrow \begin{cases} 0, & (a_z^{(new)} < 0 \text{ or } b_z^{(new)} < 0) \\ a_z^{(old)} - \Delta a^-, & \text{(otherwise)} \end{cases} \tag{20}$$

$$b_z^{(new)} \leftarrow \begin{cases} 0, & (a_z^{(new)} < 0 \text{ or } b_z^{(new)} < 0) \\ b_z^{(old)} - \Delta b^-, & \text{(otherwise)} \end{cases} \tag{21}$$

where $\Delta a^-, \Delta b^-$ are the decrement of a_z and b_z. If $a_z^{(new)}$ or $b_z^{(new)}$ becomes smaller than 0, the connection weights of neuron z are unlocked and $a_z^{(new)}$ and $b_z^{(new)}$ are set to 0.
The connection weights are updated as follows.

$$W_i(t+1) = \begin{cases} R, & (D_{zi}{}^{after} < d_{zi} \leq D_{zi}{}^{before}) \\ W_i(t), & \text{(otherwise)} \end{cases} \tag{22}$$

where R is random value. $D_{zi}{}^{before}$ is the radius of the ellipse area whose center is the neuron z for the direction to the neuron i before the area update, and $D_{zi}{}^{after}$ is the radius of the ellipse area whose center is the neuron z for the direction to the neuron i after the area update.

(1-2) When state and action are not stored

When the fired neuron is not in the areas corresponding to the stored pairs of state and action and the TD error is larger than 0, the recalled pair of state and action is regarded as an unstored data and is memorized as a new pattern.

The connection weights are updated as follows.

$$W_i(t+1) = \begin{cases} W_i(t) + \alpha(t)(X^{(tr)}(t) - W_i(t)), & (d_{ri} \leq D_{ri}) \\ W_i(t), & (\text{otherwise}) \end{cases} \tag{23}$$

where r is the center neuron of the new area, and a^{ini}, b^{ini} are the initial radius of ellipse area.

(2) When action is selected by random selection and TD error is larger than 0

When the pair of the state and the selected action are not memorized in the actor network and the TD error is larger than 0, the pair is trained as new pattern.

3.3 Reinforcement learning using KFMPAM-WD

The flow of the proposed reinforcement learning method using KFMPAM-WD is as follows:

(1) The initial values of weights in the actor network are chosen randomly.

(2) The agent observes the environment $s(t)$, and the actor $a(t)$ is selected by the actor network or the random selection.

(3) The state $s(t)$ transits to the $s(t+1)$ by action $a(t)$.

(4) The critic receives the reward $r(s(t+1))$ from the environment $s(t+1)$, and outputs the TD error δ to the actor.

$$\delta = r(s(t+1)) + \gamma V(s(t+1)) - V(s(t)) \tag{24}$$

where γ $(0 \leq \gamma \leq 1)$ is the decay parameter, and $V(s(t))$ is the value function for the state $s(t)$.

(5) The eligibility $e_t(s)$ is updated.

$$e(s) \leftarrow \begin{cases} \gamma\lambda e(s) & (\text{if} s \neq s(t+1)) \\ \gamma\lambda e(s) + 1 & (\text{if} s = s(t+1)) \end{cases} \tag{25}$$

where γ $(0 \leq \gamma \leq 1)$ is the decay parameter, and λ is the trace decay parameter.

(6) All values for states $V(s)$ are updated based on the eligibility $e_t(s)$ $(s \in S)$.

$$V(s) \leftarrow V(s) + \xi\delta e_t(s) \tag{26}$$

where ξ $(0 \leq \xi \leq 1)$ is the learning rate.

(7) The connection weights in the actor network are updated based on the TD error (See **3.2.2**).

(8) Back to (2).

4. Computer experiment results

Here, we show the computer experiment results to demonstrate the effectiveness of the proposed method.

4.1 Probablistic assocaition ability of KFMPAM-WD

Here, we examined the probabilistic association ability of the Kohonen Feature Map Probabilistic Associative Memory based on Weights Distribution (KFMPAM-WD) (Koike and Osana, 2010) which is used in the proposed method. The experiments were carried out in the KFMPAM-WD which has 800 neurons in the I/O-Layer and 400 neurons in the Map-Layer.

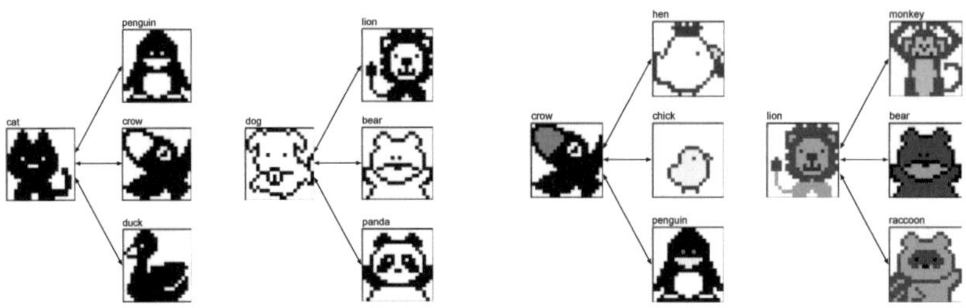

(a) Binary Patterns (b) Analog Patterns

Fig. 3. Training Pattern Pairs.

Here, we show the association result of the KFMPAM-WD for binary and analog patterns. Figure 3 shows examples of stored pattern pairs. Figure 4 (a)$\sim$(c) show a part of the association result of the KFMPAM-WD when "cat" was given during $t = 1 \sim 500$. As shown in this figure, the KFMPAM-WD could recall the corresponding patterns ("duck" ($t = 1$), "penguin" ($t = 3$),"crow" ($t = 4$)). Figure 4 (d)$\sim$(f) show a part of the association result of the KFMPAM-WD when "dog" was given during $t = 501 \sim 1000$. As shown in this figure, the proposed model could recall the corresponding patterns ("panda" ($t = 501$), "lion" ($t = 502$),"bear" ($t = 505$)).

Figure 5 shows the same association result by the direction cosine between the output pattern and each stored pattern.

Figure 6 (a)$\sim$(c) show a part of the association result of the KFMPAM-WD when "crow" was given during $t = 1 \sim 500$. As shown in this figure, the KFMPAM-WD could recall the corresponding patterns ("hen" ($t = 1$), "penguin" ($t = 2$),"chick" ($t = 3$)). Figure 6 (d)$\sim$(f) show a part of the association result of the KFMPAM-WD when "lion" was given during $t = 501 \sim 1000$. As shown in this figure, the proposed model could recall the corresponding patterns ("raccoon dog" ($t = 501$), "bear" ($t = 503$),"monkey" ($t = 504$)).

Figure 7 shows the same association result by the direction cosine between the output pattern and each stored pattern.

Figure 8 shows an example of the area representation in the Map-Layer for the training set shown in Fig.3. In this figure, light blue or green areas show area representation for each training pattern, and the red neurons show the weight-fixed neurons.

Tables 1 and 2 show the relation between the area size and the number of recall time. As shown in these tables, the KFMPAM-WD can realize probabilistic association based on the area size (that is, weights distribution).

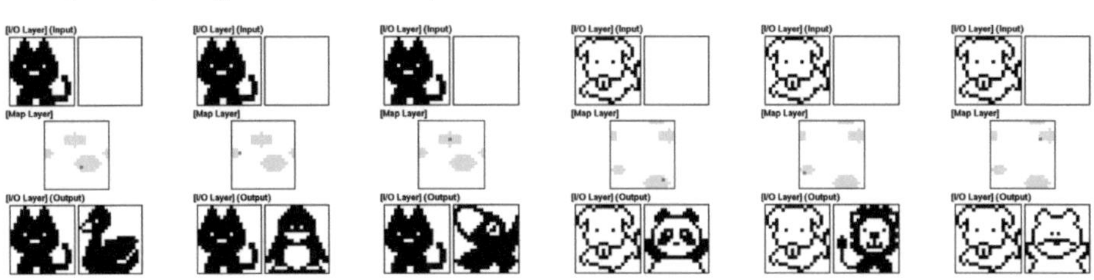

(a) $t = 1$ (b) $t = 3$ (c) $t = 4$ (d) $t = 501$ (e) $t = 502$ (f) $t = 505$

Fig. 4. Association Result (Binary Pattern).

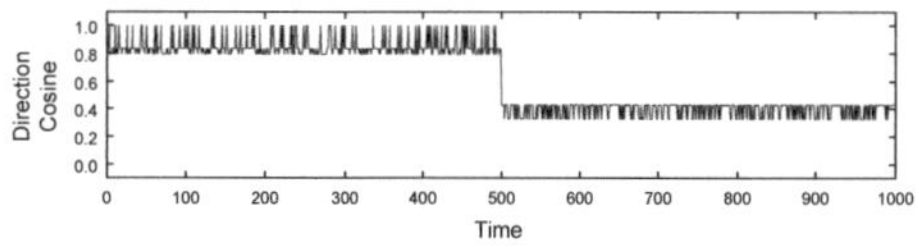

(a) cat–penguin

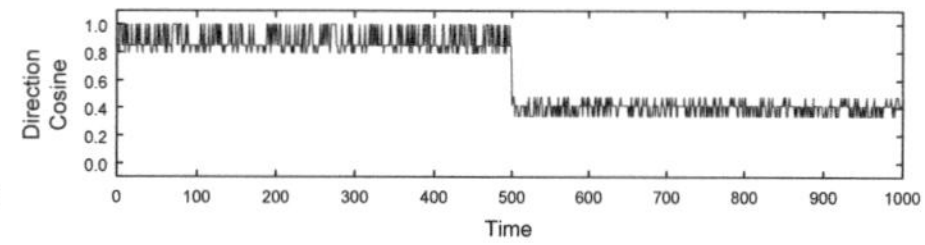

(b) cat–crow

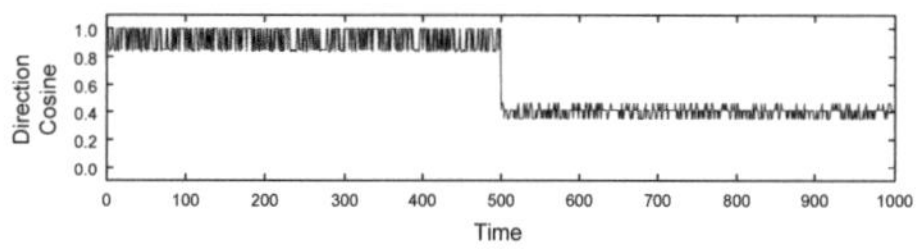

(c) cat–duck

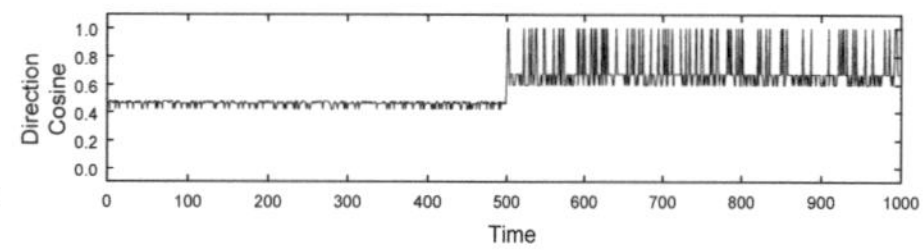

(d) dog–lion

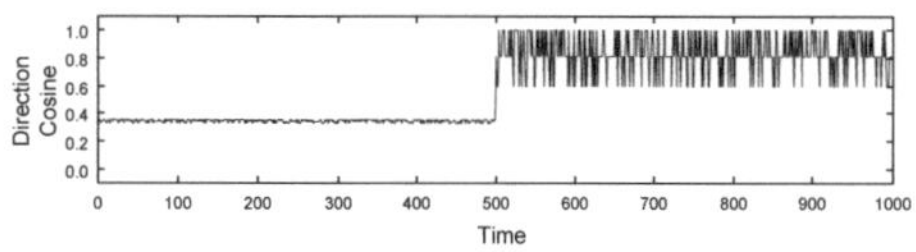

(e) dog–bear

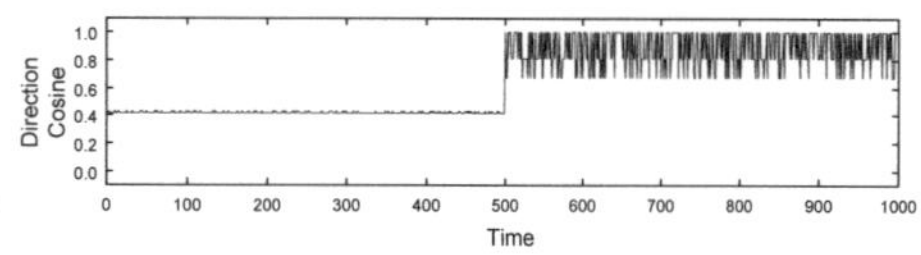

(f) dog–panda

Fig. 5. Association Result (Direction Cosine).

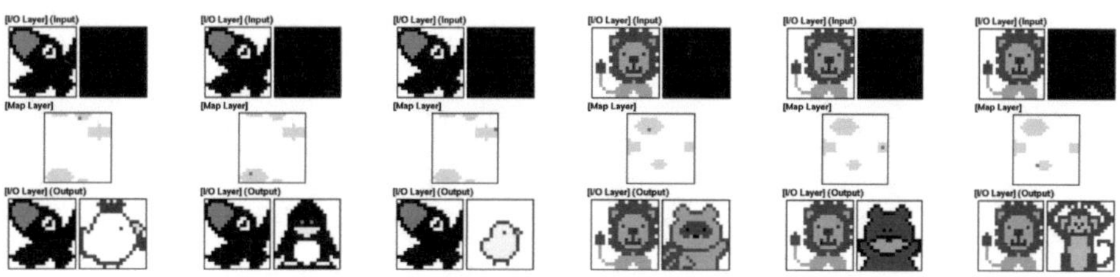

(a) $t = 1$ (b) $t = 2$ (c) $t = 3$ (d) $t = 501$ (e) $t = 503$ (f) $t = 504$

Fig. 6. Association Result (Analog Pattern).

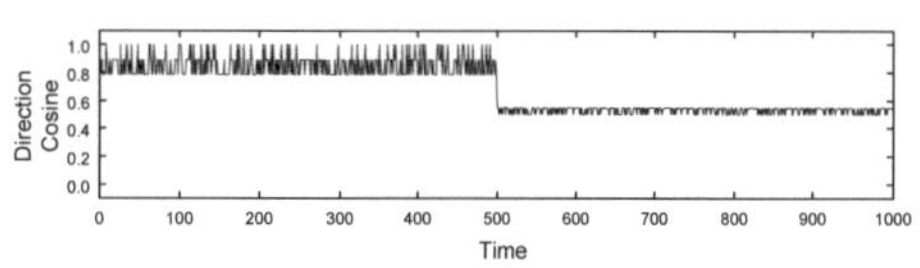

(a) crow–hen

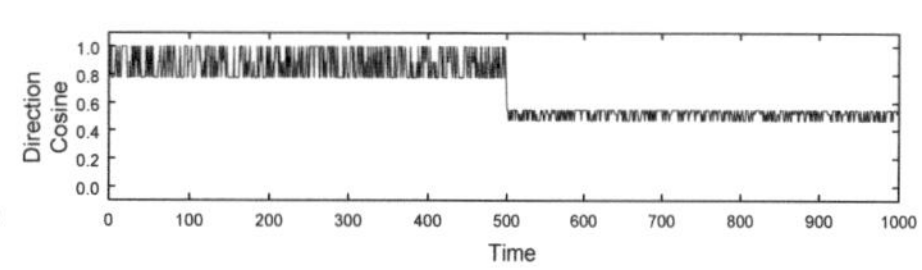

(b) crow–chick

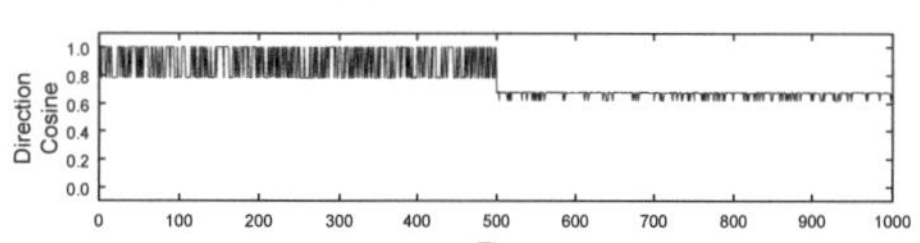

(c) crow–penguin

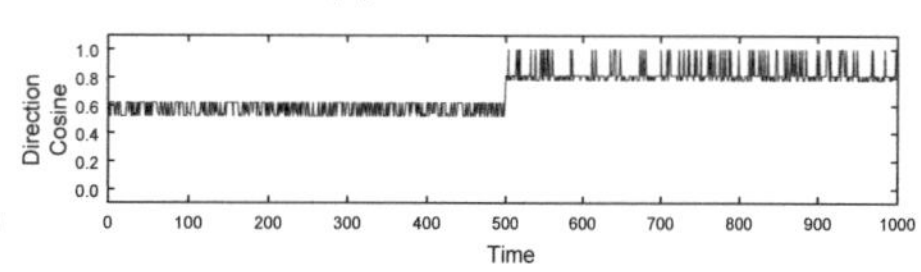

(d) lion–monkey

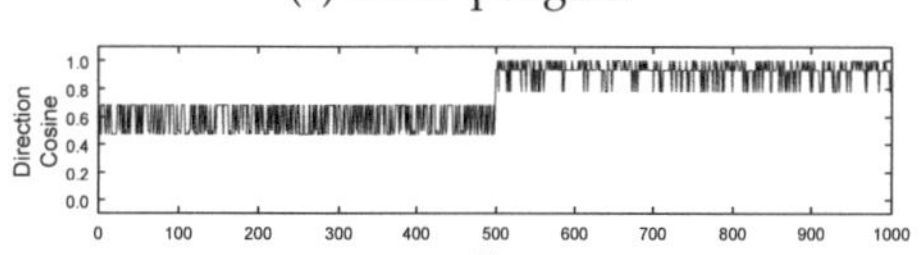

(e) lion–bear

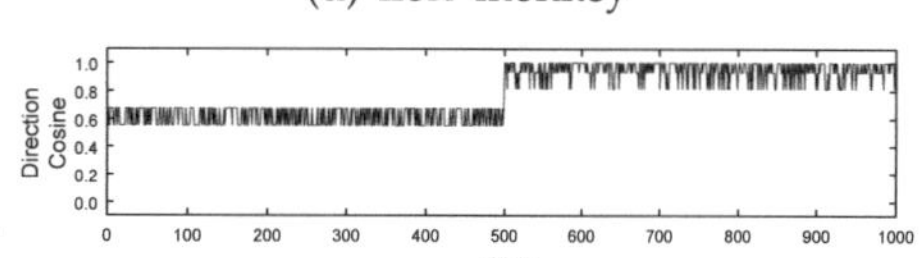

(f) lion–raccoon dog

Fig. 7. Association Result (Direction Cosine).

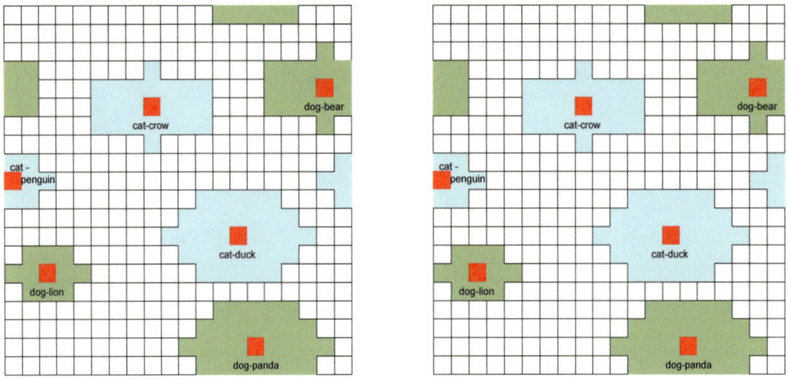

(a) Binary Pattern. (b) Analog Pattern.

Fig. 8. Area Representation for Training Set in Fig.3.

Input Pattern	Output Pattern	Area Size	Recall Time
cat	penguin	11	85
	crow	23	157
	duck	33	258
dog	lion	11	80
	bear	23	166
	panda	33	254

Table 1. Relation between Area Size and Recall Time (Binary Pattern).

Input Pattern	Output Pattern	Area Size	Recall Time
crow	hen	11	67
	chick	23	179
	penguin	33	254
lion	monkey	11	82
	bear	23	161
	raccoon dog	33	257

Table 2. Relation between Area Size and Recall Time (Analog Pattern).

4.2 Path-finding problem

We applied the proposed method to the path-finding problem. In this experiment, a agent moves from the start point (S) to the goal point (G). The agent can observe the states of three cells in the lattice, and can move forward/left/right. As the positive reward, we gave 3 when the agent arrives at the goal and 2 when the agent moves. And as the negative reward, we gave -1 when the agent hits against the wall. Table 3 shows experimental conditions. Figure 9 shows an example of maps (and the trained route (arrow)).

Parameters for Reinforcement Learning		
Decay Parameter	γ	0.7
Trace Decay Parameter	λ	0.33
Learning Rate	ξ	0.33
Parameters for Actor Network (Learning)		
Random Value	R	$0.0 < R < 1.0$
Initial Long Radius	a^{ini}	2.5
Initial Short Radius	b^{ini}	1.5
Increment of Area Size	Δa_z^+	0.01
Decrement of Area Size	Δa_z^-	0.1
Lower Limit of Long Radius	$a_z{}^{max}$	4.0
Lower Limit of Short Radius	$b_z{}^{max}$	3.0
Lower Limit of Long Radius	$a_z{}^{min}$	0.0
Lower Limit of Short Radius	$b_z{}^{min}$	0.0
Weight Update Number	T^{max}	200
Threshold for Learning	θ^l	10^{-7}
Parameters for Actor Network (Recall)		
Threshold of Neurons in Map-Layer	θ_b^{map}	0.01
Threshold of Neurons in I/O-Layer	θ_b^{in}	0.5

Table 3. Experimental Conditions.

4.2.1 Transition of number of steps

Figure 10 shows the transition of number of steps from the start to the goal. As shown in these figures, the agent can learn the route from the start to the goal by the proposed method.

4.2.2 Trained relation between state and action

Figure 11 shows an example of the trained relation between the state and the action. As shown these figures, the agent can learn the relation between state and action by the proposed method.

4.2.3 Variation of action selection method

Figure 12 shows the variation of the action selection method in the proposed method. As shown in these figures, at the beginning of the learning, the random selection is used frequently. After the learning, the action which is selected by the actor network is used frequently.

4.2.4 Use of learning information in similar environment

Here, we examined in the actor network that learns in the Map 2. Figure 13 (a) shows the transition of steps in the Map 3. As shown in this figure, the agent learn to reach the goal in few steps when the actor network that learns in the environment of the Map 2 in advance. Figure 13 (b) shows the variation of the action selection method in this experiment. Figure 14 shows the an example of the trained relation between the state and the action in this experiment.

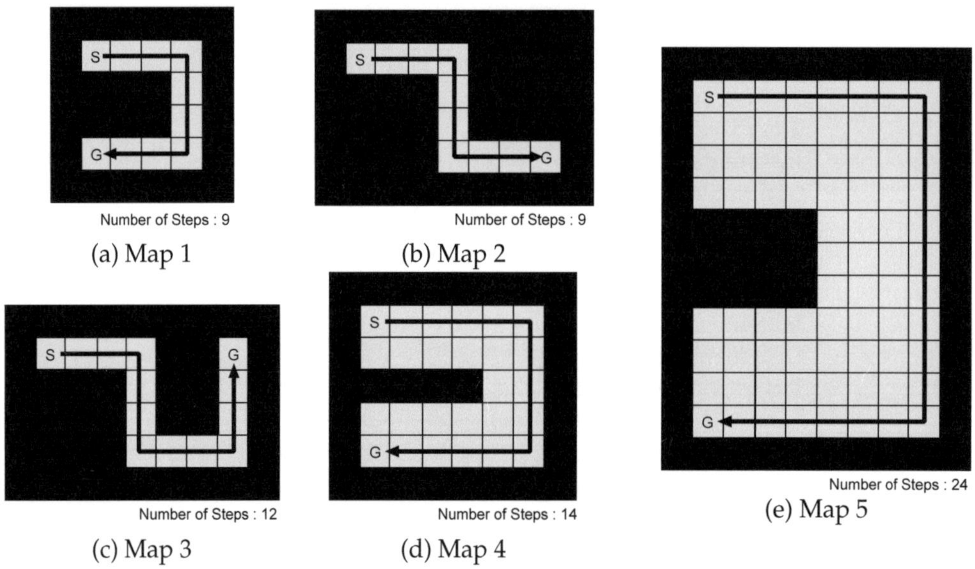

Fig. 9. Map and Trained Route.

5. Conclusion

In this research, we have proposed the reinforcement learning method using Kohonen Feature Map Probabilistic Associative Memory based on Weights Distribution. The proposed method is based on the actor-critic method, and the actor is realized by the Kohonen Feature Map Probabilistic Associative Memory based on Weights Distribution. We carried out a series of computer experiments, and confirmed the effectiveness of the proposed method in path-finding problem.

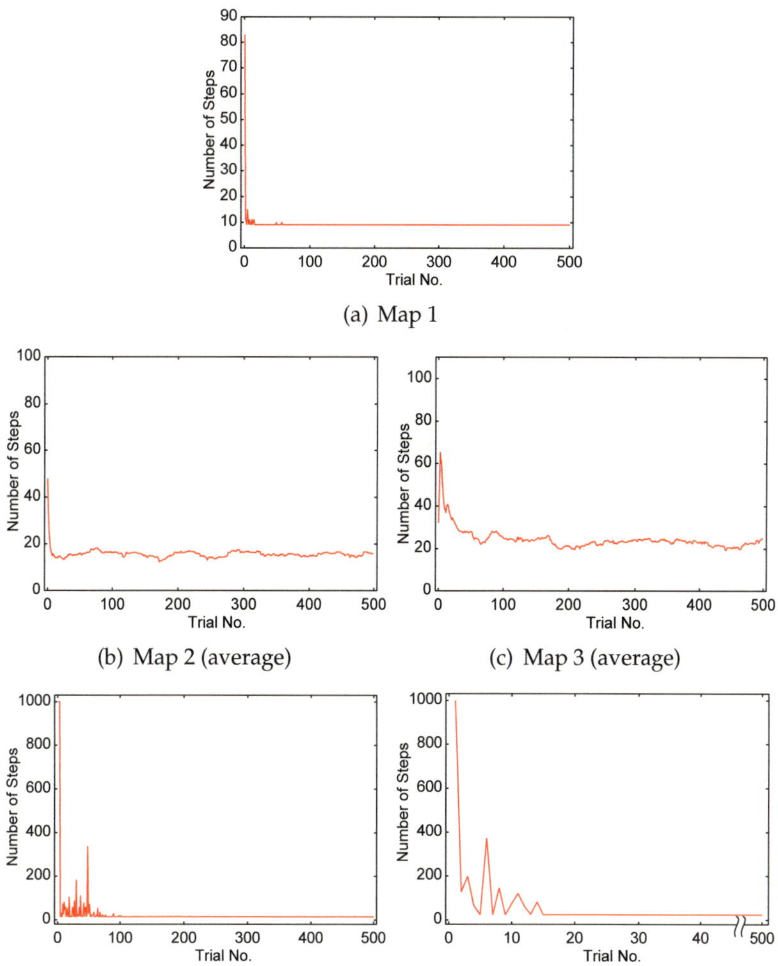

(a) Map 1

(b) Map 2 (average)

(c) Map 3 (average)

(d) Map 4

(e) Map 5

Fig. 10. Transition of Steps.

forward	forward	left	forward	right
35	11	3	35	35
a_i : 4.00	a_i : 2.56	a_i : 1.90	a_i : 4.00	a_i : 4.00
b_i : 3.00	b_i : 1.56	b_i : 0.90	b_i : 3.00	b_i : 3.00

(a) Map 1

right	forward	forward	forward	left	right
11	35	35	35	11	35
a_i : 2.51	a_i : 4.00	a_i : 4.00	a_i : 4.00	a_i : 2.23	a_i : 4.00
b_i : 1.51	b_i : 3.00	b_i : 3.00	b_i : 3.00	b_i : 1.23	b_i : 3.00

(b) Map 2

forward	forward	left	right	left	forward
35	35	11	3	11	35
a_i : 4.00	a_i : 4.00	a_i : 2.51	a_i : 1.04	a_i : 2.53	a_i : 4.00
b_i : 3.00	b_i : 3.00	b_i : 1.51	b_i : 0.04	b_i : 1.53	b_i : 3.00

(c) Map 3

left	forward	right
35	35	35
a_i : 4.00	a_i : 4.00	a_i : 4.00
b_i : 3.00	b_i : 3.00	b_i : 3.00

(d) Map 4

left	right	forward	forward
35	35	35	35
a_i : 4.00	a_i : 4.00	a_i : 4.00	a_i : 4.00
b_i : 3.00	b_i : 3.00	b_i : 3.00	b_i : 3.00

(e) Map 5

Fig. 11. An example of Trained Relation between State and Action.

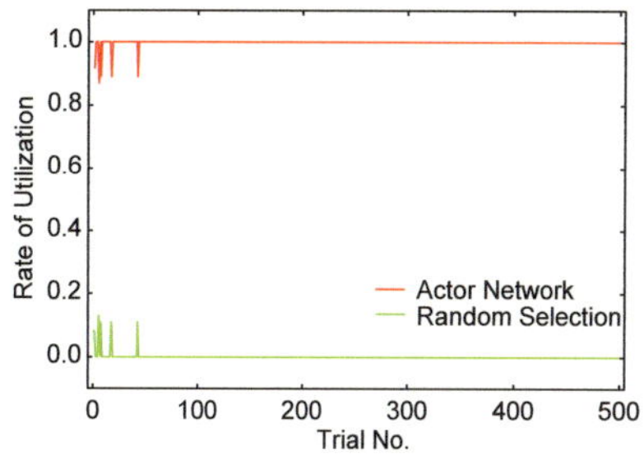

(a) Map 1

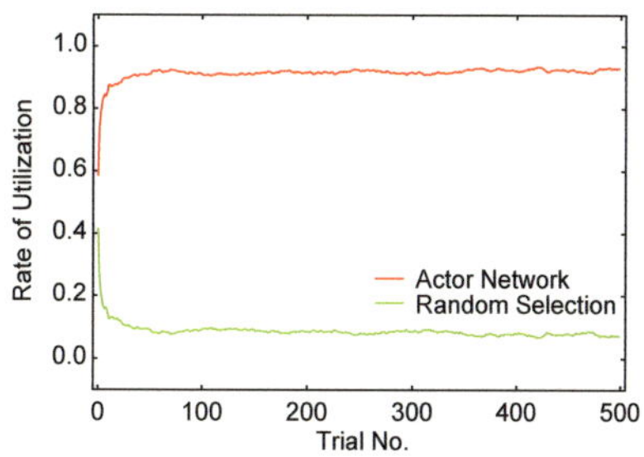

(b) Map 2 (average)

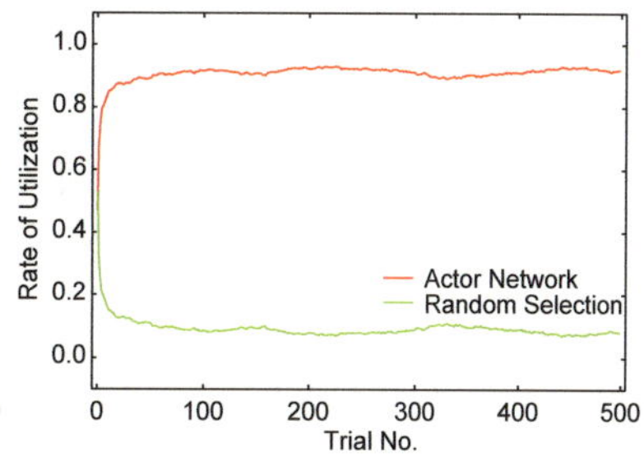

(c) Map 3 (average)

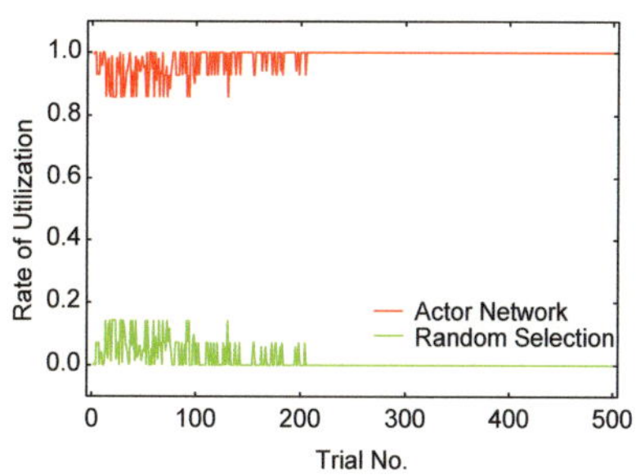

(d) Map 4

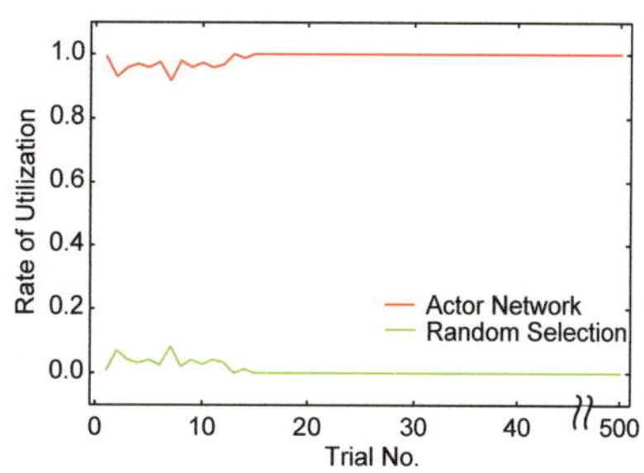

(e) Map 5

Fig. 12. Variation of Action Selection Method.

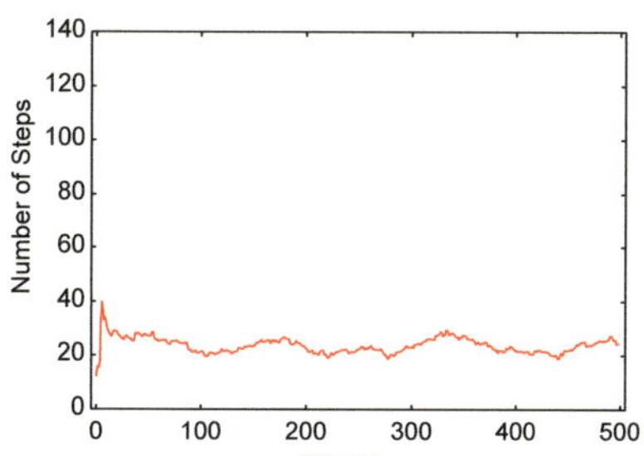

(a) Transition of Steps (average)

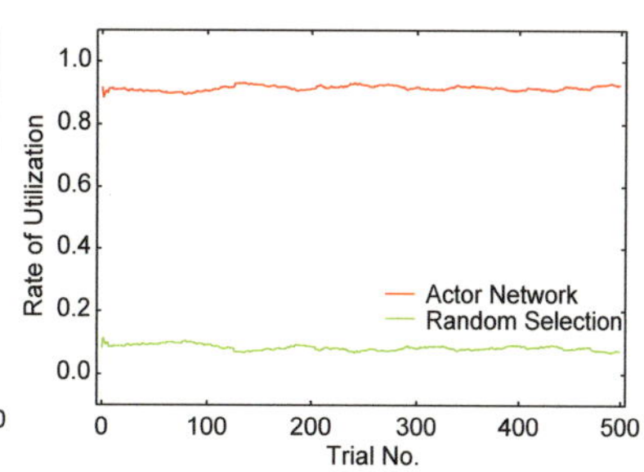

(b) Variation of Action Selection Method

Fig. 13. Use of Learning Information in Similar Environment.

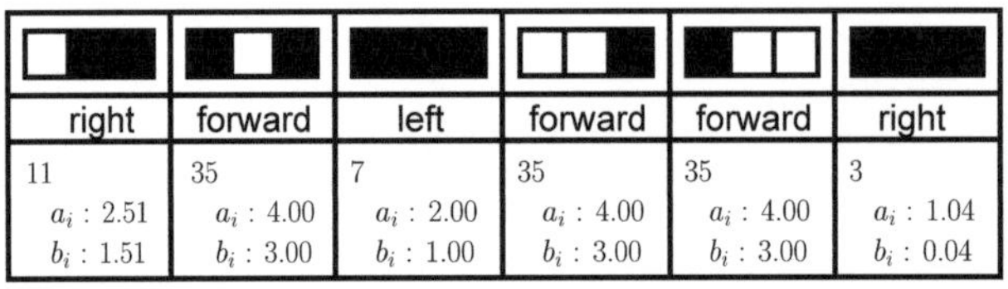

Fig. 14. An example of Trained Relation between State and Action (Map 2 $\rightarrow$ Map 3).

6. References

Ishii, S., Shidara, M. & Shibata, K. (2005) "A model of emergence of reward expectancy neurons by reinforcement learning," *Proceedings of the 10th International Sysmposium on Artificial Life and Robotics*, GS21–5.

Kohonen, T. (1994) Self-Organizing Maps, Springer.

Koike, M. & Osana, Y. (2010) "Kohonen feature map probabilistic associative memory based on weights distribution," *Proceedings of IASTED Artificial Intelligence and Applications*, Innsbruck.

Osana, Y. (2009) "Reinforcement learning using Kohonen feature map probabilistic associative Memory based on weights distribution," *Proceedings of International Symposium on Nonlinear Theory and its Applications*, Sapporo.

Shibata, K., Sugisaka, M. & Ito, K. (2001) "Fast and stable learning in direct-vision-based reinforcement learning," *Proceedings of the 6th International Sysmposium on Artificial Life and Robotics*, Vol.1, pp.200–203.

Shimizu, A. & Osana, Y. (2008) "Reinforcement learning using Kohonen feature map assocaitive memory with refractoriness based on area representation," *Proceedings of International Conference on Neural Information Processing*, Auckland.

Sutton, R. S. & Barto A. G. (1998). Reinforcement Learning, An Introduction, The MIT Press.

Witten, I. H. (1977). "An adaptive optimal controller for discrete-time Markov environments," *Information and Control*, Vol.34, pp. 286–295.

8

How to Recommend Preferable Solutions of a User in Interactive Reinforcement Learning?

Tomohiro Yamaguchi[1], Takuma Nishimura[2] and Kazuhiro Sato[3]
[1, 2]Nara National College of Technology,
[2]currently Kyoto University,
[3]FANUC Ltd
Japan

1. Introduction

In field of robot learning (Kaplan et al., 2002), interactive reinforcement learning method in that reward function denoting goal is given interactively has worked to establish the communication between a human and the pet robot AIBO. The main feature of this method is the interactive reward function setup which was fixed and build-in function in the main feature of previous reinforcement learning methods. So the user can sophisticate reinforcement learner's behavior sequences incrementally.

Shaping (Konidaris & Barto, 2006; Ng et al., 1999) is the theoretical framework of such interactive reinforcement learning methods. Shaping is to accelerate the learning of complex behavior sequences. It guides learning to the main goal by adding shaping reward functions as subgoals. Previous shaping methods (Marthi, 2007; Ng et al., 1999) have three assumptions on reward functions as following;

1. Main goal is given or known for the designer.
2. Subgoals are assumed as shaping rewards those are generated by potential function to the main goal (Marthi, 2007).
3. Shaping rewards are policy invariant (not affecting the optimal policy of the main goal) (Ng et al., 1999).

However, these assumptions will not be true on interactive reinforcement learning with an end-user. Main reason is that it is not easy to keep these assumptions while the end-user gives rewards for the reinforcement learning agent. It is that the reward function may not be fixed for the learner if an end-user changes his/her mind or his/her preference. However, most of previous reinforcement learning methods assumes that the reward function is fixed and the optimal solution is unique, so they will be useless in interactive reinforcement learning with an end-user.

To solve this, it is necessary for the learner to estimate the user's preference and to consider its changes. This paper proposes a new method how to match an end-user's preference solution with the learner's recommended solution. Our method consists of three ideas. First, we assume *every-visit-optimality* as the optimality criterion of preference for most of end-users. Including this, section 2 describes an overview of interactive reinforcement learning in our research. Second, to cover the end-user's preference changes after the reward function is given by the end-user, interactive LC-learning prepares *various policies* (Satoh &

Yamaguchi, 2006) by generating variations of the reward function under *every-visit-optimality*. It is described in section 3. Third, we propose *coarse to fine recommendation* strategy for guiding the end-user's current preference among *various policies* in section 4.
To examine these ideas, we perform the experiment with twenty subjects to evaluate the effectiveness of our method. As the experimental results, first, a majority of subjects prefer each *every-visit* plan (visiting all goals) than the *optimal* plan. Second, the majority of them prefer *shorter* plans, and the minority of them prefer *longer* plans. We discuss the reason why the end-users' preferences are divided into two groups. These are described in section 5. In section 6, the search ability of interactive LC-learning in a stochastic domain is evaluated. Section 7 describes relations between our proposed solutions and current research issues on recommendation systems. Finally, section 8 discusses our conclusions and future work.

2. Interactive reinforcement learning

This section describes the characteristics on interactive reinforcement learning in our research, and shows the overview of our system.

2.1 Interactive reinforcement learning with human

Table1 shows the characteristics on interactive reinforcement learning. In reinforcement learning, an optimal solution is decided by the reward function and the optimality criteria. In standard reinforcement learning, an optimal solution is fixed since both the reward function and the optimality criteria are fixed. On the other hand, in interactive reinforcement learning, an optimal solution may change according to the interactive reward function. Furthermore, in interactive reinforcement learning with human, various optimal solutions will occur since the optimality criteria depend on human's preference.
Then the objective of this research is to recommend preferable solutions of each user. The main problem is how to guide to estimate the user's preference? Our solution consists of two ideas. One is to prepare various solutions by *every-visit-optimality* (Satoh & Yamaguchi, 2006), another is the *coarse to fine recommendation* strategy (Yamaguchi & Nishimura, 2008).

Type of reinforcement learning	an optimal solution	reward function	optimality criteria
standard	fixed	fixed	fixed
interactive	may change	interactive	fixed
interactive with human	various optimal	may change	human's preference

Table 1. Characteristics on interactive reinforcement learning

2.2 Overview of the plan recommendation system

Fig. 1 shows an overview of the plan recommendation system. When a user input several goals to visit constantly as his/her preference goals, they are converted to the set of rewards in the plan recommendation block for the input of interactive LC-learning (Satoh & Yamaguchi, 2006) block. After *various policies* are prepared, each policy is output as a round plan for recommendation to the user. The user comes into focus on his/her preference criteria through the interactive recommendation process. The interactive recommendation will finish after the user decides the preference plan. Next section, interactive LC-Learning block is described.

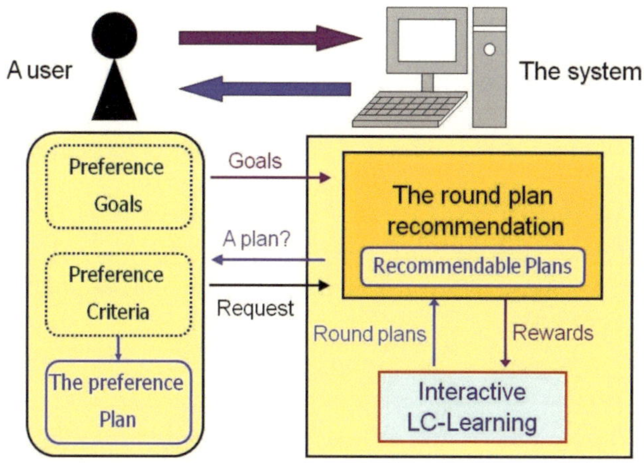

Fig. 1. The plan recommendation system

2.3 Interactive LC-Learning block

Fig. 2 shows an overview of interactive LC-Learning (Satoh & Yamaguchi, 2006) block that is extended model-based reinforcement learning. In Fig. 2, our learning agent consists of three blocks those are model identification block, optimality criterion block and policy search block. The details of these blocks are described in following section. The novelty of our method lies in optimality criterion as *every-visit-optimality* and the method of policy search collecting *various policies*.

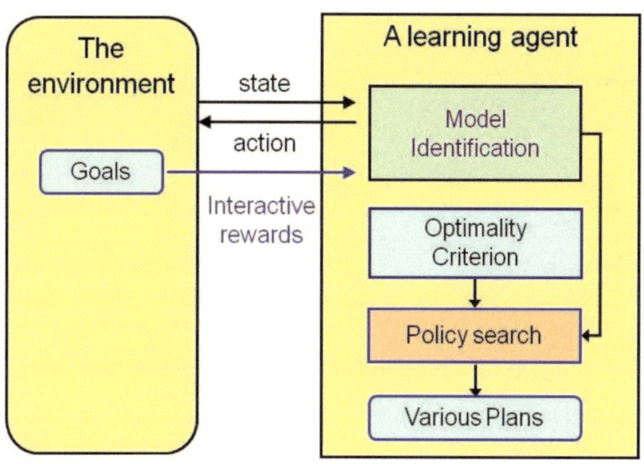

Fig. 2. Interactive LC-Learning block

2.3.1 Model identification

In model identification block, the state transition probabilities $P(s' \mid s,a)$ and reward function $R(s,a)$ are estimated incrementally by observing a sequence of (s,a,r). Note that s is an observed state, a is an executed action, and Rw is an acquired reward. This estimated model is generally assumed Markov Decision Processes (MDP) (Puterman, 2006). MDP model is defined by following four elements.

1. Set of states: $S = \{s_0, s_1, s_2, \cdots, s_n\}$
2. Set of actions: $A = \{a_0, a_1, a_2, \cdots, a_m\}$
3. State transition probabilities: $P(s' \mid s,a)$ probability of occurring state s' when execute action a at state s.
4. Reward function: $R(s,a)$ acquired reward when execute action a at state s.

2.3.2 Optimality criterion

Optimality criterion block defines the optimality of the learning policy. In this research, a policy which maximizes average reward is defined as an *optimal* policy. Eq. (1) shows the definition of average reward.

$$g^{\pi}(s) \equiv \lim_{N \to \infty} E\left(\frac{1}{N}\sum_{t=0}^{N-1} r_t^{\pi}(s)\right) \tag{1}$$

where N is the number of step, $r_\tau^{\pi}(s)$ is the expected value of reward that an agent acquired at step t where policy is π and initial state is s and $E(\;)$ denotes the expected value. To simplify, we use *gain-optimality* criterion in LC-Learning (Konda et al., 2002a). In that, average reward can be calculated by both the expected length of a reward acquisition cycle and the expected sum of the rewards in the cycle.

Then we introduce *every-visit-optimality* as the new learning criterion based on average reward. *Every-visit-optimal* policy is the *optimal* policy that visits every reward in the reward function. For example, if the reward function has two rewards, the *every-visit-optimal* policy is the largest average reward one which visits both two rewards. Fig.3 shows the example of an *every-visit-optimal* policy with two rewards.

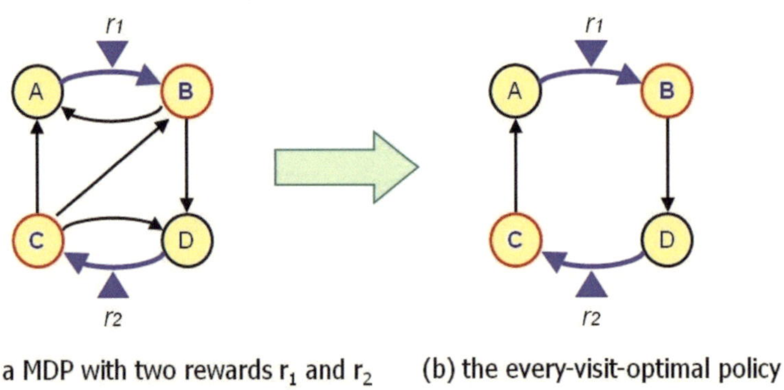

Fig. 3. An *Every-visit-optimal* policy with two rewards

2.3.3 Policy search

Policy search block searches *every-visit-optimal* policies on an identified model according to optimality of policies. Each policy is converted to a round plan by extracting a cycle. The detail of this block is described in next section.

3. Preparing various round plans

This section describes the definition of various round plans and the method for searching various policies.

3.1 Illustrated example

To begin with, we show an illustrated example. Fig.4 shows an overview of preparing various round plans within two rewards. When a MDP has two rewards as shown in Fig.4 (a), then 2^2 -1, three kinds of every-visit-optimal policies are prepared (Fig.4 (b)). Each policy is converted to a round plan by extracting a reward acquisition cycle (Fig.4 (c)), since each policy is consists of a reward acquisition cycle and some transit passes.

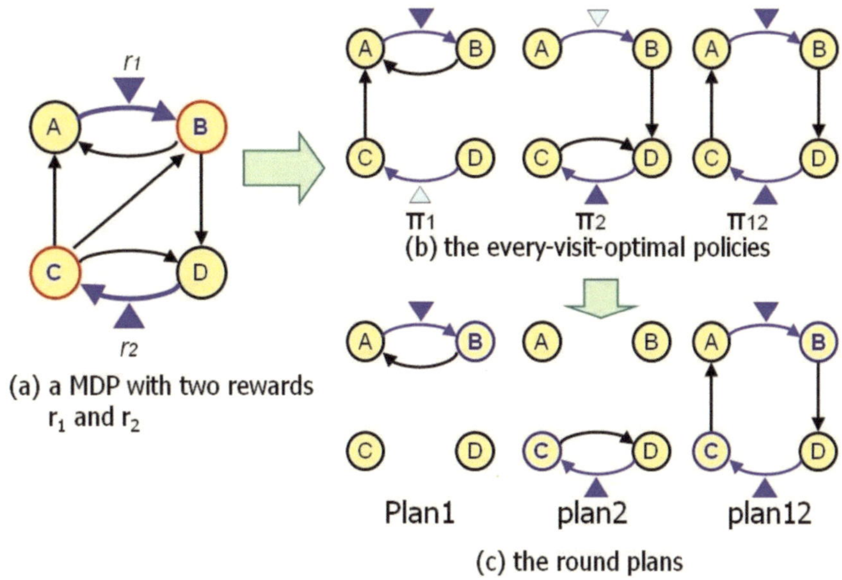

Fig. 4. Overview of preparing various round plans

3.2 Definition of various round plans by *every-visit-optimality*

Various round plans are defined by following steps.

1. Enumerate the all subsets of the reward function.
2. Search an *every-visit-optimal* policy for each subset of the reward function.
3. Collect all *every-visit-optimal* policies and convert them into round plans.

Fig. 5 illustrates the process for searching *various round plans*. When a reward function is identified as {*Rw1, Rw2*}, enumerated subsets of the function are {*Rw1*}, {*Rw2*}, {*Rw1, Rw2*} in step 1. Then an *every-visit-optimal* policy is decided for each subset of the reward function in step 2. At last, these *every-visit-optimal* policies are collected as *various round plans*. The number of plans in the *various round plans* is 2^r -1, where r is the number of rewards in the model.

3.3 Searching various policies

This section describes our *various policies* search method by interactive LC-Learning (Satoh & Yamaguchi, 2006). LC-Learning (Konda et al., 2002a; Konda et al., 2002b) is one of the average reward model-based reinforcement learning methods (Mahadevan, 1996). The features of LC-Learning are following;

1. Breadth search of an optimal policy started by each reward rule.
2. Calculating average reward by a reward acquisition cycle of each policy.

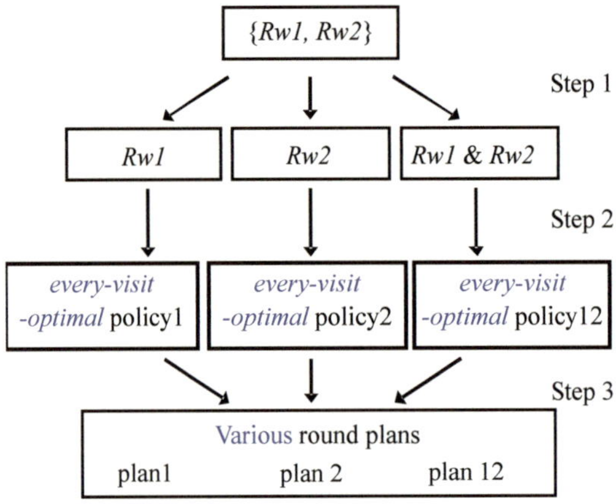

Fig. 5. Process for searching various round plans

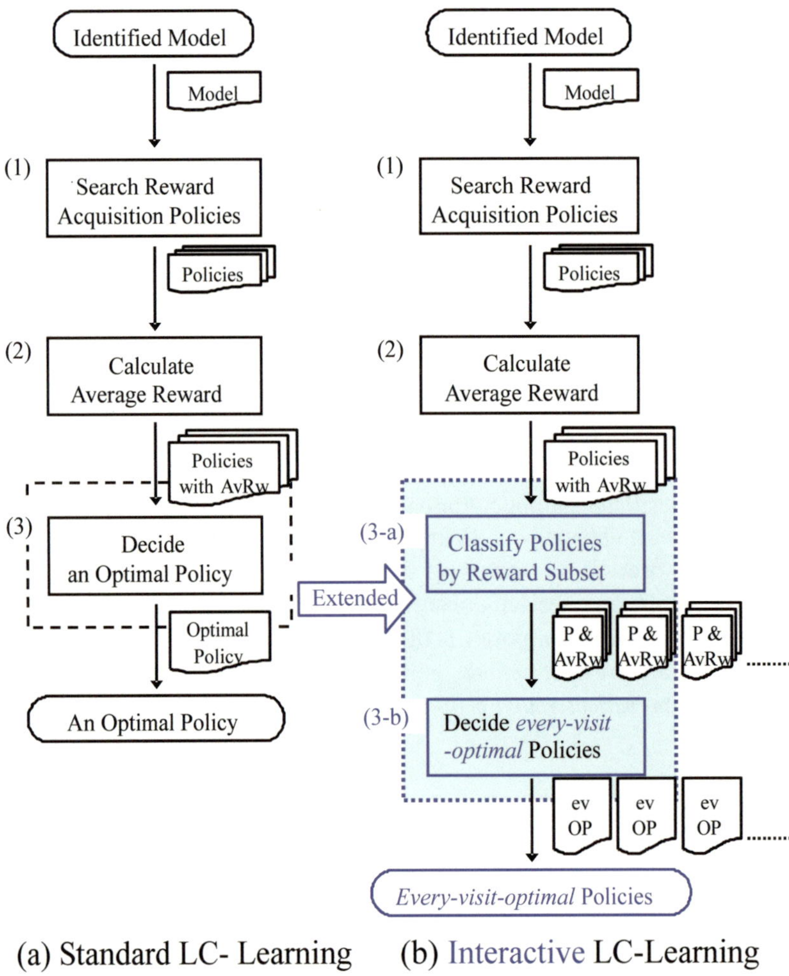

Fig. 6. Algorithm for preparing *various policies*

Fig. 6 (a) shows standard LC-Learning algorithm. Previous LC-Learning decides an optimal-policy by following three steps.

1. Search policies that have a reward acquisition cycle.
2. Calculate average reward of searched policies.
3. Decide an optimal policy that has the maximum average reward.

Fig. 6 (b) shows algorithm for interactive LC-Learning. Major differences from standard LC-Learning are following;

1. Collecting various policies by *every-visit-optimality*
2. A stochastic version based on *occurring probability*
3. Adaptable for incremental reward addition

Next, we describe the three steps for interactive LC-Learning as shown in Fig.6 (b).

(1) Search reward acquisition policies

In this step, reward acquisition policies are searched by converting a MDP into the tree structures where reward acquisition rules are root rule. We show an illustrated example. Fig. 7 shows a MDP model with two rewards r_1 and r_2. It is converted into two tree structures. Fig. 8 shows two trees. First, a tree from reward r_1 as shown in Fig. 8 (a) is generated, then a tree from reward r_2 as shown in Fig. 8 (b) is generated. In a tree structure, a policy is a path from a root node to the state that is same state to the root node. In a path, an expanded state that is same state to the previous node is pruned since it means a local cycle. In Fig.8, node D and B are pruned states.

Fig. 9 shows all reward acquisition policies in Fig. 7. In a stochastic environment, several rules branch stochastically. In such case, a path from parent node of a stochastic rule to the state that is already extracted is part of a policy that contains the stochastic rule. The policy 12 in Fig.9 is an example of this.

(2) Calculate average reward

In this step, average reward of each policy is calculated by using *occurring probability* of each state of the policy. *Occurring probability* of a state is expected value of the number of transiting the state during the agent transit from the initial state to the initial state. Eq. (2) shows definition of the *occurring probability* of state s_j where initial state is s_i. *Occurring probability* of each state is calculated approximately by value iteration using eq. (2).

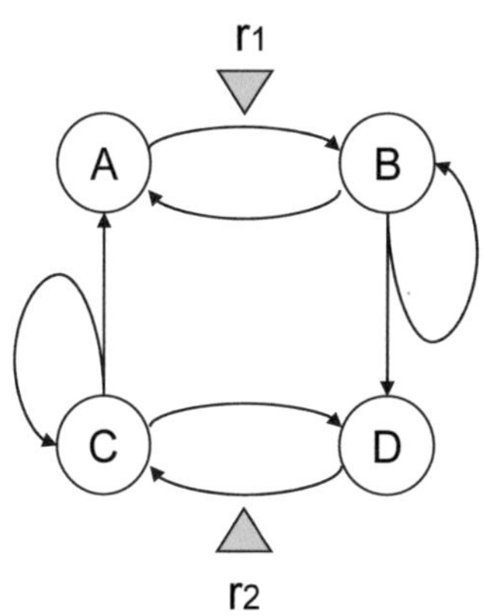

Fig. 7. An example of MDP model

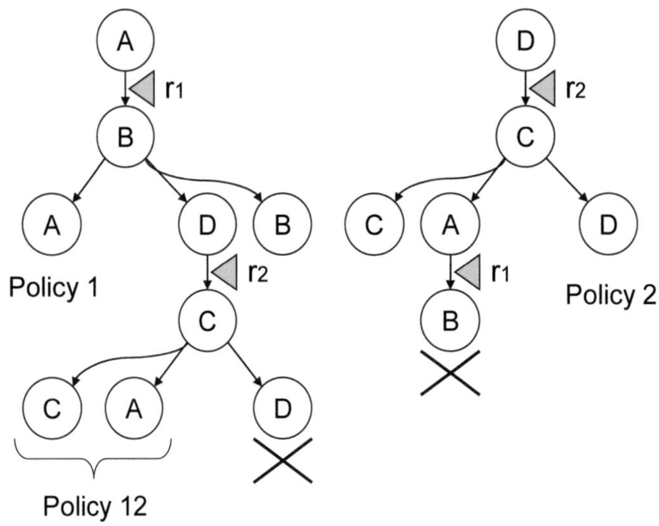

(a) A tree from reward r_1 (b) A tree from reward r_2

Fig. 8. Searching reward acquisition policies

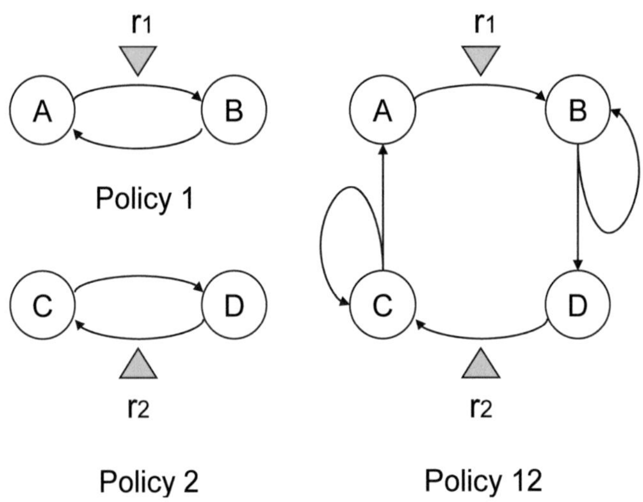

Fig. 9. Three kind of reward acquiring policies

$$P_o(s_j, s_i) = \begin{cases} 1 & (j = i) \\ \sum_{s_k} P_o(s_k, s_i) P(s_j \mid s_k, a_k) & (j \neq i) \end{cases} \tag{2}$$

Where a_k is the action that is executed at state s_k.

$$g^{\pi}(s_i) = \frac{\sum_{s_j} P_o(s_j, s_i) R(s_j, a_j)}{\sum_{s_j} P_o(s_j, s_i)} \tag{3}$$

The average reward of policies is calculated by eq. (3) using *occurring probability* calculated by eq. (2).

(3′-1) Classify policies by reward subset

In this step, all policies searched by step 1 are classified by acquisition reward set.

(3′-2) Decide *every-visit-optimal* policies

In this step, an *every-visit-optimal* policy is decided for each group classified in step (3′-1). Each *every-visit-optimal* policy is a policy that had maximum average reward in the each group.

4. Plan recommendation

This section describes the plan recommendation system and the *coarse to fine recommendation* strategy (Yamaguchi & Nishimura, 2008). In this section, a *goal* is a reward to be acquired, and a *plan* means a cycle that acquires at least one reward in a policy.

4.1 Grouping various plans by the visited goals

After preparing various round plans in section 3.3, they are merged into group by the number of acquired reward. Fig. 10 shows grouping various plans by the number of visited goals. When three goals are input by a user, they are converted into three kinds of reward as *Rw1, Rw2,* and *Rw3*. Then, Group1 in Fig. 10 holds various plans acquiring only one reward among *Rw1, Rw2,* or *Rw3*. Group2 holds various plans acquiring two kinds of reward among *Rw1, Rw2,* or *Rw3*, and Group3 holds various plans acquiring *Rw1, Rw2,* and *Rw3*.

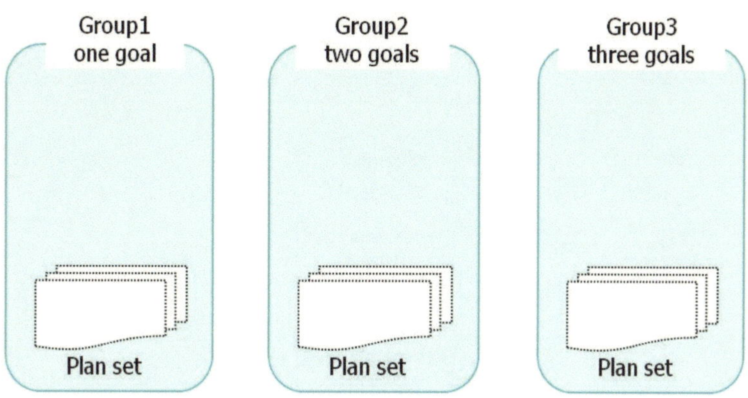

Fig. 10. Grouping various plans

4.2 Coarse to fine recommendation strategy

After grouping various plans by the number of visited goals, they are presented to the user sequentially for selecting the most preferable plan. We call the way to decide this order as recommendation strategy. In this paper, we propose *coarse to fine recommendation* strategy that consists of two steps, coarse recommendation step and fine recommendation step.

(1) Coarse recommendation step

For the user, the aim of this step is to select a preferable group. To support the user's decision, the system recommends a representative plan in each selected group to the user.

Fig. 11 shows a coarse recommendation sequence when a user changes his/her preferable group as Group1, Group2, and Group3 sequentially. When the user selects a group, the system presents the representative plan in the group as the recommended plan.

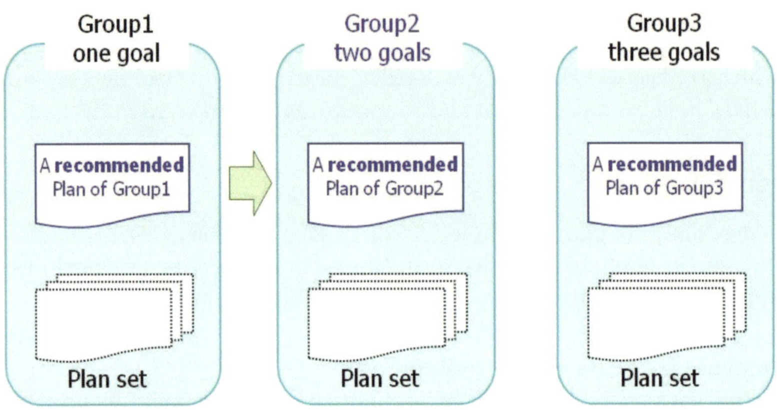

Fig. 11. Coarse recommendation

(2) Fine recommendation step

For the user, the aim of this step is to decide the most preferable plan in the selected group in previous step. To support the user's decision, the system recommends plans among his/her selected group to the user. Fig. 12 shows a fine recommendation sequence after the user selects his/her preferable group as Group2. In each group, plans are ordered according to the length of a plan.

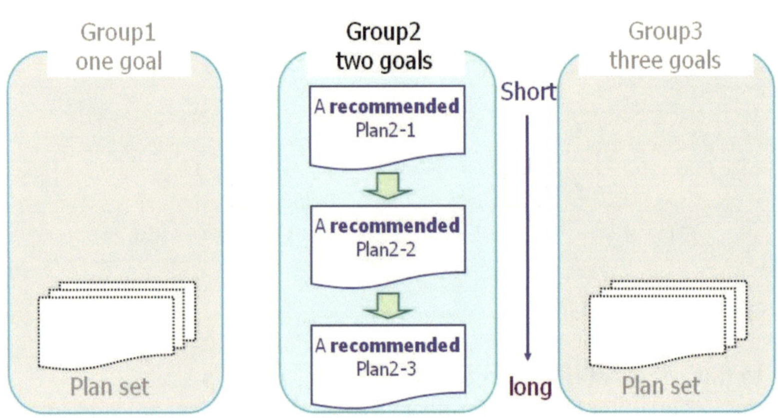

Fig. 12. Fine recommendation in the selected group

5. Experiment

We perform the experiment with twenty subjects from 19 to 21 years old to evaluate the effectiveness of our method.

5.1 The round-trip plan task

Fig. 13 shows the round-trip plan Recommendation task in Hokkaido. For a subject, this task is executed by following steps.

1. Each subject selects four cities to visit. Various round-trip plans are recommended.
2. The subject decides the most preferred round-trip plan among them. The task for a subject is to decide the most preferred round-trip plan after selecting four cities to visit among eighteen cities. The task for the system is to estimate the preferable round-trip plans to each user and to recommend them sequentially.

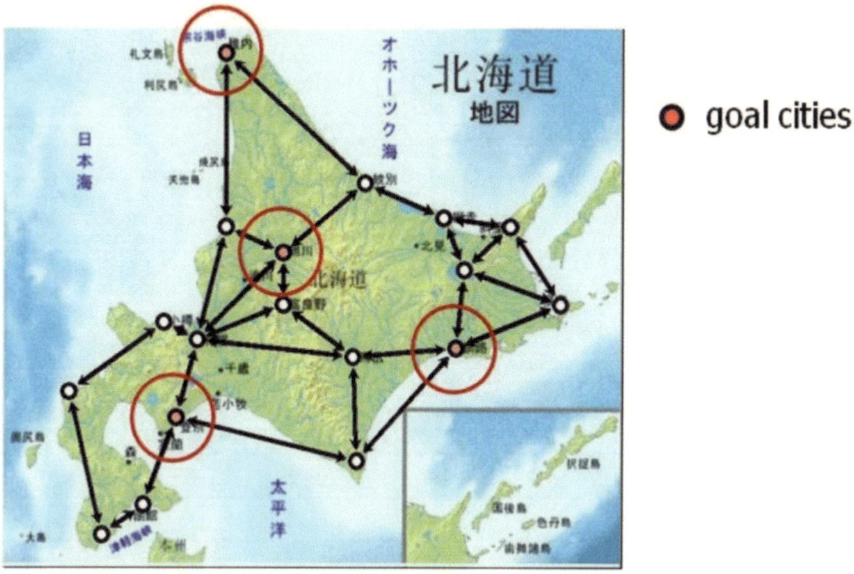

Fig. 13. The round-trip plan Recommendation task

5.2 Experimental results

Fig.14 shows the result of the most preferred plans of each twenty subjects. Horizontal axis is the number of visited cities (goals), and vertical axis is the number of subjects. The summary of the experimental result is as follows. First, the majority of subjects prefer each *every-visit* plan (visit all four cities) than the *optimal* plan. Second, majority prefers *shorter* plans, and minority prefers *longer* plans. Then we focus on these two points.

First point is the effectiveness of *every-visit* criterion. After selecting four cities, 15 (three-quarter) subjects preferred *every-visit* plans those visit selected four cities. In contrast, only 5 subjects preferred *optimal* plans with shorter length, yet these plans do not visit all four cities. This suggests that the *every-visit* criterion is preferable to the *optimality* criterion for human learners.

Second point is that the users' preferences are divided into two groups, *shorter* plans, or *longer* plans. We look more closely the preference for *every-visit* plans among 15 subjects. Among them, 10 (two-thirds) subjects preferred shorter (*every-visit-optimal*) plans, and 5 (third) subjects preferred longer (*every-visit-non-optimal*) plans. Among all 20 subjects, they indicate a similar tendency. Table 2 shows the summary of the experimental result. In table 2, a majority of subjects prefer shorter plans those are either *optimal* or *every-visit-optimal*, a minority of subjects prefer longer plans those are *every-visit-non-optimal*. The reason why the end-users' preferences are divided into two groups will be discussed in the next section.

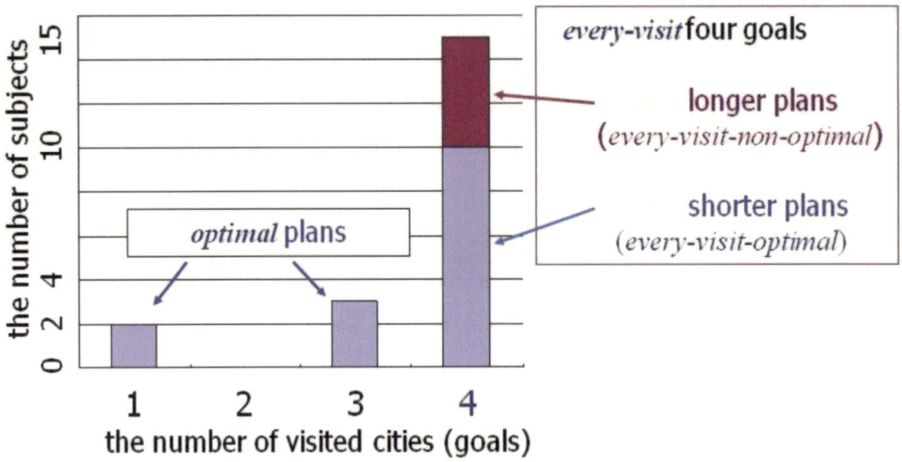

Fig. 14. The result of the most preferred plans

optimal plan	*every-visit* plan	
	every-visit-optimal	*every-visit-non-optimal*
short	shorter	long
5	10	5

Table 2. Summary of the most preferred plans

5.3 Discussions

(1) Why the end-users' preferences are divided?

We discuss the reason why the end-users' preferences are divided into two groups. Fig. 15 shows one of the *every-visit-optimal* plans those major subjects preferred. According to the results of the questionnaire survey, a majority of subjects selected an *every-visit-optimal* plan have less knowledge on Hokkaido (or no experience to visit Hokkaido).

In contrast, a minority of subjects selected *every-visit-non-optimal* plans those have additional cities to visit by the plan recommendation. Fig. 16 shows one of the *every-visit-non-optimal* plans the minority of subjects preferred. According to the results of the questionnaire survey, a majority of subjects selected an *every-visit-non-optimal* plan have much knowledge or interest on Hokkaido.

It suggests that the preference of a user depends on the degree of the user's background knowledge of the task. In other word, the change of the end-users' preference by the recommendation occurs whether they have the background knowledge of the task or not. Note that in our current plan recommendation system, no background knowledge on the recommended round-trip plan except Fig. 13 is presented to each subject. If any information about recommended plan is provided, we expect that the result on preference change of these two kinds of subjects will differ.

Fig. 15. One of the *every-visit-optimal* plans

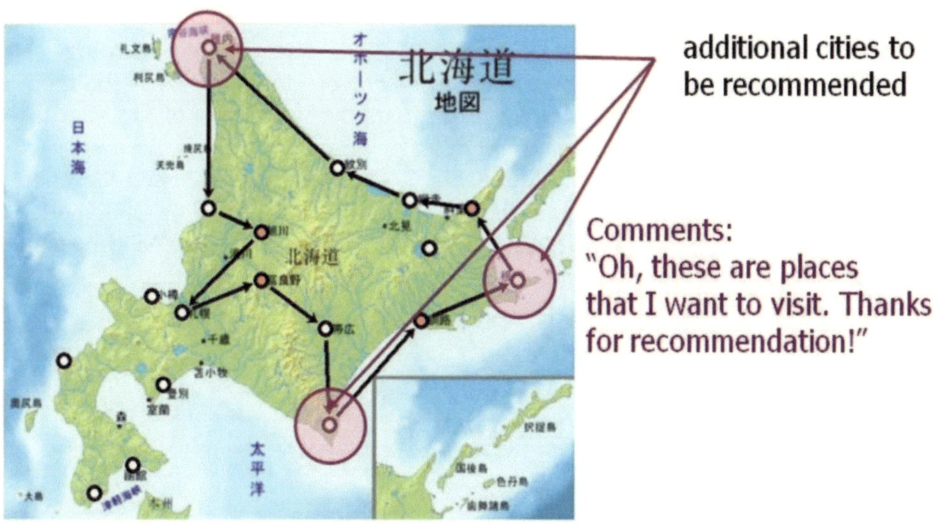

Fig. 16. One of the *every-visit-non-optimal* plans

(2) The search ability of interactive LC-learning

The computing time of the round-trip plan task in Fig. 13 including graphical output by interactive LC-learning is no more than one second or less per user input, since it is a deterministic MDP model. So we summarize the search ability of LC-Learning in a stochastic case (Satoh & Yamaguchi, 2006).

We compare two kinds of search abilities of LC-Learning to that of Modified-PIA (Puterman, 2006). First, the search cost of LC-Learning increases linearly when the number of rewards increases linearly. However, the search cost of Modified-PIA increases nonlinearly when the number of rewards increases linearly. Besides, Modified-PIA collects no *every-visit optimal* policy when the number of rewards is more than three. These suggest that our method is better than previous reinforcement learning methods for interactive reinforcement learning in which many rewards are added incrementally. We go into the comparative experiments in detail in section 6.

(3) *Every-visit-optimality* in a non-deterministic environment

In a stochastic environment, *every-visit-optimality* is defined as *p-every-visit-optimality* where each reward is visited stochastically by not less than probability p ($0 < p =< 1$). It can be calculated by *occurring probability* of each rewarded rule described in section 3.3 (2). Note that *1-every-visit-optimality* is that each reward is visited deterministically even in a stochastic environment.

6. Evaluating the search ability of interactive LC-learning

To evaluate the effectiveness of interactive LC-learning in a stochastic domain, comparative experiments with preprocessed Modified-PIA are performed when the number of rewards increases. We compare the two kinds of search abilities as follows.

1. The search cost for *every-visit optimal* policies
2. The number of collected *every-visit-optimal* policies

6.1 Preprocess for Modified-PIA

Modified-PIA(Puterman, 2006) is one of the model-based reinforcement learning methods based on PIA modified for the average reward. However Modified-PIA is the method to search an optimal policy. So it is not valid to compare the search cost of the Modified-PIA and LC-Learning that searches *various policies*. To enable to search *various policies* by Modified-PIA, following preprocess is added. Fig. 17 shows the preprocessed Modified-PIA.

1. Enumerate the models those contain the subset of reward set of the original model.
2. Search an optimal policy for each subset of the reward function using Modified-PIA.
3. Collect optimal policies.

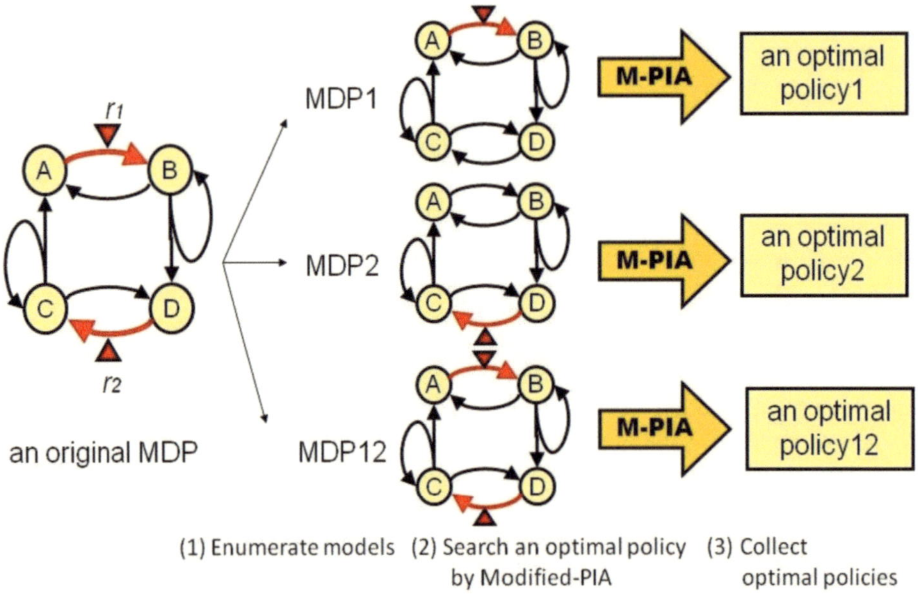

Fig. 17. The preprocessed Modified-PIA

6.2 Experimental setup

We use a hundred of MDP models those consist of randomly set state transition probability and reward function for experimental stochastic environment, in which the number of rewards is varied among 1 to 10, the number of states is 10 and the number of actions is 4. As the measure of the search cost, we used the iteration count in calculating the *occurring probability* of state for LC-Learning and we used the iteration count in calculating the value function for Modified-PIA.

6.3 The search cost for *every-visit-optimal* policies

To begin with, the search cost for *every-visit-optimal* policies is evaluated. Fig. 18 shows the comparative search cost when the number of rewards increases. The result indicates that the tendency of search cost of LC-Learning is linear and one of Modified-PIA is non-linear when the number of rewards increases.

Then we discuss the theoretical search cost. In Modified-PIA, MDP models those contain the subset of reward set of an original MDP are made and an optimal policy for each MDP is searched. So original Modified-PIA is performed 2^r-1 times where r is the number of rewards. After one reward is added, incremental search cost is following.

$$(2^{r+1}-1) - (2^r-1) = 2^r \tag{4}$$

Eq. (4) means that the search cost of Modified-PIA increases nonlinearly when the number of rewards increases. In contrast, in LC-Learning, the number of tree structure increase linearly when the number of rewards is increase. So it is considered that the search cost of LC-Learning increase linearly when the number of rewards increase.

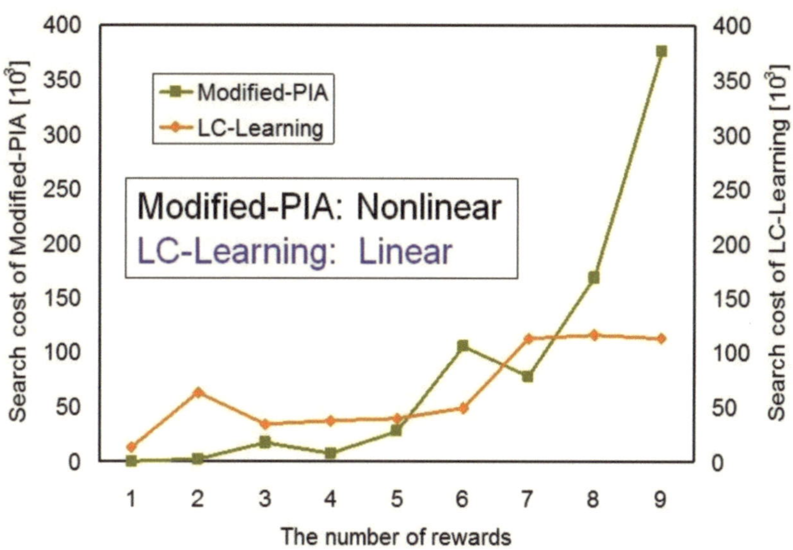

Fig. 18. Search cost when the number of rewards increases

6.4 The number of collected *every-visit-optimal* policies

To evaluate the effectiveness of interactive LC-learning, another search ability is compared with preprocessed Modified-PIA. Note that the experimental setup is same as the setup described in section 6.2. Fig. 19 shows the number of collected *every-visit-optimal* policies. Compared with LC-learning collecting all *every-visit-optimal* policies, the number of collected *every-visit-optimal* policies by preprocessed Modified-PIA is smaller than LC-learning.

Then, carefully analyzing the case of six rewards, Fig. 20 shows the rate of collected *every-visit-optimal* policies, that is percentage of LC-learning of preprocessed Modified-PIA. It

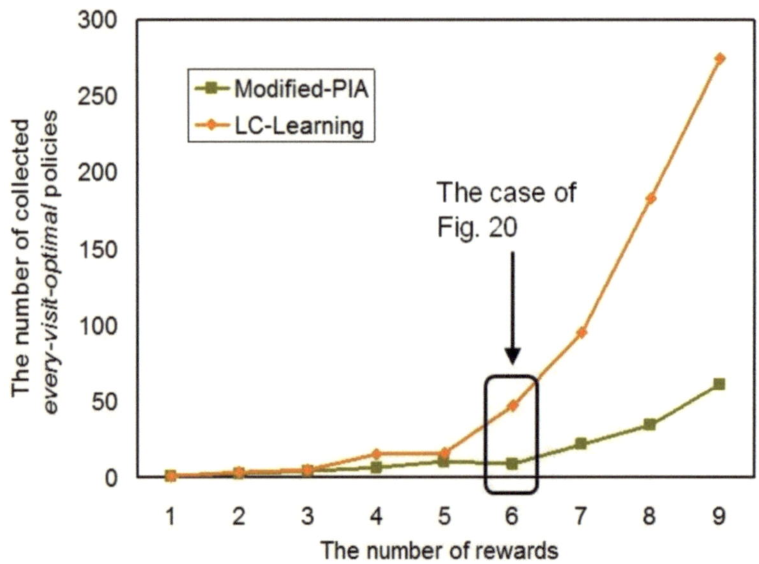

Fig. 19. The number of collected *every-visit-optimal* policies

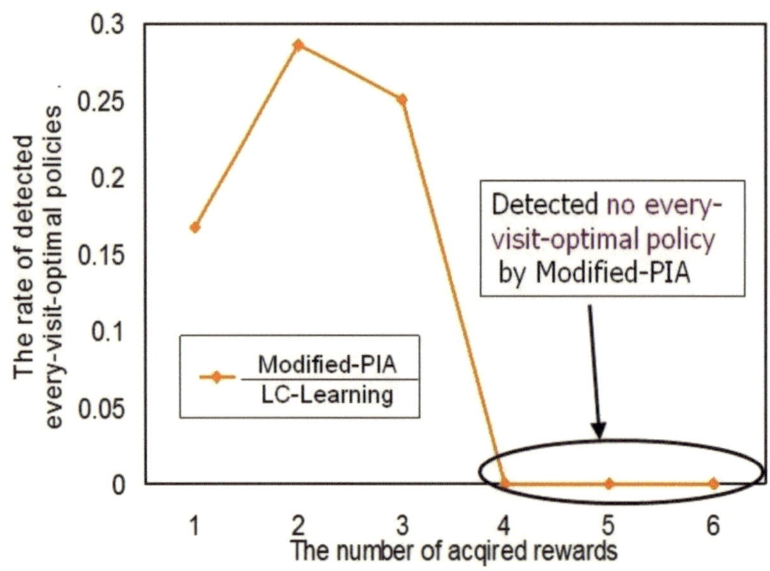

Fig. 20. The rate of collected *every-visit-optimal* policies

shows that preprocessed Modified-PIA collects no *every-visit-optimal* policy when the number of rewards is more than three.

Then we discuss the reason why the number of collected *every-visit-optimal* policies by preprocessed Modified-PIA is smaller than LC-learning. Since preprocessed Modified-PIA is based on the standard optimality, it searches an *optimal* policy in each MDP with the subset of reward set of the original model as shown in Fig.17. It means that preprocessed Modified-PIA finds an *every-visit-optimal* policy only if it is same as the *optimal* policy in each MDP model. As the number of rewards increases, the rate of *every-visit-optimal* policy that is same as the *optimal* policy decreases. In other words, the distinction between two criteria becomes larger according to the number of rewards increases.

Since most previous reinforcement learning methods including Modified-PIA are based on the standard optimality criterion, they only learn an *optimal* policy. Therefore, under *every-visit-optimality* criterion, our method is better than previous reinforcement learning methods for interactive reinforcement learning in which many rewards are added incrementally.

7. Related works on recommender systems

This section describes relations between our proposed solutions and current research issues on recommendation systems. The main feature of our recommendation system is interactive and adaptable recommendation for human users by interactive reinforcement learning. First, we describe two major problems on traditional recommenders. Second, interactive recommendation system called Conversational Recommender is summarized. At last, adaptive recommenders with learning ability are described.

7.1 Major problems on traditional recommenders

Main objective of recommender systems is to provide people with recommendations of items, they will appreciate based on their past preferences. Major approach is collaborative filtering, whether user-based or item-based (Sarwar et al., 2001) such as by Amazon.com. The common feature is that similarity is computed for users or items, based on their past preferences.

However, there are two major issues. First issue is the similar recommendations problem (Ziegler et al., 2005) in that many recommendations seem to be "similar" with respect to content. It is because of lack of novelty, serendipity (Murakami et al., 2007) and diversity of recommendations. Second issue is the preference change problem (Yamaguchi et al., 2009) that is inability to capture the user's preference change during the recommendation. It often occurs when the user is a beginner or a light user. For the first issue, there are two kinds of previous solutions. One is topic diversification (Ziegler et al., 2005) that is designed to balance and diversify personalized recommendation lists for user's full range of interests in specific topics. Another is visualizing the feature space (Hijikata et al., 2006) for editing a user's profile to search the different items on it by the user. However, these solutions do not directly considering a user's preference change. To solve this, this paper assumes a user's preference change as two-axes space, coarse and fine axes.

7.2 Interactive recommendation systems

Traditional recommenders are simple and non-interactive since they only decide which product to recommend to the user. So it is hard to support for recommending more complex products such as travel products (Mahmood et al., 2009). Therefore, conversational recommender systems (Bridge et al., 2006) have been proposed to support more natural and interactive processes. Typical interactive recommendation is the following two strategies (Mahmood et al., 2008):

1. Ask the user in detail about her preferences.
2. Propose a set of products to the user and exploit the user feedback to refine future recommendations.

A major limitation of this approach is that there could be a large number of conversational but rigid strategies for a given recommendation task (Mahmood et al., 2008).

7.3 Adaptive recommenders with learning ability

There are several adaptive recommenders using reinforcement learning. Most of them observe a user's behavior such as products the user viewed or selected, then learn the user's decision processes or preferences. To improve the rigid strategies for conversational recommenders, learning personalized interaction strategies for conversational recommender systems has been proposed (Mahmood & Ricci, 2008; Mahmood & Ricci, 2009; Mahmood et al., 2009).
Major difference from them, the feature of our approach is adaptable recommendation for human users by passive recommendation strategy called *coarse to fine recommendation*. Adaptable recommendation means that during our recommendation, a user can select these two steps (coarse step or fine step) as his/her likes before deciding the most preferable plan.

8. Conclusions

In this paper, we proposed a new method of interactive LC-learning for recommending preferable solutions of a user.

1. *Every-visit-optimality* as the optimality criterion of preference for most of end-users was assumed.
2. To cover the end-user's preference changes after the reward function is given by the end-user, interactive LC-learning prepared *various policies* by generating variations of the reward function under *every-visit-optimality*.
3. For guiding the end-user's current preference among *various policies*, *coarse to fine recommendation* strategy was proposed.

As the experimental results, first, the majority of subjects preferred each *every-visit* plan (visiting all goals) than the *optimal* plan. Second, majority preferred *shorter* plans, and minority prefers *longer* plans. We discussed the reason why the end-users' preferences are divided into two groups. Then, the search ability of interactive LC-learning in a stochastic domain was evaluated.
The future work is to assist a user for deciding the most preference plan to make his/herself known the potential preference of the user. To realize this idea, we are evaluating passive recommendation by visualizing the *coarse to fine recommendation* space and the history of the recommendation of it (Yamaguchi et al., 2009).

9. References

Bridge, D., Go"ker, M. H., McGinty, L. & Smyth, B. (2005). Case-based recommender systems, *The Knowledge Engineering Review*, Volume 20, Issue 3 (September 2005), pp.315 - 320, Cambridge University Press, ISSN:0269-8889

Hijikata, Y., Iwahama, K., Takegawa, K., Nishida, S. (2006). Content-based Music Filtering System with Editable User Profile, *Proceedings of the 21st Annual ACM Symposium on Applied Computing (ACM SAC 2006)*, pp.1050-1057, Dijon, France, April, 2006

Kaplan, F.; Oudeyer, P-Y.; Kubinyi, E. & Miklosi, A. (2002). Robotic clicker training, *Robotics and Autonomous Systems*, Dillmann, R. et al. (Eds.), pp.197-206, ELSEVIER, ISBN0921-8890, Amsterdam

Konda, T.; Tensyo, S. & Yamaguchi, T. (2002). LC-Learning: Phased Method for Average Reward Reinforcement Learning - Analysis of Optimal Criteria -, *PRICAI2002: Trends in Artificial Intelligence*, Lecture notes in Artificial Intelligence 2417, Ishizuka, M. & Sattar, A. (Eds.), pp.198-207, Springer, ISBN 3-540-44038-0, Berlin

Konda, T.; Tensyo, S. & Yamaguchi, T. (2002). LC-Learning: Phased Method for Average Reward Reinforcement Learning - Preliminary Results -, *PRICAI2002: Trends in Artificial Intelligence*, Lecture notes in Artificial Intelligence 2417, Ishizuka, M. & Sattar, A. (Eds.), pp.208-217, Springer, ISBN 3-540-44038-0, Berlin

Konidaris, G. & Barto, A. (2006). Automonous Shaping: Knowledge Transfer in Reinforcement Learning, *Proceedings of the 23rd International Conference on Machine Learning*, pp.489-496, ISBN 1-59593-383-2, Pittsburgh, June, 2006

Mahadevan, S. (1996). Average Reward Reinforcement Learning: Foundations, Algorithms, and Empirical Results, *Machine Learning*, Vol.22, No.1-3, pp.159-195, Springer (Kluwer Academic Publishers), New York

Mahmood, T. & Ricci, F. (2008). Adapting the interaction state model in conversational recommender systems, *Proceedings of the 10th international conference on Electronic commerce*, ISBN 978-1-60558-075-3, Innsbruck, August, 2008, ACM, New York

Mahmood, T. & Ricci, F. (2009). Improving recommender systems with adaptive conversational strategies, *Proceedings of the 20th ACM conference on Hypertext and hypermedia*, pp.73-82, ISBN 978-1-60558-486-7, Torino, June to July, 2009, ACM, New York

Mahmood, T.; Ricci, F.; Venturini, A. & Hopken, W. (2008). Adaptive Recommender Systems for Travel Planning, *Information and Communication Technologies in Tourism 2008*: Proceedings of ENTER 2008 International Conference in Innsbruck, Hopken, W. & Gretzel, U. (Eds.), pp.1-11, Springer, ISBN 978-3-211-77279-9, New York

Mahmood, T.; Ricci, F. & Venturini, A. (2009). Improving Recommendation Effectiveness by Adapting the Dialogue Strategy in Online Travel Planning, *International Journal of Information Technology and Tourism*, Volume 11, No.4, pp.285-302, ISSN 1098-3058, Cognizant Communication Corporation, New York

Marthi, Bhaskara. (2007). Automatic shaping and decomposition of reward functions, *Proceedings of the 24th international conference on Machine learning*, pp.601-608, ISBN 978-1-59593-793-3, Corvallis, USA, June, 2007, ACM, New York

Murakami, T.; Mori, K. and Orihara, R. (2007). Metrics for Evaluating the Serendipity of Recommendation Lists, *New Frontiers in Artifical Intelligence*, Lecture notes in Artificial Intelligence 4914, Satoh, K. et al. (Eds.), pp.40-46, Springer, ISBN 978-3-540-78196-7, Berlin

Ng, Andrew Y.; Harada, Daishi; & Russell, Stuart J. (1999). Policy Invariance Under Reward Transformations: Theory and Application to Reward Shaping, *Proceedings of the 16th International Conference on Machine Learning*, pp.278-287, Bled, Slovenia, June, 1999

Preda, M.; Mirea, A.M.; Teodorescu-Mihai, C. & Preda, D. L. (2009). Adaptive Web Recommendation Systems, *Annals of University of Craiova, Math. Comp. Sci. Ser.*, Vol. 36 (2), pp.25-34

Puterman, M. L. (1994). *Markov Decision Processes: Discrete Stochastic Dynamic Programming*, JOHN WILEY & SONS, INC, pp.385-388, ISBN 0471619779, New York

Sarwar, B.; Karypis, G.; Konstan, J. & Reidl, J. (2001). Item-Based Collaborative Filtering Recommendation Algorithms, *Proceedings of the 10th International Conference on World Wide Web*, pp.285-295, Hong Kong, May, 2001, ACM, New York

Satoh, K. & Yamaguchi, T. (2006). Preparing various policies for interactive reinforcement learning, *Proceedings of the SICE-ICASE International Joint Conference 2006 (SICE-ICCAS 2006)*, pp.2440-2444, Busan, Korea, October, 2006

Yamaguchi & T., Nishimura, T. (2008): How to recommend preferable solutions of a user in interactive reinforcement learning?, *Proceedings of the International Conference on Instrumentation, Control and Information Technology (SICE2008)*, pp.2050-2055, , Chofu, Japan, August, 2008

Yamaguchi, T.; Nishimura, T. & Takadama, K. (2009). Awareness based filtering - Toward the Cooperative Learning in Human Agent Interaction -, *Proceedings of the ICROS-SICE International Joint Conference (ICCAS-SICE 2009)*, pp.1164-1167, Fukuoka, Japan, August, 2009

Ziegler, C.N.; McNee, S.M.; Konstan, J.A. & Lausen, G. (2005). Improving Recommendation Lists Through Topic Diversification, *Proceedings of the 14th international conference on World Wide Web(WWW2005)* , pp.22-32, Chiba, Japan, May, 2005, ACM, New York

9

Reward Prediction Error Computation in the Pedunculopontine Tegmental Nucleus Neurons

Yasushi Kobayashi and Ken-ichi Okada
Osaka University, ATR Computational Neuroscience Laboratories & PRESTO JST
Japan

1. Introduction

Reinforcement learning (Houk et al., 1995; Sutton & Barto, 1998; Schultz, 2002) has been one of the central topics in a broad range of scientific fields for the last two decades. Understanding of reinforcement learning is expected to provide a systematic understanding of adaptive behaviors, including simple classical and operant conditioning of animals (Waelti et al., 2001; Richmond et al., 2003; Satoh et al., 2003; Graybiel, 2005; Samejima et al., 2005; Hikosaka et al., 2006) as well as all complex social and economical human behaviors that are desinged to maximize benefits (Montague & Berns, 2002); and is also useful in machine learning and robotics (Tesauro, 1994).

Reinforcement learning, whether performed by living organisms or computational models, involves choosing a behavior that is expected to yield the maximal reward and then revising this prediction so as to minimize the reward prediction error (Schultz, 2002), which is the difference between the predicted and actual reward.

Recent neurophysiological studies have shown that midbrain dopamine neurons encode the reward prediction error signal (Schultz et al., 1997; Hollerman & Schultz, 1998; Waelti et al., 2001; Fiorillo et al., 2003; Nakahara et al., 2004; Morris et al., 2006) and that the striatum (Hollerman & Schultz, 1998; Hikosaka et al., 2006) and cerebral cortices (Watanabe, 1996; Lee & Seo, 2007) use this signal to perform reinforcement learning with dopamine-induced synaptic plasticity (Reynolds et al., 2001; Wickens et al., 2003). Thus, computing the reward prediction error is one of the most essential aspects of reinforcement learning, however the identity of the neural structures that provide the signal s to the midbrain dopamine neurons and the mechanism by which the 'reward prediction error' is computed remain rather elusive. The pedunculopontine tegmental nucleus (PPTN) of the midbrain feeds strong excitatory inputs to dopamine neurons in the midbrain, and receives reward-related signals from various areas including the cerebral cortices and the striatum. We hypothesize that the PPTN is the key structure for computing the reward prediction error. To test this hypothesis, we recorded the activity of PPTN neurons in monkeys performing a saccade task for a juice reward (Kobayashi et al., 2002; Okada et al., 2009).

In the most recent study (Okada et al., 2009), we used multiple analytical approaches, including receiver operating characteristic (ROC) analysis (Lusted, 1978), mutual information (Werner & Mountcastle, 1963; Schreiner et al., 1978; Kitazawa et al., 1998), and correlation analyses to examine neuronal responses in the PPTN neurons in monkeys performing saccade tasks, during which the magnitudes of rewards were predicted in normal and reversed fashions. All analyses consistently indicated the existence of two neuronal groups, one signalling the expected reward magnitude predicted from the visual stimulus and the other signalling the magnitude of the actual reward, both necessary and sufficient pieces of information for computing the reward prediction error. The reward prediction error may be directly computed by subtracting the signals encoded by the two PPTN neuronal groups, or alternatively, by adding the time derivatives of the reward prediction signals to the actual reward signals, as originally hypothesized by the temporal difference reinforcement learning model. Thus, we concluded that the PPTN is indeed a key structure for computing of the reward prediction error.

2. Background

2.1 Classical view of the PPTN

The cholinergic system is one of the most important modulatory neurotransmitter systems in the brain, and controls neuronal activity that depends on selective attention. Anatomical and physiological evidence supports the idea of a 'cholinergic component' of conscious awareness (Perry et al., 1999). The PPTN in the brainstem contains both cholinergic (Mesulam et al., 1983) and non-cholinergic neurons (Jones & Beaudet, 1987; Clements & Grant, 1990; Spann & Grofova, 1992; Ford et al., 1995; Takakusaki et al., 1996; Wang & Morales, 2009), but is one of the major sources of cholinergic projections in the brainstem (Mesulam et al., 1983). The PPTN is thought to be the central part of the reticular activating system (Garcia-Rill, 1991), which provides background excitation for several sensory and motor systems essential for automatic control of movement (Takakusaki et al., 2004), perception and cognitive processes (Steckler et al., 1994). It has long been known that the PPTN is a crucial element in the regulation of the rhythms in the cortex (Steriade et al., 1990) that are associated with wakefulness and rapid eye movement sleep (Leonard & Llinas, 1994).

Anatomically, the PPTN has reciprocal connections with the basal ganglia: the subthalamic nucleus, the globus pallidus, and the substantia nigra (Edley & Graybiel, 1983; Lavoie & Parent, 1994), and more recently, was argued to form a part of the basal ganglia (Mena-Segovia et al., 2004). Further, the PPTN also has reciprocal connections with catecholaminergic systems in the brainstem: the locus coeruleus (noradrenergic) (Garcia-Rill, 1991; Garcia-Rill et al., 1995) and the dorsal raphe nucleus (serotonergic) (Steininger et al., 1992; Honda & Semba, 1994; Kayama & Koyama, 2003). This basal ganglia-PPTN-catecholaminergic complex was proposed to play an important role in gating movement, controlling several forms of attentional behavior (Garcia-Rill, 1991) and the reinforcement process (Doya, 2002). Despite these abundant anatomical findings, however, the functional importance of the PPTN is not yet fully understood.

2.2 The possible role of the PPTN in reinforcement process

Several of lesion and drug administration studies on rodents indicate that the PPTN is involved in various reinforcement processes (Bechara & van der Kooy, 1989; Kippin & van der Kooy, 2003; Alderson et al., 2006; Winn, 2006; Wilson et al., 2009). According to a physiological study in operantly conditioned cats, the PPTN relays either a reward or a salient event signal (Dormont et al., 1998). Anatomically, the PPTN receives reward input from the lateral hypothalamus (Semba & Fibiger, 1992) and the limbic cortex (Chiba et al., 2001). Conversely, the PPTN abundantly projects to midbrain dopamine neurons of the substantia nigra pars compacta and ventral tegmental area (Beckstead et al., 1979; Jackson & Crossman, 1983; Beninato & Spencer, 1987; Charara et al., 1996), which encode a reward prediction error signal for reinforcement learning (Schultz, 1998).

The PPTN is one of the strongest excitatory input sources for the dopamine neurons (Matsumura, 2005). These afferent PPTN neurons release glutamate and acetylcholine to target neurons, make glutamatergic and cholinergic synaptic connections with dopamine neurons in the midbrain (Scarnati et al., 1986; Futami et al., 1995; Takakusaki et al., 1996). In the rat, electrical stimulation of the PPTN induces a time-locked burst in dopamine neurons (Lokwan et al., 1999; Floresco et al., 2003), and chemical or electrical stimulation of the PPTN increases dopamine release in the striatum (Chapman et al., 1997; Forster & Blaha, 2003; Miller & Blaha, 2004). Other electrophysiological experiments have shown that acethylcholine acts through both nicotinic and muscarinic receptors to depolarize dopamine neurons and to alter their firing pattern (Calabresi et al., 1989; Lacey et al., 1990; Gronier & Rasmussen, 1998; Sorenson et al., 1998). Thus, PPTN activity and acethylcholine provided by the PPTN can facilitate the burst firing in dopamine neuron (Mena-Segovia et al., 2008) and appear to do so via muscarinic (Kitai et al., 1999; Scroggs et al., 2001) and nicotinic (Grenhoff et al., 1986; Pidoplichko et al., 1997; Sorenson et al., 1998; Yamashita & Isa, 2003) acethylcholine receptor activation. In addition, some of the effects induced by PPTN stimulation can be blocked by administration of the muscarinic acethylcholine receptor agonist carbachol into the PPTN (Chapman et al., 1997). This finding is consistent with the fact that cholinergic neurons in the PPTN express the inhibitory muscarinic autoreceptors (Yeomans, 1995) and suggests that activation of these receptors inhibits cholinergic inputs to the dopamine neurons (Tzavara et al., 2004; Chen et al., 2006).

Furthermore, midbrain dopamine neurons are dysfunctional following excitotoxic lesioning of the PPTN (Blaha & Winn, 1993). A number of studies have found impairments in learning following excitotoxic lesions of the PPTN (Fujimoto et al., 1989; Fujimoto et al., 1992; Steckler et al., 1994; Inglis et al., 2000; Alderson et al., 2002). Thus, abundant anatomical, electrophysiological and pharmacological studies of slice and whole animal preparations indicate that the PPTN receives signals from the reward related structures including the cerebral cortices and the striatum (Winn et al., 1997) and provides strong excitatory inputs to the dopamine neurons (Clements & Grant, 1990; Blaha & Winn, 1993; Futami et al., 1995; Oakman et al., 1995; Blaha et al., 1996; Conde et al., 1998; Dormont et al., 1998; Mena-Segovia et al., 2004; Pan & Hyland, 2005; Mena-Segovia et al., 2008). Interestingly, the dopamine/acethylcholine interaction seems to be mutual (Scarnati et al., 1987); dopmine neurons in the substantia nigra pars compacta tproject back to PPTN neurons, affecting their excitability. Even though the dopaminergic input to the PPTN is low compared with the massive cholinergic innervation of the dopamine neurons (Semba & Fibiger, 1992; Grofova & Zhou, 1998; Ichinohe et al., 2000), dopamine released within the PPTN may play an important part in controlling its activity (Steiniger & Kretschmer, 2003).

Therefore, it is plausible that the PPTN provides important information for computing reward prediction error by the dopamine neurons. Recent studies (Matsumura et al., 1997; Pan & Hyland, 2005) reported that the PPTN encodes sensory or motor rather than reward information of task events. However, using a visually guided saccade task requiring the animal to shift its gaze from a fixation to a saccade target, we demonstrated the existence of two groups of neurons within the PPTN, one whose resposes to presentation of the fixation target to initiate the task were correlated with the success and failure of individual task trials, and another that was responsive to the reward delivery (Kobayashi et al., 2002).

We hypothesized that the task performance-related neurons signal the reward prediction and the reward delivery-related neurons signal the reward outcome. This hypothesis was tested in monkeys by studying the activity of PPTN neurons during visually guided saccade tasks that were rewarded with different amonts of juice that were cued by the shape of the fixation target (Okada et al., 2009).

3. Responses of PPTN neurons to different reward magnitude

3.1 Effect of reward prediction on behavior and neuronal activity of PPTN

In this study, Japanese monkeys were trained on a visually guided saccade task that required them to maintain fixation on a central fixation target, and to make a horizontal saccade to a peripheral saccade target that was presented after the disappearance of the fixation target (Fig. 1A). Correct trials were rewarded randomly with either one or three

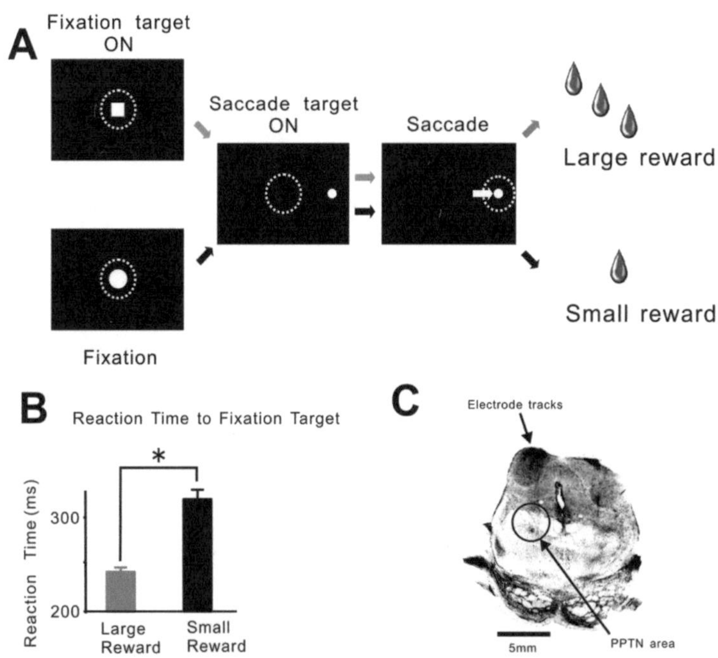

Fig. 1. Two-valued reward, visually guided saccade task.
A. Schimatic of screen views for the two-valued visually guided saccade task. A fixation target (*square or circle*) was presented for 400-1000 ms. A saccade target was presented to the left or the right of the fixation target (eccentricity, 10°) 300-500ms after fixation target offset. The monkey was required to maintain fixation on the fixation target during the entire time it was presented, and to then make a saccade to the saccade target within 500 ms after saccade target onset. They were rewarded for successful trials with either one or three drop of juice in a quasirandom fashion.
B. Mean reaction times on the the fixation target. Error bars = *SEM*, * indicates $p<0.001$ (Student's t-test).
C. Photomicrograph of a coronal section through midbrain of one monkey showing electrode tracks and the lesion (within the circle) marking the recording site in the PPTN. Figures were modified from our recent paper (Okada et al., 2009).

drops of juice; the amount (large or small) being cued at the outset by the shape of the initial central fixation target (square or circle, respectively).

The behavior of the monkeys was influenced by the reward value expectation, the percentage of successful trial being significantly higher for large rewards than for small ones. In the unsuccesful trials, three types of errors occured: monkeys failed to fixate on the fixation target (fixation error), they failed to maintain fixation until the appearance of the saccade target (fixation hold error), and they failed to make a saccade towards the saccade target (saccade error). The reaction time to fixate on the the fixation target was significantly shorter in the successful than in the unsuccesuful ones. There was also a systematic difference in the reaction time within the successful trials: those associated with large rewards were significantly shorter than those for small rewards (Fig. 1B).

One hundred fifty-three PPTN neurons (see, recording sites in Fig. 1C) exhibited significant responses to one or more task events. Of these, 30 neurons exhibited increased firing around the time of the onset of the fixation target, with significant dependency on the magnitude of the predicted reward (*fixation target* neurons), and 15 neurons exhibited increased firing only around the time of the reward delivery with significant dependency on the reward magnitude of the current reward (*reward delivery* neurons).

Figures 2A, B show raster displays and spike density functions for a representative fixation target neuron. This neuron showed elevated firing throughout the trial that was greater when the cued reward was large: compare the red raster lines and traces (large reward) with the green (small rewards). The population plot for the 30 fixation target neurons (Fig. 2C) indicates that the differences in responses to the large and small reward cues generally began to emerge about 100 ms after the cue was presented (the 1st dotted line), even though there were non-differential responses before the onset of the fixation target/cue, presumably in anticipation of its appearance. Note that the differential responses extended throughout the working memory period following offset of the fixation target/cue and lasted until and even after reward delivery (3rd dotted line), almost unaffected by other task events, such as the onset of the peripheral saccade target (black bars in Fig. 2A, 2nd dotted line in Fig. 2C) and the saccade to the saccade target (inverted triangles in Fig. 2A).

In contrast, reward delivery neurons were almost unresponsive jst before the reward was delivered, when they discharged transiently, reaching a peak discharge rate shortly after reward delivery and then rapidly declining back to baseline (Figs. 2E, F). In trial with larger rewards, the discharge rate of the transient response reached a higher peak at a slightly later time and took a few hundred milliseconds longer to decay back to baseline than did that during small reward trials.

The clear suggestion here is that the differential dependencies of the fixation target and reward delivery neurons in encode the magnitudes of the predicted and current rewards, respectively. Further, we analyzed the precision for neuronal activity to encode the reward magnitude in two ways; 1) by ROC analysis for discrimination between the small and large rewards; 2) by mutual information analysis to estimate the information contained in the spike discharges with respect to the magnitude of the reward (Werner & Mountcastle, 1963; Schreiner et al., 1978; Kitazawa et al., 1998) where. These two analyses were conducted using a sliding time window of 200 ms moved in 1 ms steps.

First, the reliability with which the activity of individual neurons encoded large or small reward was estimated by deriving an ROC value (cumulative probability of the ROC curve) that measures the accuracy by which an ideal observer could correctly distinguish between large and small reward from the neuronal signal:

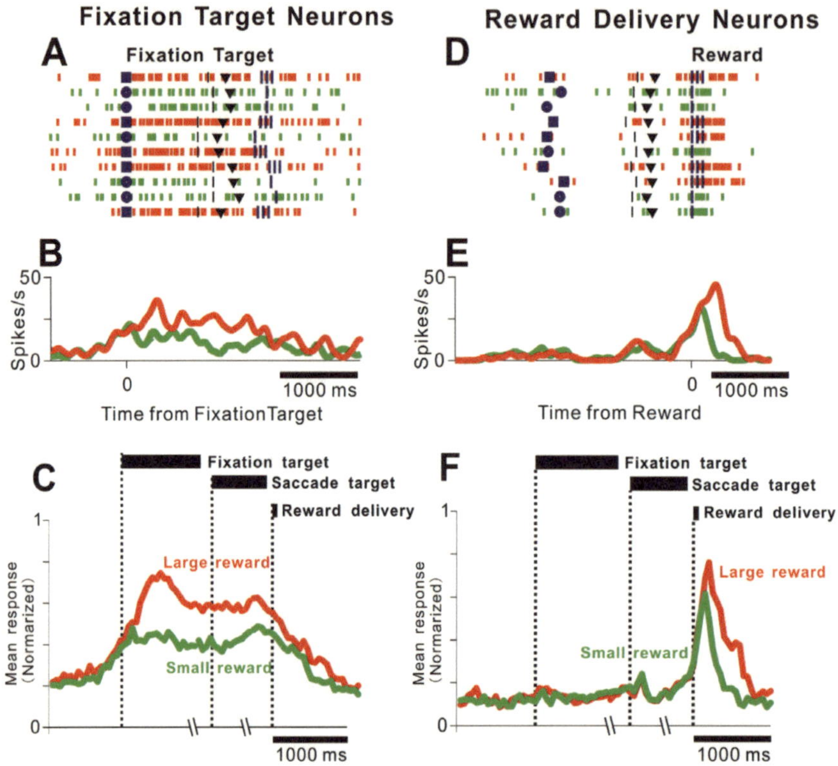

Fig. 2. Responses of the fixation target and the reward delivery neurons to task events. **A**, **B**, a rastergram and peri-task event spike density function for activities of a representative fixation target neuron over 10 successive trials, aligned to the onsetof the fixation target. Red and green rasters (**A**) and traces (**B**) indicate large and small reward trials, respectively. In (**A**) blue squares and circles indicate fixation target onset, black bars onset of the saccade target, blue triangles saccade onset and the blue lines the times at which large (three bars) and small (one bar) rewards were delivered. **C,** The population spike density function for the 30 fixation target neurons. Responses are aligned to fixation target and saccade target onsets and the moment of reward delivery (vertical dotted lines). Large and small reward trials are indicated once again with red and green, respectively, as above, and thick horizontal bars above indicate the durations of the respective events. **D-F**, a similar rastergram (**D**) and response histogram (**E**) for a representative reward delivery neuron and the population response histograms (**F**) for the 15 reward delivery neurons. Formats are the same as in **A-C**. Figures were modified from our recent paper (Okada et al., 2009).

$$ROC = \int_0^1 P(Q)dQ \tag{1}$$

$$P(x) = \int_0^x p(x)dx \tag{2}$$

$$Q(x) = \int_0^x q(x)dx \tag{3}$$

x denotes the neuronal activity sampled through the moving window. $p(x)$ and $q(x)$ denote the probability distributions for a ideal observer to answer whether the reward is large or small, respectively; $P(x)$ and $Q(x)$ denote the cumulative probability of these functions. $P(Q)$ represents an ROC curve, and the ROC value is the area under the ROC curve evaluated as $\int_0^1 P(Q)dQ$, and Q is the cumulative probability function for small reward trials that was taken as the reference distribution.

In principle, ROC analysis evaluates the reliability with which an ideal observer can tell whether the reward is large or small from the noisy signal in terms of statistical significance of the signal difference between the two rewards in comparison with the baseline noise. Therefore, an ROC value = 0.5 and > 0.56 imply that the answer is 50 and 95 % correct, respectively.

Second, the information capacity for the PPTN neuronal ensemble to signal reward magnitude during the three task periods was estimated via mutual information analysis where:

$$\begin{aligned} I_{reward} = & [-(L/N)\log_2(L/N) - (S/N)\log_2(S/N) - (High/N)\log_2(High/N) - (Low/N)\log_2(Low/N)] \\ & -[-\sum_{i=1}^{2}(l_i/N)\log_2(l_i/N) - \sum_{i=1}^{2}(s_i/N)\log_2(s_i/N)] \end{aligned} \quad (4)$$

L , S and N denote numbers of large and small reward and total trials respectively. $High$ and Low denote the numbers of trials where the neuronal response was larger and smaller than the median response for all trials, respectively. Therefore l_1 and l_2 and s_1 and s_2 represent large and small reward trials where the neuronal response was larger and smaller than the median response, respectively. Mutual information plots for individual neurons evaluate the information capacity for the neurons to express the reward magnitude in terms of a response correlation with the reward magnitude, and cumulative plots evaluate that for the ensemble neurons for an ideal case where the individual neuronal responses are perfectly independent.

Therefore, these two analyses estimate different aspects of neuronal signal precision, although they are related. Our ROC methods estimate the signal significance in comparison with the baseline noise, and the mutual information analysis evaluates the signal precision in terms of signal correlation with the reward magnitude.

We conducted an ROC analysis on the 45 fixation target and reward delivery neurons to estimate how reliably the discharges of the individual neurons indicated whether the reward was large or small. ROC values for the fixation target neurons (top 30 rows in Fig. 3A) started out near the chance level (ROC value = 0.5) and generally first acquired significance (ROC value > 0.56) during the fixation target/cue period. Most fixation target neurons continued to show significant ROC values through the working memory periods after the fixation target/cue disappeared, albeit with some substantial fluctuations, and more than half of them remained above the chance level even after reward delivery. The ROC values of the reward delivery neurons (the bottom rows in Fig. 3A), on the other hand, did not rise above chance level until after reward delivery, and then only transiently. Thus, the ROC analysis reinforced the idea that the fixation target neurons convey information about the magnitude of the predicted reward during the cue and working memory periods as well as up to and beyond the time of reward delivery and the reward delivery neurons convey information about the magnitude of the current reward only after it has been delivered. The free reward paradigm experiment also supports this view(Okada et al., 2009).

We obtained further support for this view by computing the mutual information (Kitazawa et al., 1998) in the responses about the magnitude of the reward (large or small). The cumulative plots of the mutual information conveyed by the individual fixation target neurons (cyan traces in Fig. 3B) indicated that the information grew rapidly during the fixation target/cue period, peaked roughly as the fixation target/cue disappeared, and then declined thereafter during the working memory period, but did not reach baseline in most neurons until after the reward was delivered, as did the ROC values. The mutual information conveyed by the individual reward delivery neurons (black traces in Fig. 3B) generally did not rise above the null level until after reward delivery, when it showed an abrupt substantial increase often lasting more than half a second.

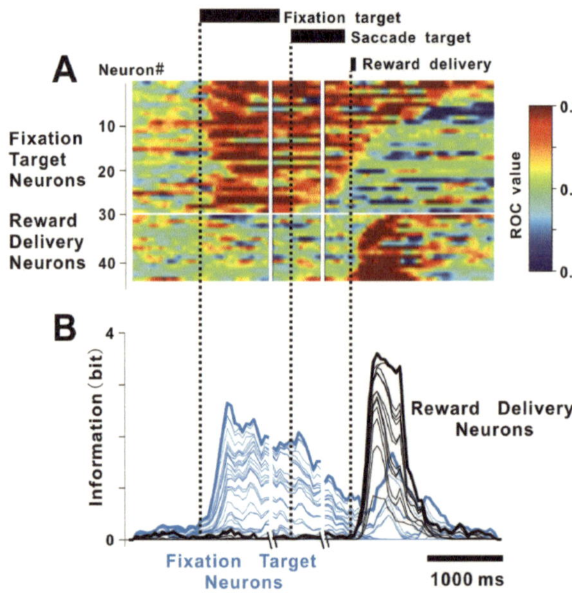

Fig. 3. Receiver operating characteristic (ROC) and mutual information analyses of responses in the fixation target and reward delivery neurons.
A, Pseudo color plots of the instantaneous ROC values (sliding time window, 200 ms) for large and small rewards indicated by activities in each of the 30 fixation target and 15 reward delivery neurons. The plots are aligned to fixation target onset and saccade target onset, and reward delivery (dotted lines) and ordered according to the neuronal ROC value after reward delivery. A white horizontal line indicates the border between the fixation target and reward delivery neurons. **B,** Cumulative plots of mutual information about reward amounts encoded by the 30 fixation target (cyan traces) and 15 reward delivery (black traces) neurons. A thick horizontal white bar indicates the duration of the respective neuronal type. Time axes in ***A*** and ***B*** are broken to align the responses to the onset of fixation, saccade target and reward delivery. Figures were modified from our recent paper (Okada et al., 2009).

Further insights were obtained by recording the activities of fixation target and reward delivery neurons in a *context reversal paradigm,* in which the meaning of the fixation target/cue was suddenly reversed while recording from a given neuron so that squares and circles indicated large and small rewards, respectively, in the first 10 trials and the opposite in the next 10 trials. The responses of the fixation target neurons during both the fixation target/cue period (Fig. 4A) and the subsequent working memory period (the maintenance period of reward prediction) (Fig. 4B) clearly reflected the context reversal with a delay of one trial, the net result being that by the second trial after the context reversal the cue predicting the larger reward was again associated with the higher discharge rate (i.e., one-trial learning). In contrast, the responses of the reward delivery neurons did not change after the reversal, so that larger rewards were still associated with larger neuronal responses even on the first trial after the context reversal (Fig. 4C).

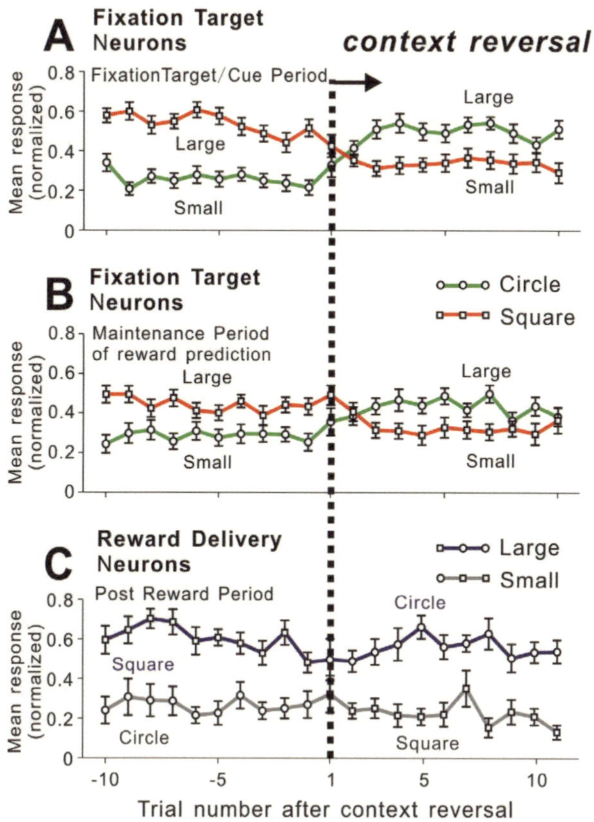

Fig. 4. Effects of context reversal on the responses of fixation target and reward delivery neurons. **A**, Responses of the fixation target neurons to fixation target (squares and circles) presentation (mean responses of 200-600 ms after fixation target on, fixation target/cue period) before and after reversal of fixation target context (from squares and circles for large and small rewards in the initial 10 trials to squares and circles for small and large rewards in the last 10 trials). **B**, Similar to **A**, but for responses after fixation target offset (maintenance period of reward prediction, 200-600 ms after fixation target off). **C**, Similar to **A** and **B** but for the responses of the reward delivery neurons to reward delivery (200-600 ms after reward delivery, post reward delivery period) to large and small rewards. Responses were estimated as the average firing frequency normalized for the peak responses of the individual neurons. Error bars indicate standard error of mean. Figures were modified from our recent paper (Okada et al., 2009).

3.2 Correlation of fixation target response with behavioral performance

In a previous study on visually guided saccade task with single-value rewards we demonstrated that PPTN neuronal responses were stronger during trials that were successfully completed (Kobayashi et al., 2002). Therefore we questioned whether the reward prediction signaled by the fixation target neuronal response might also be related to the motivation of the monkey to perform the task. We tested this in the two-value reward task by studying the correlation of the fixation target responses of the the reward magnitude-dependent fixation target neurons with the task performance. Figure 5 shows the comparison of representative and ensemble fixation target neuronal responses to large and small rewards across fixation error, fixation-hold error, and successful trials. This representative neuron (Fig. 5A) showed no significant increase in its activity during the entire period of the fixation error trials, during which the animal failed to fixate on the target. Conversely, in the fixation hold error trials during which the animal did initially fixate on the target but failed to maintain the fixation, the activity increased during the pre-cue period (onset, -100 ms from fixation target presentation) and declined roughly at the time of the fixation break (200 ms, cf. the upward arrow in the cyan eye movement trace of Fig. 5A). The pre-cue period response during thsese trials was reward magnitude-independent in that the responses during the large and small reward trials were nearly equal, while the response was magnitude-dependent during the cue period, being larger for large reward trials than for small reward ones (cf. the red and green spike density traces before the dotted line with those after the line in Fig. 5A). In the successful trials, the fixation target period responses also consisted of a reward magnitude-independent component during the pre-cue period that matched that for the fixation hold error trials (cf. cyan spike density trace with the red and green spike density traces of Fig. 5A). A late reward magnitude-dependent component that emerged during the fixation target/cue period, was much stronger than that in the fixation hold error trials and was sustained across the maintenance period until the postreward delivery period. The ensemble response for the fixation target neurons also showed a similar tendency as that of the representative neuron (Fig. 5B). The pre-cue period response was virtually absent in the fixation error trials, but there were significant pre-cue period responses in the fixation hold error and the successful trials. The magnitude-dependent response in the fixation hold error trials was small and transient, while that in the successful trials was much larger and was sustained until the post-reward delivery period.

The fact that the reward magnitude-independent pre-cue period response was absent in the fixation error trials and commonly present in both the fixation hold error and the successful trials indicates that it may reflect the monkey's motivation to fixate on the fixation target in anticipation of its presentation. Although the task intervals were quasi-randomized, monkeys appared to be able to anticipate the onset of the fixation target and to be motivated to fixate on the target in both the fixation hold error and the successful trials prior to fixation target onset, but were probably not motivated to do so in the fixation error trials.

In addition, these findings indicate that the activities of the 52 reward magnitude-independent neurons also signal the early component of the motivational drive to fixate on the fixation target in an almost equal fashion as that of the reward magnitude-dependent fixation target neurons (Fig. 5C).

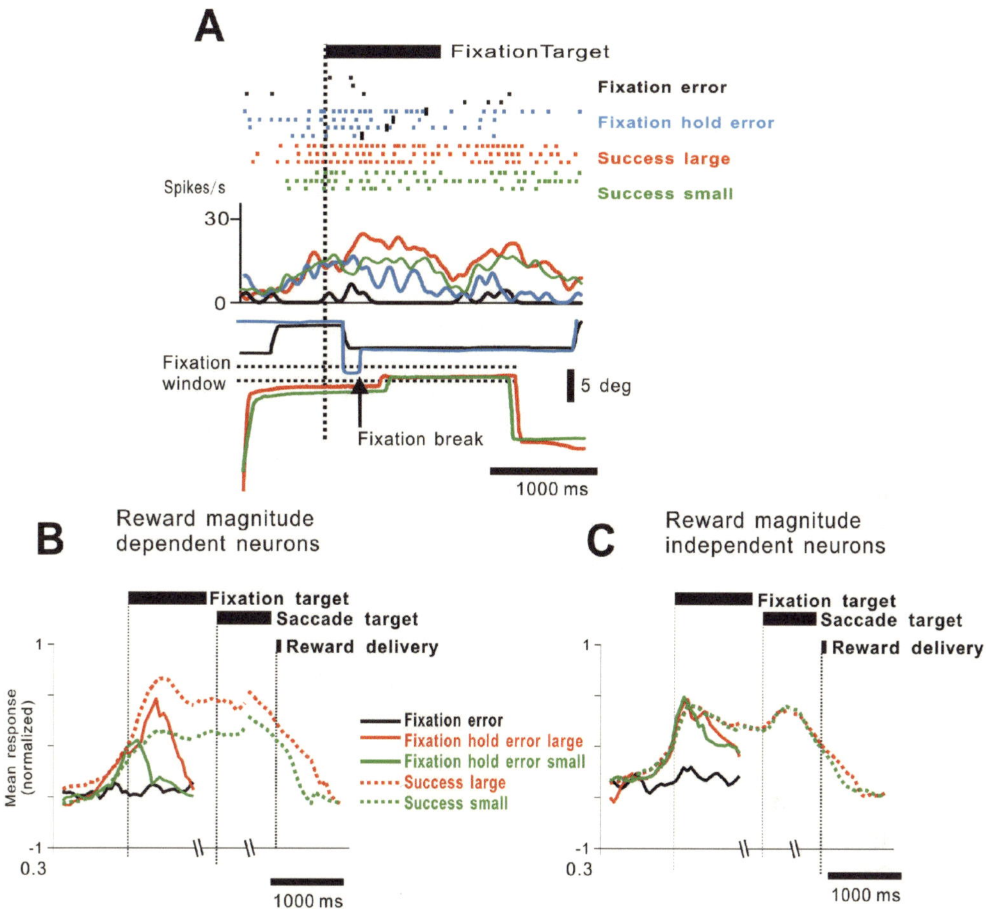

Fig. 5. Fixation target neuronal responses in unsuccessful and successful trials of the two-valued visually guided saccade task. *A*, (top and middle) Rastergram and spike density functions of a representative reward magnitude-dependent fixation target neuronal response over five success, fixation hold error and fixation error trials with normal cue (bottom) eye positions in a single representative case of each of the four trial categories. Upward arrow indicates the time of the fixation break. Two horizontal dotted lines indicate the fixation window within which the monkey was required to maintain eye position. *B*, Population spike density function of 30 reward magnitude-dependent fixation target neurons averaged for fixation error (black solid trace), fixation hold error (solid red and solid green traces for trial with large and small reward cues), and successful trials (dotted red and dotted green traces for trial with large and small reward cues), aligned to fixation target onset, saccade target onset and reward delivery. The spike density is the population average normalized for the peaks of the mean individual neuronal responses. *C*, Population spike density functions of 52 reward magnitude-independent neurons following the same format as (B). Figures were modified from our recent paper (Okada et al., 2009).

4. Computation of reward prediction error in dopamine neurons with input from the PPTN

4.1 PPTN neuronal activity for predicted and actual reward

We previously demonstrated that PPTN activity in the fixation period of a simple visually-guided saccade task predicted task outcome (Kobayashi et al., 2002). In the two-valued reward visually guided saccade task just described, we revealed new functional aspects of PPTN activity. The temporal profiles of the activities of fixation target and reward delivery neurons in this task indicated that these functional neuronal classes may encode the predicted and actual reward magnitudes, respectively. ROC analysis of the magnitude-dependent fixation target and reward delivery neuronal responses in our task revealed that most fixation target and reward delivery neurons reliably signaled whether reward is large or small. Mutual information analysis further showed that fixation target and reward delivery neurons signaled reward magnitude with high precision (maximum information capacities of 2.6 and 3.5 bits, corresponding to 0.04 and 0.25 bits/neuron), comparable to those reported for the sensory (0.2 bits/neuron (Gochin et al., 1994)) and motor systems (0.05 bits/neuron (Kitazawa et al., 1998)). The high information capacities of fixation target and reward delivery neurons imply that they are potentially capable of differentiating 6 and 11 levels of reward magnitude, respectively. Mutual information analysis also showed that fixation target neurons conveyed information about predicted reward magnitude throughout the cue and maintenance periods, with no significant attenuation until the reward delivery neurons signaled actual reward magnitude.

Finally, the fixation target neurons responded to changes in the cue-reward contingency within two trials, rapidly revising their prediction of reward magnitude following changes in cue shape. These results are consistent with a role of fixation target neurons in reward prediction error computation in reinforcement learning. Conversely, the responses of the reward delivery neurons were based on the magnitude of the rewards delivered, regardless of cue shape. These results are consistent with reward delivery neurons signalling the magnitude of the delivered reward.

4.2 PPTN neuronal activity for motivation

Consistent with previous lesion (Conde et al., 1998) and recording studies (Kobayashi et al., 2002), PPTN (the fixation target) neurons may also signal motivation to perform a given task, the monkey's reaction times to fixate on the fixation and saccade targets were significantly correlated with their subsequent successful/unsuccessful completion of the task, and the responses of the fixation target neurons were significantly smaller in the fixation error trials than in the successful trials.

We also found a significant number of reward magnitude-independent fixation target neurons whose responses were significantly correlated with the successful/unsuccessful completion of the task (Fig. 5C). The functional implication of the reward magnitude-independent fixation target neurons remains unclear, but they may represent the timestamp of the reward expectation (Pan & Hyland, 2005). The neurons responsive to reward delivery also included reward magnitude-dependent and -independent groups; however, none of these reward delivery neurons showed a response correlation with the successful/unsuccessful completion of the task, which is consistent with the view that they monitor the time and magnitude of the actual task reward. Finally, the responses of the reward magnitude-dependent fixation target and reward delivery neurons did not signal only the reward magnitude but also the timestamps of reward expectation like those found in the reward magnitude-independent fixation target and reward delivery neurons; this was reflected in the anticipatory responses preceding the onset of the fixation target and reward delivery.

4.3 Possible source of the fixation target response

We demonstrated neuronal activity within the PPTN in response to the appearence of a fixation target that was predictive of the animal's performance on the task (Fig. 5) (Kobayashi et al., 2002). This activity appeared to be related to motivation level, reward prediction and conditioned sensory responses. This last association is consistent with a previous study in cats showing that neuronal activity in the PPTN was elicited during classical conditioning tasks in response to the conditioned stimulus (Dormont et al., 1998). Our result further suggests that the salience of the conditioned stimulus in the particular task (i.e. fixation target onset in the visually guided saccade task) was influenced by the monkey's motivation for performing the task. Thus, PPTN neurons may comprise a substrate, whose role is to transform a sensory cue into a behavioral action. If this hypothesis is correct, it is quite reasonable to expect the response of a given neuron to a cue in a cue-reward association task are modulated by the magnitude of the expected reward.

From where does the PPTN receive this motivational or reward prediction signal? The fixation target neurons may receive the signals of reward prediction from the orbitofrontal cortex (Tremblay & Schultz, 1999; Hikosaka & Watanabe, 2000; Roesch & Olson, 2004; Simmons & Richmond, 2008), prefrontal cortex (Kitazawa et al., 1998; Leon & Shadlen, 1999; Roesch & Olson, 2003; Kennerley & Wallis, 2009; Luk & Wallis, 2009), cingulated cortex (Cornwall et al., 1990), striatum (Mena-Segovia et al., 2004; Hikosaka et al., 2006; Winn, 2006) or hippocampus (Yang & Mogenson, 1987).

We propose that the signals travel via 1) the ventral striatum-ventral pallidum pathway, which receives input mainly from the limbic cortex (Yang & Mogenson, 1987; Schultz et al., 1992; Brown et al., 1999), 2) the amygdala and the subthalamic nucleus (Semba & Fibiger, 1992), and 3) the cerebral cortices. Recently, Matsumura has emphasized the functional role of cortical input to the PPTN in the integration mechanism of limbic-motor control (Matsumura, 2005).

The dopamine neurons respond to expected, unexpected and salient sensory events with short latency, but little is known about the sensory systems underlying this response (Ljungberg et al., 1992). Studies of rats, cats and primates indicate that neurons in the superior colliculus, relaying visual information, make direct synaptic contacts with dopamine neurons in the substantia nigra (Comoli et al., 2003; McHaffie et al., 2006; May et al., 2009). In addition to the inputs of the substantia nigra via the superior colliculus, the dopamine neurons are also innervated by neurons, as described above. Furthermore, as the PPTN also receives input from the superior colliculus (Huerta & Harting, 1982; Redgrave et al., 1987; May & Porter, 1992). We propose that the PPTN may also relay visual information to dopamine neurons. We showed that PPTN neurons exhibited responses to the fixation target (a salient visual stimulus) that varied with subsequent performance of the task (Fig. 5). The responses of some of these neurons occurred with short latency (about 100ms), similar to the reported latency of dopamine neurons to the cue signal (50-120 ms, (Mirenowicz & Schultz, 1994; Schultz, 1998)). There have been only a few studies examining visual responses of PPTN neurons. Pan & Hyland (2005), reported visual responses of PPTN neurons in rats, which had a mean response latency to the onset of a light stimulus of 70 ms, but they observed no variable visual responses for reward prediction (Pan & Hyland, 2005). In contrast to these results, a population of our recorded PPTN neurons in primates responded differentially to a visual stimulus with dependent on motivational state. Our results may be closer to another study of PPTN neurons in cats, whose conditioned cue responses occurred with a short latency (Dormont et al., 1998). Further studies are needed to examine the effect of reward prediction on the short latency response to salient stimulus in the PPTN (Stewart & Dommett, 2006).

Interestingly, similar to the cholinergic structure PPTN, the noradrenergic locus coeruleus has been implicated in responses to both salient and motivational sensory events. Locus coeruleus neurons were phasically activated prior to behavioral responses on both correct and incorrect trials, but were not activated by stimuli that failed to elicit lever responses or by lever movements outside the task (Clayton et al., 2004). In contrast to the locus coeruleus neurons, we observed a sustained, tonic activity in the PPTN during the task. Recent pharmacological studies suggest that another monoaminergic neurotransmitter, serotonin, is also involved in reward processing. Nakamura and colleagues showed that serotonergic neurons in the dorsal raphe nucleus were tonically modulated by the size of expected reward with either a large- or small-reward preference, and after reward delivery, they were tonically modulated by the size of the received reward (Nakamura et al., 2008). Thus, dorsal raphe nucleus neurons also encode the expected and received reward value, albeit, in a different pattern than the PPTN neurons. There are reciprocal mutual, inhibitory interactions between PPTN, locus coeruleus, and dorsal raphe nucleus neurons (Koyama & Kayama, 1993). Thus, we should compare the reward-related activities of neurons in these area while controlling arousal, motivation, and learning.

4.4 Possible primary reward signal in the PPTN

In the PPTN, we observed transient reward responses for free reward and reward during the two-valued reward task(Okada et al., 2009). The reward delivery neurons may receive the actual reward signals from the lateral hypothalamus (Rolls et al., 1980; Fukuda et al., 1986; Nakamura & Ono, 1986). This pathway directly excites the PPTN (Semba & Fibiger, 1992), which responds with a brief burst and then accommodates or habituates (Takakusaki et al., 1997; Dormont et al., 1998). This brief burst, in turn, directly excites the midbrain dopamine neurons via cholinergic and glutamatergic projections (Conde, 1992) and thereby causes a phasic burst in dopamine neurons projecting to the striatum (Gerfen, 1992) for actual reward. We plan to examine whether the response properties of the PPTN fulfill the necessary features of a primary reward signal (i.e., whether the activity is related to reward occurrence, to value coding, and shows no adaptation under a fully learned condition).

4.5 Computation of reward prediction error signal in dopamine neurons

As described above, dopamine neurons have unique firing patterns related to the predicted volume and actual times of reward (Hollerman & Schultz, 1998; Schultz, 1998). Computational models (Houk et al., 1995; Montague et al., 1996; Schultz et al., 1997; Berns & Sejnowski, 1998; Suri & Schultz, 1998; Contreras-Vidal & Schultz, 1999) of dopamine firing have noted similarities between the response patterns of dopamine neurons and well-known learning algorithms, especially temporal difference reinforcement learning algorithms (Montague et al., 1996; Schultz et al., 1997; Suri & Schultz, 1998). The temporal difference model uses fast-sustained excitatory reward prediction and delayed slow-sustained inhibitory pluse signals in dopamine neurons, a sustained tonic reward prediction pulse originating from the striatum is temporally differentiated to produce an onset burst followed by an offset suppression. In the model the neurons in the striatum (the striosome) provide a significant source of GABAergic inhibition to dopamine neurons (Gerfen, 1992), and the fast excitatory, reward-predicting signals are derived via a double inhibition mechanism to dopamine neurons (matriosome-pallidum-dopamine neuron pathway (Houk et al., 1995)). Thus, the polysynaptic double inhibition pathway and monosynaptic direct inhibition may provide temporal differentiation of reward prediction in dopamine neurons. However, the model may not be realistic, because it is assumed that (1) the polysynaptic, net excitatory signal is faster than the direct monosynaptic inhibitory signal, and (2) the double inhibition pathway is required to strongly excite burst activity in dopamine neurons in response to a conditioned cue. A significant difference between the model we will propose, derived from the present findings, and the previous model is the source of excitation for dopamine neurons (Contreras-Vidal & Schultz, 1999). We propose that the excitatory PPTN neurons may send both a tonic reward prediction signal and a transient current reward signal to dopamine neurons.

Interestingly, the predictive and actual reward responses of the fixation target and reward delivery neurons follow comparable time courses to those supposed for the value function and the actual reward signals, respectively, in the temporal difference model of reinforcement learning (Houk et al., 1995; Schultz et al., 1997; Doya, 2000; Suri, 2002; Laurent, 2008). Therefore, the reward prediction error may be computed in the dopamine neurons from the fixation target and reward delivery signals, using the temporal difference algorithm, (Doya, 2000).

It is known from the classical conditioning paradigm of reinforcement learning that dopamine neurons show transient excitatory responses to cue presentation but not to reward delivery, and inhibitory responses to reward omission at the expected reward delivery time (Brown et al., 1999; Contreras-Vidal & Schultz, 1999; Doya, 2000; Fiorillo et al., 2008). The fixation target neuronal response that slowly rises at fixation target/cue presentation may be conveyed to the dopamine neurons, transformed by temporal differentiation of the temporal difference mechanism as transient excitatory (Lokwan et al., 1999) and inhibitory signals timed at fixation target presentation and reward delivery, respectively, and summed with the actual reward signals of the reward delivery neurons, for computation of reward prediction errors.

The excitatory transients impinge on the dopamine neurons in the absence of neuronal reward delivery signals, producing a sharp cue response, while upon reward delivery, the inhibitory transients are summed with the excitatory actual reward signals for computation of the reward prediction error, producing no response when the reward prediction matches with the actual one (Tobler et al., 2003; Fiorillo et al., 2008).

In our recent study, the fixation target responses in the PPTN do not primarily explain this inhibitory omission response of the dopamine neurons, as the responses of the majority of the fixation target neurons were shutdown at the actual, rather than the expected, reward delivery timing in the temporal reward omission experiments (Okada et al., 2009). Therefore, they would feed the inhibitory transients to the dopamine neurons through the temporal difference mechanism, at the time of the actual rather than the expected reward. However, a minority of fixation target neurons, whose responses were terminated at the time of the expected reward delivery (Okada et al., 2009), could convey the inhibitory transients to the dopamine neurons, producing the inhibitory omission response. It is possible that the former and latter fixation target neurons, whose responses were shutdown at the times of the actual and expected rewards, respectively, represent the value functions V(t) and V(t+1) for the current and predicted task events (Houk et al., 1995; Sutton & Barto, 1998; Doya, 2000). Furthermore GABAergic axon terminals originating from the PPTN were observed in the midbrain (Charara et al., 1996), these inhibitory connections may inhibit dopamine neurons and generate the inhibitory reward omission response. Alternatively, the inhibitory reward signals may be sent to the dopamine neurons from other neuronal structures such as the striosome (Brown et al., 1999; Contreras-Vidal & Schultz, 1999), ventral pallidum (Wu et al., 1996), habenula (Matsumoto & Hikosaka, 2007) and rostromedial tegmental nucleus (Jhou et al., 2009).

Finally, we present our hypothesis of how the PPTN drives dopamine neurons to compute the reward prediction error signal (Fig. 6). Our recent observations support the view that the fixation target and reward delivery neurons signal the predicted and actual reward magnitude, respectively. The prolonged response of the fixation target neurons indicates that they may maintain the signals of the predicted reward from the time of cue presentation until the reward delivery neurons signal the actual reward magnitude.

This study revealed that the strong excitatory inputs exerted by the PPTN on midbrain dopamine neurons (Mena-Segovia et al., 2004; Pan & Hyland, 2005; Winn, 2006) convey the memory of the predicted reward and the signals of the actual reward, two essential elements needed for computing the reward prediction error. The high information capacities of the fixation target and reward delivery neurons to signal the reward magnitude may help the dopamine neurons to accurately compute the reward prediction error and to efficiently execute reinforcement learning.

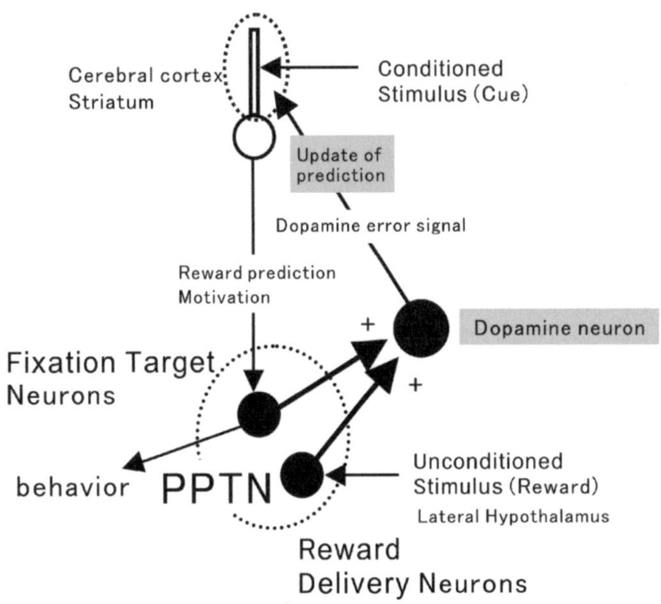

Fig. 6. Possible PPTN neuronal circuit for exciting dopamine neurons in reinforcement learning.

Computation of the reward prediction error requires a temporal memory of the predicted reward (established at cue onset and sustained until reward delivery) and a comparison of the actual reward with the predicted one. The reward predictive structures (cerebral cortex and striatum) may learn the cue-reward magnitude contingency during the training and task periods as a synaptic memory and recall that memory as the signals of the predicted reward magnitude at the time of cue presentation. These signals would then be transferred to the fixation target neurons and stored as working memory (Compte, 2006) of the reward prediction until the time of reward delivery. Thus, the PPTN is an important center, providing information of both reward prediction and actual reward to dopamine neurons.
Moreover, our study addresses the broader science of memory: we demonstrated that the memory of the task reward is recalled as neuronal activity signaling the predicted reward magnitude, which is then compared with neuronal activity signaling the actual reward magnitude. To our knowledge, the mechanism whereby past memories, engrammed in synaptic efficacy, are decoded into dynamic neural activity for comparison with the current neuronal activity, remains totally unexplored, in spite of the fact that the inverse process of encoding the firing rate of current neural events into synaptic efficacy has been extensively studied by plasticity researchers. Thus, our study is the first demonstration that structural memories of past experience are decoded into dynamic neural activity and compared with that for the present experience. And moreover, that the PPTN is the site where both signals are simultaneously represented.

5. References

Alderson, H.L.; Latimer, M.P. & Winn, P. (2006) Intravenous self-administration of nicotine is altered by lesions of the posterior, but not anterior, pedunculopontine tegmental nucleus. Eur J Neurosci 23: pp. 2169-2175.

Alderson, H.L.; Brown, V.J.; Latimer, M.P.; Brasted, P.J.; Robertson, A.H. & Winn, P. (2002) The effect of excitotoxic lesions of the pedunculopontine tegmental nucleus on performance of a progressive ratio schedule of reinforcement. Neuroscience 112: pp. 417-425.

Bechara, A. & van der Kooy, D. (1989) The tegmental pedunculopontine nucleus: a brain-stem output of the limbic system critical for the conditioned place preferences produced by morphine and amphetamine. J Neurosci 9: pp. 3400-3409.

Beckstead, R.M.; Domesick, V.B. & Nauta, W.J. (1979) Efferent connections of the substantia nigra and ventral tegmental area in the rat. Brain Res 175: pp. 191-217.

Beninato, M. & Spencer, R.F. (1987) A cholinergic projection to the rat substantia nigra from the pedunculopontine tegmental nucleus. Brain Res 412: pp. 169-174.

Berns, G.S. & Sejnowski, T.J. (1998) A computational model of how the basal ganglia produce sequences. J Cogn Neurosci 10: pp. 108-121.

Blaha, C.D. & Winn, P. (1993) Modulation of dopamine efflux in the striatum following cholinergic stimulation of the substantia nigra in intact and pedunculopontine tegmental nucleus-lesioned rats. J Neurosci 13: pp. 1035-1044.

Blaha, C.D.; Allen, L.F.; Das, S.; Inglis, W.L.; Latimer, M.P.; Vincent, S.R. & Winn, P. (1996) Modulation of dopamine efflux in the nucleus accumbens after cholinergic stimulation of the ventral tegmental area in intact, pedunculopontine tegmental nucleus-lesioned, and laterodorsal tegmental nucleus-lesioned rats. J Neurosci 16: pp. 714-722.

Brown, J.; Bullock, D. & Grossberg, S. (1999) How the basal ganglia use parallel excitatory and inhibitory learning pathways to selectively respond to unexpected rewarding cues. J Neurosci 19: pp. 10502-10511.

Calabresi, P.; Lacey, M.G. & North, R.A. (1989) Nicotinic excitation of rat ventral tegmental neurones in vitro studied by intracellular recording. Br J Pharmacol 98: pp. 135-140.

Chapman, C.A.; Yeomans, J.S.; Blaha, C.D. & Blackburn, J.R. (1997) Increased striatal dopamine efflux follows scopolamine administered systemically or to the tegmental pedunculopontine nucleus. Neuroscience 76: pp. 177-186.

Charara, A.; Smith, Y. & Parent, A. (1996) Glutamatergic inputs from the pedunculopontine nucleus to midbrain dopaminergic neurons in primates: Phaseolus vulgaris-leucoagglutinin anterograde labeling combined with postembedding glutamate and GABA immunohistochemistry. J Comp Neurol 364: pp. 254-266.

Chen, J.; Nakamura, M.; Kawamura, T.; Takahashi, T. & Nakahara, D. (2006) Roles of pedunculopontine tegmental cholinergic receptors in brain stimulation reward in the rat. Psychopharmacology (Berl) 184: pp. 514-522.

Chiba, T.; Kayahara, T. & Nakano, K. (2001) Efferent projections of infralimbic and prelimbic areas of the medial prefrontal cortex in the Japanese monkey, Macaca fuscata. Brain Res 888: pp. 83-101.

Clayton, E.C.; Rajkowski, J.; Cohen, J.D. & Aston-Jones, G. (2004) Phasic activation of monkey locus ceruleus neurons by simple decisions in a forced-choice task. J Neurosci 24: pp. 9914-9920.

Clements, J.R. & Grant, S. (1990) Glutamate-like immunoreactivity in neurons of the laterodorsal tegmental and pedunculopontine nuclei in the rat. Neurosci Lett 120: pp. 70-73.

Comoli, E.; Coizet, V.; Boyes, J.; Bolam, J.P.; Canteras, N.S.; Quirk, R.H.; Overton, P.G. & Redgrave, P. (2003) A direct projection from superior colliculus to substantia nigra for detecting salient visual events. Nat Neurosci 6: pp. 974-980.

Compte, A. (2006) Computational and in vitro studies of persistent activity: edging towards cellular and synaptic mechanisms of working memory. Neuroscience 139: pp. 135-151.

Conde, H. (1992) Organization and physiology of the substantia nigra. Exp Brain Res 88: pp. 233-248.

Conde, H.; Dormont, J.F. & Farin, D. (1998) The role of the pedunculopontine tegmental nucleus in relation to conditioned motor performance in the cat. II. Effects of reversible inactivation by intracerebral microinjections. Exp Brain Res 121: pp. 411-418.

Contreras-Vidal, J.L. & Schultz, W. (1999) A predictive reinforcement model of dopamine neurons for learning approach behavior. J Comput Neurosci 6: pp. 191-214.

Cornwall, J.; Cooper, J.D. & Phillipson, O.T. (1990) Afferent and efferent connections of the laterodorsal tegmental nucleus in the rat. Brain Res Bull 25: pp. 271-284.

Dormont, J.F.; Conde, H. & Farin, D. (1998) The role of the pedunculopontine tegmental nucleus in relation to conditioned motor performance in the cat. I. Context-dependent and reinforcement-related single unit activity. Exp Brain Res 121: pp. 401-410.

Doya, K. (2000) Reinforcement learning in continuous time and space. Neural Comput 12: pp. 219-245.

Doya, K. (2002) Metalearning and neuromodulation. Neural Netw 15: pp. 495-506.

Edley, S.M. & Graybiel, A.M. (1983) The afferent and efferent connections of the feline nucleus tegmenti pedunculopontinus, pars compacta. J Comp Neurol 217: pp. 187-215.
Fiorillo, C.D.; Tobler, P.N. & Schultz, W. (2003) Discrete coding of reward probability and uncertainty by dopamine neurons. Science 299: pp. 1898-1902.
Fiorillo, C.D.; Newsome, W.T. & Schultz, W. (2008) The temporal precision of reward prediction in dopamine neurons. Nat Neurosci 11: pp. 966-973.
Floresco, S.B.; West, A.R.; Ash, B.; Moore, H. & Grace, A.A. (2003) Afferent modulation of dopamine neuron firing differentially regulates tonic and phasic dopamine transmission. Nat Neurosci 6: pp. 968-973.
Ford, B.; Holmes, C.J.; Mainville, L. & Jones, B.E. (1995) GABAergic neurons in the rat pontomesencephalic tegmentum: codistribution with cholinergic and other tegmental neurons projecting to the posterior lateral hypothalamus. J Comp Neurol 363: pp. 177-196.
Forster, G.L. & Blaha, C.D. (2003) Pedunculopontine tegmental stimulation evokes striatal dopamine efflux by activation of acetylcholine and glutamate receptors in the midbrain and pons of the rat. Eur J Neurosci 17: pp. 751-762.
Fujimoto, K.; Ikeguchi, K. & Yoshida, M. (1992) Impaired acquisition, preserved retention and retrieval of avoidance behavior after destruction of pedunculopontine nucleus areas in the rat. Neurosci Res 13: pp. 43-51.
Fujimoto, K.; Yoshida, M.; Ikeguchi, K. & Niijima, K. (1989) Impairment of active avoidance produced after destruction of pedunculopontine nucleus areas in the rat. Neurosci Res 6: pp. 321-328.
Fukuda, M.; Ono, T.; Nishino, H. & Nakamura, K. (1986) Neuronal responses in monkey lateral hypothalamus during operant feeding behavior. Brain Res Bull 17: pp. 879-883.
Futami, T.; Takakusaki, K. & Kitai, S.T. (1995) Glutamatergic and cholinergic inputs from the pedunculopontine tegmental nucleus to dopamine neurons in the substantia nigra pars compacta. Neurosci Res 21: pp. 331-342.
Garcia-Rill, E. (1991) The pedunculopontine nucleus. Prog Neurobiol 36: pp. 363-389.
Garcia-Rill, E.; Biedermann, J.A.; Chambers, T.; Skinner, R.D.; Mrak, R.E.; Husain, M. & Karson, C.N. (1995) Mesopontine neurons in schizophrenia. Neuroscience 66: pp. 321-335.
Gerfen, C.R. (1992) The neostriatal mosaic: multiple levels of compartmental organization. J Neural Transm Suppl 36: pp. 43-59.
Gochin, P.M.; Colombo, M.; Dorfman, G.A.; Gerstein, G.L. & Gross, C.G. (1994) Neural ensemble coding in inferior temporal cortex. J Neurophysiol 71: pp. 2325-2337.
Graybiel, A.M. (2005) The basal ganglia: learning new tricks and loving it. Curr Opin Neurobiol 15: pp. 638-644.
Grenhoff, J.; Aston-Jones, G. & Svensson, T.H. (1986) Nicotinic effects on the firing pattern of midbrain dopamine neurons. Acta Physiol Scand 128: pp. 351-358.
Grofova, I. & Zhou, M. (1998) Nigral innervation of cholinergic and glutamatergic cells in the rat mesopontine tegmentum: light and electron microscopic anterograde tracing and immunohistochemical studies. J Comp Neurol 395: pp. 359-379.
Gronier, B. & Rasmussen, K. (1998) Activation of midbrain presumed dopaminergic neurones by muscarinic cholinergic receptors: an in vivo electrophysiological study in the rat. Br J Pharmacol 124: pp. 455-464.
Hikosaka, K. & Watanabe, M. (2000) Delay activity of orbital and lateral prefrontal neurons of the monkey varying with different rewards. Cereb Cortex 10: pp. 263-271.

Hikosaka, O.; Nakamura, K. & Nakahara, H. (2006) Basal ganglia orient eyes to reward. J Neurophysiol 95: pp. 567-584.

Hollerman, J.R. & Schultz, W. (1998) Dopamine neurons report an error in the temporal prediction of reward during learning. Nat Neurosci 1: pp. 304-309.

Honda, T. & Semba, K. (1994) Serotonergic synaptic input to cholinergic neurons in the rat mesopontine tegmentum. Brain Res 647: pp. 299-306.

Houk, J.C.; Adams, J.L. & Barto, A.G. (1995) A model of how the basal ganglia generate and use neural signals that predict reinforcement. In: Models of Information Processing in the Basal Ganglia, pp 249-270. New York: The MIT Press.

Huerta, M.F. & Harting, J.K. (1982) The projection from the nucleus of the posterior commissure to the superior colliculus of the cat: patch-like endings within the intermediate and deep grey layers. Brain Res 238: pp. 426-432.

Ichinohe, N.; Teng, B. & Kitai, S.T. (2000) Morphological study of the tegmental pedunculopontine nucleus, substantia nigra and subthalamic nucleus, and their interconnections in rat organotypic culture. Anat Embryol (Berl) 201: pp. 435-453.

Inglis, W.L.; Olmstead, M.C. & Robbins, T.W. (2000) Pedunculopontine tegmental nucleus lesions impair stimulus--reward learning in autoshaping and conditioned reinforcement paradigms. Behav Neurosci 114: pp. 285-294.

Jackson, A. & Crossman, A.R. (1983) Nucleus tegmenti pedunculopontinus: efferent connections with special reference to the basal ganglia, studied in the rat by anterograde and retrograde transport of horseradish peroxidase. Neuroscience 10: pp. 725-765.

Jhou, T.C.; Fields, H.L.; Baxter, M.G.; Saper, C.B. & Holland, P.C. (2009) The rostromedial tegmental nucleus (RMTg), a GABAergic afferent to midbrain dopamine neurons, encodes aversive stimuli and inhibits motor responses. Neuron 61: pp. 786-800.

Jones, B.E. & Beaudet, A. (1987) Distribution of acetylcholine and catecholamine neurons in the cat brainstem: a choline acetyltransferase and tyrosine hydroxylase immunohistochemical study. J Comp Neurol 261: pp. 15-32.

Kayama, Y. & Koyama, Y. (2003) Control of sleep and wakefulness by brainstem monoaminergic and cholinergic neurons. Acta Neurochir Suppl 87: pp. 3-6.

Kennerley, S.W. & Wallis, J.D. (2009) Reward-dependent modulation of working memory in lateral prefrontal cortex. J Neurosci 29: pp. 3259-3270.

Kippin, T.E. & van der Kooy, D. (2003) Excitotoxic lesions of the tegmental pedunculopontine nucleus impair copulation in naive male rats and block the rewarding effects of copulation in experienced male rats. Eur J Neurosci 18: pp. 2581-2591.

Kitai, S.T.; Shepard, P.D.; Callaway, J.C. & Scroggs, R. (1999) Afferent modulation of dopamine neuron firing patterns. Curr Opin Neurobiol 9: pp. 690-697.

Kitazawa, S.; Kimura, T. & Yin, P.B. (1998) Cerebellar complex spikes encode both destinations and errors in arm movements. Nature 392: pp. 494-497.

Kobayashi, Y.; Inoue, Y.; Yamamoto, M.; Isa, T. & Aizawa, H. (2002) Contribution of pedunculopontine tegmental nucleus neurons to performance of visually guided saccade tasks in monkeys. J Neurophysiol 88: pp. 715-731.

Koyama, Y. & Kayama, Y. (1993) Mutual interactions among cholinergic, noradrenergic and serotonergic neurons studied by ionophoresis of these transmitters in rat brainstem nuclei. Neuroscience 55: pp. 1117-1126.

Lacey, M.G.; Calabresi, P. & North, R.A. (1990) Muscarine depolarizes rat substantia nigra zona compacta and ventral tegmental neurons in vitro through M1-like receptors. J Pharmacol Exp Ther 253: pp. 395-400.

Laurent, P.A. (2008) The emergence of saliency and novelty responses from Reinforcement Learning principles. Neural Netw 21: pp. 1493-1499.

Lavoie, B. & Parent, A. (1994) Pedunculopontine nucleus in the squirrel monkey: distribution of cholinergic and monoaminergic neurons in the mesopontine tegmentum with evidence for the presence of glutamate in cholinergic neurons. J Comp Neurol 344: pp. 190-209.

Lee, D. & Seo, H. (2007) Mechanisms of reinforcement learning and decision making in the primate dorsolateral prefrontal cortex. Ann N Y Acad Sci 1104: pp. 108-122.

Leon, M.I. & Shadlen, M.N. (1999) Effect of expected reward magnitude on the response of neurons in the dorsolateral prefrontal cortex of the macaque. Neuron 24: pp. 415-425.

Leonard, C.S. & Llinas, R. (1994) Serotonergic and cholinergic inhibition of mesopontine cholinergic neurons controlling REM sleep: an in vitro electrophysiological study. Neuroscience 59: pp. 309-330.

Ljungberg, T.; Apicella, P. & Schultz, W. (1992) Responses of monkey dopamine neurons during learning of behavioral reactions. J Neurophysiol 67: pp. 145-163.

Lokwan, S.J.; Overton, P.G.; Berry, M.S. & Clark, D. (1999) Stimulation of the pedunculopontine tegmental nucleus in the rat produces burst firing in A9 dopaminergic neurons. Neuroscience 92: pp. 245-254.

Luk, C.H. & Wallis, J.D. (2009) Dynamic encoding of responses and outcomes by neurons in medial prefrontal cortex. J Neurosci 29: pp. 7526-7539.

Lusted, L.B. (1978) General problems in medical decision making with comments on ROC analysis. Semin Nucl Med 8: pp. 299-306.

Matsumoto, M. & Hikosaka, O. (2007) Lateral habenula as a source of negative reward signals in dopamine neurons. Nature 447: pp. 1111-1115.

Matsumura, M. (2005) The pedunculopontine tegmental nucleus and experimental parkinsonism. A review. J Neurol 252 Suppl 4: pp. IV5-IV12.

Matsumura, M.; Watanabe, K. & Ohye, C. (1997) Single-unit activity in the primate nucleus tegmenti pedunculopontinus related to voluntary arm movement. Neurosci Res 28: pp. 155-165.

May, P.J. & Porter, J.D. (1992) The laminar distribution of macaque tectobulbar and tectospinal neurons. Vis Neurosci 8: pp. 257-276.

May, P.J.; McHaffie, J.G.; Stanford, T.R.; Jiang, H.; Costello, M.G.; Coizet, V.; Hayes, L.M.; Haber, S.N. & Redgrave, P. (2009) Tectonigral projections in the primate: a pathway for pre-attentive sensory input to midbrain dopaminergic neurons. Eur J Neurosci 29: pp. 575-587.

McHaffie, J.G.; Jiang, H.; May, P.J.; Coizet, V.; Overton, P.G.; Stein, B.E. & Redgrave, P. (2006) A direct projection from superior colliculus to substantia nigra pars compacta in the cat. Neuroscience 138: pp. 221-234.

Mena-Segovia, J.; Bolam, J.P. & Magill, P.J. (2004) Pedunculopontine nucleus and basal ganglia: distant relatives or part of the same family? Trends Neurosci 27: pp. 585-588.

Mena-Segovia, J.; Winn, P. & Bolam, J.P. (2008) Cholinergic modulation of midbrain dopaminergic systems. Brain Res Rev 58: pp. 265-271.

Mesulam, M.M.; Mufson, E.J.; Wainer, B.H. & Levey, A.I. (1983) Central cholinergic pathways in the rat: an overview based on an alternative nomenclature (Ch1-Ch6). Neuroscience 10: pp. 1185-1201.

Miller, A.D. & Blaha, C.D. (2004) Nigrostriatal dopamine release modulated by mesopontine muscarinic receptors. Neuroreport 15: pp. 1805-1808.

Mirenowicz, J. & Schultz, W. (1994) Importance of unpredictability for reward responses in primate dopamine neurons. J Neurophysiol 72: pp. 1024-1027.

Montague, P.R. & Berns, G.S. (2002) Neural economics and the biological substrates of valuation. Neuron 36: pp. 265-284.

Montague, P.R.; Dayan, P. & Sejnowski, T.J. (1996) A framework for mesencephalic dopamine systems based on predictive Hebbian learning. J Neurosci 16: pp. 1936-1947.

Morris, G.; Nevet, A.; Arkadir, D.; Vaadia, E. & Bergman, H. (2006) Midbrain dopamine neurons encode decisions for future action. Nat Neurosci 9: pp. 1057-1063.

Nakahara, H.; Itoh, H.; Kawagoe, R.; Takikawa, Y. & Hikosaka, O. (2004) Dopamine neurons can represent context-dependent prediction error. Neuron 41: pp. 269-280.

Nakamura, K. & Ono, T. (1986) Lateral hypothalamus neuron involvement in integration of natural and artificial rewards and cue signals. J Neurophysiol 55: pp. 163-181.

Nakamura, K.; Matsumoto, M. & Hikosaka, O. (2008) Reward-dependent modulation of neuronal activity in the primate dorsal raphe nucleus. J Neurosci 28: pp. 5331-5343.

Oakman, S.A.; Faris, P.L.; Kerr, P.E.; Cozzari, C. & Hartman, B.K. (1995) Distribution of pontomesencephalic cholinergic neurons projecting to substantia nigra differs significantly from those projecting to ventral tegmental area. J Neurosci 15: pp. 5859-5869.

Okada, K.; Toyama, K.; Inoue, Y.; Isa, T. & Kobayashi, Y. (2009) Different pedunculopontine tegmental neurons signal predicted and actual task rewards. J Neurosci 29: pp. 4858-4870.

Pan, W.X. & Hyland, B.I. (2005) Pedunculopontine tegmental nucleus controls conditioned responses of midbrain dopamine neurons in behaving rats. J Neurosci 25: pp. 4725-4732.

Perry, E.; Walker, M.; Grace, J. & Perry, R. (1999) Acetylcholine in mind: a neurotransmitter correlate of consciousness? Trends Neurosci 22: pp. 273-280.

Pidoplichko, V.I.; DeBiasi, M.; Williams, J.T. & Dani, J.A. (1997) Nicotine activates and desensitizes midbrain dopamine neurons. Nature 390: pp. 401-404.

Redgrave, P.; Mitchell, I.J. & Dean, P. (1987) Descending projections from the superior colliculus in rat: a study using orthograde transport of wheatgerm-agglutinin conjugated horseradish peroxidase. Exp Brain Res 68: pp. 147-167.

Reynolds, J.N.; Hyland, B.I. & Wickens, J.R. (2001) A cellular mechanism of reward-related learning. Nature 413: pp. 67-70.

Richmond, B.J.; Liu, Z. & Shidara, M. (2003) Neuroscience. Predicting future rewards. Science 301: pp. 179-180.

Roesch, M.R. & Olson, C.R. (2003) Impact of expected reward on neuronal activity in prefrontal cortex, frontal and supplementary eye fields and premotor cortex. J Neurophysiol 90: pp. 1766-1789.

Roesch, M.R. & Olson, C.R. (2004) Neuronal activity related to reward value and motivation in primate frontal cortex. Science 304: pp. 307-310.

Rolls, E.T.; Burton, M.J. & Mora, F. (1980) Neurophysiological analysis of brain-stimulation reward in the monkey. Brain Res 194: pp. 339-357.

Samejima, K.; Ueda, Y.; Doya, K. & Kimura, M. (2005) Representation of action-specific reward values in the striatum. Science 310: pp. 1337-1340.

Satoh, T.; Nakai, S.; Sato, T. & Kimura, M. (2003) Correlated coding of motivation and outcome of decision by dopamine neurons. J Neurosci 23: pp. 9913-9923.

Scarnati, E.; Proia, A.; Campana, E. & Pacitti, C. (1986) A microiontophoretic study on the nature of the putative synaptic neurotransmitter involved in the pedunculopontine-

substantia nigra pars compacta excitatory pathway of the rat. Exp Brain Res 62: pp. 470-478.
Scarnati, E.; Proia, A.; Di Loreto, S. & Pacitti, C. (1987) The reciprocal electrophysiological influence between the nucleus tegmenti pedunculopontinus and the substantia nigra in normal and decorticated rats. Brain Res 423: pp. 116-124.
Schreiner, R.C.; Essick, G.K. & Whitsel, B.L. (1978) Variability in somatosensory cortical neuron discharge: effects on capacity to signal different stimulus conditions using a mean rate code. J Neurophysiol 41: pp. 338-349.
Schultz, W. (1998) Predictive reward signal of dopamine neurons. J Neurophysiol 80: pp. 1-27.
Schultz, W. (2002) Getting formal with dopamine and reward. Neuron 36: pp. 241-263.
Schultz, W.; Dayan, P. & Montague, P.R. (1997) A neural substrate of prediction and reward. Science 275: pp. 1593-1599.
Schultz, W.; Apicella, P.; Scarnati, E. & Ljungberg, T. (1992) Neuronal activity in monkey ventral striatum related to the expectation of reward. J Neurosci 12: pp. 4595-4610.
Scroggs, R.S.; Cardenas, C.G.; Whittaker, J.A. & Kitai, S.T. (2001) Muscarine reduces calcium-dependent electrical activity in substantia nigra dopaminergic neurons. J Neurophysiol 86: pp. 2966-2972.
Semba, K. & Fibiger, H.C. (1992) Afferent connections of the laterodorsal and the pedunculopontine tegmental nuclei in the rat: a retro- and antero-grade transport and immunohistochemical study. J Comp Neurol 323: pp. 387-410.
Simmons, J.M. & Richmond, B.J. (2008) Dynamic changes in representations of preceding and upcoming reward in monkey orbitofrontal cortex. Cereb Cortex 18: pp. 93-103.
Sorenson, E.M.; Shiroyama, T. & Kitai, S.T. (1998) Postsynaptic nicotinic receptors on dopaminergic neurons in the substantia nigra pars compacta of the rat. Neuroscience 87: pp. 659-673.
Spann, B.M. & Grofova, I. (1992) Cholinergic and non-cholinergic neurons in the rat pedunculopontine tegmental nucleus. Anat Embryol (Berl) 186: pp. 215-227.
Steckler, T.; Inglis, W.; Winn, P. & Sahgal, A. (1994) The pedunculopontine tegmental nucleus: a role in cognitive processes? Brain Res Brain Res Rev 19: pp. 298-318.
Steiniger, B. & Kretschmer, B.D. (2003) Glutamate and GABA modulate dopamine in the pedunculopontine tegmental nucleus. Exp Brain Res 149: pp. 422-430.
Steininger, T.L.; Rye, D.B. & Wainer, B.H. (1992) Afferent projections to the cholinergic pedunculopontine tegmental nucleus and adjacent midbrain extrapyramidal area in the albino rat. I. Retrograde tracing studies. J Comp Neurol 321: pp. 515-543.
Steriade, M.; Datta, S.; Pare, D.; Oakson, G. & Curro Dossi, R. (1990) Neuronal activities in brain-stem cholinergic nuclei related to tonic activation processes in thalamocortical systems. J Neurosci 10: pp. 2541-2559.
Stewart, R.D. & Dommett, E.J. (2006) Subcortical control of dopamine neurons: the good, the bad and the unexpected. Brain Res Bull 71: pp. 1-3.
Suri, R.E. (2002) TD models of reward predictive responses in dopamine neurons. Neural Netw 15: pp. 523-533.
Suri, R.E. & Schultz, W. (1998) Learning of sequential movements by neural network model with dopamine-like reinforcement signal. Exp Brain Res 121: pp. 350-354.
Sutton, R.S. & Barto, A.G. (1998) Reinforcement Learning. New York: The MIT Press.
Takakusaki, K.; Shiroyama, T. & Kitai, S.T. (1997) Two types of cholinergic neurons in the rat tegmental pedunculopontine nucleus: electrophysiological and morphological characterization. Neuroscience 79: pp. 1089-1109.

Takakusaki, K.; Shiroyama, T.; Yamamoto, T. & Kitai, S.T. (1996) Cholinergic and noncholinergic tegmental pedunculopontine projection neurons in rats revealed by intracellular labeling. J Comp Neurol 371: pp. 345-361.

Takakusaki, K.; Oohinata-Sugimoto, J.; Saitoh, K. & Habaguchi, T. (2004) Role of basal ganglia-brainstem systems in the control of postural muscle tone and locomotion. Progress in Brain Research 143: pp. 231-237.

Tesauro, G. (1994) TD-Gammon, a self-teaching backgammon program, achieves master-level play. Neural Computation 6: pp. 215-219.

Tobler, P.N.; Dickinson, A. & Schultz, W. (2003) Coding of predicted reward omission by dopamine neurons in a conditioned inhibition paradigm. J Neurosci 23: pp. 10402-10410.

Tremblay, L. & Schultz, W. (1999) Relative reward preference in primate orbitofrontal cortex. Nature 398: pp. 704-708.

Tzavara, E.T.; Bymaster, F.P.; Davis, R.J.; Wade, M.R.; Perry, K.W.; Wess, J.; McKinzie, D.L.; Felder, C. & Nomikos, G.G. (2004) M4 muscarinic receptors regulate the dynamics of cholinergic and dopaminergic neurotransmission: relevance to the pathophysiology and treatment of related CNS pathologies. FASEB J 18: pp. 1410-1412.

Waelti, P.; Dickinson, A. & Schultz, W. (2001) Dopamine responses comply with basic assumptions of formal learning theory. Nature 412: pp. 43-48.

Wang, H.L. & Morales, M. (2009) Pedunculopontine and laterodorsal tegmental nuclei contain distinct populations of cholinergic, glutamatergic and GABAergic neurons in the rat. Eur J Neurosci 29: pp. 340-358.

Watanabe, M. (1996) Reward expectancy in primate prefrontal neurons. Nature 382: pp. 629-632.

Werner, G. & Mountcastle, V.B. (1963) The Variability of Central Neural Activity in a Sensory System, and Its Implications for the Central Reflection of Sensory Events. J Neurophysiol 26: pp. 958-977.

Wickens, J.R.; Reynolds, J.N. & Hyland, B.I. (2003) Neural mechanisms of reward-related motor learning. Curr Opin Neurobiol 13: pp. 685-690.

Wilson, D.I.; Maclaren, D.A. & Winn, P. (2009) Bar pressing for food: differential consequences of lesions to the anterior versus posterior pedunculopontine. Eur J Neurosci 30: pp. 504-513.

Winn, P. (2006) How best to consider the structure and function of the pedunculopontine tegmental nucleus: evidence from animal studies. J Neurol Sci 248: pp. 234-250.

Winn, P.; Brown, V.J. & Inglis, W.L. (1997) On the relationships between the striatum and the pedunculopontine tegmental nucleus. Crit Rev Neurobiol 11: pp. 241-261.

Wu, M.; Hrycyshyn, A.W. & Brudzynski, S.M. (1996) Subpallidal outputs to the nucleus accumbens and the ventral tegmental area: anatomical and electrophysiological studies. Brain Res 740: pp. 151-161.

Yamashita, T. & Isa, T. (2003) Fulfenamic acid sensitive, Ca(2+)-dependent inward current induced by nicotinic acetylcholine receptors in dopamine neurons. Neurosci Res 46: pp. 463-473.

Yang, C.R. & Mogenson, G.J. (1987) Hippocampal signal transmission to the pedunculopontine nucleus and its regulation by dopamine D2 receptors in the nucleus accumbens: an electrophysiological and behavioural study. Neuroscience 23: pp. 1041-1055.

Yeomans, J.S. (1995) Role of tegmental cholinergic neurons in dopaminergic activation, antimuscarinic psychosis and schizophrenia. Neuropsychopharmacology 12: pp. 3-16.

10

Subgoal Identifications in Reinforcement Learning: A Survey

Chung-Cheng Chiu and Von-Wun Soo
National Tsing Hua University
Taiwan

1. Introduction

Designing an algorithm to build a program to solve all forms of problems is an attractive idea. The programmers don't need to spend efforts on figuring out an optimal way to solve the problem, the algorithm itself will explore the problem and automatically finds the solution to the problem. This amazing feature of automatic programming is what makes reinforcement learning so appealing, and have the potential to apply on virtually every single task of our world. Reinforcement learning is a general framework to find an optimal solution for the given task. Its generalization reduces the effort of programmers on mapping a specific task into a reinforcement learning problem, but this feature is also the main performance bottleneck of reinforcement learning. Since there are not many constraints within the framework, the search space of the policy is exponentially proportional to the dimension of the state space. When mapping a high dimensional problem into a reinforcement learning problem, the conventional reinforcement learning algorithm becomes infeasible. Most of the real world problems are high-dimensional, and it is the major limitation for reinforcement learning. Therefore, how to find a way to reduce the search space and improve the search efficiency is the most important challenge.

On dealing with a high dimensionality problem, there are two common approaches to improve the performance. One is to reduce the dimensionality; the other is to find a better optimization algorithm. The first approach has drawn much attention in recent years, and many interesting works have been proposed this way to boost the performance of reinforcement learning. This article is going to review some recent advances in the dimensionality reduction approach.

Approaches for dimensionality reduction can be classified into two categories. One is value function approximation, and the other is abstraction. The first category approximate the utility function as a specific form of function, usually linear function, and the optimization of value function becomes much more efficient when dealing with linear functions. This approximation not only reduces the cost of optimization, but also provides the abilities to dealing with continuous-variable problems and generalizing the original policy to similar problems. The second category identifies the structure of the problem, represent the problem with higher-level concepts, and remove irrelevant parameters. Approaches within this category identify the sub-spaces of the state space that do not need to include other sub-spaces when solving the problem. For example, on solving a "make-coffee" problem, we can divide the problem into two sub-problems "reach the coffee maker" and "cook coffee with coffee maker". This article is going to talk a little bit on the value function approximation, and the main focus is to review some recent advances in abstractions.

Abstraction approaches require determining sub-problems, and the sub-problems are also known as *subtasks*. On representing the original problem with subtasks, the program then can make decision among these subtasks instead of low-level actions. The new representation scales down the complexity of the problem. The problems remain to solve are how to identify these subtasks and how to learn policies of them. The second task depends on the first task: we need to construct subtasks so that to learn their policies. One way to implement this framework is to construct subtasks and define sub-policies manually. When a problem is divided into several sub-problems, it is usually easy for a programmer to implement the sub-policies, so the approach can be practical for simple problems. But when dealing with large-scale decision making problems, programming these sub-policies becomes effort demanding, and identifying a good set of subtasks is difficult if not impossible. This leads to the issue of how to identify these subtasks. Many algorithms have been proposed to attack this problem, but the complexity of these algorithms is proportional to the complexity of the problem, so they become impractical for challenging problems. How to automate these processes remains an open problem.

Even subtasks are constructed, the sub-policy learning problem is still critical. Adding subtasks to the original problem actually increases the complexity, so simply applying the conventional reinforcement learning algorithms provides no benefit. Except for implementing the sub-policies manually, the benefit of constructing subtasks comes from the potential for dimension reductions. (1) A subtask can be shared among solving different sub-problems and can save the time for learning redundant subtasks. (2) It is much easier to find irrelevant parameters within a subtask. An object can be relevant in one task and irrelevant in others; separates the problem into different subtasks allow the specific task to remove the parameters for that object. Removing irrelevant parameters reduces the dimensionality of the problems. Therefore, despite of subgoal identification issue, we will also talk about dimension reductions among subtasks.

The second section introduces existing frameworks for representing subtasks. The third section reviews existing works for subtask discovery. The fourth section discusses the issue of dimension reduction among subtasks. And the conclusions are given in the last section.

2. Subtask representation

We start the introduction for subtask representation from a widely used model, the option framework Sutton et al. (1999). The option framework defines a subtask as an option. Each option consists of three components, initiation set, terminal conditions, and the option policy function. The initiation set determines what states the option can be applied, the terminal conditions specify when the option will be terminated, and the option policy corresponds to the sub-policy of that subtask. An initiation set and terminal conditions define the scope of a subtask. The defined options are added to the action list of policies, and the decision maker can choose to apply these temporally-extended actions instead of trying a sequence of one-step actions. This approach define a general framework for defining a subtask, and the component of a subtask is simple. Due to such modulation, the option framework is widely used representation discovery algorithms.

The framework of hierarchies of abstract machines (HAM) Andre & Russell (2000); Parr & Russell (1997) is another classic approach for hierarchically structuring a task. The framework composes policies as hierarchies of stochastic finite-state machines. The root layer decision maker decides what subtask to be performed, and each subtask is one or a collection of predefined control programs. The control programs can be a simple task like moving an arm to a specific position, and the policy learning addresses how to use these abstract actions to perform the task and ignores low-level controls. The control programs are easy to be implemented, and the combination reduces the complexity of policy learning. One major difference between HAMs and option frameworks is that HAMs restrict the available choices of actions, while option framework augments the action set. Therefore, HAMs construct a more compact representation for policies. On the other hand, HAMs require more domain knowledge to define the precise architecture, and applying this framework is more challenging for subtask identification algorithms.

There are two kinds of design to learn the policy with subtasks. One is recursive optimality, the other is hierarchical optimality. In recursive optimality, each subtask performs its task without considering the context of its parent. On the other hand, the hierarchical optimality recognizes the fact that many tasks have to consider the hierarchy relation. For example, for driving to a specific point, whether you want to stop at that point or will keep driving to the other destination influences the driving behavior; you will decelerate before reaching the point in the former case, but will keep driving in an efficient speed in the latter case. Thus, the recursive optimality is a local optimal solution compared to hierarchical optimality.

The reason to seek recursive optimality is that this kind of design removes the dependency of a subtask to its parent. Without considering the context in which a subtask is executed, it is much easier to share and re-use subtasks. The design provides a more compact representation for a task, and the idea is proposed by Dietterich (2000). The algorithm, MAXQ, separates the utility values of performing the subtask and the utility within current task after the subtask is terminated (completion value): $Q_i(s, a) = V_a(s)+C_i(s, a)$ where $V_i(s)$ is the expected cumulative rewards for executing action a on state s, and $C_i(s, a)$ is the expected cumulative rewards before subtask i ends. With this form of value function decomposition and ignoring the long term expected utility after the current task, the hierarchical utility function can be computed by a compact recursive function call. Each subtask is an independent process–its execution does not need to consider the exterior variables, or the global states. Therefore, a subtask can be implemented as a function call. The concise and compact features of MAXQ lead to subsequent works Andre & Russell (2002); Marthi et al. (2006) that adopt the design of value function decomposition and extend it to achieve hierarchical optimality.

In sequential decision making, a common approach is to model the entire task with Markov decision processes (MDPs). An MPD $< S, A, P^a_{ss'}, R^a_{ss'} >$ is composed of a set of states S, a set of actions A, a transition function specifying the transition probability from s to s' with action a, and a reward function specifying the reward from s to s' with action a. In MDPs, the action execution is represented by only the sequence of these actions, and the performance time of each action is ignored. In hierarchical reinforcement learning, each subtask may take various amount of time, and ignoring the time factor becomes sub-optimal when making decisions. The semi-Markov decision process (SMDP) is a framework that extend MDPs to consider temporal-effect. Each action has an additional time variable, and the utility of an action is its expected utility over time. The Bellman equation for calculating utility values becomes

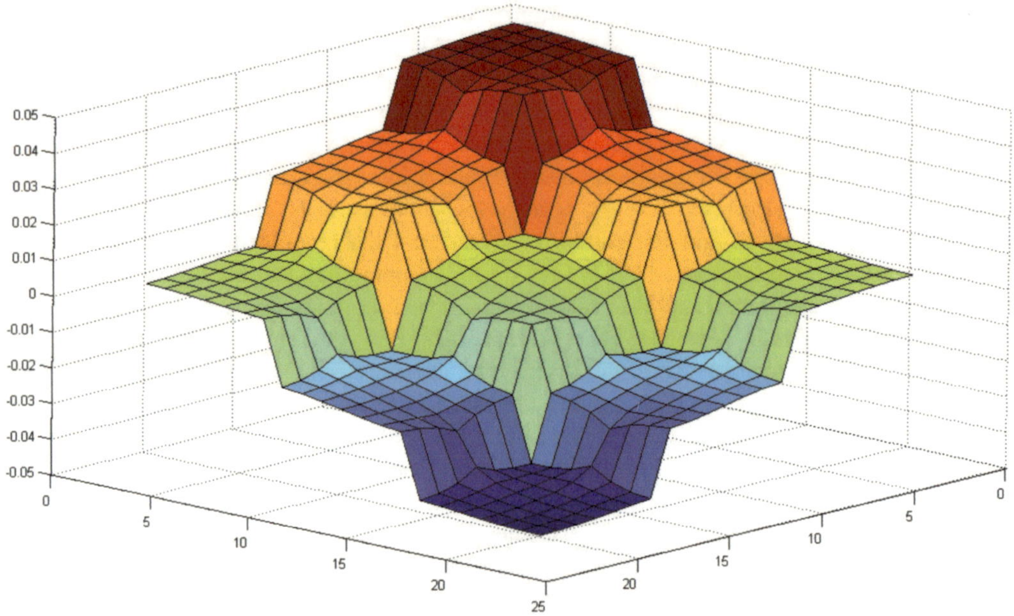

Fig. 1. The second eigenvector of the graph Laplacian on a 9-room example. Spectral graph theory has been widely applied in subgoal identification algorithms and value function approximation like Proto-value functions Mahadevan & Maggioni (2007).

$$V(s) = \max_{a \in A_s} \left[R(s,a) + \sum_{s',\tau} \gamma^{\tau} P(s',\tau | s,a) V(s') \right]$$

The policy function evaluates the utility of an action with the consideration of its various executing time, and fits the execution criterion of the subtask. Thus, this is the main model applied in hierarchical reinforcement learning.

3. Subtask identification

The fundamental works about hierarchical representation relies on manual definition for sub-tasks. This kind of design requires sufficient prior knowledge about a task, and its optimality depends on the proper construction of the hierarchical structure. Although hierarchical reinforcement learning framework provides an efficient formulation on a complex problem, the manual design requirement limits its flexibility. In many cases, we could only acquire partial solutions in problem solving that do not provide complete information for deciding a policy for states that the problem solver had not visited. These action sequences contain information for dimension reduction for the hierarchical reinforcement learning framework. The design of a HRL algorithm includes two processes, hierarchical control construction and abstractions. To formulate HRL automatically is to provide methods for performing these two processes with associated learning algorithms. This leads to researches on subtask identification and dimension reduction.

Subtask identification processes are interpreted as subgoal identification processes. Once subgoals are identified, subtasks are formulated to pursue these subgoals, and these subgoal states are the terminal conditions, and subtask policies aim for reaching the subgoals. The existing algorithms for subgoal identification can be classified into three types: (1) Identifying subgoals as states that are most relevant to a task. (2) Identifying subgoals as states that provide an easy access to the neighbor regions. (3) Constructing subtasks based on factored state space. The first case identifies subgoals as states with a high visit frequency and reward gradient Digney (1998) or as highly-visited states based on only successful trajectories McGovern & Barto (2001). Şimşek & Barto (2004) uses relative novelty as a metric to classify subgoals and non-subgoal states.

The second case defined decomposition states as access states or bottlenecks that is similar to the graph cut in graph theory. Thus, to identify bottlenecks, Menache et al. (2002) applied graph cut based on conventional network flow analysis to the whole state transition graph. Chiu & Soo (2007) use a flooding algorithm to transmit network flow between starting position and terminal position of problem solver, and take states with local maximum flood value as subgoals. Şimşek & Barto (2008) took similar idea that their approach calculates the density of shortest paths through state nodes, which is called *betweenness* in their work, and choose states with local maximum density as subgoals.

Şimşek et al. (2005) applied normalized cut based on spectral clustering approach Shi & Malik (2000) to the state transition graph updated through newly observations. The graph cut itself only provides binary separation, so they took part of state space for analysis to reduce computation complexity, and may find different results on different trials. Chiu & Soo (2010) also adopt spectral graph theory, but instead of using graph cut result, they take the smoothness property of the spectral theory. With the spectral analysis, the edges with local maximum differences are considered bottleneck edges, and their connecting nodes are bottleneck states. Mannor et al. (2004) proposed a clustering method to identify blocks which are densely connected inside but weakly connected in between. The algorithm also finds multiple separations.

HEXQ Hengst (2002) evaluates the updating frequencies of variables to rank their hierarchy. The idea is that variables which change often tend to be at lower level of hierarchy, just as variables in the inner loop will change more often. The framework constructs options based on the projected graph. The heuristic considers one variable at a time, and can not model causal relations with more than one variable. Thus, Jonsson & Barto (2006) and Mehta et al. (2008) took dynamic Bayesian network to model the causal relation. Their work requires a pre-constructed dynamic Bayesian network.

Most of works for subgoal identifications are based on discrete domains. Konidaris & Barto (2009) proposed skill chaining to find options in continuous domain. The idea is similar to the LQR-tree mechanism which builds a tree gradually via sampling points in the state space, and finds a trajectory to link to the tree. Skill chaining takes other options' boundary as terminal states and creates a new option to link to the existing option sets.

4. Redundancy reduction

Identifying subgoals from a problem only completes the half job. The benefit of constructing hierarchical reinforcement learning is its potential for redundancy reduction, and it is easier for a programmer to implement the subtask policies. Redundancy reduction scaled down the complexity of a problem in order to help the learning process, which can be done by eliminating irrelevant parameters for decision making. Givan et al. (2003) proposed a notion of equivalence in which states can be merged without losing optimality. The states are aggregated together if they have the same rewards and state transitions. The approach is applied on factored representation, and is guaranteed to be optimal. In the work of constructing basis functions for hierarchical reinforcement learning Osentoski & Mahadevan (2010), they used a graph reduction method to merge nodes connected to the same set of vertices, having the same edge labels, and a subset of their variables are the same.

Jong & Stone (2005) proposed a statistical hypothesis-testing approach to evaluate the relevance of state parameters. The method took the p-value of a single state to represent the overall projection result on a projected state. The algorithm defines the irrelevance of a state parameter if there is an action that is optimal among states that differ within only the parameter. Then all states projecting onto that state could share a unique optimal decision making without the state parameter, and the state parameters of this projection is apparently irrelevant. The irrelevant parameter analysis requires an optimal value function to determine the relevance of state parameters for decision making. Thus, the analysis can not help current problem, but the derived knowledge can be applied on similar problems to remove irrelevant parameters. The approach is applied on general MDPs, but it does not guarantee the optimality of abstractions.

Chiu & Soo (2010) proposed to use analysis of variance to derive irrelevant parameters from incomplete data, namely, a partial near-optimal solution. They defined irrelevant state parameters as parameters that do not affect the policy function. In other words, the value distribution of a policy function should be at least similar if not exactly identical among states that differ only on that state parameter. The similarity of distributions is compared via the variance analysis. The analysis estimates the policy function value distribution of a state and its projected states, and takes the mean and variance from the value distribution of the projected states onto that state. It estimates the approximate distribution before the value function is exactly calculated.

5. Conclusions

We survey some recent works about subgoal identification and redundancy reduction. Conventional reinforcement learning algorithms runs in polynomial time, but for most of the problems, this cost is not practical. Hierarchical reinforcement learning is one of the approaches to make this framework infeasible. The abstraction mechanism in hierarchical reinforcement learning not only plays the role of dimension reduction. Via assigning low level works to some simple programs, the new framework maps the problem into a architecture that closer to the style that human used to adopt for problem solving. Hierarchical reinforcement learning brings another thought of design for the programmer to define the problem, which makes problem solving much easier. Hierarchical reinforcement learning depends on temporal-extended actions, and there are many existing works proposed for constructing these actions. These works improve the performance of reinforcement learning to some extent, but the gains are not significant enough to scale down most of the complex problems. A good way to construct a compact reinforcement learning is an open problem, and is an important issue required further focus in the field of reinforcement learning.

6. References

Andre, D. & Russell, S. J. (2000). Programmable reinforcement learning agents, *in* T. K. Leen, T. G. Dietterich & V. Tresp (eds), *NIPS*, MIT Press, pp. 1019–1025.

Andre, D. & Russell, S. J. (2002). State abstraction for programmable reinforcement learning agents, *AAAI/IAAI*, pp. 119–125.

Chiu, C.-C. & Soo, V.-W. (2007). Subgoal identification for reinforcement learning and planning in multiagent problem solving, *MATES '07: Proceedings of the 5th German conference on Multiagent System Technologies*, Springer-Verlag, Berlin, Heidelberg, pp. 37–48.

Chiu, C.-C. & Soo, V.-W. (2010). Automatic complexity reduction in reinforcement learning, *Computational Intelligence* 26(1): 1–25.

Chiu, C.-C. and Soo, V.-W. (2010), AUTOMATIC COMPLEXITY REDUCTION IN REINFORCEMENT LEARNING. Computational Intelligence, 26: 1–25.

Şimşek, O. & Barto, A. G. (2004). Using relative novelty to identify useful temporal abstractions in reinforcement learning, *ICML '04: Proceedings of the twenty-first international conference on Machine learning*, ACM, New York, NY, USA, p. 95.

Şimşek, O. & Barto, A. G. (2008). Skill characterization based on betweenness, *in* D. Koller, D. Schuurmans, Y. Bengio & L. Bottou (eds), *NIPS*, MIT Press, pp. 1497–1504.

Şimşek, O., Wolfe, A. P. & Barto, A. G. (2005). Identifying useful subgoals in reinforcement learning by local graph partitioning, *ICML '05: Proceedings of the 22nd international conference on Machine learning*, ACM, New York, NY, USA, pp. 816–823.

Dietterich, T. G. (2000). Hierarchical reinforcement learning with the maxq value function decomposition, *J. Artif. Intell. Res. (JAIR)* 13: 227–303.

Digney, B. (1998). Learning hierarchical control structure for multiple tasks and changing environments, *Proceedings of the Fifth Conference on the Simulation of Adaptive Behavior: SAB 98*.

Givan, R., Dean, T. & Greig, M. (2003). Equivalence notions and model minimization in markov decision processes, *Artif. Intell.* 147(1-2): 163–223.

Hengst, B. (2002). Discovering hierarchy in reinforcement learning with hexq, *ICML '02: Proceedings of the Nineteenth International Conference on Machine Learning*, Morgan Kaufmann Publishers Inc., San Francisco, CA, USA, pp. 243–250.

Jong, N. K. & Stone, P. (2005). State abstraction discovery from irrelevant state variables, *IJCAI'05: Proceedings of the 19th international joint conference on Artificial intelligence*, Morgan Kaufmann Publishers Inc., San Francisco, CA, USA, pp. 752–757.

Jonsson, A. & Barto, A. (2006). Causal graph based decomposition of factored mdps, *J. Mach. Learn. Res.* 7: 2259–2301.

Konidaris, G. & Barto, A. (2009). Skill discovery in continuous reinforcement learning domains using skill chaining, *in* Y. Bengio, D. Schuurmans, J. Lafferty, C. K. I. Williams & A. Culotta (eds), *Advances in Neural Information Processing Systems 22*, pp. 1015– 1023.

Mahadevan, S. & Maggioni, M. (2007). Proto-value functions: A laplacian framework for learning representation and control in markov decision processes, *Journal of Machine Learning Research* 8: 2169–2231.

Mannor, S., Menache, I., Hoze, A. & Klein, U. (2004). Dynamic abstraction in reinforcement learning via clustering, *ICML '04: Proceedings of the twenty-first international conference on Machine learning*, ACM, New York, NY, USA, p. 71.

Marthi, B., Russell, S. J. & Andre, D. (2006). A compact, hierarchical q-function decomposition, *UAI*, AUAI Press.

McGovern, A. & Barto, A. G. (2001). Automatic discovery of subgoals in reinforcement learning using diverse density, *ICML '01: Proceedings of the Eighteenth International Conference on Machine Learning*, Morgan Kaufmann Publishers Inc., San Francisco, CA, USA, pp. 361–368.

Mehta, N., Ray, S., Tadepalli, P. & Dietterich, T. (2008). Automatic discovery and transfer of maxq hierarchies, *ICML '08: Proceedings of the 25th international conference on Machine learning*, ACM, New York, NY, USA, pp. 648–655.

Menache, I., Mannor, S. & Shimkin, N. (2002). Q-cut - dynamic discovery of sub-goals in reinforcement learning, *ECML '02: Proceedings of the 13th European Conference on Machine Learning*, Springer-Verlag, London, UK, pp. 295–306.

Osentoski, S. & Mahadevan, S. (2010). Basis function construction for hierarchical reinforcement learning, *AAMAS '10: Proceedings of the 9th International Conference on Autonomous Agents and Multiagent Systems*, International Foundation for Autonomous Agents and Multiagent Systems, Richland, SC, pp. 747–754.

Parr, R. & Russell, S. J. (1997). Reinforcement learning with hierarchies of machines, *in* M. I. Jordan, M. J. Kearns & S. A. Solla (eds), *NIPS*, The MIT Press.

Shi, J. & Malik, J. (2000). Normalized cuts and image segmentation, *IEEE Trans. Pattern Anal. Mach. Intell.* 22(8): 888–905.

Sutton, R. S., Precup, D. & Singh, S. P. (1999). Between mdps and semi-mdps: A framework for temporal abstraction in reinforcement learning, *Artif. Intell.* 112(1-2): 181–211.

11

A Reinforcement Learning System Embedded Agent with Neural Network-Based Adaptive Hierarchical Memory Structure

Masanao Obayashi, Kenichiro Narita, Yohei Okamoto,
Takashi Kuremoto, Kunikazu Kobayashi and Liangbing Feng
Yamaguchi University
Japan

1. Introduction

In this chapter, a way to realize intellectualization of robots (called "agents" here) is considered. We intend to achieve this by mimicing an intellectual way of human. Human learns many kinds of things from incidents driven by own actions and reflects them on the subsequent action as own experiences. These experiences are memorized in his/her brain and recollected and reused if necessary. In other words, human is not good at doing anything at first, but he/she will memory the meaningful things among his/her own experiences, at the same time oblivious of other memories without understood by him/her. He/She will accumulate knowledge gotten by experiences, and will make use of them when encounters unexperienced things.

The subject in this chapter is to realize the things mentioned above on agents. To be specific, the agent will be equipped with three main functions: "learning" taking out of the meaningful things from through experiences with trial and error, "memorization" memorizing the above meaningful things, and "the ability of associative recollection and its appropriate use" suitable for the situation. Of course, when it doesn't have such appropriate memories, the agent will learn them additively and moreover memorize them as new experiences. Repeating these processes, the agent will be more intellectual. In this intellectualization, there are a few models related to subject mentioned above, e.g., K-series model and their discrete KA-series model (D. Harter *et al.*, 2005 [1]) and DARWIN X-series models (J. L. Krichmar *et al.*, 2005 [2]). K-series and KA-series models have been developped by R. Kozuma and his colleagues. Their models are equipped with chaotic neurodynamics, which is very important to realize the brain model, hippocampal model and supervised learnimg ability. DARWIN X-series models have been developped by Edelman and his colleagues since 1981. Their models are also equipped with hippocampal model of spatial, episodic, and associative meory model. These two series models intend to realize the brain faithfully.

We have studied about this theme since 2006 [3] ~ [8]. This time our proposed model is not necessarily to realize the human brain faithfully, and intends to realize intellectualization of the agent functionally. At first we will introduce "reinforcement learning (RL, Sutton *et al.*, 1998 [9])", as experienced learning through trial and error, which is a learning algorithm based on calculation of reward and penalty given through mutual action between the agent and the environment, and which is commonly executed in living things.

In the reinforcement learning, memorizing the environment and the agent's action corresponding to it as short term memory (STM), the agent will take out the meaningful thing from them, then it will memorize its refined information as long term memory (LTM). As a medium of this LTM, we will introduce Chaotic Neural Networks (CNNs, Aihara *et al.*, 1997 [10][11]) which is generally acknowledged to be an associative memory model of the brain. The memory structure takes the form of the adaptive hierarchical memory structure so as to deal with the increase of information. The structure consists of CNNs in consideration of the adjustment to non-MDP (Markov Decision Process) environment. When the agent is placed in a certain environment, the agent will search the appropriate experienced information in LTM. In such case of searching, as the mechanism of memory search, we introduce self-organizing maps (SOM, T. Kohonen, 2001 [12]) to find the appropriate experience. In fact, during the agent's exploration of the information adapting to the environment, the time series environmental information is necessary, so, we use the feedback SOM that its output is feedback to input layer to deal with the time series information. The whole structure of the our proposed system is shown in Fig. 1. To show the example of realization of the agent composed of functions mentioned above and the effectiveness of these methods, we carried out the simulation applied to the goal-oriented maze problem shown in Figs. 11,14.

As a result, it was verified that the agent constructed by our proposed idea would work well by making use of the experienced information, refer to Fig. 14, in unexperienced large scale goal-oriented maze problems and it got the goal in just about shortest steps. See Fig. 14.

2. Proposed system structure

The proposed system consists of three parts: memory, learning and discrimination. The memory consists of short-term memory (STM) and long-term memory (LTM). Figure 1 shows these overall structure.

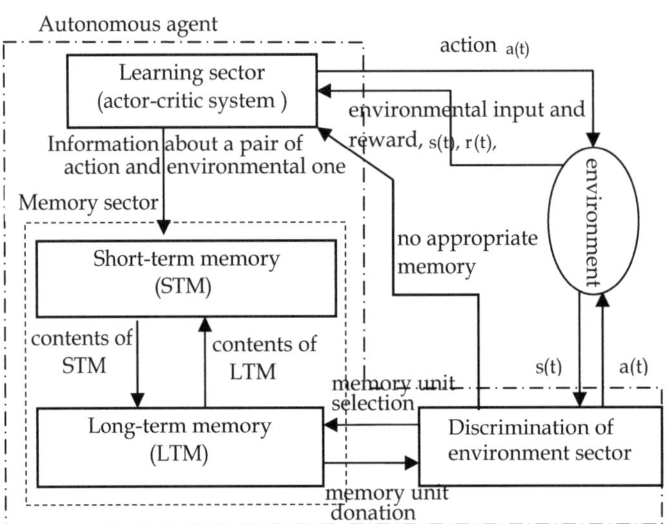

Fig. 1. Structure of the proposed RL embedded agent with adaptive hierarchical memory

Learning sector: actor-critic system is adopted. It learns the choice of appropriate actions to maximize the total predictive rewards obtained over the future considering the environmental information *s(t)* and reward *r(t)* as a result of executing action *a(t)*. Memory sector: memory setor consists of short-term-momory (STM) and long-term momory (LTM). Here, STM: it memorizes the learned path of the information (environmental information and its corresponding action) obtained in Learning sector. Unnecessary information is forgotten and only useful information is stored. LTM: it memorizes only the enough sophisticated and useful experience in STM. Environment discrimination sector: environment discrimination sector consists of initial operation part and environment discrimination part. This sector plays the role that the agent examines the environment through the agent's own behaviors and selects the memorized infromation in LTM corresponding to the current environment.

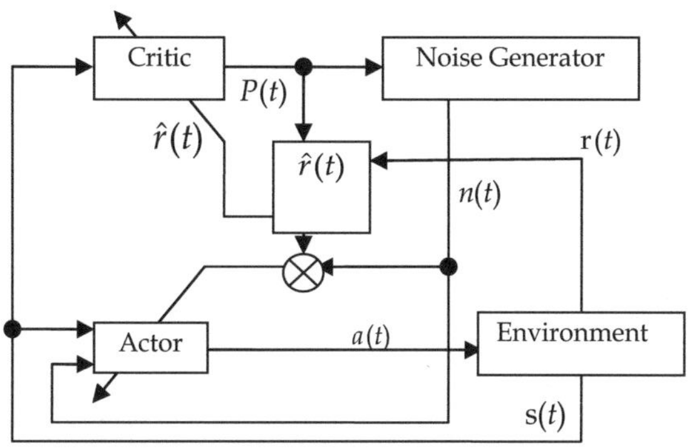

Fig. 2. The construction of the actor-critic system

3. Actor-critic reinforcement learning

Reinforcement learning (RL, Sutton *et al.*, 1998 [9]), as experienced learning through trial and error, which is a learning algorithm based on calculation of reward and penalty given through mutual action between the agent and the environment, and which is commonly executed in living things. The actor-critic method is one of representative reinforcement learning methods. We adopt it because of its flexibility to deal with both continuous and discrete state-action space environment. The structure of the actor-critic reinforcement learning system is shown in Fig. 2. The actor plays a role of a controller and the critic plays role of an evaluator in control field. Noise plays a part of roles to search the optimal action.

3.1 Structure and learning of critic

3.1.1 Structure of critic

Figure 3 shows the structure of the actor. The function of the critic is calculation of *P(t)*: the prediction value of sum of the discounted rewards that will be gotten over the future. Of course, if the value of *P(t)* becomes bigger, the performance of the system becomes better. These are shortly explained as follows:
The sum of the discounted rewards that will be gotten over the future is defined as *V(t)*.

$$V(t) \equiv \sum_{l=0}^{\infty} \gamma^{n} \cdot r(t+l), \tag{1}$$

where γ ($0 \le \gamma < 1$) is a constant parameter called discount rate.

Equation (1) is rewritten as

$$V(t) = r(t) + \gamma V(t+1). \tag{2}$$

Here the prediction value of $V(t)$ is defined as $P(t)$.
The prediction error $\hat{r}(t)$ is expressed as follows:

$$\hat{r}(t) = \hat{r}_t = r(t) + \gamma P(t+1) - P(t). \tag{3}$$

The parameters of the critic are adjusted to reduce this prediction error $\hat{r}(t)$. In our case the prediction value $P(t)$ is calculated as an output of a radial basis function neural network (RBFN) such as,

$$P(t) = \sum_{j=0}^{J} \omega_j^c y_j^c(t), \tag{4}$$

$$y_j^c(t) = \exp\left[-\sum_{i=1}^{n} (s_i(t) - m_{ij})^2 / \sigma_{ij}^2 \right]. \tag{5}$$

Here, $y_j^c(t)$: jth node's output of the middle layer of the critic at time t, ω_j^c: the weight of jth output of the middle layer of the critic, $s_i(t)$: i th state of the environment at time t, m_{ij} and σ_{ij}: center and dispersion in the i th input of j th node basis function, respectively, J: the number of nodes in the middle layer of the critic, n: the number of the states of the system (see Fig. 3).

3.1.2 Learning of parameters of critic

Learning of parameters of the critic is done by using commonly used back propagation method which makes prediction error $\hat{r}(t)$ go to zero. Updating rule of parameters are as follows:

$$\Delta\omega_i^c = -\eta_c \cdot \frac{\partial \hat{r}_t^2}{\partial \omega_i^c}, \quad (i = 1, \cdots, J). \tag{6}$$

Here η_c is a small positive value of learning coefficient.

3.2. Structure and learning of actor

3.2.1 Structure of actor

Figure 4 shows the structure of the actor. The actor plays the role of controller and outputs the control signal, action $a(t)$, to the environment. The actor basically also consists of radial basis function networks. The jth basis function of the middle layer node of the actor is as follows:

$$y_j^a(t) = \exp\left[-\sum_{i=1}^{n} (s_i(t) - m_{ij})^2 / \sigma_{ij}^2 \right], \tag{7}$$

$$a(t) = u_k(t) = \sum_{j=1}^{J} \omega_{kj} y_j^a(t) + n(t), \quad (k = 1, \cdots, K). \tag{8}$$

Here y_j^a : jth node's output of the middle layer of the actor, m_{ij} and σ_{ij} : center and dispersion in ith input of jth node basis function of the actor, respectively, K: the number of the actions, $n(t)$: additive noise, u_k : representative value of kth action, ω_{kj} : connection weight from jth node of the middle layer to kth output node. The action selection method to choose the representative u_k among all the candidates of actions is described at section 3.3.

3.2.2 Noise generator

Noise generator let selection of the output of the actor have diversity by making use of the noise. It comes to realize the learning of the trial and error according to the results of performance of the system by executing the selected action. Generation of the noise *n(t)* is as follows:

$$n(t) = n_t = noise_t \cdot \min\left(1, \exp(-P(t))\right), \tag{9}$$

where $noise_t$ is uniform random number of $[-1, 1]$, min $(\cdot)$: minimum of $\cdot$. As the $P(t)$ will be bigger (this means that the selected action goes close to the optimal action), the noise will be smaller. This leads to the stable learning of the actor.

3.2.3 Learning of parameters of actor

Parameters of the actor, ω_{kj}^a $(k = 1,...K, j = 1,\cdots,J)$, are adjusted by using the results of executing the output of the actor, i.e., the prediction error $\hat{r}_t$ and noise. k is the number of the selected and executed actions at the previous time.

$$\Delta\omega_{kj}^a = \eta_a \cdot n_t \cdot \hat{r}_t \cdot \frac{\partial u_k(t)}{\partial \omega_{kj}^a}. \tag{10}$$

$\eta_a (> 0)$ is the learning coefficient. Equation (10) means that $(-n_t \cdot \hat{r}_t)$ is considered as an error, ω_{kj}^a is adjusted as opposite to sign of $(-n_t \cdot \hat{r}_t)$. In other words, as a result of executing $u_k(t)$, e.g., if the sign of the additive noise is positive and the sign of the prediction error is positive, positive additive noise is sucess, so the value of ω_{kj}^a should be increased (see Eq. (8)), and vice versa.

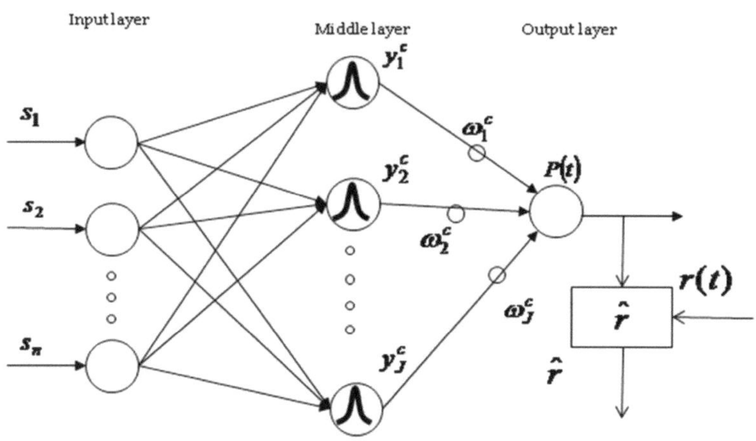

Fig. 3. Structure of the critic

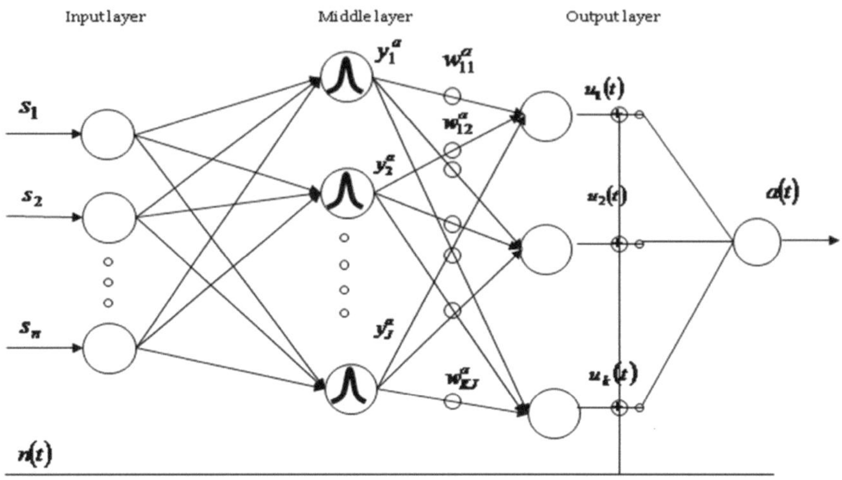

Fig. 4. Structure of the actor

3.3 Action selection method

The action u_b at time t is selected stochastically using Gibbs distribution Eq. (11).

$$P(u_b \mid \mathbf{s}(t)) = \frac{\exp(u_b(t)/T)}{\sum_{k=1}^{K} \exp(u_k(t)/T)}. \tag{11}$$

Here, $P(a_b \mid \mathbf{s}(t))$: selection probability of bth action u_b, T: a positive constant called temperature constant.

4. Hierarchical memory system

4.1 Associative Chaotic Neural Network (ACNN)

Chaotic Neural Network (CNN) has been developpped by Aihara *et al.*, 1997 [10][11]), which is generally acknowledged to be an associative memory model of the brain. CNN is constructed with chaotic neuron models that have refractory and continuous output value. Its useful usage is as an associative memory network named ACNN. The followings are the dynamics of ACNN.

$$x_i(t+1) = f(v_i(t+1) + z_i(t+1)), \tag{12}$$

$$v_i(t+1) = k_r \cdot v_i(t) - \alpha \cdot x_i(t) + a_i, \tag{13}$$

$$z_i(t+1) = k_f \cdot z_i(t) + \sum_{j=1}^{L} \omega_{ij} x_j(t), \tag{14}$$

$$\omega_{ij} = \frac{1}{U} \sum_{p=1}^{U} (x_i^p \cdot x_j^p). \tag{15}$$

$x_i(t)$: output of the ith neuron at step t, $v_i(t)$: internal state with respect to refractory of the ith neuron at step t, $z_i(t)$: internal state of the ith neuron with respect to mutual operation at step t, $f(\cdot)$: sigmoid function, ω_{ij} : connection weight from jth neuron to ith neuron, x_i^p : ith element of pth stored pattern, k_r : damping coefficient on refractory, k_f : damping coefficient on feedback, α : constant parameter, a_i : compound parameter with threshold and external input of ith neuron, $i, j = 1, \cdots, L$, L : the number of neurons in the CNN, U : the number of the stored patterns.

4.2 Network control

The dynamics of ACNN behaves chaotically or no-chaotically according to the value of the damping coefficient on refractory k_r. We would like the network to behave chaotically at first and to converge to one of the stored patterns when the state of the network becomes close to one of the stored patterns. Here, to realize this, we define network control as the control which makes transition of network from chaotic state to non-chaotic one by changing of the specified parameter k_r and vice versa. The network control algorithm of ACNN is shown in Fig. 5. The change of states of ACNN is defined by $\Delta x(t)$, total change of internal state $x(t)$ temporally, and when $\Delta x(t)$ is less than a predefined threshold value θ, the chaotic retrieval of ACNN is stopped by changing values of the parameter k_r into small one. As a result, the network converges to a stored pattern near the current network state.

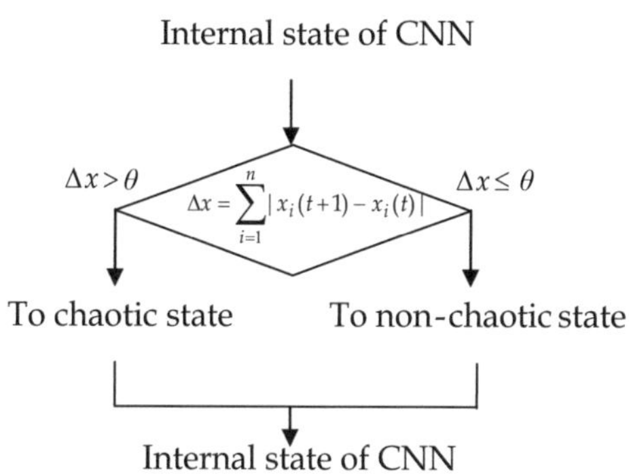

Fig. 5. Flow of the network control algorithm

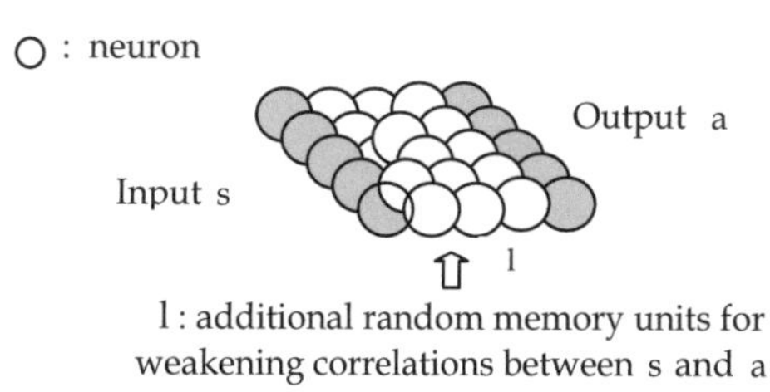

Fig. 6. Memory configuration of ACNN

4.3 Mutual associative type ACNN (MACNN)

4.3.1 Short-Term Memory (STM)

We make use of ACNN as a mutual associative memory system, called MACNN, namely, auto-associative memory matrix W_s is constructed with environmental inputs $s(t)$ and their corresponding actions $a(t)$ (refer to Fig. 6) . When $s(t)$ is set as a part of the initial states of the ACNN, the ACNN retrieves $a(t)$ with $s(t)$ and $l(t)$, using the way of the described operation at 4.2. l is a random vector to weaken the correlation between $s(t)$ and $a(t)$. The update equation of the memory matrix W_s is described as Eq. (16), here, λ_s is a forgetting coefficient, and η_s is a learning coefficient. λ_s is set to small, because that at the initial and middle learning stage W_s is not important. In case that these **s**, **l**, a are applied to MACNN, i.e., Eqs. (12) to (15), **s**, **l**, a are corresponding to $x_i(t)(i=1,..., L)$ through Eq. (15), its matrix type, Eq. (16).

$$W_S^{new} = \lambda_s \cdot W_S^{old} + \eta_S \begin{bmatrix} \mathbf{s}^T & \mathbf{l}^T & a \end{bmatrix}^T \begin{bmatrix} \mathbf{s}^T & \mathbf{l}^T & a \end{bmatrix} . \tag{16}$$

STM as one unit consists of plural MACNNs, and one MACNN memorizes information for one environmental state and action patterns (see Fig. 7). For example, STM has path information from start to goal on only one maze searching problem.

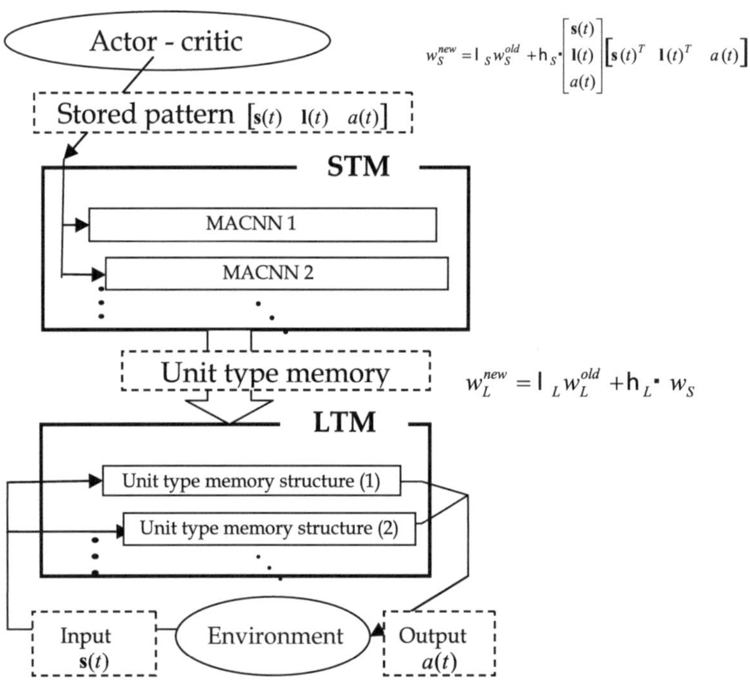

Fig. 7. Adaptive hierarchical memory structure

4.3.2 Long-Term Memory (LTM)

LTM consists of plural units. LTM memorizes enough refined information in STM as one unit (refer to Fig. 7). For example, when actor-critic learning has accomplished for a certain maze problem, information in LTM is updated as follows: In case that the current maze problem has not been experienced, the stored matrix W_L is set by Eq. (17) :

$$W_L = W_S . \tag{17}$$

In case that the current maze has been experienced and present learning is additive learning, the stored matrix is updated by Eq. (18);

$$W_L^{new} = \lambda_L \cdot W_L^{old} + \eta_L W_S \cdot \tag{18}$$

λ_L is a forgetting coefficient, and η_L is a learning coefficient. λ_L is set to large value as same as one of η_L so as not to forget previous stored patterns.

4.4 Adaptive hierarchical memory structure

Fig. 7 shows the whole configuration of the adaptive hierarchical memory structure. When an environmental state is given to the agent, at first it is sent to LTM for confirming whether it already exists in the memory or not. If it is the same as the stored information, the recalled action corresponding to it is executed, otherwise, it is used to learn at the actor-critic system. After learning the pair of the enough refined and trained environmental state s and action a in STM is sent to LTM to be stored. If it comes to be different from the stored pattern on the way to use, information about it in LTM is used to relearn at the actor-critic system in STM.

5. Discrimination of the environment

The information that the agent got through its own experienced and momorized is used to discriminate whether it is applicable to the current environment, or not. In this section, the structure of the environment discrimination and how to discriminate it are explained. The discrimination of environment is composed of the initial operation part and the memory selection part.

5.1 Initial operation

To decide whether the agent has the momory corrresponding to the current environment, the agent behaves with next features,

i. The agent behaves predefined n_{init} steps randomly without use of its own memory.
ii. The agent behaves according to two rules: One is that the agent does not return back to the paths which the agent passed during this initial operation, the other is that the agent does not strike the wall. These rules make the speedy search and collection of the information of the agent possible.

5.2 Discrimination of the environment using feedback SOM

The agent discriminates the environment by the feedback SOM. The feedback SOM consists of three layers: input layer, competition layer and output feedback layer. The sturucture of the feedback SOM is shown in Fig. 8. At first the agent investigates the evironment by executing the initial operation. In the initial opereation, during the n_{init} steps, the winner occurs every each steps, i.e., the number of n_{init} comes into winners. Using these data, the agent discriminates the environment. Concretely the agent gets these data for all the environment the agent faced and memorizes the time series of winners. When the agent is placed at the undiscriminated situation, the agent begins the initial operation and gets the above data and compares them with memorized data that is refined about specified environment through the actor-critic learning. If two data agree, after then the agent behaves using the memorized data, especially, action. In the opposite case, the agent begins learning about the current environment using the actor-critic system. The algorithm of the feedback SOM to get the time series data of the winners for each step of the initial operation about the environment is as follows:

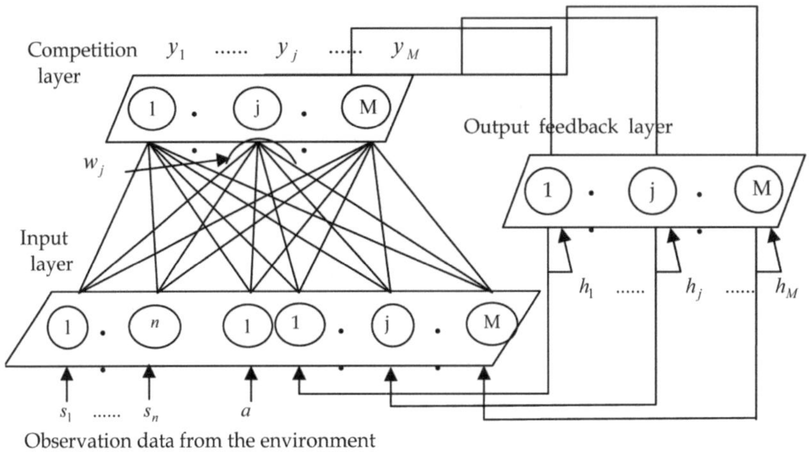

Fig. 8. The used feedback SOM

Algorithm of the feedback SOM

Step 1. Set random small values to the connenction weights

$$w_{ji}(j=1,\cdots,M, i=1,\cdots,n+M) .$$

Step 2. Give the input signal to the input layer as follows:

$$\begin{aligned} I(t) &= \{\mathbf{s}(t), a(t); \beta \mathbf{h}(t-1)\} \\ &= \{s_1(t),\cdots,s_n(t), a(t); \beta h_1(t-1),\cdots,\beta h_M(t-1)\}, \end{aligned} \tag{19}$$

where $I(t)$: input vector at time t, $s_i(t)$: ith observation data from environment, $h_j(t)$: feedaback data from competition at time, β is a positive constant representing the rate of considering the history information, n: the number of environmental states, M : the number of outputs of the competition layer.

Step 3. Calculate the distance d_j between the input vector and all the neurons in the competitive layer at time t.

$$d_j = \sqrt{\sum_{i=1}^{n+1+M} (I_i(t) - w_{ji})^2} , \quad (j=1,\cdots,M). \tag{20}$$

Step 4. Find the neuron j^* (called the winner neuron) which has the smallest distance d_{j^*} and calculate y_i as follows :

$$\begin{aligned} j^* &= \arg\min_{1\le j\le M} d_j \\ y_j(t) &= \begin{cases} 1, & j = j^*. \\ 0, & j \ne j^* \end{cases} \end{aligned} \tag{21}$$

Step 5. Calculate the output of neurons in the output feedback layer as follows :

$$h_j(t) = (1-\gamma) y_j(t) + \gamma h_j(t-1) , \tag{22}$$

where γ is a positive constant retaining the past information.

Step 6. Update the values of connection weights of the winner neuron and around it as follows :

$$w_j(k) = w_j(k-1) + \eta\Lambda(j,j^*)\{I(t) - w_j(k-1)\}$$
$$\Lambda(j,j^*) = \exp(-\frac{||j-j^*||}{\sigma^2}) \quad , \qquad (23)$$

Step 7. where $w_j(k)$: jth connection weight vector in the competition layer, η is a positive learning coefficient, k is repetition number of renewal of the weights, and σ is deviation from the center and then σ become smaller according to progress of the learning.

Step 8. Repeat Step 2 to Step 6 until the predefined times is over.

5.3 Selection of the memorized information corresponding to the current environment

Figure 9 shows the flow of the memorized environment selection in the case of $n_{init} = 5$. In the figure, during $n_{init} = 5$ steps, the number 1 and number 3 of the memorized environments were selected three times at time t, t-3, t-4 and two times at time t-1, t-2, respectively.

Threshold set algorithm of the memorized environment selection

Step 1. After learning of the feedback SOM, give the environment to the feedback SOM again to decide the value of threshold.

Step 2. Repeat the initial operation ($= n_{init}$ steps) n_{repeat} times and get the data of $n_{init} \times n_{repeat}$ neurons which won.

Step 3. Record the number of firing (winning) times of each neuron in the neurons of competition layer in $n_{init} \times n_{repeat}$ data.

Step 4. Repeat from Step 1 to Step 3 until finishing of records of above firing times for all environments.

Step 5. Fix the threshold (*threshold_win*) to decide whether the winner neuron corresponding memorized environment is adopted or not as a winner neuron.

Selection algorithm of the environment in the memorized environments in LTM

Step 1. Put the agent on the start point in the environment.

Step 2. Start the initial operation (n_{init} steps) and get the information of the observation and action at the each 1 step operation.

Step 3. Decide the winner neuron by the above information for each step.

Step 4. Calculate each total number of winner neurons which are corresponding to each memorized environment as follows:

Comparison the winner neuron in the current environment with the winner neuron in the memorized environment.

```
if (win_{i,win_neuron} > threshold_ win)
   count_i = count_i+1;
```

win_{ij} : firing number of jth neuron of the ith memory

threshold_ win: threshold to decide whether the neuron is adopted or not as a winner neuron

$count_i$: total number of winner neurons corresponding to the ith memorized environment

Step 5. Repeat from Step 3 to Step 4 until the agent finishes the initial operation of n_{init} steps.
Step 6. Select the maximum count for each memorized environment
Step 7. Distinguish whether the ith memorized environment with the selected count is able to correspond to the current environment by next process:

```
if (count_i ≥threshold_count)
    the agent may have the memory corresponding to the current
    environment , go to Step 8,
else
    the agent may not have the memory corresponding to the current
    environment, go to learning process.
    threshold_ count:  threshold to distinguish whether the selected
    memorized environment is adopted or not
```

Step 8. Request the tender of MACNN unit corresponding to the current environment.
Step 9. Start the recollection by the MACNN unit.
Step 10. When the behavior by recollection using MACNN failed, that is, the agent goes into the wall or goes over the predefined steps before arrival of the goal, Go Step 2.

Note: In the simulation of the next section, n_{init}, n_{repeat}, $threshold\_win$ and $threshold\_count$ are set to 5, 30, 10 , 4, respectively

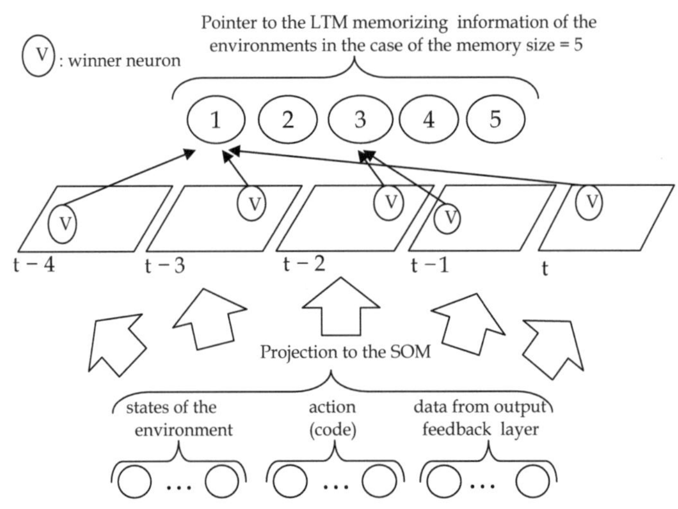

Fig. 9. Flow of the memorized environment selection in the case of n_{init}=5

6. Simulation

In this study, our proposed method is applied for the agent to find, memorize, recollect and reuse the optimal paths of the plural small and large scale mazes.

6.1 Simulation condition

An agent can perceive whether there is aisle or not at the forward, right-forward, left-forward, right, and left as the state s of the environment (refer to Fig. 10). An agent can move 1 lattice to forward, back, left, and right as action a (see Table 1). Therefore in actor-critic, a state s of the environment consists of 20 inputs (n = 5 directions ×4 lattice in Fig. 10) in Fig. 8. The content of an input is defined as the distance from the agent to wall, and has value of 1, 2, 3, and 4. In the case that there is a wall next to the agent, the content of input is value 1, and so on. The number of kinds of action a is 4 (= K in Fig. 4). The number of hidden nodes of RBFN is equal to 32 (=J) in Fig. 3 and 4. And the number of units l is equal to 21 in Fig. 6. When the agent gets the goal, it is given the reward, 1.0. For the case of a collision with wall, reward is -1.0, and for each action except for collision is - 0.1. Flow of the whole algorithm of the simulation is shown in Table 2.

	up	down	left	right
code	1000	0100	0010	0001

Table 1. Action and its code taken by the agent

<table>
<tr><td colspan="3">Flow of the whole algorithm of the simulation</td></tr>
<tr><td colspan="3">Step 1 : Set the maze to the agent.</td></tr>
<tr><td colspan="3">Step 2 : Begin the initial operation (n_{init}. steps).</td></tr>
<tr><td colspan="3">Step 3 : Distinguish whether the memorized environment selected by the result of the initial opereation is adopted or not.</td></tr>
<tr><td colspan="2">In the case of existence of
the appropriate memorized environment</td><td>In the case of absence of
the appropriate memorized environment</td></tr>
<tr><td colspan="2">Step4 : Start the behavior using the selected unit memory in LTM.</td><td>Step 4 : Switch to learn the maze by actor-critic method.</td></tr>
<tr><td>Arrival to the goal</td><td>Failure of recollecction</td><td>Step 5 : Switch to learn the MACNN and the feedback SOM by use of the data of learning sector (Step 4).</td></tr>
<tr><td>Step 5 : End of the process</td><td>Step 5 : Go back to Step 2</td><td>Step 6: Set the label of the winner neuron to select the memrized environment .</td></tr>
<tr><td colspan="2">Step 6 : Go back to Step 1</td><td>Step 7 : Go back to Step 1.</td></tr>
</table>

Table 2. Flow of the whole algorithm of the simulation

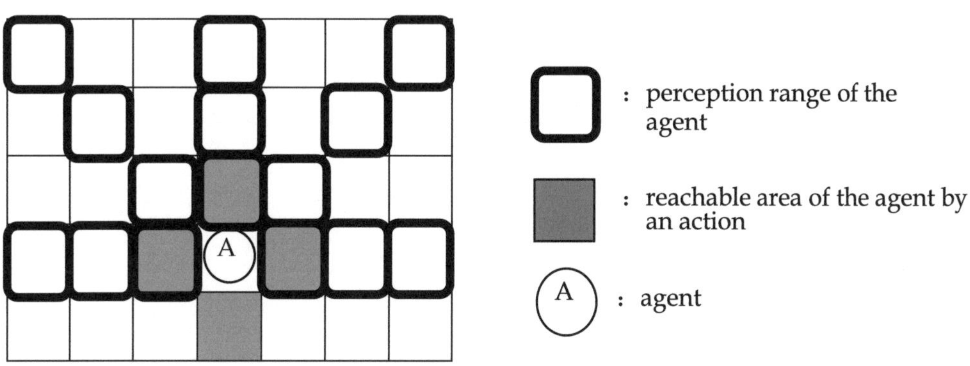

Fig. 10. Ability of perception and action of the agent

6.2 Parameters used in the simulation

Parameters used in this simulation are shown in Table 3-4. These parameters are decided by trial and error. The number of mutual retrieval Systems(MACNNs) is 11 in STM and call this layers 1
unit memory structure (see Fig. 7). LTM has 4 units type memory structure to memorize 4 mazes (see Figs. 7 and 11). Table 1 shows the number of kinds of actions and their codes taken by the agent.

Parameters used in actor-critic			
σ width coefficient	0.1	η_a learning coefficient	0.7
η_c learning coefficient	0.7	γ discount rate	0.85
T temperature coefficient	0.4 (within 3steps)	T temperature coefficient	0.1 (more than 3 steps)
Forgetting and Learning coefficients used in memory sector			
λ_S forgetting coefficient for STM	0.89	η_S learning coefficient for STM	1.00
λ_L forgetting coefficient for LTM	1.00	η_L learning coefficient for LTM	1.00
Network control parameters of MACNN			
	Chaos / Non-chaos		Chaos / Non-chaos
α constant parameter	10.0/1.00	k_r damping coefficient of refractory	0.99/0.10
ε a steepness parameter	5.0/5.0	k_f damping coefficient of feedback	0.30/030
a compound parameter	3.0/3.0	-	- -

Table 3. Parameters used in the simulations

Feedback SOM	
The number of nodes in the input layer	20+4+40
The number of nodes in the competitive layer	40
The number of nodes in the state layer	40
β : the rate of considering the past information	3.0
γ : forgetting rate	0.7
η learning coefficient	0.5 → 0.0 (linear transformation)
σ : width coefficient	0.0 → 1.0 (linear transformation)

Table 4. Parameters of the feedback SOM used in the simulations

6.3 Simulations and results

6.3.1 Confirmation of learning and recollection in the case of a simple small scale maze

At first we confirm by a simple small scale maze whether learning and recollection in our proposed system work well or not. We gave the agent a maze as shown in Fig. 11(a), and let the agent learn and memorize it. In Fig. 11(a), S means the start position of the agent and G means the goal position. I means the position where the agent begins the initial operation. Its numbered place (cell) means the position where each environment was found in LTM. Where, ■ means wall recognized as value 1, □ means aisle recognized as value 0 by the agent. The result of the simulation using the maze 1 as a simple small scale maze, the agent reached the goal through the shortest path as the real line with arrow shown in Fig. 11(a). Let us explain how the maze was solved by the agent concretely as follows:

The whole algorithm until the agent reaches to the goal in case that maze 1 is given, as follows:

Step 1. Give the maze 1 to the agent which does not learn and memorize anything.

Step 2. Switch to the learning sector because of no learned and memorized mazes, and the agent learns the maze 1 by the actor-critic method. As a result, the memory corresponding to the maze 1 is generated as the number 1 of the memory in LTM.

Step 3. The agent learns the MACNN and the feedback SOM by use of the results of learning at Step 2.

Step 4. The agent executes the initial operation (n_{init}=5 steps) n_{repeat}(=30) times and records the winner neuron number for the maze 1.

Step 5. The agent begins on the initial operation again for maze 1.

Step 6. The agent inputs the data gotten from the initial operation to the discrimination of environment sector. As a result of the discrimination, the agent gets the memory 1 (maze 1).

Step 7. The agent begins the recollection using the memory 1, i.e. MACNN1. It reaches the goal at shortest steps.

6.3.2 Generation and discrimination of plural simple small scale mazes

We consider four simple small scale mazes as shown in Fig. 11(a) to (d). At first the agent learns and memorizes the maze 1 by the way mentioned above 6.3.1, next we gave the agent the maze 2 as shown in Fig. 11(b). For the maze 2, after the agent executed the initial operation, the agent judged the memory 1 (maze 1) could not be used since the memory 1 is not corresponding to the current maze, it switched to the learning sector and memorized the maze 2 as memory 2 in LTM (refer to Table 2). Similarly, maze 3 and 4 are learned and memorized as memory 3 and 4 in LTM.

The winner neuron numbers at the each initial operation step when given the environment the same as the memory are shown in Fig. 12. In Fig. 12, it is found that though there are only four memories, the winner neuron numbers are overlapping in spite of the difference of the environments each other. Next, we check the differences of the Hamming distance between above 4 mazes each other. As mentioned at 6.3.1, ■ means wall recognized as value 1, □ means aisle recognized as value 0 by the agent. There is 15 bits (5 different directions times 3 different distances) in the perception range of the agent. The Hamming distance between the four mazes is shown in Table 5. From Table 5, it is found that there is no overlapping environments. However we encountered an example of the failure of the agent's taking the goal like following. After learning and memorizing above 4 mazes, we gave the agent maze 4 again. The situation of the failure case is shown in Fig. 13.

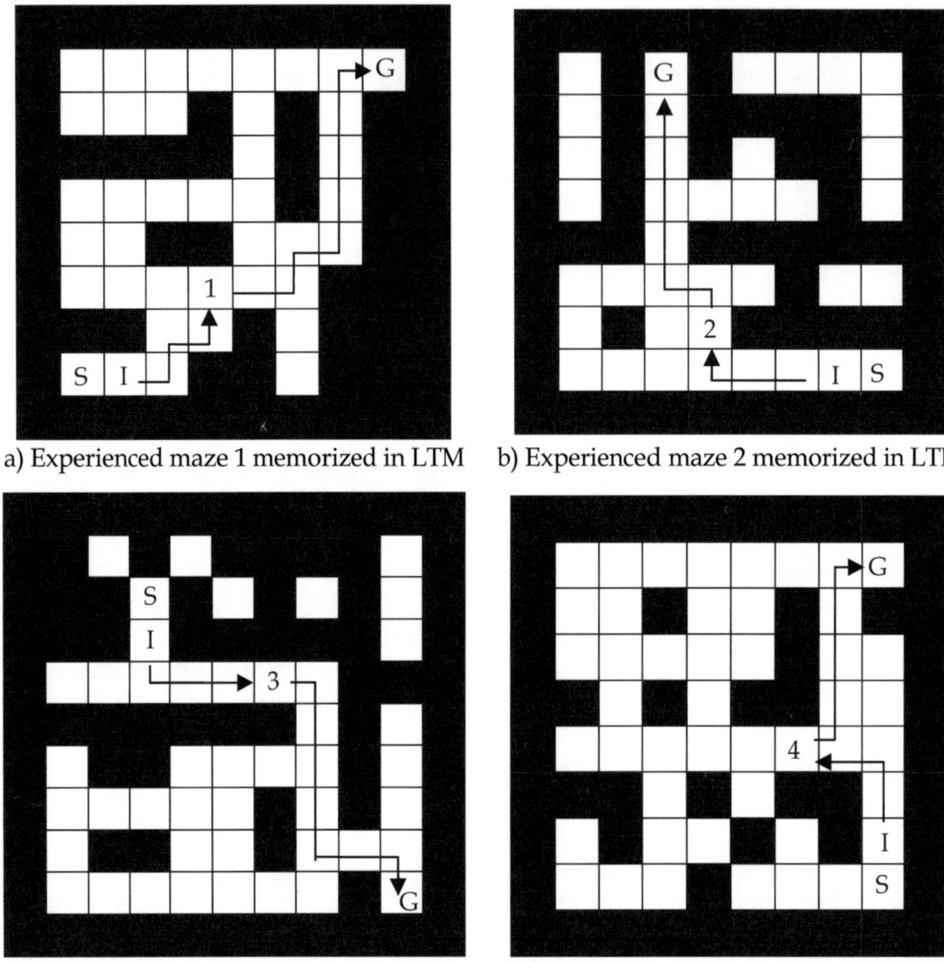

a) Experienced maze 1 memorized in LTM b) Experienced maze 2 memorized in LTM

c) Experienced maze 3 memorized in LTM d) Experienced maze 4 memorized in LTM

Fig. 11. Learned and memorized paths of the agent on the each maze.

This cause may be considered as follows: When the agent starts from start point S, it can select two directions, i.e., up and left, the agent can take move to. When the agent executes the initial operation, in other words, when the winner neuron numbers at the each initial operation are set first, if the selection rate of the upward step of the agent are biased, the upward direction are selected mainly, after memorizing of their data in LTM. However, when the agent begins the initial operation and the steps to the left are mainly selected, the winner neuron count had become less than the value of the *threshold_count* (refer to 5.3). Though the agent has the memory corresponding to the current maze, the agent judged that the agent does't have the experience of the current maze because of the small value of the *threshold_count*, and as a result, it switched to the learning sector. To solve this problem, the number of steps on the initial operation should be increased and the *threshold_count* is appropriately decided.

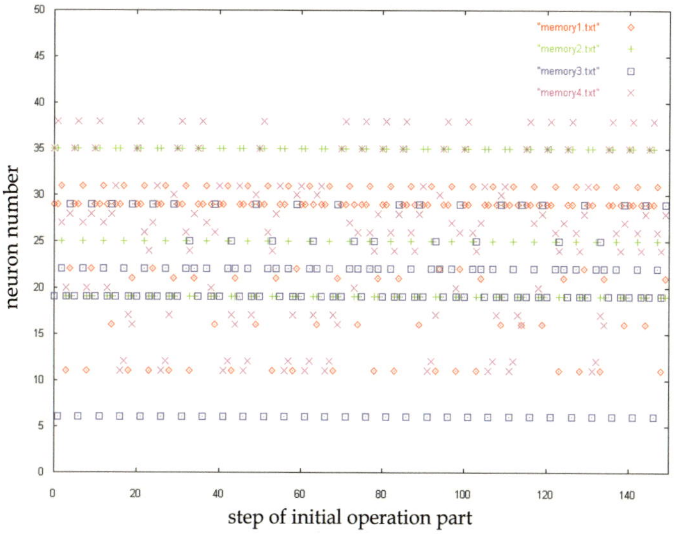

Fig. 12. The winner neuron numbers at the each initial operation step when given the environment the same as the memory

	maze 2	maze 3	maze 4
maze 1	6	6	6
maze 2		6	6
maze 3			2

a) At step 1

	maze 2	maze 3	maze 4
maze 1	8	4	8
maze 2		6	8
maze 3			8

b) At step 2

	maze 2	maze 3	maze 4
maze 1	8	10	10
maze 2		2	6
maze 3			4

c) At step 3

	maze 2	maze 3	maze 4
maze 1	10	10	10
maze 2		6	8
maze 3			6

d) At step 4

	maze 2	maze 3	maze 4
maze 1	8	4	2
maze 2		10	10
maze 3			4

e) At step 5

Table 5. Hamming distance of each other of the four mazes on the initial 5 steps

Fig. 13. The moving path in the case of failure

6.3.3 In the case of a large-scale maze

The large scale maze to be solved by the agent is shown in Fig. 14. This maze is constructed by using the four mazes shown in Fig. 11. In this maze, the shortest steps, i.e., optimal steps is 108. Before the agent tries to explore this maze, the agent learned and memorized above four mazes orderly. In the Figure, × means the position where the agent failed the choice of the memorized information in LTM, i.e., the action corresponding to the current environment under use of the learned and memorized environment. The number shows the memory number the agent selected using the initila operation. In a lot of the agent's trials to this maze, the steps until the agent got the goal is between 110 and 140. Because of the exploring steps at the initial operation process, they are more than the shortest steps. As a result, it is said that it may be possible the agent with our proposed system could reach the goal in any case of environments, by additive learning and memorizing for the unknown environment.

7. Conclusions

Living things learn many kinds of things from incidents driven by own actions and reflects them on the subsequent action as own experiences. These experiences are memorized in their brain and recollected and reused if necessary. They will accumulate knowledge gotten by experiences, and will make use of them when encounters unexperienced things.

The subject in this research was to realize the things mentioned above on an agent. In this research, we tried let the agent equip with three main functions: "learning", i.e., reinforcement learning commonly used by living things, "memorization", and "the ability of associative recollection and its appropriate use" suitable for the situation, i.e., chaotic neural network.

This time we realized a part of subjects of above functions on the agent. However, a lot of unsolved problem are still left. One of them is too difficult to decide the various kinds of parameters and thresholds approproately. Another one is to utilize the ability of feedback SOM well. SOM has the feature that input patterns similar to each other are placed in the SOM retaining the neighboring relationship. This is useful in the case of existing observation together with noise because that actually almost all observation data include noises. In such cases, making use of this characteristic of feedback SOM, the agent may realize things mentioned before.

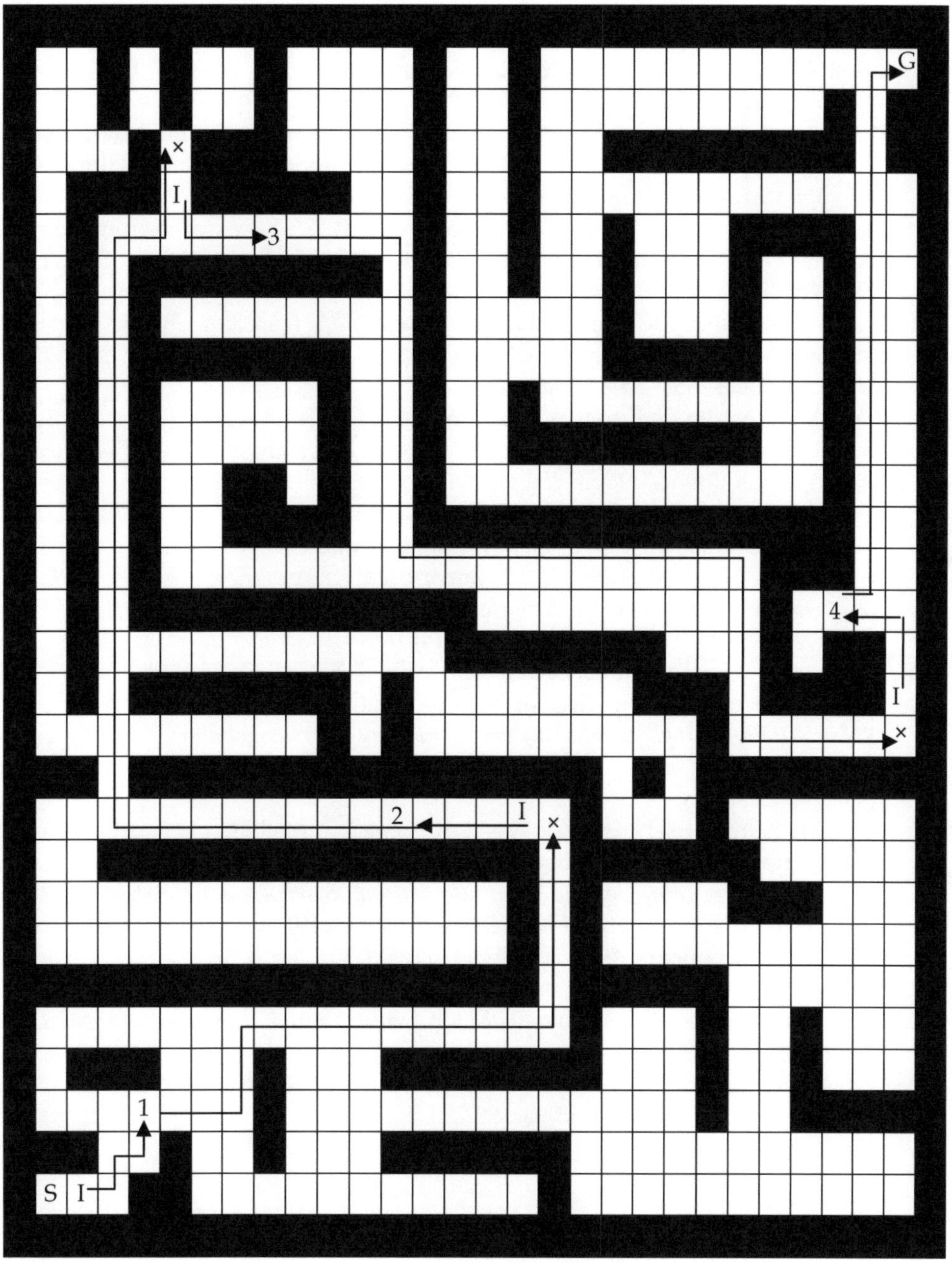

Fig. 14. The path the agent found and memorized in LTM on the large scale goal searching problem using the experienced mazes shown in Fig. 11.

8. Acknowledgements

We would like to thank that a part of this study was supported by JSPS-KAKENHI (No.20500207 and No.20500277).

9. References

[1] D. Harter, R. Kozma: "Chaotic Neurodynamics for Autonomous Agents", IEEE Trans. on *Neural Networks, Vol.* 16, pp.565-579, 2005

[2] J. L. Krichmar, K. Seth, D. G.Nitz, J. G. Fleischer, G. M. Edelman:"Spatial Navigation and Causal Analysis in a Brain-Based Device Modeling Cortical-Hippocampal Interactions", Neuroinformatics, Vol.3, No.3, pp.197-221, 2005

[3] Obayashi M., Omiya R., Kuremoto T., Kobayashi K.: "Shapes of Non-monotonous Activation Functions in Chaotic Neural Network." *IEEJ Transactions on EIS*, Vol.126, No11, pp.1401-1405, 2006 (*in Japanese*).

[4] M. Obayashi, K. Narita, K. Kobayashi, T. Kuremoto: "A Transient Chaotic Associative Memory Model with Temporary Stay Function", *IEEJ Transactions on EIS*, Vol.128, No.12, pp.1852-1858, 2008 (*in Japanese*)

[5] M. Obayashi, K. Narita, T. Kuremoto, K. Kobayashi: "A Reinforcement Learning System with Chaotic Neural Networks-Based Adaptive Hierarchical Memory Structure for Autonomous Robots", *Proceedings of International Conference on Control, Automation and Systems 2008* (*ICCAS 2008*), pp. 69-74, 2008 (Seoul, Korea)

[6] Obayashi, M., Yano, Y., Kobayashi, K., and Kuremoto, T.: "Chaotic Dynamical Associative Memory Model Using Supervised Learning". *Proceedings of the 13th International Symposium on Artificial Life and Robotics (AROB2008)*, pp.555-558, January 31-February 2, 2008 (Beppu, Japan).

[7] M. Obayashi, T. Kuremoto, K. Kobayashi: "A Self-Organized Fuzzy-Neuro Reinforcement Learning System for Continuous State Space for Autonomous Robots", *Proceedings of International Conference on Computational Intelligence for Modeling, Control and Automation 2008* (*CIMCA08*), pp.552-559, 10-12 Dec. 2008 (Vienna, Austria)

[8] Obayashi, M., Kuremoto, T., and Kobayashi, K., Feng L.: "Intelligent Agent Construction Using the Idea of the Attention Characteristic Pattern in a Chaotic Neural Network", *Proceedings of the 15th International Symposium on Artificial Life and Robotics (AROB2010)*, pp.597-600, February 4-6, 2010 (Beppu, Japan), and to be appeared as a paper of *Artificial Life and Robotics*, Vol. 15, 2010

[9] R.S. Sutton, A.G. Barto:"Reinforcement Learning", *The MIT Press,* 1998

[10] Aihara, K. and Takabe, T. and Toyoda, M.: "Chaotic Neural Networks", *Physics Letters A*, pp.333-340, 1990

[11] M. Adachi, K. Aihara:"Associative Dynamics in a Chaotic Neural Network", *Neural Networks*, Vol. 10, No. 1, pp.83-98, 1997

[12] T.kohonen: "Self-organizing Maps", *Springer*, 2001

12

Characterization of Motion Forms of Mobile Robot Generated in Q-Learning Process

Masayuki HARA[1], Jian HUANG[2] and Testuro Yabuta[3]
[1]*École Polytechnique Fédérale de Lausanne (EPFL)*
[2]*Kinki University*
[3]*Yokohama National University*
[1]*Switzerland*
[2,3]*Japan*

1. Introduction

Acquisition of unique robotic motions by machine learning is a very attractive research theme in the field of robotics. So far, various learning algorithms—e.g., adaptive learning, neural network (NN) system, genetic algorithm (GA), etc.—have been proposed and applied to the robot to achieve a target. It depends on the persons, but the learning method can be classified roughly into supervised and unsupervised learning (Mitchell, 1997). In supervised learning, the ideal output for target task is available as a teacher signal, and the learning basically proceeds to produce a function that gives an optimal output to the input; the abovementioned learning methods belong to supervised learning. Thus, the learning results should be always within the scope of our expectation. While, the teacher signal is not specifically given in unsupervised learning. Since the designers do not need to know the optimal (or desired) solution, there is a possibility that unexpected solution can be found in the learning process. This article especially discusses the application of unsupervised learning to produce robotic motions.

One of the most typical unsupervised learning is reinforcement learning that is a evolutionary computation (Kaelbling et al., 1996; Sutton & Barto, 1998). The concept of this learning method originally comes from the behavioral psychology (Skinner, 1968). As seen in animal evolution, it is expecting that applying this learning method to the robot would have a tremendous potential to find unique robotic motions beyond our expectation. In fact, many reports related to the application of reinforcement learning can be found in the field of robotics (Mahadevan & Conell, 1992; Doya, 1996; Asada et al, 1996; Mataric, 1997; Kalmar et al., 1998; Kimura & Kobayashi, 1999; Kimura et al., 2001, Peters et al., 2003; Nishimura et al., 2005). For example, Doya has succeeded in the acquistion of robotic walking (Doya, 1996). Kimura et al. have demonstrated that reinforcement learning enables the effective advancement motions of mobile robots with several degrees of freedom (Kimura & Kobayashi, 1999; Kimura et al., 2001). As a unique challenge, Nishimura et al. achieved a swing-up control of a real Acrobot—a two-link robot with a single actuator between the links—due to the switching rules of multiple controllers obtained by reinforcement learning (Nishimura et al., 2005). Among these studies, Q-learning, which is a method of reinforcement learning, is widely used to obtain robotic motions. Our previous studies have also introduced Q-learning to acquire the robotic motions, e.g., advancement motions of a caterpillar-shaped robot and a starfish-shaped robot (Yamashina et al., 2006; Motoyama et al., 2006), gymnast-like giant-swing motion of a humanoid robot (Hara et al., 2009), etc. However, most of the conventional studies have discussed the mathematical aspect such as the learning speed, the convergence of learning, etc. Very few studies have focused on the robotic evolution in the learning process or physical factor underlying the learned motions. The authors believe that to examine these factors is also challenging to reveal how the robots evolve their motions in the learning process.

This article discusses how the mobile robots can acquire optimal primitive motions through Q-learning (Hara et al., 2006; Jung et al., 2006). First, Q-learning is performed to acquire an advancement motion by using a caterpillar-shaped robot. Based on the learning results, motion forms consisting of a few actions, which appeared or disappeared in the learning process, are discussed in order to find the key factor (effective action) for performing the advancement motion. In addition to this, the environmental effect on the learning results is examined so as to reveal how the robot acquires the optimal motion form when the environment is changed. As the second step, the acquisition of a two-dimensional motion by Q-learning is attempted with a starfish-shaped robot. In the planar motion, not only translational motions in X and Y directions but also yawing motion should be included in the reward; in this case, the yawing angle have to be measured by some external sensor. However, this article proposes Q-learning with a simple reward manipulation, in which the yawing angle is included as a factor of translational motions. Through this challenge, the authors demonstrate the advantage of the proposed method and explore the possibility of simple reward manipulation to produce attractive planer motions.

2. Q-learning algorithm

Q-learning is one of reinforcement learning methods and widely used in the field of robotics. In Q-learning, an agent selects an action from all the possible actions in a state following some policy—a mapping of probability selecting action—and causes an interaction with an environment at a certain time. A reward based on the interaction and the target task is allocated to the selected action from the environment as a scalar value. At this time, the agent renews the database due to the given reward. Repeating this process, the action values are renewed and stored in each state. After the learning, an optimal motion for the desired task can be realized by just selecting the actions with the highest action value in each state. In Q-learning, the convergence to the optimal solution is promised as long as the series of learning process follows Markov Decision Process (MDP). The equation is simply expressed as follow:

$$Q(s_{t,}a_t) \leftarrow Q(s_{t,}a_t) + \alpha[r_t + \gamma \max_a Q(s_{t+1,}a) - Q(s_{t,}a_t)] \qquad (1)$$

where $Q(s_t, a_t)$ is action-value function when the agent selects an action a_t in a state s_t at time t. α and γ represent learning rate and discount rate, respectively. a $(0 < a < 1)$ dominates the learning responsiveness (speed); basically, a value near 1 is selected. On the other hand, γ is related to the convergence of learning. In general, Q-learning can be considered as a learning method to maximize the expected value of reward that will be received in the future. However, the rewards which will be given from the environment in the future are basically unknown. So, the future rewards should be estimated by using the discount rate γ, as shown in equation (2):

$$R_t = r_{t+1} + \gamma r_{t+2} + \gamma^2 r_{t+3} \cdots = \sum_{k=0}^{\infty} \gamma^k r_{t+k+1} \tag{2}$$

Without the discount rate, the agent gets interested in only the immediate rewards and this causes the myopic action selection. Therefore, the introduction of the discount rate enables Q-learning with a long-term view. Ideally, an eigenvalue near 1 is used for the discount rate, but it is pointed out that the duration until the convergence of learning becomes longer if the value is too close to 1 (Schewartz, 1993; Mahadevan, 1996). Hence, the discount rate is set at 0.8 or 0.9 in this article.

In previous studies, several augmented Q-learning methods have been proposed and discussed in order to improve the learning performance (Konda et al., 2003; Mori et al., 2005; Peter & Shaal, 2008; Juang & Lu., 2009; Rucksties et al., 2010). For example, Mori et al. demonstrated that the application of Actor–Critic using a policy gradient method is effective to the learning of CPG-Actor-Critic model even if a high-order state space is configured (Mori et al., 2005). Peters and Schaal proposed Natural Actor-Critic expanding the idea of Actor–Critic using a policy gradient method (Peter & Shaal, 2008). However, in this article, the simplest Q-learning algorithm is applied to mobile robots in order to achieve robotic primitive motions with as minimum information as possible and to facilitate the discussion of how the robots acquire the primitive motion in such the condition.

3. Experimental system

3.1 Mobile robots

As mentioned above, this article introduces the acquisition of advancement and planar motions generated by Q-learning. In Q-learning for the advancement motion, a simple caterpillar-shaped robot is designed and employed. The caterpillar-shaped robot comprises four actuators (AI-Motor, Megarobotics Co., Ltd.) as shown in Fig. 1. In this robot, two actuators on both the tips are enabled; the others are completely fixed under the position control. On the other hand, a starfish-shaped robot, which has four enabled AI-Motors as shown in Fig. 2, is applied in Q-learning for acquiring the planar motion. In these robots, the motor commands are communicated between a computer and each AI-Motor via RS232C interface.

3.2 Experimental system

A schematic diagram of experimental system is shown in Fig. 3. In the experimental system, a function that provides rewards based on the robotic actions to these robots is required in order to renew the action-value function in each state. To perform Q-learning of the advancement and planar motions, it is necessary to measure the robotic travel distance in each leaning step by using some external sensor such as a motion capture system. In this article, a position sensitive detector (PSD) system (C5949, Hamamatsu Photonics) is

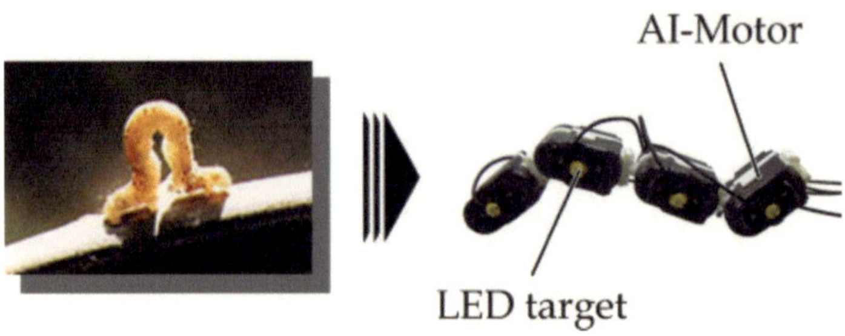

Fig. 1. Caterpillar-shaped robot for Q-learning of advancement motion: only the AI-Motors at both the sides are enabled

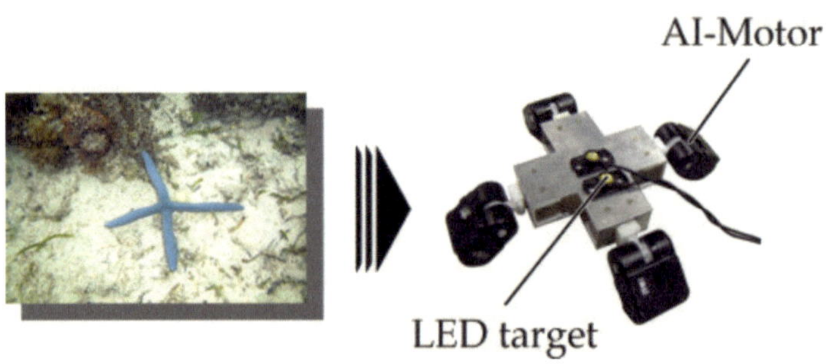

Fig. 2. Starfish-shaped robot for Q-learning of two-dimensional motions: all the AI-Motors (legs) are enabled

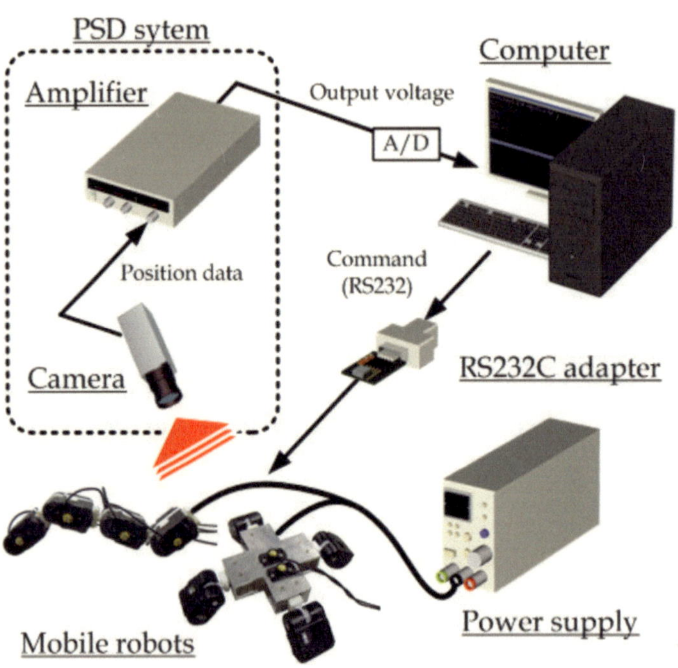

Fig. 3. A schematic diagram of experimental system: PSD system is used for motion-tracking of mobile robots

employed. The PSD system comprises a charge coupled device (CCD) camera, light-emitting diode (LED) targets, and an amplifier. In the PSD system, the CCD camera detects the LED targets which have individual IDs and the amplifier sends the two-dimensional position of each LED target to the computer as a voltage value; maximum 7 LED targets can be detected as analogue data at the same time. In Q-learning with the caterpillar-shaped robot, the CCD camera is fixed on the ground to enable tracking the LED targets attached on the side of the robot. Whereas, in Q-learning with the starfish-shaped robot, the CCD camera is attached on the ceiling to take a panoramic view of robotic two-dimensional motions. Two LED targets are attached on the top of the starfish-shaped robot; one is for measuring the robotic center position, and the other that is a bit shifted from the center of robot is for calculating the yawing angle.

3.3 Off-line Q-learning simulator based on reward database

In Q-learning, a considerable number of learning steps is required to reach an optimal solution. The long-term learning often causes the fatigue breakdown and the performance degradation in the real robot. In addition, the possibility that the mobile robots jump out of the motion-tracking-enabled area is quite high in the long-term learning; once the mobile robot gets out of the area, Q-learning has to be stopped immediately, and resumed after resetting the mobile robot within the motion-tracking-enabled area. So, the use of off-line learning is desired to facilitate Q-learning and to shorten the learning time. In general, robotic simulator is used instead of real robot to shorten the learning time. However, the robotic simulator has a technical issue related to the model error. The model error can be decreased by precisely configuring the robotic parameter in the simulator, but it causes the increase in the computational time (simulation time). Hence, this article proposes an off-line Q-learning simulator based on reward databases, which involving the real information of interaction between the robot and the environment. Here, the concept of reward-database-based Q-learning is introduced.

A flow chart of off-line Q-learning simulator is shown in Fig. 4. First, as for the reward database, ID numbers are assigned to all the action patterns and all the state transitions are performed among all the IDs several times by actually using robots. In parallel, some physical quantity related to the target motion, such as a travel distance and a yawing angle, all over the transition states are measured several times. The measured physical quantities are averaged by the number of times that the robot took the same state transition, and the averaged values are stored into a database as a representative reward data; the reward data is normalized at this time. In Q-learning with the real robots, the interaction between the robot and the environment must be simulated to allocate a reward to a selected action in each state to renew the action-value function. However, in the proposed method, once the reward database is established, the robot is not needed anymore because the reward database includes all the real interactions and related physical quantities. Hence, the proposed method can omit the computation of the interaction. In Q-learning with the reward database, a reward is just referred from the database depending on the state transition, and uses the selected reward to renew the action-value function. This is an advantage of the proposed method for the conventional methods with the robotic simulator although the preliminary experiment is needed; the conventional methods require the computation of the interaction every learning step.

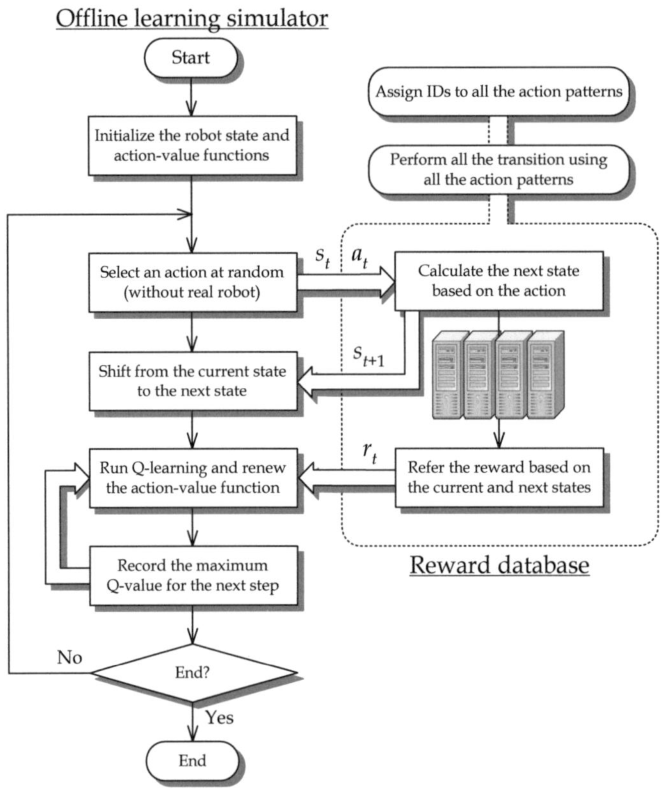

Fig. 4. A flow chart of off-line Q-learning using the reward database

4. Analysis of robotic advancement motions generated in Q-learning

4.1 Acquisition of advancement motion with the caterpillar-shaped robot

Q-learning is applied to acquire advancement motion of caterpillar-shaped robot. In this Q-learning travel distance, which is the representative data averaged by 10000 step-actions, from a state to the next state is given as reward. The action patterns of the caterpillar-shaped robot are shown in Fig. 5; the two-enabled motors at both the sides are controlled at 5 positions (0, ±26, and ±52 deg), respectively. The caterpillar-shaped robot randomly selects one of 25 actions in a learning step—random action policy. Totally, 625 ($5^2 \times 5^2$) state transitions can be selected in the learning. The learning rate and discount rate are configured at 0.9 and 0.8, respectively. Under these experimental conditions, Q-learning is performed in the proposed off-line simulator.

Fig. 6 shows the transitions of travel distances per a leaning step when only the highest Q-values are selected, i.e., when the caterpillar-shaped robot takes the greedy action; the blue, red, and green lines—in this experiment, Q-learning was performed three times—respectively indicate the relationships between the learning steps and the averaged distance traveled by the caterpillar-shaped robot in a step. From Fig. 6, it should be noted that the three trials finally reach the same performance (about 4.3 mm travel distance in a step) with the similar profile. This result also implies the good learning convergence and repeatability; all Q-learning are converged at around the 5000 learning steps in this case.

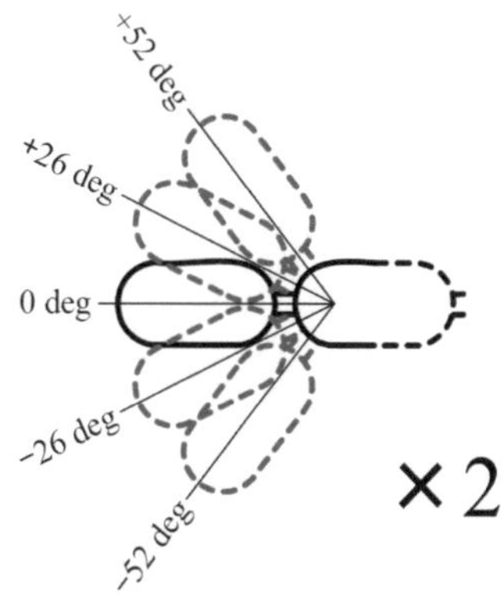

Fig. 5. Action patterns of caterpillar-shaped robot: 5^2 action patterns in each side

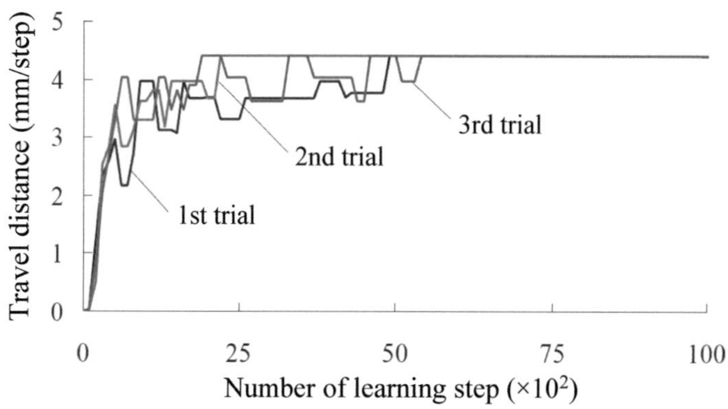

Fig. 6. Relationships between the number of learning step and averaged distance traveled by the caterpillar-shaped robot in a step under Q-learning conditions $a = 0.9$ and $\gamma = 0.8$

4.2 Transition of motion forms during Q-learning

When the caterpillar-shaped robot takes the greedy actions after Q-learning, a series of robotic actions defined by the ID numbers appear as an optimal motion. This article defines this series of robotic actions as "motion form". The motion forms consisting of a loop of a few actions appear with different patterns during Q-learning. Here, the transition of motion forms is analyzed to reveal how the caterpillar-shaped robot acquires an optimal advancement motion through the interaction with the environment. To achieve this, the motion forms are observed by extracting the learning results every 100 step until 5000 steps. Through the observation, it is found that four representative motion forms, as shown in Fig. 7, appear and disappear until the caterpillar-shaped robot reaches an optimal motion form. The number written over the robotic figure is the ID number that is allocated to the states in the database. Each motion form comprises a few actions and these actions are periodically repeated in the advancement motion. Note that these motion forms except the optimal motion form are not necessarily observed at the same timing when performing Q-learning several times because the random action policy is applied to the robot in this experiment; different environments and different learning parameters would cause other motion forms. However, since these four motion forms are frequently taken in Q-learning, this article discusses the transition of these motion forms.

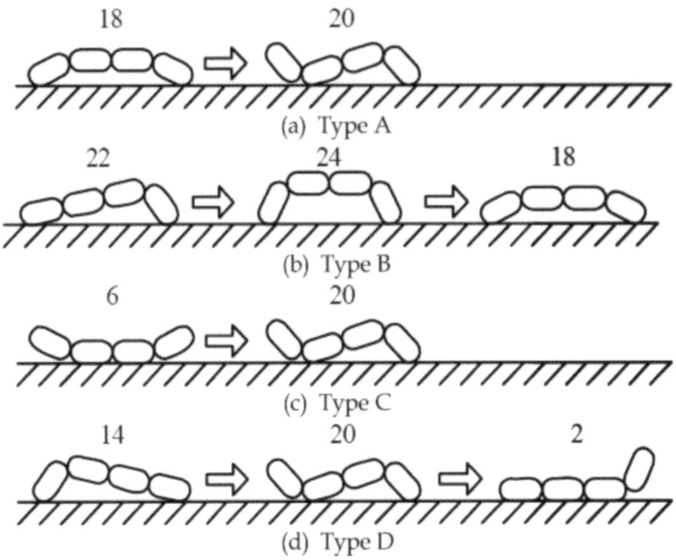

Fig. 7. Representative motion forms frequently observed in Q-learning under the conditions of $a = 0.9$ and $\gamma = 0.8$: Type D is the optimal motion form which brings the most effective advancement motion to the caterpillar-shaped robot

Fig. 8 shows a representative transition of motion forms until the caterpillar-shaped robot acquires an optimal motion form. In this learning, the optimal motion forms for the advancement motion is Type D consisting of three states (ID: 2, 14, and 20). In the early process of Q-learning, Type A, B, and C repeatedly appear and disappear until 800 steps; sometimes these motion forms are combined each other. From 800 steps to 4800 steps, major change in the motion form is not observed as shown in Fig. 8. In this phase, the states 14 and 20 are almost fixed and the subsequent state was changed variously. Through the several transitions, finally, the motion form is converged to the optimal motion form—Type D. Focusing on the transition, Q-learning might be divided into two phases based on 800 steps— early and later learning phases. In the early stage, the caterpillar-shaped robot attempts to establish some rough frameworks of motion forms for effectively performing the advancement motion. On the other hand, it seems that the robot selects a possible candidate from several key motion forms and performs the fine adjustment in the later phase. This implies the evolutionary feature of Q-learning.

Here is the discussion about the transition of motion forms. In general, the rewards possess the following relationships:

$$r_1 > r_2 > r_3 > \cdots > r_n > r_{n-1} \tag{3}$$

In a finite state, Q-learning is considered as a problem that finds out a group of actions that maximize the expected value of discount return R_t. Ideally, only the actions that have the highest Q-value should be selected in each state to maximize the expected value of R_t. However, the robot cannot take only the actions with the highest Q-value because of the finite space. So, the robot also has to select the actions with lower Q-value in some states to maximize R_t. Under this constraint, the robot attempts to find out a group of actions—motion form—with a maximum expected value of R_t. This is a big feature of unsupervised

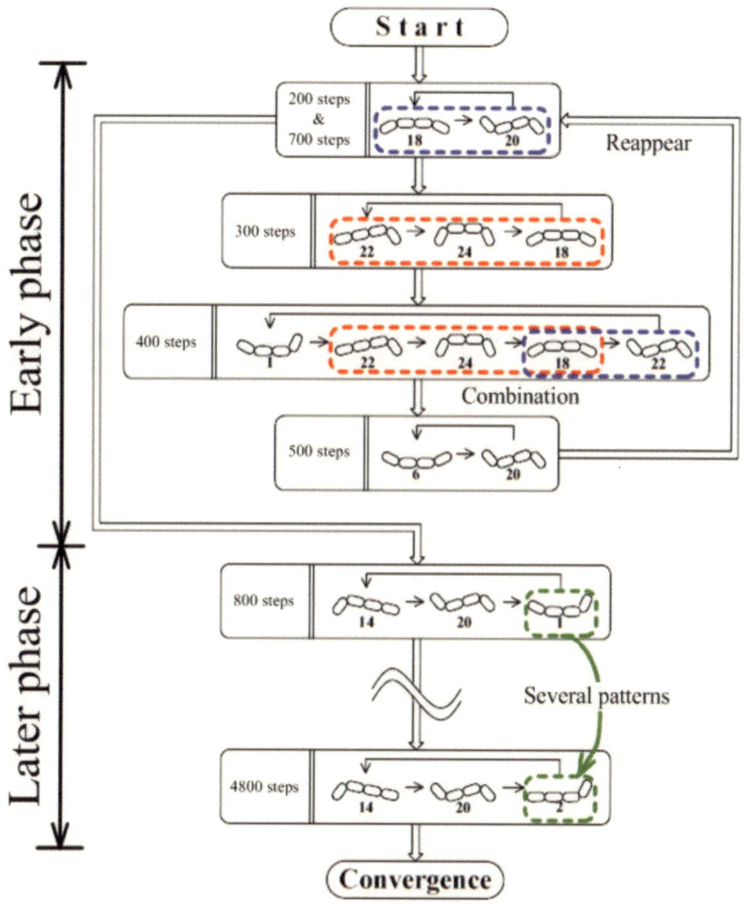

Fig. 8. A representative transition of motion forms during Q-learning process

learning; such the process cannot be found in supervised learning. Here, from equations (1) and (2), it should be noted that the discount rate γ significantly affects the transition of motion forms. In fact, our previous studies demonstrated that it is easier to produce the optimal motion form with a very few actions when γ is configured at a large value; vice versa, an inverse result is observed when γ is a smaller value (Yamashina et al., 2006; Motoyama et al., 2006). Hence, it is assumed that the discount rate is a significant factor to generate the series of motion forms in the learning process.

4.3 Environmental effect on the optimal motion form

As the next step, the environmental effect on the optimal motion form is investigated to know how Q-learning adapts to the environmental change. It is expected that Q-learning is performed involving the environmental change in the interaction and generates a motion form optimized to the given environment. In this article, ascending and descending tasks are tried by changing the inclination of floor, as shown in Fig. 9. The inclination is adjusted at ±5 deg in each task. A carpet made of the same fiber, which is used on the flat floor in the experiment of section 4.1, is attached on the slope so as to make the friction property between the caterpillar-shaped robot and the slope the same. Under this condition,

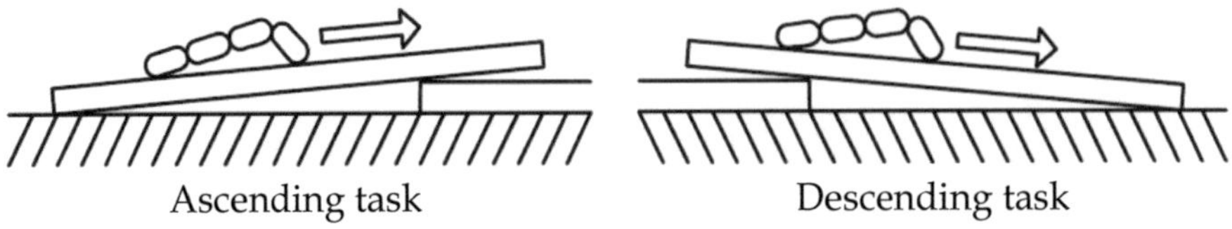

Fig. 9. Environmental changes in Q-learning: ascending and descending ±5 deg slopes

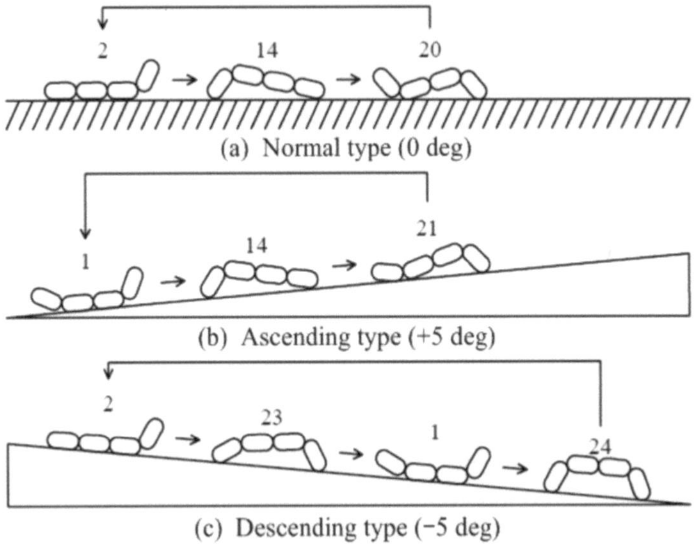

Fig. 10. Optimal motion forms in the three environments

Q-learning with the same learning parameters in section 4.1 was performed. Fig. 10 compares the optimal motion forms generated in the three environments—flat floor, uphill, and downhill. Here, let's define these optimal motion forms as normal-type, ascending-type, and descending-type motion forms, respectively. As expected, the caterpillar-shaped robot acquires different optimal motin forms. This implies that the caterpillar-shaped robot has learned the effective advancement motion in the individual environments.

The performance of each motion form is examined by comparing the travel distance in each result. The cumulative travel distances over 20 steps are shown in Fig. 11. Figs. 11 (a) and (b) show the results on the uphill and the downhill, respectively. In the case of uphill, the caterpillar-shaped robot could advance when applying the normal-type and ascending-type motion forms, whereas the robot slipped on the slope toward the opposite direction during the descending-type motion form; in this case, the ascending-type motion form demonstrated the best performance. Here, these optimal motion forms are analyzed to reveal the key factor for ascending the uphill. In the ascending task, it is considered that generating the force against the gravity and keeping the friction force not to slip on the slope would be very important. Focusing on the normal-type and ascending-type motion forms, it should be noted that the rear part pushes the caterpillar-shaped robot when the state is shifted from 14 to the next state—20 in the normal-type motion form and 21 in the ascending-type motion form. Such the state transition cannot be found during the descending-type motion form. As for the advancement motion on the uphill, this pushing action might be needed to produce the propulsion in the caterpillar-shaped robot. In adition,

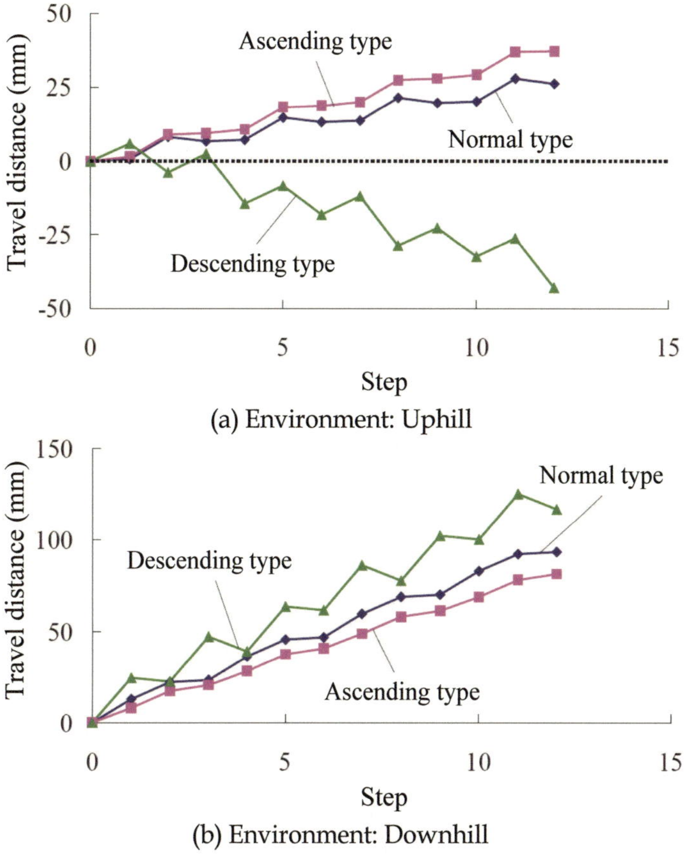

Fig. 11. Performance of optimal motion forms in several environmental conditions

the comparison of the normal-type and ascending-type motion forms tells us that the contact area between the robot and the slope is a bit larger in the ascending-type motion form after the pushing action. So, it results in larger friction force during the ascendig-type motion form and it would enable the caterpillar-shaped robot to advacne without slipping on the slope. This difference might produce the different performances of advancement motion in the normal-type and ascending-type motion forms, as shown in the blue and red lines in Fig. 11 (a). Hence, these results imply that the pushing action and large contact area after the pushing action are necessary to make the robot effectively ascend the slope. On the other hand, in the case of downhill, the robot can take advantage of slip to make a large step. In this case, it is considered that the dynamic motion and less friction force would be effective to descend the slope. The descending-type motion form shows the best performance among the three types as expected. In this motion form, the shape like a bridge is formed (23 and 24) and it is broken at the next state (1 and 2); this series of actions could be considered as a jumping. This jumping-like motion could produce the dynamic advancement motion with less friction and lead to a good performance, as shown in Fig. 11 (b).

Thus, this section demonstrated that Q-learning could find out the most optimal motion form that is peculiar to the environment. In addition, the analysis of the motion forms implies that the learned motion form is reasonable from a viewpoint of robotic kinematics.

5. Acquisition of robotic planar motion by Q-learning

5.1 Advancement motions of the starfish-shaped robot in *X* and *Y* directions

The starfish-shaped robot can basically select two actions in the horizontal and vertical directions (*X* and *Y* directions). Here, the performances of advancement motions on the flat floor in the two directions are introduced. Regarding Q-learning, four enabled motors are controlled at 3 positions (0 and ±52 deg), as shown in Fig. 12. Similar to Q-learning in the caterpillar-shaped robot, the random action policy is taken; in a learning step, the starfish-shaped robot randomly selects one of 81 actions. Totally, 6561 ($3^4 \times 3^4$) state transitions are selectable. Under the conditions $a = 0.9$ and $\gamma = 0.9$, Q-learning, whose reward databases are based on the travel distances averaged by 10000 step-actions in each direction, is performed in the proposed off-line simulator. Fig. 13 shows the optimal motion form in the *X* direction; in the *Y* direction, the optimal motion form becomes the same as that in the *X* direction that rotated by 90 deg. The transitions of travel distances in a learning step and the robotic trajectories within 20 steps are shown in Figs. 14 and 15, respectively.

As shown in Fig. 14, the performances in both the directions are almost the same. Here, the most noteworthy point is the magnitude of distance traveled in one step. The travel distance by the starfish-shaped robot (about 9.0 mm) is twice as long as that of caterpillar-shaped robot (about 4.3 mm) although each motor takes only the three positions.

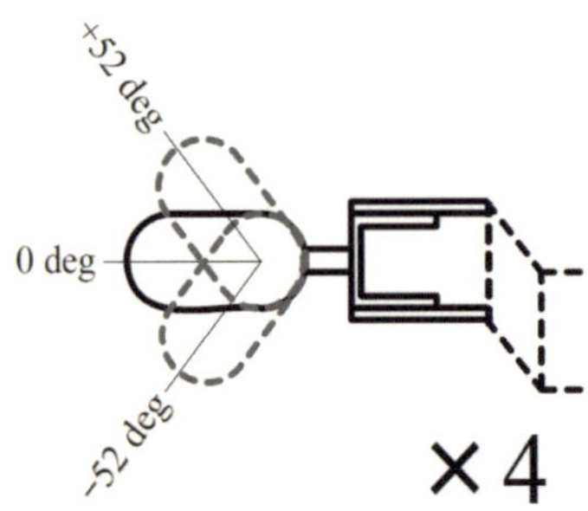

Fig. 12. Action patterns of starfish-shaped robot: 3^4 action patterns in each leg

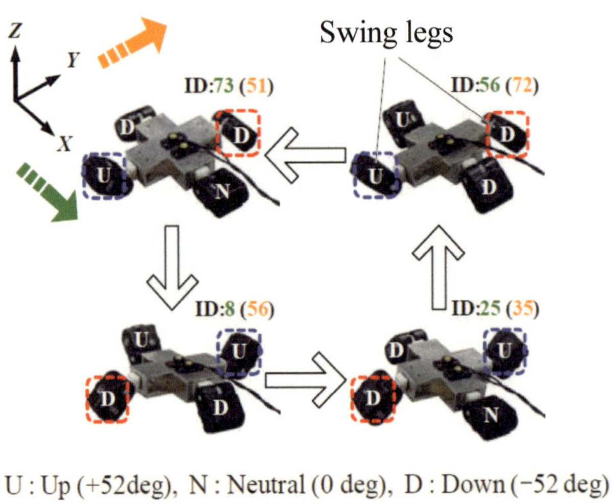

Fig. 13. Optimal motion form for the advancement motion in the *X* direction

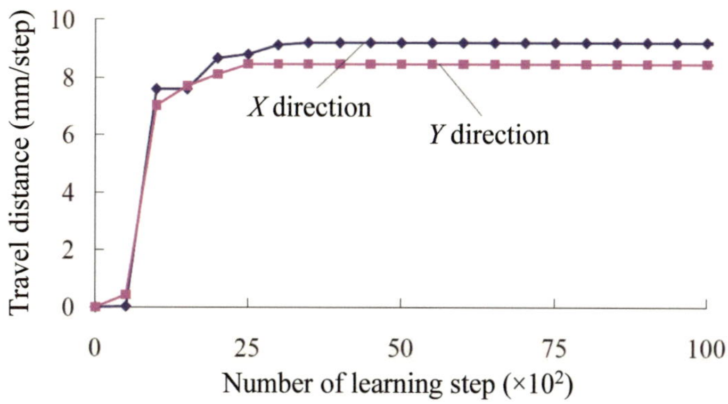

Fig. 14. Relationships between the number of learning step and averaged distance traveled by the starfish-shaped robot per a step under Q-learning conditions $a = 0.9$ and $\gamma = 0.9$

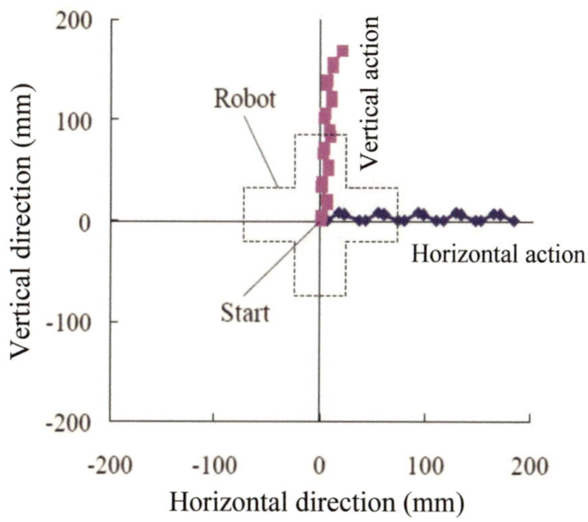

Fig. 15. Trajectories of the starfish-shaped robot in the horizontal and vertical directions

This difference would come from the availability of side legs (right and left motors); without the side legs, it can be considered that Q-learning of the starfish-shaped robot is almost the same as that of the caterpillar-shaped robot. Focusing on the motion form, it should be noted that the front and rear motors are driven for the advancement motion, whereas the right and left motors are used for helping the advancement motion. That is, it is thought that the motions of side legs prevent the starfish-shaped robot from slipping on the flat floor or moving backward. In fact, if the optimal motion form is performed without side legs, the travel distance in one step becomes significantly short. Therefore, these results imply that the starfish-shaped robot skillfully employed the advantage of the swing legs.

5.2 Planar motion by a reward manipulation

To achieve planar motion, the rewards should be configured at least including the horizontal and vertical positions and yawing angle of the starfish-shaped robot. The use of these parameters would make Q-learning complicated and it is not intuitive anymore. In this article, the possibility of producing a planar motion by a reward manipulation is discussed. Concretely, the advancement motion in an oblique direction is challenged by simply manipulating the normalized reward databases for the horizontal and vertical motions, i.e., $\boldsymbol{r}_x$ and $\boldsymbol{r}_y$ obtained in the experiment of section 5.1. This challenge can be realized only in Q-learning based on the reward database; Q-learning with the robotic simulator cannot allow this. In the reward manipulation, the following equation is employed to make a new reward database $\boldsymbol{r}_{\text{new}}$:

$$\boldsymbol{r}_{\text{new}} = w\boldsymbol{r}_x \pm \text{sgn}(w)(1-|w|)\cdot \boldsymbol{r}_y \tag{4}$$

where w ($-1 \le w \le 1$) is a weight parameter that determines the priority of the two rewards. sgn(w) represents the sign of the weight parameter. In this experiment, w is set at ±0.5 in order to achieve the advancement motions in the directions of 45 deg and 225 deg with respect to the horizontal direction. Based on $\boldsymbol{r}_{\text{new}}$, Q-learning is performed in each condition by means of the proposed off-line simulator. Fig. 16 shows the trajectories of the starfish-shaped robot traveled within 20 steps. The results show that the starfish-shaped robot could approximately advance in the directions that the authors aimed at although the directions were not able to be completely corresponding to the requested directions. Also, this demonstrates the possibility of the proposed reward manipulation to generate several planar motions. In general, the acquired Q-values should be completely renewed due to the coherence of the rewards when the agent learns new tasks, i.e., the agent cannot acquire multiple actions at a time due to the oblivion of the knowledge. Therefore, the proposed method might bring a breakthrough in generating multiple and novel motions through Q-learning.

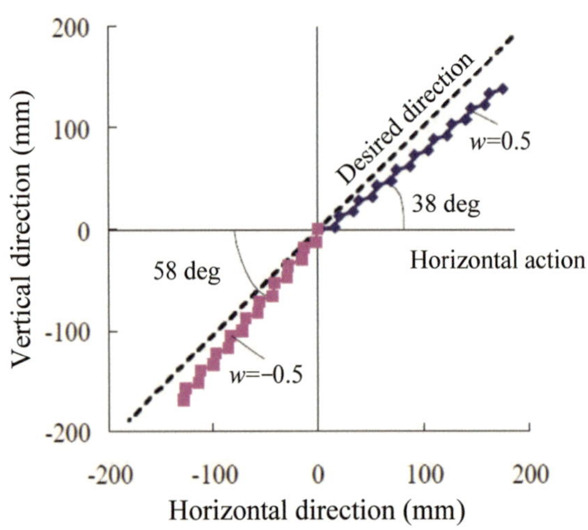

Fig. 16. Trajectories of starfish-shaped robot in the direction of 45 deg and 225 deg after Q-learning based on new reward databases manipulated by $\boldsymbol{r}_x$ and $\boldsymbol{r}_y$

6. Conclusion

In this article, the authors have focused on the key factors of robotic motions generated in Q-learning process. First, an off-line learning simulator based on the reward databases was proposed to facilitate Q-learning. Then, Q-learning was performed in the caterpillar-shaped robot to generate the advancement motion. The observation of learning process implied that some key motion forms appear or disappear in the early learning phase and Q-learning adjusts them to an optimal motion form in the later learning phase. In addition, the effect of environmental changes on the optimal motion form was discussed by using an uphill condition and a downhill condition. Even if the environment was changed, Q-learning resulted in the motion forms which are optimized for the individual environment. As the next step, the planar motion by the starfish-shaped robot was tried. The results in the horizontal and vertical actions demonstrated that the starfish-shaped robot skillfully used their advantage (side legs) to enable longer travel distance. In addition, a reward manipulation with multiple reward databases was proposed to produce the planar motions. The application implied that there is potential to yield unique robotic motions.

7. Future works

This article discussed the motion forms yielded during Q-learning by using a caterpillar-shaped robot and a starfish-shaped robot. In our future work, the authors will examine the acquisition process of a gymnast-like giant-swing motion by a compact humanoid robot and explore the key factor. Through these attempts, the authors aim at having a much better understanding of evolutionary aspect of Q-learning.

8. References

Asada, M.; Noda, S.; Tawaratsumida, S. & Hosoda, K. (1996). Purposive behaviour acquisition for a real robot by vision-based reinforcement learning. *Machine learning*, Vol. 23, pp. 279-303

Doya, K. (1996). Reinforcement learning in animals and robots. *Proceedings of International Workshop on Brainware*, pp. 69-71,

Hara, M.; Inoue, M.; Motoyama, H.; Huang, J. & Yabuta, T. (2006). Study on Motion Forms of Mobile Robots Generated by Q-Learning Process Based on Reward Database. *Proceedings of 2006 IEEE International Conference on Systems, Man and Cybernetics*, pp. 5112-5117

Hara, M.; Kawabe, N.; Sakai, N.; Huang, J. & Yabuta, T. (2009). Consideration on Robotic Giant-Swing Motion Generated by Reinforcement Learning," *Proceedings of 2009 IEEE International Conference on Intelligent Robots and Systems*, pp. 4206–4211

Juang. C. & Lu, C. (2009). Ant colony optimization incorporated with fuzzy Q-learning for reinforcement fuzzy control. *IEEE Transactions on Systems, Man, and Cybernetics, Part A: Systems and Humans*, Vol. 39, No. 3, pp. 597–608

Jung, Y.; Inoue, M.; Hara, M.; Huang, J. & Yabuta, T. (2006). Study on Motion Forms of a Two-dimensional Mobile Robot by Using Reinforcement Learning. *Proceedings of SICE-ICCAS International Joint Conference 2006*, pp. 4240-4245

Kaelbling, L. P.; Littman, M. L. & Moore, A. W. (1996). Reinforcement learning; A survey. *Journal of Artificial Intelligence Research*, Vol. 4, pp. 237-285,

Kalmar, Z.; Szepesvari, C & Lorincz, A. (1998). Module-Based Reinforcement Learning: Experiments with a Real Robot. *Autonomous Robots*, Vol. 5, pp. 273–295,

Kimura, H. & Kobayashi, S. (1999). Reinforcement learning using stochastic gradient algorithm and its application to robots. *IEE Japan Transaction on Electronics, Information and Systems*, Vol. 119-C, No. 8, pp. 931–934 (in Japanese).

Kimura, H.; Yamashita, T. & Kobayashi, S. (2001). Reinforcement Learning of Walking Behavior for a Four-Legged Robot. *Proceedings of CDC2001*, pp. 411–416

Konda, V. R. & Tsitsiklis, J. N. (2003). On Actor-Critic Algorithms. *Society for Industrial and Applied Mathematics*, Vol. 42, No. 4, pp. 1143–1166

Mahadevan, S. & Connell, J. (1992). Automatic programming of behaviour-based robots using reinforcement learning. *Artificial Intelligence*, Vol. 55, pp. 311-365

Mahadevan, S. (1996). Average Reward Reinforcement Learning: Foundations, Algorithms, and Empirical Results. *Machine Learning*, Vol. 22, pp. 159-196.

Mataric, M. J. (1997). Reinforcement learning in the multi-robot domain. *Autonomous Robots*, Vol. 4, pp. 73-83

Mitchell, T. (1997). Machine Learning, MacGraw-Hill Science

Mori, T; Nakamura, Y. & Ishii, S. (2005). Reinforcement Learning Based on a Policy Gradient Method for a Biped Locomotion. *Transactions of the IEICE*, Vol. J88-D-II, No. 6, pp. 1080–1089

Motoyama, H.; Yamashina, R.; Hara, M.; Huang, J. & Yabuta, T. (2006). Study on Obtained Advance Motion Forms of a Caterpillar Robot by using Reinforcement Learning. *Transaction of JSME*, Vol. 72, No. 723, pp. 3525-3532 (in Japanese)

Nishimura, M.; Yoshimoto, J.; Tokita, Y.; Nakamura, Y. & Ishii, S. (2005). Control of Real Acrobot by Learning the Switching Rule of Multiple Controllers. Transactions of the IEICE, Vol. J88-A, No. 5, pp. 646-657 (in Japanese)

Peters, J.; Vijayakumar, S. & Shcaal, S. (2003). Reinforcement Learning for Humanoid Robotics. *Proceedings of Humanoids 2003*

Peters. J. & Schaal, S. (2008). Natural Actor-Critic. *Neurocomputing*, Vol. 71, pp. 1180–1190

Rucksties, T.; Sehnke, F.; Schaul, T.; Wierstra, J.; Sun, Y. & Schmidhuber, J. (2010). Exploring Parameter Space in Reinforcement Learning. *Journal of Behavioral Robotics*, Vol.1, No. 1, pp. 14–24

Schwartz, A. (1993). A Reinforcement Learning Method for Maximizing Undiscounted Rewards. *Proceedings of the 10th International Conference, on Machine Learning*, pp. 298-305

Skinner, B. F. (1968). The technology of teaching. Prentice Hall College Div

Sutton, R. S. & Barto, A. G. (1998). Reinforcement Learning: An Introduction. MIT Press

Yamashina, R.; Maehara, S.; Urakawa, M.; Huang, J. & Yabuta, T. (2006). Advance Motion Acquisition of a Real Robot by Q-learning Using Reward Change. *Transaction of JSME*, Vol. 72, No. 717, pp. 1574-1581 (in Japanese)

13

A Robot Visual Homing Model that Traverses Conjugate Gradient TD to a Variable λ TD and Uses Radial Basis Features

Abdulrahman Altahhan
Yarmouk Private University
Syria

1. Introduction

The term 'homing' refers to the ability of an agent - either animal or robot - to find a known goal location. It is often used in the context of animal behaviour, for example when a bird or mammal returns 'home' after foraging for food, or when a bee returns to its hive. Visual homing, as the expression suggests, is the act of finding a home location using vision. Generally it is performed by comparing the image currently in view with 'snapshot' images of the home stored in the memory of the agent. A movement decision is then taken to try and match the current and snapshot images (Nehmzow 2000).

A skill that plays a critical role in achieving robot autonomy is the ability to *learn* to operate in previously unknown environments (Arkin 1998; Murphy 2000; Nehmzow 2000). Furthermore, learning to home in unknown environments is a particularly desirable capability. If the process was automated and straightforward to apply, it could be used to enable a robot to reach any location in any environment, and potentially replace many existing computationally intensive homing and navigation algorithms. Numerous models have been proposed in the literature to allow mobile robots to navigate and home in a wide range of environments. Some focus on learning (Kaelbling, Littman et al. 1998; Nehmzow 2000; Asadpour and Siegwart 2004; Szenher 2005; Vardy and Moller 2005), whilst others focus on the successful application of a model or algorithm for a specific environment and ignore the learning problem (Simmons and Koenig 1995; Thrun 2000.; Tomatis, Nourbakhsh et al. 2001).

Robotic often borrow conceptual mechanisms from animal homing and navigation strategies described in neuroscience or cognition literature (Anderson 1977; Cartwright and Collett 1987). Algorithms based on the snapshot model use various strategies for finding features within images and establishing correspondence between them in order to determine home direction (Cartwright and Collett 1987; Weber, Venkatesh et al. 1999; Vardy and Moller 2005). Block matching, for example, takes a block of pixels from the current view image and searches for the best matching block in stored images within a fixed search radius (Vardy and Oppacher 2005).

Most robot homing models proposed in the literature have the limitations of either depending upon landmarks (Argyros, Bekris et al. 2001; Weber, Wermter et al. 2004; Muse, Weber et al. 2006), which makes them environment-specific, or requiring pre-processing stages, in order for them to learn or perform the task (Szenher 2005; Vardy 2006). These assumptions restrict the employability of such models in a useful and practical way. Moreover, new findings in cognition suggest that humans are able to home in the absence of feature-based landmark information (Gillner, Weiß et al. 2008). This biological evidence suggests that in principle at least the limitations described are unnecessarily imposed on existing models.

This chapter describes a new visual homing model that does not require either landmarks or pre-processing stages. To eliminate the landmarks requirement, and similarly to what (Ulrich and Nourbakhsh 2000) have devised to do localization, a new measure that quantifies the overall similarity between a current view and a stored snapshot is used to aid the homing model. To eliminate the pre-processing requirement it was necessary to employ a general learning process capable of capturing the specific characteristics of any environment, without the need to customise the model architecture. Reinforcement learning (RL) provides such a capability, and tackling visual homing based on RL coupled with radial basis features and whole image measure forms the first novelty of the work.

RL has been used previously in robot navigation and control, including several models inspired by biological findings (Weber, Wermter et al. 2004; Sheynikhovich, Chavarriaga et al. 2005). However some of those models lack the generality and/or practicality, and some are restricted to their environment; the model proposed by (Weber, Wermter et al. 2004; Muse, Weber et al. 2006; Weber, Muse et al. 2006), for example, depends on object recognition of a landmark in the environment to achieve the task. Therefore, the aim of the work described in this chapter was to exploit the capability of RL as much as possible by general model design, as well as by using a whole image measure. RL advocates a general learning approach that avoids human intervention of supervised learning and, unlike unsupervised learning, has a specific problem-related target that should be met. Furthermore, since RL deals with reward and punishment it has strong ties with biological systems, making it suitable for the homing problem. Whilst environment-dynamics or map-building may be necessary for more complex or interactive forms of navigation or localization, visual homing based on model-free learning can offer an adaptive form of local homing. In addition, although the immediate execution of model-based navigation can be successful (Thrun, Liu et al. 2004; Thrun, Burgard et al. 2005), RL techniques have the advantage of being model-free i.e. no knowledge needed about the environment. The agent learns the task by learning the best policy that allows it to collect the largest sum of rewards from its environment according to the environment dynamics.

The second novelty of this work is related to enhancing the performance of the an existing RL method. Reinforcement learning with function approximation has been shown in some cases to learn slowly (Bhatnagar, Sutton et al. 2007). Bootstrapping methods like temporal difference (TD) (Sutton 1988) although was proved to be faster than other RL methods, such as residual gradient established by Baird (Baird 1995), it can still be slow ((Schoknecht and Merke 2003). Slowness in TD methods can occur due to different reasons. The frequent cause is when the state space is big, high-dimensional or continuous. In this case, it is hard to maintain the value of each state in a tabular form. Even when the state space is

approximated in some way, using artificial neural networks (ANN) for example, the learning process can become slow because it is still difficult to generalize in such huge spaces. In order for TD to converge when used for prediction, all states should be visited frequently enough. For large state spaces this means that convergence may involve many steps and will become slow.
Numerical techniques have been used with RL methods to speed up its performance. For example, (Ziv and Shimkin 2005) used a multi-grid framework which is originated in numerical analysis to enhance the iterative solution of linear equations. Whilst, others attempted to speed up RL methods performance in multi-agent scenario, (Zhang, Abdallah et al. 2008), by using a supervised approach combined with RL to enhance the model performance. TD can be speed up by using it with other gradient types. In (Bhatnagar, Sutton et al. 2007), for example, TD along with the natural gradient has been used to boost learning.
(Falas and Stafylopatis 2001; Falas and Stafylopatis 2002) have used conjugate gradient with TD. Their early experiments confirmed that using such a combination can enhance the performance of TD. Nevertheless, no formal theoretical study has been conducted which disclose the intrinsic properties of such a combination. The present work is an attempt to fill this gap. It uncover an interseting property of combining TD method with the conjugate gradient which simplifies the implementation of the conjugate TD.
The chapter is structured as follows. Firstly an overview of TD and function approximation is presented, followed by the deduction of the TD-conj learning and its novel equivalency property. Then a detail describtion of the novel visual homing model and its components is presneted. The results of extensive simulations and experimental comparisons are shown, followed by conclusions and recommendations for further work.

2. TD and function approximation

When function approximation techniques are used to learn a parametric estimate of the value function $V^{\pi}(s)$, $V_t(s_t)$ should be expressed in terms of some parameters $\vec{\theta}_t$. The mean squared error performance function can be used to drive the learning process:

$$F_t = MSE(\vec{\theta}_t) = \sum_{s \in S} pr(s)\left[V^{\pi}(s) - V_t(s)\right]^2 \tag{1}$$

pr is a probability distribution weighting the errors $Er_t^2(s)$ of each state, and expresses the fact that better estimates should be obtained for more frequent states where:

$$Er_t^2(s) = \left[V^{\pi}(s) - V_t(s)\right]^2 \tag{2}$$

The function F_t needs to be minimized in order to find a global optimal solution $\vec{\theta}^*$ that best approximates the value function. For on-policy learning if the sample trajectories are being drawn according to pr through real or simulated experience, then the update rule can be written as:

$$\vec{\theta}_{t+1} = \vec{\theta}_t + \frac{1}{2}\alpha_t \vec{d}_t \tag{3}$$

$\vec{d}_t$ is a vector that drives the search for $\vec{\theta}^*$ in the direction that minimizes the error function $Er_t^2(s)$, and $0 < \alpha_t \le 1$ is a step size. Normally going opposite to the gradient of a function leads the way to its local minimum. The gradient $\vec{g}_t$ of the error $Er_t^2(s)$ can be written as:

$$\vec{g}_t = \nabla_{\vec{\theta}_t} Er_t^2(s_t) = 2\left[V^\pi(s_t) - V_t(s_t)\right] \cdot \nabla_{\vec{\theta}_t} V_t(s_t) \tag{4}$$

Therefore, when $\vec{d}_t$ is directed opposite to $\vec{g}_t$, i.e. $\vec{d}_t = -\vec{g}_t$, we get the gradient descent update rule:

$$\vec{\theta}_{t+1} = \vec{\theta}_t + \alpha_t\left[V^\pi(s_t) - V_t(s_t)\right] \cdot \nabla_{\vec{\theta}_t} V_t(s_t) \tag{5}$$

It should be noted that this rule allows us to obtain an estimate of the value function through simulated or real experience in a supervised learning (SL) fashion. However, even for such samples the value function V^π can be hard to be known in a priori. If the target value function V^π of policy π is not available, and instead some other approximation of it is, then an approximated form of rule (5) can be realized. For example, replacing $R_t = \sum_{i=1}^{\infty} \gamma^{i-1} r_{t+i}$ by V^π for an infinite horizon case produces the Monte Carlo update $\vec{\theta}_{t+1} = \vec{\theta}_t + \alpha_t[R_t - V_t(s_t)] \cdot \nabla_{\vec{\theta}_t} V_t(s_t)$. By its definition R_t is an unbiased estimate for $V^\pi(s_t)$, hence this rule is guaranteed to converge to a local minima. However, this rule requires waiting until the end of the task to obtain the quantity R_t to perform the update. This demand can be highly restrictive for the practical application of such rule. On other hand, if the n-step return $R_t^{(n)} = \sum_{i=1}^{n} \gamma^{i-1} r_{t+i} + \gamma^n V_t(s_{t+n})$ is used to approximate $V^\pi(s_t)$, then from (5) we obtain the rule $\vec{\theta}_{t+1} = \vec{\theta}_t + \alpha_t\left[R_t^{(n)} - V_t(s_t)\right] \cdot \nabla_{\vec{\theta}_t} V_t(s_t)$ which is less restrictive and of more practical interest than rule (5) since it requires only to wait n steps to obtain $R_t^{(n)}$. Likewise, any averaged mixture of $R_t^{(n)}$ (such as $\frac{1}{2}R_t^{(1)} + \frac{1}{2}R_t^{(3)}$) can be used, as long as the coefficients sum up to 1. An important example of such averages is the sum $R_t^\lambda = (1-\lambda)\sum_{n=1}^{\infty} \lambda^{n-1} R_t^{(n)}$ which also can be used to get the update rule:

$$\vec{\theta}_{t+1} = \vec{\theta}_t + \alpha_t\left[R_t^\lambda - V_t(s_t)\right] \cdot \nabla_{\vec{\theta}_t} V_t(s_t) \tag{6}$$

Unfortunately, however, $R_t^{(n)}$ (and any of its averages including R_t^λ) is a biased approximation of $V^\pi(s_t)$ for the very reason that makes it practical (which is not waiting until the end of the task to obtain $V^\pi(s_t)$). Hence rule (6) does not necessary converge to a local optimum solution $\vec{\theta}^*$ of the error function F_t. The resultant update rule (6) is in fact the forward view of the TD(λ) method where no guarantee of reaching $\vec{\theta}^*$ immediately follows. Instead, under some conditions, and when linear function approximation are used, then the former rule is guaranteed to converge to a solution $\vec{\theta}_\infty$ that satisfies (Tsitsiklis and Van Roy 1997) $MSE^{\frac{1}{2}}(\vec{\theta}_\infty) \le \frac{1-\gamma\lambda}{1-\gamma} MSE^{\frac{1}{2}}(\vec{\theta}^*)$.

The theoretical forward view of the TD updates involves the quantity R_t^λ which is, in practice, still hard to be available because it needs to look many steps ahead in the future.

Therefore, it can be replaced by the mechanistic backward view involving eligibility traces. It can be proved that both updates are equivalent for the off-line learning case (Sutton and Barto 1998) even when λ varies from one step to the other as long as $\lambda \in [0,1]$. The update rules of TD with eligibility traces, denoted as TD(λ) are:

$$\vec{\theta}_{t+1} = \vec{\theta}_t + \alpha_t \delta_t \cdot \vec{e}_t \tag{7}$$

$$\vec{e}_t = \gamma\lambda\vec{e}_{t-1} + \nabla_{\vec{\theta}_t} V_t(s_t) \tag{8}$$

$$\delta_t = r_{t+1} + \gamma V_t(s_{t+1}) - V_t(s_t) \tag{9}$$

It can be realized that the forward and backward rules become identical for TD(0). In addition, the gradient can be approximated as:

$$\vec{g}_t = 2\delta_t \cdot \nabla_{\vec{\theta}_t} V_t(s_t) \tag{10}$$

If linear neural network is used to approximate $V_t(s_t)$, then it can be written as $V_t(s_t) = \vec{\varphi}_t^T \vec{\theta}_t = \vec{\theta}_t^T \vec{\varphi}_t$. In this case, we obtain the update rule:

$$\vec{e}_t = \gamma\lambda\vec{e}_{t-1} + \vec{\phi}_t \tag{11}$$

It should be noted that all of the former rules starting from (4) depend on the gradient decent update. When the quantity $V^\pi(s_t)$ was replaced by some approximation the rules became impure gradient decent rule. Nevertheless, such rules can still be called gradient decent update rules since they are derived according to it. Rules that uses its own approximation of $V^\pi(s_t)$ are called bootstrapping rules. In particular, TD(0) update is a bootstrapping method since it uses the term $r_{t+1} + \gamma V_t(s_{t+1})$ which involves its own approximation of the value of the next state to approximate $V^\pi(s_t)$. In addition, the gradient $\vec{g}_t$ can be approximated in different ways. For example, if we approximate $V^\pi(s_t)$ by $r_{t+1} + \gamma V_t(s_{t+1})$ first then calculate the gradient we get the residual gradient temporal difference, which in turn can be combined with TD update in a weight averaged fashion to get the residual TD (Baird 1995).

3. TD and conjugate gradient function approximation

3.1 Conjugate gradient extension of TD

We turn our attention now for an extension of TD(λ) learning using function approximation. We will direct the search for the optimal points of the error function $Er_t^2(s)$ along the conjugate direction instead of the gradient direction. By doing so an increase in the performance is expected. In fact, more precisely a decrease of the number of steps to reach optimality is expected. This is especially true for cases where the number of distinctive eigenvalues of the matrix H (matrix of second derivatives of the performance function) is less than n the number of parameters $\vec{\theta}$. To direct the search along the conjugate gradient direction, $\vec{p}$ should be constructed as follows:

$$\vec{p}_t = -\vec{g}_t + \beta_t \vec{p}_{t-1} \tag{12}$$

$\vec{p}_0$ is initiated to the gradient of the error (Hagan, Demuth et al. 1996; Nocedal and Wright 2006); $\vec{p}_0 = -\vec{g}_0$. Rule (12) ensures that all $\vec{p}_t \; \forall t$ are orthogonal to $\Delta\vec{g}_{t-1} = \vec{g}_t - \vec{g}_{t-1}$. This can be realized by choosing the scalar β_t to satisfy the orthogonality condition:

$$\Delta\vec{g}_{t-1} \cdot \vec{p}_t = 0 \Rightarrow \Delta\vec{g}_{t-1}^T \vec{p}_t = 0 \Rightarrow \Delta\vec{g}_{t-1}^T(-\vec{g}_t + \beta_t \vec{p}_{t-1}) = 0 \Rightarrow \beta_t = \frac{\Delta\vec{g}_{t-1}^T \vec{g}_t}{\Delta\vec{g}_{t-1}^T \vec{p}_{t-1}} \tag{13}$$

In fact, the scalar β_t can be chosen in different ways that should produce equivalent results for the quadratic error functions (Hagan, Demuth et al. 1996), the most common choices are:

$$\beta_t^{(HS)} = \frac{\Delta\vec{g}_{t-1}^T \vec{g}_t}{\Delta\vec{g}_{t-1}^T \vec{p}_{t-1}} \tag{14}$$

$$\beta_t^{(FR)} = \frac{\vec{g}_t^T \vec{g}_t}{\vec{g}_{t-1}^T \vec{g}_{t-1}} \tag{15}$$

$$\beta_t^{(PR)} = \frac{\Delta\vec{g}_{t-1}^T \vec{g}_t}{\vec{g}_{t-1}^T \vec{g}_{t-1}} \tag{16}$$

due to Hestenes and Steifel, Fletcher and Reeves, and Polak and Ribiere respectively.
From equation (4) the conjugate gradient rule (12) can be rewritten as follows:

$$\vec{p}_t = 2\left[V^\pi(s_t) - V_t(s_t)\right] \cdot \nabla_{\vec{\theta}_t} V_t(s_t) + \beta_t \vec{p}_{t-1} \tag{17}$$

By substituting in (3) we obtain the pure conjugate gradient general update rule:

$$\vec{\theta}_{t+1} = \vec{\theta}_t + \frac{1}{2}\alpha_t\left[2\left[V^\pi(s_t) - V_t(s_t)\right]\nabla_{\vec{\theta}_t} V_t(s_t) + \beta_t \vec{p}_{t-1}\right] \tag{18}$$

3.2 Forward view of conjugate gradient TD

Similar to TD(λ) update rule (6), we can approximate the quantity $V^\pi(s_t)$ by R_t^λ, which does not guarantee convergence, because it is not unbiased (for $\lambda < 1$), nevertheless it is more practical. Hence, we get the theoretical forward view of TD-conj(λ); the TD(λ) conjugate gradient update rules:

$$\vec{p}_t = 2\left[R_t^\lambda - V_t(s_t)\right] \cdot \nabla_{\vec{\theta}_t} V_t(s_t) + \beta_t \vec{p}_{t-1} \tag{19}$$

$$\vec{\theta}_{t+1} = \vec{\theta}_t + \alpha_t\left[\left[R_t^\lambda - V_t(s_t)\right]\nabla_{\vec{\theta}_t} V_t(s_t) + \frac{1}{2}\beta_t \vec{p}_{t-1}\right] \tag{20}$$

If the estimate $r_{t+1} + \gamma V_t(s_{t+1})$ is used to estimate $V^\pi(s_t)$ (as in TD(0)), then we can obtain the TD-conj(0) update rules; where rules (19) and (20) are estimated as:

$$\vec{p}_t = 2\delta_t \cdot \nabla_{\vec{\theta}_t} V_t(s_t) + \beta_t \vec{p}_{t-1} \tag{21}$$

$$\vec{\theta}_{t+1} = \vec{\theta}_t + \alpha_t \left[\delta_t \nabla_{\vec{\theta}_t} V_t(s_t) + \frac{1}{2} \beta_t \vec{p}_{t-1} \right] \tag{22}$$

It should be noted again that those rules are not pure conjugate gradient but nevertheless we call them as such since they are derived according to the conjugate gradient rules.

3.3 Equivalency of TD(λ t≠0) and TD-conj(λ=0)

Theorem 1:

TD-conj(0) is equivalent to a special class of TD(λ_t) that is denoted as TD($\lambda_t^{(conj)}$), under the condition: $0 \le \lambda_t^{(conj)} = \frac{\beta_t}{\gamma} \frac{\delta_{t-1}}{\delta_t} \le 1; \forall t$, regardless of the approximation used. The equivalency is denoted as TD-conj(0)$\equiv$TD($\lambda_t^{(conj)}$) and the bound condition is called the equivalency condition.

Proof:

We will proof that TD-conj(0) is equivalent to a backward view of a certain class of TD(λ_t), denoted as TD($\lambda_t^{(conj)}$). Hence, by the virtue of the equivalency of the backward and forward views of all TD(λ_t) for the off-line case, the theorem follows. For the on-line case the equivalency is restricted to the backward view of TD($\lambda_t^{(conj)}$).
The update rule (22) can be rewritten in the following form:

$$\vec{\theta}_{t+1} = \vec{\theta}_t + \alpha_t \delta_t \left[\nabla_{\vec{\theta}_t} V_t(s_t) + \frac{\beta_t}{2\delta_t} \vec{p}_{t-1} \right] \tag{23}$$

where it is assumed that $\delta_t \ne 0$ because otherwise it means that we reached an equilibrium point for $V_t(s_t)$, meaning the rule has converged and there is no need to apply any learning rule any more. Now we introduce the conjugate eligibility traces vector $\vec{e}_t^{(conj)}$ that is defined as follows:

$$\vec{e}_t^{(conj)} \quad = \frac{1}{2\delta_t} \vec{p}_t \tag{24}$$

By substituting (21) in (24) we have that

$$\vec{e}_t^{(conj)} = \nabla_{\vec{\theta}_t} V_t(s_t) + \frac{\beta_t}{2\delta_t} \vec{p}_{t-1} \tag{25}$$

From (25) we proceed in two directions. First, by substituting (25) in (23) we obtain an update rule identical to rule (11):

$$\vec{\theta}_{t+1} = \vec{\theta}_t + \alpha_t \delta_t \vec{e}_t^{(conj)} \tag{26}$$

Second, from (24) we have that:

$$\vec{p}_{t-1} = 2\delta_{t-1} \vec{e}_{t-1}^{(conj)} \tag{27}$$

Hence, by substituting (27) in (25) we obtain:

$$\vec{e}_t^{(conj)} = \nabla_{\vec{\theta}_t} V_t(s_t) + \frac{\delta_{t-1}}{\delta_t} \beta_t \vec{e}_{t-1}^{(conj)} \tag{28}$$

By conveniently defining:

$$\gamma \lambda_t^{(conj)} = \beta_t \frac{\delta_{t-1}}{\delta_t} \tag{29}$$

we acquire an update rule for the conjugate eligibility traces $\vec{e}_t^{(conj)}$ that is similar to rule (8):

$$\vec{e}_t^{(conj)} = \gamma \lambda_t^{(conj)} \vec{e}_{t-1}^{(conj)} + \nabla_{\vec{\theta}_t} V_t(s_t) \tag{30}$$

Rules (26) and (30) are almost identical to rules (8) and (9) except that λ is variable in (29). Hence, they show that TD-conj(0) method can be equivalent to a backward update of TD(λ) method with a variable λ. In addition, rule (29) establishes a canonical way of varying λ; where we have:

$$\lambda_t^{(conj)} = \frac{\beta_t}{\gamma} \frac{\delta_{t-1}}{\delta_t} \tag{31}$$

The only restriction we have is that there is no immediate guarantee that $\lambda_t^{(conj)} \in [0,1]$. Hence, the condition for full equivalency is that $\lambda_t^{(conj)}$ satisfies:

$$0 \le \lambda_t^{(conj)} = \frac{\beta_t}{\gamma} \frac{\delta_{t-1}}{\delta_t} \le 1 \tag{32}$$

According to (31) and by substituting (14), (15) and (16) we obtain the following different ways of calculating $\lambda_t^{(conj)}$:

$$^{1}\lambda_t^{(conj)} = \frac{\left(\delta_t \cdot \nabla_{\vec{\theta}_t} V_t(s_t) - \delta_{t-1} \cdot \nabla_{\vec{\theta}_{t-1}} V_{t-1}(s_{t-1})\right)^T \nabla_{\vec{\theta}_t} V_t(s_t)}{\gamma\left(\delta_t \cdot \nabla_{\vec{\theta}_t} V_t(s_t) - \delta_{t-1} \cdot \nabla_{\vec{\theta}_{t-1}} V_{t-1}(s_{t-1})\right)^T \vec{e}_{t-1}^{(conj)}} \tag{33}$$

$$^{2}\lambda_t^{(conj)} = \frac{\delta_t \left\| \nabla_{\vec{\theta}_t} V_t(s_t)_t \right\|^2}{\gamma \delta_{t-1} \left\| \nabla_{\vec{\theta}_{t-1}} V_{t-1}(s_{t-1}) \right\|^2} \tag{34}$$

$$^{3}\lambda_t^{(conj)} = \frac{\left(\delta_t \cdot \nabla_{\vec{\theta}_t} V_t(s_t) - \delta_{t-1} \cdot \nabla_{\vec{\theta}_{t-1}} V_{t-1}(s_{t-1})\right)^T \nabla_{\vec{\theta}_t} V_t(s_t)}{\gamma \delta_{t-1} \left\| \nabla_{\vec{\theta}_{t-1}} V_{t-1}(s_{t-1}) \right\|^2} \tag{35}$$

which proves our theorem □.
There are few things to be realized from Theorem 1:

$\lambda_t^{(conj)}$ should be viewed as a more general form of λ which can magnify or shrink the trace according to how much it has confidence in its estimation. TD with variable λ has not been studied before (Sutton and Barto 1998), and $\lambda_t^{(conj)}$ gives for the first time a canonical way to vary λ depending on conjugate gradient directions.

From (31) it can be realized that both δ_t and δ_{t-1} are involved in the calculations of the eligibility traces. This means that the division cancels the direct effect of an error δ and leaves the relative rate-of-changes between consequent steps of this error to play the big role in changing $\lambda_t^{(conj)}$ according to (31).

Since $\gamma \in [0,1]$ and $\lambda_t^{(conj)}$ should satisfy that $\lambda_t^{(conj)} \in [0,1]$, so as the term $\gamma\lambda_t^{(conj)}$ should satisfy $0 \le \gamma\lambda_t^{(conj)} \le 1$. Therefore, condition (32) can be made more succinct:

$$0 \le \beta_t \frac{\delta_{t-1}}{\delta_t} \le \gamma \le 1 \tag{36}$$

The initial eligibility trace is:

$$\vec{e}_0^{(conj)} = \frac{1}{2\delta_0}\vec{p}_0 = \frac{1}{2\delta_0} 2\delta_0 \nabla_{\vec{\theta}_t} V_0(s_0) \Rightarrow \qquad \vec{e}_0^{(conj)} = \nabla_{\vec{\theta}_t} V_0(s_0) \tag{37}$$

From an application point of view, it suffices for $\lambda_t^{(conj)}$ value to be forced to this condition whenever its value goes beyond 1 or less than 0:

$$if(\lambda_t^{(conj)} > 1) \Rightarrow \lambda_t^{(conj)} \leftarrow 1, \qquad if(\lambda_t^{(conj)} < 0) \Rightarrow \lambda_t^{(conj)} \leftarrow 0 \tag{38}$$

If $V_t(s_t)$ is approximated by a linear approximation $V_t(s_t) = \vec{\theta}_t^T \vec{\varphi}_t$ then: $\nabla_{\vec{\theta}_t} V_t(s_t) = \vec{\varphi}_t$, in this case we have from (30) that:

$$\vec{e}_t^{(conj)} = \gamma\lambda_t^{(conj)} \vec{e}_{t-1}^{(conj)} + \vec{\phi}_t \tag{39}$$

λ can be defined by substituting $\nabla_{\vec{\theta}_t} V_t(s_t) = \vec{\phi}_t$ in (33), (34) and (35) respectively as follows:

$$^{1}\lambda_t^{(conj)} = \frac{\left(\delta_t\vec{\phi}_t - \delta_{t-1}\vec{\phi}_{t-1}\right)^T \vec{\phi}_t}{\left(\delta_t\vec{\phi}_t - \delta_{t-1}\vec{\phi}_{t-1}\right)^T \vec{e}_{t-1}}, \; ^{2}\lambda_t^{(conj)} = \frac{\delta_t \left\|\vec{\phi}_t\right\|^2}{\delta_{t-1}\left\|\vec{\phi}_{t-1}\right\|^2}, \; ^{3}\lambda_t^{(conj)} = \frac{\left(\delta_t\vec{\phi}_t - \delta_{t-1}\vec{\phi}_{t-1}\right)^T \vec{\phi}_t}{\delta_{t-1}\left\|\vec{\phi}_{t-1}\right\|^2} \tag{40}$$

Any method that depends on TD updates such as Sarsa or Q-learning can take advantage of these new findings and use the new update rules of TD-conj(0).

This concludes our study of the properties of TD-conj(0) method and we move next to the model.

4. The visual homing Sarsa-conj(0) model

For visual homing it is assumed that the image at each time step represents the current state, and the state space S is the set of all images, or views, that can be taken for any location (with specific orientation) in the environment. This complex state space has two problems. Firstly, each state is of high dimensionality, i.e. it is represented by a large number of pixels. Secondly, the state space is huge, and a policy cannot be learned directly for each state.

Instead, a feature representation of the states is used to reduce the high-dimensionality of the state space and to gain the advantages of coding that allows a parameterized representation to be used for the value function (Stone, Sutton et al. 2005). In turn, parameterization permits learning a general value function representation that can easily accommodate for new unvisited states by generalization. Eventually, this helps to solve the second problem of having to deal with a huge state space.

The feature representation can reduce the high-dimensionality problem simply by reducing the number of components needed to represent the views. Hence, reducing dimensionality is normally carried out at the cost of less distinctiveness for states belonging to a huge space. Therefore, the features representation of the state space, when successful, strikes a good balance between distinctiveness of states and reduced dimensionality. This assumption is of importance towards the realization of any RL model with a high-dimensional states problem.

4.1 State representation and home information

One representation that maintains an acceptable level of distinctiveness and reduces the high-dimensionality of images is the histogram. A histogram of an image is a vector of components, each of which contains the number of pixels that belong to a certain range of intensity values. The significance of histograms is that they map a large two-dimensional matrix to a smaller one-dimensional vector. This effectively encodes the input state space into a coarser feature space. Therefore, if the RGB (Red, Green, and Blue) representation of colour is used for an image the histogram of each colour channel is a vector of components, each of which is the number of pixels that lie in the component's interval. The interval each component represents is called the bin, and according to a pre-specified bin size of the range of the pixel values, a pre-specified number of bins will be obtained.

A histogram does not preserve the distinctiveness of the image, i.e. two different images can have the same histogram, especially when low granularity bin intervals are chosen. Nevertheless, histograms have been found to be widely acceptable and useful in image processing and image retrieval applications (Rubner and et al. 2000). Other representations are possible, such as the one given by the Earth Mover's Distance (Rubner and et al. 2000). However, such mapping is not necessary for the problem here since the model will be dealing with a unified image dimension throughout its working life, because its images are captured by the same robot camera.

The feature representation approach does not give a direct indication of the distance to the goal location. Although the assumption that the goal location is always in the robot's field of view will *not* be made, by comparing the current view with the goal view(s) the properties of distinctiveness, distance and orientation can be embodied to an extent in the RL model. Since the home location can be approached from different directions, the way it is represented should accommodate for those directions. Therefore, a home (or goal) location is defined by m snapshots called the stored views. A few snapshots (normally $m \geq 3$) of the home location are taken at the start of the learning stage, each from the same fixed distance but from a different angle. These snapshots define the home location and are the only information required to allow the agent to learn to reach its home location starting from any arbitrary position in the environment (including those from which it cannot see the home, i.e. the agent should be able to reach a hidden goal location). Fig. 1 shows a sample of a three-view representation of a goal location taken in a simulated environment.

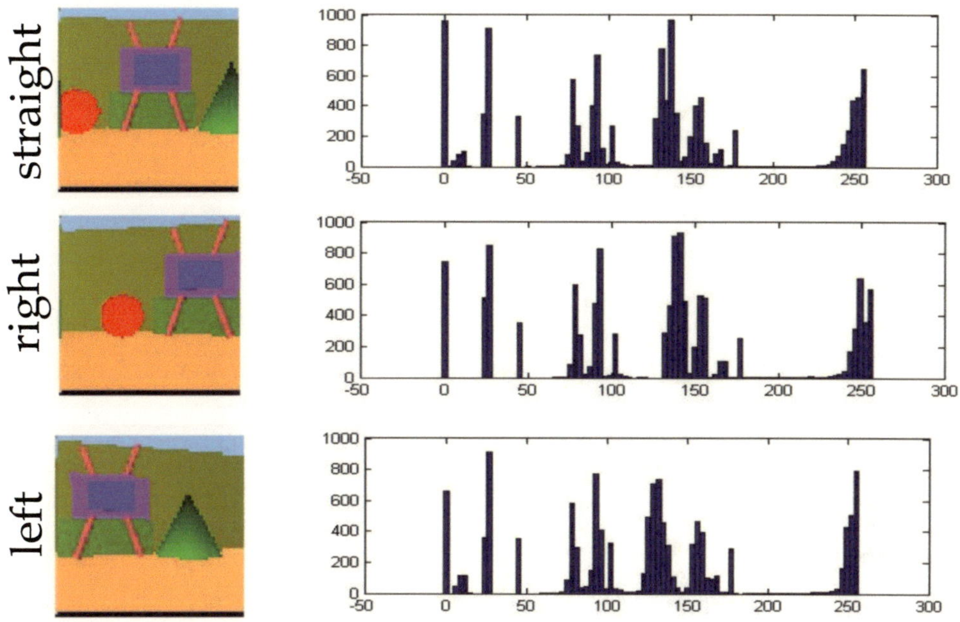

Fig. 1. Sample of a three-view representation taken from three different angles for a goal location with their associated histograms in a simulated environment.

4.2 Features vectors and radial basis representation

A histogram of each channel of the current view is taken and compared with those of the stored views through a radial basis function (RBF) component. This provides the features space $\Phi : S \rightarrow \Re^n$ representation (41) which is used with the Sarsa-conj algorithm, described later:

$$\phi_i\left(s_t(c,j)\right) = \exp\left(-\frac{\left(h_i\left(s_t(c)\right) - h_i\left(v(c,j)\right)\right)^2}{2\hat{\sigma}_i^2} \right) \tag{41}$$

Index t stands for the time step j for the jth stored view, and c is the index of the channel, where the RGB representation of images is used. Accordingly, $v(c,j)$ is the channel c image of the jth stored view, $h_i\left(v(c,j)\right)$ is histogram bin i of image $v(c,j)$, and $h_i\left(s_t(c)\right)$ is histogram bin i of channel c of the current (t) view. The number of bins will have an effect on the structure and richness of this representation and hence on the model. It should be noted that the radial basis feature extraction used here differs from the radial basis feature extraction used in (Tsitsiklis and Van Roy 1996). The difference is in the extraction process and not in the form. In their feature extraction, certain points s_i are normally chosen from the input space $\Re^n$ to construct a linear combination of radial basis functions. Those points in that representation are replaced in this work by the bins themselves.
Further, the variance of each bin will be substituted by a global average of the variances of those bins.

$$\hat{\sigma}_i^2 = (1/T-1)\sum_{t=1}^{T}\Delta h_i^2(t) \tag{42}$$

$$\Delta h_i^2(t) = \left(h_i\left(s_t(c)\right) - h_i\left(v(c,j)\right)\right)^2 \tag{43}$$

where T is the total number of time steps. To normalize the feature representation the scaled histogram bins $h_i\left(s_t(c)\right)/H$ are used, assuming that n is the number of features we have:

$$\sum_i^n h_i\left(v(c,j)\right) = \sum_i^n h_i\left(s_t(c)\right) = H \tag{44}$$

where it can be realized that H is a constant and is equal to the number of all pixels taken for a view. Hence, the final form of the feature calculation is:

$$\phi_i\left(s_t(c,j)\right) = \exp\left(-\frac{\left(h_i\left(s_t(c)\right) - h_i\left(v(c,j)\right)\right)^2}{2H^2\hat{\sigma}^2}\right) \tag{45}$$

It should be noted that this feature representation has the advantage of being in the interval [0 1], which will be beneficial for the reasons discussed in the next section.
The feature vector of the current view (state) is a union of all of the features for each channel and each stored view, as follows:

$$\Phi(s_t) = \bigoplus_{j=1}^{m}\bigoplus_{c=1}^{3}\bigoplus_{i=1}^{B}\varphi_i\left(s_t(c,j)\right) = (\phi_1,\ldots,\phi_i,\ldots,\phi_n) \tag{46}$$

where m is the number of stored views for the goal location, 3 channels are used, and B is the number of bins to be considered. Since an RGB image with values in the range of [0 255] for each pixel will be used, the dimension of the feature space is given by:

$$n = C \times B \times m = C \times (round(\frac{256}{b}) + 1) \times m \tag{47}$$

where b is the bin's size and $C = 3$ is the number of channels. Different bin sizes give different dimensions, which in turn give different numbers of parameters $\vec{\theta}$ that will be used to approximate the value function.

4.3 NRB similarity measure and the termination condition

To measure the similarity between two images, the sum of all the Normalized Radial Basis (NRB) features defined above can be taken and then divided by the feature dimension. The resultant quantity is scaled to 1 and it expresses the overall belief that the two images are identical:

$$NRB(s_t) = \sum_{i=1}^{n}\vec{\phi}_i\left(s_t\right)/n \tag{48}$$

For simplicity the notation $NRB(s_t)$ and NRB_t will be used interchangeably. Other measures can be used (Rubner and et al. 2000). In previous work the Jeffery divergence measure was used (Altahhan Burn, et al. 2008). However the above simpler measure was adopted because it is computationally more efficient for the proposed model since it only requires an extra sum and a division operations. JDM has its own logarithmic calculation which cost additional computations.

Another benefit of NRB is that it is scaled to 1 - a uniform measure can be interpreted more intuitively. On the other hand, it is impractical to scale Jeffery Divergence Measure because although the maximum is known to be 0 there is no direct indication of the minimum. Fig. 2 demonstrates the behaviour of NRB; the robot was placed in front of a goal location and the view was stored. The robot then has been let to rotate in its place form -90° (left) to +90° (right); in each time step the current view has been taken and compared with the stored view and their NRB value was plotted. As expected the normal distribution shape of those NRB values provide evidence for its suitability.

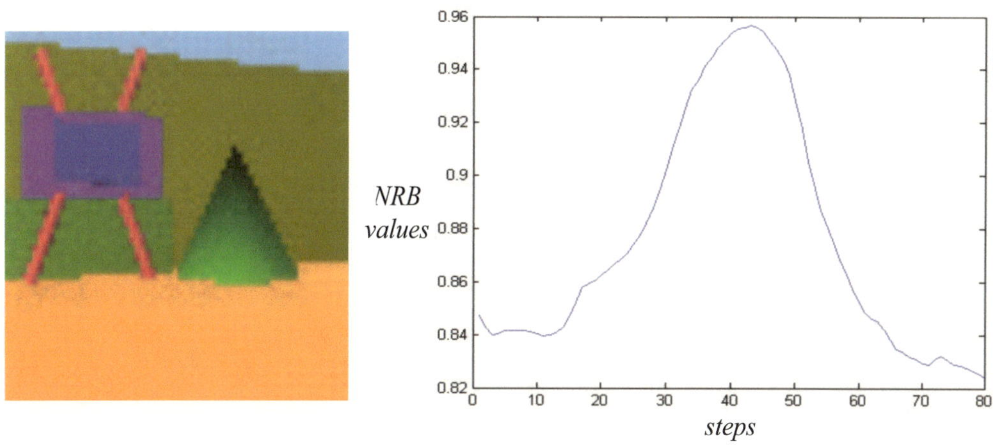

(a) (b)

Fig. 2. (a): Current view of agent camera. (b) The plotted values of the normalized radial bases similarity measure of a sample π rotation.

An episode describes the collective steps of an agent starting from any location and navigating in the environment until it reaches the home location. The agent is assumed to finish an episode and be at the home location (final state) if its similarity measure indicates with high certainty ψ_{upper} that its current view is similar to one of the stored views. This specifies the episode termination condition of the model.

$$If\ NRB(s_t) \geq \psi_{upper} \Rightarrow \text{Terminate Episode}$$

Similarly, the agent is assumed to be in the neighbourhood of the home location with the desired orientation $If\ NRB(s_t) \geq \psi_{lower}$ where $\psi_{upper} \geq \psi_{lower}$. This situation is called home-at-perspective and the interval $[\psi_{upper}, \psi_{lower}]$ is called the home-at-perspective confidence interval.

4.4 The action space

In order to avoid the complexity of dealing with a set of actions each with infinite resolution speed values (which in effect turns into an infinite number of actions), the two differential wheel speeds of the agent are assumed to be set to particular values, so that a set of three actions with fixed values is obtained. The set of actions is A = [Left_Forward, Right_Forward, Go_Forward]. The acceleration of continuous action space cannot be obtained using this limited set of actions. Nevertheless, by using actions with a small differential speed (i.e. small thrust rotation angle) the model can still get the effect of continuous rotation by repeating the same action as needed. This is done at the cost of more action steps.

A different set of actions than the limited one used here could be used to enhance the performance. For example, another three actions [Left_Forward, Right_Forward, Go_Forward] with double the speed could be added, although more training would be a normal requirement in this case. One can also add a layer to generalize towards other actions by enforcing a Gaussian activation around the selected action and fade it for other actions, as in (Lazaric, Restelli et al. 2007). In this work, however, the action set was kept to a minimum to concentrate on the effect of other components of the model.

4.5 The reward function

The reward function r depends on which similarity or dissimilarity function was used, and it consists of three parts:

$$r_{NRB} = \text{cost} + \Delta NRB_{t-1} + NRB_t \quad (49)$$

The main part is the cost, which is set to -1 for each step taken by the robot without reaching the home location. The other two parts are to augment the reward signal to provide better performance. They are:

Approaching the goal reward. This is the maximum increase in similarity between the current step and the previous step. This signal is called the differential similarity signal and it is defined as:

$$\Delta NRB_{t-1} = \left(NRB_t - NRB_{t-1}\right) \quad (50)$$

The Position signal, which is simply expressed by the current similarity NRB_t. Thus, as the current location differs less from the home location, this reward will increase. Hence, the reward can be rewritten in the following form:

$$r_{NRB} = \text{cost} + 2NRB_t - NRB_{t-1} \quad (51)$$

The two additional reward components above will be considered only if the similarity of t and t-1 steps are both beyond the threshold ψ_{lower} to ensure that home-at-perspective is satisfied in both steps. This threshold is empirically determined, and is introduced merely to enhance the performance.

4.6 Variable eligibility traces and update rule for TD($\lambda_t^{(conj)}$)

An eligibility trace constitutes a mechanism for temporal credit assignment. It indicates that the memory parameters associated with the action are eligible for undergoing learning changes (Sutton and Barto 1998). For visual homing, the eligibility trace for the current action a is constructed from the feature vectors encountered so far. More specifically, it is the discounted sum of the feature vectors of the images that the robot has seen previously when the very same action a had been taken. The eligibility trace for other actions which have not been taken while in the current state is simply its previous trace but discounted, i.e. those actions are now less accredited, as demonstrated in the following equation.

$$\vec{\mathbf{e}}_t(a) \leftarrow \begin{cases} \gamma\lambda\vec{\mathbf{e}}_{t-1}(a)+\vec{\boldsymbol{\varphi}}(s_t) & \text{if } a=a_t \\ \gamma\lambda\vec{\mathbf{e}}_{t-1}(a) & \text{otherwise} \end{cases} \tag{52}$$

λ is the discount rate for eligibility traces $\vec{\mathbf{e}}_t$ and γ is the rewards discount rate . The eligibility trace components do not comply with the unit interval i.e. each component can be more than 1. The reward function also does not comply with the unit interval. The update rule that uses the eligibility trace and the episodically changed learning rate α_{ep} is as follows:

$$\vec{\boldsymbol{\theta}}(a_t) \leftarrow \vec{\boldsymbol{\theta}}(a_t) + \alpha_{ep} \cdot \vec{\mathbf{e}}_t(a_t) \cdot \delta_t \tag{53}$$

As it was shown above and in (Altahhan 2008) the conjugate gradient TD-conj(0) method is translated through an equivalency theorem into a TD(λ) method with variable λ denoted as TD($\lambda_t^{(conj)}$) with the condition that $0 \le \lambda_t^{(conj)} \le 1$. Therefore, to employ conjugate gradient TD, equation (52) can be applied to obtain the eligibility traces for TD-conj. The only difference is that λ is varying according to one of the following possible forms:

$$^1\lambda_t^{(conj)} = \frac{\left(\delta_t\vec{\phi}_t - \delta_{t-1}\vec{\phi}_{t-1}\right)^T \vec{\phi}_t}{\gamma\left(\delta_t\vec{\phi}_t - \delta_{t-1}\vec{\phi}_{t-1}\right)^T \vec{e}_{t-1}^{(conj)}},\ ^2\lambda_t^{(conj)} = \frac{\delta_t\left\|\vec{\phi}_t\right\|^2}{\gamma\delta_{t-1}\left\|\vec{\phi}_{t-1}\right\|^2},\ \text{or}\ ^3\lambda_t^{(conj)} = \frac{\left(\delta_t\vec{\phi}_t - \delta_{t-1}\vec{\phi}_{t-1}\right)^T \vec{\phi}_t}{\gamma\delta_{t-1}\left\|\vec{\phi}_{t-1}\right\|^2} \tag{54}$$

TD-conj(0) (and any algorithm that depends on it such as Sarsa-conj(0) (Altahhan 2008) is a family of algorithms, not because its λ is changed automatically from one step to the other, but because λ can be varied using different types of formulae. Some of those formulae are outlined in (25) for linear function approximation.
In addition, those values of $\lambda_t^{(conj)}$ that do not satisfy $0 \le \lambda_t^{(conj)} \le 1$, can be forced according to the following:

$$if(\lambda_t^{(conj)} > 1) \Rightarrow \lambda_t^{(conj)} \leftarrow 1, \qquad if(\lambda_t^{(conj)} < 0) \Rightarrow \lambda_t^{(conj)} \leftarrow 0$$

The eligibility traces can be written as:

$$\vec{\mathbf{e}}_t^{(conj)}(a) \leftarrow \begin{cases} \gamma\lambda_t^{(conj)}\vec{\mathbf{e}}_{t-1}^{(conj)}(a)+\vec{\boldsymbol{\varphi}}(s_t) & \text{if } a=a_t \\ \gamma\lambda_t^{(conj)}\vec{\mathbf{e}}_{t-1}^{(conj)}(a) & \text{otherwise} \end{cases} \tag{55}$$

For episodic tasks γ can be set to 1 (absence). Finally the update rule is identical to (52), where the conjugate eligibility trace is used instead of the fixed λ eligibility trace:

$$\vec{\boldsymbol{\theta}}(a_t) \leftarrow \vec{\boldsymbol{\theta}}(a_t) + \alpha_{ep} \cdot \vec{\mathbf{e}}_t^{(conj)}(a_t) \cdot \delta_t \tag{56}$$

4.7 The policy used to generate actions

A combination of the ε-greedy policy and Gibbs soft-max (Sutton and Barto 1998) policy is used to pick up an action and to strike a balance between exploration and exploitation.

$$\pi_{\varepsilon+Gibbs}(a_i,\vec{\varphi}(s_t)) = Gibbs(a_i,\vec{\varphi}(s_t)) + \Pr(a_i,\vec{\varphi}(s_t)) \tag{57}$$

Using ε-greedy probability allows exploration to be increased as needed by initially setting ε to a high value then decreasing it through episodes.

$$\Pr(a,\vec{\phi}(S_t)) = \begin{cases} 1-\varepsilon+\dfrac{\varepsilon}{|A|} & if a = \arg\max\left[\vec{\phi}(S_t)^T \cdot \vec{\theta}(a_i)\right] \\ \dfrac{\varepsilon}{|A|} & otherwise \end{cases} \tag{58}$$

The Gibbs soft-max probability given by equation (59) enforces the chances of picking the action with the highest value when the differences between the values of it and the remaining actions are large, i.e. it helps in increasing the chances of picking the action with the highest action-value function when the robot is sure that this value is the right one.

$$Gibbs(a_i,\vec{\phi}(s_t)) = \frac{\exp\left[\vec{\phi}(s_t)^T \cdot \theta(a_i)\right]}{\sum_{j=1}^{|A|}\exp\left[\vec{\phi}(s_t)^T \cdot \theta(a_j)\right]} \tag{59}$$

4.8 The learning method

The last model component to be discussed is the learning algorithm. The basis of the model learning algorithm is the Sarsa(λ) control algorithm with linear function approximation (Sutton and Barto 1998). However, this algorithm was adapted to use the TD-conj(0) instead of the TD(λ) update rules. Hence, it was denoted as Sarsa-conj(0). From a theoretical point of view, TD-conj(0)- and any algorithm depending on its update such as Sarsa-conj(0) – uses the conjugate gradient direction in conjunction with TD(0) update. While, from an algorithm implementation point of view, according to the equivalency theorem, TD-conj(0) and Sarsa-conj(0) have the same skeleton of TD(λ) and Sarsa(λ) (Sutton and Barto 1998) with the difference that TD-conj(0) and Sarsa-conj(0) use the variable eligibility traces $\lambda_t^{(conj)}$ (Altahhan 2008). The benefit of using TD-conj(0) update is to optimize the learning process (in terms of speed and performance) by optimizing the depth of the credit assignment process according to the conjugate directions, purely through automatically varying λ in each time step instead of assigning a fixed value to λ manually for the duration of the learning process.

Sarsa is an on-policy bootstrapping algorithm that has the properties of (a) being suitable for control, (b) providing function approximation capabilities to deal with huge state space, and (c) applying on-line learning. These three properties are considered ideal for the visual robot homing (VRH) problem. The ultimate goal for VRH is to control the robot to achieve the homing task, the state space is huge because of the visual input, and on-line learning was chosen because of its higher practicality and usability in real world situations than off-line learning.

Initialization

initialize b, m, *and* $final\_episode$

$$n \leftarrow \approx 3 \times \frac{256}{b} \times m$$

$$\vec{\theta}_0(a_i) \leftarrow \vec{1} \qquad i = 1:|A|$$

$$a_0 \leftarrow 2$$

Repeat for each episode

$$\vec{\mathbf{e}}_0(a_i) \leftarrow \vec{\mathbf{0}} \qquad i = 1:|A|$$

$s_0 \leftarrow$ Initial robot view, $t \leftarrow 1$

Generate a_0 using sampling of probability $\pi(\vec{\varphi}(s_0), a)$

Repeat (for each step of episode)

Take action a_t, Observe r_{t+1}, $\vec{\varphi}(s_{t+1})$,

Generate a_{t+1} using sampling of probability $\pi(\vec{\varphi}(s_{t+1}), a)$.

$$\delta_t \leftarrow \left[r_{t+1} + \gamma\, \vec{\varphi}(s_{t+1})^T \cdot \vec{\theta}(a_{t+1}) - \vec{\varphi}(s_t)^T \cdot \vec{\theta}(a_t) \right]$$

$${}^{1}\lambda_t^{(conj)} \leftarrow \frac{\left(\delta_t \vec{\varphi}_t - \delta_{t-1}\vec{\varphi}_{t-1}\right)^T \vec{\varphi}_t}{\gamma\left(\delta_t \vec{\varphi}_t - \delta_{t-1}\vec{\varphi}_{t-1}\right)^T \vec{\mathbf{e}}_{t-1}}, \quad {}^{2}\lambda_t^{(conj)} \leftarrow \frac{\delta_t \left\|\vec{\varphi}_t\right\|^2}{\gamma\delta_{t-1}\left\|\vec{\varphi}_{t-1}\right\|^2}, \text{ or } \quad {}^{3}\lambda_t^{(conj)} \leftarrow \frac{\left(\delta_t \vec{\varphi}_t - \delta_{t-1}\vec{\varphi}_{t-1}\right)^T \vec{\varphi}_t}{\gamma\delta_{t-1}\left\|\vec{\varphi}_{t-1}\right\|^2}$$

$$\vec{\mathbf{e}}_t^{(conj)}(a) \leftarrow \begin{cases} \gamma\lambda_t^{(conj)} \vec{\mathbf{e}}_{t-1}^{(conj)}(a) + \vec{\varphi}(s_t) & \text{if } a = a_t \\ \gamma\lambda_t^{(conj)} \vec{\mathbf{e}}_{t-1}^{(conj)}(a) & \text{otherwise} \end{cases}$$

$$\vec{\theta}(a_t) \leftarrow \vec{\theta}(a_t) + \alpha_{ep} \cdot \vec{\mathbf{e}}_t^{(conj)}(a_t) \cdot \delta_t$$

$$\vec{\varphi}(s_t) \leftarrow \vec{\varphi}(s_{t+1}), \; \vec{\varphi}(s_{t-1}) \leftarrow \vec{\varphi}(s_t)$$

$$\delta_{t-1} \leftarrow \delta_t, \quad a_t \leftarrow a_{t+1}$$

until $\frac{1}{n}\sum_{i=1}^{n} \phi_i(s_t) < \psi_{upper}$

until *episode* $==$ $final\_episode$

Fig. 3. Dynamic-policy Sarsa-conj(0) control, with RBF features extraction, linear action-value function approximation and Policy Improvement. The approximate Q is implicitly a function of $\vec{\theta}$. $\lambda_t^{(conj)}$ can be assigned to any of the three forms calculated in the preceding step.

The action-value function was used to express the policy, i.e. this model uses a critic to induce the policy. Actor-critic algorithms could be used, which have the advantage of simplicity, but the disadvantage of high variance in the TD error (Konda and Tsitsiklis 2000). This can cause both high fluctuation in the values of the TD error and divergence. This limitation was addressed in this model by carefully designing a suitable scheme to balance exploration and exploitation according to a combination of Gibbs distribution and ε-greedy policy. The Gibbs exponential distribution has some important properties which helped in realizing the convergence. According to (Peters, Vijayakumar et al. 2005) it helps the TD error to lie in accordance with the natural gradient.

In that sense this model is a hybrid model. Like any action-value model it uses the action-value function to induce the policy, but not in a fixed way. It also changes the policy preferences (in each step or episode) towards a more greedy policy like any actor-critic model. So it combines with and varies between action-value and actor-critic models. It is felt that this hybrid structure has its own advantages and disadvantages, and the convergence properties of such algorithms need to be studied further in the future.
TD-conj(0) learns on-line through interaction with software modules that feed it with the robot visual sensors (whether from simulation or from a real robot). The algorithm coded as a controller returns the chosen action to be taken by the robot, and updates its policy through updating its set of parameters used to approximate the action-value function Q. Three linear networks are used to approximate the action-value function for the three actions.

$$\vec{\boldsymbol{\theta}}(a_{(i)}) = (\theta_1^{a(i)},\ldots,\theta_i^{a(i)},\ldots,\theta_n^{a(i)}) \qquad i = 1,..|A|$$

The current image was passed through an RBF layer, which provides the feature vector $\vec{\boldsymbol{\varphi}}(s_t) = (\phi_1,\ldots,\phi_i,\ldots,\phi_n)$. The robot was left to run through several episodes. After each episode the learning rate was decreased, and the policy was improved further through general policy improvement theorem (GPI). The overall algorithm is shown in Fig. 3.
The learning rate was the same used by (Boyan 1999)

$$\alpha_{ep} = \alpha_0 \cdot \frac{n_0 + 1}{n_0 + episode} \tag{60}$$

This rate starts with the same value as α_0 then is reduced exponentially from episode to episode until the final episode. n_0 is a constant that specifies how quickly α_{ep} is reduced. It should be noted that the policy is changing during the learning phase. The learning algorithm evaluates the same policy that it generates the samples from, i.e. it is an on-policy algorithm. It uses the same assumption of the general policy improvement principle to anticipate that even when the policy is being changed (improved towards a more greedy policy) the process should lead to convergence to optimal policy. It moves all the way from being arbitrarily stochastic to becoming only ε-greedy stochastic.

5. Experimental results

The model was applied using a simulated Khepera (Floreano and Mondada 1998) robot in Webots™ (Michel 2004) simulation software. The real Khepera is a miniature robot, 70 mm in diameter and 30 mm in height, and is provided with 8 infra-red sensors for reactive behaviour, as well as a colour camera extension.
A (1.15 m x 1 m) simulated environment has been used as a test bed for the model. The task is to learn to navigate from any location in the environment to a home location (without using any specific object or landmark). For training, the robot always starts from the same location, where it cannot see the home location, and the end state is the target location. After learning the robot can be placed in any part of the environment and should be able to find the home location.
Fig. 4 shows the environment used. The home is assumed to be in front of the television set. A cone and ball of different colours are included to enrich and add more texture to the home location. It should be re-emphasized that no object recognition techniques were used, only

the whole image measure. This allows the model to be applied to any environment with no constraints and with minimal prior information about the home. The controller was developed using a combination of C++ code and Matlab Engine code.

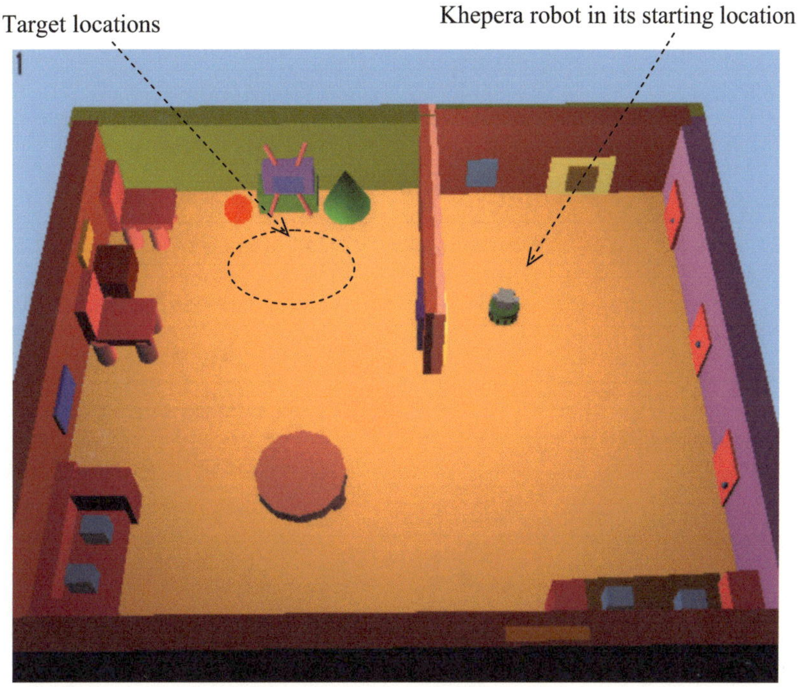

Fig. 4. A snapshot of the realistic simulated environment.

The robot starts by taking three (m=3) snapshots for the goal location. It then undergoes a specific number (EP) of episodes that are collectively called a run-set or simply a run. In each episode the robot starts from a specific location and is left to navigate until it reaches the home location. The robot starts with a random policy, and should finish a run set with an optimised learned policy.

5.1 Practical settings of the model parameters

Table 1 summarises the various constants and parameters used in the Sarsa-conj(0) algorithm and their values/initial values and updates. Each run lasts for 500 episodes (EP=500), and the findings are averaged over 10 runs to insure validity of the results. The feature space parameters were chosen to be b=3, m=3. Hence, $n = 3\times(\mathit{round}(256/3)+1)\times 3 = 774$. This middle value for b, which gives a medium feature size (and hence medium learning parameters dimension), together with the relatively small number of stored views (m=3), were chosen mainly to demonstrate and compare the different algorithms on average model settings. However, different setting could have been chosen.

The initial learning rate was set to $\alpha_0 = (1/EP)\times(1/n) \approx (1/500)\times(1/1000) = 2\times 10^{-6}$ in accordance with the features size and the number of episodes. This is to divide the learning between all features and all episodes to allow for good generalization and stochastic variations. The learning rate was decreased further from one episode to another, equation (59), to facilitate learning and to prevent divergence of the policy parameters $\vec{\theta}$ (Tsitsiklis and Van Roy 1997) (especially due to the fact that the policy itself is changing). Although factor $\lambda_t^{(conj)}$ in TD-conj(0) is a counterpart of fixed λ in conventional TD(λ), in contrast with λ it varies from one step to another to achieve better results. The discount constant was set to $\gamma = 1$, i.e. the rewards sum does not need to be discounted through time because it is bounded, given that the task ends after reaching the final state at time T.

Symbol	Value	Description
EP	500	Number of episodes in each run
α_0	$\alpha_0 = 2\times10^{-6} \approx (1/EP)\times(1/n)$	Initial learning rate
α_{ep}	$\alpha_{ep} = \alpha_0\left((n_0 \times EP + 1)/(n_0 \times EP + ep)\right)$	Episode learning rate
n_0	$75\% EP$	Start episode for decreasing α_{ep}
ε_0	0.5	Initial exploration rate
ε_{ep}	$\varepsilon_{ep} = \varepsilon_0\left((n_0 \times EP + 1)/(n_0 \times EP + ep)\right)$	Episodic exploration rate
$n_{0\varepsilon}$	$50\% EP$	Start episode for decreasing ε_{ep}
γ	1	The reward discount factor
m	3	Number of snapshots of the home
b	3	Features histograms bin size

Table 1. The model different parameters, their values and their description.

$\psi_{upper}, \psi_{lower}$ are determined empirically and were set to 0.96 and 0.94 respectively when using the NRB measure and b=m=3. These setting simply indicate that to terminate the episode the agent should be ≥ 96% sure (using the NRB similarity measure) that its current view corresponds with one (or more) of the stored views in order to assume that it has reached the home location. Furthermore, they indicate that the agent should be ≥ 94% sure that its current view is similar to the stored views to assume that it is in the home-at-perspective region.

5.2 Convergence results

Fig. 5. shows the learning plots for the TD-conj(0) ≡ TD(λ_t^{conj}) where the ${}^1\lambda_t^{conj}$ was used. Convergence is evident by the exponential shape of all of the plots. In particular the cumulative rewards converged to an acceptable value. The steps plot resonates with the rewards plot, i.e. the agent attains gradually good performance in terms of cumulative rewards and steps-per-episode. The cumulative changes made to the policy parameters have also a regular exponential shape, which suggests the minimization of required learning from one episode to another. It should be noted that although the learning rate is decreased through episodes, if the model were not converging then more learning could have occurred in later episodes, which would have deformed the shape of the changes in the policy parameters plot.

λ can take any value in the [0 , 1] interval. It has been shown by (Sutton and Barto 1998) that the best performance for TD(λ) is expected to be when λ has a high value close to 1, such as

0.8 or 0.9 depending on the problem. λ=1 is not a good candidate as it approximates Monte Carlo methods and has noticeably inferior performance than smaller values (Sutton and Barto 1998). It should also be noted that the whole point of the suggested TD-conj(0) method is to optimize and automate the selection of λ in each step to allow TD to perform better and avoid trying different values for λ.

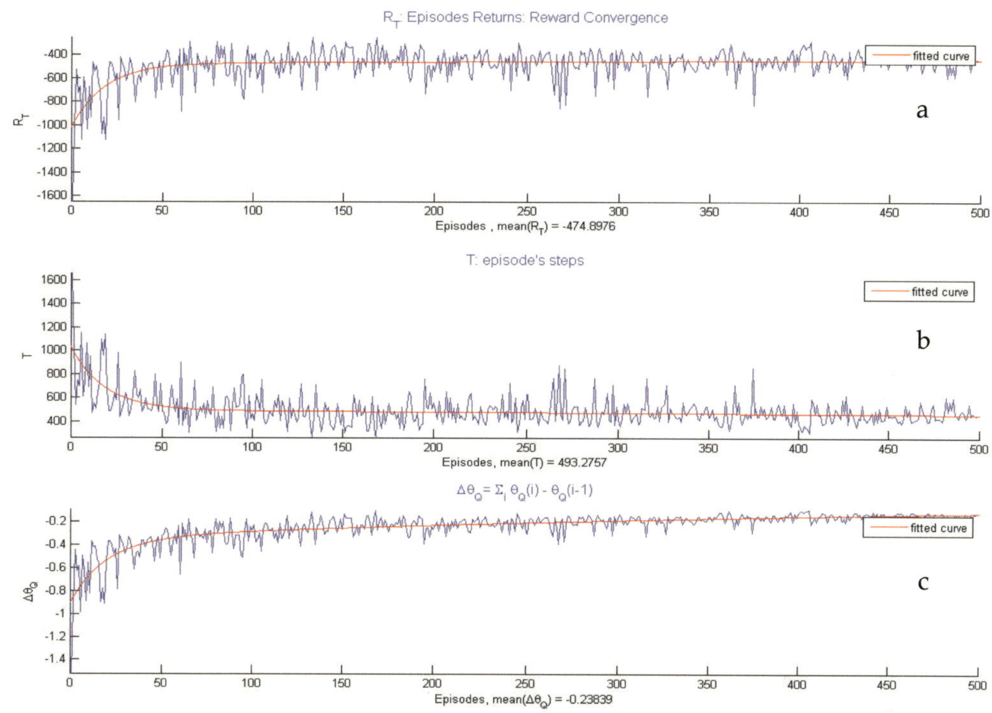

Fig. 5. TD($^1\lambda_t^{(conj)}$) algorithm's performance (a) The cumulative rewards. (b) The number of steps. (c): The cumulative changes of the learning parameters.

Fig. 6. shows that the learning rate decreased per episode. The exploration factor rate was decreased using a similar method. The overall actual exploration versus exploitation percentage is shown in Fig. 6(c). The Temporal error for a sample episode is shown in Fig. 6(d). Fig. 6(e) shows the trace decay factor $^1\lambda_t^{(conj)}$ for the same sample episode. It can be seen that for $^1\lambda_t^{(conj)}$, most of the values are above 0.5. As has been stated in the Equivalency Theorem, there is no guarantee that $\lambda_t^{(conj)}$ satisfies the condition $0 \le \lambda_t^{(conj)} \le 1$. Nevertheless, for most of the values this form of $\lambda_t^{(conj)}$ does satisfy this condition. For those values that did not, it is sufficient to apply the following rule on them:

$$if(\lambda_t^{(conj)} > 1) \Rightarrow \lambda_t^{(conj)} \leftarrow 1, \qquad if(\lambda_t^{(conj)} < 0) \Rightarrow \lambda_t^{(conj)} \leftarrow 0 \tag{61}$$

It should be noted that better performance could have been achieved by the following rule:

$$if(\lambda_t^{(conj)} > 1) \Rightarrow \lambda_t^{(conj)} \leftarrow 1 - \xi, \qquad if(\lambda_t^{(conj)} < 0) \Rightarrow \lambda_t^{(conj)} \leftarrow 0 \tag{62}$$

However, using this rule would mean that the results shown for TD($\lambda_t^{(conj)}$) might have been affected by the higher performance expected for TD update when $\lambda_t^{(conj)}$ is close (but not equal)

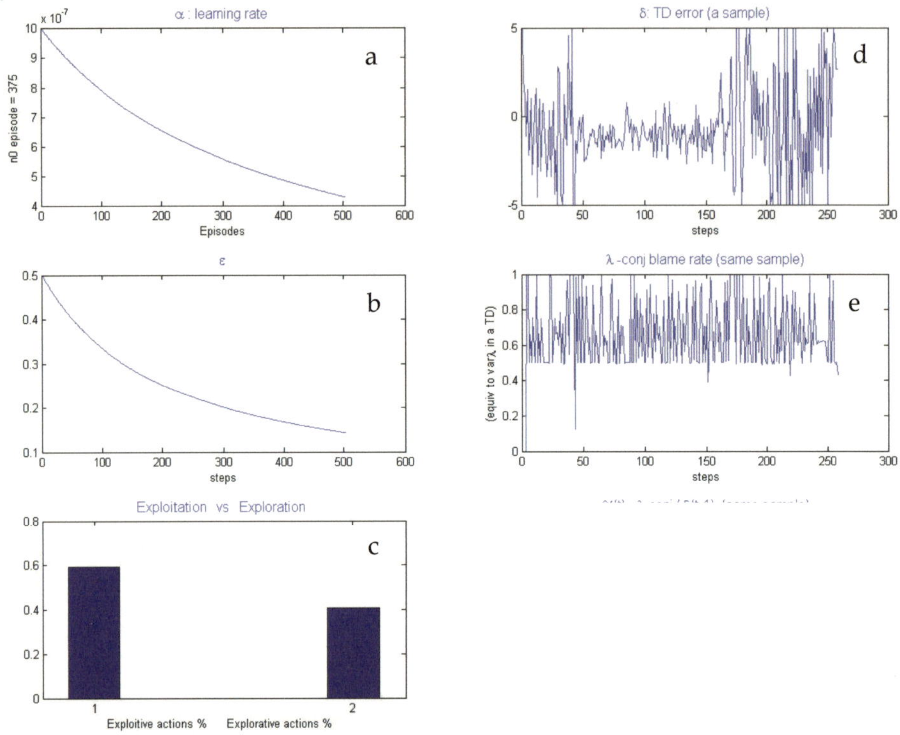

Fig. 6. TD($^1\lambda_t^{(conj)}$) algorithm internal variables (a): The learning rate. (b): the exploration factor rate. (c): the overall exploration versus exploitation. (d)): the temporal error for a sample episode. (e): the trace decay factor $\lambda_t^{(conj)}$

to 1. This is because for one single update at some time step t TD(λ) and TD($\lambda_t^{(conj)}$) are identical for the same $\lambda_t^{(conj)}$ value. It is the collective variation from one TD(λ) update to another at each time step that makes TD($\lambda_t^{(conj)}$) different from TD(λ). Therefore, better performance could have been achieved by following rule (62). Hence the performance of TD($\lambda_t^{(conj)}$) could be questionable and shaken when this rule is used. Few values did not satisfy the Equivalency Theorem condition - the percentage was 0.0058% for TD($^1\lambda_t^{(conj)}$). To show the path taken by the robot in each episode, the Global Positioning System (GPS) was used to register the robot positions (but not to aid the homing process in any way). Fig. 7. shows the evident improvements that took place during the different learning stages.

5.3 Action space and setting exploitation versus exploration

Since action space is finite, and to avoid fluctuation and overshoot in the robot behaviour, low wheel speeds were adopted for these actions. This in turn required setting the exploration to a relatively high rate (almost 50%) during the early episodes. It was then dropped gradually through episodes, in order to make sure that most of the potential paths were sufficiently visited. Setting exploration high also helps to decrease the number of episodes needed before reaching an acceptable performance. This explains the exponential appearance of the different learning curves.

The features variance also played a role in the exploration/exploitation rates. This was because $\hat{\sigma}_0^2$ was initialized in the first episode with $\sigma^2(im)$, the variance of the goal location snapshots, then it was updated in subsequent episodes until it was stable. This encourages the agent to explore the environment more in the first episode than any other, which results in big differences between the first and the rest of the episodes. Therefore, it should be noted that all of the episodic figures have been plotted excluding the first episode, to prevent the graphs from being unnecessarily mis-scaled.

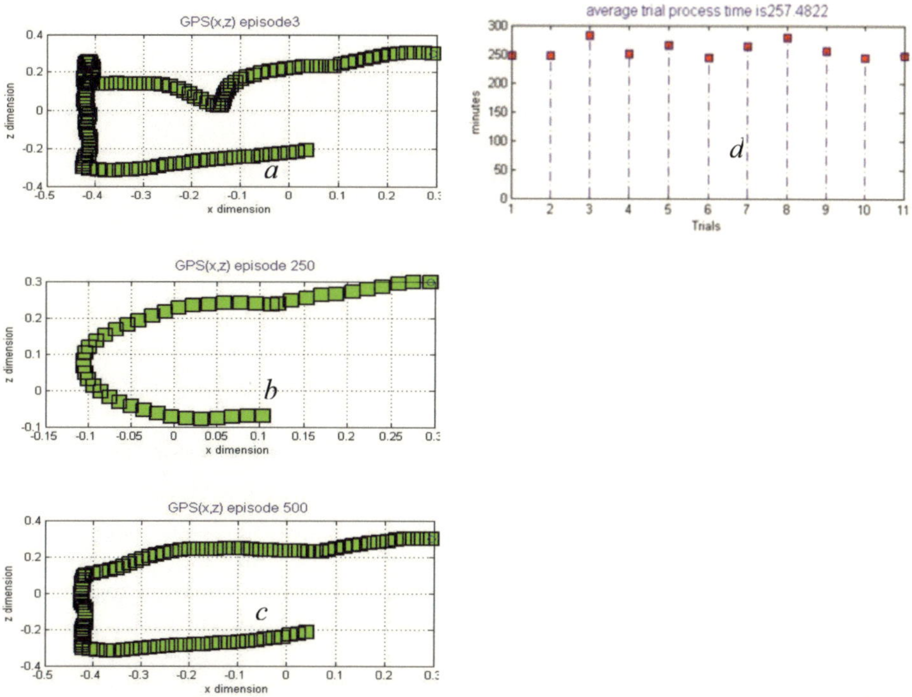

Fig. 7. TD($^{1}\lambda_t^{(conj)}$) algorithm performance for the homing problem (a, b, c): GPS plots for early, middle and last episodes, they show the trajectory improvement that took place during learning. (d): the timing plot of the 10 run sets (trials).

6. TD($\lambda_t^{(conj)}$) and TD(λ) comparisons study

6.1 Rewards comparison

Fig. 8. shows the fitted curves for the rewards plots of the different TD(λ) and TD($\lambda_t^{(conj)}$) algorithms. It summarizes the experiments conducted on the model and its various algorithms in terms of the gained rewards. The model uses Sarsa(λ), and Sarsa($\lambda_t^{(conj)}$), algorithms with a dynamic-policy. It should be recalled that the only difference between the two algorithms is that one uses TD(λ) update and the other uses TD($\lambda_t^{(conj)}$) update. Therefore, the comparisons highlight the differences between TD(λ) and TD($\lambda_t^{(conj)}$) updates, and the collective study highlights the dynamic-policy algorithm behaviour.

Several interesting points can be realized in this figure: The three TD($\lambda_t^{(conj)}$) algorithms climb quicker and earlier (50-150 episodes) than the five TD(λ) algorithms then: TD($^{1}\lambda_t^{(conj)}$) and TD($^{2}\lambda_t^{(conj)}$) keeps a steady performance to finally dominate the rest of the algorithms. While, although the fastest (during the first 150 episodes), TD($^{3}\lambda_t^{(conj)}$) deteriorates after that. TD(λ) algorithms performances varied but they were slower and in general performed

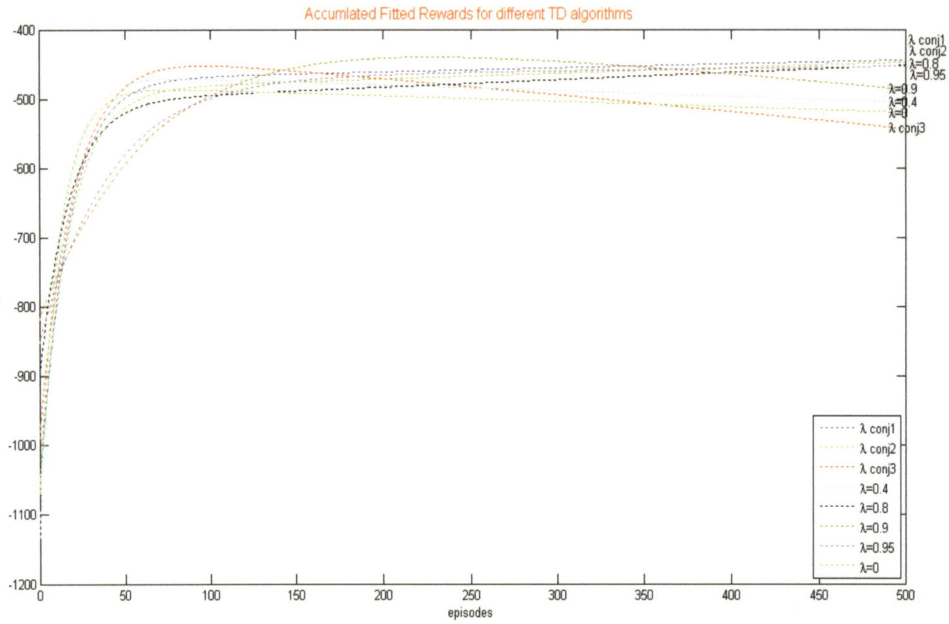

Fig. 8. Overall comparisons of different TD(λ) methods for λ = 0, 0.4, 0.8 and TD($\lambda_t^{(conj)}$) for ${}^1\lambda_t^{(conj)}$, ${}^2\lambda_t^{(conj)}$ and ${}^3\lambda_t^{(conj)}$ using the fitted returns curves for 10 runs each with 500 episodes.

worse than TD($\lambda_t^{(conj)}$) algorithms: TD(0.4) climbed quickly and its performances declined slightly at the late episodes (after 350 episodes). TD(0) did the same but was slower. TD(0.95, 0.8) climbed slowly but kept a steady improvement until they came exactly under TD(${}^1\lambda_t^{(conj)}$) and TD(${}^2\lambda_t^{(conj)}$). TD(0.9) performed slightly better than TD($\lambda_t^{(conj)}$) at a middle stage (150-350), then it declined after that. TD(0.9) was similar to TD(${}^3\lambda_t^{(conj)}$) although it was slower at the rise and the fall.

Therefore, for the fastest but short term performance TD(${}^3\lambda_t^{(conj)}$) is a good candidate. For a slower and good performance on the middle run TD(0.9) might still be a good choice. For a slower and long term performance TD(0.8) and TD(0.95) is a good choice.

For both the fastest and best overall performance in the long term TD(${}^1\lambda_t^{(conj)}$) and TD(${}^2\lambda_t^{(conj)}$) are the best choices. Nevertheless, those findings are guidelines and even for the tackled problem they do not tell the whole story. As will be shown in the following section, other performance measure can further give a better picture about those algorithms.

6.2 Comparisons beyond the rewards

Fig. 9. summarizes different comparisons between the different algorithms using averages of different performance measures for the same run sets mentioned in the previous section.

6.2.1 The figure structure

The set of algorithms that uses TD(λ) updates is shown in blue dots (connected), while the set of the new proposed TD($\lambda_t^{(conj)}$) is shown in red squares (not connected). Each measure has been demonstrated in an independent plot. The horizontal axes were chosen to be the λ value for TD(λ), while for TD($\lambda_t^{(conj)}$) there is no specific value for λ as it is varying from one step to another (therefore disconnected). However, for the purpose of comparing TD(${}^1\lambda_t^{(conj)}$), TD(${}^2\lambda_t^{(conj)}$) and TD(${}^3\lambda_t^{(conj)}$) algorithms, their measures were chosen to be correlate with

TD(0.8), TD(0.9) and TD(0.95) respectively. The arrow to the left of each plot refers to the direction of good performance. The figure is divided horizontally into two collections; one that is concerned with the during-learning measures and contains six plots distributed along two rows and three columns. The other collection is concerned with the after-learning measures and contains three plots that are distributed over one row.

The first row of the during-learning collection contains measures that are RL related such as the rewards and the parameters changes. The second row of the first collection is associated with the problem under consideration, i.e. the homing task. For testing purposes, the optimal route of the homing task can be designated in the studied environment. The difference between the current and the desired positions can be used to calculate the root mean squared error (RMS) of each time step, which are then summed to form the RMS for each episode, and those in turn can be summed to form the run set RMS. Two different performance measures were proposed using the GPS; their results are included in the second row of the figure. The first depends on the angular difference between the current and the desired orientations and is called the angular RMS. The second depends on the difference between the current and the desired movement vectors, and is called vectorial RMS. All of these measures was taken during learning (performing 500 episodes) hence the name. All of the during-learning measures in this figure were averaged over 10 run sets each with 500 episodes.

The second collection are measures that have been taken after the agent finished the 500 (learning episodes) ×10 (run sets); where it was left to go through 100 episodes without any learning. In those episodes the two policy components (Gibbs and ε-greedy) were restricted to an ε-greedy component only and the policy parameters used are the averaged parameters of all of the previous 10 run sets (performed during-learning). The Gibbs component was added initially to allow the agent to explore the second best guess more often than the third guess (action). Nevertheless, keeping this component after learning would increase the arbitrariness and exploration of the policy which is not desired anymore therefore it was removed.

The three measures in the after-learning collection are related to the number of steps needed to complete the task. The steps average measures the average number of steps needed by the agent to complete the task. Another two scales measures the rate of successes of achieving the task within a pre-specified number of steps (175 and 185 steps[1]).

6.2.2 The algorithms assessment

To assess the performance of the algorithms TD(λ) algorithms will be analyzed first then the focus is switched to TD($\lambda_t^{(conj)}$). Apparently, when the blue dots are examined in the first row, it can be seen that (a and b) appears to have a theme for TD(λ); the number of steps and the accumulated rewards both have a soft peak. The best TD(λ) algorithm is TD(0.9). This suggests that the peak of TD(λ) for the particular studied homing task is near that value. During-learning TD(0.9) could collect the most rewards in the least number of steps, however it caused more changes than the rest (except for TD(0.95)).

When the red squares are examined in the first row of plots it can be seen that TD($^1\lambda_t^{(conj)}$) and TD($^2\lambda_t^{(conj)}$) performed best in terms of the gained rewards (as was already pointed out in the previous subsection). What is more, they incurred less changes than any other algorithm which is an important advantage over other algorithms.

---

[1] These two numbers were around the least number of steps that could be realized by the agent without highly restricting its path, they were empirically specified

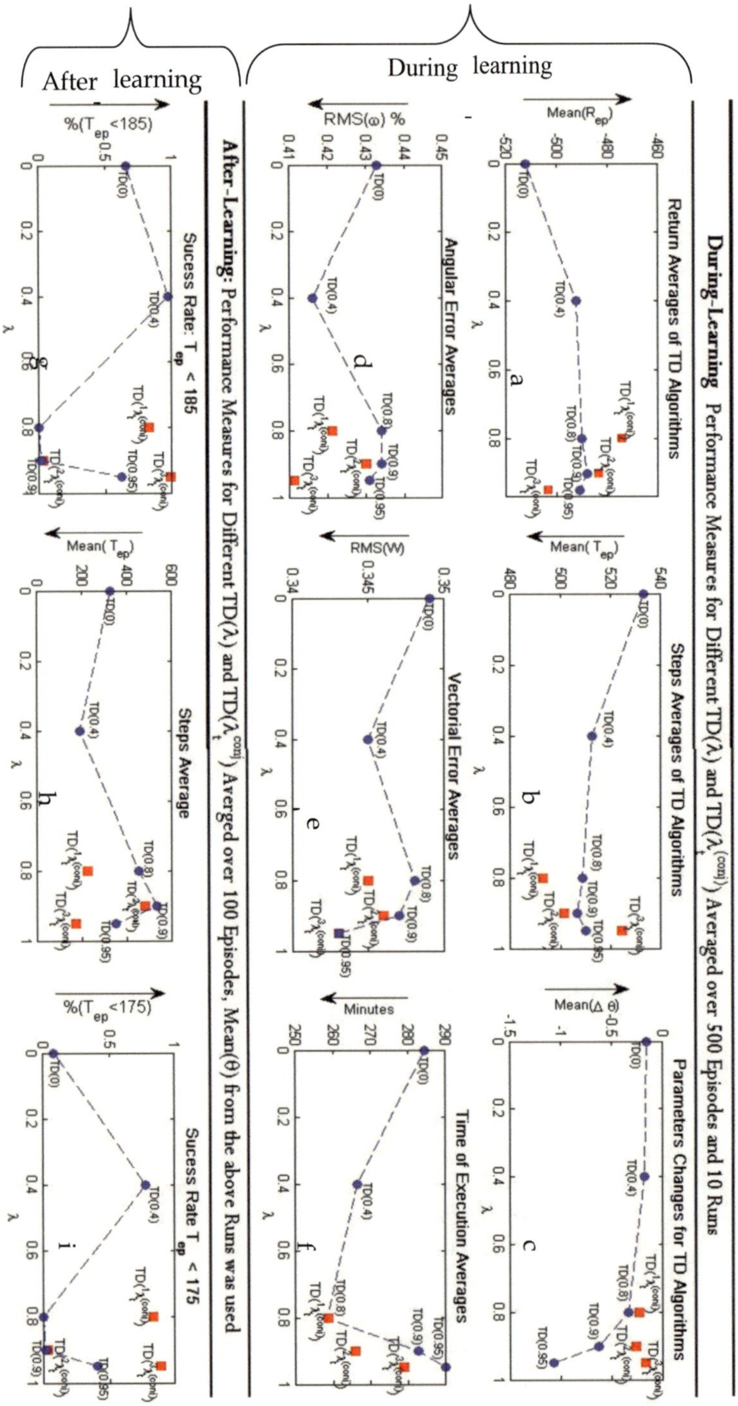

Fig. 9. Overall comparisons of different TD(λ) methods for λ = 0, 0.4, 0.8, 0.9, 0.95 and TD($\lambda_t^{(conj)}$) for ${}^1\lambda_t^{(conj)}$, ${}^2\lambda_t^{(conj)}$ and ${}^3\lambda_t^{(conj)}$. The arrows refer to the direction of better performance.

6.2.3 Calculations efficiency and depth of the blame

There are some interesting points to note when examining the changes in the policy parameters. Mean $\Delta\theta$ appears to have a theme for TD(λ); the changes to θ increase with λ. When the Mean $\Delta\theta$ is compared for the best two algorithms (during learning) TD(${}^{1}\lambda_t^{(conj)}$) and TD(λ=0.9), it can be seen that TD(${}^{1}\lambda_t^{(conj)}$) caused less changes to the learning parameters but still outperformed TD(λ=0.9). TD(${}^{1}\lambda_t^{(conj)}$) avoids the unnecessary changes for the policy parameters and hence avoids fluctuations of performance during learning. It only performed the necessary changes. On the other hand TD(λ=0.9) always 'blames' the previous states trace equally for all steps (because λ is fixed) and maximally (because λ=0.9 has a high value). TD(${}^{1}\lambda_t^{(conj)}$) gets the right balance between deep and shallow blame (credit) assignment by varying the deepness of the trace of states to be blamed and incurs changes according to the conjugate gradient of the TD error.

6.2.4 Time efficiency

The execution time Mean(Time) provides even more information than Mean $\Delta\theta$. Both TD(${}^{1}\lambda_t^{(conj)}$) and TD(λ=0.9) have almost identical execution times, although the execution time for TD(${}^{1}\lambda_t^{(conj)}$) was initially anticipated to be more than any TD(λ) because of the extra time for calculating $\lambda_t^{(conj)}$. This means that with no extra time cost or overhead TD(${}^{1}\lambda_t^{(conj)}$) achieved the best performance, which are considered to be important results.

TD(${}^{2}\lambda_t^{(conj)}$) performed next best, after TD(${}^{1}\lambda_t^{(conj)}$), according to the Mean(R_T) and Mean(T) performance measures, but not in terms of policy parameters changes or execution time; for those, TD(λ=0.9) still performed better. This means that this form of ${}^{2}\lambda_t^{(conj)}$ achieved better performance than λ=0.9, but at the cost of extra changes to the policy parameters, and incurred extra time overhead for doing so.

6.2.5 ε-Greedy divergence

ε-greedy divergence is a divergence that occurs after learning when the agent changes from the decreasing ε-greedy-Gibbs policy to a fixed ε-greedy policy. It has occurred sometimes especially when the agent had to switch from the reinforcement learning behaviour to the reactive behaviour near the walls and obstacles. For example the TD(λ=0.9) and TD(${}^{2}\lambda_t^{(conj)}$) diverged in this way. Also using the walls more is the likely cause that made the RMS(w) of TD(0.95) to beat the RMS(w) of TD(0.4).

7. Summary and conclusion

So Who Wins? In summary, TD(${}^{1}\lambda_t^{(conj)}$) outperformed all of the described algorithms during learning, while TD(${}^{3}\lambda_t^{(conj)}$) outperformed all of the described algorithms after learning. TD(${}^{1}\lambda_t^{(conj)}$) and TD(${}^{2}\lambda_t^{(conj)}$) suite more a gradual learning process while TD(${}^{3}\lambda_t^{(conj)}$) suits quick and more aggressive learning process. TD(${}^{1}\lambda_t^{(conj)}$) might still be preferred over the other updates because it preformed collectively best in all of the proposed measures (during and after learning). This demonstrates that using the historically oldest form of conjugate factor β to calculate ${}^{1}\lambda_t^{(conj)}$, proposed by Hestenes and Steifel, has performed the best of the three proposed TD($\lambda_t^{(conj)}$) algorithms. The likely reason is that this form of $\lambda_t^{(conj)}$ uses the preceding eligibility trace in its denominator, equation (40), not only the current and previous gradients.

The TD-conj methods has the important advantage over TD(λ) of automatically setting the learning variable $\lambda_t^{(conj)}$ equivalent to λ in TD(λ), without the need to manually try different λ values. This is the most important contribution of this new method which has been verified by the experimental comparisons. TD-conj gives a canonical way of automatically setting λ to the value which yields the best overall performance.

Conclusions and future work

A new robust learning model for visual robot homing (VRH) has been developed, which reduces the amount of required a priori knowledge and the constraints associated with the robot's operating environment. This was achieved by employing a reinforcement learning method for control and appropriate linear neural networks, in combination with a reward signal and termination condition based on a whole image measure.

The proposed model is an attempt to address the lack of models for homing that are fully adaptive to any environment in which a robot operates. It does not require human intervention in the learning process, nor does it assume that those environments should be artificially adapted for the sake of the robot. This study shows that visual homing based on RL and whole image techniques can offer generality and automated learning properties. There are various aspects of novelty, but the two main ones are concerned with the learning method and the model. The new TD-conj method is used in an existing RL control algorithm, namely Sarsa. The algorithm is applied in a novel RL model designed for visual robot homing.

The use of a whole image measure as a means of termination and to augment the reward signal coming from the environment is one element of novelty. The simple NRB is a newly established measure shown to be effective. This conforms with the latest findings in cognition which asserts that landmarks are not necessary for homing (Gillner, Weiß et al. 2008). The home location is defined through m snapshots. This, together with the use of a whole image measure, allows for robust task execution with minimal required knowledge about the target location and its environment.

Furthermore, it was realized that there is a need to boost RL algorithms that use function approximation. A new family of RL methods, TD-conj(λ), has been established (Altahhan 2008) by using the conjugate gradient direction instead of the gradient direction in the conventional TD(λ) with function approximation. Since TD-conj(0) is proved to be equivalent to TD(λ) where λ is variable and is denoted as $\lambda_t^{(conj)}$(Altahhan 2008), this family is used in the proposed model as the learning algorithm.

Some of the advantages of the novel method and model can be summarized in the following points. Simplicity of learning: the robot can learn to perform its visual homing (sub-navigation) task in a simple way, without a long process of map building. Only limited storage of information is required in the form of m stored views. No pre- or manual processing is required. No a priori knowledge about the environment is needed in the form of landmarks. An important advantage of the proposed model over MDP model-based approaches is that abduction of the robot is solved directly, i.e. the robot can find its way and recover after it has been displaced from its current position and put in a totally different position. Other models that use algorithms such as the particle filter (Thrun, Burgard et al. 2005) can recover from this problem but not as quickly as the proposed model. This is because the current view, alone, gives enough information for the trained neural network to decide immediately on which action to take, while multimode filters (such as the particle filter, or an unscented Kalman filter) may take two or more steps to know where the agent is, and then to take a suitable action depending on its location.

In future research, a number of enhancements are planned to the model. Although setting up a suitable exploration/exploitation was automated in the model and required only the specification of ε0 and n0ε prior to execution, finding the best balance between these parameters will be a topic for future research. Finally, reducing the number of the learning parameters is another issue that is being investigated.

8. Reference

Altahhan, A. (2008). Conjugate Gradient Temporal Difference Learning for Visual Robot Homing. Faculty of Computing and Engineering. Sunderland, University of Sunderland. Ph.D.: 206.

Altahhan, A., K. Burn, et al. (2008). Visual Robot Homing using Sarsa(λ), Whole Image Measure, and Radial Basis Function. International Joint Conference on Neural Networks (IJCNN), Hong Kong.

Anderson, A. M. (1977). "A model for landmark learning in the honey-bee." Journal of Comparative Physiology A 114: 335-355.

Argyros, A. A., K. E. Bekris, et al. (2001). Robot Homing based on Corner Tracking in a Sequence of Panoramic Images. 2001 IEEE Computer Society Conference on Computer Vision and Pattern Recognition (CVPR'01)

Arkin, R. C. (1998). Behavior-Based Robotics, MIT Press.

Asadpour, M. and R. Siegwart (2004). "Compact Q-learning optimized for micro-robots with processing and memory constraints." Robotics and Autonomous Systems, Science Direct, Elsevier.

Baird, L. C. (1995). Residual Algorithms: Reinforcement Learning with Function Approximation. International Conference on Machine Learning, proceedings of the Twelfth International Conference, San Francisco, CA, Morgan Kaufman Publishers.

Bhatnagar, S., R. S. Sutton, et al. (2007). Incremental Natural Actor-Critic Algorithms. Neural Information Processing Systems (NIPS19).

Boyan, J. A. (1999). Least-squares temporal difference learning Proceedings of the Sixteenth International Conference on Machine Learning San Francisco, CA Morgan Kaufmann.

Cartwright, B. A. and T. S. Collett (1987). "Landmark maps for honeybees." Biological Cybernetics 57: 85-93.

Falas, T. and A.-G. Stafylopatis (2001). Temporal differences learning with the conjugate gradient algorithm. Neural Networks, 2001. Proceedings. IJCNN '01. International Joint Conference on, Washington, DC, USA.

Falas, T. and A.-G. Stafylopatis (2002). Temporal differences learning with the scaled conjugate gradient algorithm. Neural Information Processing ICONIP 2002.

Floreano, D. and F. Mondada (1998). Hardware solutions for evolutionary robotics. First European Workshop on Evolutionary Robotics, Berlin, Springer-Verlag.

Gillner, S., A. M. Weiß, et al. (2008). "Visual homing in the absence of feature-based landmark information." Cognition 109(1): 105-122.

Hagan, M. T., H. B. Demuth, et al. (1996). Neural Network Design, PWS Publishing Company.

Kaelbling, L. P., M. L. Littman, et al. (1998). "Planning and acting in partially observable stochastic domains." Artificial Intelligence 101: 99–134.

Konda, V. and J. Tsitsiklis (2000). Actor-critic algorithms. . NIPS 12.

Lazaric, A., M. Restelli, et al. (2007). Reinforcement Learning in Continuous Action Spaces through Sequential Monte Carlo Methods. NIPPS 2007.

Michel, O. (2004). "Webots: Professional Mobile Robot Simulation." International Journal of Advanced Robotic Systems 1: 39-42.

Murphy, R. R. (2000). Introduction to AI Robotics. Cambridge, Massachusetts., The MIT Press.
Muse, D., C. Weber, et al. (2006). "Robot docking based on omnidirectional vision and reinforcement learning." Knowledge-Based Systems, Science Direct, Elsevier 19(5): 324-332
Nehmzow, U. (2000). Mobile robotics: A Practical Introduction, Springer-Verlag.
Nocedal, J. and S. J. Wright (2006). Numerical Optimization. New York, Springer.
Peters, J., S. Vijayakumar, et al. (2005). "Natural Actor-Critic." Proceedings of the Sixteenth European Conference on Machine Learning: 280–291.
Rubner, Y. and et al. (2000). "The Earth Mover's Distance as a Metric for Image Retrieval." International Journal of Computer Vision 40(2): 99-121.
Schoknecht, R. and A. Merke (2003). "TD(0) Converges Provably Faster than the Residual Gradient Algorithm." Machine Learning 20(2): 680-687.
Sheynikhovich, D., R. Chavarriaga, et al. (2005). Spatial Representation and Navigation in a Bio-inspired Robot. Biomimetic Neural Learning for Intelligent Robots. S. Wermter, M. Elshaw and G. Palm, Springer: 245-265.
Simmons, R. and S. Koenig (1995). Probabilistic Robot Navigation in Partially Observable Environments. Proc. of the International Joint Conference on Artificial Intelligence.
Stone, P., R. S. Sutton, et al. (2005). "Reinforcement learning for robocup soccer keepaway." International Society for Adaptive Behavior 13(3): 165–188.
Sutton, R. S. (1988). "Learning to predict by the methods of temporal differences." Machine Learning 3: 9–44.
Sutton, R. S. and A. Barto (1998). Reinforcement Learning, an introduction. Cambridge, Massachusetts, MIT Press.
Szenher, M. (2005). Visual Homing with Learned Goal Distance Information. Proceedings of the 3rd International Symposium on Autonomous Minirobots for Research and Edutainment (AMiRE 2005), Awara-Spa, Fukui, Japan, Springer.
Thrun, S. (2000.). Probabilistic Algorithms in Robotics, CMU-CS-00-126.
Thrun, S., W. Burgard, et al. (2005). Probabilistic Robotics. Cambridge, Massachusetts; London, England, The MIT Press.
Thrun, S., Y. Liu, et al. (2004). "Simultaneous localization and mapping with sparse extended information filters." International Journal of Robotics Research 23(7-8): 693–716.
Tomatis, N., I. Nourbakhsh, et al. (2001). Combining Topological and Metric: a Natural Integration for Simultaneous Localization and Map Building. Proc. Of the Fourth European Workshop on Advanced Mobile Robots (Eurobot 2001).
Tsitsiklis, J. N. and B. Van Roy (1996). "Feature-based methods for large scale dynamic programming. ." Machine Learning 22: 59-49.
Tsitsiklis, J. N. and B. Van Roy (1997). "An analysis of temporal-difference learning with function approximation." IEEE Transactions on Automatic Control 42(5): 674–690.
Ulrich, I. and I. Nourbakhsh (2000). Appearance-Based Place Recognition for Topological Localization IEEE International Conference on Robotics and Automation San Francisco, CA.
Vardy, A. (2006). Long-Range Visual Homing. IEEE International Conference on Robotics and Biomimetics, 2006. ROBIO '06., Kunming.
Vardy, A. and R. Moller (2005). "Biologically plausible visual homing methods based on optical flow techniques." Connection Science 17(1–2): 47–89.
Vardy, A. and F. Oppacher (2005). A scale invariant local image descriptor for visual homing. Biomimetic neural learning for intelligent robots. G. Palm and S. Wermter, Springer.

14

Complex-Valued Reinforcement Learning: A Context-based Approach for POMDPs

Takeshi Shibuya[1] and Tomoki Hamagami[2]
[1]*University of Tsukuba*
[2]*Yokohama National University*
[1,2]*Japan*

1. Introduction

Reinforcement learning (RL) algorithms are representative active learning algorithms that can be used to decide suitable actions on the basis of experience, simulations, and searches (Sutton & Barto, 1998; Kaelbling et al., 1998). The use of RL algorithms for the development of practical intelligent controllers for autonomous robots and multiagent systems has been investigated; such controllers help in realizing autonomous adaptability on the basis of the information obtained through experience. For example, in our previous studies on autonomous robot systems such as an intelligent wheelchair, we used RL algorithms for an agent in order to learn how to avoid obstacles and evolve cooperative behavior with other robots (Hamagami & Hirata, 2004; 2005). Furthermore, RL has been widely used to solve the elevator dispatching problem (Crites & Barto, 1996), air-conditioning management problem (Dalamagkidisa et al., 2007), process control problem (S.Syafiie et al., 2008), etc.

However, in most cases, RL algorithms have been successfully used only in ideal situations that are based on Markov decision processes (MDPs). MDP environments are controllable dynamic systems whose state transitions depend on the previous state and the action selected. On the other hand, because of the limited number of dimensions and/or low accuracy of the sensors used, real-world environments are considered to be partially observable MDPs (POMDPs). In a POMDP environment, the agent faces a serious problem called perceptual aliasing, i.e., the agent cannot distinguish multiple states from one another on the basis of perceptual inputs. Some representative approaches have been adopted to solve this problem (Mccallum, 1995; Wiering & Schmidhuber, 1996; Singh et al., 2003; Hamagami et al., 2002). The most direct representative approach involves the use of the memory of contexts called episodes to disambiguate the current state and to keep track of information about the previous state (Mccallum, 1995). The use of this memory-based approach can ensure high learning performance if the environment is stable and the agent has sufficient memory. However, since most real-world environments belong to the dynamic class, the memory of experience has to be revised frequently. Therefore, the revised algorithm often becomes complex and task-dependent.

Another approach for addressing perceptual aliasing involves treatment of the environment as a hierarchical structure (Wiering & Schmidhuber, 1996). In this case, the environment is divided into small sets without perceptual aliasing, so that the agent can individually learn each small set. This approach is effective when the agent knows how to divide the environment into sets with non-aliasing states. However, the agent must learn to divide the environment accurately and to apply a suitable policy to each divided set. This process is time-consuming.

In this paper, we introduce a new RL algorithm developed by using a complex-valued function that represents each state-action value as a complex value. The most important advantage of using complex values in RL is to use time series information. This simple extension allows for compensation of the perceptual aliasing problem and ensures that mobile robots exhibit intelligent behavior in the real world. The complex-valued RL algorithm has two practical advantages. First, it can be easily combined with conventional simple algorithms such as Q-learning and Profit Sharing; this is because the proposed algorithm uses the same framework as do the aforementioned conventional algorithms. Second, the proposed algorithm does not memorize episodes of experience directly, i.e., the learning/control system does not require a large memory space.

In the remainder of this paper, we describe the basic idea of complex-valued reinforcement. In this study, we extend this idea to conventional RL algorithms such as Q-learning and Profit Sharing. We also perform simulation experiments to demonstrate the effectiveness of the method in environments involving perceptual aliasing problems.

2. Reinforcment learning with complex-valued function

2.1 Basic idea

Complex-valued neural networks (CVNNs) (Hirose, 2003) are extensions of conventional real-valued neural networks. In a CVNN, the inputs, outputs, and parameters such as weights and thresholds are expressed as complex numbers, and hence, the activation function is inevitably a complex-valued function. The advantage of such a network is that it allows one to represent the context dependence of information on the basis of both amplitude and phase structure. The amplitude corresponds to the energy, while the phase represents time lag and time lead.

The idea of complex-valued RL has been proposed on the basis of the abovementioned features of CVNNs. In other words, similar to the case of a CVNN, the complex values used in complex-valued reinforcement learning (CVRL) are expansions of the real values in used ordinary RL. One of the reasons for introducing complex values in RL is to compensate for perceptual aliasing by employing the phase representing the context in which the behavior is observed.

In CVRL, the value function or action-value function is defined as a complex value. Although we discuss only action-value functions in the following sections, the same idea may be applied to state-value functions as well. These complex values are revised by the proposed learning algorithm, whose framework is almost the same as that of a conventional algorithm. The main difference between the proposed algorithm and a conventional algorithm is that the former shifts the phase during the exploration of the environment.

The proposed RL algorithm does not select the best action but returns the most appropriate action for the given context. This properness is evaluated by using a complex-valued action-value function and an internal reference value that holds the context of the agent. The context is a series of observations and actions which the agent has obtained and taken. A complex-valued action value function is a function of state and action but not of time. The internal reference value is time-dependent and is updated step-by-step. Namely, our algorithm separates a time-dependent value function into two parts: a complex-valued action value function and an internal reference value.

In the following sections, we describe more specific algorithms that use the complex-valued function based on Q-learning and PS.

2.2 Basic implementations

2.2.1 Complex-valued Q-learning

Q-learning is a typical RL algorithm that learns the manner in which an environment state can be identified (C.J.C.H.Watkins, 1989). $Q(s,a)$ indicates the expected value of the reward when an agent selects action a at state s. In the learning phase, $Q(s,a)$ is revised as follows:

$$Q(s_t,a_t) \leftarrow (1-\alpha)Q(s_t,a_t) + \alpha(r + \gamma \max_{a'} Q(s_{t+1},a')) \tag{1}$$

where α denotes the learning rate; γ, the discount rate; and r, the reward.
The agent decides the next action on the basis of a function named policy. Policy is defined as a probability distribution over the action set for a given agent state. In this study, the Boltzmann policy, which gives probability of selecting action according to the Boltzmann distribution, is employed as a softmax policy.

$$\pi(s_t,a) = \frac{\exp(Q(s_t,a)/T)}{\sum_{a' \in \mathcal{A}(s_t)} \exp(Q(s_t,a')/T)} \tag{2}$$

where T denotes a scale parameter that controls randomness of the policy.
As mentioned above, the agent cannot observe its state directly in POMDPs. The agent can obtain the observation value x instead of the state s. Therefore, the value function is defined as a function of a pair of x and a.
The proposed algorithm named $\dot{\text{Q}}$-learning causes the action-value function to expand to a complex value as follows:

$$\dot{Q}(x_t,a_t) \leftarrow (1-\alpha)\dot{Q}(x_t,a_t) + \alpha(r_{t+1} + \gamma \dot{Q}^{(t)}_{\max})\dot{\beta} \tag{3}$$

$$\dot{Q}^{(t)}_{\max} = \dot{Q}(x_{t+1},a) \tag{4}$$

$$a = \operatorname*{argmax}_{a' \in \mathcal{A}(x_{t+1})} \left(Re\left[\dot{Q}(x_{t+1},a')\overline{\dot{I}_t} \right] \right) \tag{5}$$

The *dot* mark ($\dot{}$) indicates that the value is complex. $\dot{\beta}$ is the degree of rotation of the phase. $\dot{Q}^{(t)}_{\max}$ is the most appropriate complex-valued action-value in the given context. $\overline{\dot{I}_t}$ indicates the complex conjugate of the internal reference value $\dot{I}_t$. In this study, we assume that the agent receives a positive reward if it reaches the terminal state.
We employ the following equation to determine the value of $\dot{I}_t$.

$$\dot{I}_t = \dot{Q}(x_t,a_t)/\dot{\beta} \quad t \geq 0 \tag{6}$$

(6) shows that $\dot{Q}$-value and the rotational amount give the internal reference value used in the next action selection. When this equation is employed, the phase difference between the internal reference value and the selected action value becomes zero in the MDP environment. For the first action selection, we cannot determine the internal reference value since there is no previously selected action value. Therefore, we employ the following heuristics to determine the internal reference value.

$$\dot{I}_{-1} = \dot{Q}(x_0,a) \tag{7}$$

$$a = \operatorname*{argmax}_{a' \in \mathcal{A}(x_0)} |\dot{Q}(x_0,a')| \tag{8}$$

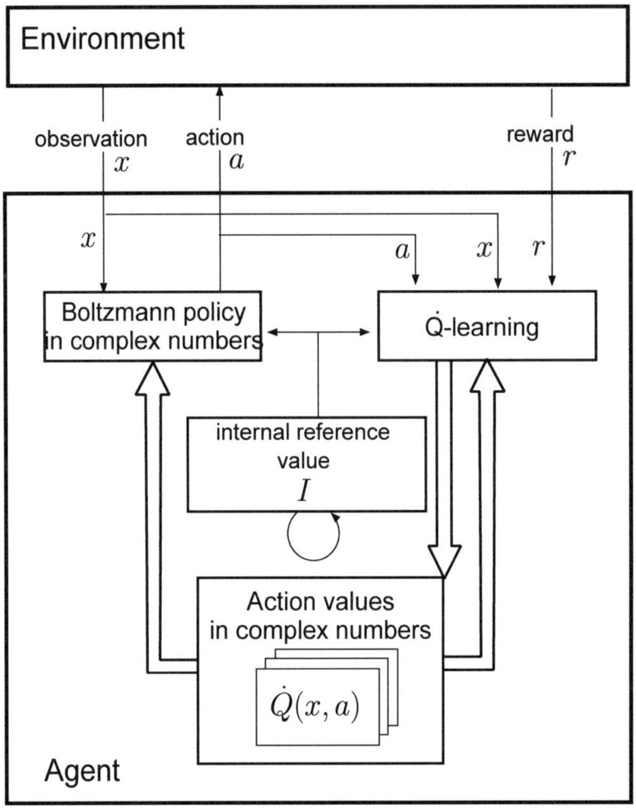

Fig. 1. Complex-valued reinforcement learning using Q̇-learning and Boltzmann policy.

Furthermore, in order to improve the learning efficiency, we use the concept of eligibility trace (A.G.Barto et al., 1983).

$$\dot{Q}(x_{t-k}, a_{t-k}) \leftarrow (1-\alpha)\dot{Q}(x_{t-k}, a_{t-k}) + \alpha(r_{t+1} + \gamma\dot{Q}^{(t)}_{\max})\dot{u}(k) \tag{9}$$

where $\dot{u}(k)$ denotes an eligibility parameter. In this study, we employ

$$\dot{u}(k) = \dot{\beta}^{k+1}. \tag{10}$$

where $k = 0,1,\cdots,$ and $N_e - 1$ is the index used for updating the action-values. N_e is the number of traces. Equation (9) is reduced to (3) if $N_e = 1$.

In order to select an action, the agent evaluates the action according to the stochastic policy, as follows:

$$\pi_{\dot{I}_{t-1}}(x_t, a) = \frac{\exp\left(Re\left[\dot{Q}(x_t, a)\overline{\dot{I}_{t-1}}\right]/T\right)}{\sum_{a' \in \mathcal{A}(x_t)} \exp\left(Re\left[\dot{Q}(x_t, a')\overline{\dot{I}_{t-1}}\right]/T\right)} \tag{11}$$

With this Boltzmann selection, there is a higher probability of the agent choosing the action corresponding to the Q̇-value, which not only has a greater norm $|\dot{Q}|$ but is also closer in phase to $\dot{I}_{t-1}$. Figure 1 shows an overview of our algorithm.

2.2.2 Complex-valued profit sharing

based on the method of learning experience reinforcement. The basic idea of this learning is to share profits on the basis of the evaluation value for action selection $v(s,a)$ when the agent receives a reward and to reinforce the successful episodes.

$$v(s_t,a_t) \leftarrow v(s_t,a_t) + f_t \quad (t = W-1, W-2, \cdots, 0) \tag{12}$$

$$f_t = \begin{cases} r & (t = W-1) \\ \gamma f_{t+1} & (t = W-2, W-3, \cdots, 0) \end{cases} \tag{13}$$

where f_t denotes the reinforcement function; W, the length of the episode; and γ, the discount rate.

Then, simple complex-valued profit sharing(scPS) is defined as the extension of these functions, as follows:

$$\boldsymbol{v}(x_t,a_t) \leftarrow \boldsymbol{v}(x_t,a_t) + \boldsymbol{f}_t \quad (t = W-1, W-2, \cdots, 0) \tag{14}$$

$$\boldsymbol{f}_t = \begin{cases} r \ (t = W-1) \\ \gamma e^{j\omega_t} \boldsymbol{f}_{t+1} & (t = W-2, W-3, \cdots, 0) \end{cases} \tag{15}$$

where W is the length of each episode. In this section, variables represented in bold face denote that they are complex.

Fig. 2 shows a comparison of the conventional function f_t and the complex-valued function $\boldsymbol{f}_t$. Similar to f_t, $\boldsymbol{f}_t$ is attenuated, and the plot of the complex-valued function is a spiral around the time axis. The continuity of the phase on the spiral is expected to represent a context in which the agent receives a reward. In other words, depending on whether the context phase is continuous or not, the agent can identify identical state-action pairs that would cause perceptual aliasing. After learning, the following probability provides the agent's action. We employ a roulette selection scheme $V(x_t,a) = \mathrm{Re}\left[\boldsymbol{v}(x_t,a)\bar{\boldsymbol{i}}(t)\right]$. Since in the roulette selection scheme, every weight of the action is considered to be positive, a subset of the action set is considered:

$$\mathcal{A}_{sub}(x_t) = \{a \in \mathcal{A}(x_t) | V(x_t,a) \geq 0\} \tag{16}$$

and the policy is defined as follows:

$$P(x_t,a) = \begin{cases} \dfrac{V(x_t,a)\delta(x_t,a)}{\sum_{a' \in \mathcal{A}_{sub}(x_t)} \left(V(x_t,a')\right)} & for \quad |\mathcal{A}_{sub}(x_t)| > 0 \\ \dfrac{1}{|\mathcal{A}(x_t)|} & \text{otherwise} \end{cases} \tag{17}$$

$$\delta(x,a) = \begin{cases} 1 & \text{if} \quad a \in \mathcal{A}_{sub}(x_t) \\ 0 & \text{otherwise} \end{cases} \tag{18}$$

Equation (17) provides a roulette selection scheme in which actions s.t. $V(x,a) < 0$. If all the actions are ignored, the agent chooses an action with the equal probability.

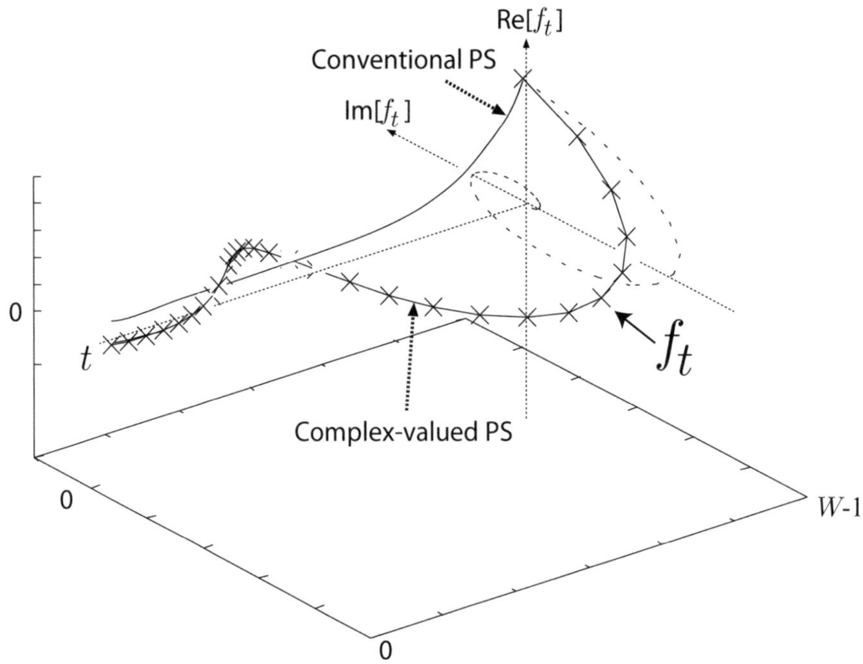

Fig. 2. An example of the complex-valued reinforcement function $\boldsymbol{f}$ for scPS.

$\boldsymbol{i}$ represents an internal reference value that is expressed as follows:

$$\boldsymbol{i}(t) = \begin{cases} \exp(j\theta_0) & (t = 0) \\ \exp\left(j\left(\theta_0 + \sum_{k=1}^{t}(-\omega_{k-1})\right)\right) & \\ & (t = 1, 2, \cdots, W-1) \end{cases} \tag{19}$$

where θ_0 represents the initial phase $\boldsymbol{i}(0)$.

2.3 Advanced implementations

2.3.1 Multiple action values

The aim of CVRL is to solve the perceptual aliasing problem by using the context of the agent. As described below, some of the experimental results obtained support the fact that CVRL can be successfully used to solve the perceptual aliasing problem. However, it is not possible for the agent to re-visit given a state many times and take the same action every time in that state. This is because that the internal reference value changes from the ideal value. Figure 3 illustrates this problem from the point of view of the action values. Figure 3(a) shows an example of the complex-valued action value corresponding to an observation. In Fig.3(b), the horizontal axis represents the phase of the internal reference value and the vertical axis represents effectiveness of the action values in the context. We assume that action a_1 is the suitable action. When the internal reference value is in area A or C, the probability of action a_1 being selected is high. However, as mentioned above, the internal reference value is so revised that the phase of the value varies along the horizontal axis in each step. In this case, the agent chooses the undesired action a_0 when the phase of the internal reference value is in area B.

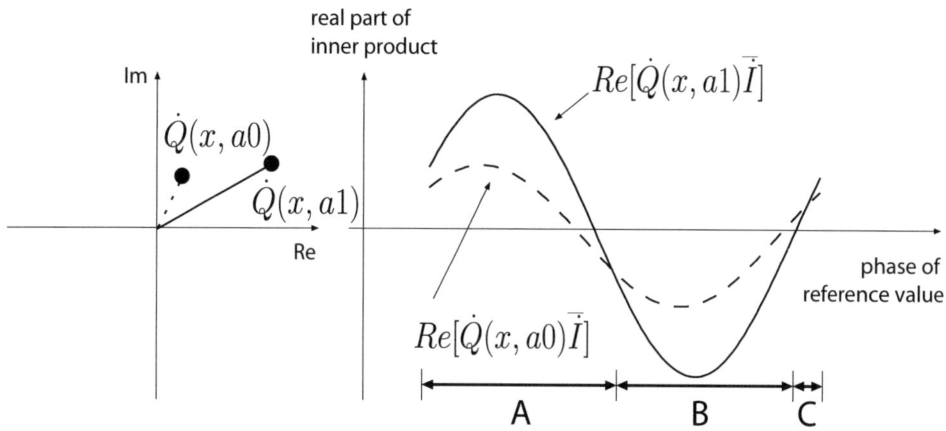

(a) Action values (b) Plot of phase of reference value vs real part of inner product

Fig. 3. Relation between conventional complex-valued action values and internal reference value ($|\dot{I}|$ is normalized)

In order to resolve this problem, the use of multiple action values has been proposed (Shibuya & Hamagami, 2009). In this case, we assign multiple values to each action. Formally, we consider a virtual action set $\mathcal{A}^+(x)$ for the original action set $\mathcal{A}(x)$ and assume that there exists a corresponding action in $\mathcal{A}(x)$ for every action in $\mathcal{A}^+(x)$. We define action values for the virtual actions. The agent uses the virtual action set $\mathcal{A}^+(x)$ for computing the value function. Namely, the value function is defined on the $\mathcal{X} \times \mathcal{A}(x)$. The agent executes an original action with respect to the virtual action. Although $\mathcal{A}^+(x)$ can be learnt from the agent-environment interaction, we set $\mathcal{A}^+(x)$ by using a priori knowledge. In this study, we multiply the action values by an experimental parameter named *multiple degree*. For example, when we use 2 as the multiple degree, the agent uses the virtual action set $\mathcal{A}^+(x) = \{a_{00}, a_{01}, a_{10}, a_{11}\}$ for the original action set $A(x) = \{a_0, a_1\}$. Figure 4 shows the case

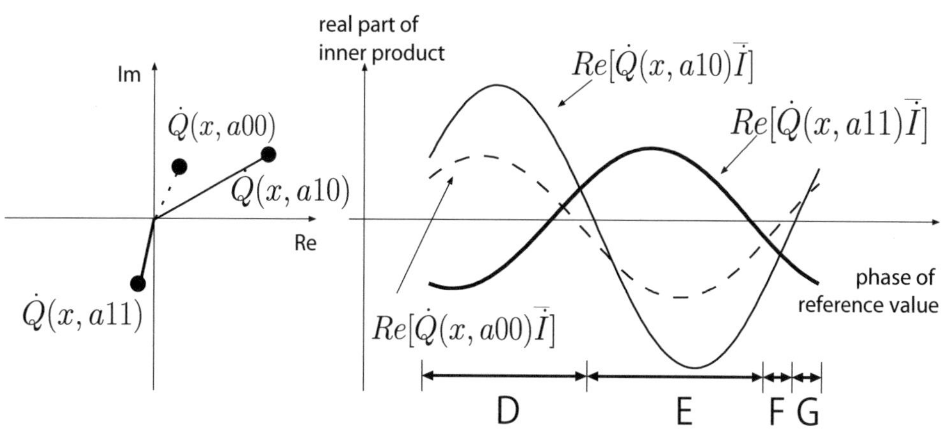

(a) Action values (b) Plot of phase of reference value vs. real part of inner product

Fig. 4. Relation between multiple complex-valued action values and the internal reference value ($|\dot{I}|$ is normalized)

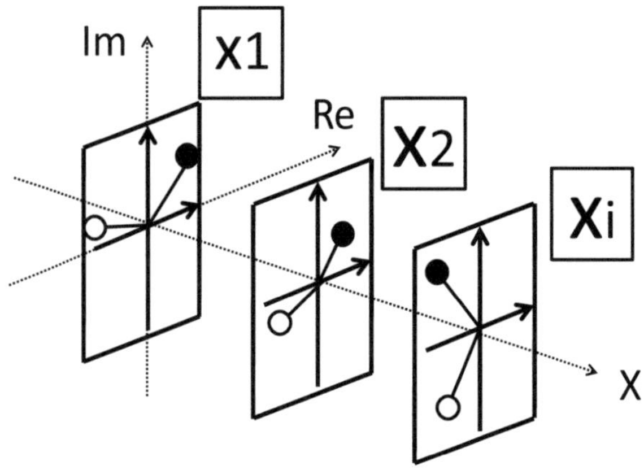

Fig. 5. Idea of conventional complex-valued reinforcement learning.

of that multiple action value is employed. In Fig. 4(b), horizontal and vertical axis is same as Fig.3(b). Action a_{10} is taken in the area D or G. Action a_{11} is taken in the area E. In this way, a method of multipe actoin value contributes to widen area where a_1 is taken.

An important advantage of using multiple action values is that it is not necessary to update the method of obtaining the action values, and hence, only virtual action values need to be determined.

2.3.2 Complex-valued RBF network for continuous environment

For using RL in real-world applications, it is important that continuous state spaces are efficiently handled. Fuchida et al. showed that in the case of (real-valued) RL, continuous state spaces can be efficiently handled without the need for mesh size parameters if the continuous action value function is approximated by using the radial basis function (RBF) (Fuchida et al., 2000; Samejima & T.Omori, 1999; Li & Duckett, 2005). In this section, approximation of the complex-valued action value function for continuous action spaces with perceptual aliasing is discussed, as shown in Fig.6. The aforementioned approximation method enables the treatment of the continuous state space without discretization in complex-valued RL.

In this section, we assume that an observation is a vector in the vector space $\mathbb{R}^M$. We employ

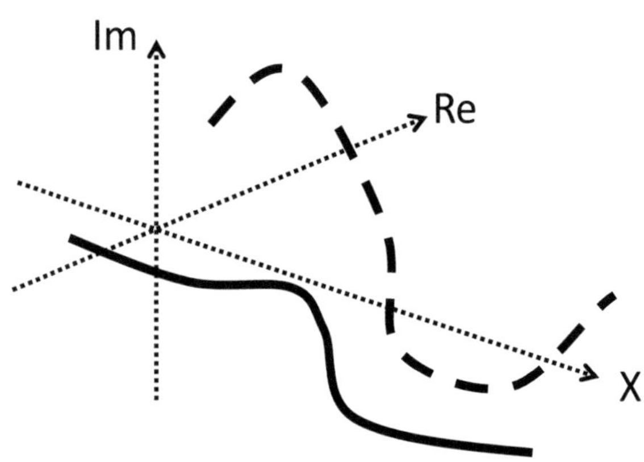

Fig. 6. Idea of complex-valued reinforcement learning using a complex-valued RBF network.

two RBF networks corresponding to two components of $\dot{Q}(\boldsymbol{x},a)$: a real part and an imaginary part. The complex-valued action value function is then represented as follows:

$$\dot{Q}(\boldsymbol{x},a) = Q_{Re}(\boldsymbol{x},a) + jQ_{Im}(\boldsymbol{x},a) \tag{20}$$

$$Q_{Re}(\boldsymbol{x},a) = \sum_{n=1}^{N_a} \omega_{Re,a,n}\phi_{Re,a,n}(\boldsymbol{x}) \tag{21}$$

$$\phi_{Re,a,n}(\boldsymbol{x}) = \prod_{m=1}^{M} \exp\left(-\frac{(x_m - \mu_{Re,a,n,m})^2}{\sigma^2_{Re,a,n,m}}\right) \tag{22}$$

$$Q_{Im}(\boldsymbol{x},a) = \sum_{n=1}^{N_a} \omega_{Im,a,n}\phi_{Im,a,n}(\boldsymbol{x}) \tag{23}$$

$$\phi_{Im,a,n}(\boldsymbol{x}) = \prod_{m=1}^{M} \exp\left(-\frac{(x_m - \mu_{Im,a,n,m})^2}{\sigma^2_{Im,a,n,m}}\right) \tag{24}$$

Note that n is the index of the RBF, and m is the dimension index; $\phi_{Re,a,n}$ and $\phi_{Im,a,n}$ are the RBFs. N_a is the number of RBFs in each component. $\omega_{Re,a,n}$ and $\omega_{Im,a,n}$ are the weight parameters. $\sigma_{Re,a,n}$ and $\sigma_{Im,a,n}$ are the variance parameters. $\mu_{Re,a,n,m}$ and $\mu_{Im,a,n,m}$ are the mean parameters. In this section, variables represented in bold face denote that they are vector.

$$\dot{\delta}_t = (r_{t+1} + \gamma\dot{Q}^{(t)}_{\max})\dot{\beta} - \dot{Q}(\boldsymbol{x}_t,a_t) \tag{25}$$

$$= \delta_{Re,t} + j\delta_{Im,t} \tag{26}$$

1. Real part

$$\omega_{Re,a,n} \leftarrow \omega_{Re,a,n} + \alpha_\omega \delta_{Re,t}\phi_{Re,a,n}(\boldsymbol{x}_t) \tag{27}$$

$$\sigma_{Re,a,n,m} \leftarrow \sigma_{Re,a,n,m} + \alpha_\sigma \delta_{Re,t}\omega_{Re,a,n} \times \frac{(x_{t,m} - \mu_{Re,a,n,m})^2}{\sigma^3_{Re,a,n,m}}\phi_{Re,a,n}(\boldsymbol{x}_t) \tag{28}$$

$$\mu_{Re,a,n,m} \leftarrow \mu_{Re,a,n,m} + \alpha_\mu \delta_{Re,t}\omega_{Re,a,n} \times \frac{x_{t,m} - \mu_{Re,a,n,m}}{\sigma_{Re,a,n,m}}\phi_{Re,a,n}(\boldsymbol{x}_t) \tag{29}$$

2. Imaginary part

$$\omega_{Im,a,n} \leftarrow \omega_{Im,a,n} + \alpha_\omega \delta_{Im,t}\phi_{Im,a,n}(\boldsymbol{x}_t) \tag{30}$$

$$\sigma_{Im,a,n,m} \leftarrow \sigma_{Im,a,n,m} + \alpha_\sigma \delta_{Im,t}\omega_{Im,a,n} \times \frac{(x_{t,m} - \mu_{Im,a,n,m})^2}{\sigma^3_{Im,a,n,m}}\phi_{Im,a,n}(\boldsymbol{x}_t) \tag{31}$$

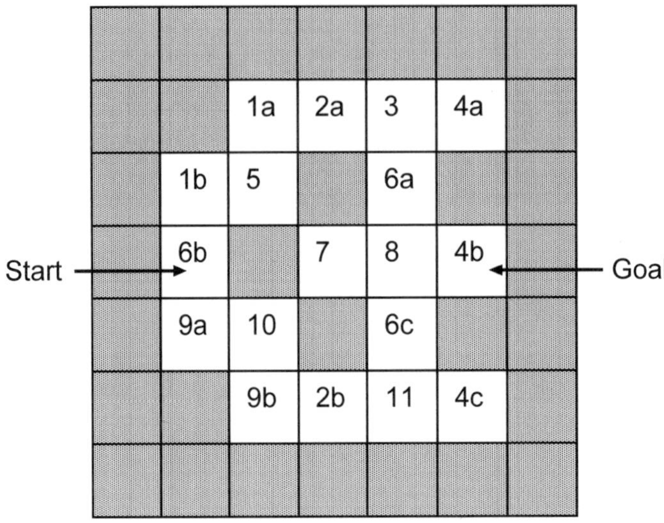

Fig. 7. Maze problems involving perceptual aliasings. Each cell is a state of the agent. The number on a cell indicates the observation. That is, the agent cannot distinguish between state 2a and 2b.

$$\begin{aligned}\mu_{Im,a,n,m} \leftarrow\ & \mu_{Im,a,n,m} \\ & +\alpha_{\mu}\delta_{Im,t}\omega_{Im,a,n} \\ & \times \frac{x_{t,m} - \mu_{Im,a,n,m}}{\sigma_{Im,a,n,m}}\phi_{Im,a,n}(\boldsymbol{x}_t)\end{aligned} \tag{32}$$

The method of updating the complex-valued RBF network is the same as that of updating the RBF network.

3. Experiments and results

Three simple experiments are conducted to evaluate the algorithms by using the proposed complex-valued functions. First, $\dot{\text{Q}}$-learning is used to solve simple maze problems associated with perceptual aliasing Then, Miyazaki's environment (Miyazaki & Kobayashi, 2003) is learnt in the case of scPS. Finally, an experiment in a chained state environment which is useful type of environment for evaluating various intervals of perceptual aliasings is conducted for the multiple action values.

3.1 Maze problems

Figure 7 shows the maze environment involving a certain degree of perceptual aliasing. An agent starts from the cell marked "Start" and attempts to reach the cell marked "Goal." However, the agent cannot distinguish between some of the cells in the maze because the sensors detect only the existence of the walls around the agent. Thus, the agent faces a serious problem of having to change its action according to the context.
Q-learning, Q(λ)(Sutton & Barto, 1998), $\dot{\text{Q}}$-learning ($N_e = 1$) and $\dot{\text{Q}}$-learning ($N_e = 2$) are evaluated in the maze. The parameter conditions are shown in Table 1. The agent can choose an action from north, east, south, or west but cannot choose the action that makes it move

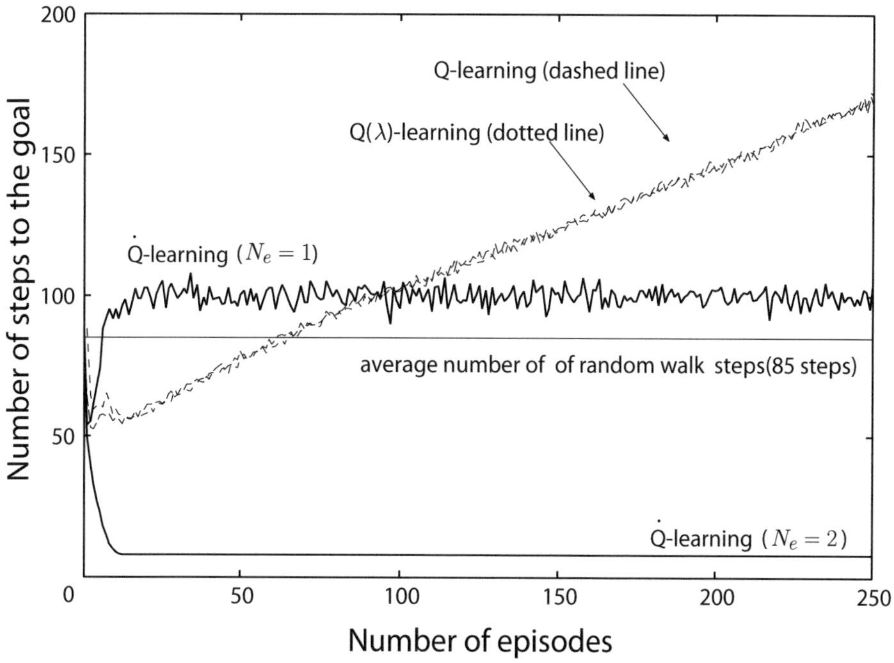

Fig. 8. Result in the POMDPs maze. This graph shows average steps over 1000 learning.

toward the walls. The agent obtains an r value of 100 if it achieves the goal. Each learning action consists of 100 episodes, and each episode consists of a series of steps from the start to the goal. If the agent cannot achieve the goal within 5000 steps, we restart the learning. Figure 8 shows the average number of steps in the POMDP environment shown in Fig.7. None of the algorithms are restarted in this case. In Q-learning and Q(λ), the average number of steps begins to increase after approximately 30 episodes because of the effect of perceptual aliasing. A greater number of steps are required in $\dot{\text{Q}}$-learning ($N_e = 1$) than in random walk. In contrast to these algorithms, the $\dot{\text{Q}}$-learning ($N_e = 2$) curve shows a sharp descent, and the number of learning steps converges to 12.

Q-learning, Q(λ)	
α	0.001 × (500 - episode)
γ	0.9
T	100 × (1.0/(1+episode))
λ	0.9 (for Q(λ))
$\dot{\text{Q}}$-learning	
α	0.25
$\dot{\beta}$	$\exp(j\pi/6)$
γ	0.9
T	20
N_e	1 (eligibility trace is not used) 2 (eligibility trace is used)

Table 1. experimental parameters for the maze tasks.

Figure 9 shows the acquired typical action sequence from the point of view of using the context. Figure 9(a) shows the case of using Q-learning. The two state-action pairs in the initial state cannot reach the goal because of the perceptual aliasing between 6a, 6b, and 6c. For instance, if the agent has learnt to choose north in the initial state, the agent tries to choose north in the state 6a. However, the north action in this state 6a is not suitable. The agent has to learn this contradiction. Figure 9(b) shows the case of using $\dot{Q}$-learning . In contrast to the case of Q-learning, both the state-action pairs in the initial state in $\dot{Q}$-learning can reach the goal. Furthermore, we can see that the number of state-action pairs that can reach the goal is greater in $\dot{Q}$-learning than in Q-learning. Since $\dot{Q}$-learning employs the idea of context, action selection depends on the history of the state-action pair. Context-based action selection involves the use of the internal reference value shown in (6) and (7) and depends on the previous state-action pair only. Thus, the proposed method enables the agent to take a context-dependent action to achieve the goal even if several perceptual aliasing problems exist.

3.2 Miyazaki's environment

We compare scPS, PS-r*, and $\dot{Q}$-learning in Miyazaki's simulation experiment(Miyazaki & Kobayashi, 2003), as shown in Fig.10. The agent obtains the same observation Z in four states Z_a, Z_b, Z_c, Z_d. Thus, we conclude that the agent obtains identical observations in n states $S_1, S_2, \cdots, S_n$. In other words, n in the figure indicates the number of states that the agent can distinguish between. When the agent takes action a in state X, it reaches state S_1 with probability p or state X with probability $1 - p$. The agent repeatedly takes an action from the initial state X to the terminal state Z_d. The agent obtains the reward 100 iff the agent take action b at the state Z_d. We employ the parameters $n = 7$ and $p = 0.9$. We set the minimum number of steps from the start to the goal as 12.

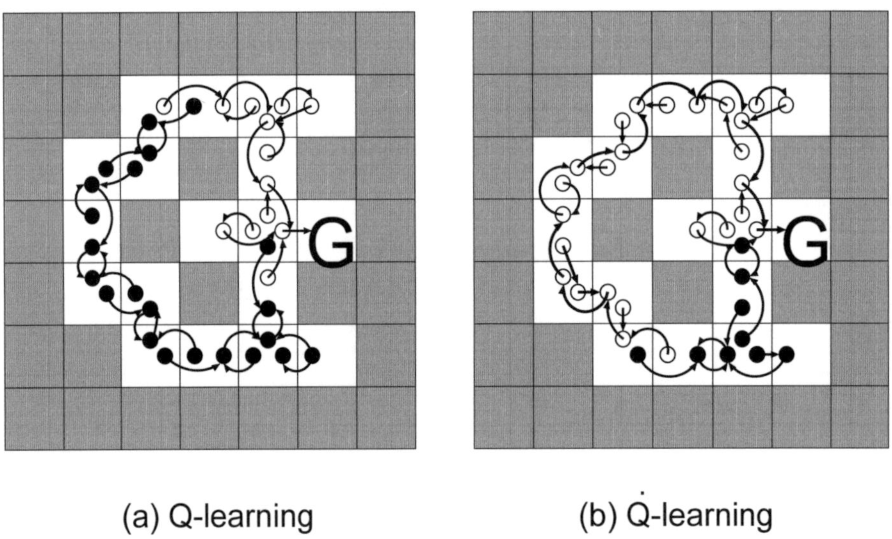

Fig. 9. Acquired action sequences. White and black bullets show the state-action pairs that can or cannot reach the goal, respectively. The location of a bullet is directly indicative of the corresponding action. For example, a bullet located in the upper region of a cell indicates the state-action pair of the cell and north action.

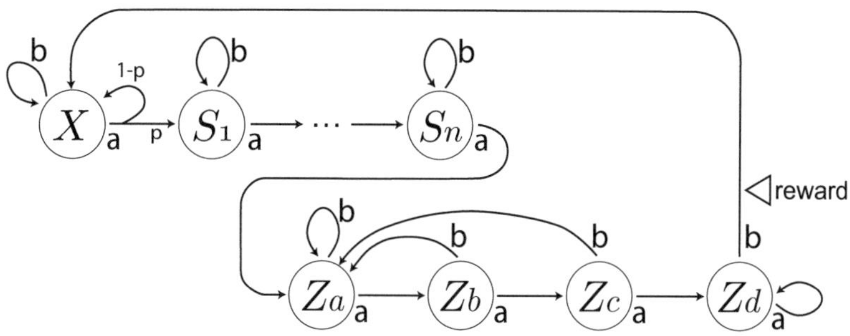

Fig. 10. Miyazaki's simulation environment (Miyazaki & Kobayashi, 2003).

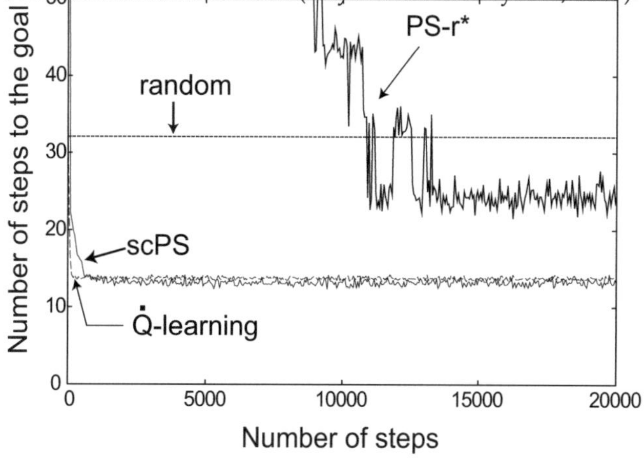

Fig. 11. Learning performance in Miyazaki's environment. The horizontal axis indicates the number of action selection. The vertical axis indicates the average number of steps if the agent uses the policy in each step.

We perform a total of 50 experiments, each of which consists of 20000 action selection steps. The experimental parameters are shown in Table 2.

scPS	
initial evaluation values	1.0×10^{-10}
discount factor γ	0.5
phase change ω[deg]	30
PS-r*	
initial evaluation values	0.8
significance level α	0.05
$\dot{Q}$-learning	
initial action values	0.0
learning rate α	0.8
phase rotation $\dot{\beta}$	$e^{j\pi/6}$
discount factor γ	0.9
number of traces N_e	3

Table 2. Parameter setting for Miyazaki's experiment.

The results of our experiments are shown in Fig.11. From the results, scPS a acquires suitable policy for a short term. Table 2 shows that state transition and series of selected actions acquired by the policy in the case of scPS. Between states X and S_7, the phase of the selected complex-valued evaluation value rotates by 30 degree. The phases of the selected evaluation values are almost equal to the phase of the internal reference value at a given time. From Z_a to Z_c, the selected evaluation values remain unchanged since the same evaluation value is selected. However, the internal reference value changes continuously. This causes the agent to take another action in state Z_d. In this experiment, the agent learns $V(Z,a) > V(Z,b)$ for $Z = Z_a, Z_b, Z_c$ and $V(Z,a) < V(Z,b)$ for $Z = Z_d$.

3.3 Chained state problems

Figure 12 shows an example of a simulation environment performed to evaluate the multiple action values. In Fig. 12, $s_0, s_1, \cdots, s_7$ denote the states of the agent. States s_0 and s_7 are the initial state and terminal state, respectively. The agent's objective is to learn to go from the start s_0 to the goal s_7. a_0 and a_1 denote the actions. Note that the agent is required to take action a_1 in all the states in order to achieve the goal s_7.
The agent obtains a reward r if it achieves the goal s_7. We assume that the state transition and observation are both deterministic. Additionally, we assume the state space and observation space to be both finite and countable. We compare the performance of $\dot{Q}$-learning with and without the multiple complex-valued action value. The multiplexing degree is employed is 2. In each experiment, we consider all possible types of aliasing. Namely, each experiment comprises a series of sub-experiments ranging from no aliasing (the agent can distinguish all the states.) to full aliasing (the agent is confused and cannot distinguish between any of

x	a	arg$\boldsymbol{v}$ [deg]	arg$\boldsymbol{i}$ [deg]
X	a	337.5	337.5
S_1	a	309.5	307.5
S_2	a	279.5	277.5
S_3	a	249.5	247.5
S_4	a	219.6	217.5
S_5	a	189.4	187.5
S_6	a	159.4	157.5
S_7	a	128.6	127.5
Z_a	a	50.2	97.5
Z_b	a	50.2	67.5
Z_c	a	50.2	37.5
Z_d	b	0.7	7.5

Table 3. Comparison between the phase of complex-valued evaluation values and the phase of the internal reference value.

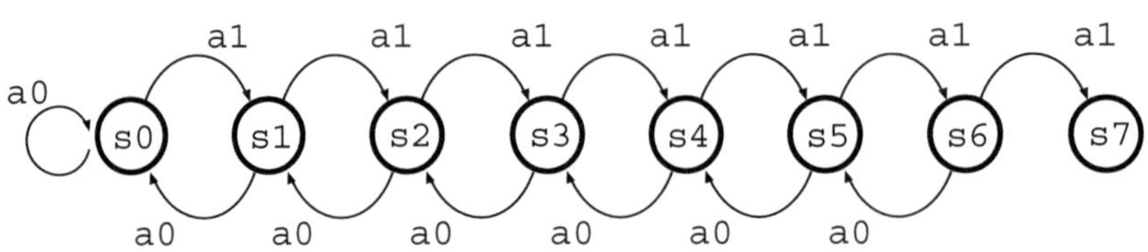

Fig. 12. An eight-state environment.

the states). In order to identify a task, we define certain observation patterns. An observation pattern is a set of relationships between the states and the observations and is represented by a sequence of numbers from the observation of the initial state to the observation of the terminal state. The appearance of the same sequence of numbers is indicative of perceptual aliasing. We ignore the numerical values in the pattern and simply focus on whether the values are the "same or different." For instance, the observation pattern 0-1-2-3-4-5-6-7 indicates that there is no perceptual aliasing, while 0-0-0-0-0-0-0-0 implies that the agent confuses between all the states; further, 0-1-2-3-4-0-5-6 implies that the agent confuses between s_0 and s_5. We perform five learning experiments in each observation pattern. Each learning action consists of 100 episodes, each of which consists of a series of steps from the start to the goal; here, each transition is called a step. The other experimental parameters are shown in Table 4. It is difficult for the $\dot{Q}$-learning agent to take the same action in several states where the obtained observation is the same. For example, we assume that the agent cannot distinguish between s_0 and s_5. In other words, the agent can distinguish between all the states except for the s_0/s_5 pair. The internal reference value in the s_0 stage differs from that in the s_5 stage because either (6) or (7) is used to move the internal reference value in the complex plane at each step. Because of this difference, the agent takes different actions. When the same action is suitable for the abovementioned two states, CVRL is effective. However, when the actions suitable for the two states are different, CVRL is ineffective.

Figure 13 shows the average learning curves in each environment. The number of steps in the conventional method converges to 15, while the number of steps in the multiple action value method converges to approximately 9.1. These results reveal that fewer steps are required in the case of $\dot{Q}$-learning with the multiple action value method than in the case of $\dot{Q}$-learning without the multiple action value method. We use the average number of steps in the final episode. We define the scores of the proposed method and conventional method as f_m and f_s, respectively. We evaluate the learning performance on the basis of the ratio f_m/f_s.

Figure 14 shows the experimental results. The vertical axis on the left indicates the final number of average steps f_m & f_s, while the vertical axis on the right indicates the ratio f_m/f_s. The horizontal axis indicates the tasks sorted on the basis of the ratio f_m/f_s. We group the observation patterns under three classes on the basis of the fm/fs value. Classes 1, 2, and 3 are sets of observation patterns for which $f_m/f_s < 1$, $f_m/f_s = 1$, and $f_m/f_s > 1$, respectively. We show the typical examples for each class in Table 5. Classes 1, 2, and 3 account for 32%, 59%, and 9.1% of the total number of observation patterns, respectively.

In class 1, the proposed method is superior to the conventional method. The observation patterns in this class are characterized on the basis of the time interval between the perceptual aliasing states. Every third or fourth state appearing in a given time interval is found to be a perceptual aliasing state. The results show that the use of multiple action values enables the agent to show a suitable behavior.

$\dot{Q}$-learning	
α	0.25
$\dot{\beta}$	$\exp(j\pi/6)$
γ	0.9
T	20
N_e	2
r	100.0

Table 4. Experimental parameters for chained state environment.

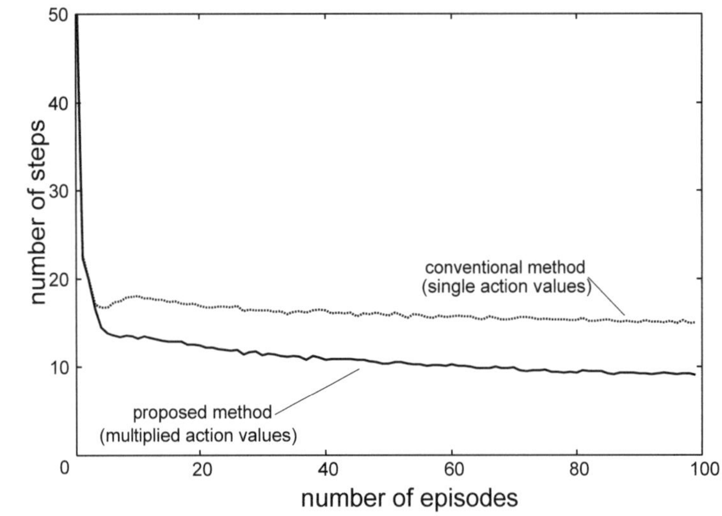

Fig. 13. Simulation results obtained for eight-state environment.

In class 2, the proposed method is as efficient as the conventional method. An observation pattern 0-1-2-3-4-5-6-7, which represents no perceptual aliasing, is included in this class. Another observation pattern 0-0-0-0-0-0-0, which represents that the agent confuses all the states, is also included in this class. Consequently, the performance of $\dot{Q}$-learning depends on the time intervals between the perceptual states and not on the number of perceptual states alone.

In class 3, the conventional method is superior to the proposed method. In the case of the conventional method, the observation patterns require a greater number of episodes to acquire a suitable behavior in class 3 than in class 2. We conducted an additional experiment with 500

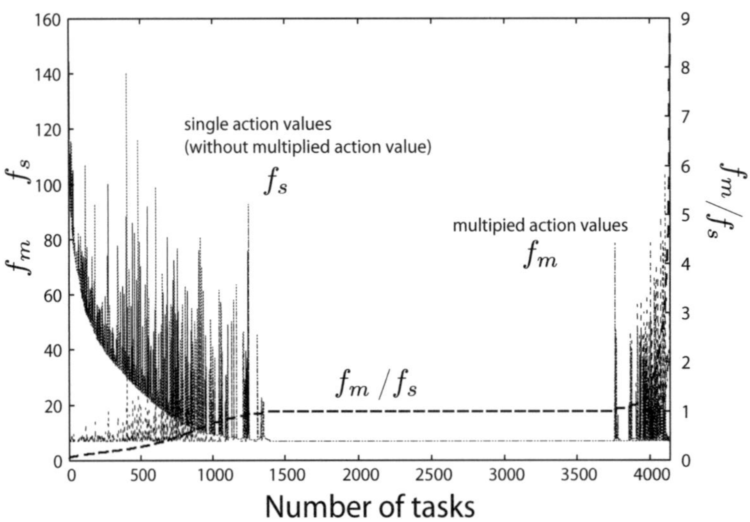

Fig. 14. Rules for interaction between complex-valued action values and internal reference values.

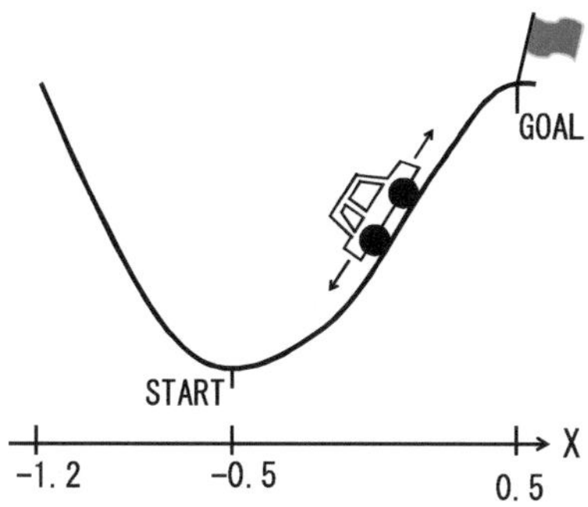

Fig. 15. Mountain car task.

episodes in the observation patterns of this class (shown in Table 5). The experimental results show that $f_m = 7.0$ in the three observation patterns. Therefore, we assume that the proposed method requires a greater number of episodes than does the conventional method; this is probably because of the greater number of action values in the former case.
As mentioned above, the proposed method can be used to improve the learning performance. On the other hand, it causes to increase the number of episodes.

3.4 Mountain car task with perceptual aliasing

We compare the method based on the complex-valued RBF network with three conventional methods, that is, random walk, dQ-learning without the RBF network, and Q-learning with the RBF network. We conduct a simulation experiment involving a mountain car task. The agent that uses $\dot{Q}$-learning without the RBF network divides the state space into 10 equal parts.

	observation pattern	f_m	f_s	f_m/f_s
class 1	0-1-2-3-0-4-0-4	7.0	147.8	0.047
	0-1-2-3-4-1-5-4	7.0	125.0	0.056
	0-1-2-3-4-0-5-5	7.0	118.6	0.059
class 2	0-1-2-0-3-4-2-4	7.0	7.0	1.0
	0-0-0-0-0-0-0-0	7.0	7.0	1.0
	0-1-2-3-4-5-6-7	7.0	7.0	1.0
class 3	0-0-1-2-3-1-1-2	54.0	7.0	7.7
	0-1-2-3-2-1-0-1	57.2	7.0	8.2
	0-1-2-1-0-0-0-3	60.8	7.0	8.7

Table 5. Comparison of performance of the proposed method and that of the conventional method.

discount rate γ	0.7
reward r	100
Boltzmann temperature T	150/(1+episode)
learning rate of μ α_μ	0.001
learning rate of σ α_σ	0.001
learning rate of ω α_ω	0.001

Table 6. Parameters for Q-learning with RBF network.

discount rate γ	0.7
reward r	100
Boltzmann temperature T	0.5
rotational value of phase $\dot{\beta}$	exp(1j[deg])
learning rate α	0.1
discreted state number D	10 at even intervals

Table 7. Parameters for $\dot{Q}$-learning

Figure 15 shows the mountain car task. The possible actions for an agent that controls the car are forward(a=+1), neutral(a=0) and reverse(a=-1). The agent aims to reach the goal from the start. However, the output power is not sufficiently high for the car to climb up the anterior mountain in one trip. Therefore, the car should climb a posterior mountain and climb the anterior mountain swiftly. The agent observes only the position of the car. The subsequent state is derived from the following equation:

$$v \leftarrow v + 0.001a - 0.0025\cos(3x) \tag{33}$$

$$x \leftarrow x + v \tag{34}$$

Note that $x(-1.2 \leq x \leq 0.5)$ and $v(-0.07 \leq v \leq 0.07)$ indicate the position and velocity of the car, respectively. The agent obtains a reward if and only if the car reaches the goal. Tables 6, 7 and 8 show the parameters for Q-learning with the RBF network, $\dot{Q}$-learning , and complex-valued RBF network, respectively. Each step corresponds to an action of the car, and each episode consists of a series of steps from the start to the goal. One learning action consists of 300 episodes.

discount rate γ	0.7
reward r	100
Boltzmann temperature T	0.5
rotational value of phase $\dot{\beta}$	exp(1j[deg])
learning rate of μ α_μ	0.001
learning rate of σ α_σ	0.001
learning rate of ω α_ω	0.01

Table 8. Parameters for complex-valued RBF network

Figure 16 shows the average number of steps for 20 learnings. The horizontal axis indicates the number of episodes, and the vertical axis indicates the number of steps from the start to the goal. Since Q-learning cannot be used to address perceptual aliasing, the results show that the learning behavior is better in the case of $\dot{Q}$-learning without the RBF network than in the case of Q-learning with the RBF network. The result also shows that the use of the complex-valued RBF network in these methods enables the agent to learn the best behavior quickly. When the RBF network is used, the learning efficiency is improved because the value function is extrapolated to the unsampled states.

4. Conclusion and future plans

A new reinforcement learning algorithm that uses complex-valued functions is proposed. This algorithm can be used to expand typical learning algorithms such as Q-learning and

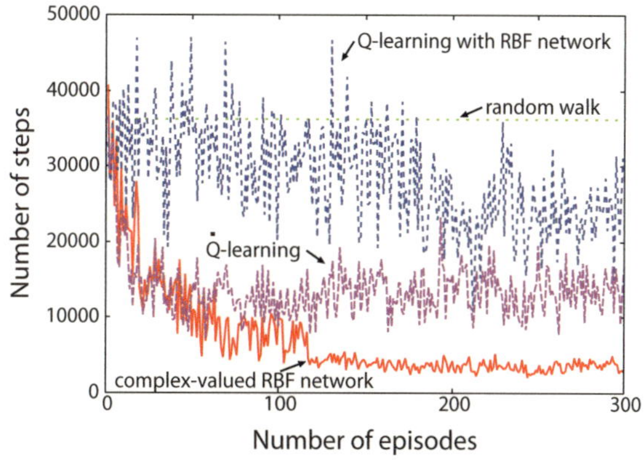

Fig. 16. Simulation result obtained for mountain car task with perceptual aliasing.

profit sharing and can allow for an agent to deal with time series or context. From the results of simulation experiments, we confirm that the algorithms generate redundant contexts to compensate for perceptual aliasing.

In the future, we plan to expand the proposed learning algorithm and compare the performance of this algorithm with that of other reinforcement learning algorithms. We also plan to make the following improvements to the proposed learning method:

- Implementation of the phase of the internal reference value as a time-varying function so that the method can be used in a dynamic environment
- Extension of the method to more complex and high-dimensional space
- Improvement of the method so that it can be applied to real autonomous robots in an uncertain environment

5. References

A.G.Barto, R.S.Sutton & C.W.Anderson (1983). Neuronlike elements that can solve difficult learning control problems, *IEEE Transactions on Systems, Man, and Cybernetics* 13: 835–846.

C.J.C.H.Watkins (1989). *Learning from Delayed Rewards*, PhD thesis, Cambridge University.

Crites, R. H. & Barto, A. G. (1996). Improving elevator performance using reinforcement learning, *Advances in Neural Information Processing Systems 8* pp. 1017–1023.

Dalamagkidisa, K., Kolokotsab, D., K.Kalaitzakisc & Stavrakakisc, G. (2007). Reinforcement learning for energy conservation and comfort in buildings, *Building and Environment* 42(7): 2686–2698.

Fuchida, T., Maehara, M., Mori, K. & Murashima, S. (2000). A learning method of RBF network using reinforcement leaning method(in Japanese), *IEICE technical report. Neurocomputing* 99(684): 157–163.

Hamagami, T. & Hirata, H. (2004). Development of intelligent wheelchair acquiring autonomous, cooperative, and collaborative behavior, *Proceedings of IEEE International Conference on Systems, Man and Cybernetics*, pp. 3235–3530.

Hamagami, T. & Hirata, H. (2005). State space partitioning and clustering with sensor alignment for autonomous robots, *Proceedings of IEEE International Conference on Systems, Man and Cybernetics*, pp. 2655–2660.

Hamagami, T., Koakutsu, S. & Hirata, H. (2002). Reinforcement learning to compensate for perceptual aliasing using dynamic additional parameter: Motivational value, *Proceedings of IEEE International Conference on Systems, Man and Cybernetics*, pp. 1–6.

Hirose, A. (ed.) (2003). *Complex-Valued Neural Networks : Theories and Applications*, Series on Innovative Intelligence, World Scientific Publishing Co. Pte. Ltd.

Kaelbling, L. P., Littman, M. L. & Cassandra, A. R. (1998). Planning and acting in partially observable stochastic domains, *Artificial Intelligence* 101: 99–134.

Li, J. & Duckett, T. (2005). Q-learning with a growing RBF network for behavior learning in mobile robotics, *Proceedings of the IASTED International Conference on Robotics and Applications*.

Mccallum, R. A. (1995). Instance-based utile distinctions for reinforcement learning with hidden state, *Proceedings of the 12th International Conference on Machine Learning*, pp. 387–395.

Miyazaki, K. & Kobayashi, S. (2003). An extention of profit sharing to partially observable markov decision processes : Proposition of ps-r* and its evaluation, *Transactions of the Japanese Society for Artificial Intelligence* 18(5): 286–296.

Samejima, K. & T.Omori (1999). Adaptive internal state space construction method for reinforcement learning of a real-world agent, *Neural Networks* 12: 1143–1155.

Shibuya, T. & Hamagami, T. (2009). Multiplied action values for complex-valued reinforcement learning, *Proceedings of the International Conference on Electrical Engineering*, pp. I9FP0491_1–6.

Singh, S., Littman, M. L., Jong, N. K., Pardoe, D. & Stone, P. (2003). Learning predictive state representations, *Proceedings of the 20th International Conference on Machine Learning*, pp. 712–719.

Syafiie, S., Tadeo, F., Martinez, E., Weber, C., Elshaw, M. & Mayer, N. M. (eds) (2008). Model-free learning control of chemical processes, *in Reinforcement Learning*, I-Tech Education and Publishing, Austria, chapter 16.

Sutton, R. S. & Barto, A. G. (1998). *REINFORCEMENT LEARNING: An Introduction*, MIT Press.

Wiering, M. & Schmidhuber, J. (1996). HQ-learning, *Adaptive Behavior* 6(2): 219–246.

15

Adaptive PID Control of a Nonlinear Servomechanism Using Recurrent Neural Networks

Reza Jafari[1] and Rached Dhaouadi[2]
[1]Oklahoma State University, Stillwater, OK 74078,
[2]American University of Sharjah, Sharjah,
[1]USA
[2]UAE

1. Introduction

Recent progress in the theory of neural networks played a major role in the development of new tools and techniques for modelling, identification and control of complex nonlinear dynamic systems. Intelligent control, with a special focus on neuro-control has been used successfully to solve difficult real control problems which are nonlinear, noisy and relatively complex. This is due to the fact that neural networks have an inherent ability to learn from input-output data and approximate an arbitrarily nonlinear function well. The inclusion of semi-linear sigmoid activation functions offers nonlinear mapping ability for solving highly nonlinear control problems (Omatu et al., 1995).

A large number of identification and control structures have been proposed on the basis of neural networks in recent years (Jain & Medsker, 1999). Most of the developed neural networks use a feed-forward structure along with the back-propagation training algorithm. Recently, more research interest is given to recurrent networks with special application to dynamic systems. A Recurrent Neural Network (RNN) exhibits internal memory due to its feedback structure, which gives the network the possibility of retaining information to be used later. By their inherent characteristic of memorizing past information, for long or short-term periods, RNNs are good candidates for nonlinear system identification and control (Narendra & Pathasarathy, 1990).

Although control theory has made great advances in the last few decades, which has led to many sophisticated control schemes, PID control remains the most popular type of control being used in industry today. This popularity is partly due to the fact that PID controllers have simple structures that are easily implemented. On-line self-tuning PID controller offer an advantage for plants that have uncertain dynamics, time varying parameters, and nonlinearities. Recently a lot of attentions have been focused on neural based PID controller, and many efforts have been done to investigate different aspects of deploying neural networks in the area of adaptive PID control (Puskorius & Feldkamp, 1993), (Saikalis, 2001)

The concept of adaptive PID control was introduced to compensate the drawbacks of the fixed-gains PID controller. For example, if the operating point of a process is changed due to disturbances, there is a need to adjust the controller parameters manually in order to keep the optimal settings. Usually this procedure known as tuning is difficult and time consuming for systems with interacting loops. In addition to these difficulties, the conventional PID tuning methods have major drawbacks. For example, the Ziegler-Nichols (Astrom & Wittenmark, 1989) tuning method is sensitive to disturbances because of its reliance on open loop experiments. The tuning method proposed by Nishikawa (Nishikawa et al. 1989) requires man-machine interaction in which the operator needs to generate input signals every time the parameters have to be modified in order to adapt to changes in the process dynamics. Adaptive controller with the ability of self-tuning is therefore the ideal solution to all these difficulties.

Substantial research effort is also ongoing in the general area of adaptive control with neural networks, both in designing structures and learning algorithms (Chang et al. 2003), (Kuc & Gie, 2000), (Ranger & Desbiens, 2003), (Liu, 2001), (Mandic & Chamers, 2001). The design and implementation of adaptive control for nonlinear dynamic systems is challenging and extremely difficult. In most cases, developing adaptive control strategies depend on the particular information of the nonlinear structure of the plant that needs to be controlled. Neural networks with the ability to deal with nonlinearities can be used to develop an adaptive controller for unknown systems. If the relationship between the input and the output of an unknown nonlinear plant is modeled by an appropriate neural network, the model obtained can be used to construct a proper controller. The whole procedure of training and construction of a neural based controller can be implemented on-line. The neural network model is updated by measured plant input and output data and then the controller parameters are directly tuned using the updated model.

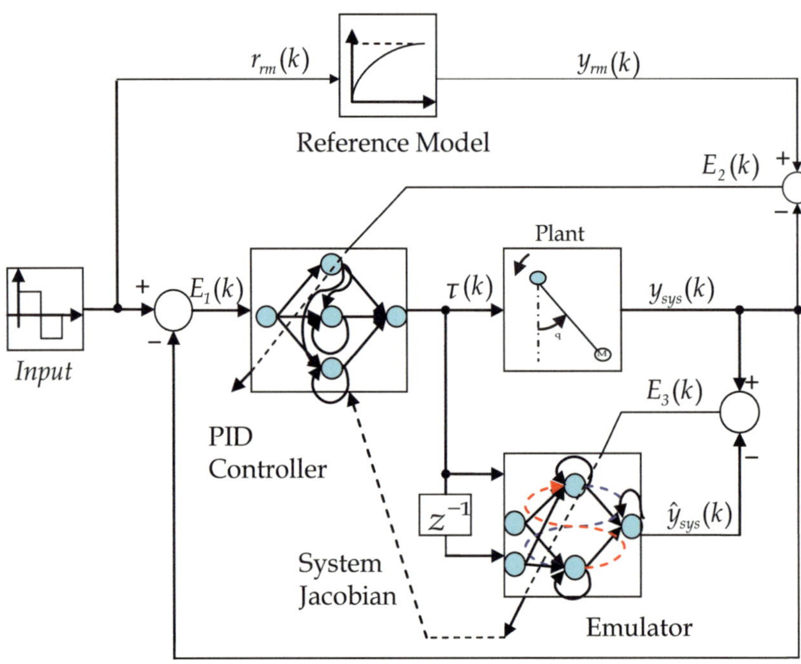

Fig. 1.1 Adaptive PID with RNN based emulator

In this chapter RNNs are used in system modeling and in the design of an adaptive PID controller for nonlinear electromechanical systems such as servo drives in robot

manipulators. The design of a servo drive system represents a difficult problem in most cases because of troublesome characteristics such as severe friction nonlinearities, variable parameters, time-varying process dynamics and unobservable system states and disturbances.
The proposed adaptive control scheme studied in this chapter is based on a RNN-PID controller combined with a RNN system emulator as shown in Fig. 1.1 (Dhaouadi & Jafari, 2007). The RNN-PID controller is designed based on the discrete equations of the PID controller transfer function. The parameters K_p, K_i and K_d of the partially connected RNN are regarded as the gains of the PID controller. These gains are not fixed, but can be adjusted on-line based on an adaptation law so as to achieve the desired control objectives. The plant direct model is constructed with the RNN emulator as shown in Fig. 1. The network is tuned online to provide the Jacobian coefficients of the system which are needed to adapt the PID gains. The self-tuning RNN will be trained using the gradient decent RTRL algorithm, (Kuc & Gie, 2000). The training of the RNN emulator will be first performed off-line so as to learn the dynamics of the plant and will be next optimized on-line.
Such control approach can be classified as indirect adaptive control, as the parameters of the plant model are adapted and control is computed based on the current model, rather than directly adapting the controller parameters.
Global asymptotic stability of the closed loop system is a challenging problem. Absolute stability analysis of RNN in general is investigated via Linear Matrix Inequality (LMI) (Barbanov & Prokhorov 2002). Barabanov and Prokhorov derived a sufficient condition for the network parameters which guarantees the absolute stability of RNN in a general form. The method is based on the sector condition. Barabanov and Prokhorov introduced later a new algorithm for global asymptotic stability of nonlinear discrete-time systems (Barbanov & Prokhorov, 2003). The new method, for reduction of a dissipativity domain of a discrete-time system, approximates level surface of Lyapunov function. In this paper, we develop a criterion to prove the stability of the RNN-PID controller in the sense of Lyapunov.
In summary, the analysis presented in this chapter shows that appropriately structured recurrent neural networks can provide conveniently parameterized dynamic models of nonlinear systems for use in adaptive PID control. The main features of the proposed new adaptive PID controller are

- Compensation of different process and unmodelled uncertainties,
- Simple to configure since it does not require a process model.
- Could track changes of process dynamics on-line.
- Has all the properties of PID control.

The chapter is organized as follows: section 1 gives a literature review and introduces a general overview of the control methodology used. The main contribution of this work is represented in section 2 where an adaptive RNN-PID controller is developed for Reference Model Control. Stability analysis of the designed controller is investigated via Lyapunov theory in section 3. Finally, discussion of simulation results and conclusions are given in section 4.

2. Adaptive RNN-PID design

The PID controller is one of the most useful and familiar controller used in industry. PI and PID controllers have been proven to be remarkably effective in regulating a wide range of processes. However, the PID controller may give low performance when dealing with highly nonlinear and uncertain systems. The abilities of neural networks in dealing with nonlinear dynamical systems make them a viable alternative approach to deal with complex systems. RNNs will be used next to develop an adaptive PID controller which is robust to system parameters variation and uncertain dynamics.

In this section, we will develop an adaptive RNN based PID controller for nonlinear dynamic systems. The parameters of the proposed RNN-PID controller are adjusted on-line. A single-axis servomechanism is used as a case study to study the performance of the PID controller and validate the proposed adaptive control scheme.

2.1 Discrete-time PID controller

The design of the RNN based PID controller starts by deriving the discrete-time PID equation. From this difference equation the network can be designed accordingly. The general PID transfer function in the s-domain is given by

$$\frac{U(s)}{E(s)} = K_p + \frac{K_i}{s} + K_d\left(\frac{s}{1+\tau s}\right). \tag{2.1}$$

For practical applications, an approximate derivative term is introduced to reduce the effect of measurement noise. Next, the discrete-time representation of the PID controller is obtained by mapping the transfer function from the s-domain to the z-domain using the bilinear transformation.

$$s \Leftrightarrow \frac{2}{T}\left(\frac{1-z^{-1}}{1+z^{-1}}\right), \tag{2.2}$$

The discrete-time control signal $u(n)$ is derived from the error signal $e(n)$ as follows.

$$u(n) = K_p e(n) + K_i v(n) + K_d w(n), \tag{2.3}$$

where $v(n)$ is the integral term, and $w(n)$ is the derivative term.

$$\frac{V(s)}{E(s)} = \frac{1}{s}, \tag{2.4}$$

$$\frac{W(s)}{E(s)} = \frac{s}{1+\tau s}, \tag{2.5}$$

$$\frac{V(z)}{E(z)} = \frac{T}{2}\left(\frac{1+z^{-1}}{1-z^{-1}}\right), \tag{2.6}$$

The difference equation of the integral term $v(n)$ is

$$v(n) = v(n-1) + \frac{T}{2}[e(n) + e(n-1)], \tag{2.7}$$

Similarly,

$$\frac{W(z)}{E(z)} = \frac{2(1-z^{-1})}{(2\tau+T)-(2\tau-T)z^{-1}}, \tag{2.8}$$

Defining

$$\alpha_0 = 2\tau + T \text{ and } \alpha_1 = 2\tau - T \tag{2.9}$$

The difference equation of the approximate derivative term is

$$\frac{\alpha_0}{2} w(n) = \frac{\alpha_1}{2} w(n-1) + e(n) - e(n-1), \tag{2.10}$$

This equation is written next in a modified form through a change of variables. Let's define $p(n) = \frac{\alpha_0}{2} w(n)$, then

$$p(n) = \frac{\alpha_1}{\alpha_0} p(n-1) + e(n) - e(n-1), \tag{2.11}$$

The PID derivative gain will be therefore changed accordingly

$$K_d w(n) = \left(\frac{2K_d}{\alpha_0}\right) p(n), \tag{2.12}$$

2.2 RNN controller design

Combining the derived discrete-time equations (2.5-2.12) of the PID controller, the corresponding recurrent neural network can be designed accordingly. The input to the network is the error signal and the output of the network is the control signal. There are several ways of designing the network architecture to represent the PID controller. In our approach, a partially connected recurrent neural network is used with a single hidden layer and three hidden neurons as shown in Fig. 2.1. The activation function is assumed to be linear. The feedback connections between the neurons in the hidden layer have one sampling time delay. The network parameters are clustered in three matrices W_{hi}, R_h, W_{ch}.

$$W_{hi} = \begin{bmatrix} 1 \\ \frac{T}{2} \\ 1 \end{bmatrix}, \ R_h = \begin{bmatrix} 0 & 0 & 0 \\ \frac{T}{2} & 1 & 0 \\ -1 & 0 & \frac{\alpha_1}{\alpha_0} \end{bmatrix}, \ W_{oh} = \begin{bmatrix} K_p & K_i & \frac{2K_d}{\alpha_0} \end{bmatrix}, \tag{2.13}$$

where, W_{hi} represents the RNN gains between the input layer and the hidden layer, W_{ch} represents the RNN gains between the hidden layer and the output layer, and R_h represents the RNN feedback gains between the neurons in the hidden layer. T is the sampling time, and K_p, K_i and K_d are the controller gains.

One of the major advantages of the designed network is the simplicity of the designed controller. The training procedure of the proposed controller is relatively easy due to the linearity of the activation functions.

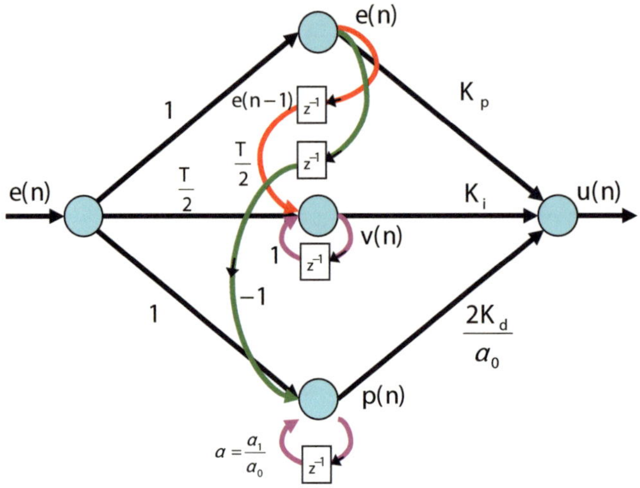

Fig. 2.1 Partially connected RNN-based PID controller

2.3 PID update equations

As it is shown in Fig. 2.1, the network includes four weights K_p, K_i, $\frac{2K_d}{\alpha_0}$, and $\frac{\alpha_1}{\alpha_0}$, which need to be tuned. The rest of the weights are fixed. The network output can be computed using the forward equations as follows

$$e(n) = O_1(n) \tag{2.14}$$

$$v(n) = O_2(n) = O_2(n-1) + \frac{T}{2}[e(n) + e(n-1)] \tag{2.15}$$

$$p(n) = O_3(n) = \alpha O_3(n-1) + e(n) - e(n-1) \tag{2.16}$$

$$u(n) = K_p O_1(n) + K_i O_2(n) + K_d^* O_3(n) \tag{2.17}$$

where the gains α and K_d^* are defined by

$$\alpha = \frac{\alpha_1}{\alpha_0}, \; K_d^* = \frac{2K_d}{\alpha_0} \tag{2.18}$$

The training algorithm of the RNN-PID controller is based on the gradient descent method and uses the output error signal $e(n)$, which is the difference between the actual RNN output and the desired output.

$$\varepsilon(n) = d(n) - u(n) \tag{2.19}$$

For offline training, the data set $(\varepsilon(n), d(n))$ is generated from the simulated PID control system and is used to train the RNN. The performance index to be minimized is the sum of squares of errors $E_{sq}(n)$ of the training data set.

$$E_{sq}(n)=\frac{1}{2}\sum_{n=1}^{N}\varepsilon(n)^2 \tag{2.20}$$

According to the gradient-descent method, the weights are updated by performing the following derivations.

$$K_p(n+1)=K_p(n)-\eta\frac{\partial E_{sq}(n)}{\partial K_p} \tag{2.21}$$

$$K_i(n+1)=K_i(n)-\eta\frac{\partial E_{sq}(n)}{\partial K_i} \tag{2.22}$$

$$K_d^*(n+1)=K_d^*(n)-\eta\frac{\partial E_{sq}(n)}{\partial K_d^*} \tag{2.23}$$

$$\alpha(n+1)=\alpha(n)-\eta\frac{\partial E_{sq}(n)}{\partial \alpha} \tag{2.24}$$

where η is the learning ratio. The chain rule is used to back propagate the error to find the terms to minimize the performance index. The derivative of the sum squares errors with respect to the network parameters can be written as

$$\frac{\partial E_{sq}(n)}{\partial K_p}=-\varepsilon(n)\frac{\partial u(n)}{\partial K_p}=-\varepsilon(n)O_1(n) \tag{2.25}$$

$$\frac{\partial E_{sq}(n)}{\partial K_i}=-\varepsilon(n)\frac{\partial u(n)}{\partial K_i}=-\varepsilon(n)O_2(n) \tag{2.26}$$

$$\frac{\partial E_{sq}(n)}{\partial K_d^*}=-\varepsilon(n)\frac{\partial u(n)}{\partial K_d^*}=-\varepsilon(n)O_3(n) \tag{2.27}$$

$$\frac{\partial E_{sq}(n)}{\partial \alpha}=-\varepsilon(n)\frac{\partial u(n)}{\partial \alpha}=-\varepsilon(n)K_d^*\frac{\partial O_3(n)}{\partial \alpha} \tag{2.28}$$

Based on the normal RTRL algorithm the derivative terms in equations 2.25-2.28 will be computed recursively at every time step and the network parameters are updated accordingly.

2.4 Adaptive PID controller

This section presents two direct and indirect adaptive control schemes for a PID controller using RNN. The first control scheme is based on one neural network to implement the RNN-PID, and the system Jacobian is computed by approximation. In the second control scheme, an RNN emulator is added to the system for the exact computation of the system Jacobian.

2.4.1 Adaptive PID controller without emulator

In the first control scheme, we consider only a RNN-PID controller in the system as shown in Fig. 2.2. According to the desired response of the system, the reference model is chosen to obtain the desired settling time and damping characteristics. The RNN-PID controller is trained first off-line and is placed next in series with the system for on-line tuning. The system output is fed-back to be compared with the reference signal and form the error $e_1(k)$. This error is the input signal to the RNN-PID controller. On the other hand the system output is compared with the reference model output to form the second error $e_2(k)$. By minimizing this error the system response will become closer to the model response. This minimization is done by tuning the RNN-PID parameters as discussed in the following section.

2.4.1.1 Update equations

The adaptation procedure of the PID controller is quite different from that done in off-line learning. Here the error which needs to be minimized is not immediately after the network. The objective here is to minimize the performance index function

$$I(n) = \frac{1}{2} e_2(n)^2 \tag{2.29}$$

To be able to do this minimization, we need to differentiate (2.29) with respect to the network parameters. By applying the chain rule

$$\frac{\partial I(n)}{\partial K_p} = \frac{\partial I(n)}{\partial y(n)} \times \frac{\partial y(n)}{\partial u(n)} \times \frac{\partial u(n)}{\partial K_p} = -e_2(n) J_p(n) \frac{\partial u(n)}{\partial K_p} \tag{2.30}$$

$$\frac{\partial I(n)}{\partial K_i} = \frac{\partial I(n)}{\partial y(n)} \times \frac{\partial y(n)}{\partial u(n)} \times \frac{\partial u(n)}{\partial K_i} = -e_2(n) J_p(n) \frac{\partial u(n)}{\partial K_i} \tag{2.31}$$

$$\frac{\partial I(n)}{\partial K_d^*} = \frac{\partial I(n)}{\partial y(k)} \times \frac{\partial y(n)}{\partial u(n)} \times \frac{\partial u(n)}{\partial K_d^*} = -e_2(n) J_p(n) \frac{\partial u(n)}{\partial K_d^*} \tag{2.32}$$

$$\frac{\partial I(n)}{\partial \alpha} = \frac{\partial I(n)}{\partial y(n)} \times \frac{\partial y(n)}{\partial u(n)} \times \frac{\partial u(n)}{\partial \alpha} = -e_2(n) J_p(n) \frac{\partial u(n)}{\partial \alpha} \tag{2.33}$$

where $J_p(n)$ is the system Jacobian. The terms $\frac{\partial u(n)}{\partial K_p}$, $\frac{\partial u(n)}{\partial K_i}$, $\frac{\partial u(n)}{\partial K_d^*}$, and $\frac{\partial u(n)}{\partial \alpha}$ can be calculated similar to equation 2.25-2.28 in section 2.3.

The major difference between the above difference equations and the off-line training equations is the multiplication with two additional terms which are $e_2(n)$ and $J_p(n)$. This is due to the fact that the error which needs to be minimized is not placed immediately after the network. Here the plant is placed between the error and the network. So the error should be back-propagated through the plant to reach to the networks parameters. This error back propagation through the plant requires the knowledge of the system Jacobian $J_p(n)$.

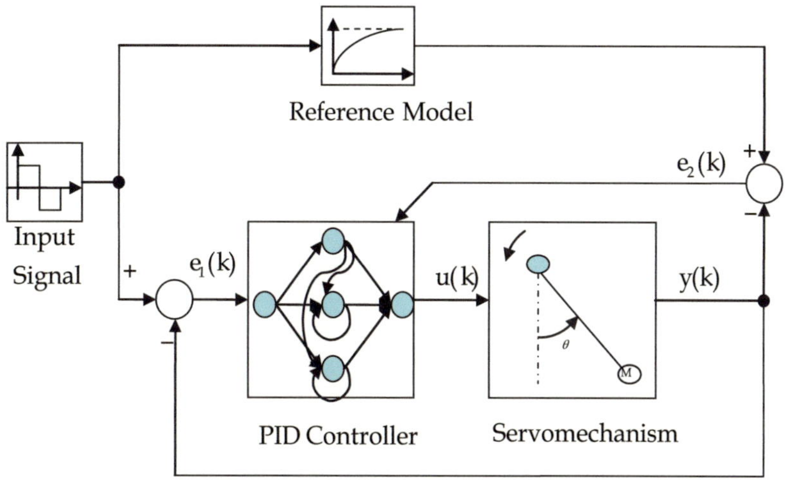

Fig. 2.2 Adaptive PID without emulator

2.4.1.2 System Jacobian

For MIMO system with n inputs and m outputs, the Jacobian is defined by the following matrix equation.

$$J_p = \frac{\partial y}{\partial u} = \begin{bmatrix} \frac{\partial y_1}{\partial u_1} & \cdots & \frac{\partial y_1}{\partial u_n} \\ \vdots & \ddots & \vdots \\ \frac{\partial y_m}{\partial u_1} & \cdots & \frac{\partial y_m}{\partial u_n} \end{bmatrix} \tag{2.34}$$

where $y = [y_1 y_2 \cdots y_n]^T$ is the output vector and $u = [u_1 u_2 \cdots u_n]^T$ is the input vector to the system.

In this work, because we are dealing with only one input and one output, the system Jacobian is a scalar. One way to approximate this term is by taking the ratio of the difference between the current and previous input/output signals of the system. This approximation can be considered to be sufficiently precise if the sampling time is made sufficiently small.

$$J_p(n) = \frac{\partial y(n)}{\partial u(n)} \approx \frac{y(n) - y(n-1)}{u(n) - u(n-1)} \tag{2.35}$$

An alternative way to compute the Jacobian more accurately is by building an emulator of the system. This will be discussed in section 2.4.2.

With this approximation, the system Jacobian is used in (2.30)-(2.33) to perform the RNN-PID gains tuning and minimize the reference model error in the least squares sense.

2.4.1.3 Reference model difference equation

In the system simulation, the reference model is generated on-line within the control algorithm, so we need to find the difference equation for the desired model. Our desired model here is a second order model. With the general transfer function

$$G_{rm}(s) = \frac{\omega_n^{\ 2}}{s^2 + 2\xi\omega_n s + \omega_n^{\ 2}} \tag{2.36}$$

By considering $\tau^2 = \frac{1}{\omega_n^2}$

$$G_{rm}(s) = \frac{1}{\tau^2 s^2 + 2\tau\xi s + 1} \tag{2.37}$$

Considering the bilinear approximation rule $\left(s \rightarrow \frac{2}{T}\frac{1-z^{-1}}{1+z^{-1}} \right)$,

$$\frac{y_{rm}(z)}{r_m(z)} = \frac{1}{\tau^2 \left(\frac{2}{T}\frac{1-z^{-1}}{1+z^{-1}} \right)^2 + 2\tau\xi \left(\frac{2}{T}\frac{1-z^{-1}}{1+z^{-1}} \right) + 1} \tag{2.38}$$

$$\frac{y_{rm}(z)}{r_m(z)} = \frac{1 + 2z^{-1} + z^{-2}}{\left(\frac{4\tau^2}{T^2} + \frac{4\tau\xi}{T^2} + 1 \right) + \left(\frac{-8\tau^2}{T^2} + 2 \right) z^{-1} + \left(\frac{4\tau^2}{T^2} - \frac{4\tau\xi}{T^2} + 1 \right) z^{-2}} \tag{2.39}$$

The overall difference equation will be

$$y_{rm}(n) = -\frac{c_1}{c_0} y_{rm}(n-1) - \frac{c_2}{c_0} y_{rm}(n-2) + \frac{1}{c_0}\left[r_m(n) + 2r_m(n-1) + r_m(n-2) \right] \tag{2.40}$$

where r_m and y_{rm} are the input and output of the model and

$$c_0 = \frac{4\tau^2}{T^2} + \frac{4\tau\xi}{T^2} + 1$$

$$c_1 = \frac{-8\tau^2}{T^2} + 2 \tag{2.41}$$

$$c_2 = \frac{4\tau^2}{T^2} - \frac{4\tau\xi}{T^2} + 1$$

2.4.1.4 Simulation results with constant mass

To verify the performance of the adaptive RNN-PID controller and check whether it can force the servomechanism response to follow the reference model system, a multi-level step input signal is applied as shown in Figure 2.3.

Figure 2.3 shows the input signal and the system response before adaptation, and Figure 2.4 shows the response after 100 iterations. The sum of squares of errors is also illustrated in Figure 2.4. These Figures show clearly that the controller gains are adequately tuned to force the system output to follow closely the reference model output.

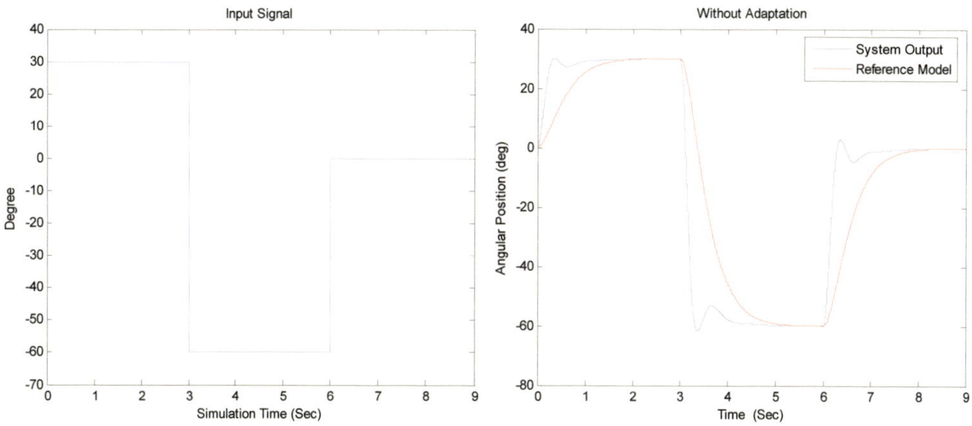

Fig. 2.3 Input signal and initial system response

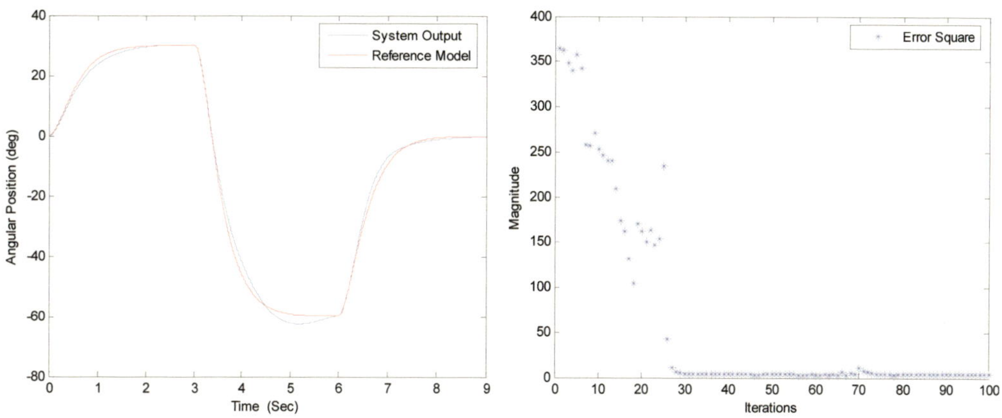

Fig. 2.4 System responses and sum of squares of errors after 100 iterations

The system parameters and are summarized in Table 2.1.

Simulation Parameters		
Simulation Time	t	9 sec
Sampling Time	T_S	0.001 sec
Reference Time Constant	τ_{rm}	0.2 sec
Damping Coefficient	ξ	1
Mass	M	2 Kg
Length	L	0.2 m
Damping Coefficient	B	1

Table 2.1 Simulation parameters for the adaptive PID controller with constant mass

The PID gains variation during the last cycle after 100 iterations is shown in Figure 2.5. It is shown that the gains, K_i, K_d*, andα, have stabilized to nearly constant values, while the gain K_p is continuously tuned around an optimum value as the reference signal is changed.

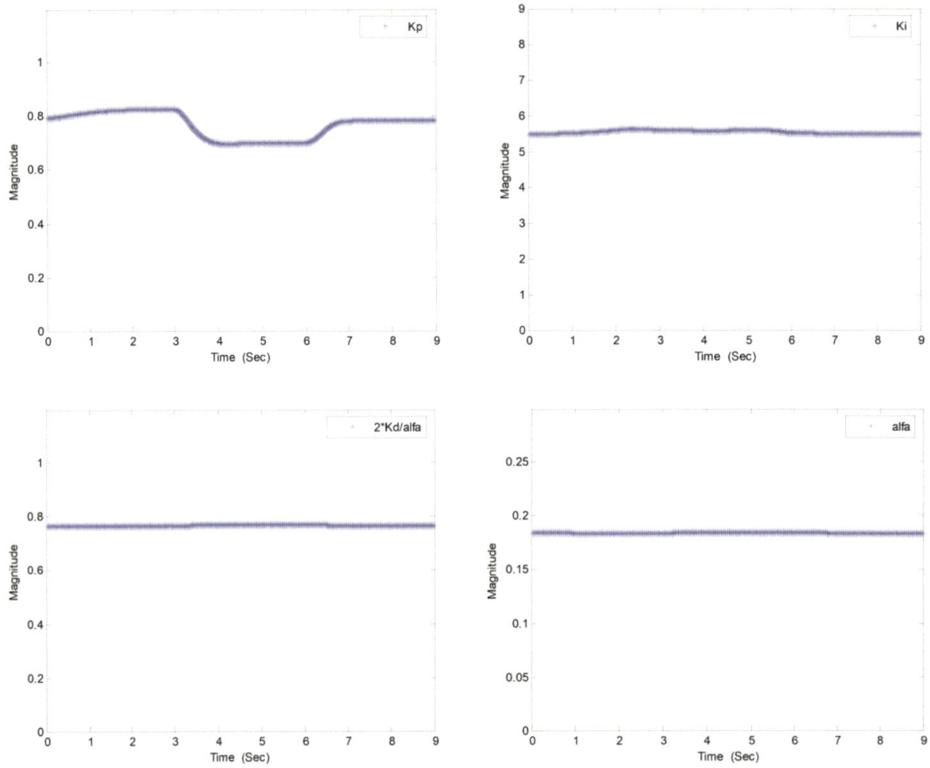

Fig. 2.5 PID gains variation for last iteration

2.4.2 Adaptive PID controller with emulator

Usually, back-propagating the error through the hybrid system results in some errors due to the approximation of the system Jacobian. To avoid these errors it is better to model the plant with a neural network. This neural network is called an emulator. By adding a neuro-emulator in parallel with the plant, the emulator will be trained to learn the dynamics of the system. So by having an RNN based plant, the system Jacobian can be computed more accurately. The emulator will be trained first off-line to make sure the RNN model is very close to the actual system. Next, the emulator will be trained on-line and will be used to compute the system Jacobian.

The servomechanism under consideration is of a second order type. The corresponding difference equation will include inputs and outputs delayed with two sampling times. We need therefore to construct a recurrent network which can memorize inputs and outputs up to two samples back in time. Figure 2.6 shows the proposed RNN to represent the pendulum system. In this partially connected network there are no recurrent connections between the output layer and the input layer. The only connections are between the output layer and the hidden layer and some internal connections within the hidden layers. The input signal includes only the current signal x(n) and the delayed signal x(n-1).

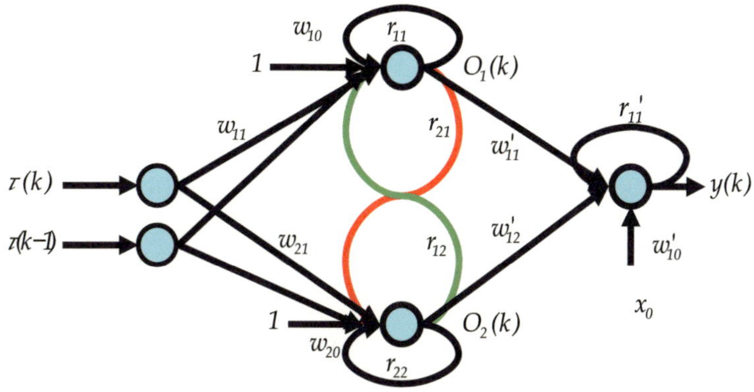

Fig. 2.6 RNN Architecture for Pendulum Identification

Figure 2.7 shows the general layout of the complete control system. As we can see from this figure the RNN based emulator is placed in parallel with the plant and is trained on-line to allow the computation of the system Jacobian.

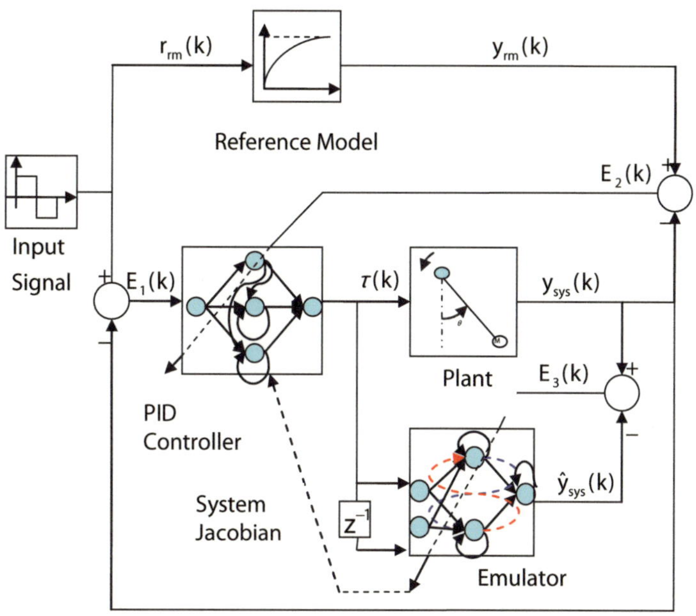

Fig. 2.7 Adaptive PID with RNN based emulator

2.4.3 Jacobian computation

For the exact calculation of the system Jacobian, there is a need to differentiate the plant output $y(k)$ with respect to the control signal $\tau(k)$. According to Figure 2.7, the forward equations of the emulator are written as

$$O_1(k) = w_{10} + w_{11}\tau(k) + w_{12}\tau(k-1) + r_{11}O_1(k-1) + r_{12}O_2(k-1) \tag{2.42}$$

$$O_2(k) = w_{20} + w_{21}\tau(k) + w_{22}\tau(k-1) + r_{21}O_1(k-1) + r_{22}O_2(k-1) \tag{2.43}$$

$$y(k) = w'_{10} + w'_{11}O_1(k) + w'_{12}O_2(k) + r'_{11}y(k-1) \tag{2.44}$$

By differentiating (2.44) with respect to $\tau(k)$

$$\frac{\partial y(k)}{\partial \tau(k)} = w'_{11}\frac{\partial O_1(k)}{\partial \tau(k)} + w'_{12}\frac{\partial O_2(k)}{\partial \tau(k)} + r'_{11}\frac{\partial y(k-1)}{\partial \tau(k)} \tag{2.45}$$

$\frac{\partial O_1(k)}{\partial \tau(k)}$ and $\frac{\partial O_2(k)}{\partial \tau(k)}$ can be derived by differentiating (2.42) and (2.43) with respect to $\tau(k)$

$$\frac{\partial O_1(k)}{\partial \tau(k)} = w_{11} + w_{12}\frac{\partial \tau(k-1)}{\partial \tau(k)} + r_{11}\frac{\partial O_1(k-1)}{\partial \tau(k)} + r_{12}\frac{\partial O_2(k-1)}{\partial \tau(k)} \tag{2.46}$$

$$\frac{\partial O_2(k)}{\partial \tau(k)} = w_{21} + w_{22}\frac{\partial \tau(k-1)}{\partial \tau(k)} + r_{11}\frac{\partial O_1(k-1)}{\partial \tau(k)} + r_{12}\frac{\partial O_2(k-1)}{\partial \tau(k)} \tag{2.47}$$

To compute $\frac{\partial \tau(k-1)}{\partial \tau(k)}$ another approximation is used

$$\frac{\partial \tau(k-1)}{\partial \tau(k)} \approx \frac{\tau(k-1) - \tau(k-2)}{\tau(k) - \tau(k-1)} \tag{2.48}$$

Using (2.48), the terms in (2.46) and (2.47) are calculated recursively and are used to determinethe system Jacobian with a better approximation. The accuracy of the Jacobian depends on how good the emulator is trained. Consequently the overall performance of the controller will be improved.

With the RNN based emulator, the update equations are the same as those derived in the previous section. Because the controller and emulator are both tuned on-line during each iteration, it is better to make the emulator training procedure faster than the controller. This will help to increase the PID controller performance.

The flowchart of the program adaptive PID controller algorithm with an RNN based emulator is shown in Figure 2.8. The program starts with some initializations such as allocating random weights, learning ratio and momentum term. Initially $\tau(k)$ which is the control signal, is assumed to be zero. $\tau(k)$ is feeding system and emulator to generate $y_{sys}(k)$ and $\hat{y}_{sys}(k)$. Based on these two values $E_3(k)$ is calculated. The input signal is sent to the reference model to generate $y_{rm}(k)$. Based on the difference between $y_{rm}(k)$ and $y_{sys}(k)$, $E_2(k)$ is calculated. Finally $y_{sys}(k)$ is compared with the reference point to form $E_1(k)$. By finding all errors the RTRL adaptation mechanism will tune the parameters accordingly. After adaptation and before executing the program for the next sample , the old values are updated. This procedure is repeated till the total number of samples is reached. The whole procedure is again executed for the given number of iterations.

Figure 2.9 shows the initial system response before tuning and Figure 2.10 show the results after adaptation. Due to the better approximation of the Jacobian the controller tuning is faster. The simulation parameters are shown in Table 2.2. Since the control scheme is based on two separate RNN's that are tuned online the stability of overall system becomes a main issue. Each RNN with its inherent feed-back connections may cause one the networks to be unstable. Instability of one the networks make the whole control system to become unstable. The brief stability analysis of the designed controller will be discussed in section 3.

Simulation Parameters		
Simulation Time	t	9 sec
Sampling Time	T_s	0.001 sec
Reference Time Constant	τ_{rm}	0.2 sec
Damping Coefficient	ξ	1
Mass	M	2 Kg
Length	L	0.2 m
Damping Coefficient	B	1
Controller Parameters		
Controller Gain	K_p	7.2464
Controller Gain	K_i	18.8667
Controller Gain	K_d*	0.7668
Controller parameter	α	0.1826
Learning ratio	η	1e-5
Momentum term	ϑ	0.06
Emulator Parameters		
Learning ratio	η	0.09
Momentum term	ϑ	0

Table 2.2 Simulation parameters for the adaptive PID controller with emulator

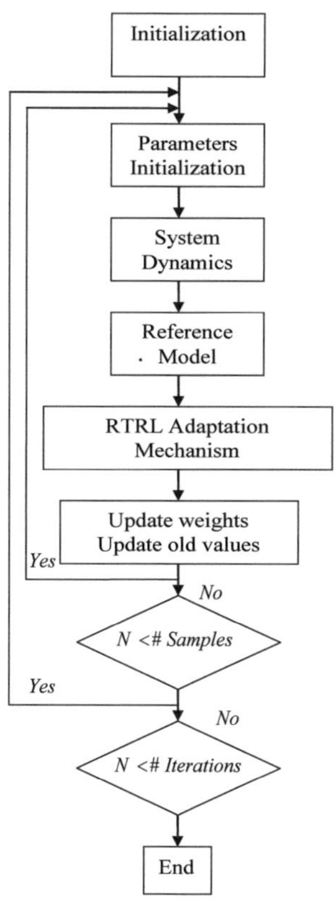

Fig. 2.8 Control program flowchart

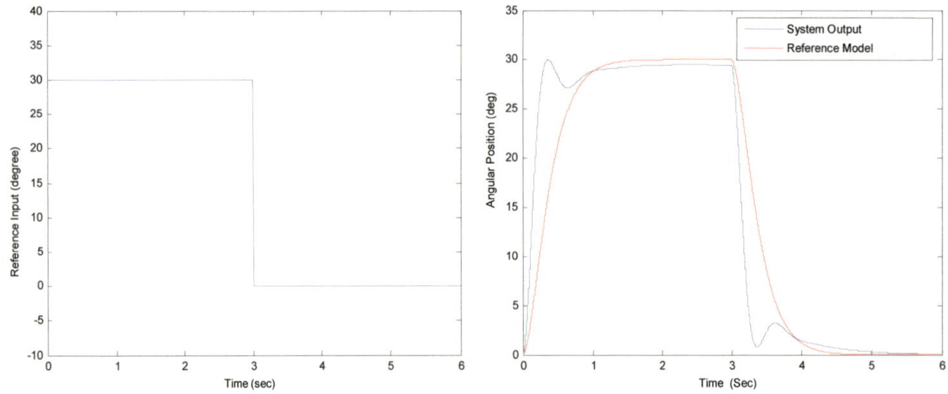

Fig. 2.9 Input signal and initial system response

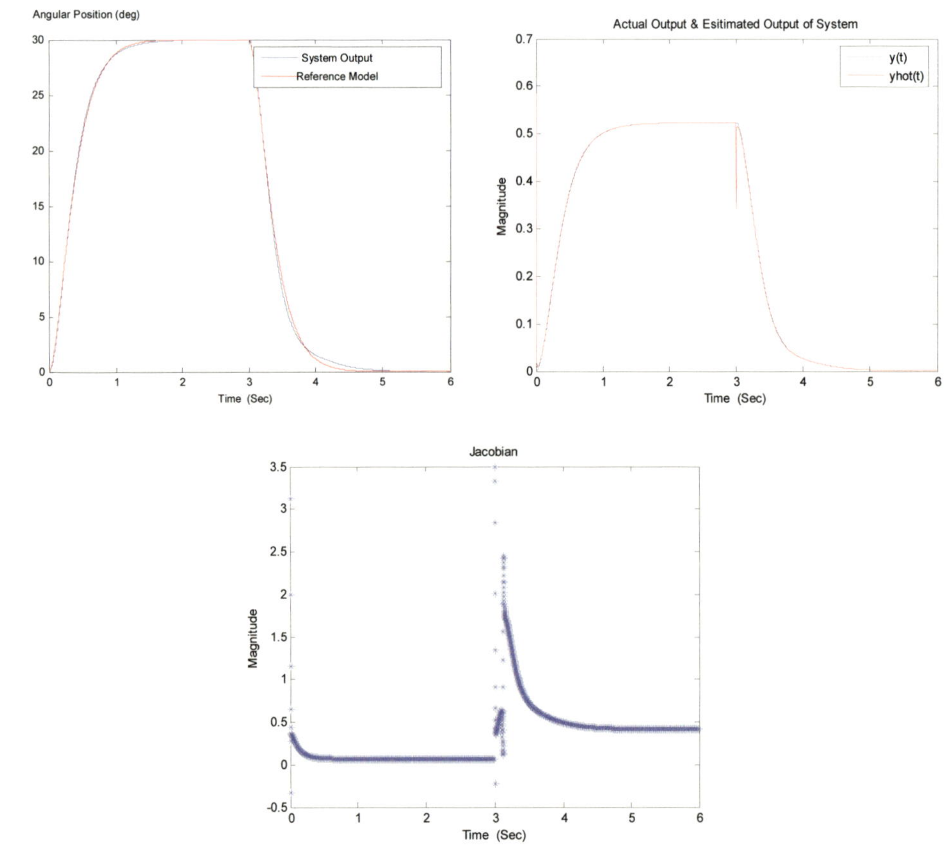

Fig. 2.10 Results after adaptation with $\tau_{rm} = 0.2$ sec

2.4.4 Robot arm control

A one-degree of freedom robot arm can be modelled as a pendulum system with a servomechanism at the joint. Controlling the robot arm position with variable load is a challenging problem. In this section, the RNN based PID controller will be deployed to control the robot arm to follow a desired trajectory which consists of moving a load from one location to another location as shown in Figure 2.11.

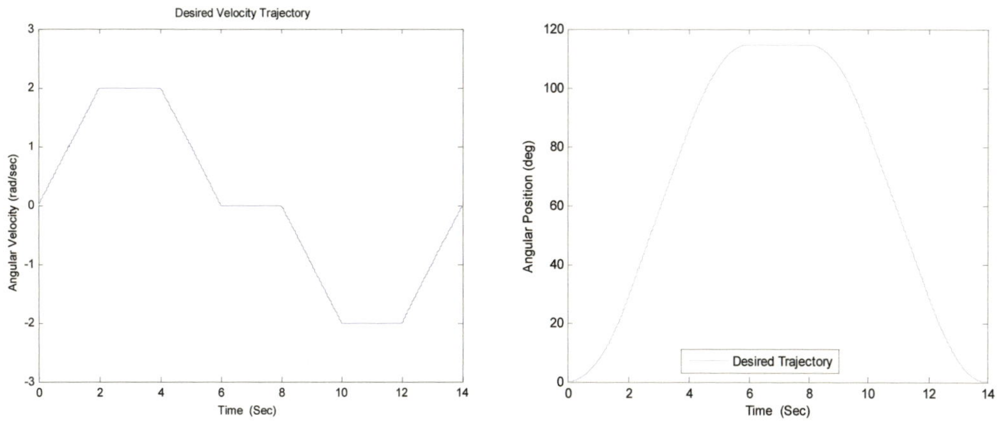

Fig. 2.11 Robot arm desired velocity and position

Assume that the robot arm starts to move from the 0° initial position. During the first 2 seconds the arm velocity will increase with a constant slope in the positive direction. In the next two seconds the velocity becomes constant which means the arm will move at constant velocity in the same direction. In the third two seconds when the arm is close to the target, it needs to decelerate or decrease its velocity. In the next two seconds the arm should stop (velocity become zero) to pick an object. Then this procedure will be repeated in the opposite direction till reaching to the initial position. As it can be observed form Figure 2.12 which illustrates the system response without adaptation, at t=6 sec there is a disturbance applied to the system by picking up an object. It is assumed that the object mass is 10% of the initial system mass.

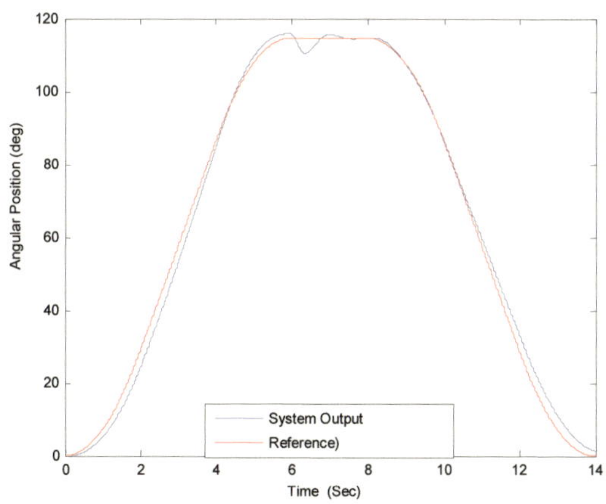

Fig. 2.12 Initial system response with disturbance

Our goal here is to verify whether the designed RNN based PID controller can tune its parameters to tolerate these disturbances or not. The tuning procedure is done on-line while the arm is moving. If the controller is capable to control the arm for the desired trajectory with the consideration of mass disturbance, it means that our designed adaptive PID controller works fine. As it is shown in Figure 2.13 after 2 iterations the sum of squares of errors which was initially 1042 reaches to 0.092. The PID gains are successfully adapted in order to make the robot arm follow the desired trajectory.

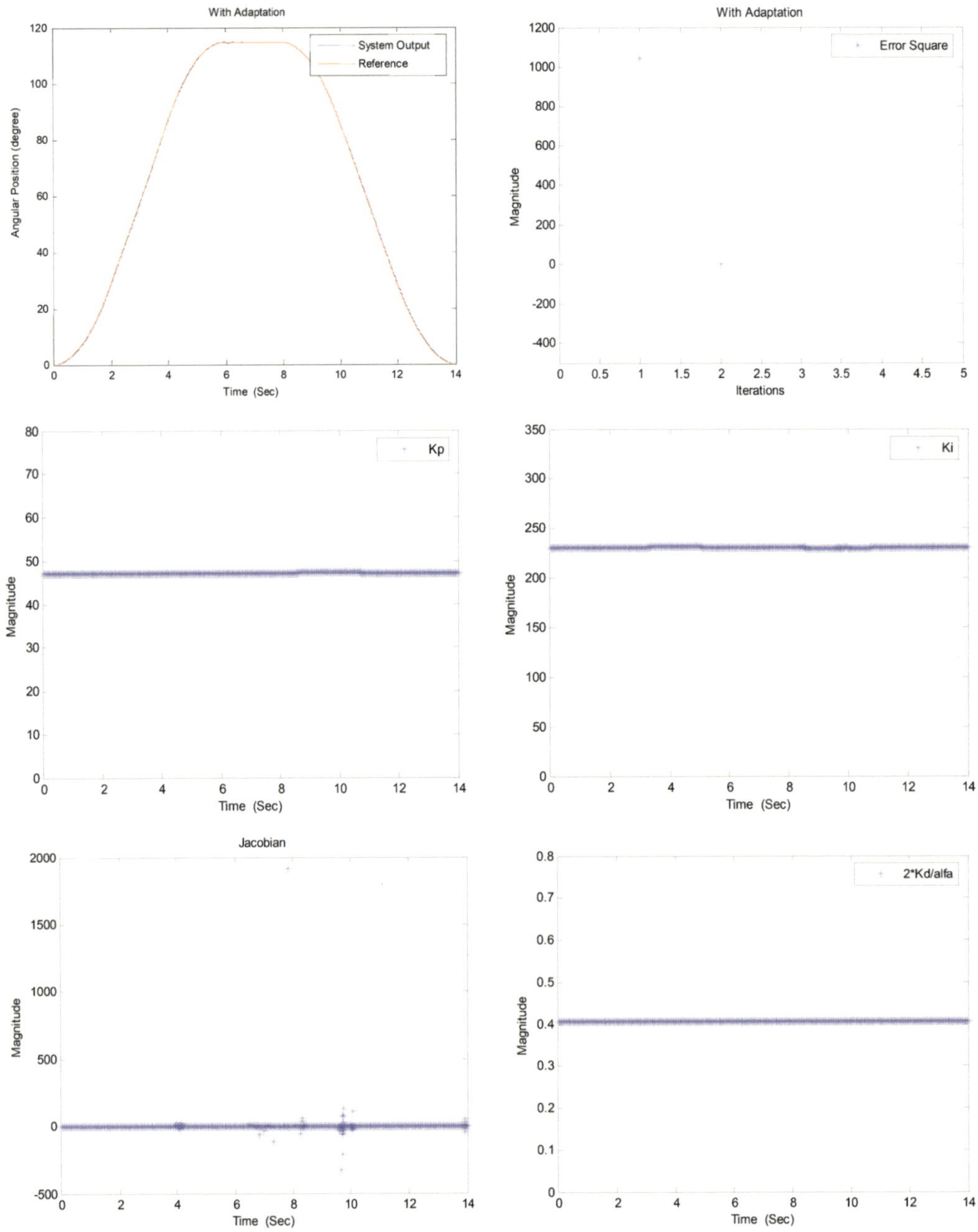

Fig. 2.13 Results after adaptation

3. Stability analysis

Global Asymptotic Stability (GAS) is a desired goal in designing any control system. However, this desired goal may not be easily achieved for systems involved with RNN. The inherent feedback properties of RNN make the analysis of this kind of systems complex. Several researches have been done to derive necessary and sufficient conditions for stability of RNN. Suykens (Suykens 2002) derived a necessary and sufficient condition for global stability of a specific class of RNN. The weak point of his criterion was due to the elimination of biases in the stability analysis. Barabanov and Prokhorov (Barbanov & Prokhorov 2002) observed that ignoring biases not only severely limits the mapping capabilities of RNN but also almost always results in extremely conservative stability criterion. They used the Linear Matrix Inequality (LMI) approach to derive a sufficient condition for the absolute stability of a given RNN. Their criterion was more useful compared to (Suykens 2002) due to the consideration of biases but still was not efficient. The derivation could not confirm the stability of many stable systems which are actually globally stable. Barabanov and Prokhorov later on proposed a new method of stability by approximating Lyapunov surface (Barbanov & Prokhorov 2003). The new method which is based on the reduction of a dissipativity domain can be applied to all bounded and differentiable systems. The proposed method can give the largest space of stable RNN parameters compared to all the previous studies.

The designed RNN-PID controller in this work is fairly easy for stability analysis because of using linear functions in the hidden layer. In this section we will put the RNN-PID controller dynamics into a state equation to derive the stability criterion.

Denote the output of the controller (control signal) as *y(k)* and the input to the controller (error) *u(k)*. Define the output of the hidden layer as the state vector (shown in Figure 3.1)

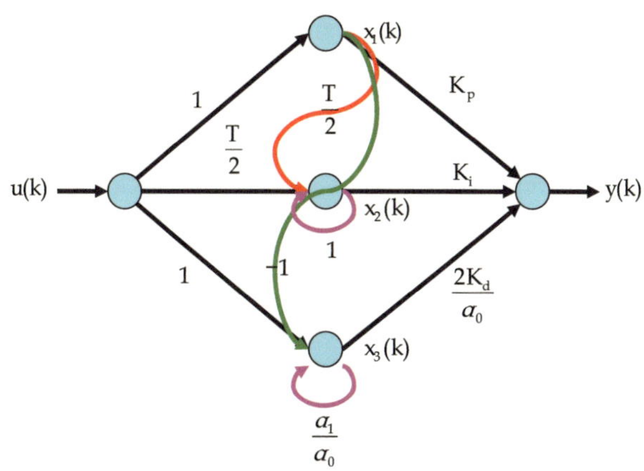

Fig. 3.1 RNN based PID controller in state space form

$$X(k) = [x_1(k) \quad x_2(k) \quad x_3(k)]^T \tag{3.1}$$

Hence the controller dynamics can be written as

$$\begin{aligned} X(k+1) &= AX(k) + Bu(k) \\ y(k) &= CX(k) \end{aligned} \tag{3.2}$$

Where

$$A=\begin{bmatrix} 0 & 0 & 0 \\ \frac{T}{2} & 1 & 0 \\ -1 & 0 & \frac{\alpha_1}{\alpha_0} \end{bmatrix},\ B=\begin{bmatrix} 1 \\ \frac{T}{2} \\ 1 \end{bmatrix},\ C=\begin{bmatrix} K_p & K_i & \frac{2K_d}{\alpha_0} \end{bmatrix} \tag{3.3}$$

System (3.2) is considered to be slowly varying if $\|\Delta u(k)\|$ is sufficiently small. Considering the slow change in the rate of $u(k)$ then the above system would be globally asymptotically stable if and only if the eigenvalues satisfy the following condition

$$|\lambda_i|<1,\ i=1,2,3 \tag{3.4}$$

Where λ_i is the ith eigenvalue of A. The eigenvalue of A are $\lambda_1=0, \lambda_2=1, \lambda_3=\frac{\alpha_1}{\alpha_0}$. Since one of the eigenvalue is located on the unit circle then the designed controller cannot be asymptotically stable. However the controller can be stable in the sense of Lyapunov if and only if

$$-1\le\frac{\alpha_1}{\alpha_0}\le 1 \tag{3.5}$$

Substituting for α_0 and α_1 from equation (2.9) the stability criterion for the controller can be written as

$$-T-2\tau\le -T+2\tau\le T+2\tau \tag{3.6}$$

4. Conclusion

This work investigates the application of artificial neural networks for system identification and control of nonlinear dynamic systems with a special focus on Recurrent Neural Networks (RNNs). This work mainly focused on developing a RNN-based adaptive PID controller. The corresponding algorithms are developed and tested.

The adaptive controller was designed to compensate the drawbacks of the conventional PID controller in controlling nonlinear dynamic systems. Two major control approaches have been verified. First, when the plant is known and we have some information about it in advance. The second control approach assumes a completely unknown plant. The comprehensive control approach for the second case contains two RNNs. One of them acts as a controller and the other one as an emulator. It has been shown that the control system with two networks is more efficient, reliable and accurate. However, with the RNN it has been observed that the system becomes more sensitive which needs careful tuning of the learning ratio and momentum terms.

In this research, the significant contribution is in the development of the RNN based controller with the self-tuning ability. Controlling unknown complex systems is a challenging problem, especially when the black-box system is highly nonlinear and the output is contaminated with disturbances. The authors have shown the power of RNNs to overcome these difficulties.

In the tuning process of the RNN-based controller with emulator, it is found that increasing the learning ratio and momentum term minimizes the error faster, but may deteriorate the network stability.

5. References

Sigeru Omatu, Marzuki Khalid and Rubiyah Yusof, (1995), Neuro-Control and its applications, Springer, TJ217.5.053

L. C. Jain and L. R. Medsker, (1999), Recurrent Neural Networks: Design and Applications, CRC Press, ISBN 0849371813.

Narendra, M. and K. Parthasarathy, (1990), "Identification and Control of Dynamical Systems using Neural Networks," IEEE Trans. on Neural Networks, Vol. 1, No. 1, pp. 4-27.

G. V. Puskorius and L. A. Feldkamp, (1993) "Automotive Engine Idle Speed Control with Recurrent Neural Networks " Research Laboratory, Ford Motor Company, pp 48124,

George Saikalis, (2001), "A Neural Network Control by Adaptive Interaction," in Proceedings of the American Control Conference, Arlington, VA, June 25-27, 2001, pp. 1247-1252.

Wei-Der Chnag, Rey-Chue Hwang, Jer-Guang Hsieh, (2003), "A multivariable on-line adaptive PID controller using auto-tuning neurons," Engineering Applications of Artificial Intelligence, Vol.16, No.1, pp. 57-63, February 2003.

Tae-Yong Kuc, Woong-Gie Han, (2000) "An Adaptive PID learning control of Robot manipulators," Automatica, Vol. 36, pp. 717-725, May 2000.

Phlippe Ranger and Andre Desbiens, (2003), "Improved Back stepping-based adaptive PID control," in Proceedings of the 4th International Conference on Control and Automation ICCA'03, pp. 123-127.

G.P.Liu, "Nonlinear Identification and Control, (2001), A neural Network Approach". Springer, TJ213 .L522.

Danilo P. Mandic and Jonathon A. Chambers, (2001)," Recurrent Neural Networks for Prediction", Chichester, New York, John Wiley & Sons, Q325.5 .M36.

R. Dhaouadi and R. Jafari, "Adaptive PID Neuro-Controller for a Nonlinear Servomechanism," (2007), Proc. of the 2007 IEEE International Symposium on Industrial Electronics (ISIE07), Vigo, Spain, June 4-7, 2007.

Ronald J. Williams and Jing Peng, (1990), "An Efficient Gradient-Based Algorithm for on-line Training of Recurrent Network Trajectories," College of Computer Science Northeastern University, Boston, MA 02115, pp 490-501. 3

Ronald J. Wiliams and David Zipser, (1989), "A Learning Algorithm for Continually Running Fully Recurrent Neural Networks," MIT Press Journals, Neural Computation, Summer 1989, Vol. 1, No. 2, pp. 270-280, (doi: 10.1162/neco.1989.1.2.270).

Gaviphat Lekutai, (1997), "Adaptive Self-Tuning Neuro Wavelet Network Controllers," Doctorial thesis, Electrical Engineering Department, Blacksburg, Virginia.

Astrom K.J. and B. Wittenmark, (1989), "Adaptive Control" Addison Wesley, USA,

Nishikawa, Y., N. Sanomiya, T. Ohta, and H. Tanaka, (1984), "A method for Auto-Tuning of PID control parameters," Automatica, Vol. 20, pp. 321-332.

Feng Lin, Robert D. Brandt, and George Saikalis, (2000), "Self-Tuning of PID Controllers by Adaptive Interaction," in Proceedings of the American Control Conference, Chicago, Illinois, June 2000.

Shen Dongkai and Wang Zhanlin, "An Adaptive Controller Based On Neural Networks for Motor-Drive Load Simulator", College of Automation Science and Electrical Engineering, Beijing University of Aeronautics and Astronautics Beijing 10083, PR. China.

Wiliam H. Press, Saul A. Teukolsky, Wiliam T. Vetterling and Brain P. Flannery, (2002), "Numerical Recipe in C", Cambridge Pres.

A. Scottedward Hodel and Chales E.Hall, (2001), "Variable-Structure PID Control to Prevent Integrtator Windup", IEEE Transaction on Industrial Electronics, Vol.48, No.2, April 2001.

Haykin, S., (1994), Neural Networks A Comprehensive Foundation. Upper Saddle River, NJ: Prentice Hall,.

Hassoun, M. H., (1995), Fundamentals of Artificial Neural Networks. Cambridge, MA: MIT Press.

Smith, Bradley R., (1997), "Neural Network Enhancement of Closed-Loop Controllers for Ill-Modeled Systems with Unknown Nonlinearities," PhD Dissertation, URN: etd-111597- 81423, Mechanical Engineering, Virginia Tech. University.

Tanomaru, J. and S. Omatu, (1991), "On the Application of Neural Networks to Control and Inverted Pendulum: an Overview," Proceedings of the 30th SICE Annual Conference, pp. 1151-1154.

Greene, M.E. and H. Tan, (1991)," Indirect Adaptive Control of a Two-Link Robot Arm Using Regularization Neural Networks," Proceedings of the International Conference on Industrial Electronics, Control and Instrumentation, Vol.2, pp. 952-956 .

N. E. Barbanov and D. V. Prokhorov, (2002), "Stability Analysis of Discrete-Time Recurrent Neural Networks," IEEE Transactions on Neural Networks, Vol. 13, No.2 March.

N. E. Barbanov and D. V. Prokhorov, (2003), "A New Method for Stability of Nonlinear Discrete-Time Systems," IEEE Transactions on Automatic Control, Vol. 48, No.12 Dec. 2003.

John A. K. Suykens, Joos P. L. Vandewalle and Bart L. R. De Moor, (1996), "Artificial Neural Networks for Modeling and Control of Nonlinear Systems," Kluwer Academic Publishers, Boston.

16

Robotic Assembly Replanning Agent Based on Neural Network Adjusted Vibration Parameters

Lejla Banjanovic-Mehmedovic and Senad Karic
Faculty of Electrical Engineering University of Tuzla, H&HInc.
Bosnia and Herzegowina

1. Introduction

The applications of robot are very extended and have already become classic in different branches of mass industrial production such as welding, painting by spraying, antirust protection, etc. Though the operations performed by robots in these fields are very complex, the operations of assembly are even more complex. In fact, robot assembly operations involve the process of direct solving the conflicting situations being not within the classic repetitive work.

Investigations treating typical assembly duties started forty years ago (Bohman, 1994). In the meantime, it was offered a series of control mechanism of mating date. Performing assemblies depends on sensation of and appropriate reaction to the forces of contact between mating components date (Wei, 2001).

It is shown that with the intelligent techniques, example components can be assembled faster, gentle and more reliably. In order to create robot behaviours that are similarly intelligent, we seek inspiration from human strategies date (Chan, 1995). The working theory is that the human accomplishes an assembly in phases, with a defined behaviour and a subgoal in each phase. The human changes behaviours according to events that occur during the assembly and the behaviour is consistent between the events. The human's strategy is similar to a discrete event system in that the human progresses through a series of behavioural states separated by recognizable physical events.

In achieving acceptably fast robot behavior with assuring contact stability, many promising intelligent-control methods have been investigated in order to learn unstructured uncertainties in robot manipulators date (Chan, 1995), (Miyazaki et al., 1993), (Brignone et al., 2001). For example, (Newman et al., 2001) work describes intelligent mechanical assembly system. First phase for assembly is blind search. In this phase multiple parameters are assigned to rotational search attractor. If sensors register force values higher then thresholds, new parameters are assigned. Intelligent layer is represented on 22-dimensional space of trajectories, and based on blind search parameters (correct and incorrect) neural network is made. Correct assembly path is chosen by using form of Genetic algorithm search, so the new vectors are evolved from most successful "parents". Using this process, the robot was allowed to generate and test its own program modifications.

The primary source of difficulty in automated assembly is the uncertainty in the relative position of the parts being assembled (Vaaler, 1991). The crucial thing in robot assembly is how to enable a robot to accomplish a task successfully in spite of the inevitable uncertainties

(Xiao & Zhang, 1995). Often a robot motion may fail and result in some unintended contact between the part held by the robot and the environment. There are generally three types of approaches to tackle this problem. One is to model the effect of uncertainties in the off-line planning process, but computability is the crucial issue. A different approach is to rely on-line sensing to identify errors caused by uncertainties in a motion process and to replann the motion in real-time based on sensed information The third approach is to use task-dependent knowledge to obtain efficient strategies for specific tasks rader than focusing on generic strategies independent of tasks.
(Xiao & Zhang, 1995) introduced a systematic replanning approach which consisted of patch-planning based on contact analyses and motion strategy planning based on constraints on nominal and uncertainty parameters of sensing and motion. In order to test the effectiveness of the replanning approach, they have developed a general geometric simulator SimRep on a SUN SPAR@ Station which implements the replanning algorithms, allows flexible design of task environments and modeling of nominal and uncertainty parameters to run the algorithms and simulates the kinematics' robot motions guided by the replanning algorithms in the presence of uncertainties.
In our paper, we present the complex robot assembly of miniature parts in the example of mating the gears of one multistage planetary speed reducer. Assembly of tube over the planetary gears was noticed as the most difficult problem of overall assembly and favourable influence of vibration and rotation movement on compensation of tolerance was also observed. There were extensive experimental complex investigations made for the purpose of finding the optimum solution, because many parameters had to be specified in order to complete assembly process in defined real-time. But, tuning those parameters through experimental discovering for improved performance was time consuming process.
The main contribution of this work is the use of a task replanning approach in combination with robot learning from experimental setup. We propose neural network based learning which gives us new successful vibration solutions for each stage of reducer. With this extended optimal vibration values as source information, we introduce Deterministic search strategy in scope of Robot Assembly Replanning Agent.

2. Machine learning

Machine learning usually refers to the changes in systems that perform tasks associate with artificial intelligence date. The changes might be either enhancement to already performing systems or synthesis of new system. A learning method is an algorithm (usually implemented in software) that estimates an unknown mapping between a systems input and outputs from the available data set. Learning is required when these mappings cannot be determined completely in advanced because of a priory uncertainty date (Farrell & Baker, 1993).
Generally speaking, there are two types of learning: supervised and unsupervised. These algorithms vary in their goals, in the available training data sets, in the learning strategies and representation of data.
Supervised learning requires a trainer, who supplies the input-output training instances. The learning system adapts its parameters by some algorithms to generate the desired output patterns from a given input pattern. In absence of trainers, the desired output for a given input instance is not known, and consequently the learner has to adapt its parameters autonomously. Such type of learning is termed unsupervised learning.

When the data are preprocessed and when we know what kind of learning task is defined for our application, it is important to make decision about the application of one or more of machine learning approaches. The most frequently used techniques include statistical methods (involve Bayesian inference), symbolic, inductive learning algorithms (decision building tree), cluster analysis, multiple-layered, feed-forward neural networks such as Backpropagation networks, fuzzy logic and evolution-based genetic algorithms (Kantardzic, 2001). These techniques are robust in their ability to analyze user queries, identify users' information needs and suggest alternatives for search.

3. Robot learning

Over the last few years, a number of studies were reported concerning machine learning and how it has been applied to help robots to improve their operational capabilities. Typical "things" that are learnt by robots are "how" to perform various behaviors: obstacle avoidance, navigation problems, planning robot control, etc. Imitation learning has helped significantly to start learning with reasonable initial behaviour.

It is difficult to define a coherent experimental method for robot learning (Wyatt et al., 1999). That is partly because the robot's behaviour may be the product of the robot's learning algorithm, it's initial knowledge, some property of the it's sensors, limited training time, stochastic actions, real-time responses, online learning, the environment or of an interaction between some subset of these. All of this makes it very difficult to interpret results. The robot learning experiments must be designed so as to generate meaningful results in the face of such complexity.

Essentially, we can define the robot learning as one of learning a policy function π from some set of sensory states S to some set of actions A. In order words, a task-dependent control policy π maps a continuous-valued state vector **x** of a controlled system and its environment, possibly in a time t dependent way, to a continuous-valued control vector **u**:

$$u = \pi(x,t,\theta) \tag{1}$$

The parameter vector θ contains the problem-specific parameters in the policy π that need to be adjusted by the learning system. Examples of policy functions include desired control behaviours for mobile robots, such as avoiding obstacles, following walls, moving a robot arm to pick up some object.

Approaches to robot learning can be classified using three dimensions: *direct versus indirect control, the used learning method* and *the class of tasks* in question (Schaal, Atkenson, 2010).

How the control policy is learned, can be proceed in many different ways. Assuming that the model equation (1) is unknown, one classical approach is to learn these models using methods of function approximation and then compute a controller based on the estimated model, which is often discussed as the certainty-equivalence principle in the adaptive control. Such techniques are summarized under the name *model-based learning*, or *indirect learning* or *internal model learning*. Alternatively, *model-free learning* of the policy is possible given an optimization or reward criterion, usually using methods from optimal control or reinforcement learning. Such model-free learning is also known as direct learning, since the policy is learned directly, i.e., without a detour through model identification.

From the viewpoint of machine learning, robot learning can be classified as *supervised learning, reinforcement learning, learning modularizations or learning feature representations that subserve learning.*

We can distinguish two supervised paradigms, inductive concept learning and explanation-based learning (Mahadevan, 1996). Inductive concept learning, assumes that a teacher presents examples of the target function for the robot. In this paradigm, the temporal credit assignment problem is non-existent, since the teacher is essentially telling the robot what action to perform, in some situation. In explanation-based learning, the teacher not only supplies the robot with example of the target function, but also provides a domain theory for determining the range of sensory situations over which the example action is useful. It can be a logical function or a neural network, or even an approximate qualitative physics based theory.

The unsupervised paradigms involve reinforcement learning and evolutionary learning. In *reinforcement learning*, the learner does not explicitly know the input-output instances, but it receives some form of feedback from its environment. The feedback signals help the learner to decide whether its action on the environment is rewarding or punishable. The learner thus adapts its parameters based on the states (rewarding/punishable) of its actions. Intuitively, RL is a process of trial and error, combined with learning. There are several popular methods of approaching model-free robot learning. Value function-based methods are discussed in the context of actor-critic methods, temporal difference (TD) learning and Q learning. A novel wave of algorithms avoids value functions and focuses on directly learning the policy, either with gradient methods or probability methods.

The evolutionary learning is very similar to reinforcement learning, in that the robot is only provided with a scalar feedback signal, but the differences is in term of learning (online vs. offline), etc.

It is useful too to distinguish between several general classes of motor tasks that could be the goal of learning. *Regulator tasks* keep the system at a particular set point of operation-a typical example is a balancing a pole on a finger tip or standing upright on two legs. *Tracking tasks* require the control system to follow a given desired trajectory within the abilities of the control system. *Discrete movement tasks*, also called one-shot tasks, are defined by achieving a particular goal at which the motor skill terminates (basketball foul shot). *Periodic movement tasks* are typical in domain of locomotion. *The complex movement tasks* are composed of sequencing and superimposing simpler motor skills, e.g. leading to complex manipulation skills like assembling a bookshelf etc.

In order to achieve faster and reliable above specified complex robot assembly process in this research, we validate the results concerning the robotic assembly by introducing of learning strategies. First, the supervised (neural network) based learning is capable to reproduce the training data and to form clutter of adjustable vibrations for assembly process. Second, the unsupervised form of learning is used to reach a goal matting point using minimal path searching actions. It is equipped with reinforcement signal detection, which can measure physical aspect of mating process (model-free learning). The robot moves with reward in case of tolerance compensation. In case of jamming, Robot Assembly Replanning Agent uses this signal as error detection in system and replanns actions in order to achieve a goal position.

4. Planning agents

Intelligent agents are able to perceive their environment and respond in a timely fashion to changes that occur in it in order to satisfy their design objectives (Wooldridge, 2008). They are able to exhibit goal-directed behaviour by taking the initiative in order to satisfy their

design objectives. But for non-functional systems, the simple model of goal-directed programming is not acceptable, as it makes some important limiting assumptions. In particular, it assumes that the environment does change and if the assumptions underlying the procedure become false while the procedure is executing, then the behaviour of the procedure may not be defined and it will be crash. In such environment, blindly executing a procedure without regard is poor strategy. In such dynamic environments, an agent must be reactive, i.e. it must be responsive to events that occur in its environment.
Building purely goal-directed systems is not hard, but it is hard building a system that achieves balance goal-directed and reactive behaviour. The agents must achieve their goals systematically using complex procedure-like patterns of action.
We assume that the environment may be in any of a finite set E of discrete, instantaneous states:

$$E = \left\{ e, e', \ldots \right\} \tag{2}$$

Agents are assumed to have a finite repertoire of possible actions available to them, which transform the state of the environment

$$A_c = \left\{ a_0, a_1, \ldots \right\} \tag{3}$$

A run r of the agent in an environment is thus a sequence of interleaved environment states and actions:

$$r : e_0 \xrightarrow{a_0} e_1 \xrightarrow{a_1} e_2 \xrightarrow{a_2} e_3 \xrightarrow{a_3} \ldots \xrightarrow{a_{n-1}} e_n \tag{4}$$

We model agents as functions which map runs to actions:

$$A_g : R^E \rightarrow A_C \tag{5}$$

where R^E is subset of these that end with environment state.
Means-ends reasoning is the process of deciding how to achieve an end using the available means (actions that can perform). *Means-ends reasoning is known as planning.*
A *planner* is system that takes as input the following: representation of a goal, the current state of the environment and the actions available to the agent. As output, a planning algorithm generate a plan P. A plan P is a sequence of actions:

$$P = \left\{ a_1, \ldots a_n \right\} \tag{6}$$

Many agents must have reactive role in order to achieve goal, i.e. agent must *replann*. In this case agent has next structure:

$$P' = \left\{ a_1, a_i', a_{i+1}' \ldots a_n \right\} \tag{7}$$

In practical reasoning agents, the plan function is implemented by giving the agent a plan library. The plan library is a collection of plans, which an agent designer gives to an agent. The control cycle of decision-making process of agent is a loop, in which the agent

continually observes the world, decides what intention to achieve, uses means-ends reasoning to find a plan to achieve these intentions and execute the plan (replann).
Learning has an advantage that it allows the agents to initially operate in unknown environments and to become more competent than its initial knowledge alone might allow. The agent decides on actions based on the current environmental state and through feedback in terms of the desirability of the action (reward), learns from interaction with the environment.
Examples of reaching a desired goal, avoiding obstacles, self-collisions, etc. using a combination of robot learning and task replanning are presented in (Banjanović-Mehmedovic, et.al., 2008), (Ekvall & Kragic, 2008).

5. Robot assembly system

5.1 Assembly system

The main difficulty in assembly of planetary speed reducers is the installation of tube over planetary wheels. Namely, the teeth of all three planetary wheels must be mated with toothed tube. Fig. 1. presents a). only one stage of planetary reducer, and b). planetary speed reducer (cross-section 20mm, height five degrees 36mm), which has been used for experiments.

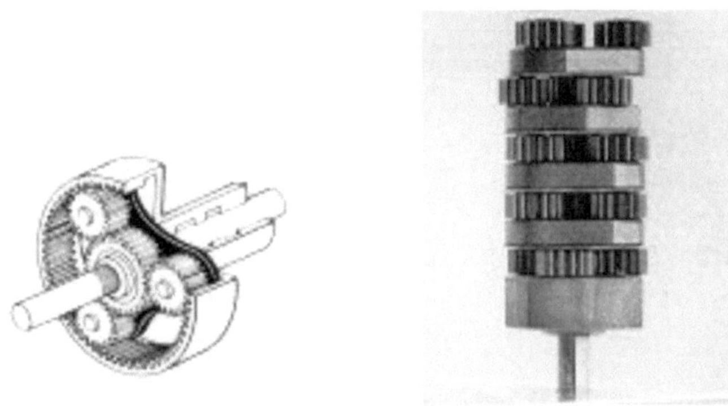

Fig. 1. One stage of planetary reducer, b). View inside of planetary speed reducer.

In this research has not been considered the complete assembly of each part of planetary reducer but only the process of connecting the toothed tube to five-stage planetary reducer. By solving the problem of assembly the gears, there will be no problem to realise complete assembly of planetary speed reducer.
For the process of assembly, the vertical-articulated robot with six-degrees of freedom, type S-420i of the firm FANUC has been used, completed by vibration module (Fig. 2.), developed at Fraunhofer- Institut für Produktionstechnik and Automatisierung (IPA) in Stuttgart, Germany. Total form of movement should be produced by vibration module to allow the fastest possible way of mating the tube with base part of planetary reducer respectively to compensate tolerance by vibration (Schweigert, 1995).
According to the functioning the individual systems of tolerance compensation can be divided into (Bernhart & Steck, 1992):

- controllable (active) system for tolerance compensation in which, on base of sensor information on tolerance, the correction of movement is made for the purpose of tolerance compensation

- uncontrollable (passive) system for tolerance compensation in which the orientation of external parts is achieved by the means of advanced determined strategy of searching or forced by connection forces
- combination of above two cases.

For this system of assembly (Banjanovic-Mehmedovic, 1999), the passive mechanism of tolerance compensation has been used with specially adjusted vibration of installation tools. The assembly process starts with gripe positioning together with toothed tube exactly 5mm above the base part of planetary reducer and than moving in direction of negative z-axis in order to start assembly (Fig. 2.).

Fig. 2. Particular phases of assembly process.

The analysis of assembly process shows that movement based on vibration and rotation act positively on the course of process. Vibration module should be able to produce vibration in x- and y- direction, and rotation around the z-axis. Sensors (inductive sensor of passed way and vicinity) necessary in process of assembly ware mounted on vibration module. There was a special controlling card developed for control by step-motor and magnets for generating vibrations on vibration module.

5.2 Search strategy

The complex systems are often modelled according to either state-based or an event-based paradigm. While in state-based model, the system is characterized by states and states changes, in the latter case is characterized by event (actions) that can be performed to move from one state to another (H.ter Beek et.al., 2008).

Transition system is described with quadruple (S, s_0, A_C, R), where S is set of states, s_0 is initial state, A are transition from one state to another and R is transition relation. In our research, we used this concept in order to describe the relationships between the parts being assembled. Namely, the states are assembly parameters–vibration amplitudes and frequencies for each planetary reducer stage and transition action are used to move through assembly process from one stage to another of planetary reducer.

During the robot assembly of two or more parts we encounter the problem of tolerance compensation. For automatic assembly the tolerance is especially difficult problem because in process of mating it must be compensated but it takes time and requires corresponding algorithms.

In order to compensate tolerance during robot assembly, we use the *'search strategy'*, which adjusted amplitudes and frequencies to optimal values gained from experimental experience (amplitude of upper plate, amplitude of down plate, frequency of upper plate, frequency of down plate) (Fig. 3.). In case of jamming from different physical reasons (position, friction, force etc.), robot returned to beginning of current reducer stage, where the jamming was made. The search strategy tried three times to continue assembly process with another optimal assembly vibration parameter stage set values. It exploited the technique of blind search in optimal parameter space with repeated trials at manipulation tasks. When the jamming has been overcome, robot kept moving until it reached the final point in assembly. On the opposite, flashing of red lamp informed the personnel that there has been a jamming.

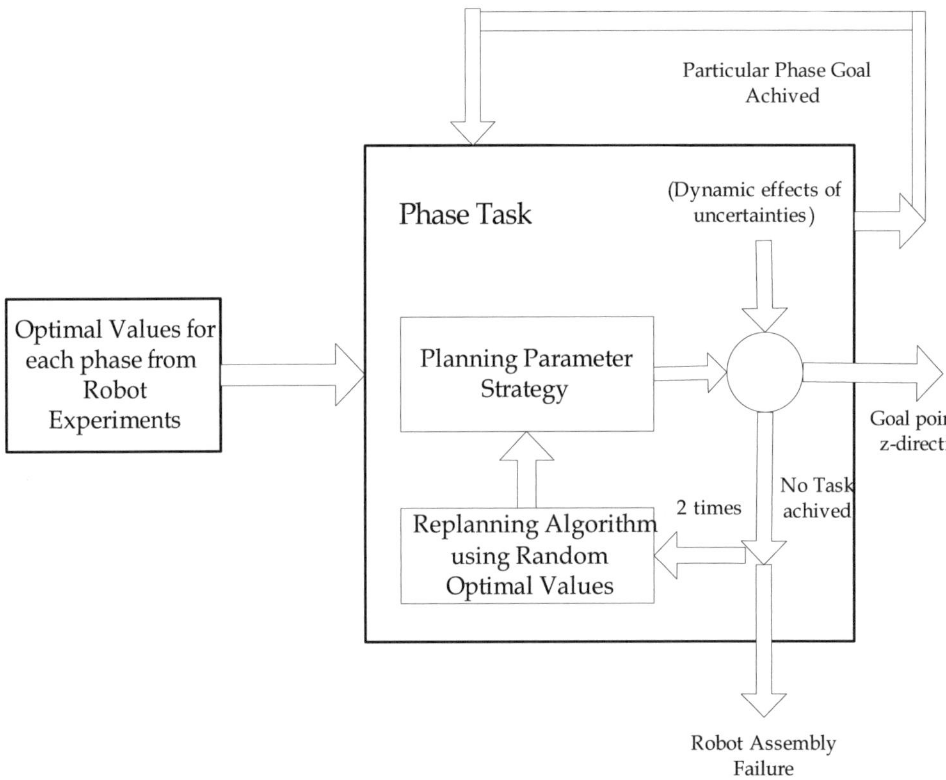

Fig. 3. Search strategy in experimental robot assembly.

There were extensive experimental complex investigations made for the purpose of finding the optimum solution, because many parameters had to be specified in order to complete assembly process in defined real-time. But, tuning those parameters through experimental discovering for improved performance is time consuming process.

The search strategy involved in assembly experiments exploited the technique of blind search of optimal vibration values in repeated trials in each stage. If selected optimal value is in discontinuity area, then the path between one selected optimal stage parameter set and another will be outside of cone (Fig. 4.).

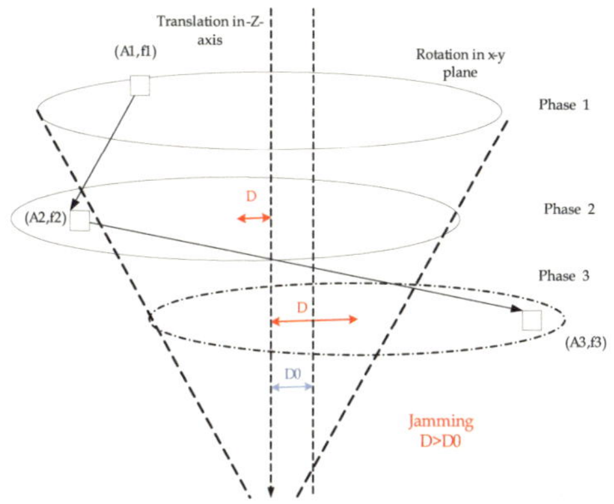

Fig. 4. Transition problems between states inside Search Strategy.

In this case, the tolerance compensation isn't achieved, because position tolerance of some stage D is greater than admitted position tolerance D0. What is solution for this? In order the path between two phases would be in cone towards stable tolerance compensation, we need *deterministic transition action* (directed path between vibration states based on minimal path finding).

To make this search strategy more intelligent, additional learning software was created to enable improvements of performance.

6. Robot assembly replanning agent

Today robot need to react to stochastic and dynamic environments, i.e., they need to learn how to optimally adapt to uncertainty and unforeseen changes (Schaal&Atkenson, 2010). The robot learning covers a rather large field, from learning to perceive, to plan, to make decisions etc.

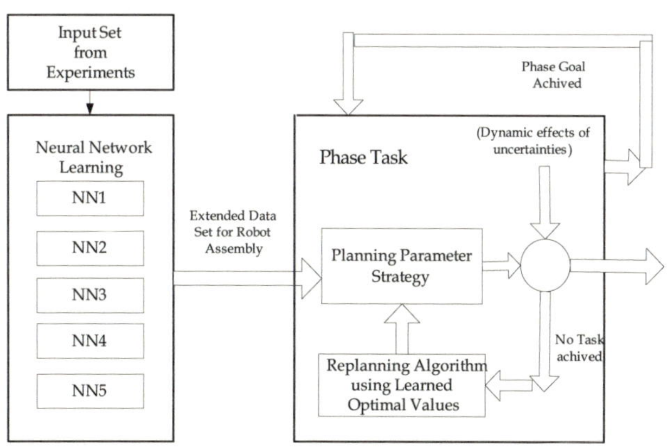

Fig. 5. Robot Assembly Replanning Agent.

Learning control is concerned with learning control in simulated or actual physical robots. It refers to the process of acquiring a control strategy for a particular control system and particular task by trial and error.

Task planning is the problem of finding a sequence of actions to reach a desired goal state. This is a classical AI problem that is commonly formalized using a suitable language to

represent task relevant actions, states and constraints (Ekvall & Kragic, 2008). The robot has to be able to plan the demonstrated task before executing it if the state of the environment has changed after the demonstration took place. The objects to be manipulated are not necessarily at the same positions as during the demonstration and thus the robot may be facing a particular starting configuration it has never seen before.
In this paper, we present a learning method in combination with robot path planning/replanning agent system. The performance of this method is demonstrated on a simulated robot assembly through intelligent agent system (Fig. 5.). We propose neural network based learning which gives us new successful vibration solutions for each stage of reducer. With this extended vibration parameters as source information for Planning/Replanning Task, we introduce advanced search strategy of robot assembly.
In the replanning scheme, the error model is used to model various dynamic effects of uncertainties and physical constraints by jamming. Combing the efforts of the planner and learned optimal values, the replanner is expected to guarantee that agent system enters the region of convergence of its final target location.

6.1 Neural network based vibration parameters learning

The artificial neural networks (ANN), with their remarkable ability to derive meaning from complicated or imprecise data, can be used to extract patterns and detect trends that are too complex to be noticed by either humans or other computer techniques. A trained neural network can be thought of as an "expert" in the category of information it has been given to analyze. This expert can then be used to provide projections given new situations of interest and answer to question "what if" (Stergiou & Siganos, 1996). Another reason that justifies the use of ANN technology, is the ability of ANNs to provide fusion of different information in order to learn complex relationships among the individual values, which would otherwise be lost if the values were individually analyzed.
There exist many types of neural networks, but the basic principles are very similar. Each neuron in the network is able to receive input signals, to process them and to send an output signal. The neural network has the power of a universal approximator, i.e., it can realize an arbitrary mapping of one vector space onto another vector space. The main advantage of neural networks is that they are able to use some a priori unknown information hidden in data, but they aren't able to extract it. Process of 'capturing' the unknown information is called 'learning of neural network' or 'training of neural network'. In mathematical formalism to learn means to adjust the free parameters (synaptic weight coefficients and bias levels) in such a way that some conditions are fulfilled (Svozil et al., 1997).
Neural network based learning is used in this research to generate wider scope of parameters in order to improve the robot behaviour. The parameter vector θ contains the problem-specific parameters in the policy π that need to be adjusted by the learning system. The amplitude and frequencies vibration data is collected during assembly experiments and is used as sources of information for the learning algorithm.

$$u = \pi\left(x, t, A, f_r\right) \tag{8}$$

By starting the robot work, vibration module vibrated with determined amplitude (to +/-2mm) and frequency (to max. 10Hz) for each stage of reducer. For those experiments, the vibration figure horizontal EIGHT (Fig. 6) is used (the frequency ratio between down and above plate is $f_D/f_U=2$).

As optimum values of amplitudes of down and above plate that were valid for all stages of reducer are $A_D=A_U=0.8$mm. From experiments, we gained that smaller frequencies of vibration were better ($f_D/f_U=4/2$ or $6/3$) for 1-2 stage (counting of stages starts from up to down), while for each next stage the assembly process was made better with higher frequencies ($f_D/f_U=8/4$ or $10/5$).

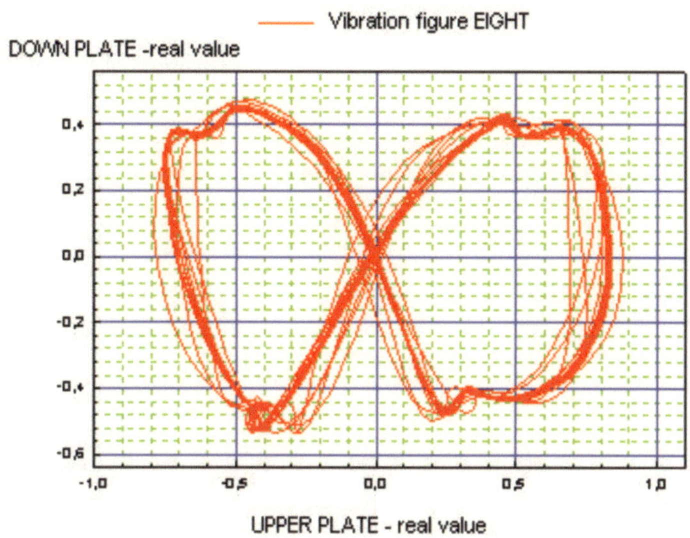

a)

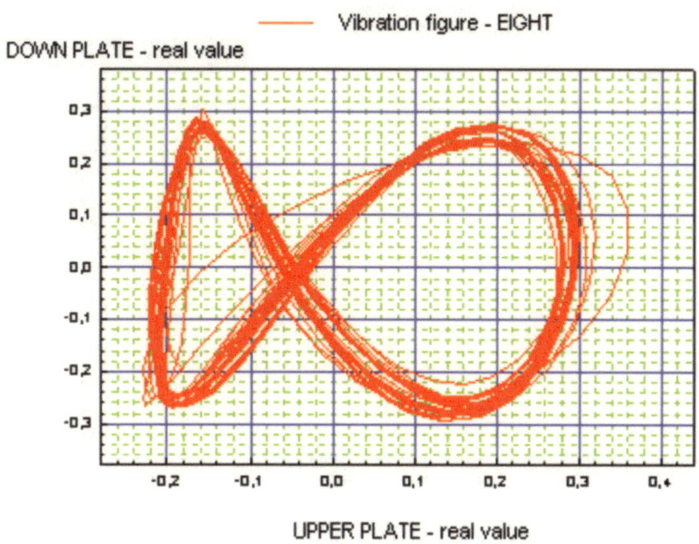

b)

Fig. 6. Vibration figure-EIGHT: a) (1-2 stage; $f_D/f_U=4/2$ $A_D/A_U=1.4/1.4$); b) (3-4 stage; $f_D/f_U=10/5$ $A_D/A_U=0.5/0.5$).

Multi-layer feed-forward neural networks (MLF), trained with a back-propagation learning algorithm, are the most popular neural networks. In our research we used MLF neural network contains 10 tansig neurons in hidden layer and 1 purelin neuron in its output layer. The feed-forward neural networks were formed and tested for each stage of assembly process. Each one was initialized with random amplitudes $A_U=A_D=A_i$ between 0 and 2 and frequencies values f_i between 0 through 4. Namely, the range of the frequencies measurement is normalized by mapping from frequencies ratio f_D/f_U=(4/2, 6/3, 8/4,10/5) onto the range of the state frequencies values (0 through 4). To training the MLF network, we used 35 vibrations sets for each 5 phases of assembly. The mean square errors (MSE) during the training of 5 MLF networks were achieved for 7-10 epochs. Two thousand data points were taken as a testing sample.

The following picture (Fig. 7.) presents network's trying to learn the new optimal stage vibration sets indicated by their respective picture. Each frame consists of the network's training true regions (circles mark) and network's training bad regions (rectangle marks).

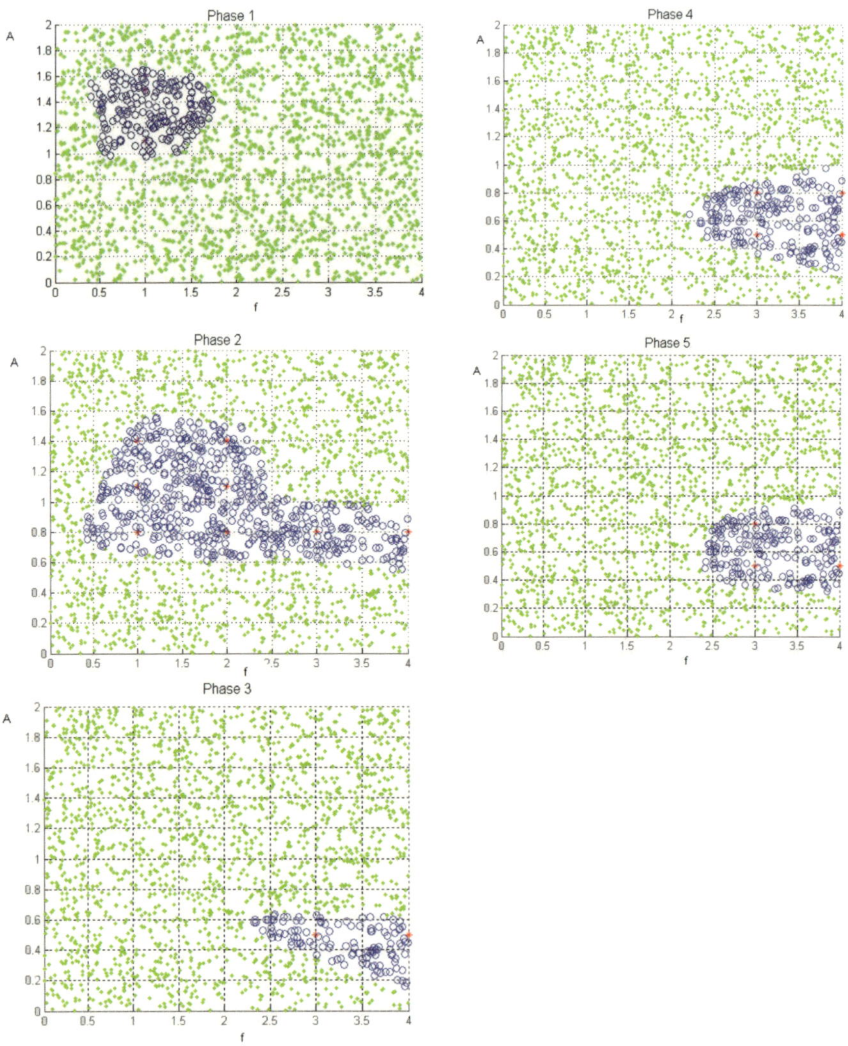

Fig. 7. Results of neural network training for all 5 stages

The results show that the scope of adjusted vibration parameters obtained from autonomous learning is extended in respect to adjusted vibration sets from experimental robot assembly. We can see that critical moment in assembly process is second phase, which presents medium clutter position of optimal vibration parameter sets through stages. Phases 2 presents discontinuity between first and third phase in clutter space. It can be reason for advanced form of planning/replanning too.

6.2 Advanced replanning strategy

The problem with applied search strategy in experiments was in case of behaviour switching (case of assembly jamming). The search strategy tried to continue assembly process with another optimal, but blind chosen parameter state value. With updated search strategy, named *Deterministic search strategy*, we propose next paradigm:

1. In order to have *deterministic transition action (DTA)*, minimal distance is used between vibration state sets. DTA finds *minimal distance vector* from selected optimal value (A(i),f(i)), i=1,..N from current extended vibration state s(k) gained from learning process towards next vibration state s(k+1).

$$V_{path}(k) = \min\big(\big(A_o(k), f_o(k)\big) - \big(A_i(k+1), f_i(k+1)\big)\big), k = 1,..4 \tag{9}$$

The minimal path between two phase is in cone and we have compensated tolerance (D<D0), see Fig. 8.

2. In case of jamming (in our simulator: *error event signal*), we propose *Replanning Algorithm with Learned Optimal values*, which offers new plan for path tracking during simulation of robot assembly. Fig. 8. presents next situation: system detect error event during second state of assembly and strategy try to continue assembly process with another optimal set value (A2′,f2′) from state s(2). This another value is optimal parameter value, with mean value of distance from state s(1) to state s(2). We make enough offset from this critical optimal point to another optimal solution. After that, strategy establishes action between values (A2′, f2′) and (A3′, f3′).

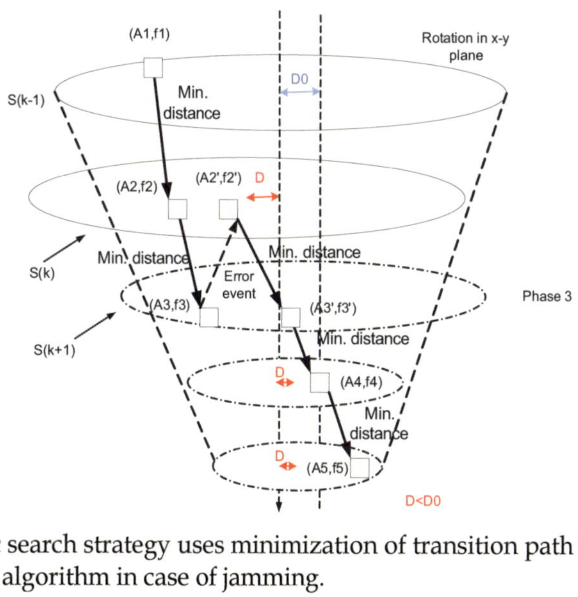

Fig. 8. Deterministic search strategy uses minimization of transition path between states and recovery parameter algorithm in case of jamming.

To demonstrate the validity of this paradigm, we present test results obtained by implementation of Robot Assembly Replanning Agent in Matlab. We use random start point in vibration parameter space (1.0,1.0), but system detects error event signal and tries assembly with new start vibration value (1.53, 1.27) (Fig. 9.).

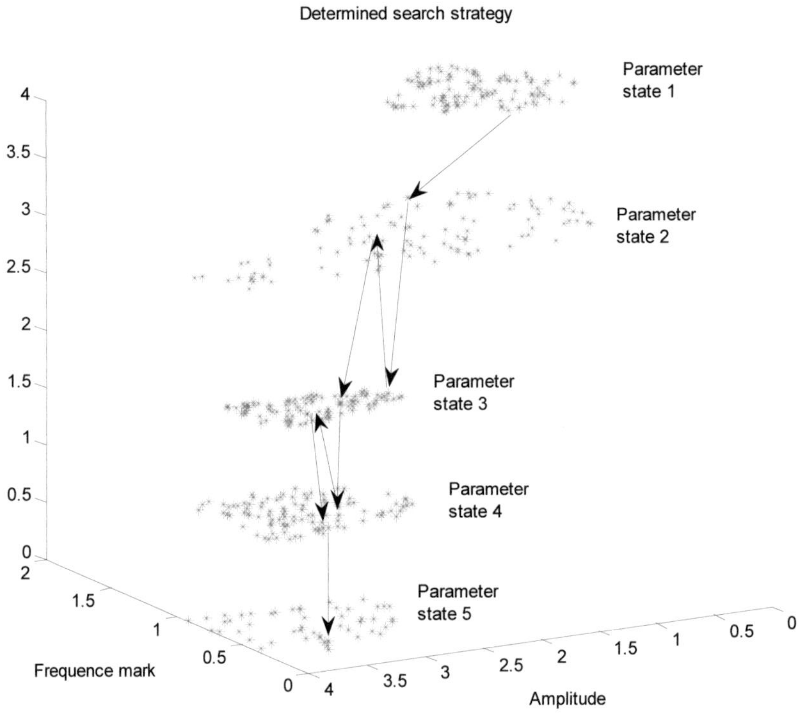

Fig. 9. Presentation of advanced search strategy in case of detecting error event signals.

In case of detecting of error event signal in second state, deterministic search strategy tries instead optimal value (0.52,2.72) to continue assembly process with another optimal assembly vibration parameter stage set value (0.49, 3.19). New transition action is made from this new optimal value from current state with minimal path distance towards optimal vibration parameter stage set in next state. But here, system detects new error event and tries assembly instead (0.52,3.14) with (0.36,3.42), until it reaches the final point in assembly simulation process.

7. Conclusion

There is enough space for investigation in this class of robot assembly search strategy, because the selection of assembly strategy is based on inspiration from human strategies. As an example of robot assembly, it was researched the complex assembly of toothed tube over planetary gears. Important contribution of paper is combination replanning task approach with learning approach in order to accommodate the uncertainty in complex assembly of tube over planetary gears. Two form of learning are proposed in state and action domain.

First, supervised neural network based learning is used to generate wider scope of state parameters in order to improve the robot behaviour. Second, the unsupervised learning is used to reach a goal matting point. Using Deterministic search strategy based on minimal path tracking as transition action between vibration states and replanning of actions in case of error signal detection in system, it is possible to involve intelligent control of robot assembly. Simulations were performed in domain of robot assembly to demonstrate usefulness of the presented method. Robotic provides an excellent test-bench for studying different techniques of computational intelligence.
Recent trends in robot learning are to use trajectory-based optimal control techniques and reinforcement learning to scale complex robotic systems. Future work in domain of replanning agent is research with genetic based replanning agent in order to accelerate the optimization speed of path planning technique.

8. References

Banjanovic-Mehmedovic, L. (1999). Robot Assembly of planetary motor speed reducer, *Proceedings of the VIII IEEE Electrotechnical and Computer Science Conference ERK '99;* Portoroz, Slowenia, pp.267-270

Banjanovic-Mehmedovic, L.; Karic, S.; Jasak, Z. (2008), Learning of Robotic Assembly based on Specially Adjustable Vibrations Parameters, *IEEE Symposium on Signal Processing and Information Technology (ISSPIT),pp. 123-128,* ISBN 978-1-4244-3555-5

Bernhart, W. & Steck, W. (1992). Vibration macht's möglich. *Technische Rundschau,* Vol.16, (1992) pp. 48-51

Bohman, J. (1994). *Mathematische Algorithmen für Fügeprozesse mit minimalen Rektionskräften und ihre Umsetzung in der Robotertechnik,* Doktor-Dissertation, Fakultät für Technische Wissenschaften der Technischen Universität Ilmenau

Brignone, L.; Sivayoganathan, K.; Balendran, V. & Horwarth, M. (2001). Contact localisation: a novel approach to intelligent robotic assembly, *Proceedings of International Joint Conference of Neural Networks,* pp. 2182-2187

Chan, S.P. (1995). A neural network compensator for uncertainties in robotic assembly. Journal of Intelligent and Robotic Systems, Vol 13., No.2, (June, 1995) pp. 127-141

Ekvall, S.; Kragic, D. (2008). Robot learning from demonstration: A Task-level Planning Approach, *International Journal of Advanced Robotic Systems,* Vol.5, No.3 (2008), pp. 223-234, ISSN 1729-8806

Farrell, J. & Baker, W. (1993). Learning Control Systems, In: *Introduction to Intelligent and autonomous Control,* Antsaklis, P. J. & Passino, K. M), (Ed.), Kluwer Academic Publisher

Kantardzic, M. (2001). *Data Mining, Concepts, Models, methods and Algorithms,* A John Wiley & Sons, Inc. Publication

H. ter Beek, M.; Fantechi, A.; Gnesi, S.; Mazzanti, F. (2008). *An Action/State-Based Model-Checking Approach for the Analysis of Communication Protocols for Service-Oriented Applications,* In: Lecture Notes in Computer Science, Vol. 4916/2008, pp. 133-148, DOI:10.11007/978-3-540-79707-4_11

Mahadevan, S. (1996). Machine learning for Robots: A Comparison of Different Pardigms, *Proceedings of IEEE/RSJ International Conference on Intelligent Robots and Systems (IROS-96),* Japan

Miyazaki, F.; Ide, K.; Masutani, Y.; Ahn, D.S. (1993). Learning of robotic assembly based on force information, In: Experimental Robotics II, Lecture Notes in Control and Information Sciences, Volume 190/193, pp. (78-88), Publisher Springer Berlin/Heidelberg

Newman, W.S.; Branicky, M. & Pao, J.-H. (2001). Intelligent Strategies for Compliant Robotic Assembly, *Proceedings of 11th Yale Workshop on Adaptive and Learning Systems*, pp. 139-146, Yale

Schaal, S.; Atkenson, C.A. (2010) Learning Control in Robotics, *IEEE Robotics and Automation Magazine*, Vol.17, No.2, June 2010, pp. 20-29, ISSN 1070-9932

Siegwart, U. (1995). Taktile Präzisionsmontage mit Industrierobotern in der Feinwerktechnik. *wt-Produktion und Menagment 85,* (1995) pp. 33-36

Svozil, D.; Kvasnička, J. & Pospichal, J. (1997). Introduction to multi-layer feed-forward neural networks. *Elsevier Chemometrics and Intelligent Systems 39,* (1996), pp. (43-62).

Stergiou, C. & Siganos, D. (1996). Neural Networks. *SURPRISE 96*, Vol.4

Vaaler, E.G. (1991). *A machine Learning Based Logic Branching Algorithm for Automated Assembly,* PhD, MIT

Wai, J. (2001). *Intelligent Robotic Learning using Guided Evolutionary Simulated Annealing,* MSc. Thesis, Case Western Reserve University

Wyatt, J.; Hoar, J.; Hayes, G. (1999). *Experimantal methods for robot learning,* In: Towards Intelligent Mobile Robots - Scientific Methods in Mobile Robotics, Nehmzow U.; Recce, M. & Bisset, D., (Ed.), Department of Computer Science

Xiao, J.; Zhang, L. (1995). A Geometric Simulator SimRep for Testing the Replanning Approach toward Assembly Motions in the Presence of Uncertainties, *Proceedings of the 1995 IEEE International Symposium on Assembly and Task Planning (ISATP'95),* pp.171-177

Wooldridge, M. (2008). *An Introduction to MultiAgent Systems,* John Wiley & Sons , Inc. Publication, ISBN 978-0-471-49691-5

17

Integral Reinforcement Learning for Finding Online the Feedback Nash Equilibrium of Nonzero-Sum Differential Games

Draguna Vrabie and Frank L. Lewis
University of Texas at Arlington
United States

1. Introduction

Adaptive/Approximate Dynamic Programming (ADP) is the class of methods that provide online solution to optimal control problems while making use of measured information from the system and using computation in a forward in time fashion, as opposed to the backward in time procedure that is characterizing the classical Dynamic Programming approach (Bellman, 2003). These methods were initially developed for systems with finite state and action spaces and are based on Sutton's temporal difference learning (Sutton, 1988), Werbos' Heuristic Dynamic Programming (HDP) (Werbos, 1992), and Watkins' Q-learning (Watkins, 1989).

The applicability of these online learning methods to real world problems is enabled by approximation tools and theory. The value that is associated with a given admissible control policy will be determined using value function approximation, online learning techniques, and data measured from the system. A control policy is determined based on the information on the control performance encapsulated in the value function approximator. Given the universal approximation property of neural networks (Hornik et al., 1990), they are generally used in the reinforcement learning literature for representation of value functions (Werbos, 1992), (Bertsekas and Tsitsiklis, 1996), (Prokhorov and Wunsch, 1997), (Hanselmann et al., 2007). Another type of approximation structure is a linear combination of a basis set of functions and it has been used in (Beard et al., 1997), (Abu-Khalaf et al., 2006), (Vrabie et al. 2009).

The approximation structure used for performance estimation, endowed with learning capabilities, is often referred to as a critic. Critic structures provide performance information to the control structure that computes the input of the system. The performance information from the critic is used in learning procedures to determine improved action policies. The methods that make use of critic structures to determine online optimal behaviour strategies are also referred to as adaptive critics (Prokhorov and Wunsch, 1997), (Al-Tamimi et al., 2007), (Kulkarni & Venayagamoorthy, 2010).

Most of the previous research on continuous-time reinforcement learning algorithms that provide an online approach to the solution of optimal control problems, assumed that the dynamical system is affected only by a single control strategy. In a game theory setup, the controlled system is affected by a number of control inputs, computed by different controllers that try to optimize individual performance functions. In these situations the control problem is formulated with the purpose of finding the set of control policies that are admissible, i.e. control policies that guarantee the stability of the controlled dynamical system, and minimize the individual performance functions in a Nash equilibrium sense. This kind of solution is characterized by the fact that any change in the policy of any given player (in the space of admissible policies) will result in a worse performance for that player, relative to the performance that it receives by means of the Nash equilibrium solution policy.

Nash differential games have been originally introduced in (Starr & Ho, 1969). Their study is highly relevant as they have a number of potential applications in control engineering and economics (see e.g. (Abou-Kandil et al., 2003); (Engwerda, 2005)). The underlying game theory formulation appears also in the study of coupled large scale systems (Mukaidani, 2007-a), e.g. networking and wireless communication systems (Shah, 1998).

This chapter is presenting an Adaptive Dynamic Programming (ADP) algorithm, formulated using the continuous-time mathematical framework, that provides, in an online manner, the Nash equilibrium solution of two-player nonzero-sum differential games with linear dynamics and infinite horizon quadratic cost. The main advantage of this ADP approach consists in the fact that neither of the two participants in the game makes use of explicit knowledge on the model of the drift dynamics of the system that they influence through their behavior policy. This means that the two players will learn online the most effective behavior policies that correspond to the Nash equilibrium while using no explicit knowledge on the drift dynamics of the differential game. This results in two clear benefits when compared with model based procedures:

- conducting identification experiments for finding the drift term that describes the system dynamics is not required, while this lack of knowledge does not have any impact on the obtained equilibrium solution,
- the resulting equilibrium behavior policies of the two players will not be affected by any error differences between the dynamics of a model of the system and the dynamics of the real system.

For the case when the system has linear dynamics and the cost indices are quadratic and have infinite horizon, it is known that finding the Nash equilibrium to the game problem is equivalent with calculating the solution of a set of coupled algebraic Riccati equations (ARE) (see e.g. (Starr and Ho, 1969), (Abou-Kandil et al., 2003), (Basar and Olsder, 1999), (Engwerda, 2005)). The solution of the coupled ARE has been approached in (Cherfi et al., 2005-a), (Cherfi et al., 2005-b), (Jungers et al., 2007), (Freiling, 1996), (Li and Gajic, 1995) by means of iterative procedures. These algorithms construct sequences of cost functions, or matrices, which converge to the equilibrium solution of the game. In the case of (Cherfi et al., 2005-a), (Cherfi et al., 2005-b), (Freiling et al., 1996), and (Jungers et al., 2007), convergence results of these procedures are still to be determined. It is important to note that all above mentioned algorithms require exact and complete knowledge of the system dynamics and the solution is obtained by means of offline iterative computation procedures.

An ADP procedure that provides solution to the Hamilton-Jacobi-Isaacs equation, associated with the two-player zero-sum nonlinear differential game, has been introduced in (Wei and Zhang, 2008). The ADP algorithm involves calculation of two sequences of cost functions, the upper and lower performance indices, sequences that converge to the saddle point solution of the game. The adaptive critic structure that is required for learning the saddle point solution is comprised by four action networks and two critic networks. The requirement of full knowledge on the system dynamics is still present in the case of that algorithm.

The result presented in this chapter is the first reinforcement learning approach to the saddle point solution of a two player nonzero-sum differential game. By virtue of the online ADP method, that makes use of the integral reinforcement learning (IRL) approach (Vrabie et al., 2009), exact knowledge of part of the system dynamics is not required. To our knowledge, there exists no ADP algorithm that provides the Nash equilibrium solution of the two-player nonzero-sum differential game in an online fashion and without using complete information on the model of the dynamical system to be controlled.

The main traits of this new online procedure are the following:

- It involves the use of ADP techniques that will determine the Nash equilibrium solution of the game in an online data-based procedure that does not require full knowledge of the system dynamics.
- It is the online version of a mathematical algorithm that solves the underlying set of coupled algebraic Riccati equations of the game problem. The equivalent algorithm makes use of offline procedures and requires full knowledge of the system dynamics to determine the Nash equilibrium of the game.

In this ADP approach both game players are actively learning and improving their policy. The algorithm is built on interplay between

- a learning phase, and
- a policy update step.

During the learning phase each of the players is learning the value function that it associates with the use of a given pair of admissible policies. Both players are learning simultaneously. During the policy update step both players are changing their feedback control policies in the sense of performance improvement. That means that each player will change its policy such that it will minimize his cost in front of the previous policy of their opponent.

For learning the value that each player associates with a given admissible pair of control policies we will use value function approximation. In this chapter we will consider the case in which the critic is represented as a linear combination of a set of basis functions which spans the space of value functions to be approximated, see e.g. (Beard et al., 1997). The learning technique that is here employed for value function approximation uses the concept of minimization of the temporal difference error and has been described in (Vrabie, 2009).

The objective of this chapter is to present an online algorithm that makes use of ADP techniques to provide the solution to the two-player differential nonzero-sum game. It will also show that the foundation of the novel online procedure that will be described here is the mathematical result introduced in (Li and Gajic, 1995). That algorithm involves solving a sequence of Lyapunov equations in order to build a sequence of control policies that converges to the Nash equilibrium solution of the game, and thus requires full knowledge on the system dynamics. Herein we will show how, by means of ADP techniques, the solution of these game optimal control problems can be obtained in an online fashion, using measured data from the system, and reduced information on the system dynamics.

We begin our investigation by providing the formulation of the two player nonzero-sum game problem. We then provide an overview of the online integral reinforcement learning (IRL) method that can be used online to determine the value associated with a given pair of admissible control strategies. In Section 3 we describe the online method that provides the Nash equilibrium solution of the two-player nonzero-sum game. The adaptive critic structure associated with the online solution of the game will also be discussed. It will be important to note that in this case, each of the two players will make use of a critic structure that will use reinforcement learning ideas to learn online the value that the player associates with a given admissible control strategy. Section 4 will investigate the convergence properties of the online reinforcement learning algorithm. It will be shown that the ADP procedure introduced in this chapter is theoretically equivalent with the iterative procedure introduced in (Li & Gajic, 1995), and thus has the same convergence properties. A formulation of the algorithm in the form of a quasi-Newton method will also be provided. Section 5 will present a simulation result.

2. Preliminaries

2.1 Problem formulation

We consider the system described by the equation:

$$\begin{aligned} \dot{x} &= Ax + B_1 u_1 + B_2 u_2 \\ x(t_0) &= x_0 \end{aligned} \tag{1}$$

where $x \in \mathbb{R}^n, u_i \in \mathbb{R}^{m_i}$ for $i = 1,2$, and A, B_1 and B_2 are matrices of appropriate dimensions. Each player i, $i = 1,2$, desires to determine the feedback control strategy $u_i = K_i x$ such that the quadratic performance index, where $Q_i \geq 0, R_{ij} \geq 0 (i \neq j), R_{ii} > 0$,

$$J_i = \frac{1}{2} \int_{t_0}^{\infty} (x^T Q_i x + u_1{}^T R_{i1} u_1 + u_2{}^T R_{i2} u_2) d\tau \tag{2}$$

is minimized.

Definition 1

A feedback control pair (u_1, u_2) is admissible if the dynamics of the closed loop system (1) are stable and the performance indices (2) calculated for the given control pair have finite values.

The two-player game problem is defined as follows:

Given the continuous-time system (1), the cost functions $J_i, i = 1,2$ defined by (2), and the set of admissible control inputs $U \subset \mathbb{R}^{m_1} \times \mathbb{R}^{m_2}$, determine the state-feedback admissible control policies such that the closed loop system is stable and the cost functions attain the minimum possible value.

These control strategies corresponds to the Nash equilibrium of the two-player differential game. Thus, the pair of feedback control policies that is sought, denoted (u_1^*, u_2^*), satisfies the following relations for any admissible control pair $(u_1, u_2) \in U$

$$\begin{aligned} J_1(u_1, u_2^*) &\geq J_1(u_1^*, u_2^*) \\ J_2(u_1^*, u_2) &\geq J_2(u_1^*, u_2^*) \end{aligned} . \tag{3}$$

For $i = 1,2$ and $j = 1,2$ $j \neq i$, let us define the minimum cost function by:

$$V_i(x) = \min_{u_i \in U_i} J_i(u_i, u_j{}^*, x) \quad \forall x \in \mathbb{R}^n . \tag{4}$$

Assuming that the optimal value function is differentialble, we can then write two coupled equations, for $i, j = 1,2, j \neq i$,

$$0 = \min_{(u_i, u_j^*)\in U} \left\{ x^T Q_i x + u_i^T R_{i1} u_i + u_j^{*T} R_{i2} u_j^* + \nabla^T V_i [Ax + B_j u_j^* + B_i u_i] \right\} \quad \forall x \in \mathbb{R}^n, \tag{5}$$

that we shall refer to as the Hamilton-Jacobi-Bellman equations.
After performing the minimization in (5) we obtain that the two elements of the closed loop optimal control pair (u_1^*, u_2^*) will have the state feedback form

$$u_i^* = -R_{ii}^{-1} B_i^T P_i^* x = K_i^* x \quad i = 1,2 \tag{6}$$

where the values of the two matrices P_i^*, $i = 1,2$ satisfy the necessary conditions for finding the Nash equilibrium, i.e. the two matrices $P_i^*, i = 1,2$ must be positive definite solutions to the coupled algebraic Riccati equations (ARE)

$$\begin{aligned} N_1(P_1^*, P_2^*) &\triangleq A^T P_1^* + P_1^* A + Q_1 + P_2^* S_{12} P_2^* - P_1^* S_1 P_1^* - P_2^* S_2 P_1^* - P_1^* S_2 P_2^* = 0 \\ N_2(P_1^*, P_2^*) &\triangleq A^T P_2^* + P_2^* A + Q_2 + P_1^* S_{21} P_1^* - P_2^* S_2 P_2^* - P_1^* S_1 P_2^* - P_2^* S_1 P_1^* = 0 \end{aligned} \tag{7}$$

where $S_i = B_i R_{ii}^{-1} B_i^T$, $i = 1,2$ and $S_{ij} = B_j R_{jj}^{-1} R_{ij} R_{jj}^{-1} B_j^T$, $i,j = 1,2,\ j \neq i$.
Finding Nash equilibrium solutions of the game (u_1^*, u_2^*), defined through (6) by the pair of matrices (P_1^*, P_2^*), resumes to finding solutions to the coupled AREs (7) such that the closed loop system dynamics will be stable, i.e. $A - S_1 P_1^* - S_2 P_2^*$ is Hurwitz.

2.2 Integral reinforcement learning

The online iterative procedure that will be presented in Section 3 relies heavily on value function estimation. Thus the goal of this section is to briefly present the online procedure, introduced in (Vrabie et al., 2009), that uses reinforcement learning ideas to find the value of the parameters of the infinite horizon cost associated with a quadratic cost function such as $J_i, i = 1,2$. We refer to this online method as integral reinforcement learning (IRL).
As stated above, the procedure presented herein is used to find the value of the parameters of the infinite horizon cost associated with a cost function that has a quadratic nature, such as $J_i, i = 1,2$. To bring the general theoretical concept into specific, let us formulate the following problem: Given the dynamical system (1) and an admissible pair of linear state-feedback control policies $(u_1, u_2) = (K_1 x, K_2 x) \subset U$, determine the parameters of the infinite horizon cost function J_i, that player i associates with this admissible control pair.
Before giving an online procedure for solving this problem one needs to choose a parametric representation for the value function to be determined. In this particular case the cost functions are quadratic and the control policies have linear state-feedback structure. Thus a quadratic representation in the initial state can provide an exact representation for each of the two cost functions. One can write:

$$J_i = x_0^T P_i x_0 = \frac{1}{2} \int_{t_0}^{\infty} x^T \overline{Q_i} x \, d\tau \tag{8}$$

where $\overline{Q_i} = Q_i + K_1^T R_{i1} K_1 + K_2^T R_{i2} K_2$, i = 1,2.
After choosing a parametric representation for the value function one has to determine the values of its parameters, namely the matrix P_i. The integral reinforcement learning algorithm that will be used for finding the parameters of the value function, i.e. the value of the matrix P_i, is based on the following equation that is satisfied for every time sample $T_0 > 0$

$$x_t^T P_i x_t = \int_t^{t+T_0} x_\tau^T \overline{Q}_i x_\tau d\tau + x_{t+T_0}^T P_i x_{t+T_0} \quad (9)$$

where x_τ denotes the state of the system described by $\dot{x} = (A + B_1K_1 + B_2K_2)x$ with initial condition x_t, and x_{t+T_0} is the value of the state at time $t+T_0$.
The online implementation of the algorithm is given next.
The solution of (9) consists of the value of the matrix P_i that is parameterizing the cost function. The quadratic cost functions will be written as:

$$x_t^T P_i x_t = \overline{p}_i^T \overline{x}_t \quad (10)$$

where $\overline{x_t}$ denotes the Kronecker product quadratic polynomial basis vector with the elements $\{x_k(t)x_l(t)\}_{k=1,n;l=k,n}$ and $\overline{p} = v(P)$ with $v(.)$ a vector valued matrix function that acts on symmetric matrices and returns a column vector by stacking the elements of the diagonal and upper triangular part of the symmetric matrix into a vector, where the off-diagonal elements are taken as $2P_{ij}$, (Brewer, 1978). Denote the integral reinforcement over the time interval $[t, t+T_0]$ by:

$$d(\overline{x}_t, K_1, K_2) \equiv \int_t^{t+T_0} x_\tau^T \overline{Q}_i x_\tau d\tau \,. \quad (11)$$

Based on these notations and structures, (9) is rewritten as:

$$\overline{p}_i^T (\overline{x}_t - \overline{x}_{t+T_0}) = d(\overline{x}_t, K_1, K_2) \,. \quad (12)$$

In (12) the vector of unknown parameters is $\overline{p}_i$ and $\overline{x}_t - \overline{x}_{t+T_0}$ acts as a regression vector. The right hand side target integral reinforcement function is measured based on the state trajectories over the time interval $[t, t+T_0]$.
The parameter vector $\overline{p}_i$ is found by minimizing, in the least-squares sense, the error between the target expected cost over the finite horizon, and the measured cost, $d(\overline{x}_t, K_1, K_2)$. Thus the sought parameters satisfy

$$\overline{p}_i = \arg\min_{\eta} (d(\overline{x}_t, K_1, K_2) - \eta^T (\overline{x}_t - \overline{x}_{t+T_0}))^2 \,. \quad (13)$$

The solution can be obtained online based on data measured along the trajectories of the system, and using batch least squares or the recursive least squares algorithm.
It is important to note that this online algorithm for value function approximation is a data-based approach that uses reinforcement learning ideas. Also, this value function approximation technique does not require explicit knowledge of the model of the controlled system's drift dynamics, i.e. matrix A, or input to state matrices B_1, B_2.

3. Online iterative algorithm that solves the coupled algebraic Riccati equations of the nonzero-sum game

3.1 Initialization of the online algorithm

Before we proceed with the description of the online algorithm, we give a necessary assumption.

Assumption 1 The triples $(A, B_i, \sqrt{Q_i})$, $i = 1,2$ are stabilizable and detectable.
Under this assumption one can reasonably say that initial state feedback control strategies $u_i^{(0)} = K_i^{(0)} x \quad i = 1,2$ exist such that closed loop system matrix $A - B_1 K_1^{(0)} - B_2 K_2^{(0)}$ is Hurwitz.
A procedure for obtaininig the two controllers such that the closed loop system is stable is described next. The procedure has two steps and it can be execute in an online manner without using knowledge on the drift dynamics of the system (1), i.e. without knowing the matrix A.

Step 1

Let Player 2 use the "no control" policy corresponding to $u_2(x) = 0$, and determine the optimal control strategy of Player 1 with respect to the cost index J_1.
This is a classical linear quadratic regulation problem and the optimal control strategy will have the form $u_1^{(0)}(x) = K_1^{(0)} x = -R_{11}^{-1} B_1^T P_1^{(0)} x$ where $P_1^{(0)}$ is the solution of the ARE

$$A^T P_1^{(0)} + P_1^{(0)} A + Q_1 - P_1^{(0)} B_1 R_{11}^{-1} B_1^T P_1^{(0)} = 0 . \tag{14}$$

Note that the solution of this single player optimal control problem can be obtained by solving (14) by means of the online ADP technique introduced in (Vrabie et al., 2009), without using any knowledge on the drift dynamics described by matrix A.
For completeness we outline the procedure herein.

a. We start from the assumption that an initial stabilizing state-feedback control policy $u_1^{(00)}(x) = -K_1^{(00)} x$ is available such that the matrix describing the closed loop system $A - B_1 K_1^{(00)}$ is Hurwitz.
b. For $k \geq 0, k \in \mathrm{N}$, determine the value function defined as:

$$x_0^T P_1^{(0,k+1)} x_0 = \frac{1}{2} \int_{t_0}^{\infty} x^T(\tau) \left(Q_1 + K_1^{(0,k)} R_{11} K_1^{(0,k)} \right) x(\tau) d\tau , \tag{15}$$

function that is associated with the use of the stabilizing state-feedback controller $u_1^{(0,k)}(x) = -K_1^{(0,k)} x = -R_{11}^{-1} B_1^T P_1^{(0,k)} x$, where $x_0 = x(0)$ is an initial state.
The sequence of matrices $P_1^{(0,k)}$, $k \geq 0, k \in \mathrm{N}$ can be determined using integral reinforcement learning, as described in Section 2.2, using discrete-time data measured from the system and without using any knowledge on the dynamics of the system (1).
Finding this value via de online model free algorithm is equivalent with solving the Lyapunov equation

$$(A - B_1 K_1^{(0,k)})^T P_1^{(0,k+1)} + P_1^{(0,k+1)} (A - B_1 K_1^{(0,k)}) + Q_1 + K_1^{(0,k)} R_{11} K_1^{(0,k)} = 0 , \tag{16}$$

equation that requires complete knowledge on the model of the system.

c. The iterative procedure described in b) has as result a convergent sequence of positive definite matrices, as shown in (Kleinman, 1968), such that $P_1^{(0,k)} \underset{k \to \infty}{\to} P_1^{(0)}$. A stop criterion can be defined as:

$$\left\| P_1^{(0,k+1)} - P_1^{(0,k)} \right\| \leq \varepsilon \tag{17}$$

or:

$$\left\| A^T P_1^{(0,k)} + P_1^{(0,k)} A + Q_1 - P_1^{(0,k)} B_1 R_{11}^{-1} B_1^T P_1^{(0,k)} \right\| \le \varepsilon , \qquad (18)$$

for a prespecified value of ε, where $\| \ \|$ denotes a matrix norm. The latter expression, although it requires knowledge of the system dynamics, can be checked using online measured data and equation (12) such as

$$\left(\overline{p}_1^{(0,k)} \right)^T (\overline{x_t} - \overline{x_{t+T_0}}) - d(\overline{x_t}, K_1^{(0,k)}, 0) \le \varepsilon \qquad (19)$$

The result is that the dynamics of the system (1) with the control pair $(u_1^{(0)}(x),0)$ are stable, i.e. $A - S_1 P_1^{(0)}$ is Hurwitz.

Step 2

Let Player 1 use the stabilizing control policy $u_1^{(0)}(x) = K_1^{(0)} x$, and determine the optimal control strategy of Player 2 with respect to the cost index J_2.

Again, this is a classical linear quadratic regulation problem and the optimal control strategy will have the form $u_2^{(0)}(x) = K_2^{(0)} x = -R_{22}^{-1} B_2^T P_2^{(0)} x$ where $P_2^{(0)}$ is the solution of the ARE

$$(A - S_1 P_1^{(0)})^T P + P(A - S_1 P_1^{(0)}) + Q_2 + P_1^{(0)} S_{21} P_1^{(0)} - P B_2 R_{22}^{-1} B_2^T P = 0 . \qquad (20)$$

Similarly to Step 1, the solution of this single player optimal control problem can be obtained by means of the online ADP IRL technique, introduced in (Vrabie et al., 2009) and outlined above, without using any knowledge on the drift dynamics of the system described by the matrix A.

The resulting control pair $(u_1^{(0)}(x), u_2^{(0)}(x))$ is admissible, i.e. $A - S_1 P_1^{(0)} - S_2 P_2^{(0)}$ is Hurwitz. At this point we are in the possession of an initial admissible pair of feedback control strategies $(u_1^{(0)}, u_2^{(0)}) = (K_1^{(0)} x, K_2^{(0)} x)$, that we shall also represent by $(P_1^{(0)}, P_2^{(0)})$.

It is worth noting that the Step 1 above can also be executed with respect to Player 2, followed by Step 2 that will now be relative to Player 1. Also in this case, a pair of admissible control policies will be obtained.

In the following we formulate the iterative algorithm that learns online the Nash equilibrium solution of the two-player zero-sum differential game. At every step of the iterative procedure each player uses reinforcement learning to estimate the infinite horizon value function that it associates with the current admissible control pair. Following the value function estimation procedure each of the two players makes a decision to improve its control policy. The end result is an online algorithm which leads to the saddle point solution of the differential game while neither of the two players uses any knowledge on the drift dynamics of the environment.

3.2 Online partially model free algorithm for solving the nonzero-sum differential game

Initialization

Start with initial matrices $(P_1^{(0)}, P_2^{(0)})$ such that $A - S_1 P_1^{(0)} - S_2 P_2^{(0)}$ is Hurwitz (i.e. initial control policies for both players are available such that the closed loop dynamics of the system are stable). Let $k = 0$.

Itterative procedure

For $k \geq 0, k \in \mathrm{N}$, let two critic structures use the integral reinforcement learning procedure described in Section 2.2 to determine the value that each of the two players is associating with the control policies described by the matrix pair $(P_1^{(k)}, P_2^{(k)})$. Namely each of the two critics will determine the matrices $P_i^{(k+1)}, i=1,2, k \geq 0$ that satisfy

$$x_0^T P_i^{(k+1)} x_0 = \frac{1}{2} \int_{t_0}^{\infty} x^T \overline{Q_i}^{(k)} x d\tau \tag{21}$$

where $\overline{Q_i}^{(k)} = Q_i + P_i^{(k)} S_i P_i^{(k)} + P_j^{(k)} S_{ij} P_j^{(k)} \quad i=1,2, j \neq i$.

Each of the two players will update their control policies such that the new control policy pair is characterized by $(P_1^{(k+1)}, P_2^{(k+1)})$, i.e.

$$\begin{aligned} u_1^{(k+1)}(x) = K_2^{(k+1)} x = -R_{11}^{-1} B_1^T P_1^{(k+1)} x \\ u_2^{(k+1)}(x) = K_2^{(k+1)} x = -R_{22}^{-1} B_2^T P_2^{(k+1)} x \end{aligned}. \tag{22}$$

Stop criterion

Stop the online algorithm when the following criterion is satisfied for a specified value of the number ε

$$\max(\left\| N_1(P_1^{(k+1)}, P_2^{(k+1)}) \right\|, \left\| N_2(P_1^{(k+1)}, P_2^{(k+1)}) \right\|) \leq \varepsilon, \tag{23}$$

where $\| \ \|$ denotes a matrix norm. The latter expression can be checked using online measured data and the following relation

$$\left\| \left(\left(\overline{p_1}^{(k+1)}\right)^T (\overline{x_t} - \overline{x_{t+T_0}}) - d(\overline{x_t}, K_1^{(k+1)}, K_2^{(k+1)}), \left(\overline{p_2}^{(k+1)}\right)^T (\overline{x_t} - \overline{x_{t+T_0}}) - d(\overline{x_t}, K_1^{(k+1)}, K_2^{(k+1)}) \right) \right\| \leq \varepsilon . \tag{24}$$

3.3 Adaptive critic structure for solving the two-player Nash differential game

The adaptive critic structure that represents the implementation of this algorithm is given in Figure 1.

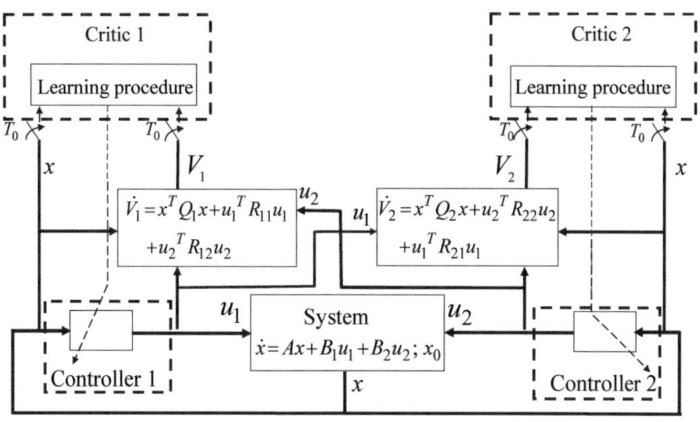

Fig. 1. Adaptive critic structure for the ADP game with IRL.

An important aspect that is revealed by the adaptive critic structure is the fact that this ADP algorithm is now using three time scales:

a. the continuous-time scale, represented by the full lines, that is connected with the continuous-time dynamics of the system and the continuous-time computation performed by the two players;
b. a discrete time scale given by T_0. This time scale is connected with the online learning procedure that is based on discrete-time measured data;
c. a slower, discrete-time scale that is a multiple of T_0. This time scale, indicated by the dashed lines, is connected with the update procedure of the control policies of the two players. The update procedure is performed only after the value function learning procedure, that uses integral reinforcement information, has converged.

The values of the time periods T_0 can be variable and are controlled by the two learning critics. Each critic will output a matrix $P_i^{(k)}, i=1,2$, in a synchronous fashion, after both online learning algorithms for the value functions have converged. Each controller will use the information from its corresponding critic to calculate and then implement a new control policy.

From the perspective of two-player games, the proposed online algorithm can be presented as follows:

Initialization

Let the initial policy of Player 2 be zero $u_2^{(00)}=0$.

Let Player 1 determine its optimal control policy $K_1^{(0)}=-R_{11}^{-1}B_1^T P_1^{(0)}$ in an online optimization procedure while Player 2 is not playing the game.

Let Player 2 determine its optimal control policy $K_2^{(0)}=-R_{22}^{-1}B_2^T P_2^{(0)}$ in an online optimization procedure while Player 1 is playing the game using $K_1^{(0)}$.

Iterative procedure

For $k \ge 0$, let both players determine online, using the integral reinforcement learning procedure, the values that they associate with the use of the policy pair $(K_1^{(k)}, K_2^{(k)})$, namely the pair of matrices $(P_1^{(k+1)}, P_2^{(k+1)})$.

Let both players update their control policies using

$$K_i^{(k+1)} = -R_{ii}^{-1}B_i^T P_i^{(k+1)}. \tag{25}$$

Stop criterion

Let both players stop this iterative procedure when there is no change in the control policies is observed at two successive steps (i.e. the Nash equilibrium has been obtained and both players can not further improve their cost function by changing their behavior policy).

4. Analysis of the online learning algorithm

In this section we are providing an analysis for the online algorithm that was introduced in section 3.

4.1 Mathematical formulation of the online algorithm

Using the notation $A^{(k)} = A - S_1P_1^{(k)} - S_2P_2^{(k)}$, it can be shown that equations (21) can be written as:

$$\left(A^{(k)}\right)^T P_i^{(k+1)} + P_i^{(k+1)}A^{(k)} = -\overline{Q}_i^{(k)} \tag{26}$$

where $i = 1,2$.
Thus the online algorithm described in Section 3.2 is equivalent with the following procedure:

Initialization

Start with initial matrices $(P_1^{(0)}, P_2^{(0)})$ such that $A - S_1P_1^{(0)} - S_2P_2^{(0)}$ is Hurwitz.

Iterative procedure

For $k \geq 0, k \in \mathrm{N}$, solve the Lyapunov equations (25).

Stop criterion

Stop the online algorithm when the criterion (23) is satisfied for a user specified value of ε.
This offline algorithm that uses iterations on Lyapunov equations has been proposed and analysed in (Li & Gajic, 1995) and its convergence has been further discussed in (Mukaidani, 2006) and (Mukaidani, 2007-b). Considering the mathematical equivalence between the algorithm introduced in (Li & Gajic, 1995) and the online procedure based on reinforcement learning that we proposed in Section 3, we can conclude that the online, partially model free, algorithm that we presented herein has the same convergence properties.

4.2 Analysis of the online algorithm

It is interesting to see that, similarly to the Newton method proposed in (Kleinman, 1968) for solving the classical continuous-time algebraic Riccati equation, the algorithm presented in this chapter relies on iterations on Lyapunov equations. However, the online procedure introduced here, and its underlying algorithm, is not a Newton method for finding the solution of the coupled ARE given in (7). This shall be clarified by means of the next two propositions.
First let us look at the formulation of the Newton method that determines the unique positive definite solution of the classical continuous-time algebraic Riccati equation

$$A^T P + PA + Q - PBR^{-1}B^T P = 0 . \tag{27}$$

Denote with $Ric(P_k)$ the matrix valued function defined as

$$Ric(P_k) = A^T P_k + P_k A + Q - P_k BR^{-1}B^T P_k \tag{28}$$

and let Ric'_{P_k} denote the Frechet derivative of $Ric(P_k)$ taken with respect to P_k. The matrix function Ric'_{P_k}, evaluated at a given matrix *M*, will thus be

$$Ric'_{P_k}(M) = (A - BR^{-1}B^T P_k)^T M + M(A - BR^{-1}B^T P_k) . \tag{29}$$

Proposition 1 The unique positive solution of (27) can be determined by Newton's method given by:

$$P_k = P_{k-1} - (Ric'_{P_{k-1}})^{-1} Ric(P_{k-1}) , \tag{30}$$

provided that the initial matrix P_0 is such that $A - BR^{-1}B^T P_0$ is Hurwitz; and considering that the regular conditions for existence and uniqueness of positive definite solution are satisfied. For a proof see (Vrabie et al., 2009).
Next we will use the same mathematical tools to provide formulation to the algorithm used herein.

Consider the notations introduced in (7) for the two coupled algebraic Riccati equations, and let $N_{1}{}'_{P_1^{(k)}}$ and $N_{2}{}'_{P_2^{(k)}}$ denote the Frechet derivatives of $N_1(P_1^{(k)},P_2^{(k)})$ and $N_2(P_1^{(k)},P_2^{(k)})$, taken with respect to $P_1^{(k)}$ and respectively $P_2^{(k)}$, such that

$$\begin{aligned} N_{1}{}'_{P_1^{(k)}}(M) &= (A^{(k)})^T M + MA^{(k)} \\ N_{2}{}'_{P_2^{(k)}}(M) &= (A^{(k)})^T M + MA^{(k)}{}' \end{aligned} \tag{31}$$

where $A^{(k)} = A - S_2P_2^{(k)} - S_1P_1^{(k)}$.

Proposition 2 Consider that the regular conditions for existence and uniqueness of solution of the infinite horizon nonzero-sum differential game with quadratic performance are satisfied. Then, provided that an initial pair $(P_1^{(0)},P_2^{(0)})$ is such that $A^{(0)} = A - S_2P_2^{(0)} - S_1P_1^{(0)}$ is Hurwitz, the online algorithm described in Section 3.2, that provides the Nash equilibrium solution of (7), can be formulated as the following quasi-Newton method

$$\begin{aligned} P_1^{(k+1)} &= P_1^{(k)} - (N_{1}{}'_{P_1^{(k)}})^{-1} N_1(P_1^{(k)},P_2^{(k)}) \\ P_2^{(k+1)} &= P_2^{(k)} - (N_{2}{}'_{P_2^{(k)}})^{-1} N_2(P_1^{(k)},P_2^{(k)}) \end{aligned}. \tag{32}$$

Proof We first show that the two equations (26)

$$\left(A^{(k)}\right)^T P_i^{(k+1)} + P_i^{(k+1)}A^{(k)} = -\overline{Q}_i^{(k)} \tag{33}$$

can be written in the form:

$$(P_1^{(k+1)} - P_1^{(k)})A^{(k)} + (A^{(k)})^T(P_1^{(k+1)} - P_1^{(k)}) + N_1(P_1^{(k)},P_2^{(k)}) = 0 \tag{34}$$

and respectively:

$$(P_2^{(k+1)} - P_2^{(k)})A^{(k)} + (A^{(k)})^T(P_2^{(k+1)} - P_2^{(k)}) + N_2(P_1^{(k)},P_2^{(k)}) = 0\,. \tag{35}$$

For i=1, we write (33) as:

$$\left(A^{(k)}\right)^T P_1^{(k+1)} + P_1^{(k+1)}A^{(k)} = -(Q_1 + P_1^{(k)}S_1P_1^{(k)} + P_2^{(k)}S_{12}P_2^{(k)})\,. \tag{36}$$

Using the definition of $N_1(P_1^{(k)},P_2^{(k)})$ we can write:

$$\begin{aligned} N_1(P_1^{(k)},P_2^{(k)}) = {} & (A - S_1P_1^{(k)} - S_2P_2^{(k)})^T P_1^{(k)} + P_1^{(k)}(A - S_1P_1^{(k)} - S_2P_2^{(k)}) + \\ & + Q_1 + P_2^{(k)}S_{12}P_2^{(k)} + P_1^{(k)}S_1P_1^{(k)} \end{aligned} \tag{37}$$

and thus we have

$$N_1(P_1^{(k)},P_2^{(k)}) - \left(A^{(k)}\right)^T P_1^{(k)} - P_1^{(k)}A^{(k)} = Q_1 + P_2^{(k)}S_{12}P_2^{(k)} + P_1^{(k)}S_1P_1^{(k)}\,. \tag{38}$$

Adding equations (36) and (38) we obtain

$$\left(P_1^{(k+1)}-P_1^{(k)}\right)A^{(k)}+\left(A^{(k)}\right)^T\left(P_1^{(k+1)}-P_1^{(k)}\right)+N_1(P_1^{(k)},P_2^{(k)})=0\,. \tag{39}$$

Similarly, for i=2, one can obtain (35) using (33) and the definition of $N_2(P_1^{(k)},P_2^{(k)})$.
Using (31) we write

$$N'_{1\,P_1^{(k)}}(P_1^{(k+1)}-P_1^{(k)})=(A^{(k)})^T\left(P_1^{(k+1)}-P_1^{(k)}\right)+\left(P_1^{(k+1)}-P_1^{(k)}\right)A^{(k)} \tag{40}$$

and thus (39) becomes

$$N'_{1\,P_1^{(k)}}(P_1^{(k+1)}-P_1^{(k)})=-N_1(P_1^{(k)},P_2^{(k)}), \tag{41}$$

and the sequence of matrices $\left\{P_1^{(k)}\right\}$ will be determined using the iterative relation

$$P_1^{(k+1)}=P_1^{(k)}-(N'_{1P_1^{(k)}})^{-1}N_1(P_1^{(k)},P_2^{(k)})\,. \tag{42}$$

In a similar fashion we can show that the sequence of matrices $\left\{P_2^{(k)}\right\}$ is the result of the iterative procedure $P_2^{(k+1)}=P_2^{(k)}-(N'_{2P_2^{(k)}})^{-1}N_2(P_1^{(k)},P_2^{(k)})$.

5. Simulation result for the online algorithm

This section presents the results that were obtained in simulation while finding the state-feedback controllers that correspond to the Nash equilibrium solution of the differential game.

Here we considered the system used in Example 1 in (Jungers et al., 2007). The purpose of the design method is to allow the two players to determine by means of online measurements and reinforcement learning techniques the control strategies that satisfy the equilibrium characterized by (3). It is important to emphasize that the equilibrium result will be obtained without making use of any knowledge on the drift dynamics of the system, matrix A.

The matrices of the model of the plant, that are used in this simulation are:

$$A_{nom}=\begin{bmatrix}-0.0366 & 0.0271 & 0.0188 & -0.4555\\ 0.0482 & -1.0100 & 0.0024 & -4.0208\\ 0.1002 & 0.2855 & -0.7070 & 1.3229\\ 0 & 0 & 1.0000 & 0\end{bmatrix} \tag{43}$$

$$\begin{aligned}B_1&=\begin{bmatrix}0.4422 & 3.0447 & -5.52 & 0\end{bmatrix}^T\\ B_2&=\begin{bmatrix}0.1761 & -7.5922 & 4.99 & 0\end{bmatrix}^T\end{aligned} \tag{44}$$

The following cost function parameters were chosen $Q_1=diag(3.5;2;4;5)$, $Q_2=diag(1.5;6;3;1)$, $R_{11}=1$, $R_{22}=2$, $R_{12}=0.25$, $R_{21}=0.6$.

For the purpose of demonstrating the online learning algorithm the closed loop system was excited with an initial condition, the initial state of the system being $x_0=\begin{bmatrix}0 & 0 & 0 & 1\end{bmatrix}$. The simulation was conducted using data obtained from the system at every 0.2s. The value of the stop criterion ε was 10^{-6}.

The algorithm was initialized using the matrices $P_i^{(0)}, i=1,2$ that were calculated using the initialization procedure that was outlined above. It is important to mention here that the two admissible control policies $K_i^{(0)}, i=1,2$ corresponding to the solutions $P_i^{(0)}, i=1,2$ can also be determined online by means of the online policy iteration algorithm introduced in (Vrabie et al., 2009), a procedure that does not require knowledge on the drift dynamics of the system, namely matrix A.

In order to solve online for the values of the $P_i^{(k)}, i=1,2$, a least-squares problem of the sort described in Section 2.2 was set up before each iteration step in the online algorithm. Since there are 10 independent elements in the symmetric matrices $P_i^{(k)}, i=1,2$ the setup of the least-squares problem requires at least 10 measurements of the cost function associated with the given control policy and measurements of the system's states at the beginning and the end of each time interval, provided that there is enough excitation in the system. Here we chose to solve a least squares problem after a set of 15 data samples was acquired and thus the policy of the controller was updated every 3 sec.

Figure 2 and Figure 3 present the evolution of the parameters of the value of the game seen by Player 1 and Player 2 respectively.

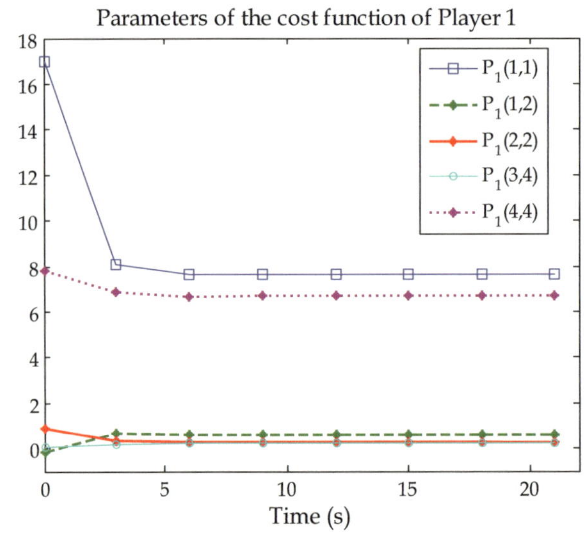

Fig. 2. Convergence of the cost function of Player 1 using the ADP method with integral reinforcement learning technique.

The matrices that are characterizing the equilibrium solution were obtained in simulation after 7 iteration steps. These are:

$$P_1^{(7)} = \begin{bmatrix} 7.6586 & 0.6438 & 0.6398 & -3.0831 \\ 0.6438 & 0.2878 & 0.2855 & -0.0945 \\ 0.6398 & 0.2855 & 0.5620 & 0.2270 \\ -3.0831 & -0.0945 & 0.2270 & 6.6987 \end{bmatrix} \tag{45}$$

and

$$P_2^{(7)} = \begin{bmatrix} 3.4579 & 0.1568 & 0.2047 & -1.8480 \\ 0.1568 & 0.6235 & 0.2889 & -0.0711 \\ 0.2047 & 0.2889 & 0.4014 & 0.0729 \\ -1.8480 & -0.0711 & 0.0729 & 3.7850 \end{bmatrix}. \tag{46}$$

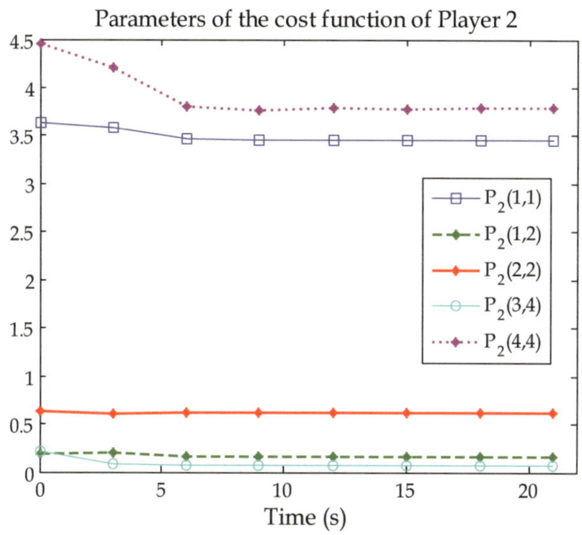

Fig. 3. Convergence of the cost function of Player 2 using the ADP method with integral reinforcement learning technique

The same results have been obtained in (Freiling et al., 1996) by means of a different iterative method.

The two saddle point control policies are:

$$K_1^{(7)} = [-1.8151 \quad 0.4150 \quad 1.9501 \quad 2.9041] \tag{47}$$

and

$$K_2^{(7)} = [-0.22 \quad 1.6323 \quad 0.0772 \quad -0.2891]. \tag{48}$$

It is important to note that the ADP online gaming method described in Section 3, uses measurements from the system and does not require any knowledge of the matrix A. Nonetheless, the resulting solution is close to the exact solution of the game problem that can be obtained via numerical methods that require an exact model of the system.

6. Conclusion

This chapter introduced an online data-based approach that makes use of reinforcement learning techniques to determine in an online fashion the solution of the two-player nonzero-sum differential game with linear dynamics. The algorithm is suitable for online implementation and furthermore does not require exact knowledge of the system drift dynamics given by matrix A.

The two participants in the continuous-time differential game are competing in real-time and the feedback Nash control strategies will be determined based on online measured data from the system. The algorithm is built on interplay between a learning phase, where each of the players is learning online the value that they associate with a given set of play policies, and a policy update step, performed by each of the payers towards decreasing the value of their cost. The players are learning concurrently.

It was shown that the online procedure is based on a mathematical algorithm that solves offline the coupled ARE associated with the differential game problem and involves iterations on Lyapunov equations to build a sequence of controllers. The Lyapunov equations that appear at each step of the iteration are solved online using measured data by means of an integral reinforcement learning procedure.

Here we considered the infinite horizon, state-feedback, linear-quadratic case of the problem. Ideas related with the extension of this result to the more general case of a game with nonlinear dynamics will be pursued in detail in a future research. Also, herein we restricted the discussion to the case of two-player games. However it is straightforward to formulate the ADP algorithm for the general case with N players.

7. References

Abou-Kandil, H.; Freiling, G. & Jank, G. (2003). Necessary and sufficient conditions for constant solutions of coupled Riccati equations in Nash games, *Systems and Control Letters*, 21, pp. 295-306.

Abu-Khalaf, M., Lewis, F. L. & Huang, J. (2006). Policy Iterations and the Hamilton-Jacobi-Isaacs Equation for H-infinity State-Feedback Control with Input Saturation, *IEEE Transactions on Automatic Control*, pp. 1989- 1995.

Al-Tamimi, A., Abu-Khalaf, M. & Lewis F. L. (2007). Adaptive Critic Designs for Discrete-Time Zero-Sum Games with Application to H-infinity Control, *IEEE Transactions on Systems, Man, and Cybernetics, Part B*, 37, 1, pp. 240-247.

Basar, T. & Olsder, G. J. (1999). *Dynamic Noncooperative Game Theory*, 2nd ed., (Classics in Applied Mathematics; 23), SIAM.

Beard, R., Saridis, G., & Wen, J., (1997). Galerkin approximations of the generalized Hamilton-Jacobi-Bellman equation, *Automatica*, 33, 11, pp. 2159-2177, ISSN:0005-1098.

Bellman, R. (2003). *Dynamic Programming*, Dover Publications, ISBN 0-486-42809-5, Mineola, New York.

Bertsekas D. P. & Tsitsiklis J. N. (1996). *Neuro-Dynamic Programming*, Athena Scientific, ISBN: 1-886529-10-8, Massachusetts.

Brewer J. W. (1978). Kronecker Products and Matrix Calculus in System Theory, *IEEE Trans. on Circuit and System*, 25, 9, pp. 772–781, ISSN: 0098-4094.

Cherfi L., Abou-Kandil H. & Bourles H. (2005-a). Iterative method for general algebraic Riccati equation, *Proceedings ACSE'05*, pp. 1-6, December 2005.

Cherfi L., Chitour Y. & Abou-Kandil H. (2005-b). A new algorithm for solving coupled algebraic Riccati equations, *Proceedings of CIMCA'05*, pp. 83 - 88.

Engwerda J.C. (2005). *LQ dynamic optimization and differential games*, Chichester: Wiley.

Freiling G., Jank G. & Abou-Kandil H. (1996). On Global Existence of Solutions to Coupled Matrix Riccati Equations in Closed-Loop Nash Games, *IEEE Transaction on Automatic Control*, 41, 2, pp. 264-269.

Hanselmann T., Noakes L. & Zaknich A. (2007). Continuous-time adaptive critics, *IEEE Transactions on Neural Networks*, 18, 3, pp. 631-647, ISSN: 1045-9227.

Hornik, K., Stinchcombe M. & White H. (1990). Universal approximation of an unknown mapping and its derivatives using multilayer feedforward networks, *Neural Networks*, 3, 5, pp. 551-560, ISSN:0893-6080.

Jungers M., De Pieri E. & Abou-Kandil H. (2007). Solving Coupled Riccati Equations for Closed-Loop Nash Strategy, by Lack of Trust Approach, *International Journal of Tomography and Statistics*, 7, F07, pp. 49-54.

Kleinman, D. (1968). On an Iterative Technique for Riccati Equation Computations, *IEEE Trans. on Automatic Control*, 13, 1, pp. 114 - 115, ISSN: 0018-9286.

Kulkarni, R. V. & Venayagamoorthy, G. K. (2010), Adaptive critics for dynamic optimization, *Neural Networks*, 23, 5, pp. 587-591.

Li, T. & Gajic, Z. (1995). Lyapunov iterations for solving coupled algebraic Riccati equations of Nash differential games and algebraic Riccati equations of zero-sum games, In: *New Trends in Dynamic Games*, G. Olsder (Ed.), Birkhauser, pp. 333-351.

Mukaidani, H. (2006). Optimal numerical strategy for Nash games of weakly coupled large scale systems, *Dynamics of Continuous, Discrete and Impulsive Systems, Series B: Applications and Algorithms*, 13, pp. 249-268.

Mukaidani, H. (2007-a). Newton's method for solving cross-coupled sign-indefinite algebraic Riccati equations for weakly coupled large-scale systems, *Applied Mathematics and Computation*, 188, pp. 103-115.

Mukaidani, H. (2007-b). Numerical computation of sign-indefinite linear quadratic differential games for weakly coupled large scale systems, *International Journal of Control*, 80, 1, pp. 75-86.

Prokhorov D. & Wunsch D. (1997). Adaptive critic designs, *IEEE Trans. on Neural Networks*, 8, 5, pp. 997-1007.

Shah, V. (1998). *Power control for wireless data services based on utility and pricing*, M.S. thesis, Rutgers University.

Starr, A. & Ho Y. (1969). Nonzero-sum differential games, *Journal of Optimization Theory and Applications*, 3, 3, pp. 184-206.

Sutton, R. (1988). Learning to predict by the method of temporal differences, *Machine Learning*, 3:9-44, ISSN: 0885-6125.

Vrabie D., Pastravanu O., Lewis F., Abu-Khalaf, M. (2009). Adaptive Optimal Control for Continuous-Time Linear Systems Based on Policy Iteration, *Automatica*, 45, 2, pp. 477-484, February 2009, ISSN:0005-1098.

Watkins, C. (1989). *Learning from Delayed Rewards*, Ph.D. Thesis, Cambridge University, Cambridge, England.

Werbos, P. J. (1992). Approximate dynamic programming for real-time control and neural modelling, In: *Handbook of Intelligent Control, Neural, Fuzzy, and, Adaptive Approaches*, White D. & Sofge D. (Eds.), New York: Van Nostrand.

Wei, Q. & Zhang, H. (2008). A new approach to solve a class of continuous-time nonlinear quadratic zero-sum game using ADP, *Proceedings of IEEE International Conference on Networking, Sensing and Control (ICNSC'08)*, 6, 8, pp. 507 - 512, ISBN: 978-1-4244-1685-1

18

Online Gaming: Real Time Solution of Nonlinear Two-Player Zero-Sum Games Using Synchronous Policy Iteration

Kyriakos G. Vamvoudakis and Frank L. Lewis
Automation and Robotics Research Institute, The University of Texas at Arlington, USA

1. Introduction

Games provide an ideal environment in which to study computational intelligence, offering a range of challenging and engaging problems. Game theory (Tijs, 2003) captures the behavior in which a player's success in selecting strategies depends on the choices of other players. One goal of game theory techniques is to find (saddle point) equilibria, in which each player has an outcome that cannot be improved by unilaterally changing his strategy (e.g. Nash equilibrium). The H_∞ control problem is a *minimax* optimization problem, and hence a zero-sum game where the controller is a minimizing player and the disturbance a maximizing one. Since the work of George Zames in the early 1980s, H_∞ techniques have been used in control systems, for sensitivity reduction and disturbance rejection. This chapter is concerned with 2-player zero-sum games that are related to the H_∞ control problem, as formulated by (Basar & Olsder, 1999; Basar & Bernard, 1995; Van Der Shaft, 1992).

Game theory and H-infinity solutions rely on solving the Hamilton-Jacobi-Isaacs (HJI) equations, which in the zero-sum linear quadratic case reduce to the generalized game algebraic Riccati equation (GARE). In the nonlinear case the HJI equations are difficult or impossible to solve, and may not have global analytic solutions even in simple cases (e.g. scalar system, bilinear in input and state). Solution methods are generally offline and generate fixed control policies that are then implemented in online controllers in real time.

In this chapter we provide methods for online gaming, that is for solution of 2-player zero-sum infinite horizon games *online*, through learning the saddle point strategies in real-time. The dynamics may be nonlinear in continuous-time and are assumed known. A novel neural network adaptive control technique is given that is based on reinforcement learning techniques, whereby the control and disturbance policies are tuned online using data generated in real time along the system trajectories. Also tuned is a 'critic' approximator structure whose function is to identify the value or outcome of the current control and disturbance policies. Based on this value estimate, the policies are continuously updated. This is a sort of indirect adaptive control algorithm, yet, due to the direct form dependence of the policies on the learned value, it is affected online as direct ('optimal') adaptive control.

Reinforcement learning (RL) is a class of methods used in machine learning to methodically modify the actions of an agent based on observed responses from its environment (Doya,

2001; Doya et al 2001; Howard, 1960; Barto et al 2004; Sutton & Barto, 1998). The RL methods have been developed starting from learning mechanisms observed in mammals. Every decision-making organism interacts with its environment and uses those interactions to improve its own actions in order to maximize the positive effect of its limited available resources; this in turn leads to better survival chances. RL is a means of *learning optimal behaviors by observing the response from the environment to non-optimal control policies.* In engineering terms, RL refers to the learning approach of an actor or agent which modifies its actions, or control policies, based on stimuli received in response to its interaction with its environment. This learning can be extended along two dimensions: i) nature of interaction (competitive or collaborative) and ii) the number of decision makers (single or multi agent).

In view of the advantages offered by the RL methods, a recent objective of control systems researchers is to introduce and develop RL techniques which result in optimal feedback controllers for dynamical systems that can be described in terms of ordinary differential or difference equations. These involve a computational intelligence technique known as Policy Iteration (PI) (Howard, 1960; Sutton & Barto, 1998; D. Vrabie et al, 2009), which refers to a class of algorithms built as a two-step iteration: *policy evaluation* and *policy improvement.* PI provides effective means of learning solutions to HJ equations online. In control theoretic terms, the PI algorithm amounts to learning the solution to a nonlinear Lyapunov equation, and then updating the policy through minimizing a Hamiltonian function. PI has primarily been developed for discrete-time systems, and online implementation for control systems has been developed through approximation of the value function based on work by (Bertsekas & Tsitsiklis, 1996) and (Werbos, 1974; Werbos 1992). Recently, online policy iteration methods for continuous-time systems have been developed by (D. Vrabie et al, 2009).

In recent work (Vamvoudakis & Lewis, 2010), we developed an online approximate solution method based on PI for the (1-player) infinite horizon optimal control problem for continuous-time nonlinear systems with known dynamics. This is an optimal adaptive controller that uses two adaptive structures, one for the value (cost) function and one for the control policy. The two structures are tuned simultaneously online to learn the solution of the HJ equation and the optimal policy.

This chapter presents an optimal adaptive control method that converges online to the solution to the 2-player differential game (and hence the solution of the bounded L_2 gain problem). Three approximator structures are used. Parameter update laws are given to tune critic, actor, and disturbance neural networks simultaneously online to converge to the solution to the HJ equation and the saddle point policies, while also guaranteeing closed-loop stability. Rigorous proofs of performance and convergence are given.

The chapter is organized as follows. Section 2 reviews the formulation of the two-player zero-sum differential game. A policy iteration algorithm is given to solve the HJI equation by successive solutions on nonlinear Lyapunov-like equations. This essentially extends Kleinman's algorithm to nonlinear zero-sum differential games. Section 3 develops the synchronous zero-sum game PI algorithm. Care is needed to develop suitable approximator structures for online solution of zero-sum games. First a suitable 'critic' approximator structure is developed for the value function and its tuning method is pinned down. A persistence of excitation is needed to guarantee proper convergence. Next, suitable 'actor' approximator structures are developed for the control and disturbance policies. Finally in section 4, the main result is presented in Theorem 2, which shows how to tune all three approximators simultaneously by using measurements along the system trajectories in real time and Theorem 3, which proves exponential convergence to the critic neural network and convergence to the approximate Nash solution. Proofs using Lyapunov techniques guarantee convergence and closed-loop stability. Section 5 presents simulation examples that show the effectiveness of the online synchronous zero-sum game CT PI algorithm in learning the optimal value, control and disturbance for both linear and nonlinear systems. Interestingly, a simulation example shows that the two-player online game converges faster than an equivalent online 1-player (optimal control) problem when all the neural networks are tuned simultaneously in real time. Therefore, it is indicated that one learns faster if one has an opponent and uses synchronous policy iteration techniques.

2. Background: Two player differential game, and policy iteration

In this section is presented a background review of 2-player zero-sum differential games. The objective is to lay a foundation for the structure needed in subsequent sections for online solution of these problems in real-time. In this regard, the Policy Iteration Algorithm for 2-player games presented at the end of this section is key.

Consider the nonlinear time-invariant affine in the input dynamical system given by

$$\dot{x} = f(x) + g(x)u(x) + k(x)d(x) \tag{1}$$

where state $x(t) \in \mathbb{R}^n$, control $u(x) \in \mathbb{R}^m$, and disturbance $d(x) \in \mathbb{R}^q$, Assume that $f(x)$ is locally Lipschitz, $\|f(x)\| < b_f \|x\|$, and $f(0) = 0$ so that $x = 0$ is an equilibrium point of the system. Furthermore take $g(x), k(x)$ as continuous.

Define the performance index (Lewis & Syrmos, 1995)

$$J(x(0),u,d) = \int_0^\infty \left(Q(x) + u^T Ru - \gamma^2 \|d\|^2\right) dt \equiv \int_0^\infty r(x,u,d)\, dt \tag{2}$$

for $Q(x) \geq 0$, $R = R^T > 0$, $r(x,u,d) = Q(x) + u^T Ru - \gamma^2 \|d\|^2$ and $\gamma \geq \gamma^* \geq 0$, where γ^* is the smallest γ for which the system is stabilized (Van Der Shaft, 1992). For feedback policies $u(x)$ and disturbance policies $d(x)$, define the value or cost of the policies as

$$V(x(t),u,d) = \int_t^\infty \left(Q(x) + u^T Ru - \gamma^2 \|d\|^2\right) dt \tag{3}$$

When the value is finite, a differential equivalent to this is the nonlinear Lyapunov-like equation

$$0 = r(x,u,d) + (\nabla V)^T (f(x) + g(x)u(x) + k(x)d(x)),\ V(0) = 0 \tag{4}$$

where $\nabla V = \partial V / \partial x \in R^n$ is the (transposed) gradient and the Hamiltonian is

$$H(x,\nabla V,u,d) = r(x,u,d) + (\nabla V)^T (f(x) + g(x)u(x) + k(x)d) \tag{5}$$

For feedback policies (Basar & Bernard, 1995), a solution $V(x) \geq 0$ to (4) is the value (5) for given feedback policy $u(x)$ and disturbance policy $d(x)$.

2.1 Two player zero-sum differential games and Nash equilibrium

Define the 2-player zero-sum differential game (Basar & Bernard, 1995; Basar & Olsder, 1999)

$$V^*(x(0)) = \min_u \max_d J(x(0),u,d) = \min_u \max_d \int_0^\infty \left(Q(x) + u^T Ru - \gamma^2 \|d\|^2 \right) dt \tag{6}$$

subject to the dynamical constraints (1). Thus, u is the minimizing player and d is the maximizing one. This 2-player optimal control problem has a unique solution if a game theoretic saddle point exists, i.e., if the Nash condition holds

$$\min_u \max_d J(x(0),u,d) = \max_d \min_u J(x(0),u,d) \tag{7}$$

To this game is associated the Hamilton-Jacobi-Isaacs (HJI) equation

$$0 = Q(x) + \nabla V^T(x) f(x) - \frac{1}{4}\nabla V^T(x) g(x) R^{-1} g^T(x) \nabla V(x) + \frac{1}{4\gamma^2}\nabla V^T(x) kk^T \nabla V(x), \qquad V(0) = 0 \tag{8}$$

Given a solution $V^*(x) \geq 0 : \mathbb{R}^n \to \mathbb{R}$ to the HJI (8), denote the associated control and disturbance as

$$u^* = -\tfrac{1}{2} R^{-1} g^T(x) \nabla V^* \tag{9}$$

$$d^* = \frac{1}{2\gamma^2} k^T(x) \nabla V^* \tag{10}$$

and write

$$0 = H(x,\nabla V,u^*,d^*) = Q(x) + \nabla V^T(x) f(x) - \frac{1}{4}\nabla V^T(x) g(x) R^{-1} g^T(x) \nabla V(x) + \frac{1}{4\gamma^2}\nabla V^T(x) kk^T \nabla V(x) \tag{11}$$

Note that global solutions to the HJI (11) may not exist. Moreover, if they do, they may not be smooth. For a discussion on viscosity solutions to the HJI, see (Ball & Helton, 1996; Bardi & Capuzzo-Dolcetta, 1997; Basar & Bernard, 1995). The HJI equation (11) may have more than one nonnegative local smooth solution $V(x) \geq 0$. A minimal nonnegative solution $V_a(x) \geq 0$ is one such that there exists no other nonnegative solution $V(x) \geq 0$ such that $V_a(x) \geq V(x) \geq 0$. Linearize the system (1) about the origin to obtain the Generalized ARE (See Section IV.A). Of the nonnegative solutions to the GARE, select the one corresponding to the stable invariant manifold of the Hamiltonian matrix. Then, the minimum nonnegative solution of the HJI is the one having this stabilizing GARE solution as its Hessian matrix evaluated at the origin (Van Der Shaft, 1992).

It is shown in (Basar & Bernard, 1995) that if $V^*(x)$ is the minimum non-negative solution to the HJI (11) and (1) is locally detectable, then (9), (10) given in terms of $V^*(x)$ are in Nash equilibrium solution to the zero-sum game and $V^*(x)$ is its value.

2.2 Policy iteration solution of the HJI equation

The HJI equation (11) is usually intractable to solve directly. One can solve the HJI iteratively using one of several algorithms that are built on iterative solutions of the Lyapunov equation

(4). Included are (Feng et al. 2009) which uses an inner loop with iterations on the control, and (Abu-Khalaf, Lewis, 2008; Abu-Khalaf et al. , 2006; Van Der Shaft, 1992) which uses an inner loop with iterations on the disturbance. These are in effect extensions of Kleinman's algorithm (Kleinman, 1968) to nonlinear 2-player games. The complementarity of these algorithms is shown in (Vrabie, 2009). Here, we shall use the latter algorithm (e.g. (Abu-Khalaf, Lewis, 2008; Abu-Khalaf et al., 2006; Van Der Shaft, 1992)).

Policy Iteration (PI) Algorithm for 2-Player Zero-Sum Differential Games (Van Der Shaft, 1992)

Initialization: Start with a stabilizing feedback control policy u_0

1. For $j = 0,1,...$ given u_j
2. For $i = 0,1,...$ set $d^0 = 0$, solve for $V_j^i(x(t))$, d^{i+1} using

$$0 = Q(x) + \nabla V_j^{iT}(x)(f + gu_j + kd^i) + u_j^T R u_j - \gamma^2 \left\| d^i \right\|^2 \quad (12)$$

$$d^{i+1} = \arg\max_d [H(x, \nabla V_j^i, u_j, d)] = \frac{1}{2\gamma^2} k^T(x) \nabla V_j^i \quad (13)$$

On convergence, set $V_{j+1}(x) = V_j^i(x)$

3. Update the control policy using

$$u_{j+1} = \arg\min_u [H(x, \nabla V_{j+1}), u, d] = -\tfrac{1}{2} R^{-1} g^T(x) \nabla V_{j+1} \quad (14)$$

Go to 1.

■

Nota Bene: In practice, the iterations in i and j are continued until some convergence criterion is met, e.g. $\left\| V_j^{i+1} - V_j^i \right\|$ or, respectively $\left\| V_{j+1} - V_j \right\|$ is small enough in some suitable norm.

Given a feedback policy $u(x)$, write the Hamilton-Jacobi (HJ) equation

$$0 = Q(x) + \nabla V^T(x)\big(f(x) + g(x)u(x)\big) + u^T(x)Ru(x) + \frac{1}{4\gamma^2} \nabla V^T(x) k k^T \nabla V(x), \qquad V(0) = 0 \quad (15)$$

for fixed $u(x)$. The minimal non negative solution $V(x)$ to this equation is the so-called available storage for the given $u(x)$ (Van Der Shaft, 1992). Note that the inner loop of this algorithm finds the available storage for u_j, where it exists.

Assuming that the available storage at each index j is smooth on a local domain of validity, the convergence of this algorithm to the minimal nonnegative solution to the HJI equation is shown in (Abu-Khalaf & Lewis, 2008; Van Der Shaft, 1992). Under these assumptions, the existence of smooth solutions at each step to the Lyapunov-like equation (12) was further shown in (Abu-Khalaf et al., 2006). Also shown was the asymptotic stability of $(f + gu_j + kd^i)$ at each step. In fact, the inner loop yields $V_j^{i+1}(x) \geq V_j^i(x), \forall x$ while the outer loop yields $V_{j+1}(x) \leq V_j(x), \forall x$ until convergence to V^*.

Note that this algorithm relies on successive solutions of nonlinear Lyapunov-like equations (12). As such, the discussion surrounding (4) shows that the algorithm finds the value $V_j^i(x(t))$ of successive control policy/disturbance policy pairs.

3. Approximator structure and solution of the Lyapunov equation

The PI Algorithm is a *sequential* algorithm that solves the HJI equation (11) and finds the Nash solution (u^*, d^*) based on sequential solutions of the nonlinear Lyapunov equation (12). That is, while the disturbance policy is being updated, the feedback policy is held constant. In this section, we use PI to lay a rigorous foundation for the NN approximator structure required *on-line solution of the 2-player zero-sum differential game in real time.* In the next section, this structure will be used to develop an adaptive control algorithm of novel form that converges to the ZS game solution. It is important to define the neural network structures and the NN estimation errors properly or such an adaptive algorithm cannot be developed.

The PI algorithm itself is not implemented in this chapter. Instead, here one implements both loops, the outer feedback control update loop and the inner disturbance update loop, *simultaneously* using neural network learning implemented as differential equations for tuning the weights, while simultaneously keeping track of and learning the value $V(x(t),u,d)$ (3) of the current control and disturbance by solution of the Lyapunov equation (4)/(12). We call this *synchronous PI* for zero-sum games.

3.1 Value function approximation: Critic Neural Network Structure

This chapter uses nonlinear approximator structures (e.g. neural networks) for Value Function Approximation (VFA) (Bertsekas & Tsitsiklis, 1996; Werbos, 1974; Werbos, 1992), therefore sacrificing some representational accuracy in order to make the representation manageable in practice. Sacrificing accuracy in the representation of the value function is not so critical, since the ultimate goal is to find a good policy and not necessarily an accurate value function. Based on the structure of the PI algorithm in Section IIB, VFA for online 2-player games requires three approximators, which are taken as neural networks (NN), one for the value function, one for the feedback control policy, and one for the disturbance policy. These are motivated respectively by the need to solve equations (12), (14), and (13).

To solve equation (12), we use VFA, which here requires approximation in Sobolev norm (Adams & Fournier, 2003), that is, approximation of the value $V(x)$ as well as its gradient $\nabla V(x)$. The following definition describes uniform convergence that is needed later.

Definition 2. (uniform convergence). A sequence of functions $\{p_n\}$ converges uniformly to p if $\forall \varepsilon > 0, \exists N(\varepsilon): \sup\|p_n(x) - p(x)\| < \varepsilon, n > N(\varepsilon)$.

Assumption 1. For each feedback control and disturbance policy the nonlinear Lyapunov equation (12) has a smooth local solution $V(x) \geq 0$.

According to the Weierstrass higher-order approximation Theorem (Abu-Khalaf & Lewis, 2005; Finlayson, 1990; Hornik et al., 1990), there exists a complete independent basis set $\{\varphi_i(x)\}$ such that the solution $V(x)$ to (4) and its gradient are uniformly approximated, that is, there exist coefficients c_i such that

$$V(x) = \sum_{i=1}^{\infty} c_i \varphi_i(x) = \sum_{i=1}^{N} c_i \varphi_i(x) + \sum_{i=N+1}^{\infty} c_i \varphi_i(x)$$

$$V(x) \equiv C_1^T \phi_1(x) + \sum_{i=N+1}^{\infty} c_i \varphi_i(x) \tag{16}$$

$$\frac{\partial V(x)}{\partial x} = \sum_{i=1}^{\infty} c_i \frac{\partial \varphi_i(x)}{\partial x} = \sum_{i=1}^{N} c_i \frac{\partial \varphi_i(x)}{\partial x} + \sum_{i=N+1}^{\infty} c_i \frac{\partial \varphi_i(x)}{\partial x} \tag{17}$$

where $\phi_1(x) = [\varphi_1(x)\,\varphi_2(x) \cdots \varphi_N(x)]^T : \mathbb{R}^n \to \mathbb{R}^N$, and the second terms in these equations converge uniformly to zero as $N \to \infty$. Specifically, the linear subspace generated by the basis set is dense in the Sobolev norm $W^{1,\infty}$ (Adams, Fournier, 2003).

Therefore, assume there exist NN weights W_1 such that the value function $V(x)$ is approximated as

$$V(x) = W_1{}^T \phi_1(x) + \varepsilon(x) \tag{18}$$

with $\phi_1(x) : \mathbb{R}^n \to \mathbb{R}^N$ the NN activation function vector, N the number of neurons in the hidden layer, and $\varepsilon(x)$ the NN approximation error. For approximation in Sobolev space, the NN activation functions $\{\varphi_i(x) : i = 1, N\}$ should be selected so that $\{\varphi_i(x) : i = 1, \infty\}$ provides a complete independent basis set such that $V(x)$ and its derivative are uniformly approximated, e.g., additionally

$$\frac{\partial V}{\partial x} = \left(\frac{\partial \phi_1(x)}{\partial x} \right)^T W_1 + \frac{\partial \varepsilon}{\partial x} = \nabla \phi_1{}^T W_1 + \nabla \varepsilon \tag{19}$$

Then, as the number of hidden-layer neurons $N \to \infty$, the approximation errors $\varepsilon \to 0$, $\nabla \varepsilon \to 0$ uniformly (Abu-Khalaf & Lewis, 2005; Finlayson, 1990). In addition, for fixed N, the NN approximation errors $\varepsilon(x)$, and $\nabla \varepsilon$ are bounded by constants locally (Hornik et al., 1990).

We refer to the NN with weights W_1 that performs VFA as the *critic* NN.

Standard usage of the Weierstrass high-order approximation Theorem uses polynomial approximation. However, non-polynomial basis sets have been considered in the literature (e.g. (Hornik et al., 1990; Sandberg, 1997)). The NN approximation literature has considered a variety of activation functions including sigmoids, tanh, radial basis functions, etc.

Using the NN VFA, considering fixed feedback and disturbance policies $u(x(t)), d(x(t))$, equation (4) becomes

$$H(x, W_1, u, d) = Q(x) + u^T R u - \gamma^2 \|d\|^2 + W_1{}^T \nabla \phi_1 (f(x) + g(x)u(x) + k(x)d(x)) = \varepsilon_H \tag{20}$$

where the residual error is

$$\varepsilon_H = -(\nabla \varepsilon)^T (f + gu + kd)$$

$$= -(C_1 - W_1)^T \nabla \phi_1 (f + gu + kd) - \sum_{i=N+1}^{\infty} c_i \nabla \varphi_i(x)(f + gu + kd) \tag{21}$$

Under the Lipschitz assumption on the dynamics, this residual error is bounded locally.

The following Proposition has been shown in (Abu-Khalaf & Lewis, 2005; Abu-Khalaf & Lewis, 2008).
Define $|v|$ as the magnitude of a scalar v, $\|x\|$ as the vector norm of a vector x, and $\| \|_2$ as the induced matrix 2-norm.
Proposition 1. For any policies $u(x(t)), d(x(t))$ the least-squares solution to (20) exists and is unique for each N. Denote this solution as W_1 and define

$$V_1(x) = W_1^T \phi_1(x) \tag{22}$$

Then, as $N \to \infty$:

a. $\sup|\varepsilon_H| \to 0$
b. $\sup\|W_1 - C_1\|_2 \to 0$
c. $\sup|V_1 - V| \to 0$
d. $\sup\|\nabla V_1 - \nabla V\| \to 0$

■

This result shows that $V_1(x)$ converges uniformly in Sobolev norm $W^{1,\infty}$ (Adams & Fournier, 2003) to the exact solution $V(x)$ to (4) as $N \to \infty$, and the weights W_1 converge to the first N of the weights, C_1, which exactly solve (4).
The effect of the approximation error on the HJI equation (8) is

$$Q(x) + W_1^T \nabla\varphi_1(x) f(x) - \frac{1}{4} W_1^T \nabla\varphi_1(x) g(x) R^{-1} g^T(x) \nabla\varphi_1^T W_1 + \frac{1}{4\gamma^2} W_1^T \nabla\varphi_1(x) kk^T \nabla\varphi_1^T W_1 = \varepsilon_{HJI} \tag{23}$$

where the residual error due to the function approximation error is

$$\varepsilon_{HJI} \equiv -\nabla\varepsilon^T f + \tfrac{1}{2} W_1^T \nabla\varphi_1 g R^{-1} g^T \nabla\varepsilon + \tfrac{1}{4} \nabla\varepsilon^T g R^{-1} g^T \nabla\varepsilon - \tfrac{1}{2\gamma^2} W_1^T \nabla\varphi_1 kk^T \nabla\varepsilon - \tfrac{1}{4\gamma^2} \nabla\varepsilon^T kk^T \nabla\varepsilon \tag{24}$$

It was also shown in (Abu-Khalaf & Lewis, 2005; Abu-Khalaf & Lewis, 2008) that this error converges uniformly to zero as the number of hidden layer units N increases. That is, $\forall \varepsilon > 0, \exists N(\varepsilon): \sup\|\varepsilon_{HJI}\| < \varepsilon, N > N(\varepsilon)$.

3.2 Tuning and convergence of the critic neural network

In this section are addressed the tuning and convergence of the critic NN weights when fixed feedback control and disturbance policies are prescribed. Therefore, the focus is on solving the nonlinear Lyapunov-like equation (4) (e.g. (12)) for a fixed feedback policy u and fixed disturbance policy d.
In fact, this amounts to the *design of an observer for the value function*. Therefore, this algorithm is consistent with adaptive control approaches which first design an observer for the system state and unknown dynamics, and then use this observer in the design of a feedback control.
The ideal weights of the critic NN, W_1 which provide the best approximate solution for (20) are unknown. Therefore, the output of the critic neural network is

$$\hat{V}(x) = \hat{W}_1^T \phi_1(x) \tag{25}$$

where $\hat{W}_1$ are the current estimated values of W_1. The approximate nonlinear Lyapunov-like equation is then

$$H(x,\hat{W}_1,u,d)=\hat{W}_1{}^T\nabla\phi_1(f+gu+kd)+Q(x)+u^T Ru-\gamma^2\|d\|^2=e_1 \tag{26}$$

with e_1 a residual equation error. In view of Proposition 1, define the critic weight estimation error

$$\tilde{W}_1=W_1-\hat{W}_1.$$

Then,

$$e_1=-\tilde{W}_1{}^T\nabla\phi_1(f+gu)+\varepsilon_H.$$

Given any feedback control policy u, it is desired to select $\hat{W}_1$ to minimize the squared residual error

$$E_1=\tfrac{1}{2}e_1{}^T e_1.$$

Then $\hat{W}_1(t)\to W_1$ and $e_1\to\varepsilon_H$. Select the tuning law for the critic weights as the normalized gradient descent algorithm

$$\dot{\hat{W}}_1=-a_1\frac{\partial E_1}{\partial\hat{W}_1}=-a_1\frac{\sigma_1}{(1+\sigma_1{}^T\sigma_1)^2}[\sigma_1{}^T\hat{W}_1+h^T h+u^T Ru-\gamma^2\|d\|^2] \tag{27}$$

where $\sigma_1=\nabla\phi_1(f+gu+kd)$. This is a nonstandard modified Levenberg-Marquardt algorithm where $(\sigma_1^T\sigma_1+1)^2$ is used for normalization instead of $(\sigma_1^T\sigma_1+1)$. This is required in the theorem proofs, where one needs both appearances of $\sigma_1/(1+\sigma_1^T\sigma_1)$ in (27) to be bounded (Ioannou & Fidan, 2006; Tao, 2003).
Note that, from (20),

$$Q(x)+u^T Ru-\gamma^2\|d\|^2=-W_1{}^T\nabla\varphi_1(f+gu+kd)+\varepsilon_H. \tag{28}$$

Substituting (28) in (27) and, with the notation

$$\bar{\sigma}_1=\sigma_1/(\sigma_1^T\sigma_1+1)\ ,\ m_s=1+\sigma_1^T\sigma_1 \tag{29}$$

we obtain the dynamics of the critic weight estimation error as

$$\dot{\tilde{W}}_1=-a_1\bar{\sigma}_1\bar{\sigma}_1{}^T\tilde{W}_1+a_1\bar{\sigma}_1\frac{\varepsilon_H}{m_s}. \tag{30}$$

To guarantee convergence of $\hat{W}_1$ to W_1, the next Persistence of Excitation (PE) assumption and associated technical lemmas are required.
Persistence of Excitation (PE) Assumption. Let the signal $\bar{\sigma}_1$ be persistently exciting over the interval $[t,t+T]$, *i.e.* there exist constants $\beta_1>0$, $\beta_2>0$, $T>0$ such that, for all t,

$$\beta_1 \mathrm{I} \le S_0 \equiv \int_t^{t+T} \bar{\sigma}_1(\tau)\bar{\sigma}_1^{\mathrm{T}}(\tau)d\tau \le \beta_2 \mathrm{I}. \tag{31}$$

with I the identity matrix of appropriate dimensions.
The PE assumption is needed in adaptive control if one desires to perform system identification using e.g. RLS (Ioannou & Fidan, 2006; Tao, 2003). It is needed here because one effectively desires to identify the critic parameters to approximate $V(x)$.
The properties of tuning algorithm (27) are given in the subsequent results. They are proven in (Vamvoudakis & Lewis, 2010).
Technical Lemma 1. Consider the error dynamics system with output defined as

$$\dot{\tilde{W}}_1 = -a_1\bar{\sigma}_1\bar{\sigma}_1^{\mathrm{T}}\tilde{W}_1 + a_1\bar{\sigma}_1\frac{\varepsilon_H}{m_s}$$

$$y = \bar{\sigma}_1^{T}\tilde{W}_1 . \tag{32}$$

The PE condition (31) is equivalent to the uniform complete observability (UCO) (Lewis, Jagannathan, Yesildirek, 1999) of this system, that is there exist constants $\beta_3 > 0$, $\beta_4 > 0$, $\mathrm{T} > 0$ such that, for all *t*,

$$\beta_3 \mathrm{I} \le S_1 \equiv \int_t^{t+T} \Phi^T(\tau,t)\bar{\sigma}_1(\tau)\bar{\sigma}_1^{\mathrm{T}}(\tau)\Phi(\tau,t)d\tau \le \beta_4 \mathrm{I}. \tag{33}$$

with $\Phi(t_1,t_0), t_0 \le t_1$ the state transition matrix of (32) and I the identity matrix of appropriate dimensions.

■

Technical Lemma 2. Consider the error dynamics system (32). Let the signal $\bar{\sigma}_1$ be persistently exciting. Then:

a. The system (32) is exponentially stable. In fact if $\varepsilon_H = 0$ then $\left\|\tilde{W}(k\mathrm{T})\right\| \le e^{-\alpha kT}\left\|\tilde{W}(0)\right\|$ with

$$\alpha = -\frac{1}{\mathrm{T}}\ln(\sqrt{1-2a_1\beta_3}) . \tag{34}$$

b. Let $\left\|\varepsilon_H\right\| \le \varepsilon_{\max}$ and $\left\|y\right\| \le y_{\max}$. Then $\left\|\tilde{W}_1\right\|$ converges exponentially to the residual set

$$\tilde{W}_1(t) \le \frac{\sqrt{\beta_2 \mathrm{T}}}{\beta_1}\left\{\left[y_{\max} + \delta\beta_2 a_1\left(\varepsilon_{\max} + y_{\max}\right)\right]\right\} . \tag{35}$$

where δ is a positive constant of the order of 1.

■

The next result shows that the tuning algorithm (27) is effective under the PE condition, in that the weights $\hat{W}_1$ converge to the actual unknown weights W_1 which solve the nonlinear Lyapunov-like equation (20) in a least-squares sense for the given feedback and disturbance policies $u(x(t)), d(x(t))$. That is, (25) converges close to the actual value function of the current policies. The proof is in (Vamvoudakis & Lewis, 2010).

Theorem 1. Let $u(x(t)), d(x(t))$ be any bounded policies. Let tuning for the critic NN be provided by (27) and assume that $\bar{\sigma}_1$ is persistently exciting. Let the residual error in (20) be bounded $\|\varepsilon_H\| < \varepsilon_{\max}$. Then the critic parameter error converges exponentially with decay factor given by (34) to the residual set

$$\tilde{W}_1(t) \leq \frac{\sqrt{\beta_2 \mathrm{T}}}{\beta_1}\left\{\left[1 + 2\delta\beta_2 a_1\right]\varepsilon_{\max}\right\}. \tag{36}$$

■

Remark 1. Note that, as $N \rightarrow \infty$, $\varepsilon_H \rightarrow 0$ uniformly (Abu-Khalaf & Lewis, 2005; Abu-Khalaf & Lewis, 2008). This means that $\varepsilon_{\max}$ decreases as the number of hidden layer neurons in (25) increases.

Remark 2. This theorem requires the assumption that the feedback policy $u(x(t))$ and the disturbance policy $d(x(t))$ are bounded, since the policies appear in (21). In the upcoming Theorems 2 and 3 this restriction is removed.

3.3 Action and disturbance neural network

It is important to define the neural network structure and the NN estimation errors properly for the control and disturbance or an adaptive algorithm cannot be developed. To determine a rigorously justified form for the actor and the disturbance NN, consider one step of the Policy Iteration algorithm (12)-(14). Suppose that the solution $V(x)$ to the nonlinear Lyapunov equation (12) for given control and disturbance policies is smooth and given by (16). Then, according to (17) and (13), (14) one has for the policy and the disturbance updates:

$$u = -\frac{1}{2}R^{-1}g^T(x)\sum_{i=1}^{\infty} c_i \nabla\varphi_i(x) \tag{37}$$

$$d = \frac{1}{2\gamma^2}k^T(x)\sum_{i=1}^{\infty} c_i \nabla\varphi_i(x) \tag{38}$$

for some unknown coefficients c_i. Then one has the following result.

The following proposition is proved in (Abu-Khalaf & Lewis, 2008) for constrained inputs. Non-constrained inputs are easier to prove.

Proposition 2. Let the least-squares solution to (20) be W_1 and define

$$u_1 = -\frac{1}{2}R^{-1}g^T(x)\nabla V_1(x) = -\frac{1}{2}R^{-1}g^T(x)\nabla\phi_1{}^T(x)W_1 \tag{39}$$

$$d_1 = \frac{1}{2\gamma^2}k^T(x)\nabla V_1(x) = \frac{1}{2\gamma^2}k^T(x)\nabla\phi_1{}^T(x)W_1 \tag{40}$$

with V_1 defined in (22). Then, as $N \rightarrow \infty$:

a. $\sup\|u_1 - u\| \rightarrow 0$

b. $\sup\|d_1 - d\| \rightarrow 0$

c. There exists a number of NN hidden layer neurons N_0 such that u_1 and d_1 stabilize the system (1) for $N>N_0$.

■

In light of this result, the ideal feedback and disturbance policy updates are taken as (39), (40) with W_1 unknown. Therefore, define the feedback policy in the form of an action neural network which computes the control input in the structured form

$$\hat{u}(x) = -\tfrac{1}{2}R^{-1}g^T(x)\nabla\phi_1{}^T\hat{W}_2, \tag{41}$$

where $\hat{W}_2$ denotes the current estimated values of the ideal NN weights W_1. Define the actor NN estimation error as

$$\tilde{W}_2 = W_1 - \hat{W}_2 \tag{42}$$

Likewise, define the disturbance in the form of a disturbance neural network which computes the disturbance input in the structured form

$$\hat{d}(x) = \tfrac{1}{2\gamma^2}k^T(x)\nabla\phi_1{}^T\hat{W}_3, \tag{43}$$

where $\hat{W}_3$ denotes the current estimated values of the ideal NN weights W_1. Define the disturbance NN estimation error as

$$\tilde{W}_3 = W_1 - \hat{W}_3 \tag{44}$$

4. Online solution of 2-player zero-sum games using neural networks

This section presents our main results. An online adaptive PI algorithm is given for online solution of the zero-sum game problem which involves simultaneous, or synchronous, tuning of critic, actor, and disturbance neural networks. That is, the weights of all three neural networks are tuned at the same time. This approach is a version of Generalized Policy Iteration (GPI), as introduced in (Sutton & Barto, 1998). In the standard Policy Iteration algorithm (12)-(14), the critic and actor NNs are tuned sequentially, e.g. one at a time, with the weights of the other NNs being held constant. By contrast, we *tune all NN simultaneously in real-time.*

The next definition and facts complete the machinery required for the main results.

Definition 3. (Lewis, Jagannathan, Yesildirek, 1999) (UUB) A time signal $\zeta(t)$ is said to be uniformly ultimately bounded (UUB) if there exists a compact set $S \subset \mathbb{R}^n$ so that for all $\zeta(0) \in S$ there exists a bound B and a time $T(B,\zeta(0))$ such that $\|\zeta(t)\| \le B$ for all $t \ge t_0 + T$.

Facts 1.

a. $g(.), k(.)$ are bounded by constants:

$$\|g(x)\| < b_g, \quad \|k(x)\| < b_k$$

b. The NN approximation error and its gradient are bounded locally so that

$$\|\varepsilon\| < b_\varepsilon, \quad \|\nabla\varepsilon\| < b_{\varepsilon_x}$$

c. The NN activation functions and their gradients are bounded locally so that

$$\|\phi_1(x)\| < b_\phi, \; \|\nabla\phi_1(x)\| < b_{\phi_x}$$

■

The main Theorems are now given, which provide the tuning laws for the actor, critic and disturbance neural networks that guarantee convergence of the synchronous online zero-sum game PI algorithm in real-time to the game saddle point solution, while guaranteeing closed-loop stability.

Theorem 2. System stability and convergence of NN weights. Let the dynamics be given by (1), the critic NN be given by (25), the control input be given by actor NN (41) and the disturbance input be given by disturbance NN (43). Let tuning for the critic NN be provided by

$$\dot{\hat{W}}_1 = -a_1 \frac{\sigma_2}{(\sigma_2^T\sigma_2+1)^2}[\sigma_2{}^T\hat{W}_1 + Q(x) - \gamma^2\left\|\hat{d}\right\|^2 + \hat{u}^T R\hat{u}] \tag{45}$$

where $\sigma_2 = \nabla\phi_1(f + g\hat{u} + k\hat{d})$. Let the actor NN be tuned as

$$\dot{\hat{W}}_2 = -\alpha_2\left\{(F_2\hat{W}_2 - F_1\bar{\sigma}_2^T\hat{W}_1) - \frac{1}{4}\bar{D}_1(x)\hat{W}_2 m^T(x)\hat{W}_1\right\} \tag{46}$$

and the disturbance NN be tuned as

$$\dot{\hat{W}}_3 = -\alpha_3\left\{\left(F_4\hat{W}_3 - F_3\bar{\sigma}_2^T\hat{W}_1\right) + \frac{1}{4\gamma^2}\bar{E}_1(x)\hat{W}_3 m^T\hat{W}_1\right\} \tag{47}$$

where $\bar{D}_1(x) \equiv \nabla\phi_1(x)g(x)R^{-1}g^T(x)\nabla\phi_1{}^T(x)$, $\bar{E}_1(x) \equiv \nabla\phi_1(x)kk^T\nabla\phi_1{}^T(x)$, $m \equiv \dfrac{\sigma_2}{(\sigma_2{}^T\sigma_2+1)^2}$, and $F_1 > 0, F_2 > 0, F_3 > 0, F_4 > 0$ are tuning parameters. Let Facts 1 hold and let $Q(x) > 0$. Suppose that $\bar{\sigma}_2 = \sigma_2/(\sigma_2^T\sigma_2+1)$ is persistently exciting. Let the tuning parameters be selected as detailed in the proof. Then there exists an N_0 such that, for the number of hidden layer units $N > N_0$ the closed-loop system state, the critic NN error $\tilde{W}_1$, the actor NN error $\tilde{W}_2$ and the disturbance NN error $\tilde{W}_3$ are UUB.

Proof: See appendix.

■

Remark 3. See the comments following equation (24). Let $\varepsilon > 0$ and let N_0 be the number of hidden layer units above which $\sup\|\varepsilon_{HJI}\| < \varepsilon$. In the proof it is seen that the theorem holds for $N > N_0$.

Remark 4. The theorem shows that PE is needed for proper identification of the value function by the critic NN, and that nonstandard tuning algorithms are required for the actor and the disturbance NN to guarantee stability.

Remark 5. The assumption $Q(x) > 0$ is sufficient but not necessary for this result. If this condition is replaced by zero state observability, the proof still goes through, however it is tedious and does not add insight. The method used would be the technique used in the proof of technical Lemma 2 Part a in (Vamvoudakis & Lewis), or the standard methods of (Ioannou & Fidan, 2006; Tao, 2003).

Remark 6. The tuning parameters F_1, F_2, F_3, F_4 in (46), and (47) must be selected to make the matrix M in (A.10) positive definite.

Theorem 3. Exponential Convergence and Nash equilibrium. Suppose the hypotheses of Theorem 1 and Theorem 2,. Then Theorem 1 holds with

$$\varepsilon_{\max} > \frac{1}{4}\left\|\tilde{W}_2\right\|^2\left\|\frac{\bar{D}_1}{m_s}\right\| - \frac{1}{4\gamma^2}\left\|\tilde{W}_3\right\|^2\left\|\frac{\bar{E}_1}{m_s}\right\| + \varepsilon\left\|\frac{1}{m_s}\right\|$$

where $m_s = \sigma_2{}^T\sigma_2 + 1$, so that exponential convergence of $\hat{W}_1$ to the approximate optimal critic value W_1 is obtained. Then:

a. $H(x,\hat{W}_1,\hat{u}_1,\hat{d}_1)$ is UUB. That is, $\hat{W}_1$ converges to the approximate HJI solution, the value of the ZS game. Where

$$\hat{u}_1 = -\frac{1}{2}R^{-1}g^T(x)\nabla\phi_1{}^T(x)\hat{W}_1 \tag{48}$$

$$\hat{d}_1 = \frac{1}{2\gamma^2}k^T(x)\nabla\phi_1{}^T(x)\hat{W}_1 \tag{49}$$

b. $\hat{u}(x),\hat{d}(x)$ (see (41) and (43)) converges to the approximate Nash equilibrium solution of the ZS game.

Proof. Consider the UUB weights $\tilde{W}_1$, $\tilde{W}_2$ and $\tilde{W}_3$ as proved in Theorem 2.

a. The approximate HJI equation is

$$H(x,\hat{W}_1) = Q(x) + \hat{W}_1{}^T\nabla\varphi_1(x)f(x) - \frac{1}{4}\hat{W}_1{}^T D_1\hat{W}_1 + \frac{1}{4\gamma^2}\hat{W}_1{}^T E_1\hat{W}_1 - \hat{\varepsilon}_{HJI} \tag{50}$$

After adding zero we have

$$H(x,\hat{W}_1) = \tilde{W}_1{}^T\nabla\varphi_1(x)f(x) - \frac{1}{4}\tilde{W}_1{}^T D_1\tilde{W}_1 - \frac{1}{2}\tilde{W}_1{}^T D_1\hat{W}_1 + \frac{1}{4\gamma^2}\tilde{W}_1{}^T E_1\tilde{W}_1 + \frac{1}{2\gamma^2}\tilde{W}_1{}^T E_1\hat{W}_1 - \varepsilon_{HJI} \tag{51}$$

But

$$\hat{W}_1 = -\tilde{W}_1 + W_1 \tag{52}$$

After taking norms in (52) and letting $\left\|W_1\right\| < W_{1\max}$ one has

$$\left\|\hat{W}_1\right\| = \left\|-\tilde{W}_1 + W_1\right\| \le \left\|\tilde{W}_1\right\| + \left\|W_1\right\| \le \left\|\tilde{W}_1\right\| + W_{\max} \tag{53}$$

Now (51) becomes by taking into account (53),

$$\left\|H(x,\hat{W}_1)\right\| \le \left\|\tilde{W}_1\right\|\left\|\nabla\varphi_1(x)\right\|\left\|f(x)\right\| - \frac{1}{4}\left\|\tilde{W}_1\right\|^2\left\|\bar{D}_1\right\| - \frac{1}{2}\left\|\tilde{W}_1\right\|\left\|\bar{D}_1\right\|\left(\left\|\tilde{W}_1\right\| + W_{\max}\right)$$

$$+\frac{1}{4\gamma^2}\left\|\tilde{W}_1\right\|^2\left\|\bar{E}_1\right\|+\frac{1}{2\gamma^2}\left\|\tilde{W}_1\right\|\left\|\bar{E}_1\right\|\left(\left\|\tilde{W}_1\right\|+W_{\max}\right)+\left\|\varepsilon_{HJI}\right\| \quad (54)$$

Let Facts 1 hold and also $\sup\left\|\varepsilon_{HJI}\right\|<\varepsilon$ then (54) becomes

$$\begin{aligned}\left\|H(x,\hat{W}_1)\right\| \le b_{\phi_x} b_f \left\|\tilde{W}_1\right\|\left\|x\right\|+\frac{1}{4}\left\|\tilde{W}_1\right\|^2\left\|\bar{D}_1\right\|+\frac{1}{2}\left\|\tilde{W}_1\right\|\left\|\bar{D}_1\right\|\left(\left\|\tilde{W}_1\right\|+W_{\max}\right)\\ +\frac{1}{4\gamma^2}\left\|\tilde{W}_1\right\|^2\left\|\bar{E}_1\right\|+\frac{1}{2\gamma^2}\left\|\tilde{W}_1\right\|\left\|\bar{E}_1\right\|\left(\left\|\tilde{W}_1\right\|+W_{\max}\right)+\varepsilon\end{aligned} \quad (55)$$

All the signals on the right hand side of (55) are UUB. So $\left\|H(x,\hat{W}_1)\right\|$ is UUB and convergence to the approximate HJI solution is obtained.

b. According to Theorem 1 and equations (39), (40) and (41), (43), $\left\|\hat{u}-u_1\right\|$ and $\left\|\hat{d}-d_1\right\|$ are UUB because $\left\|\hat{W}_2-W_1\right\|$ and $\left\|\hat{W}_3-W_1\right\|$ are UUB

So the pair $\hat{u}(x),\hat{d}(x)$ gives the Nash equilibrium solution of the zero-sum game.
This completes the proof.

■

Remark 7. The theorems make no mention of finding the minimum nonnegative solution to the HJI. However they do guarantee convergence to a solution $(u(x),d(x))$ such that $(f(x)+g(x)u(x)+k(x)d(x))$ is stable. This is only accomplished by the minimal nonnegative HJI solution. Practical implementation, in view of the Policy Iteration Algorithm, would start with initial weights of zero in the disturbance NN (43). NN usage suggests starting with the initial control NN weights in (41) randomly selected and nonzero.
Note that the dynamics is required to be known to implement this algorithm in that $\sigma_2=\nabla\phi_1(f+g\hat{u}+k\hat{d})$, $\bar{D}_1(x)$, $\bar{E}_1(x)$ and (41), (43) depend on *f(x), g(x), k(x)*.

5. Simulations

Here we present simulations of a linear and a nonlinear system to show that the game can be solved ONLINE by learning in real time, using the method of this chapter. We also present Simulation B to show that that one learns FASTER if one has an opponent. *That is, the two-player online game converges faster than an equivalent online 1-player (optimal control) problem when all the NNs are tuned online in real time.*

5.1 Linear system

Consider the continuous-time F16 aircraft plant with quadratic cost function used in (Stevens & Lewis, 2003). The system state vector is $x=[\alpha \quad q \quad \delta_e]$, where α denotes the angle of attack, q is the pitch rate and δ_e is the elevator deflection angle. The control input is the elevator actuator voltage and the disturbance is wind gusts on angle of attack. One has the dynamics $\dot{x}=Ax+Bu+Kd$,

$$\dot{x}=\begin{bmatrix}-1.01887 & 0.90506 & -0.00215\\ 0.82225 & -1.07741 & -0.17555\\ 0 & 0 & -1\end{bmatrix}x+\begin{bmatrix}0\\0\\1\end{bmatrix}u+\begin{bmatrix}1\\0\\0\end{bmatrix}d$$

where Q and R in the cost function are identity matrices of appropriate dimensions and $\gamma = 5$. In this linear case the solution of the HJI equation is given by the solution of the game algebraic Riccati equation (GARE)

$$A^T P + PA + Q - PBR^{-1}B^T P + \frac{1}{\gamma^2} PKK^T P = 0$$

Since the value is quadratic in the LQR case, the critic NN basis set $\phi_1(x)$ was selected as the quadratic vector in the state components $x \otimes x$ with $\otimes$ the Kronecker product. Redundant terms were removed to leave $n(n+1)/2 = 6$ components. Solving the GARE gives the parameters of the optimal critic as $W_1^* = [1.6573 \quad 1.3954 \quad -0.1661 \quad 1.6573 \quad -0.1804 \quad 0.4371]^T$ which are the components of the Riccati solution matrix P.

The synchronous zero-sum game PI algorithm is implemented as in Theorem 2. PE was ensured by adding a small probing noise to the control and the disturbance input. Figure 1 shows the critic parameters, denoted by $\hat{W}_1 = [W_{c1} \quad W_{c2} \quad W_{c3} \quad W_{c4} \quad W_{c5} \quad W_{c6}]^T$ converging to the optimal values. In fact after 600s the critic parameters converged to $\hat{W}_1(t_f) = [1.7090 \quad 1.3303 \quad -0.1629 \quad 1.7354 \quad -0.1730 \quad 0.4468]^T$. The actor parameters after 600s converge to the values of $\hat{W}_2(t_f) = [1.7090 \quad 1.3303 \quad -0.1629 \quad 1.7354 \quad -0.1730 \quad 0.4468]^T$. The disturbance parameters after 600s converge to the values of $\hat{W}_3(t_f) = [1.7090 \quad 1.3303 \quad -0.1629 \quad 1.7354 \quad -0.1730 \quad 0.4468]^T$.

Then, the actor NN is given as

$$\hat{u}_2(x) = -\frac{1}{2} R^{-1} \begin{bmatrix} 0 \\ 0 \\ 1 \end{bmatrix}^T \begin{bmatrix} 2x_1 & 0 & 0 \\ x_2 & x_1 & 0 \\ x_3 & 0 & x_1 \\ 0 & 2x_2 & 0 \\ 0 & x_3 & x_2 \\ 0 & 0 & 2x_3 \end{bmatrix}^T \begin{bmatrix} 1.7090 \\ 1.3303 \\ -0.1629 \\ 1.7354 \\ -0.1730 \\ 0.4468 \end{bmatrix}.$$

Then, the disturbance NN is given as

$$\hat{d}(x) = \frac{1}{2\gamma^2} \begin{bmatrix} 0 \\ 0 \\ 1 \end{bmatrix}^T \begin{bmatrix} 2x_1 & 0 & 0 \\ x_2 & x_1 & 0 \\ x_3 & 0 & x_1 \\ 0 & 2x_2 & 0 \\ 0 & x_3 & x_2 \\ 0 & 0 & 2x_3 \end{bmatrix}^T \begin{bmatrix} 1.7090 \\ 1.3303 \\ -0.1629 \\ 1.7354 \\ -0.1730 \\ 0.4468 \end{bmatrix}.$$

The evolution of the system states is presented in Figure 2. One can see that after 300s convergence of the NN weights in critic, actor and disturbance has occurred.

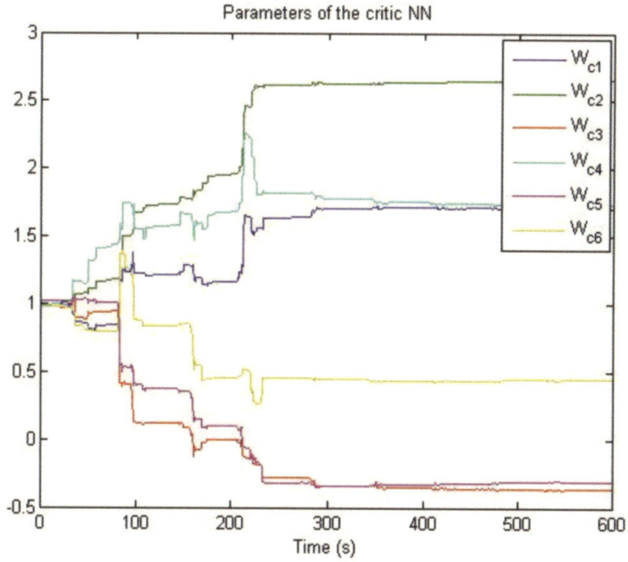

Fig. 1. Convergence of the critic parameters to the parameters of the optimal critic.

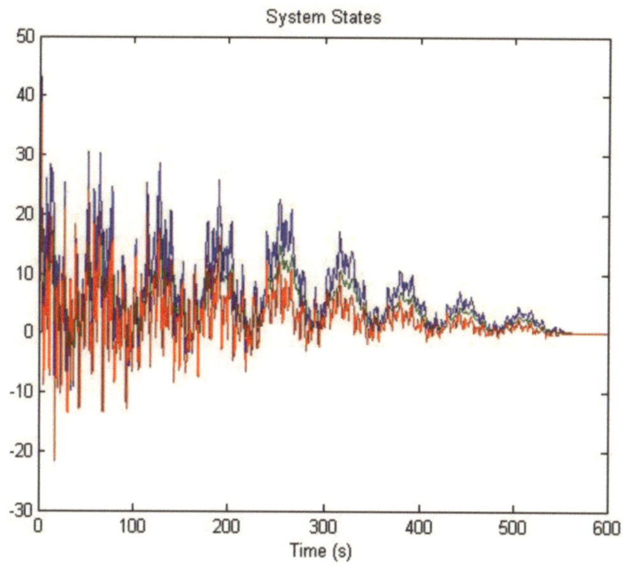

Fig. 2. Evolution of the system states for the duration of the experinment.

5.2 Single player linear system

The purpose of this example is to show that one learns FASTER if one has an opponent. That is, the online two-player game converges faster than an equivalent online 1-player (optimal control) problem. In this example, we use the method for online solution of the optimal control problem presented in (Vamvoudakis & Lewis, 2010). That is, Theorem 2 without the disturbance NN (47).

Consider the continuous-time F16 aircraft plant described before but with $d = 0$. Solving the ARE with Q and R identity matrices of appropriate dimensions, gives the parameters of the optimal critic as

$$W_1^* = [1.4245 \quad 1.1682 \quad -0.1352 \quad 1.4361 \quad -0.1516 \quad 0.4329]^T .$$

Figure 3 shows the critic parameters, denoted by $\hat{W}_1 = [W_{c1} \quad W_{c2} \quad W_{c3} \; W_{c4} \quad W_{c5} \quad W_{c6}]^T$ converging to the optimal values. In fact after 800s the critic parameters converged to $\hat{W}_1(t_f) = [1.4270 \quad 1.1654 \quad -0.1367 \quad 1.4387 \quad -0.1496 \; 0.4323]^T$. The actor parameters after 800s converge to the values of $\hat{W}_2(t_f) = [1.4270 \quad 1.1654 \quad -0.1367 \quad 1.4387 \quad -0.1496 \; 0.4323]^T$.
In comparison with part A, it is very clear that the two-player zero-sum game algorithm has faster convergence skills than the single-player game (e.g. optimal control problem) by a factor of two. As a conclusion the critic NN learns faster when there is an oponent for the control input, namely a disturbance.

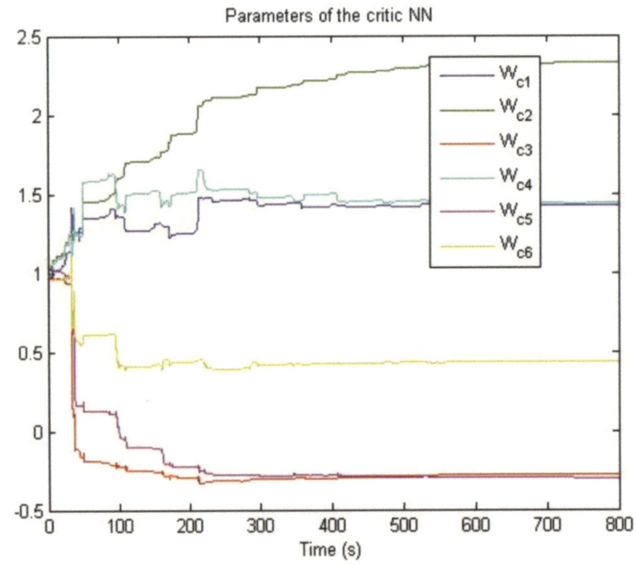

Fig. 3. Convergence of the critic parameters to the parameters of the optimal critic.

5.3 Nonlinear system

Consider the following affine in control input nonlinear system, with a quadratic cost constructed as in (Nevistic & Primbs, 1996; D. Vrabie, Vamvoudakis & Lewis, 2009)

$$\dot{x} = f(x) + g(x)u + k(x)d, \; x \in \mathbb{R}^2$$

where

$$f(x) = \begin{bmatrix} -x_1 + x_2 \\ -x_1^3 - x_2^3 + 0.25x_2(\cos(2x_1)+2)^2 - 0.25x_2 \frac{1}{\gamma^2}(\sin(4x_1)+2)^2 \end{bmatrix}$$

$$g(x) = \begin{bmatrix} 0 \\ \cos(2x_1)+2 \end{bmatrix}, \quad k(x) = \begin{bmatrix} 0 \\ (\sin(4x_1)+2) \end{bmatrix}.$$

One selects $Q = \begin{bmatrix} 1 & 0 \\ 0 & 1 \end{bmatrix}, R = 1, \gamma = 8.$

The optimal value function is $V^*(x) = \frac{1}{4}x_1^{\ 4} + \frac{1}{2}x_2^{\ 2}$ the optimal control signal is $u^*(x) = -(\cos(2x_1) + 2)x_2$ and $d^*(x) = \frac{1}{\gamma^2}(\sin(4x_1) + 2)x_2$.

One selects the critic NN vector activation function as

$$\varphi_1(x) = [x_1^{\ 2} \quad x_2^2 \quad x_1^{\ 4} \quad x_2^{\ 4}]$$

Figure 4 shows the critic parameters, denoted by

$$\hat{W}_1 = [W_{c1} \quad W_{c2} \quad W_{c3} \quad W_{c4}]^T$$

by using the synchronous zero-sum game algorithm. After convergence at about 80s have

$$\hat{W}_1(t_f) = [0.0008 \quad 0.4999 \quad 0.2429 \quad 0.0032]^T$$

The actor parameters after 80s converge to the values of

$$\hat{W}_2(t_f) = [0.0008 \quad 0.4999 \quad 0.2429 \quad 0.0032]^T,$$

and the disturbance parameters after 300s converge to the values of

$$\hat{W}_3(t_f) = [0.0008 \quad 0.4999 \quad 0.2429 \quad 0.0032]^T.$$

So that the actor NN

$$\hat{u}_2(x) = -\tfrac{1}{2}R^{-1}\begin{bmatrix} 0 \\ \cos(2x_1) + 2 \end{bmatrix}^T \begin{bmatrix} 2x_1 & 0 \\ 0 & 2x_2 \\ 4x_1^3 & 0 \\ 0 & 4x_2^3 \end{bmatrix}^T \begin{bmatrix} 0.0008 \\ 0.4999 \\ 0.2429 \\ 0.0032 \end{bmatrix}$$

also converged to the optimal control, and the disturbance NN

$$\hat{d}(x) = \frac{1}{2\gamma^2}\begin{bmatrix} 0 \\ \sin(4x_1) + 2 \end{bmatrix}^T \begin{bmatrix} 2x_1 & 0 \\ 0 & 2x_2 \\ 4x_1^3 & 0 \\ 0 & 4x_2^3 \end{bmatrix}^T \begin{bmatrix} 0.0008 \\ 0.4999 \\ 0.2429 \\ 0.0032 \end{bmatrix}$$

also converged to the optimal disturbance.

The evolution of the system states is presented in Figure 5. Figure 6 shows the optimal value function. The identified value function given by $\hat{V}_1(x) = \hat{W}_1^T \phi_1(x)$ is virtually indistinguishable from the exact solution and so is not plotted. In fact, Figure 7 shows the 3-

D plot of the difference between the approximated value function and the optimal one. This error is close to zero. Good approximation of the actual value function is being evolved. Figure 8 shows the 3-D plot of the difference between the approximated control, by using the online algorithm, and the optimal one. This error is close to zero.
Finally Figure 9 shows the 3-D plot of the difference between the approximated disturbance, by using the online algorithm, and the optimal one. This error is close to zero.

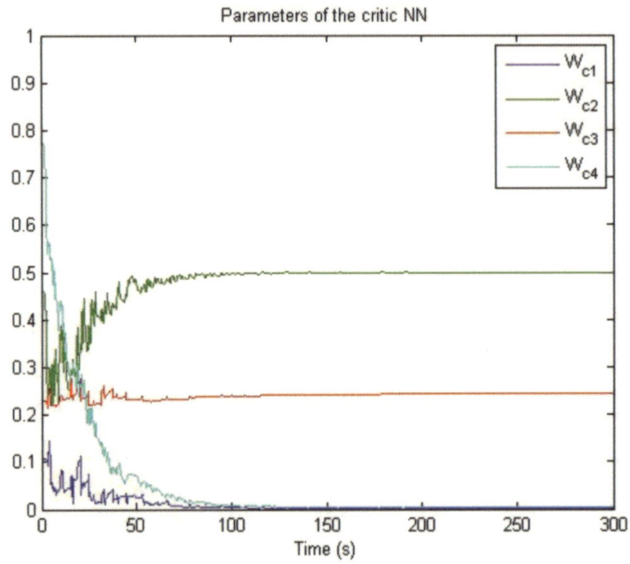

Fig. 4. Convergence of the critic parameters.

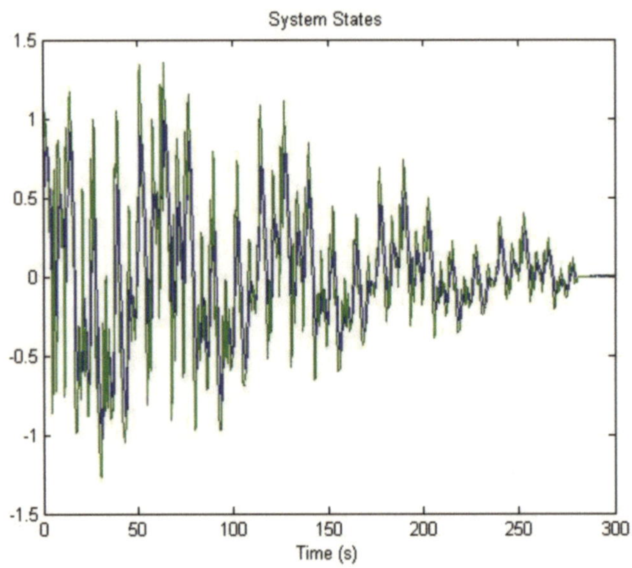

Fig. 5. Evolution of the system states.

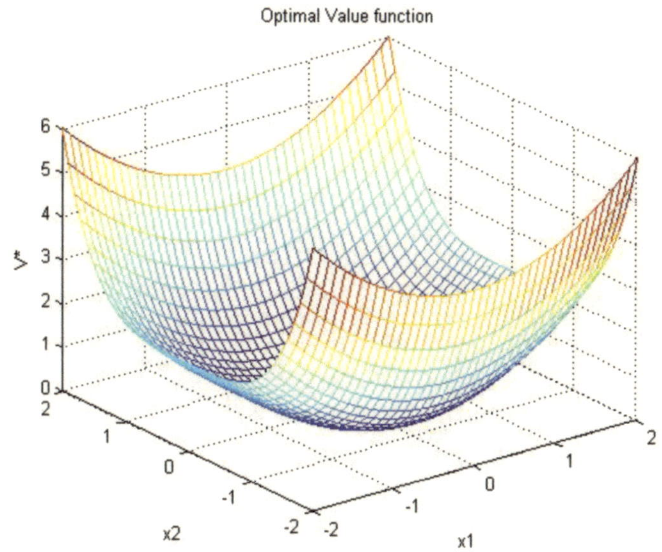

Fig. 6. Optimal Value function.

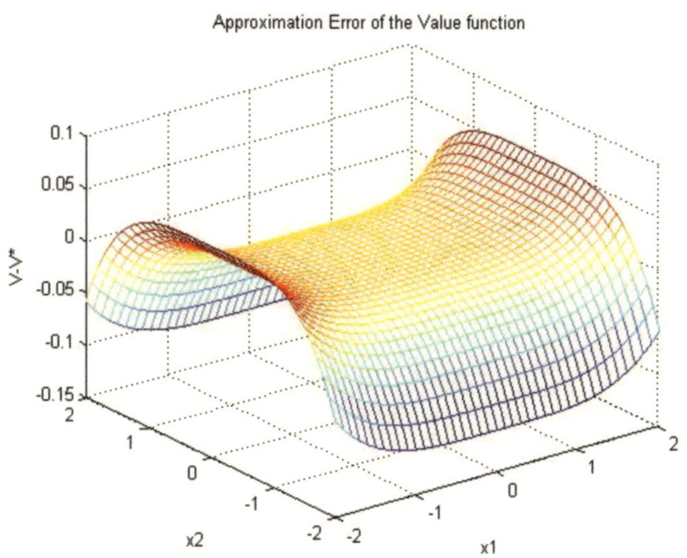

Fig. 7. 3D plot of the approximation error for the value function.

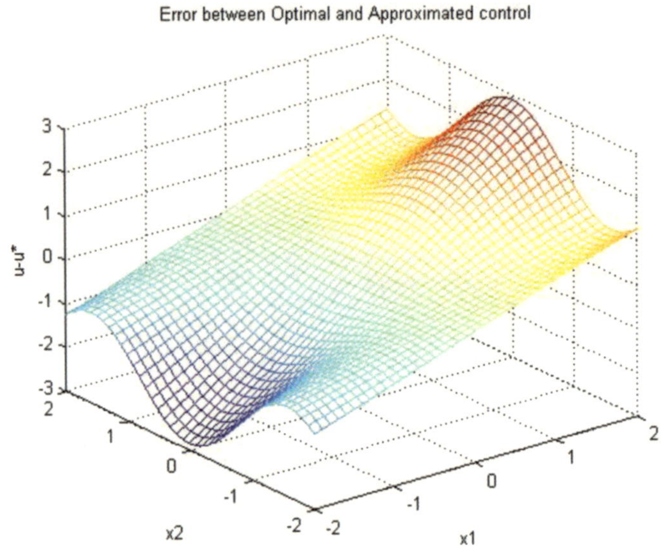

Fig. 8. 3D plot of the approximation error for the control.

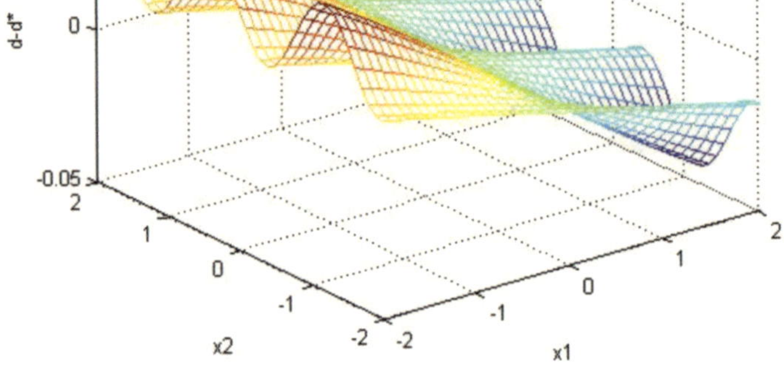

Fig. 9. 3D plot of the approximation error for the disturbance.

6. Appendix

Proof for Theorem 2: The convergence proof is based on Lyapunov analysis.
We consider the Lyapunov function

$$L(t) = V(x) + \frac{1}{2}tr(\tilde{W}_1^{\ T} a_1^{-1}\tilde{W}_1) + \frac{1}{2}tr(\tilde{W}_2^{\ T} a_2^{-1}\tilde{W}_2) + \frac{1}{2}tr(\tilde{W}_3^{\ T} a_3^{-1}\tilde{W}_3). \quad \text{(A.1)}$$

The derivative of the Lyapunov function is given by

$$\dot{L}(x) = \dot{V}(x) + \tilde{W}_1^{\ T}\alpha_1^{-1}\dot{\tilde{W}}_1 + \tilde{W}_2^{\ T}\alpha_2^{-1}\dot{\tilde{W}}_2 + \tilde{W}_3^{\ T}\alpha_3^{-1}\dot{\tilde{W}}_3 \quad \text{(A.2)}$$

First term is,

$$\dot{V}(x) = W_1^{\ T}\left(\nabla\phi_1 f(x) - \frac{1}{2}\bar{D}_1(x)\hat{W}_2 + \frac{1}{2\gamma^2}\bar{E}_1(x)\hat{W}_3\right) + \nabla\varepsilon^T(x)\left(f(x) - \frac{1}{2}g(x)R^{-1}g^T(x)\nabla\phi_1^{\ T}\hat{W}_2 + \frac{1}{2\gamma^2}kk^T\nabla\phi_1^{\ T}\hat{W}_3\right).$$

Then

$$\begin{aligned}\dot{V}(x) &= W_1^{\ T}\left(\nabla\phi_1 f(x) - \frac{1}{2}\bar{D}_1(x)\hat{W}_2 + \frac{1}{2\gamma^2}\bar{E}_1(x)\hat{W}_3\right) + \varepsilon_1(x)\\ &= W_1^{\ T}\nabla\phi_1 f(x) + \frac{1}{2}W_1^{\ T}\bar{D}_1(x)\left(W_1 - \hat{W}_2\right) - \frac{1}{2}W_1^{\ T}\bar{D}_1(x)W_1\\ &\quad - \frac{1}{2\gamma^2}W_1^{\ T}\bar{E}_1(x)\left(W_1 - \hat{W}_3\right) + \frac{1}{2\gamma^2}W_1^{\ T}\bar{E}_1(x)W_1 + \varepsilon_1(x)\end{aligned}$$

$$\begin{aligned}&= W_1^{\ T}\nabla\phi_1 f(x) + \frac{1}{2}W_1^{\ T}\bar{D}_1(x)\tilde{W}_2 - \frac{1}{2}W_1^{\ T}\bar{D}_1(x)W_1 - \frac{1}{2\gamma^2}W_1^{\ T}\bar{E}_1(x)\tilde{W}_3 + \frac{1}{2\gamma^2}W_1^{\ T}\bar{E}_1(x)W_1 + \varepsilon_1(x)\\ &= W_1^{\ T}\sigma_1 + \frac{1}{2}W_1^{\ T}\bar{D}_1(x)\tilde{W}_2 - \frac{1}{2\gamma^2}W_1^{\ T}\bar{E}_1(x)\tilde{W}_3 + \varepsilon_1(x)\end{aligned}$$

where $\varepsilon_1(x) \equiv \dot{\varepsilon}(x) = \nabla\varepsilon^T(x)(f(x) - \frac{1}{2}g(x)R^{-1}g^T(x)\nabla\phi_1^{\ T}\hat{W}_2 + \frac{1}{2\gamma^2}kk^T\nabla\phi_1^{\ T}\hat{W}_3)$.

From the HJI equation $W_1^{\ T}\sigma_1 = -h^T h - \frac{1}{4}W_1^{\ T}\bar{D}_1(x)W_1 + \frac{1}{4\gamma^2}W_1^{\ T}\bar{E}_1(x)W_1 + \varepsilon_{HJI}(x)$.

Then

$$\begin{aligned}\dot{L}_V(x) &= -h^T h - \frac{1}{4}W_1^{\ T}\bar{D}_1(x)W_1 + \frac{1}{4\gamma^2}W_1^{\ T}\bar{D}_1(x)W_1 + \frac{1}{2}W_1^{\ T}\bar{E}_1(x)\tilde{W}_2 - \frac{1}{2\gamma^2}W_1^{\ T}\bar{E}_1(x)\tilde{W}_3 + \varepsilon_{HJI}(x) + \varepsilon_1(x)\\ &\equiv \dot{\bar{L}}_V(x) + \frac{1}{2}W_1^{\ T}\bar{D}_1(x)\tilde{W}_2 - \frac{1}{2\gamma^2}W_1^{\ T}\bar{E}_1(x)\tilde{W}_3 + \varepsilon_1(x). \end{aligned} \quad \text{(A.3)}$$

where $\dot{\bar{L}}_V(x) = -h^T h - \frac{1}{4}W_1^T \bar{D}_1(x) W_1 + \frac{1}{4\gamma^2} W_1^T \bar{D}_1(x) W_1 + \varepsilon_{HJI}(x) + \varepsilon_1(x)$

Second term is,

$$\dot{L}_1 = \tilde{W}_1^T \alpha_1^{-1} \dot{\tilde{W}}_1 = \tilde{W}_1^T \alpha_1^{-1} \alpha_1 \frac{\sigma_2}{\left(\sigma_2^T \sigma_2 + 1\right)^2} (\sigma_2^T \hat{W}_1 + Q(x) + \frac{1}{4} \hat{W}_2^T \bar{D}_1 \hat{W}_2 - \frac{1}{4\gamma^2} \hat{W}_3^T \bar{\mathrm{E}}_1 \hat{W}_3)$$

$$\dot{L}_1 = \tilde{W}_1^T \frac{\sigma_2}{\left(\sigma_2^T \sigma_2 + 1\right)^2} (-\sigma_2^T \tilde{W}_1 + \frac{1}{4} \tilde{W}_2^T \bar{D}_1(x) \tilde{W}_2 - \frac{1}{4\gamma^2} \tilde{W}_3^T \bar{\mathrm{E}}_1 \tilde{W}_3 + \varepsilon_{HJI}(x))$$

$$= \dot{\bar{L}}_1 + \frac{1}{4} \tilde{W}_1^T \frac{\sigma_2}{\left(\sigma_2^T \sigma_2 + 1\right)^2} \left(\tilde{W}_2^T \bar{D}_1(x) \tilde{W}_2 - \frac{1}{\gamma^2} \tilde{W}_3^T \bar{\mathrm{E}}_1 \tilde{W}_3 \right) \tag{A.4}$$

where $\dot{\bar{L}}_1 = \tilde{W}_1^T \frac{\sigma_2}{\left(\sigma_2^T \sigma_2 + 1\right)^2} \left(-\sigma_2^T \tilde{W}_1 + \varepsilon_{HJI}(x) \right) = \tilde{W}_1^T \bar{\sigma}_2 \left(-\sigma_2^T \tilde{W}_1 + \frac{\varepsilon_{HJI}(x)}{m_s} \right)$.

By adding the terms of (A.3) and (A.4) we have

$$\dot{L}(x) = -Q(x) - \frac{1}{4} W_1^T \bar{D}_1(x) W_1 + \frac{1}{4\gamma^2} W_1^T \bar{E}_1(x) W_1 + \frac{1}{2} W_1^T \bar{D}_1(x) \tilde{W}_2 - \frac{1}{2\gamma^2} W_1^T \bar{E}_1(x) \tilde{W}_3 + \varepsilon_{HJI}(x) + \varepsilon_1(x)$$
$$+ \tilde{W}_1^T \frac{\sigma_2}{\left(\sigma_2^T \sigma_2 + 1\right)^2} (-\sigma_2^T \tilde{W}_1 + \frac{1}{4} \tilde{W}_2^T \bar{D}_1(x) \tilde{W}_2 - \frac{1}{4\gamma^2} \tilde{W}_3^T \bar{\mathrm{E}}_1 \tilde{W}_3 + \varepsilon_{HJI}(x)) + \tilde{W}_2^T \alpha_2^{-1} \dot{\tilde{W}}_2 + \tilde{W}_3^T \alpha_3^{-1} \dot{\tilde{W}}_3$$

$$\dot{L}(x) = \dot{\bar{L}}_1 + \dot{\bar{L}}_V(x) + \varepsilon_1(x) - \frac{1}{4} \tilde{W}_2^T \bar{D}_1(x) W_1 \frac{\bar{\sigma}_2^T}{m_s} W_1 + \frac{1}{4} \tilde{W}_2^T \bar{D}_1(x) W_1 \frac{\bar{\sigma}_2^T}{m_s} \tilde{W}_1$$
$$+ \frac{1}{4} \tilde{W}_2^T \bar{D}_1(x) \tilde{W}_2 \frac{\bar{\sigma}_2^T}{m_s} W_1 + \frac{1}{4} \tilde{W}_2^T \bar{D}_1(x) \hat{W}_2 \frac{\bar{\sigma}_2^T}{m_s} \hat{W}_1 - \frac{1}{4\gamma^2} \tilde{W}_3^T \bar{E}_1(x) W_1 \frac{\bar{\sigma}_2^T}{m_s} \tilde{W}_1$$
$$- \frac{1}{4\gamma^2} \tilde{W}_3^T \bar{E}_1(x) \tilde{W}_3 \frac{\bar{\sigma}_2^T}{m_s} W_1 - \frac{1}{4\gamma^2} \tilde{W}_3^T \bar{E}_1(x) \hat{W}_3 \frac{\bar{\sigma}_2^T}{m_s} \hat{W}_1 + \frac{1}{2} \tilde{W}_2^T \bar{D}_1(x) W_1 - \frac{1}{2\gamma^2} \tilde{W}_3^T \bar{\mathrm{E}}_1(x) W_1$$
$$+ \frac{1}{4\gamma^2} \tilde{W}_3^T \bar{E}_1(x) W_1 \frac{\bar{\sigma}_2^T}{m_s} W_1 - \tilde{W}_2^T \alpha_2^{-1} \dot{\hat{W}}_2 - \tilde{W}_3^T \alpha_3^{-1} \dot{\hat{W}}_3 \tag{A.5}$$

where $\bar{\sigma}_2 = \frac{\sigma_2}{\sigma_2^T \sigma_2 + 1}$ and $m_s = \sigma_2^T \sigma_2 + 1$.

In order to select the update law for the action neural networks, write (A.5) as

$$\dot{L}(x) = \dot{\bar{L}}_V + \dot{\bar{L}}_1 + \varepsilon_1(x) - \tilde{W}_2^T \left[\alpha_2^{-1} \dot{\hat{W}}_2 - \tfrac{1}{4} \bar{D}_1(x) \hat{W}_2 \frac{\bar{\sigma}_2^T}{m_s} \hat{W}_1 \right] - \tilde{W}_3^T \left[\alpha_3^{-1} \dot{\hat{W}}_3 + \tfrac{1}{4\gamma^2} \bar{\mathrm{E}}_1(x) \hat{W}_3 \frac{\bar{\sigma}_2^T}{m_s} \hat{W}_1 \right]$$

$$+\frac{1}{2}\tilde{W}_2^T\bar{D}_1(x)W_1+\frac{1}{4}\tilde{W}_2^T\bar{D}_1(x)W_1\frac{\bar{\sigma}_2^T}{m_s}\tilde{W}_1-\frac{1}{4}\tilde{W}_2^T\bar{D}_1(x)W_1\frac{\bar{\sigma}_2^T}{m_s}W_1+\frac{1}{4}\tilde{W}_2^T\bar{D}_1(x)W_1\frac{\bar{\sigma}_2}{m_s}\tilde{W}_2$$

$$-\frac{1}{2\gamma^2}\tilde{W}_3^T\bar{E}_1(x)W_1-\frac{1}{4\gamma^2}\tilde{W}_3^T\bar{E}_1(x)W_1\frac{\bar{\sigma}_2^T}{m_s}\tilde{W}_1+\frac{1}{4\gamma^2}\tilde{W}_3^T\bar{E}_1(x)W_1\frac{\bar{\sigma}_2^T}{m_s}W_1-\frac{1}{4\gamma^2}\tilde{W}_3^T\bar{E}_1(x)W_1\frac{\bar{\sigma}_2}{m_s}\tilde{W}_3$$

Now define the actor tuning law as

$$\dot{\hat{W}}_2=-\alpha_2\left\{\left(F_2\hat{W}_2-F_1\bar{\sigma}_2^T\hat{W}_1\right)-\frac{1}{4}\bar{D}_1(x)\hat{W}_2m^T\hat{W}_1\right\} \tag{A.6}$$

and the disturbance tuning law as

$$\dot{\hat{W}}_3=-\alpha_3\left\{\left(F_4\hat{W}_3-F_3\bar{\sigma}_2^T\hat{W}_1\right)+\frac{1}{4\gamma^2}\bar{E}_1(x)\hat{W}_3m^T\hat{W}_1\right\}. \tag{A.7}$$

This adds to $\dot{L}$ the terms

$$\begin{aligned}&\tilde{W}_2^TF_2W_1-\tilde{W}_2^TF_2\tilde{W}_2-\tilde{W}_2^TF_1\bar{\sigma}_2^TW_1+\tilde{W}_2^TF_1\bar{\sigma}_2^T\tilde{W}_1\\&+\tilde{W}_3^TF_4W_1-\tilde{W}_3^TF_4\tilde{W}_3-\tilde{W}_3^TF_3\bar{\sigma}_2^TW_1+\tilde{W}_3^TF_3\bar{\sigma}_2^T\tilde{W}_1\end{aligned}$$

Overall

$$\begin{aligned}\dot{L}(x)=&-Q(x)-\frac{1}{4}W_1^T\bar{D}_1(x)W_1+\frac{1}{4\gamma^2}W_1^T\bar{E}_1(x)W_1+\varepsilon_{HJI}(x)+\tilde{W}_1^T\bar{\sigma}_2\left(-\bar{\sigma}_2^T\tilde{W}_1+\frac{\varepsilon_{HJI}(x)}{m_s}\right)+\varepsilon_1(x)\\&+\frac{1}{2}\tilde{W}_2^T\bar{D}_1(x)W_1+\frac{1}{4}\tilde{W}_2^T\bar{D}_1(x)W_1\frac{\bar{\sigma}_2^T}{m_s}\tilde{W}_1-\frac{1}{4}\tilde{W}_2^T\bar{D}_1(x)W_1\frac{\bar{\sigma}_2^T}{m_s}W_1\\&+\frac{1}{4}\tilde{W}_2^T\bar{D}_1(x)W_1\frac{\bar{\sigma}_2}{m_s}\tilde{W}_2-\frac{1}{2\gamma^2}\tilde{W}_3^T\bar{E}_1(x)W_1-\frac{1}{4\gamma^2}\tilde{W}_3^T\bar{E}_1(x)W_1\frac{\bar{\sigma}_2}{m_s}\tilde{W}_3\\&-\frac{1}{4\gamma^2}\tilde{W}_3^T\bar{E}_1(x)W_1\frac{\bar{\sigma}_2^T}{m_s}\tilde{W}_1+\frac{1}{4\gamma^2}\tilde{W}_3^T\bar{E}_1(x)W_1\frac{\bar{\sigma}_2^T}{m_s}W_1\\&+\tilde{W}_2^TF_2W_1-\tilde{W}_2^TF_2\tilde{W}_2-\tilde{W}_2^TF_1\bar{\sigma}_2^TW_1+\tilde{W}_2^TF_1\bar{\sigma}_2^T\tilde{W}_1\\&+\tilde{W}_3^TF_4W_1-\tilde{W}_3^TF_4\tilde{W}_3-\tilde{W}_3^TF_3\bar{\sigma}_2^TW_1+\tilde{W}_3^TF_3\bar{\sigma}_2^T\tilde{W}_1\end{aligned} \tag{A.8}$$

Now it is desired to introduce norm bounds. It is easy to show that under the Facts 1

$$\|\varepsilon_1(x)\|<b_{\varepsilon_x}b_f\|x\|+\tfrac{1}{2}b_{\varepsilon_x}b_g^2b_{\phi_x}\sigma_{\min}(R)\left(\|W_1\|+\|\tilde{W}_2\|\right)+\tfrac{1}{2\gamma^2}b_{\varepsilon_x}b_k^2b_{\phi_x}\left(\|W_1\|+\|\tilde{W}_3\|\right)$$

Also since $Q(x)>0$ there exists q such that $x^Tqx<Q(x)$ locally. It is shown in (Abu-Khalaf & Lewis, 2008; Abu-Khalaf et al. 2006) that ε_{HJI} converges to zero uniformly as N increases.

Select $\varepsilon > 0$ and $N_0(\varepsilon)$ such that $\sup\left\|\varepsilon_{HJI}\right\| < \varepsilon$ (see comments after (24)). Then assuming $N > N_0$ and writing in terms of $\tilde{Z} = \begin{bmatrix} x \\ \bar{\sigma}_2{}^{\mathrm{T}}\tilde{W}_1 \\ \tilde{W}_2 \\ \tilde{W}_3 \end{bmatrix}$, (A.8) becomes

$$\dot{L} < \frac{1}{4}\left\|W_1\right\|^2\left\|\bar{D}_1(x)\right\| + \frac{1}{4\gamma^2}\left\|W_1\right\|^2\left\|\bar{E}_1(x)\right\| + \varepsilon + \tfrac{1}{2}\,||\,W_1\,||\,b_{\varepsilon_x}b_{\varphi_x}b_g{}^2\sigma_{\min}(R) + \tfrac{1}{2\gamma^2}\,||\,W_1\,||\,b_{\varepsilon_x}b_k^2 b_{\phi_x}$$

$$-\tilde{Z}^T\begin{bmatrix} qI & 0 & 0 & 0 \\ 0 & I & \left(\frac{1}{2}F_1 - \frac{1}{8m_s}\bar{D}_1W_1\right)^T & \frac{1}{2}F_3 + \left(\frac{1}{8\gamma^2 m_s}\bar{\mathrm{E}}_1W_1\right) \\ 0 & \frac{1}{2}F_1 - \left(\frac{1}{8m_s}\bar{D}_1W_1\right) & F_2 - \frac{1}{8}\left(\bar{D}_1W_1m^{\mathrm{T}} + mW_1^T\bar{D}_1\right) & 0 \\ 0 & \frac{1}{2}F_3 + \left(\frac{1}{8\gamma^2 m_s}\bar{\mathrm{E}}_1W_1\right) & 0 & F_4 + \frac{1}{8\gamma^2}\left(\bar{\mathrm{E}}_1W_1m^{\mathrm{T}} + mW_1^T\bar{\mathrm{E}}_1\right) \end{bmatrix}\tilde{Z}$$

$$+\tilde{Z}^T\begin{bmatrix} b_{\varepsilon_x}b_f \\ \dfrac{\varepsilon}{m_s} \\ (\frac{1}{2}\bar{D}_1 + F_2 - F_1\bar{\sigma}_2^T - \frac{1}{4}\bar{D}_1W_1m^T)W_1 + \frac{1}{2}b_{\varepsilon_x}b_g^2b_{\phi_x}\sigma_{\min}(R) \\ (-\frac{1}{2\gamma^2}\bar{\mathrm{E}}_1 + F_4 - F_3\bar{\sigma}_2^T + \frac{1}{4\gamma^2}\bar{\mathrm{E}}_1W_1m^T)W_1 + \frac{1}{2\gamma^2}b_{\varepsilon_x}b_k^2b_{\phi_x} \end{bmatrix} \tag{A.9}$$

Define

$$M = \begin{bmatrix} qI & 0 & 0 & 0 \\ 0 & I & \left(\frac{1}{2}F_1 - \frac{1}{8m_s}\bar{D}_1W_1\right)^T & \frac{1}{2}F_3 + \left(\frac{1}{8\gamma^2 m_s}\bar{\mathrm{E}}_1W_1\right) \\ 0 & \frac{1}{2}F_1 - \left(\frac{1}{8m_s}\bar{D}_1W_1\right) & F_2 - \frac{1}{8}\left(\bar{D}_1W_1m^{\mathrm{T}} + mW_1^T\bar{D}_1\right) & 0 \\ 0 & \frac{1}{2}F_3 + \left(\frac{1}{8\gamma^2 m_s}\bar{\mathrm{E}}_1W_1\right) & 0 & F_4 + \frac{1}{8\gamma^2}\left(\bar{\mathrm{E}}_1W_1m^{\mathrm{T}} + mW_1^T\bar{\mathrm{E}}_1\right) \end{bmatrix} \tag{A.10}$$

$$d = \begin{bmatrix} b_{\varepsilon_x}b_f \\ \dfrac{\varepsilon}{m_s} \\ (\frac{1}{2}\bar{D}_1 + F_2 - F_1\bar{\sigma}_2^T - \frac{1}{4}\bar{D}_1W_1m^T)W_1 + \frac{1}{2}b_{\varepsilon_x}b_g^2b_{\phi_x}\sigma_{\min}(R) \\ (-\frac{1}{2\gamma^2}\bar{\mathrm{E}}_1 + F_4 - F_3\bar{\sigma}_2^T + \frac{1}{4\gamma^2}\bar{\mathrm{E}}_1W_1m^T)W_1 + \frac{1}{2\gamma^2}b_{\varepsilon_x}b_k^2b_{\phi_x} \end{bmatrix}$$

$$c = \frac{1}{4}\|W_1\|^2 \left\|\bar{D}_1(x)\right\| + \frac{1}{4\gamma^2}\|W_1\|^2 \left\|\bar{E}_1(x)\right\| + \tfrac{1}{2}\,||W_1||\,|b_{\varepsilon_x} b_{\varphi_x} b_g{}^2 \sigma_{\min}(R) + \tfrac{1}{2\gamma^2}\,||W_1||\,|b_{\varepsilon_x} b_k^2 b_{\phi_x}$$

Let the parameters be chosen such that $M > 0$. Now (A.9) becomes

$$\dot{L} < -\left\|\tilde{Z}\right\|^2 \sigma_{\min}(M) + \|d\|\left\|\tilde{Z}\right\| + c + \varepsilon$$

Completing the squares, the Lyapunov derivative is negative if

$$\left\|\tilde{Z}\right\| > \frac{\|d\|}{2\sigma_{\min}(M)} + \sqrt{\frac{d^2}{4\sigma_{\min}^2(M)} + \frac{c+\varepsilon}{\sigma_{\min}(M)}} \equiv B_Z. \tag{A.11}$$

It is now straightforward to demonstrate that if L exceeds a certain bound, then, $\dot{L}$ is negative. Therefore, according to the standard Lyapunov extension theorem (Lewis, Jagannathan, Yesildirek, 1999) the analysis above demonstrates that the state and the weights are UUB.
To show this from (A.1), one has,

$$\sigma_{\min}(P)\|x\|^2 + \frac{1}{2a_1}\left\|\tilde{W}_1\right\|^2 + \frac{1}{2a_2}\left\|\tilde{W}_2\right\|^2 + \frac{1}{2a_3}\left\|\tilde{W}_3\right\|^2 \le L \le$$

$$\le \sigma_{\max}(P)\|x\|^2 + \frac{1}{2a_1}\left\|\tilde{W}_1\right\|^2 + \frac{1}{2a_2}\left\|\tilde{W}_2\right\|^2 + \frac{1}{2a_3}\left\|\tilde{W}_3\right\|^2 \tag{A.12}$$

$$\tilde{Z}^T \underbrace{\begin{bmatrix} \sigma_{\min}(P) & & & \\ & \dfrac{1}{2\|\bar{\sigma}_2\|^2 a_1} & & \\ & & 1/2a_2 & \\ & & & 1/2a_3 \end{bmatrix}}_{S_1} \tilde{Z} \le L \le \tilde{Z}^T \underbrace{\begin{bmatrix} \sigma_{\max}(P) & & & \\ & \dfrac{1}{2\|\bar{\sigma}_2\|^2 a_1} & & \\ & & 1/2a_2 & \\ & & & 1/2a_3 \end{bmatrix}}_{S_2} \tilde{Z} \tag{A.13}$$

Equation (A.13) is equivalent to

$$\tilde{Z}^T \sigma_{\min}(S_1)\tilde{Z} \le L \le \tilde{Z}^T \sigma_{\max}(S_2)\tilde{Z}$$

Then

$$\sigma_{\min}(S_1)\left\|\tilde{Z}\right\|^2 \le L \le \sigma_{\max}(S_2)\left\|\tilde{Z}\right\|^2.$$

Therefore,

$$L > \sigma_{\max}(S_2)\left(\frac{\|d\|}{2\sigma_{\min}(M)} + \sqrt{\frac{\|d\|^2}{4\sigma_{\min}^2(M)} + \frac{c+\bar{\varepsilon}_1+\bar{\varepsilon}_2}{\sigma_{\min}(M)}}\right)^2 \tag{A.14}$$

implies (A.11).

Note that condition (A.11) holds if the norm of any component of $\tilde{Z}$ exceeds the bound, i.e. specifically $x > B_Z$ or $\bar{\sigma}_2^{\mathrm{T}}\tilde{W}_1 > B_Z$ or $\tilde{W}_2 > B_Z$ or $\tilde{W}_3 > B_Z$ (Khalil, 1996).
Now consider the error dynamics and the output as in Technical Lemmas 1, 2 and assume $\bar{\sigma}_2$ is persistently exciting

$$\dot{\tilde{W}}_1 = -a_1\bar{\sigma}_2\bar{\sigma}_2^{\mathrm{T}}\tilde{W}_1 + a_1\bar{\sigma}_2\frac{\varepsilon_{HJI}}{m_s} + \frac{a_1}{4m_s^2}\tilde{W}_2^T\bar{D}_1(x)\tilde{W}_2 - \frac{a_1}{4\gamma^2 m_s^2}\tilde{W}_3^T\bar{\mathrm{E}}_1\tilde{W}_3$$

$$y = \bar{\sigma}_2^T\tilde{W}_1 . \tag{A.15}$$

Then Theorem 1 is true with

$$\left\|\frac{\sigma_2^T}{m_s}\tilde{W}_1\right\| > \varepsilon_{\max} > \frac{1}{4}\left\|\tilde{W}_2\right\|^2\left\|\frac{\bar{D}_1}{m_s}\right\| - \frac{1}{4\gamma^2}\left\|\tilde{W}_3\right\|^2\left\|\frac{\bar{\mathrm{E}}_1}{m_s}\right\| + \varepsilon\left\|\frac{1}{m_s}\right\|$$

This provides an effective practical bound for $\left\|\bar{\sigma}_2^T\tilde{W}_1\right\|$.

This completes the proof.

■

6. References

Abu-Khalaf, M. & Lewis, F. L. (2005). Nearly Optimal Control Laws for Nonlinear Systems with Saturating Actuators Using a Neural Network HJB Approach. *Automatica*, Vol. 41, No. 5, pp. 779-791.

Abu-Khalaf, M. & Lewis, F. L. (2008). Neurodynamic Programming and Zero-Sum Games for Constrained Control Systems. *IEEE Transactions on Neural Networks*, Vol. 19, No. 7, pp. 1243-1252.

Abu-Khalaf, M.; Lewis, F. L. & Huang, J. (2006). Policy Iterations on the Hamilton-Jacobi-Isaacs Equation for H_∞ State Feedback Control With Input Saturation. *IEEE Transactions on Automatic Control*, Vol. 51, No. 12, pp. 1989-1995.

Adams R. & Fournier J. (2003). *Sobolev spaces*, New York: Academic Press.

Ball J.& Helton W. (1996). Viscosity solutions of Hamilton-Jacobi equations arising in nonlinear H_∞-control. *J. Math Syst., Estimat., Control*, Vol. 6, No.1, pp. 1-22.

Bardi M. & Capuzzo-Dolcetta I. (1997). *Optimal Control and Viscosity Solutions of Hamilton-Jacobi-Bellman Equations*. Boston, MA: Birkhäuser.

Başar T. & Olsder G. J. (1999). *Dynamic Noncooperative Game Theory*, 2nd ed. Philadelphia, PA: SIAM, Vol. 23, SIAM's Classic in Applied Mathematics.

Başar T. & Bernard P. (1995). *H_∞ Optimal Control and Related Minimax Design Problems*. Boston, MA: Birkhäuser.

Bertsekas D. P. & Tsitsiklis J. N. (1996). *Neuro-Dynamic Programming*, Athena Scientific, MA.

Doya K. (2000). Reinforcement Learning In Continuous Time and Space. *Neural Computation*, Vol. 12, No. 1, pp. 219-245.

Doya K., Kimura H. & Kawato M. (2001). Neural Mechanisms of Learning and Control. *IEEE Control Syst. Mag.*, Vol. 21, No. 4, pp. 42-54.

Feng Y., Anderson B. D. & M. Rotkowitz. (2009). A game theoretic algorithm to compute local stabilizing solutions to HJBI equations in nonlinear H∞ control. *Automatica,* Vol. 45, No. 4, pp. 881-888.

Finlayson B. A. (1990). *The method of weighted residuals and variational principles.* New York: Academic Press, 1990.

Hanselmann T., Noakes L. & Zaknich A. (2007). Continuous-Time Adaptive Critics. *IEEE Transactions on Neural Networks,* Vol. 18, No. 3, pp. 631-647.

Hornik K., Stinchcombe M. & White H. (1990). Universal Approximation of an unknown mapping and its derivatives using multilayer feedforward networks, *Neural Networks,* Vol. 3, pp. 551-560.

Howard R. A. (1960). *Dynamic Programming and Markov Processes,* MIT Press, Cambridge, Massachusetts.

Ioannou P. & Fidan B. (2006). *Adaptive Control Tutorial,* SIAM, Advances in Design and Control, PA.

Khalil H. K. (1996). *Nonlinear Systems.* Prentice-Hall.

Kleinman D. (1968). On an Iterative Technique for Riccati Equation Computations. *IEEE Transactions on Automatic Control,* Vol. 13, pp. 114- 115, February.

Lewis F.L., Jagannathan S., Yesildirek A. (1999). *Neural Network Control of Robot Manipulators and Nonlinear Systems.* Taylor & Francis.

Lewis F. L., Syrmos V. L. (1995). *Optimal Control,* John Wiley.

Nevistic V., Primbs J. A. (1996). Constrained nonlinear optimal control: a converse HJB approach. *Technical Report 96-021,* California Institute of Technology.

Van Der Shaft A. J. (1992). L_2-gain analysis of nonlinear systems and nonlinear state feedback H_∞ control. *IEEE Transactions on Automatic Control,* Vol. 37, No. 6, pp. 770-784.

Sandberg E. W. (1997). Notes on uniform approximation of time varying systems on finite time intervals. *IEEE Transactions on Circuits and Systems-1: Fundamental Theory and Apprications,* Vol. 45, No. 8, pp. 863-865.

Stevens B. & Lewis F. L. (2003). *Aircract Control and Simulation,* 2nd edition, John Willey, New Jersey.

Si J., Barto A., Powel W. & Wunch D. (2004). *Handbook of Learning and Approximate Dynamic Programming,* John Wiley, New Jersey.

Sontag E. D. & Sussman H. J. (1995). Nonsmooth control Lyapunov functions. *IEEE Proc. CDC95,* pp. 2799-2805.

Sutton R. S. & Barto A. G. (1998). *Reinforcement Learning – An Introduction,* MIT Press, Cambridge, Massachusetts.

Tao G. (2003). *Adaptive Control Design and Analysis,* Adaptive and Learning Systems for Signal Processing, Communications and Control Series, Hoboken, NJ: Wiley-Interscience.

Tijs S. (2003). *Introduction to Game Theory,* Hindustan Book Agency, India.

Vamvoudakis K. G. & Lewis F. L. (2010). Online Actor-Critic Algorithm to Solve the Continuous-Time Infinite Horizon Optimal Control Problem. *Automatica,* Vol. 46, No. 5, pp. 878-888.

Vrabie D., Pastravanu O., Lewis F. & Abu-Khalaf M. (2009). Adaptive Optimal Control for Continuous-Time Linear Systems Based on Policy Iteration. *Automatica,* Vol. 45, No. 2, pp. 477-484.

Vrabie D., Vamvoudakis K. & Lewis F. (2009). Adaptive optimal controllers based on generalized policy iteration in a continuous-time framework. *Proc. of the IEEE Mediterranean Conf. on Control and Automation*, pp. 1402-1409.

Vrabie D. (2009) *Online Adaptive Optimal Control for Continuous Time Systems*, Ph.D. Thesis, Dept. of Electrical Engineering, Univ. Texas at Arlington, Arlington, TX, USA.

Werbos P.J. (1974). *Beyond Regression: New Tools for Prediction and Analysis in the Behavior Sciences*, Ph.D. Thesis.

Werbos P. J. (1992). Approximate dynamic programming for real-time control and neural modeling. *Handbook of Intelligent Control*, ed. D.A. White and D.A. Sofge, New York: Van Nostrand Reinhold.

19

Hybrid Intelligent Algorithm for Flexible Job-Shop Scheduling Problem under Uncertainty

Guojun Zhang, Haiping Zhu and Chaoyong Zhang
School of Mechanical Science & Engineering,
Huazhong University of Science & Technology
Wuhan
P.R. China

1. Introduction

Production scheduling plays an important role in improving efficiency and reducing cost. One of its core technologies is the establishment of an effective scheduling model and its corresponding optimization algorithms. However, most researches focus on scheduling optimization in static environment, less concern of the uncertainty and complexity in the real job-shop. It must be different from the exact solution if some situations are ignored or not considered in scheduling problem such as changing processing time, uncertain capability of storage, possibility of human decision, unpredicted accident and so on.
Inchoate research on FJSP (Flexible Job-Shop Scheduling Problem) concentrated on the simple application of integer programming and simulation, which can hardly be used to solve the complex scheduling problem. With the development of related fields and theory of optimization, a great many methods and techniques have been adopted into JSP. Operational research predigests the JSP into a mathematical programming model, using branch-and-bound method and dynamic programming algorithm to realize optimization or approximate optimization. However, OR only suits to simple scheduling problem (Philips et al., 1987). Based on theory of control, Gershwin and his fellows expatiate comprehensively the adoption of theory of control in manufacturing system. Limited to the capability of modeling, a lot of predigestion to the environment is a must; the practice to get the optimum solution expands with a exponential characteristic (Juanqi, 1998). AI (Artificial Intelligence) is a combination of all the methods for JSP, which aim at enhancing the intelligence of scheduling method. It can smooth the disadvantages of mathematical programming and simulation. Based on the system status and deterministic objective of optimization, effective heuristic research and concurrent fuzzy reasoning are conducted to choose the optimum solution and support online decision. Nevertheless, AI is weak in adapting to new environment, and there are 3 main limitations of this method: low speed of operation, insensitive to asynchronisic event in the environment, the system can't be universally adopted (Juanqi, 1998). In a job-shop DEDS (Discrete Event Dynamic System), the JSP can be

solved by its parsing model and method, such as Petri net. The Petri net can precisely reflect the characteristics of discrete and stochastic etc. in job-shop scheduling (Hongsen, 1994). But it's hard to present a model when the principle and methodology are complex. The complexity of manufacturing system makes it hard to express and analyze by a precise analytical model. While simulation can provide an ideal model for quantitative evaluation to guide the scheduling (Law, 1986). Whereas, the experimental characteristic make it hard to figure out the general rule, and the value and credibility of the result have much to do with the simulation model, simulation method and the data input. Uncertain theory has also been adopted into the scheduling problem for its stochastic and fuzzy characteristics (Zhaoqiang & Yiren, 2002). Just as AI, it needs a long development cycle time as well as abundant experience etc. Soft computing is also widely adopted into scheduling, such as genetic algorithm (Croee & Tadei, 1995), Tabu searching (Taillard, 1990), simulated annealing (Van Laarhoven, 1992), neural network (Foo & Takefuji, 1998), particle swarm optimization etc. Based on the aforementioned methodologies, we can find that each method has its own limit, so researchers start to combine the approximate algorithms to solve scheduling problem. This paper proposed a compounding method which syncretises simulation and soft computing to solve FJSP (flexible job-shop scheduling problem) under uncertain environment.

As the execution layer between the ERP/MRPII for planning and job-shop layer for operation and control, MES (Manufacturing Execution System) focuses on how to optimize the job-shop scheduling (Shuxia, 2004). The essence of scheduling is a decision making constrained by multi-objectives and multi-priorities. The multi-objectives here focuses on the combination of less production time, less total cost and equilibrium of production ability while the multi-constraints focuses on the constraints of process route, machines and delivery time of order in which the priorities differ on different types of work pieces.

Information is the basis of decision making. The scheduling models in previous research are proposed with all the information deterministically given, for example, taking the process time of the work piece on specific machine as deterministic information without considering the priority. Actually, the stochastic information floods the real job-shop, which makes getting the satisfied scheduling a difficult job. In recent years, job-shop scheduling in uncertain environment gradually arouses the attention of researchers, such as study on scheduling problem with fuzzy characteristic. However, in discrete event dynamic system, more parameters are suited to be described by stochastic variable rather than fuzzy variable, such as the process time of work piece, the frequency of machine fault and the interval of order, which can be thought to obey an exponential distribution (Peigen, 1998), so it is of great significance to study scheduling under stochastic constraints.

In this paper, describing the uncertain information in the real job-shops with several stochastic variables, a stochastic multi-objectives and multi-priorities programming model for Flexible job-shop scheduling is proposed, in which Time, Cost and Equilibrium serve as the three basic objectives for scheduling. The credibility of the delivery time of different types of work pieces serve as the scheduling constraints. In order to obtain the approximate optimum solution, a hybrid intelligent algorithm which combines Stochastic Simulation (SS), Neural Network (NN) with Genetic Algorithm (GA) is proposed. The feasibility of the model and its corresponding hybrid intelligent algorithm is validated through some instances.

2. The stochastic programming model with chance-constraint

Generally, job-shop problem is depicted by a non-linear programming model. If certain stochastic factors being taken into account, the programming model would differ from the classical model. The concept of chance-constraint and stochastic programming proposed by Liu (Baoding et al., 2003) is depicted as follows:

Assume that X is a decision-making vector; E is a stochastic vector with deterministic distribution. There are r objective functions decided by X and E:$f_i(X, E)$, $1 \le i \le r$, constrained to p constrained function: $g_j(X, E)$, $1 \le j \le p$. The objective functions and constrained functions are stochastic, so they can be depicted only by the credibility as follows: $P\{ g_j(X, E) \le 0\} \ge \alpha_j$, $1 \le j \le p$, P represent the probability of the stochastic event $g_j(X, E) \le 0$, α_j is the credibility. If the objective of programming is to minimize $f_i(X, E)$, $1 \le i \le r$, choose β_i as the credibility, the objective function would be:

$$\begin{cases} \min \overline{f_i} \\ s.t. \;\; P\{f_i(X,E) \le \overline{f_i}\} \ge \beta_i \end{cases} ,1 \le i \le r$$

Above all, the stochastic programming model with multi-chance-constraints and multi objectives is:

$$\begin{cases} \min[\overline{f_1}, \overline{f_2}, ..., \overline{f_r}] \\ s.t. \\ \quad P\{f_i(X,E) \le \overline{f_i}\} \ge \beta_i, 1 \le i \le r \\ \quad P\{g_j(X,E) \le 0\} \ge \alpha_j, 1 \le j \le p \end{cases}$$

$[\overline{f_1}, \overline{f_2}, ..., \overline{f_r}]$ stands for the weighted sum of the r variables.

3. Multi-objectives and multi-priorities flexible job-shop scheduling strategy

In the Flexible job-shop with several pieces of machines, after receiving the production order assigned by the planning section, production process would be arranged and optimized by reasonable scheduling. The scheduling parameter can be depicted by the mathematical format:

There are m pieces of machine available: $\{R_1, R_2, \ldots. R_m\}$

There are n work pieces' task included in the order:$\{T_1, T_2, \ldots T_m\}$ $T_i(1 \le i \le n)$ is a operation sequence decided by the process route programming, which includes K_i $(1 \le K_i \le m)$ operations and recorded as follows: $T_i = \{OP_{i1}, OP_{i2}, \ldots, OP_{iK}\}$, each operation OP_{ik} can be processed on several machines, and operation on each machine R_j would take you certain time and cost, time function be depicted as $et(OP, R)$, cost function be depicted as $ec(OP, R)$. In the uncertain informative environment, when operation $OP_{ik}(1 \le i \le n, 1 \le k \le K_i)$ is being processed on machine R_j $(1 \le j \le m)$, $et(OP_{ik}, R_j)$ and $ec(OP_{ik}, R_j)$ are two stochastic constants with deterministic distribution, else $et(OP_{ik}, R_j) = ec(OP_{ik}, R_j) \equiv 0$.

3.1 Work piece priority and chance constraint

On the premise of following the demand of process route, MES would assign appropriate machine for each operation of each work piece, making sure that the delivery time of order can be met. That is to say, the delivery time is a key constraint in scheduling. As the production order is formed by a consideration of customer order, enterprise planning and operation. The tasks included in the order can be divided into many priorities for many factors such as importance of customer, quantity of order, and the degree of emergency of the requirement. For example, if we divide the work pieces into two group, in one of which the delivery time should be precisely met (called critical work piece) while there can be a flexible space in the other group of work pieces (called ordinary work piece). On this condition, the job-shop resources should satisfy the needs of critical work pieces on first hand to meet the delivery time. The remained resources can then be assigned to the ordinary work pieces. Literature 4 adopted by-directional scheduling strategy, for the critical work piece, reverse order scheduling is adopted, while for the ordinary work piece, sequential scheduling is adopted. However, for uncertain environment in which processing time is stochastic, this strategy for scheduling will bring out many problems. That means the result of the scheduling can hardly meet the delivery time.

In real job-shop, the processing time of work piece on each machine is a stochastic variable obeying certain distribution (exponential distribution in general), that leads to the stochastic characteristic of the production cycle of work piece. We can describe the constraint of delivery time as a chance constraint. The priority of the work pieces can be divided into r subclasses by a high-low order (the element in the same subclass share the same priority): $S_1, S_2, \ldots, S_r$, each subclass has the corresponding credibility of meeting delivery time: $\alpha_1, \alpha_2, \ldots \alpha_r (\alpha_1 > \alpha_2 > \ldots > \alpha_r)$. The delivery time of each task is deterministic as: $dt_1, dt_2, \ldots, dt_n$, the real production cycle time of each task(including the total processing time and total waiting time) can be calculated and depicted as $pt_1, pt_2, \ldots, pt_n$. The delivery constraint described by chance constraint is:

$$\forall T_i \in S_j, P\{pt_i - dt_i \le 0\} \ge \alpha_j, 1 \le i \le n, 1 \le j \le r \tag{1}$$

There would be a queue waiting when several work pieces are assigned to the same machine, the sequence of processing should be determined by the principle of scheduling. Generally, FIFS (first in first serviced) principle is adopted. Towards different priorities, serving the task with higher priority on first hand is more reasonable to actual demand. At this moment, if there is a queue on a machine waiting for processing while a piece is being processed, after it is processed, the piece in queue with highest priority should be chosen to be processed. The piece of longer waiting time should be processed first within the same priority.

3.2 Proposing a multi-objectives function

Shorter production time and lower cost is two basic objectives. For an order to be scheduled, with the complexity of process route of each component differing from others, we can aim at minimize the total production cycle time of the task for all work pieces. η as the credibility, the time objective function can be depicted by chance constraint as follows:

$$\begin{cases} \min \overline{pt} \\ s.t.\ P\{\sum_{i=1}^{n} pt_i \le \overline{pt}\} \ge \eta \end{cases} \tag{2}$$

Meanwhile, we can aim at minimizing the total production cost of the task for all work pieces, taking γ as credibility. The cost objective function can be depicted by chance constraint as follows:

$$\begin{cases} \min \overline{ec} \\ s.t.\ P\{\sum_{i=1}^{n}\sum_{k=1}^{K_i} ec(OP_{ik}, R_j) \le \overline{ec}\} \ge \gamma \end{cases} \tag{3}$$

Another objective of scheduling is the equilibrium of the schedule, which has long been ignored. According to a schedule, if the average load of machine is floating dramatically, we call it an unbalanced scheduling. The disequilibrium of scheduling would cause a loss in coping with the emergency. We introduce the standard deviation in statistics to quantify the equilibrium of scheduling, dividing the whole production cycle time into several isometric time segment, figure out the total working time of the machine in each time segment, than calculate the standard deviation between this total working time and average working time. The smaller the standard deviation, the better the equilibrium of the schedule is.

Assume that the production cycle time is OT, obviously, $OT = \max_{1 \le i \le n} pt_i$, divide OT into N isometric time segments, in each of which the total processing time of all the machines is $\Delta RT_s (1 \le s \le N)$, the standard deviation is $D^2 = \sum_{s=1}^{N} (\Delta RT_s - \frac{1}{N}\sum_{s=1}^{N} \Delta RT_s)^2$, with credibility ν, the objective of equilibrium of schedule is depicted as:

$$\begin{cases} \min \overline{rt} \\ s.t.\ P\{\sum_{s=1}^{N} (\Delta RT_s - \frac{1}{N}\sum_{s=1}^{N} \Delta RT_s)^2 \le \overline{rt}\} \ge \nu \end{cases} \tag{4}$$

3.3 Stochastic programming model of job-shop scheduling with multi-objectives and multi-priorities

The process route of each work piece and the machines available for each operation are known according to (1) (2) (3) (4), the machines available to operation OP_{ik} is $AR_{ik} = \{R_{ik}^1, R_{ik}^2, ..., R_{ik}^{H_{ik}}\}$, including H_{ik} elements, the principle for scheduling of task waiting in queue is Higher Priority First Served. The stochastic programming model of job-shop scheduling in uncertain environment is proposed as follows:

$$\begin{cases} \min[\overline{pt},\overline{ec},\overline{rt}] \\ s.t.\ \ P\{\sum_{i=1}^{n} pt_i \le \overline{pt}\} \ge \eta \\ P\{\sum_{i=1}^{n}\sum_{k=1}^{K_i} ec(OP_{ik},R_j) \le \overline{ec}\} \ge \gamma \\ P\{\sum_{s=1}^{N}(\Delta RT_s - \frac{1}{N}\sum_{s=1}^{N}\Delta RT_s)^2 \le \overline{rt}\} \ge \nu \\ P\{pt_i - dt_i \le 0\} \ge \alpha_j, 1 \le i \le n, 1 \le j \le r, T_i \in S_j \end{cases} \tag{5}$$

4. The design and implementation of hybrid intelligent algorithm

4.1 Basic procedures of hybrid intelligent algorithm

Model (5) is too complex to be solved by traditional algorithm, so we adopt the hybrid intelligence which syncretizes stochastic simulation, neural network, genetic algorithm and other critical techniques. The algorithm includes 3 major steps:

Step 1. based on the quantity and capability of machine in job-shop, as well as the distribution characteristics of stochastic variables as time and cost etc. Present a simulation model; collect quantities of data samples by simulating.

Step 2. Present the three-layer feed-forward neural networks, use the samples acquired in simulation to weight-train the neural network to approach the stochastic functions in model(5).

Step 3. apply the genetic algorithm to solve the optimization problem, including definition of rules for chromosome coding/encoding, initialization and selection of population, the calculation and evaluation of individual fitness, crossover and mutation etc. The calculation of individual fitness will utilize the trained neural network in step2.

4.2 Stochastic simulations

Stochastic simulations(Monte Carlo simulation) is one of the stochastic system modeling techniques focuses on sample test, the sample of the stochastic variables is based on their probabilistic distribution. There are a lot of complex calculations for probabilities of stochastic variables in model (5), as for the complexity of multi-priorities scheduling, even a schedule sequence is determined, the stochastic variables such as the completion period of each work piece can not be expressed by a explicit. So the stochastic simulation should be integrated with simulation analysis to get the approximate sample data.

According to experience, we can assume the operation time et(OP_{ik}, R_j) comply with the exponential distribution with λ_{ikj} as its exponent, depicted as:

$$\text{et}(OP_{ik},R_j)\sim\exp(\lambda_{ikj}).$$

The cost of processing is influenced by many uncertain factors, ec($OPik,Rj$) can be assumed to comply with normal distribution depicted as:

$$\text{ec}(OP_{ik},R_j)\sim \text{N}(\mu_{ikj},\sigma_{ikj}^2).$$

Given a schedule sequence (the concrete machine for each operation) and a group of deterministic sample values for all stochastic variables, which work pieces are being processed is available on theory. Therefore, to present stochastic simulation model on platform of SIMUL8, then run simulation and statistically analyze the critical data acquired, including:

1. Production time of each work piece pt_i
2. The processing cost of each work piece $\sum_{k=1}^{K_i} ec(OP_{ik}, R_j)$
3. The total working time of all devices in each time segment (N segment in all) is ΔRT_s

4.3 Neural network approach to the stochastic functions

Take the schedule sequence as Vector Y, the four constraints in model (5) can be depicted by Y's stochastic function, definition as the following $n+3$ functions:

$$\begin{cases} U_1(Y) = \min\{\overline{pt} \mid P\{\sum_{i=1}^{n} pt_i \le \overline{pt}\} \ge \eta\} \\ U_2(Y) = \min\{\overline{ec} \mid P\{\sum_{i=1}^{n}\sum_{k=1}^{K_i} ec(OP_{ik}, R_j) \le \overline{ec}\} \ge \gamma\} \\ U_3(Y) = \min\{\overline{rt} \mid P\{\sum_{s=1}^{N}(\Delta RT_s - \frac{1}{N}\sum_{s=1}^{N}\Delta RT_s)^2 \le \overline{rt}\} \ge \nu\} \\ U_4^{(i)}(Y) = P\{pt_i - dt_i \le 0\}, 1 \le i \le n \end{cases} \tag{6}$$

The stochastic simulation provides abundant data samples, which are used to train a neural network to approach the $n+3$ uncertain functions in (6). The neural network is three-layer feed-forward with $\sum_{i=1}^{n} K_i$ input neurons (data input is Y), 18 hidden layer neurons and $n+3$ output neurons (data output are $U1(Y)$, $U2(Y)$, $U3(Y)$, $u_4^{(i)}$ (Y)).

4.4 Genetic algorithm of multi-objectives optimization

Coding, encoding of chromosome and initialization of population. Besides being simple, the principle for coding of chromosome should also assure any of the chromosomes can get a permissive schedule sequence by encoding. Permissive means meeting the requirements of constraints of process route and process machine. Here designed a coding method for positive integer:

The total length of coding is, each bit represents an operation: the first bit represents the first operation of work piece 1, the second bit represents the second operation of work piece 1,..., the K_{1+1} represents the first operation of work piece 2, the rest may be deduced by analogy. If bit j represents operation k of work piece of I, the range of value for bit j is $[1,H_{ik}]$, H_{ik} represents the number of machine available for operation k of work piece i. Looking on the coding principle, once given the collection of machine for each operation and the accurate process time, each chromosome can be precisely mapped into a schedule sequence, meanwhile the process details (when and where) of each operation can be calculated which is solely determined. Also, during the initialization of population, once length bits stochastic positive integers are created with value-range of each bit in $[1,H_{ik}]$, the coding of chromosome is permissive.

The calculation and evaluation of fitness. Individual fitness can be calculated using the trained neural network, if we take $\sum_{i=1}^{n} K_i$ bits coding of random chromosomes as the input of neural network, n+3 output would be acquired. Contraposing data output first prove whether $U_4^{(i)}(Y) \geq \alpha_j, T_i \in S_j$ is right, if not, the delivery time can not be satisfied which means the schedule is not donable. The fitness of chromosome is 0, the corresponding individual being eliminated. Else when $U_4^{(i)}(Y) \geq \alpha_j, T_i \in S_j$ proves to be true, then *U1(Y), U2(Y)* and *U3(Y)* can figure out $\overline{pt}, \overline{ec}, \overline{rt}$, giving the weight of the three objectives(time, cost and equilibrium) w_1, w_2, w_3 on preferential relationship, then calculate $w_1 \overline{pt} + w_2 \overline{ec} + w_3 \overline{rt}$, the smaller the value, the higher the individual fitness is.

Operator of cross and mutation. The cross between two parents is operated as follows: exchange the codes presenting the same operation sequence in two chromosomes, and then we will get two sons.

The mutation process is as fig. 2, bit *j* of parent's chromosome mutates stochastically by certain probability. Notes: if bit j stands for the operation *k* of work piece I, the value range of bit *j* after mutation is $[1, H_{ik}]$.

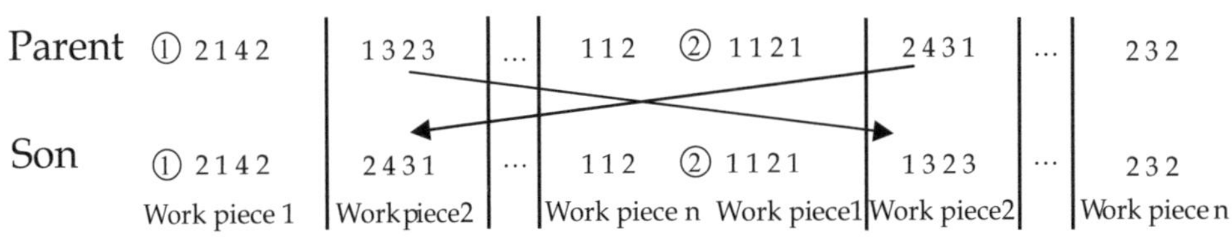

Fig. 1. Process of crossing

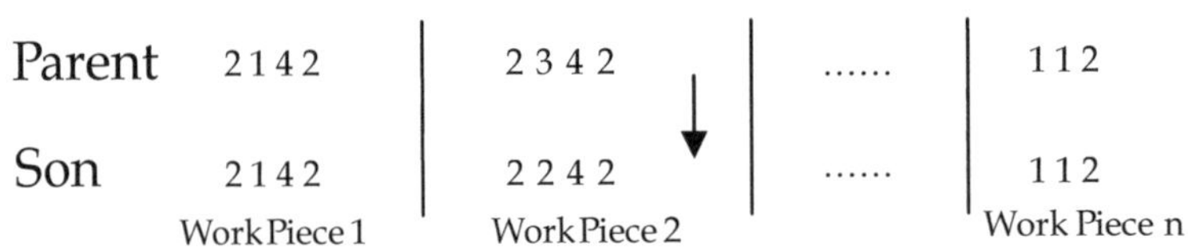

Fig. 2. Process map of mutation

5. Case study

We apply our study to a car manufacturing enterprise. The mold job-shop accepts the orders for manufacturing of molds, which include orders from both enterprise itself and other company. The manufacturing resources in the job-shop is enough with all necessary machine for mold processing, which include lathe, milling machine, grinding machine, numeral control machine, process center, electric discharge machine etc.(the serial number of machines are $R_1, R_2, \ldots, R_{35}$). Table 1 shows a piece of production order, which includes 3 work pieces waiting for process with delivery time of 270,300,320 respectively. The delivery time of work piece 1 and 2 should be strictly met with credibility99%, while work piece 3 is more flexible with a 50% credibility to meet the delivery time. So, there are two priorities of scheduling. Three work pieces have fixed process route, each operation has many devices available for processing which differ in time and cost. According to experience and historical statistically analysis, the time and cost spent on each machine for one operation are stochastic variables. The time comply with exponential distribution while cost obeys normal distribution, whose parameters are shown in table 1. Take "R_2/20/(18,6)"as an example, it means work piece being processed on machine R_2 with processing time obeying exponential distribution exp(20), cost obeying normal distribution N(18,6). We need to schedule for the order and implement optimum scheduling.

Work piece	Operation	Class of machine available		
		Resource1	Resource2	Resource3
Work piece 1	Lathing	R_2/20/(18,6)	R_3/25/(17,5)	
	Milling	R_7/35/(39,1)	R_8/30/(45,2)	R_{10}/40/(37,1)
	Surface process	R_{30}/100/(125,8)	R_{31}/90/(140,6)	R_{32}/110/(120,8)
	Lineation,Drilling Assembling,Adjustment	R_{20}/40/(50,4)	R_{22}/42/(55,3)	
	Line incision	R_{17}/40/(45,4)	R_{18}/45/(49,3)	
Work piece 2	Lathing	R2/25/(19,2)	R_3/33/(18,2)	R_5/30/(18,1)
	Drilling,Milling	R_8/40/(55,4)	R_{10}/50/(50,3)	
	Surface process	R_{30}/70/(85,8)	R_{31}/67/(90,6)	
	Grinding	R_{25}/50/(60,6)	R_{26}/52/(60,5)	
	Repairing Assembling	R_{20}/100/(110,10)	R_{21}/115/(117,10)	R_{22}/110/(121,9)
Work piece 3	Milling	R_8/60/(102,5)	R_9/70/(85,7)	R_{11}/55/(127,9)
	Surface process	R_{31}/50/(93,6)	R_{32}/60/(55,2)	R_{33}/58/(60,2)
	Electrode NC process	R_{35}/33/(36,4)	R_{30}/30/(42,3)	
	Electric-charge Process	R_{19}/40/(50,4)	R_{16}/39/(60,4)	
	Repairing ,assembling	R_{21}/160/(220,12)	R_{22}/150/(240,10)	

Table 1. Operations and machines available for work pieces

First, present a stochastic programming model, believable probabilities are:

$$\eta = \gamma = \nu = 0.8, \alpha_1 = 0.99, \alpha_2 = 0.5$$

Then use hybrid intelligent algorithm with weights of three objectives being 1/3 respectively to solve the problem. Get 200 groups of data samples through stochastic simulation (each group of data should be acquired by 500 times simulation), train the neural network with these data (15 input units, 18 hidden layer units and 6 output units), and calculate the weight. Finally, using genetic algorithm to find the optimum solution with 15 bits code, cross rate 0.5 and mutation rate 0.01. After 30 generations' evolution, the result of schedule is as follows:

Work piece 1(2,7,30,22,17), work piece 2(5,8,30,25,20), work piece 3(8,32,35,19,22). The numbers in the bracket represent the serial number of machine for each operation. According to experience, this schedule sequence is a approximate optimum solution which has satisfied the requirements of all the chance constraints.

6. Conclusions

After analyzing the stochastic factors as time and cost in production process, we have proposed stochastic programming model based on chance constraints to describe the multi-priorities Flexible Job-Shop Scheduling problem aiming at objectives of shorter production time, lower cost and equilibrium of schedule. The advantage of this model is that it reflects the stochastic condition in real job-shop and proposes a hybrid intelligent algorithm which syncretizes many critical techniques such as the stochastic simulation, neural network and genetic algorithm etc., finally, a case study shows that our study can be applied to FJSP to get a approximate optimum solution.

7. References

Baoding, L.; Ruiqing, Z. & Gang, W. (2003). Uncertain programming and application. In Chinese. Tsinghua University Press, Beijing

Croee, F. D. & Tadei, R. (1995). A genetic algorithm for the Job Shop problem. Computer Ops. Res.vol.22(1), pp.15—24.

Foo, Y. S. & Takefuji, Y. (1998). Integer linear programming neural networks for job-shop scheduling. In: IEEE Int Conf on NNS, San Diego,pp.320—332

Hongsen, Y. (1994). Research and Application of FMS Modeling, Scheduling, Controlling and Simulating. In Chinese. Harbin Institute of Technology.

Juanqi, Y. (1998). Synthetically Description and development of FMS Scheduling Research. In Chinese. Journal of Shanghai Jiaotong University,vol.32 (5),pp.124--127

Law, M. (1986). Simulation series: Part I: Introducing simulation: A tool for analyzing complex systems. Ind. Eng., May,: pp.46—63.

Peigen, L. (1998). Manufacturing System Performance Analysis Modeling - Theory and Methods. In Chinese. Huazhong University of Science and Technology, Wuhan

Philips, T.; Revenderen, A. etc. (1987). Theory and Practice of Operational Research, China Commercial Press, pp. 282--346. Beijing

Shuxia, L. (2004). MES certain technologies research under complex information environment. In Chinese. [Doctoral dissertation]. Wuhan

Taillard, E. (1990). Some efficient heuristic methods for the flow shop sequencing problem. Euro Operation Res. vol. 47(1), pp. 65—74.

Van Laarhoven. (1992). Job shop scheduling by simulated annealing, Operations Research.vol.40, pp.113--125

Zhaoqiang, G. & Yiren, Z. (2002). Study on Job Shop Fuzzy Scheduling Problem Based on Genetic Algorithm. In Chinese. CIMS, 8 (8),pp.616—620.

20

Adaptive Critic Designs-Based Autonomous Unmanned Vehicles Navigation: Application to Robotic Farm Vehicles

Daniel Patiño[1] and Santiago Tosetti
Instituto de Automática, Advanced Intelligent Systems Laboratory, Universidad Nacional de San Juan
Av. Lib. San Martín 1109 (O), 5400 San Juan, Argentina.
Argentina

1. Introduction

Unmanned vehicles like Unmanned Aerial Vehicles (UAV) and Unmanned Ground Vehicles (UGV) are mechanical devices capable of moving in some environment with a certain degree of autonomy. These vehicles use IMU (Inertial Measurement Unit), high precision GPS RTK (Global Positioning Systems, Real-Time Kinematics), encoders, compass, and tilt sensors, to position them self and follow waypoints. A picture of a vehicle with these characteristics is shown in Figure 1. Its use is becoming more frequent for both intensive and extensive agriculture, in the precision agriculture context. For example, in USA or Argentina with millions of arable hectares is essential to have autonomous farm machines for handling and managing growth, quality, and yield of the crops.

Fig. 1. Prototype of a UGV equipped with a number of sensors. This prototype belongs to the Instituto the Automática of the Universidad Nacional de San Juan.

[1] dpatino@inaut.unsj.edu.ar

The environment where these vehicles are used can be classified as:

- Structured or partially structured when it is well known and the motion can be planned in advance. In general, this is the case of navigation and guide of mobile robots.
- Not structured, when there are uncertainties which imply some on-line planning of the motion, this is the case of navigation and guide of robotic aerial vehicles.

In general, the objective of controlling the autonomous vehicles implies solving the problems of sensing, path planning and kinematic and dynamic control. Autonomy of a vehicle is related to determine its own position and velocity without external aids. Autonomy is very important to certain military vehicles and to civil vehicles operating in areas of inadequate radio-navigation coverage. Regarding the trajectory planning, there are many approaches (Aicardi et al., 1995). Many works have been published on the control of autonomous vehicles, mainly in the UGV or mobile robots. Some of them propose stable control algorithms which are based on Lyapunov theory (Singh & Fuller, 2001). Others have focused on optimization planning and control (Kuwata et al., 2005) and (Patiño et al., 2008).

In this paper we propose the use of ACDs to design autonomously an optimal path planning and control strategy for robotic unmanned vehicles, in particular for a mobile robot, following a previous work (Liu & Patiño, 1999a), and (Liu & Patiño, 1999b).

We consider a mobile robot with two actuated wheels and the autonomous control system is designed for kinematic and dynamic model. The kinematic mobile robot model for the so-called kinematic wheels under the nonholonomic constrain of *pure rolling* and *nonslipping*, is given by,

$$\dot{q} = S(q)v(t)\,, \tag{1}$$

Where $q(t), \dot{q}(t) \in \Re^3$ are defined as

$$q = [x, y, \theta]^T, \qquad \dot{q} = [\dot{x}, \dot{y}, \dot{\theta}]^T, \tag{2}$$

$x(t), y(t),$ and $\theta(t) \in \Re^3$ denote the linear position, and orientation respectively of the center of mass of the mobile vehicle; $\dot{x}(t), \dot{y}(t),$ denote the Cartesian components of the linear velocity of the vehicle; $\dot{\theta}(t),$ denotes the angular velocity of the mobile robot; the matrix $S(q) \in \Re^{3\times 2}$, is defined as,

$$S(q) = \begin{bmatrix} cos(\theta) & 0 \\ sin(\theta) & 0 \\ 0 & 1 \end{bmatrix}, \tag{3}$$

and the velocity vector $v(t) \in \Re^2$, is defined as

$$v = [v_l, w]^T\,, \tag{4}$$

with $v_l \in \Re$ denoting the constant straight line velocity, and $w(t) \in \Re$ is the angular velocity of the mobile robot.

Considering the dynamics of the car-driving device which contains a dc motor, a dc amplifier, and a gear transmission system,

$$w = \frac{Ka}{s^2 + bs + a} \cdot w_R\,, \tag{5}$$

where $w_R \in \Re$, is the reference angular velocity, and $K, a, b \in \Re^+$ are the car-driving device parameters.

The state of the mobile vehicle is given by (cf. Figure 1) the coordinates of the robot (x, y), the orientation of the vehicle, θ, and the actual turning rate of the robot, $\dot{\theta}$. The *control signal* is the *desired turning* rate of the mobile vehicle, w_R.

1.2 Control problem formulation

As was previously defined, the reference trajectory is generated via a reference vehicle which moves according to the following dynamic trajectory,

$$\dot{q}_R = S(q_R)v(t), \tag{6}$$

Where $S(\cdot)$ was defined in (3), $q_R = [x_R, y_R, \theta_R]^T \in \Re^3$ is the desired time-varying position and orientation trajectory, and $v_R = [v_l, w_l]^T \in \Re^2$ is the reference time-varying velocity. With regard to (5), it is assumed that the signal $v_R(t)$ is constructed to produce the desired motion, and that $v_R(t)$, $\dot{v}_R(t)$, $q_R(t)$, and $\dot{q}_R(t)$ are bounded for all time.

In general the vehicle motion control can be classified in: i) Positioning without prescribing orientation: in this case a final destination point is specified; ii) Positioning with prescribed orientation: in this case a destination point has to be achieved with a desired orientation; and iii) Path following: here, the path is defined through a sequence of waypoints.

In the first experiment, the *control objective* is limited to the first case, that is, given a reference point located at the workspace, (x_R, y_R), and considering the vehicle dynamical model, it is desired to obtain autonomously a *sequence of optimal control actions* (values of the turning rate) such that the vehicle achieves the target point as fast as possible (cf. Figure 2), and with minimum energy consumption. Since the mobile robot´s speed, v_l, is taken as constant, minimum-time control is equivalent to shortest-path control.

The design of the control system will be based on adaptive critic designs, in particular HDP (Werbos, 1992) and (Bellman, 1957). Next Section shows the background material needed for the present work.

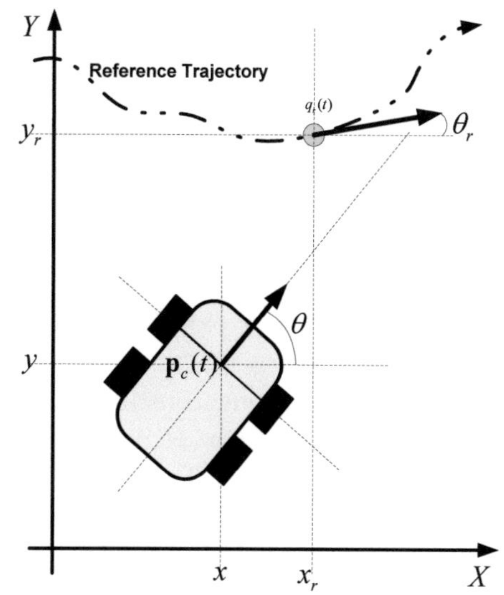

Fig. 1. The state of the unmanned ground vehicle.

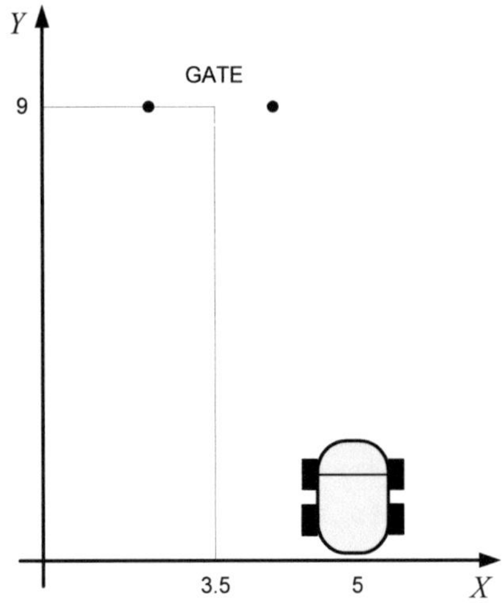

Fig. 2. The gate for the unmanned ground vehicle to go through.

2. Background in adaptive critic designs

2.1 Introduction to dynamic programming

Suppose that it is given a discrete-time nonlinear (time-varying) system,

$$x(k+1) = F[x(k),u(k),k]\,, \tag{7}$$

where, $x \in \Re^n$ represents the (complete) state vector of the system and $u \in \Re^m$ denotes the control action. Suppose that it is desired to minimize for (7) a performance index (or cost),

$$J[x(i),i] = \sum_{k=i}^{\infty} \gamma^{k-i} U[x(k),u(k),k], \tag{8}$$

where U is called the utility function or local cost function, and γ is the discount factor with $0 \le \gamma \le 1$. Note that J is dependent on the initial time i and the state $x(i)$, and it is referred to as the cost-to-go of the state $x(i)$. The objective is to choose the control sequence $u(k), k = i, i+1, \ldots$ so that the J function (the cost) in (8) is minimized. The cost in this case accumulates indefinitely; these kinds of problems are referred to as *infinite horizon problems* in Dynamic Programming. On the other hand, in finite horizon problems, the cost will accumulate over a finite number of steps. Dynamic programming is based on Bellman's *principle of optimality*, (Lewis & Syrnos, 1995), (Prokhorov & Wunsch, 1997), and establishes that an optimal (control) policy has the property that no matter what previous decisions (i.e., controls) have been, the remaining decisions must constitute an optimal policy with regard to the state resulting from those previous decisions.

Suppose that we have computed the optimal cost $J^*[x(k+1),k+1]$, from time $k+1$ to the terminal time for possible states $x(k+1)$, and that we have also found the optimal control sequences from time $k+1$ on. The optimal cost results when the optimal control sequence $u^*(k+1), u^*(k+2), \ldots,$ is applied to the system with initial state $x(k+1)$. Note that the optimal control sequence depends on $x(k+1)$. If we apply an arbitrary control $u(k)$ at time k and then use the known optimal control sequence from $(k+1)$ on, the resulting cost will be

$$J[x(k),k] = U[x(k),u(k),k] + \gamma J^*[x(k+1),k+1],$$

where, $x(k)$ is the state at time k and is determined by (2). According to Bellman, the optimal cost from time k on is equal to

$$\begin{aligned} J^*[x(k),k] &= \min_{u(k)} J[x(k),k] = \\ &= \min_{u(k)}\left(U[x(k),u(k),k] + \gamma J^*[x(k+1),k+1]\right). \end{aligned} \tag{9}$$

The optimal control $u^*(k)$ at time k is the $u(k)$ that achieves the minimum. Equation (9) is the principle of optimality for discrete-time systems. Its importance lies in the fact that it allows us to optimize over only one control vector at a time by working *backward* in time. Dynamic programming is a very useful tool in solving optimization and optimal control problems. In particular, it can easily be applied to nonlinear systems with constraints on the control and state variables, and arbitrary performance indexes.

2.2 Adaptive critic designs

In the computations in (9), whenever one knows the function J and the model F in (7), it is a simple problem in function minimization to pick the actions $u^*(k)$ which minimize J. However, due to the backward numerical process required, it is too computationally expensive to determine the exact J function for most real problems, even when the scales of the problems are considered to be small. Therefore, approximation methods are demanding in practice when performing dynamic programming (Werbos, 1992), (Bellman, 1957), (Balakrishnan & Biega, 1995).

Instead of solving for the value of J function for every possible state, one can use a function approximation structure such as a neural network to approximate the J function. There are three basic methods proposed in the literature for approximating the dynamic programming. They are collectively called Adaptive Critic Designs, which include Heuristic Dynamic Programming (HDP), Dual Heuristic Programming (DHP), and Globalized Dual Heuristic Programming (GDIHP) (Bellman, 1957), (Werbos, 1990), (Balakrishnan & Biega, 1995).

A typical adaptive critic design consists of three modules —Critic, Model, and Action. The present work considers the case where each module is a neural network; the designs in this case are referred to as neural network--based adaptive critic designs. The following introduces the HDP. In HDP (Werbos, 1990), (Werbos, 1992), (Lewis & Syrnos, 1995), (Balakrishnan & Biega, 1995, the critic network output estimates J function in equation (7). This is done by minimizing the following error measure over time,

$$\|E_1\| = \sum_k E_1(k) = \frac{1}{2}\sum_k [J(k) - U(k) - \gamma J(k+1)]^2 \tag{10}$$

where, $J(k) = J[x(k),t,W_C]$ and W_C represents the parameters of the critic network. The function U is chosen as a utility function which indicates the performance of the overall system (see examples in (Balakrishnan & Biega, 1995), (Werbos, 1990)). It is usually a function of $x(k)$, $u(k)$, and k, i.e., $U(k)=[x(k),u(k),k]$. When $E_1(k)=0$ for all k, (10) implies that

$$J(k)=U(k)+\gamma J(k+1)= \\ =U(k)+\gamma[U(k+1)+\gamma J(k+2)]=\ldots=\sum_{l=k}^{\infty}\gamma^{l-k}U(k) \tag{11}$$

which is exactly the same as in dynamic programming [cf. (8)]. In Eq. (11), it is assumed that $J(k)<\infty$ which can usually be guaranteed by choosing the discount factor γ such that $0<\gamma<1$. The training samples for the critic network are obtained over a trajectory starting from $x(0)=x_0$ at $k=0$.The trajectory can be either over a fixed number of time steps [e.g., 300 consecutive points] or from $k=0$ until the final state is reached. The training process will be repeated until no more weight update is needed.
The weight update, during the pth training iteration, is given by

$$W_{C,i}^{(p+1)}=W_{C,i}^{(p)}-\eta_1\frac{\partial E_1(k)}{\partial W_{C,i}^{(p)}}= \\ =W_{C,i}^{(p)}-\eta_1[J(k)-U(k)-\gamma J(k+1)]\frac{\partial J(k)}{\partial W_{C,i}^{(p)}} \tag{12}$$

where, $\eta_1>0$ is the learning rate and $W_{C,i}$, the ith component of W_C. Note that the gradient method is used in (12) and that the pth corresponds to certain time instant k [hence the use $E_1(k)$ in (12)]. The weight update can also be performed in batch mode, e.g., after the completion of each trajectory. The model network in an adaptive critic design predicts $x(k+1)$ given $x(k)$ and $u(k)$; it is needed for the computation of

$$J(k+1)=J[x(k+1),k+1,W_C^{(p-1)}]$$

in (12) for the weight update. The model network learns the mapping given in equation (7); it is trained previously off-line (Werbos, 1992), (Bellman, 1957), (Balakrishnan & Biega, 1995), or trained in parallel with the critic and action networks. Here, $J(k+1)$ is calculated using $W_C^{(p-1)}$ and its dependence on $W_C^{(p)}$ is not considered, according to (Liu & Patiño, 1999a). After the critic network's training is finished, the action network's training starts with the objective of minimizing $J(k+1)$. The action network generates an action signal $u(k)=[x(k),k,W_A]$; its training follows a similar procedure to the one for the critic network's training. The training process will be repeated until no more weight update is needed while keeping the critic network's weights fixed. During the pth training iteration, the weight update is given by

$$W_{A,i}^{(p+1)}=W_{A,i}^{(p)}-\alpha_1\frac{\partial J(k+1)}{\partial W_{A,i}^{(p)}}= \\ =W_{A,i}^{(p)}-\alpha_1\sum_{j=1}^{n}\frac{\partial J(k+1)}{\partial x_j(k+1)}\sum_{k=1}^{m}\frac{\partial x_j(k+1)}{\partial u_k(k)}\cdot\frac{\partial u_k(k)}{\partial W_{A,i}^{(p)}} \tag{13}$$

where, $\alpha_1 > 0$. Again, the model network is required for the computation of $\partial x_i(k)/\partial u_k(k)$ in the above weight update. It can be seen in (13) that information is propagated backward through the critic network to the model network and then to the action network, as if three networks formed one large feedforward network. After action network's training cycle is completed, one may check its performance, then stop or continue the training procedure entering the critic network's training cycle again, if the performance is not acceptable yet.
It is emphasized that in the methods described above, the knowledge of desired target values for the function J and the action signal $u(k)$ is not required in the neural net-work training. In conventional applications of neural networks for function approximation, the knowledge of the desired target values of the function to be approximated is required. It should also be emphasized that the nature of the present methodology is to iteratively build a link between present actions and future consequences via an estimate of the utility function J.

3. Main results

A simulation study has been carried out using the mobile vehicle model presented in Section I. The set of parameters for this vehicle model used are the following: $K = 0.45$, $a = 102.6$, $b = 9.21$, $vl = 0.2m/s$. The three networks (critic, action, and model) are all implemented using multilayer feedforward neural networks. Each neural network has six inputs, $(x_R, y_R, x, y, \theta, w)$, where x_R and y_R denote the desired target gate. The critic network output J, the action network output w_R, and the model network is trained according to equation (1) and (5). The training samples for the critic network are obtained over trajectories starting from $x(0) = 0.5$ at $k = 0$, initial position of the vehicle, and a reference point located at position $(8m, 3.5m)$.
The discount factor is chosen as $\gamma = 0.8$, and the utility function is chosen as

$$U(k) = \frac{1}{2}\left[q\left(\tilde{x}^2(k) + \tilde{y}^2(k)\right) + rw_R^2(k)\right]$$

where, $\tilde{x} = x - x_R$ and $\tilde{y} = y - y_R$ are position errors with respect to the target point (x, y), and $q > 0$ and $r > 0$ are positive weight constants. As described previously, the training takes place in two stage: the training of model network, and then the training of critic network and action network. The objective for the training of the critic network is to match $J(k)$ with $U(k) + \gamma J(k+1)$. The objective for the training of the action network la minimize $J(k+1)$. The procedures for the training of critic and action networks are similar, and they are repeated iteratively. Figure 3 shows the result for the mobile vehicle when reaching the reference point, after 10 trials (learning cycles), and Figure 4 passing through one gate from two different initial conditions. Figure 5 shows the result for the mobile vehicle through two gates.
A second simulation study was performed using the kinematic model of both the robot and the reference trajectory virtual robot. In his case the mathematical model of the systems are defined as in Equations (1), (2) and (3) under the non-holonomic restriction

$$\theta(t) = tan^{-1}\frac{\dot{y}(t)}{\dot{x}(t)}. \tag{14}$$

In this case both the linear and angular velocities are variable, and the mobile robot follows a reference trajectory given by the equations

$$\begin{aligned} \dot{x}_r &= v_r \cos\theta_r \\ \dot{y}_r &= v_r \sin\theta_r \; . \\ \dot{\theta}_r &= \omega_r \end{aligned} \tag{15}$$

Once the reference trajectory is stated, the tracking error can be defined as (Kanayama et al. 1990)

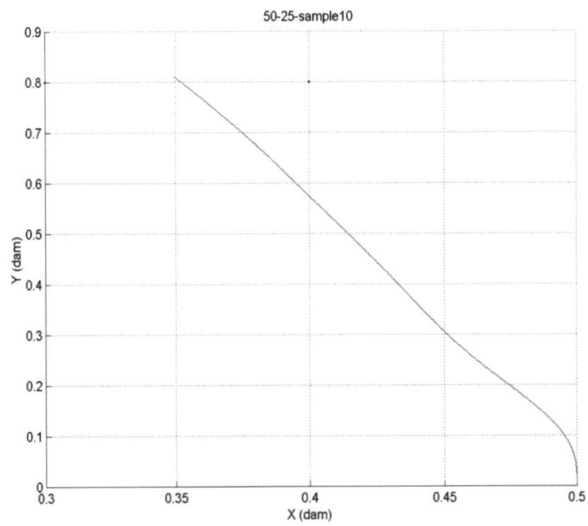

Fig. 3. Result for passing through the gate.

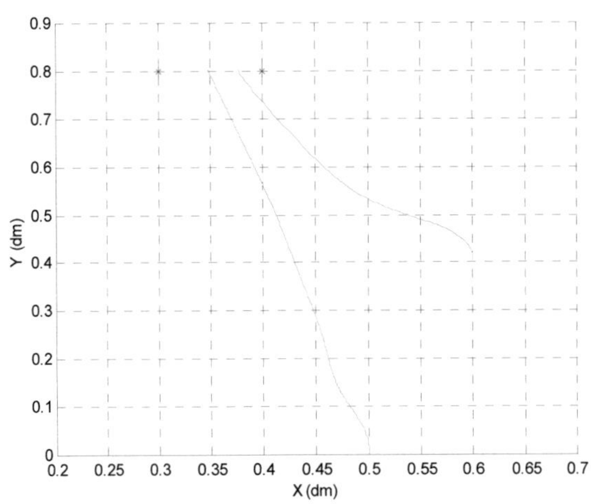

Fig. 4. Result for passing through one gate from two different initial conditions.

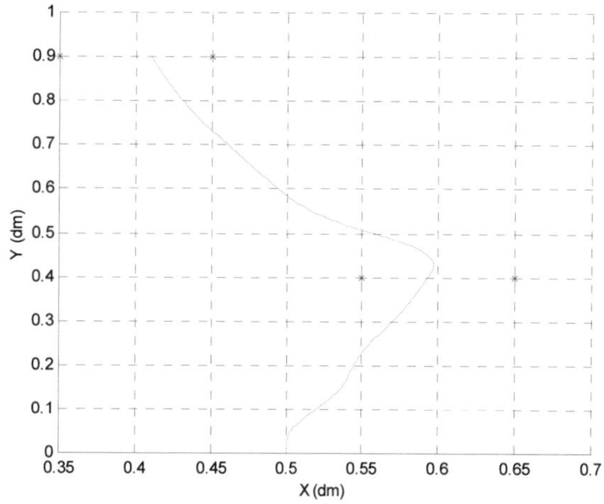

Fig. 5. Result for passing through two gates.

$$\begin{bmatrix} x_e \\ y_e \\ \theta_e \end{bmatrix} = \begin{bmatrix} \cos\theta & \sin\theta & 0 \\ -\sin\theta & \cos\theta & 0 \\ 0 & 0 & 1 \end{bmatrix} \begin{bmatrix} x_r - x \\ y_r - y \\ \theta_r - \theta \end{bmatrix}, \tag{16}$$

and combining equations (1), (14) and (15), the tracking error model is

$$\begin{aligned} \dot{x}_e &= \omega y_e - v_r + v_r \cos\theta_e \\ \dot{y}_e &= -\omega x_e + v_r \sin\theta_e \\ \dot{\theta}_e &= \omega_r - \omega \end{aligned} . \tag{17}$$

Figure 6 shows all the variables presented in the previous equations.

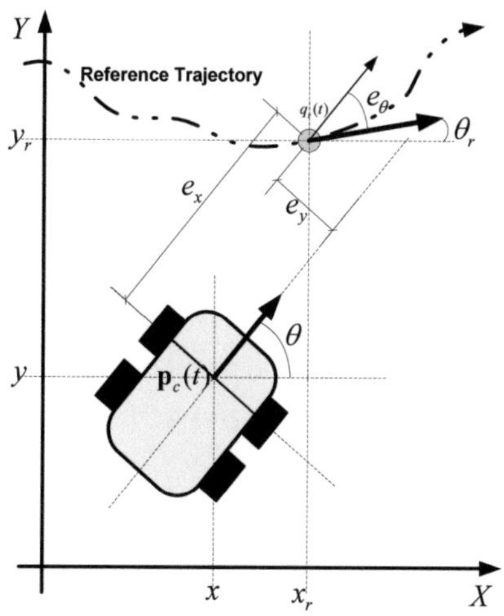

Fig. 6. Representation of the robot and virtual robot state variables.

For the sake of simplicity, a new set of coordinates is chosen, defined as

$$\begin{bmatrix} x_0 \\ x_1 \\ x_2 \end{bmatrix} = \begin{bmatrix} \theta_e \\ y_e \\ -x_e \end{bmatrix}, \begin{bmatrix} u_0 \\ u_1 \end{bmatrix} = \begin{bmatrix} \omega_r - \omega \\ v - v_r \cos x_0 \end{bmatrix}. \tag{18}$$

Finally, equation (16) can be written as

$$\begin{aligned} \dot{x}_0 &= u_0 \\ \dot{x}_1 &= (\omega_r - u_1)x_2 + v_r \sin x_0 \\ \dot{x}_2 &= -(\omega_r - u_0)x_1 + u_1 \end{aligned} . \tag{19}$$

With this change of coordinates the tracking problem is turned into a regulation one. In this experiment the control action is given by

$$\begin{bmatrix} u_0 \\ u_1 \end{bmatrix} = K \begin{bmatrix} x_0 \\ x_1 \\ x_2 \end{bmatrix}. \tag{20}$$

Figure 7 shows the overall block diagram of the control system.

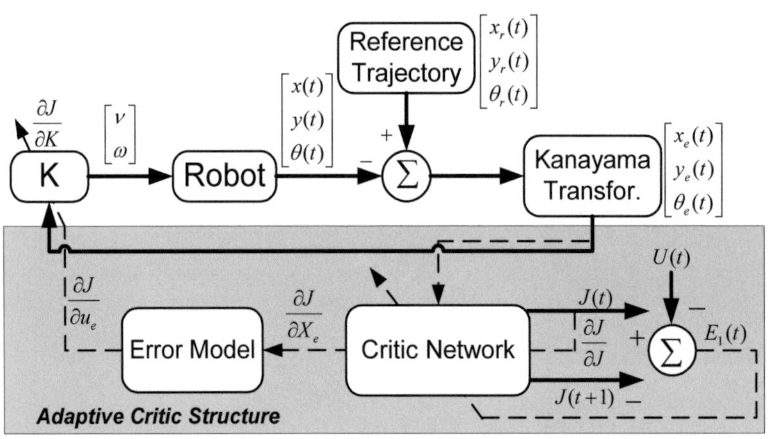

Fig. 7. Block diagram of the control system.

The virtual robot describes a circular trajectory given by the equations:

$$\begin{aligned} x_r &= x_c + R \sin(ct) \\ y_r &= y_c - R \cos(ct) \\ \theta_r &= tan^{-1} \frac{\dot{y}_r}{\dot{x}_r} = ct \\ v_r &= \sqrt{\dot{x}_r^2 + y_r^2} = cR \\ \omega_r &= \dot{\theta}_r = c \end{aligned}$$

Where $(x_c, y_c) = (0,0)$ is the center of the trajectory, $R = 0.5$ is the radius, $c = 0.2$ and t is the time.
The utility function given for this experiment is

$$U(k) = \frac{1}{2}\left[\left(x^T(k)Qx(k)\right) + u^T(k)Ru(k)\right],$$

with

$$Q = \begin{bmatrix} 0.1 & 0 & 0 \\ 0 & 0.1 & 0 \\ 0 & 0 & 0.1 \end{bmatrix} \text{ and } R = \begin{bmatrix} 0.1 & 0 \\ 0 & 0.1 \end{bmatrix}$$

The experience begins with a K matrix stable but not adjusted, given the results shown in Figures 8 and 9.
After 11 iterations of the training algorithm, the control system guides the robot to track the reference trajectory, as can be seen in Figures 10 and 11.

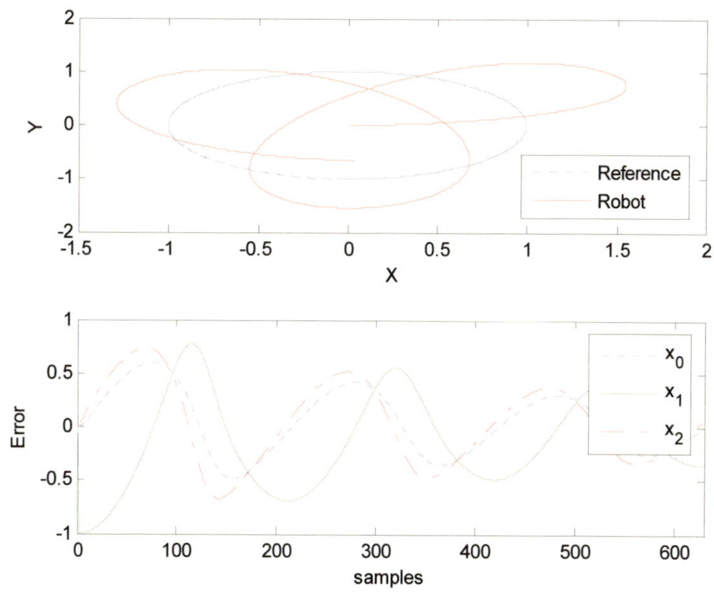

Fig. 8 Reference trajectory and initial performance of the robot.

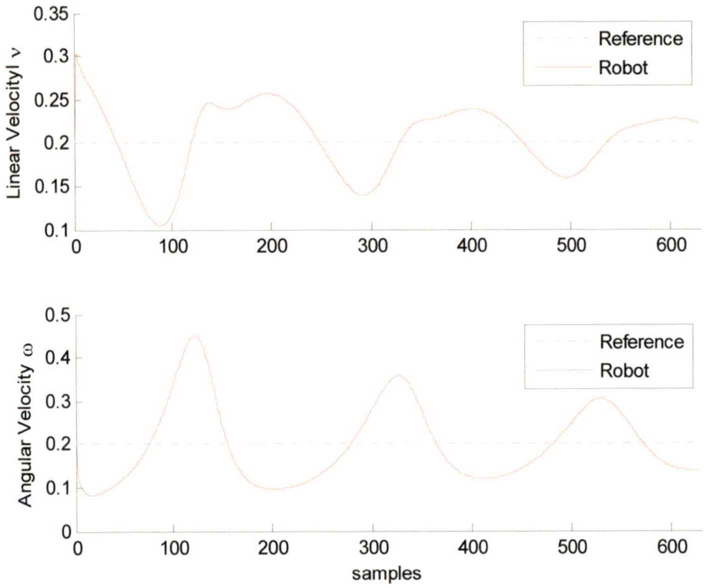

Fig. 9. Linear and angular velocity for the first trial.

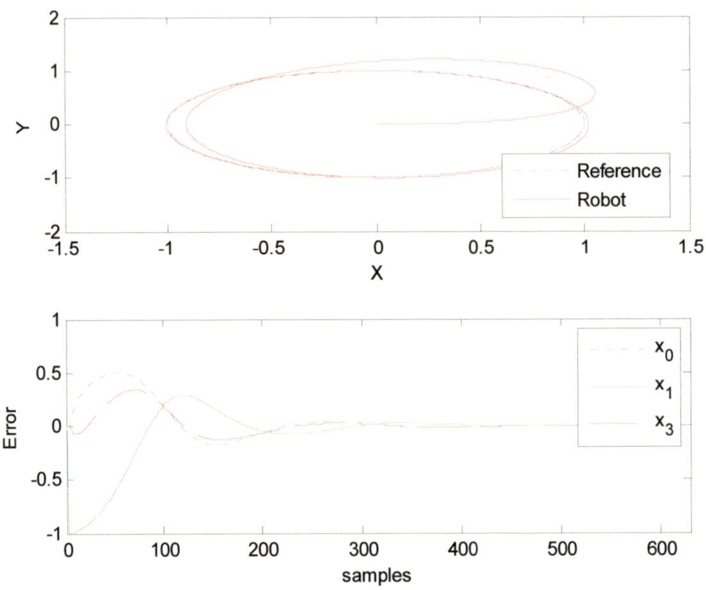

Fig. 10. Performance of the control system after 11 training iterations.

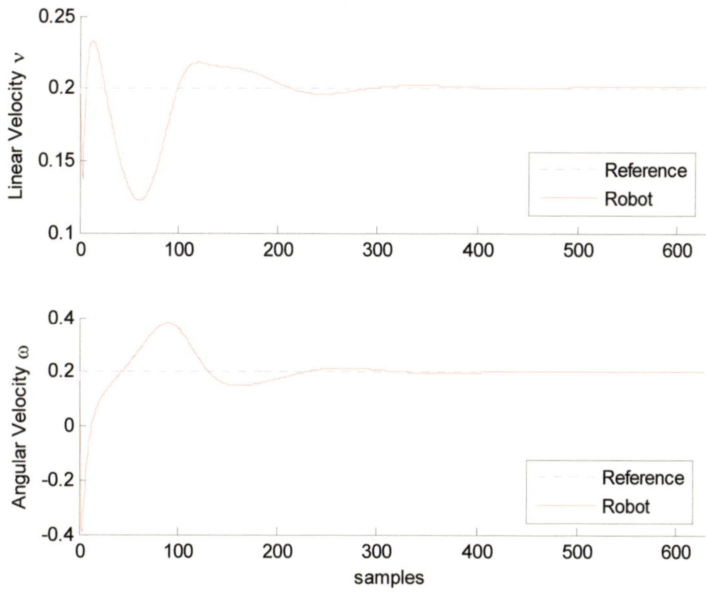

Fig. 11. Linear and angular velocity after 11 training iterations.

4. Conclusions

A solution to the problem of generating autonomously optimal control action sequence for a mobile robot control based on Adaptive Critic Designs approach has been presented. The proposed controller based on adaptive critic designs learns to guide the robot to a final point autonomously. It has been shown that using this technique we can obtain near optimal control actions which requires no external training data and gives an optimal control law for the entire range of operation. This work is extensible to UAV, assuming that is flying at a constant altitude, so the mission will be restricted to a planar motion around of a target point, and the kinematic equation of motion is similar to a UGV, see (Patiño et al., 20008). Future directions of research will be oriented to reach a final point with orientation with application to UAV. In addition, the problem of obstacle avoidance will be addressed. It will be also researched with other structures as DHP and GDHP, to use different local cost functions, and to consolidate formally a systematic design principle. From a theoretical point of view the efforts will be placed on the robustness issues of optimal control systems using adaptive critic designs.

5. Acknowledgements

This work was supported by Universidad Nacional de San Juan, and Agency for Scientific and Technological Promotion (ANPCyT), Argentina, under grant PICT/04 N° 21592, and PICT/05 Start-up N° 35398.

6. References

Aicardi M., Casalino G., Bicchi A., and Balestrino A. (1995). Closed Loop Steering of Unicycle-Like Vehicles via Lyapunov Techniques. *IEEE Robotics and Automation Magazine*, Vol. 2, No. 1, pp. 27-35.

Balakrishnan S. N., and Biega V. (1995). Adaptive critic based neural networks for control (low order systems applications). *Proceedings 1995 American Control Conference*, 335-339, Seattle, WA, 1995.

Bellman R. E., . (1957). Dynamic Programming*Princeton University Press*, Princeton, NJ.

Kanayama, Yukata, Yoshihiko Kimura, Fumio Miyazaki and Tetsuo Noguchi (1990). A stable tracking control method for an autonomous mobile robot. Proceedings IEEE International Conference on Robotics and Automation 1, 384-389.

Kuwata Y., Schouwenaars T, Richards A., and How J. (2005). Robust Constrained Receding Horizon Control for Trajectory Planning. *AIAA Guidance, Navigation, and Control Conference*, San Francisco, California, August.

Lewis F. and Syrnos V. L. (1995). Optimal Control. *John Wiley*, New York, NY, 1995.

Liu D. and Patiño H. D. (1999a). Adaptive Critic Designs for Self-Learning Ship Steering Control. *Proceedings of the 1999 IEEE, International Symposium on Intelligent Control/Intelligent Systems and Semiotics,* Cambridge, MA September, pp. 15-17.

Liu D, and Patiño H. D. (1999b) A Self-Learning Ship Steering Controller Based on Adaptive Critic Designs. *14th World Congress of IFAC*, Beijing, P.R. China, pp. 367-372.

Patiño H. D., Tosetti S., and Martinez M. (2008). A New Kinematics-Based Tracking Control for UAV using a Reference Virtual Aerial Robot Approach, *2º Conferencia/Workshop de Vehículos/Sistemas No-Tripulados (UVS) de América Latina*, Ciudad de Panamá, Panamá, Aug. 2008, pp. 5-7.

Prokhorov D. V., and Wunsch D. (1997). Adaptive Critic Designs, *IEEE Tranactions on Neural Networks*, Vol. 8, No. 5, Sep. 1997, pp. 997-1007.

Singh L. and Fuller J. (2001).Trajectory generation for a UAV in Urban Terrain, using nonlinear MPC, *Proceedings of American Control Conference,* Arlington, VA, 2001, pp. 2301-08.

Werbos P. (1990a). Consistency of HDP applied to a simple reinforcement learning problem. *Neural Networks*, 3, 1990, pp. 179-189.

Werbos P. (1990b). A menu of designs for reinforcement learning over time. *Neural Networks for Control* (W.T. Miller III, R.S. Sutton, and P.J. Werbos, Eds.). Chapter 3. The MIT Press, Cambridge, MA, 1990.

Werbos P. (1992a). Neurocontrol and supervised learning: An overview and evaluation. In: Handbook of Intelligent Control. *Neural, Fuzzy, and Adaptive Approaches* (D.A. White aud D.A. Sofge, Eds.). Chapter 3, Van Nostrand Reinhold, New York, NY, 1992.

Werbos P. (1992b).Approximate dynamic programming for real-time control and neural modeling. *Handbook of Intelligent Control Neural, Fuzzy, and Adaptive Approaches* (D.A. White and D.A. Sofge, Eds.). Chapter 13. Van Nostrand Reinhold, New York, NY, 1992.

21

DAQL-Enabled Autonomous Vehicle Navigation in Dynamically Changing Environment

Chi Kit Ngai and Nelson H. C. Yung
The University of Hong Kong, Hong Kong, China

1. Introduction

Many autonomous tasks can be considered as having to satisfy multiple goals simultaneously. In particular, Autonomous Vehicle (AV) navigation can be considered as a task having to satisfy at least two goals in an environment. The first goal is to plan a path for an agent to move from an origin to a destination that takes the shortest number of navigation steps. If the environment is static and the destination is stationary, then this shortest path is constant and can be planned in advance if the environment is known a priori, or estimated as the agent explores the environment if it is initially unknown. If the environment or the destination is dynamically changing, then the shortest path is no longer constant. This problem may still be considered as a path planning issue if the environment at each sampled time is known. However, the problem is more appropriately dealt with by incorporating a second goal that aims to avoid collisions between the agent and its neighboring obstacles while executing an overall shortest path strategy towards the destination. The collision avoidance (CA) problem has been well studied in the context of static known or unknown environments (Latombe, 1991; Ge & Cui, 2000; Oriolo et al., 1998; Ye et al., 2003). In the case of dynamic environments (DE) (Stentz, 1994; Stentz, 1995; Yang & Meng, 2003; Minguez & Minguez, 2004; Minguez, 2005), the focus at present is on dynamic environment (DE) that is slowly changing with fairly low obstacle density.

In theory, if the agent samples the environment fast enough, any environment would appear as a static environment and the navigation problem can be solved using existing solutions for static environments. In practice, this condition is difficult to achieve particularly when obstacles are moving at speeds higher than the agent or sampling rate is low. To deal with this situation, an obvious approach is to explicitly consider obstacle motions. Fiorini & Shiller (Fiorini & Shiller, 1998) proposed the concept of Velocity Obstacles that enables obstacle motions between two time steps to be considered in their formulation. Like other similar algorithms (Mucientes e al., 2001; Yamamoto et al., 2001; Feng et al., 2004; Qu et al., 2004), they assumed that objects move in a constant velocity. Shiller et al. (Shiller et al., 2001; Large et al., 2002) further proposed the non-linear velocity obstacle concept which assumes that obstacles can have variable speed. Moreover, they described the obstacles' trajectories using circular approximation. Although it may not always capture the correct movement of obstacles, it is an attempt to predict obstacle motions between two time steps. Similarly, Zhu's hidden Markov model (Zhu, 1991) and Miura's probabilistic model (Miura et al., 1999) also attempted the same. The idea of considering obstacles motion within two time steps explicitly proves to be vital in enhancing the agent's CA ability in reality. Motivated by this idea, we propose in this chapter a new approach, which incorporates two major features that are not found in solutions for static environments: (1) actions performed by obstacles are taken into account when the agent determines its own action; and (2) reinforcement learning is adopted by the agent to handle destination seeking (DS) and obstacle actions.

Reinforcement Learning (RL) (Sutton & Barto, 1998) aims to find an appropriate mapping from situations to actions in which a certain reward is maximized. It can be defined as a class of problem solving approaches in which the learner (agent) learns through a series of trial-and-error searches and delayed rewards (Sutton & Barto, 1998; Kaelbling, 1993; Kaelbling et al., 1996; Sutton, 1992). The purpose is to maximize not just the immediate reward, but also the cumulative reward in the long run, such that the agent can learn to approximate an optimal behavioral strategy by continuously interacting with the environment. This allows the agent to work in a previously unknown environment by learning about it gradually. In fact, RL has been applied in various CA related problems (Er & Deng, 2005; Huang et al., 2005; Yoon & Sim, 2005) in static environments. For RL to work in a DE containing multiple agents, the consideration of actions of other agents/obstacles in the environment becomes necessary (Littman, 2001). For example, Team Q-learning (QL) (Littman, 2001; Boutilier, 1996) considered the actions of all the agents in a team and focused on the fully cooperative game in which all agents try to maximize a single reward function together. For agents that do not share the same reward function, Claus and Boutilier (Claus & Boutilier, 1998) proposed the used of JAL. Their results showed that by taking into account the actions of another agent, JAL performs somewhat better than the traditional QL. However, JAL depends crucially on the strategy adopted by the other agents and it assumes that other agents maintain the same strategy throughout the game. While this assumption may not be valid, Hu and Wellman proposed Nash Q-learning (Hu & Wellman, 2004) which focuses on a general sum game that the agents are not necessarily working cooperatively. Nash equilibrium is used for the agent to adopt a strategy which is the best response to the other's strategy. This approach requires the agent to learn others Q-value by assuming that the agent can observe other's rewards.

In this chapter, we propose an improved QL method called Double Action Q-Learning (DAQL) (Ngai & Yung, 2005a; Ngai & Yung, 2005b) that similarly considers the agent's own action and other agents' actions simultaneously. Instead of assuming that the rewards of other agents can be observed, we use a probabilistic approach to predict their actions, so that they may work cooperatively, competitively or independently. Based on this, we further develop it into a solution for the two goal navigation problem in a dynamically changing environment, and generalize it for solving multiple goal problems. The solution uses DAQL when it is required to consider the responses of other moving agents/obstacles. If agent action would not cause the destination to move, then QL (Watkins & Dayan, 1992) would suffice for DS. Given two actions from two goals, a proportional goal fusion function is employed to maintain a balance in the final action decision. Extensive simulations of the proposed method in environments with single constant speed obstacle to multiple obstacles at variable speed and directions indicate that the proposed method is able to (1) deal with single obstacle at any speed and directions; (2) deal with two obstacles approaching from different directions; (3) cope with large sensor noise; (4) navigate in high obstacle density and high relative velocity environments. Detailed comparison with the Artificial Potential Field method (Ratering & Gini, 1995) reveals that the proposed method improves path time and the number of collision-free episodes by 20.6% and 23.6% on average, and 27.8% and 115.6% at best, respectively.

The rest of this chapter is organized as follows: Section 2 introduces the concept of the proposed DAQL-enabled reinforcement learning framework. Section 3 describes the implementation method of the proposed framework in solving the autonomous vehicle navigation problem. Section 4 presents the simulation procedures and results with comparisons with related method. Finally, conclusions are given in Section 5.

2. DAQL-enabled multiple goal reinforcement learning

2.1 General overview

Autonomous navigation is inherently a multiple goal problem involving destination seeking, collision avoidance, lane/wall following and others. Fig. 1 depicts the concept of multiple goal Reinforcement Learning with totally G goals. A multiple-goal scenario can be generalized such that both conventional QL and DAQL can be used for learning depending on the nature of the environment. The individual Q-values are eventually fused to produce a final action. For instance, limit the vehicle navigation problem to two goals: DS and CA. If obstacles and destination are non-stationary, then both goals can be dealt with by DAQL, whereas if they are all stationary, then QL suffice. Here, this general concept is illustrated by assuming that the destination is stationary and the obstacles are mobile. As such, QL is used for DS and DAQL is used for CA.

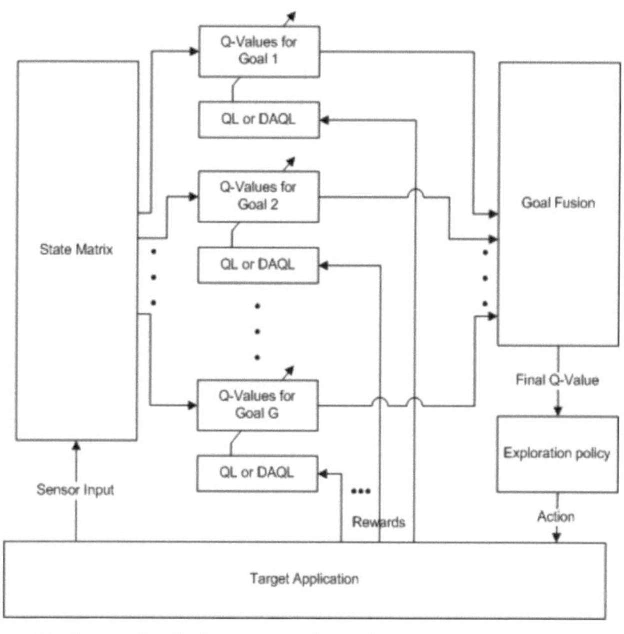

Fig. 1. Concept of multiple goal reinforcement learning.

2.2 Reinforcement learning framework

An effective tool for mapping states (that describe the environment) to actions (that are taken by an agent) and carrying out appropriate optimization (based on a value function) is the Markov Decision Process (MDP) model. It is a model for sequential decision making under uncertainty. In an MDP, the transition probability and the reward function are determined by the current state and the action selected by the agent only (Puterman, 1994). It can be explained by considering a specific time instant of an agent and its environment as depicted in Fig. 2. At each time step t, the agent observes the state $s_t \in S$, where S is the set of possible states, then chooses an action $a_t \in A(s_t)$, where $A(s_t)$ is the set of actions available in s_t, based on s_t and an exploration policy (e.g. greedy policy). The action causes the environment to change to a new state (s_{t+1}) according to a transition probability, $P^a_{ss'} = \Pr\{s_{t+1} = s' \mid s_t = s, a_t = a\}$. At the end of a sampling time T, the environment returns a reward or penalty to the agent according to a reward function, $R^a_{ss'} = E\{r_{t+1} \mid a_t = a, s_t = s, s_{t+1} = s'\}$. The agent then faces a similar situation in the next time instant.

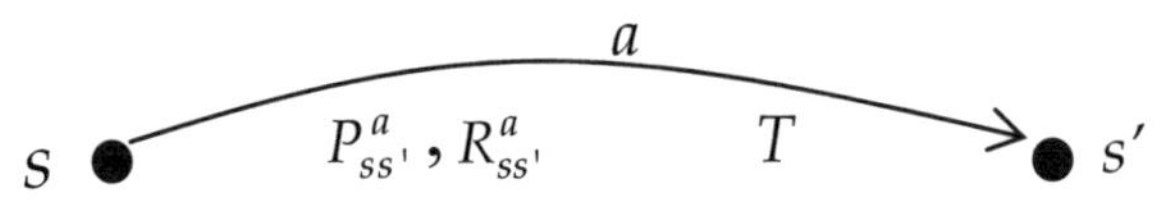

Fig. 2. State diagram of the MDP model given that s_t=s, s_{t+1}=s', and a_t=a.

In RL, the value function is introduced to estimate the value for the agent to be in a given state. It is the expected infinite discounted sum of reward that the agent will gain as follows (Sutton & Barto, 1998):

$$V^{\pi}(s) = E_{\pi}\{R_t \mid s_t = s\} = E_{\pi}\left\{\sum_{k=0}^{\infty} \gamma^k r_{t+k+1} \mid s_t = s\right\} \tag{1}$$

where $E_\pi\{\}$ is the expected value when policy π is adopted and R_t is the discounted sum of future rewards; γ is the discounting factor and r_{t+k+1} is the reward (or penalty) received at time (t+k+1). Policy π is a mapping from each state-action pair to the probability $\pi(s,a)$ of taking action a when in state s. To solve the RL task, an optimal policy should be determined that would result in an a_t with the highest expected discounted reward from s to the end of the episode. The optimal value function corresponding to the optimal policy is then achieved by maximizing the value function that represents the expected infinite discounted sum of reward:

$$V^*(s) = \max_{a \in A(s)} \sum_{s'} P^a_{ss'}\left(R^a_{ss'} + \gamma V^{\pi}(s')\right) \tag{2}$$

The corresponding action-value function is given as:

$$Q^{\pi}(s,a) = E_{\pi}\{R_t \mid s_t = s, a_t = a\} = E_{\pi}\left\{\sum_{k=0}^{\infty} \gamma^k r_{t+k+1} \mid s_t = s, a_t = a\right\} \tag{3}$$

and the optimal action-value function is given as:

$$Q^*(s,a) = E\left\{r_{t+1} + \gamma \max_{a'} Q^*(s_{t+1}, a') \mid s_t = s, a_t = a\right\} = \sum_{s'} P^a_{ss'}\left[R^a_{ss'} + \gamma \max_{a'} Q^*(s', a')\right] \tag{4}$$

2.3 Q-learning

Q-Learning (Watkins & Dayan, 1992) is one of the efficient methods for solving the RL problem through the action-value function in Eqt. (4). In QL, the agent chooses a_t according to policy π and the Q-values corresponding to state s_t. After performing action a_t in state s_t and making the transition to state s_{t+1}, it receives an immediate reward (or penalty) r_{t+1}. It then updates the Q-values for a_t in s_t using the Q-values of the new state, s_{t+1}, and the reward r_{t+1} as given by the update rule:

$$Q(s_t,a_t) \leftarrow Q(s_t,a_t) + \alpha\left[r_{t+1} + \gamma \max_{a_{t+1}} Q(s_{t+1},a_{t+1}) - Q(s_t,a_t)\right] \tag{5}$$

QL has been proven to converge to optimal action-value with probability one if each action is executed in each state an infinite number of times (Kaelbling et al., 1996; Watkins & Dayan, 1992), and works reasonably well in single agent environment, where the agent is the only object that is able to evoke a state transition.

2.4 Double action Q-learning

In general, it is fair to assume that a DE consists of static obstacles (e.g. walls) and dynamic agents/obstacles. In this case, the assumption that state transition is solely caused by an agent is not exactly appropriate (Littman, 2001; Boutilier, 1995; Claus & Boutilier, 1998). In other words, state transition in a DE may be caused by the action taken by the agent, $a^1_t \in A_1(s_t)$, and a collective action taken by the other agents/obstacles, $a^2_t \in A_2(s_t)$, where $A_1(s_t)$ and $A_2(s_t)$ are the set of actions available in s_t for the agent and the obstacle in the environment respectively. Fig. 3 depicts a new MDP that reflects this relationship, whereas a^2_t describes the action performed by an obstacle. The net state transition at each time step is the result of all the action pairs taken together.

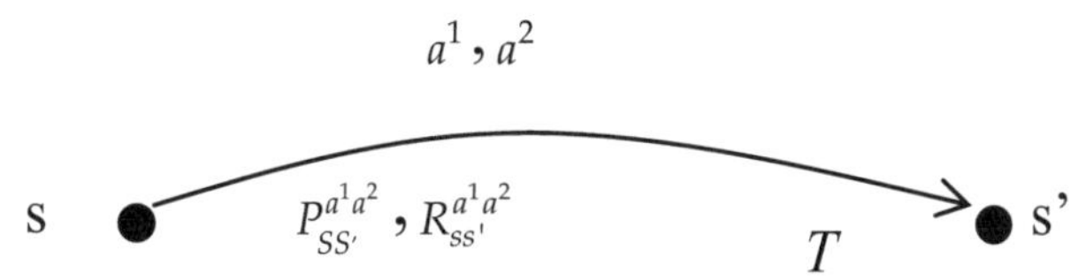

Fig. 3. State diagram of the new MDP model given that $s_t = t$, $s_{t+1} = s'$, $a^1_t = a^1$, and $a^2_t = a^2$.

The seven parameters of the new MDP are: T, s_t, s_{t+1}, a^1_t, a^2_t, $P^{a^1a^2}_{ss'}$ and $R^{a^1a^2}_{ss'}$, where $P^{a^1a^2}_{ss'} = \Pr\{s_{t+1} = s' \mid s_t = s, a^1_t = a^1, a^2_t = a^2\}$ is the transition probability from s to s′, when the agent takes action a^1 and the environment takes action a^2; and $R^{a^1a^2}_{ss'} = E\{r_{t+1} \mid a^1_t = a^1, a^2_t = a^2, s_t = s, s_{t+1} = s'\}$ is the reward received as a result.

In this new model, state changes when either (or both) the agent or the environment has taken its action. To reflect the fact that state transition is now determined by a^1 and a^2, the new value function is formulated below:

$$\begin{aligned} V^{\pi^1\pi^2}(s_t) &= E_{\pi^1,\pi^2}\{R_t \mid s_t = s\} = E_{\pi^1,\pi^2}\left\{\sum_{k=0}^{\infty}\gamma^k r_{t+k+1} \mid s_t = s\right\} = E_{\pi^1,\pi^2}\left\{r_{t+1} + \gamma\sum_{k=0}^{\infty}\gamma^k r_{t+k+2} \mid s_t = s\right\} \\ &= \sum_{a^1}\pi^1(s,a^1)\sum_{a^2}\pi^2(s,a^2)\sum_{s'}P^{a^1a^2}_{ss'}\left[R^{a^1a^2}_{ss'} + \gamma E_{\pi^1,\pi^2}\left\{\sum_{k=0}^{\infty}\gamma^k r_{t+k+2} \mid s_{t+1} = s'\right\}\right] \\ &= \sum_{a^1}\pi^1(s,a^1)\sum_{a^2}\pi^2(s,a^2)\sum_{s'}P^{a^1a^2}_{ss'}\left[R^{a^1a^2}_{ss'} + \gamma V^{\pi^1\pi^2}(s')\right] \end{aligned} \tag{6}$$

where $E_{\pi^1,\pi^2}\{\}$ represents the expected value when policy π^1 is adopted by the agent and policy π^2 is adopted by the environment. Similarly, there exists an optimal value function when an optimal policy pair π^1 and π^2 is applied. Although there may be more than one pair, we called all the optimal pairs π^{1*} and π^{2*}. They have the optimal value function $V^*(s)$ defined as:

$$
\begin{aligned}
V^*(s_t) &= \max_{a^1\in A_1(s),a^2\in A_2(s)} E_{\pi^{1*},\pi^{2*}}\left\{R_t \mid s_t=s,a_t^1=a^1,a_t^2=a^2\right\} \\
&= \max_{a^1a^2} E_{\pi^{1*},\pi^{2*}}\left\{\sum_{k=0}^{\infty}\gamma^k r_{t+k+1} \mid s_t=s,a_t^1=a^1,a_t^2=a^2\right\} \\
&= \max_{a^1a^2} E_{\pi^{1*},\pi^{2*}}\left\{r_{t+1}+\gamma\sum_{k=0}^{\infty}\gamma^k r_{t+k+2} \mid s_t=s,a_t^1=a^1,a_t^2=a^2\right\} \\
&= \max_{a^1a^2} E\left\{r_{t+1}+\gamma V^*(s_{t+1}) \mid s_t=s,a_t^1=a^1,a_t^2=a^2\right\} \\
&= \max_{a^1a^2}\sum_{s'}P_{ss'}^{a^1a^2}\left[R_{ss'}^{a^1a^2}+\gamma V^*(s')\right]
\end{aligned}
\tag{7}
$$

The corresponding optimal action-value function is given as:

$$
\begin{aligned}
Q^*(s,a^1,a^2) &= E\left\{r_{t+1}+\gamma\max_{a^1{}',a^2{}'}Q^*(s_{t+1},a^1{}',a^2{}') \mid s_t=s,a_t^1=a^1,a_t^2=a^2\right\} \\
&= \sum_{s'}P_{ss'}^{a^1,a^2}\left[R_{ss'}^{a^1,a^2}+\gamma\max_{a^1{}',a^2{}'}Q^*(s',a^1{}',a^2{}')\right]
\end{aligned}
\tag{8}
$$

Using the same technique as QL, the function $Q^*(s_t,a^1_t,a^2_t)$ can be updated continuously that fulfils the purpose of RL. The QL type update rule for the new MDP model is given below:

$$
Q(s_t,a_t^1,a_t^2)\leftarrow Q(s_t,a_t^1,a_t^2)+\alpha\left[r+\gamma\max_{a_{t+1}^1,a_{t+1}^2}Q^*(s_{t+1},a_{t+1}^1,a_{t+1}^2)-Q(s_t,a_t^1,a_t^2)\right] \tag{9}
$$

Although a^2_t is involved in calculating Eqt. (7), (8) & (9), it is inherently uncontrollable by the agent and therefore maximizing a^2_t in (7) and a^2_{t+1} in (8) & (9) is meaningless. Instead, an approximation to the optimal action-value function by using the observed a^2_{t+1} is found and maximizing Eqt. (8) by a^1_{t+1} subsequently. As such, the new update rule for DAQL is:

$$
Q(s_t,a_t^1,a_t^2)\leftarrow Q(s_t,a_t^1,a_t^2)+\alpha\left[r_{t+1}+\gamma\max_{a_{t+1}^1}Q(s_{t+1},a_{t+1}^1,a_{t+1}^2)-Q(s_t,a_t^1,a_t^2)\right] \tag{10}
$$

where s_t, a^1_t are known in t, a^2_t , s_{t+1}, and r_{t+1} are known in t+1, and a^2_{t+1} can only be known in t+2. Therefore, the learning is delayed by two time steps when compared with conventional QL, but with a^2_t and a^2_{t+1} appropriately included.
When comparing Eqt. (5) with (10), the difference between DAQL and QL is that action a^2_t has been explicitly specified in the update rule. The optimal value function as a result of maximizing a^1_t only, while a^2_t is considered explicitly but unknown is given below:

$$
\begin{aligned}
V^*{}'(s) &= \max_{a^1}E_{\pi^{1*}\pi^2}\left\{R_t \mid s_t=s,a_t^1=a^1\right\} = \max_{a^1}E_{\pi^{1*}\pi^2}\left\{\sum_{k=0}^{\infty}\gamma^k r_{t+k+1} \mid s_t=s,a_t^1=a^1\right\} \\
&= \max_{a^1}E_{\pi^{1*}\pi^2}\left\{r_{t+1}+\gamma\sum_{k=0}^{\infty}\gamma^k r_{t+k+2} \mid s_t=s,a_t^1=a^1\right\} = \max_{a^1}E_{\pi^2}\left\{r_{t+1}+\gamma V^*{}'(s_{t+1}) \mid s_t=s,a_t^1=a^1\right\} \\
&= \max_{a^1}\sum_{a^2}\pi^2(s,a^2)\sum_{s'}P_{ss'}^{a^1a^2}\left[R_{ss'}^{a^1a^2}+\gamma V^*{}'(s')\right]
\end{aligned}
\tag{11}
$$

The corresponding optimal action-value function is:

$$\begin{aligned} Q^{*\prime}(s,a^1,a^2) &= E_{\pi^2}\left\{ r_{t+1} + \gamma \max_{a^{1\prime}} Q^{*}(s_{t+1},a^{1\prime},a^{2\prime}) \mid s_t = s, a_t^1 = a^1, a_t^2 = a^2 \right\} \\ &= \sum_{s'}\sum_{a^{2\prime}} \pi^2(s',a^{2\prime}) P_{ss'}^{a^1a^2}\left[R_{ss'}^{a^1a^2} + \gamma \max_{a^{1\prime}} Q^{*\prime}(s',a^{1\prime},a^{2\prime}) \right] \end{aligned} \quad (12)$$

It can be seen that Eqt. (4) is a special case of Eqt. (12). The DAQL formulation learns the expected Q-values by maximizing the future Q-values with a^1_t over actual a^2_{t+1} through time iterations. Therefore, if the current state is known and a^2_t can be predicted, a^1_t can be selected by using proper exploration policy (e.g. greedy policy):

$$a_t^1 = \arg\max_{a_t^1}(Q(s_t,a_t^1,a_t^2)) \quad (13)$$

To predict obstacles' action, an AR model is applied, which allows the calculation of the expected Q-value. In case that other obstacles' actions are not predictable, such as when they move randomly, we assumed that a^2_t has equal probability in taking any of the $|A_2(s)|$ actions.

2.5 Goal fusion

The purpose of goal fusion (GF) is to derive a single final action from the actions of different goals. Available methods for the coordination of goals include simple summation or switch of action value function (Uchibe et al., 1996), mixtures of local experts by supervised learning (Jacobs et al., 1991), and multiple model based reinforcement learning (Doya et al., 2002). Here, we adopt a modified summation method to coordinate multiple goals. A GF function based on this is formulated as follow:

$$Q_{final}(a_t^1) = \left[\frac{Q_1(a_t^1)}{\sum_{a^1}|Q_1(a^1)|} \quad \frac{Q_2(a_t^1)}{\sum_{a^1}|Q_2(a^1)|} \quad \cdots \quad \frac{Q_G(a_t^1)}{\sum_{a^1}|Q_G(a^1)|} \right] \begin{bmatrix} \beta_1 \\ \beta_2 \\ \vdots \\ \beta_G \end{bmatrix} \quad (14)$$

Where $\beta_1+\beta_2+\ldots+\beta_G=1$, G is the number of goals to be achieved and $Q_1(a^1_t),\ldots,Q_G(a^1_t)$ are the Q-values of the G goals respectively. The importance of the goals with respect to the whole task is represented by the value of β. A more important goal is represented by a larger β while a less important goal is represented by a smaller β.

3. Autonomous navigation through moving obstacles

3.1 Geometrical relations between agent and environment

The control variables of the agent and the ith obstacle at time t are depicted in Fig.4. It is assumed that there are N moving obstacles in the environment and that obstacle distances can be sensed by distance sensors on the agent, which have a minimum and maximum detectable distance of $d_{s,min}$ (10cm) and $d_{s,max}$ (500cm) respectively. Further assume that only M obstacles in the environment can be detected, where $M \le N$. The location of the ith obstacle is denoted by distance $d_i \in D_o$ where $D_o=[d_{s,min}, d_{s,max}] \subset \Re$ and angle $\theta_i \in \Theta$ where $\Theta=[0,2\pi] \subset \Re$.

We assume that the agent is $d_{dest} \in \Re^+$ away from the destination and is at an angle $\phi \in \Theta$. The four parameters: d_i, θ_i, d_{dest}, and ϕ are quantized into states. The state set for the relative location of the destination is $l_{dest} \in L_{dest}$ where $L_{dest} = \left\{ \left(\tilde{d}_{dest}, \tilde{\varphi} \right) | \tilde{d}_{dest} \in D_{dest} \text{ and } \tilde{\varphi} \in \Theta_q \right\}$, $D_{dest}=\{i \mid i=0,1,\cdots,11\}$ and $\Theta_q=\{j \mid j=0,1,\cdots,15\}$. The state set for obstacle location is $s_i \in S_i$ where $S_i = \left\{ \left(\tilde{d}_i, \tilde{\theta}_i \right) | \tilde{d}_i \in D_q \text{ and } \tilde{\theta}_i \in \Theta_q \right\}$, $D_q=\{k \mid k=0,1,\ldots,9\}$ and $\Theta_q=\{j \mid j=0,1,\ldots,15\}$. Quantization is achieved as follows and depicted in Fig. 5 for ϕ and θ_i:

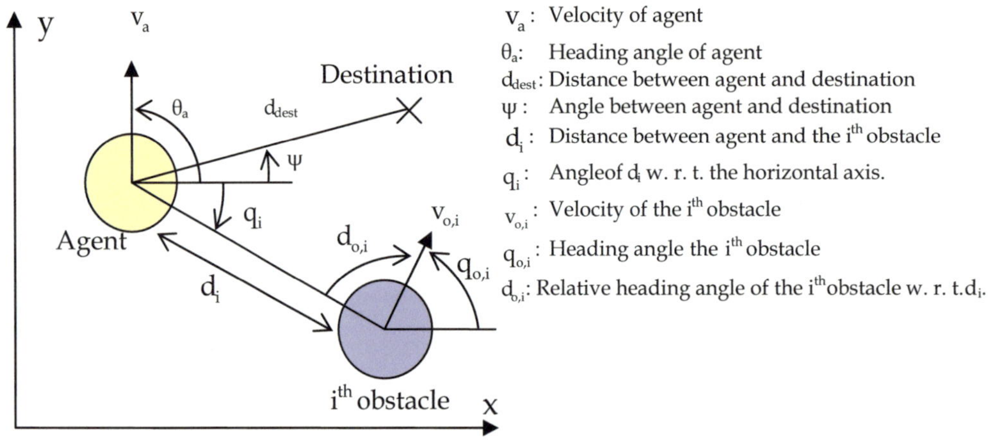

Fig. 4. Control variables of agent and the ith obstacle.

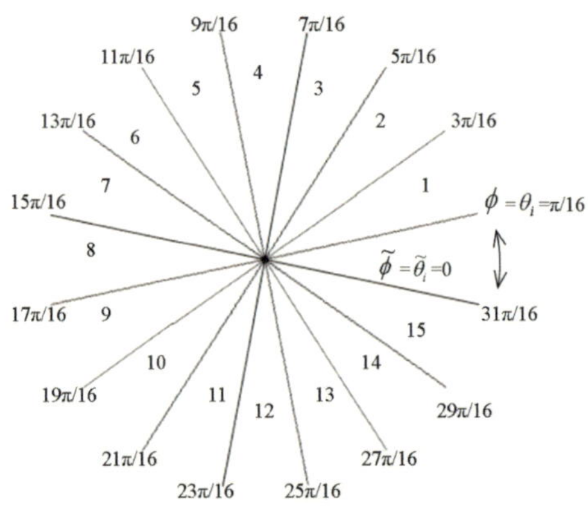

Fig. 5. Quantization of ϕ and θ_i into $\tilde{\phi}$ and $\tilde{\theta}_i$ respectively.

$$\tilde{d}_{dest} = \begin{cases} \lfloor d_{dest} / 5 \rfloor & \text{for } d_{dest} < 10 \\ \lfloor d_{dest} / 10 \rfloor + 1 & \text{for } 10 \le d_{dest} < 100 \\ 11 & \text{for } d_{dest} \ge 100 \end{cases} \tag{15}$$

$$\tilde{\phi} = \begin{cases} \left\lfloor \dfrac{\phi + \pi/16}{\pi/8} \right\rfloor & \text{for } 0 \le \phi < 31\pi/16 \\ 0 & \text{for } 31\pi/16 \le \phi < 2\pi \end{cases} \tag{16}$$

$$\tilde{d}_i = \lfloor d_i / 5 \rfloor \quad (17)$$

$$\tilde{\theta}_i = \begin{cases} \left\lfloor \dfrac{\theta_i + \pi/16}{\pi/8} \right\rfloor & \text{for } 0 \le \theta_i < 31\pi/16 \\ 0 & \text{for } 31\pi/16 \le \theta_i < 2\pi \end{cases} \quad (18)$$

There are altogether 192 states for L_{dest} and 160 states for S_i. The output actions are given by $a \in A$ where $A=\{(|v_a|,\theta_a) \mid |v_a| \in V_a$ and $\theta_a \in \Theta\}$, $V_a=\{m \times v_{max}/5 \mid m=0,1,...,15\}$, $\Theta_a=\{n\pi/8 \mid n=0,1,\cdots,15\}$, and v_{max} is the maximum agent speed. For $|\vec{v}_a|=0$, the agent is at rest despite of θ_a, resulting in only 81 actions. For DAQL, we assume that obstacles have speed $v_o \in \Re^+$ and heading angle $\theta_o \in \Theta$. They are quantized to $a^2_i \in A_o$ where $A_o = \{(\tilde{v}_o, \tilde{\theta}_o) \mid \tilde{v}_o \in V_q \text{ and } \tilde{\theta}_o \in \Theta_q\}$, $V_q=\{l \mid l=0,1,...,10\}$, and $\Theta_q=\{j \mid j=0,1,\cdots,15\}$. Quantization is achieved as follows:

$$\tilde{v}_o = \begin{cases} \lfloor v_o + 5 \rfloor & \text{for } 0 \le v_o < 105 \\ 100 & \text{for } v_o \ge 105 \end{cases} \quad (19)$$

$$\tilde{\theta}_o = \left\lfloor \frac{\theta_o}{\pi/8} \right\rfloor \quad (20)$$

where there are altogether 161 actions for each obstacle as observed by the agent. The concept of factored MDP (Boutilier et al., 2000; Guestrin et al. 2001) can be applied if necessary to reduce the number of states required.

3.2 Destination seeking

For convenience, destination is assumed stationary here, otherwise actions performed by the moving destination may be considered as in the case of obstacles, which the same DAQL formulation applies.

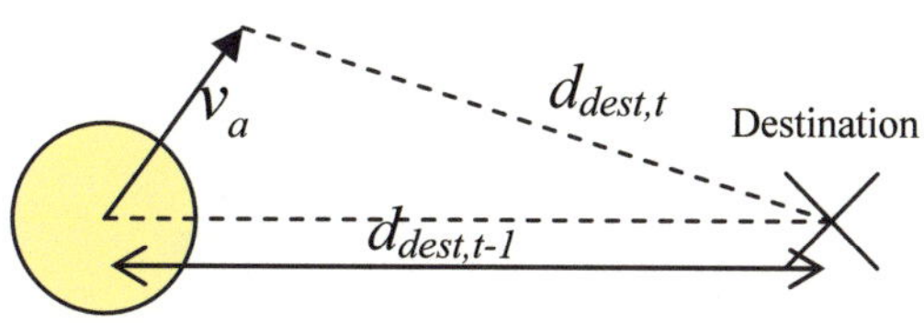

Fig. 6. Change in d_{dest} from t-1 to t.

The purpose of using reinforcement learning in destination seeking is for the agent to learn the limitation of the underlying vehicle mechanics such as limited acceleration and deceleration. The crux of the QL formulation for DS is that the agent is punished if its trajectory towards the destination contains more steps than necessary. With reference to Fig. 6, let us define $\Delta d_{dest}=d_{dest,t-1}-d_{dest,t}$, where $d_{dest,t-1}$ is the distance between the agent and destination at t-1, $d_{dest,t}$ is the distance at t; and the agent travels at v_a from t-1 to t. If the agent performs a shortest path maneuver, then $|v_a|T=\Delta d_{dest}$, otherwise $|v_a|T>\Delta d_{dest}$ and the worst case is when the agent has moved away from the destination, i.e., $\Delta d_{dest}=-|v_a|T$. Let us define d_{extra} as:

$$d_{extra} = |v_a|T - \Delta d_{dest} \quad (21)$$

where $0 \le d_{extra} \le 2\,|\,v_a\,|\,T$. The normalized reward function of the agent is thus defined as:

$$r_{DS,t} = (\Delta d_{dest} - d_{extra}) \,/\, (v_{a,\max} T) \tag{22}$$

where $-3 \le r_{DS,t} \le 1$. In Eqt. (22), d_{extra} is a penalty to the agent in order to ensure that it follows the shortest path to travel to the destination. The reward function is further shifted to $1 \le r_{DS,t} \le 0$ by $r_{DS,t} \leftarrow (r_{DS,t} - 1)/4$, so that the Q-values calculated are in line with those from CA. By using the QL update rule, the agent can learn to use the most appropriate action in the current state to reach the destination using the most direct path, as depicted in Fig. 7.

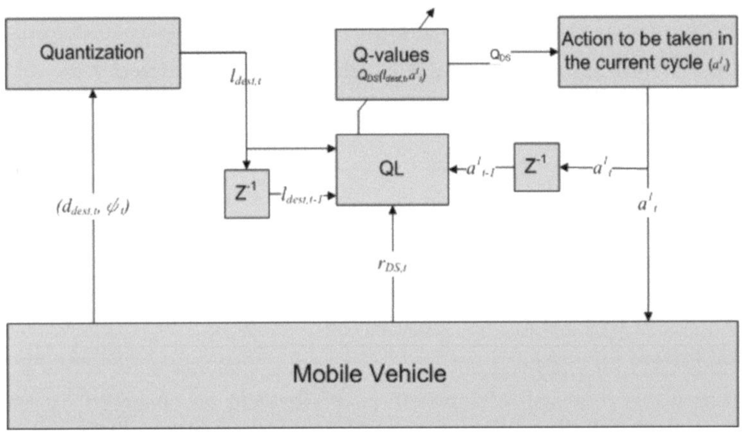

Fig. 7. QL for destination seeking.

3.3 Collision avoidance

Given multiple mobile obstacles in the environment, DAQL is most applicable here. The reward function adopted by DAQL represents punishment (-1) to the agent when collision occurs:

$$r_{CA,i,t} = \begin{cases} 0 & \text{if no collision occured} \\ -1 & \text{if collision occured} \end{cases} \tag{23}$$

When $r_{CA,i,t}$ is available, the agent uses the DAQL update rule to learn CA, as depicted in Fig. 8. Given obstacles' actions in two time steps (t-2 & t-1), the agent updates its Q-values ($q_i(s_{i,t}, a^1_t, a^2_{i,t})$) at t. If there are M obstacles that are detectable by the agent, the DAQL update rule is applied M times and the results are combined based the parallel learning concept introduced by Laurent & Piat (Laurent & Piat, 2001; Laurent & Piat, 2002). Their proposal of taking the sum of all the Q-values from all the obstacles is used, as oppose to taking the maximum Q-value over all the obstacles, as given in the following:

$$Q_{CA}(a^1_t) = \sum_i q_i(s_{i,t}, a^1_t, a^2_{i,t}) \tag{24}$$

where $Q_{CA}(a^1_t)$ is the overall Q-value set for the entire obstacle population when the agent takes a^1_t; $q_i(s_{i,t}, a^1_t, a^2_{i,t})$ is the Q-value set due to the ith obstacle; $s_{i,t}$ is the state of the ith obstacle observed by the agent at time t; and $a^2_{i,t}$ is the action performed by the ith obstacle at t. Since all M obstacles share a single set of Q-values, the Q-values are updated M times in one time step. As a^2_t is not known at t, it has to be predicted, which can be treated independently from RL, i.e. the agent predicts from the environment's historical information, or it can be based on concepts (rules learn from examples) and instances (pools of examples). To incorporate the predicted $a^2{}_t$, Eqt. (24) is modified as follows:

$$q_i(a_t^1) = \sum_{a_{i,t}^2} p_{a_{i,t}^2} q_i(s_{i,t}, a_t^1, a_{i,t}^2) \tag{25}$$

$$Q_{CA}(a_t^1) = \sum_i q_i(a_t^1) \tag{26}$$

where $p_{a_{i,t}^2}$ is the probability that the environment takes action $a^2{}_{i,t}$. The expected value of the overall Q-value is obtained by summing the product of the Q-value of each obstacle when they take action $a^2{}_{i,t}$ with their probability of occurrence. The combined Q-value for the entire DE, $Q_{CA}(a^1{}_t)$, is the summation of Q-values of each obstacle.

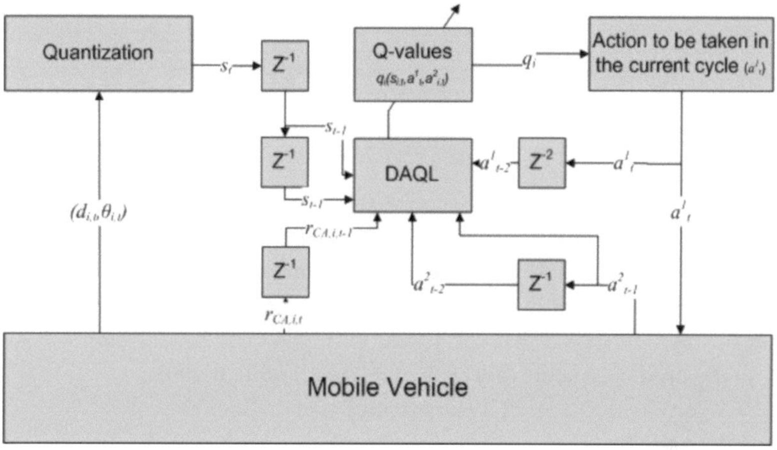

Fig. 8. DAQL for single obstacle.

3.4 Prediction

To predict $a^2{}_{i,t}$, a linear prediction technique based on the autoregressive (AR) model is adopted. We assume that the accelerations of obstacles are slowly changing in the time interval T between two time steps. A 1st order AR model (Kehtarnavaz & Li, 1988; Ye, 1999) is used to model the acceleration $a_i(t)$:

$$a_i(t) = B_{i,t} a_i(t-1) + e(t) \tag{27}$$

where $e(t)$ is the prediction error and $B_{i,t}$ is a time-dependent coefficient and is estimated adaptively according to the new distance measurements. The acceleration is thus approximated by a combination of velocity and position representations:

$$\begin{aligned} a_i(t) &= \frac{1}{T}[v_i(t) - v_i(t-1)] \\ &= \frac{1}{T^2}\{[r_i(t) - r_i(t-1)] - [r_i(t-1) - r_i(t-2)]\} \\ &= \frac{1}{T^2}[r_i(t) - 2r_i(t-1) + r_i(t-2)] \end{aligned} \tag{28}$$

where $v_i(t)$ and $r_i(t)$ are the velocity and position of the ith obstacle at time step t, respectively. Substituting Eqt. (28) into (27) gives a 3rd order AR model:

$$r_i(t)-(2+B_{i,t})r_i(t-1)+(2B_{i,t}+1)r_i(t-2)-B_{i,t}r_i(t-3)=e(t) \tag{29}$$

Therefore, the next position of the ith obstacle at time t+1 can be predicted by the following equation if the coefficient $B_{i,t}$ is known:

$$\hat{r}_i(t+1)=r_i(t)+v_k(t)T+\hat{B}_{i,t}a_k(t)T^2 \tag{30}$$

where $\hat{B}_{i,t}$ is time-dependent and is updated by the adaptive algorithm in (Shensa, 1981). The coefficient $\hat{B}_{i,t}$ can thus be determined by the following equations:

$$\hat{B}_{i,t}=\Delta_{i,t}R_{i,t}^{-1} \tag{31}$$

$$\Delta_{i,t}=\lambda\Delta_{i,t-1}+a_k(t)a_k^T(t-1) \tag{32}$$

$$R_{i,t}=\lambda R_{i,t-1}+a_k(t-1)a_k^T(t-1) \tag{33}$$

where $0<\lambda\leq 1$ is a weighting factor close to 1. Since $a_k(t)$, $\Delta_{k,t}$, $R_{k,t}$ and λ are all known, $\hat{B}_{i,t}$ can be predicted and thus $\hat{r}_i(t+1)$ can be predicted, from which the action performed by the ith obstacle at t can be predicted and the probability $p_{a_{i,t}^2}$ can be determined. A probability of 1 is given to the predicted action and 0 is given to all other actions.

3.5 Fusion of DS and CA

Given two sets of Q values from DS and CA, they are combined by using β - a parameter that varies between 0 and 1, to balance the influence of the two goals, as given in Eqt. (34), where $Q_{CA}(a^1_t)$) and $Q_{DS}(a^1_t)$ are normalized.

$$Q_{final}(a_t^1)=(1-\beta)\frac{Q_{CA}(a_t^1)}{\sum_{a^1}|Q_{CA}(a^1)|}+\beta\frac{Q_{DS}(a_t^1)}{\sum_{a^1}|Q_{DS}(a^1)|} \tag{34}$$

For β closer to 1, $Q_{final}(a^1_t)$ is biased towards DS, giving the agent better DS performance but poorer CA performance. Conversely, for β closer to 0, $Q_{final}(a^1_t)$ is biased towards CA, giving the agent poorer DS performance but better CA performance. The final decision of the agent is made by using the ε-greedy policy as shown in Eqt. (35). Fig. 9 and Fig. 10 depict the functional diagram and pseudo code of the proposed method respectively for multiple obstacles.

$$a_t^1=\begin{cases}\arg\max_{a_t^1} Q_{final}(a_t^1) & \text{with probability } 1\text{-}\varepsilon\\ \text{random} & \text{with probability } \varepsilon\end{cases} \tag{35}$$

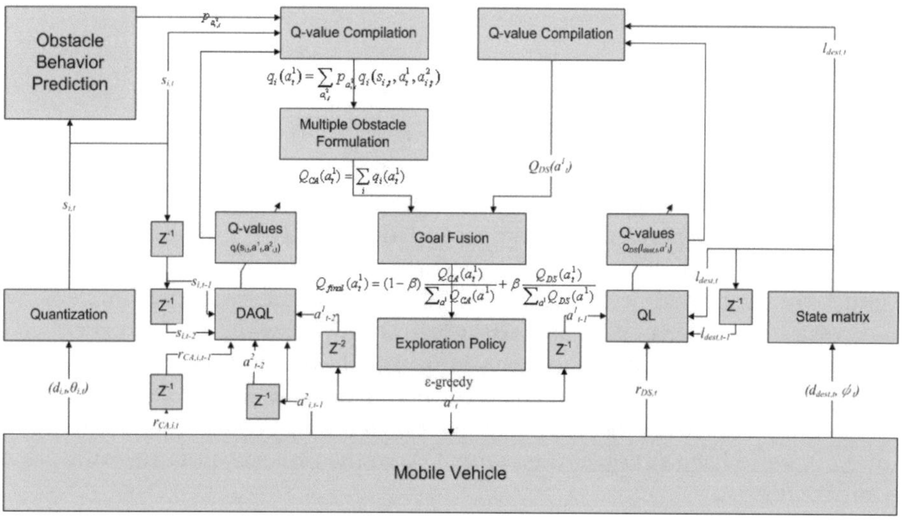

Fig. 9. Functional diagram of the proposed method.

Initialize $q_i(s,a^1,a^2)$ arbitrarily
Repeat (for each episode)
    Initialize a^1, a^2, r, l_{dest}, s_i, and s_i'
    Repeat (for each step of episode):
        Get $p_{a_i^2{}'}$ by predicting the action $a^2_i{}'$ that will be performed by the ith obstacle

$$\text{Calculate } q_i(a^1{}') = \sum_{a_i^2{}'} p_{a_i^2} q_i(s_i, a^1{}', a_i^2{}')$$

$$\text{Calculate } Q_{CA}(a^1{}') = \sum_i q_i(a^1{}')$$

$$\text{Determine } Q_{DS}(a^1{}')$$

$$\text{Calculate } Q_{final}(a^1{}') = (1-\beta)\frac{Q_{CA}(a^1{}')}{\sum_{a^1}\left|Q_{CA}(a^1)\right|} + \beta\frac{Q_{DS}(a^1{}')}{\sum_{a^1}\left|Q_{DS}(a^1)\right|}$$

        Choose $a^{1'}$ from s using policy derived from $Q_{final}(a^1{}')$
        Take action $a^1{}'$ using ε-greedy exploration policy
        Observe the new state l_{dest}', s_i'', r' and $a^2_i{}'$
        Determine the action a^2_i that have been performed by the ith obstacle

$$q_i(s_i,a^1,a_i^2) \leftarrow q_i(s_i,a^1,a_i^2) + \alpha\left[r_{CA,i} + \gamma \max_{a^1{}'} q_i(s',a^1{}',a_i^2{}') - q_i(s,a^1,a_i^2)\right]$$

$$Q_{DS}(l_{dest},a) \leftarrow Q_{DS}(l_{dest},a) + \alpha\left[r_{DS} + \gamma \max_{a'} Q_{DS}(l_{dest}{}',a') - Q_{DS}(l_{dest},a)\right]$$

        $l_{dest} \leftarrow l_{dest}'$, $s_i \leftarrow s_i'$, $s_i' \leftarrow s_i''$, $a^1 \leftarrow a^1{}'$, $a^2 \leftarrow a^2{}'$, $r_{CA,i} \leftarrow r_{CA,i}'$
    until l_{dest}' is terminal

Fig. 10. Pseudo code of the proposed method.

4. Simulations and results

4.1 Simulation conditions

In this simulation, length has unit of cm and time has unit of second. The agent and obstacles are assumed to be circular with diameter of 100 cm, and the environment is 2500×2500 (cm^2), as depicted in Fig. 11. The numbers in the figure represent the location of the agents and targets in every 10 s. The maximum speed of the agent ($v_{a,max}$) is assumed to be 50 cm/s, with a maximum acceleration and deceleration of 20 cm/s^{-2}. The agent is required to start from rest, and decelerate to 0 cm/s when it reaches the destination.
To acquire environmental information, a sensor simulator has been implemented to measure distances between agent and obstacles. The sensor simulator can produce either accurate or erratic distance measurements of up to 500 cm, at T interval (typically 1s) to simulate practical sensor limitations. The other parameters are set as follows: α for both DS and CA learning is set to 0.6 for faster update of Q-values; γ is set to 0.9 for CA and 0.1 for DS; β of 0.1 is set to have strong bias towards CA, in the expense of longer path; ε is set 0.5 for DS and 0.1 for CA.

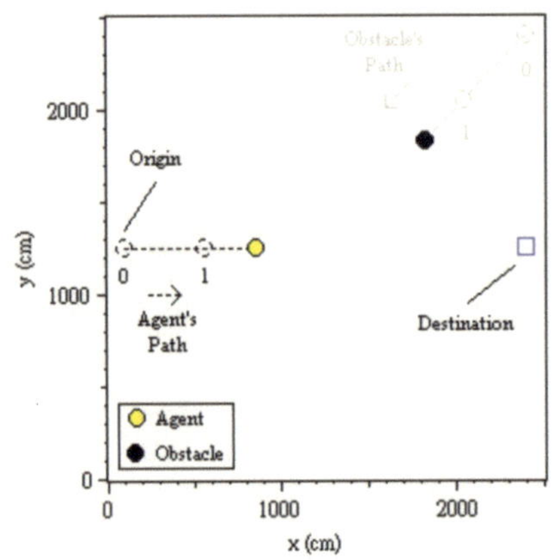

Fig. 11. Simulation environment.

4.2 Factors affecting navigation performance

The factors that affect an agent's performance in a DE are: relative velocity, relative heading angle; separation; and obstacle density. They define the bounds within which the agent can navigate without collision from an origin to a destination. The relative velocity of obstacle as observed by the agent can be defined as: $\vec{v}_{r,i} = \vec{v}_{o,i,\max} - \vec{v}_{a,\max}$, where $\vec{v}_{o,i,\max}$ and $\vec{v}_{a,\max}$ are velocity vectors of the ith obstacle (O_i) and agent (A) respectively. In essence, $\vec{v}_{r,i}$ represents the rate of change in separation between A and O_i. Given , heading angle of O_i w.r.t. the line joining the centres of O_i and A, and δ_a, heading angle of A as depicted in Fig.12, relative heading angle is defined as $\psi=\pi-(\delta_a+\delta_{o,i})$. It should be noted that ψ equals π when A and O_i are moving towards each other, $-\pi$ when A and O_i are moving away from each other, and 0 when both are moving in the same direction. Let d_i be the separation between A and O_i. It determines the priority A would adopt when considering O_i among other obstacles. If $d_{s,max}$ is the maximum sensor measurement range of A, and if $d_{s,max}<d_i$ then O_i simple does not exist from A's point of view. Obstacle density can be defined as $D=N\pi r_o^2/(A_{env}-\pi r_a^2)$, where N

is the number of obstacle in the environment and A_{env} is the area of the closed environment. We also assume that the obstacles are identical and have a radius of r_o, and A has a radius of r_a. Given A_{env}=25002, r_o=r_a=50, D=0.00125N.

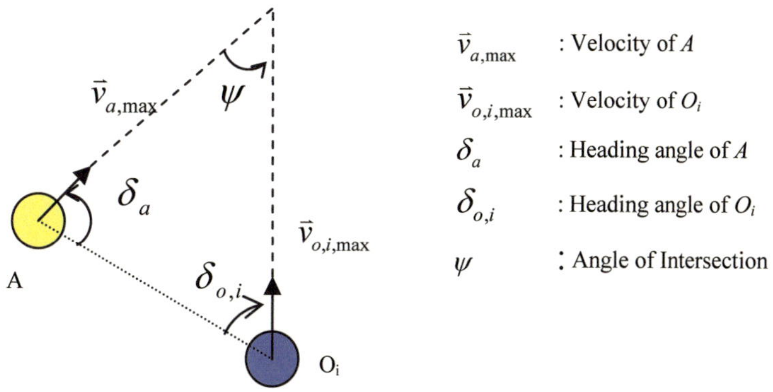

Fig. 12. Heading angles of O_i and A.

4.3 Training for destination seeking

First, the agent was trained by randomly generated origin and destination (O-D) pairs in the environment without obstacles, where each training episode consisted of the agent successfully travelled from O to D. Second, 100 episodes were used to train the agent to obtain a set of Q-values and another 100 episodes of different O-D pairs were used to evaluate the path length versus the shortest path based on the trained Q-values without learning and exploration. Step 2 was repeated 100 times to get an average performance over 10,000 episodes. Fig.13 depicts the mean % difference between the actual and the shortest paths.

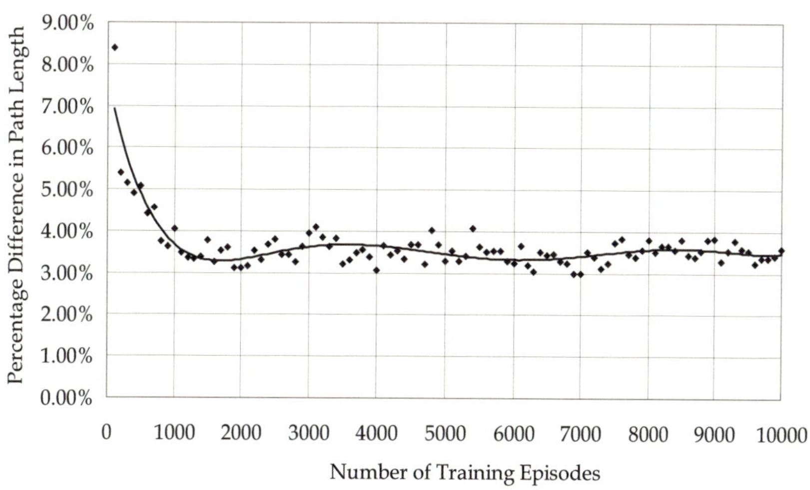

Fig. 13. Percentage difference in path length.

It can be seen that given sufficient training, the agent achieves a path difference of 3-4%. This is so because of the discrete actions the agent adopted in the simulation. In Fig.13, the data are curve fitted with a 6th order polynomial (solid line), from which a cost function is applied to determine the optimal number of training required. The cost function is defined as $C=f(x)\times\ln(E)$ and plotted in Fig. 14, where $f(x)$ is the polynomial function for the mean % difference and E is the number of episodes. From Fig. 14, minimum cost is achieved when the number of training episodes is around 1500. The Q-values for DS that correspond to this are used in all subsequent simulations.

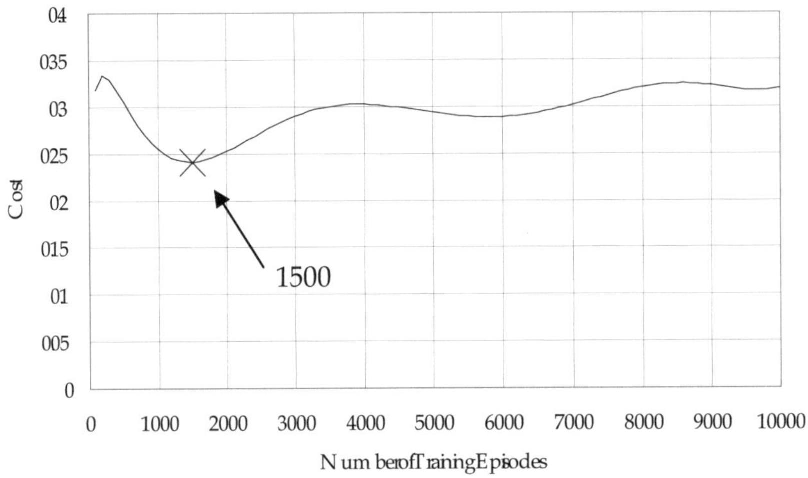

Fig. 14. Cost function.

4.4 Training for collision avoidance

For different environmental factors, we trained the agent with Q-values for CA set to zeros initially for 10000 episodes in each case. After training, simulation results are obtained by allowing the agent to maneuver in an environment with the same set of environmental factors without learning and exploration. When obstacles are present, the agent travels between a fixed OD pair. The agent learnt from the rewards or punishments when it interacted with the obstacle. When the agent reached the destination, an episode was terminated and the agent and obstacle were returned to their origins for the next episode.
Furthermore, to illustrate the behavior of the agent in a more complex environment which involves multiple sets of different environmental factors at the same time, environments with randomly moving obstacles are constructed. Q-values for CA are set to zeros initially and the agent is trained for 10000 episodes in each test case. After training, simulation results are obtained by allowing the agent to maneuver in the same environment without learning ability and exploration. In each training episode, the agent was required to travel to a fixed destination from a fixed origin through the crowd of randomly moving obstacles which were randomly placed in the environment, and the termination condition was the same as before.

4.5 Obstacles at constant velocity

This simulation investigates how the agent reacts to one or more obstacles at constant velocity with an initial separation of larger than 500 cm. The AR model in Section 3.4 was used for obstacle action prediction. For one obstacle, two v_o values and two ψ were considered: 50 cm/s and 100 cm/s; and π and $\frac{3}{4}\pi$. The simulation was repeated for v_o=50 cm/s when two obstacles were present at different heading angles. It was also repeated for a group of obstacles having the same heading angle. These cases are tabulated in Tables 1 to 3.

Case	ψ (rad)	v_o (cm/s)	$\lvert \vec{v}_{r,i} \rvert$ (cm/s)
A	π	50	100
B	π	100	150
C	$3\pi/4$	50	92.39
D	$3\pi/4$	100	139.90

Table 1. Summary of simulation parameters with ONE obstacle.

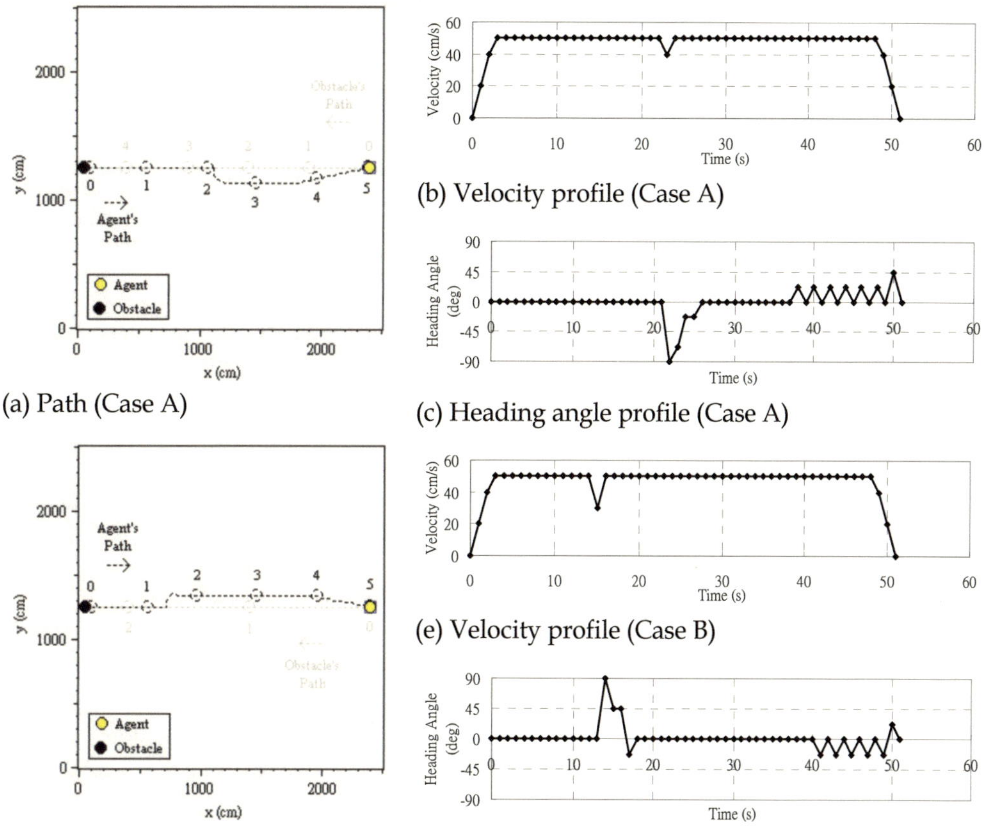

(a) Path (Case A)
(b) Velocity profile (Case A)
(c) Heading angle profile (Case A)
(d) Path (Case B)
(e) Velocity profile (Case B)
(f) Heading angle profile (Case B)

Fig. 15. Simulation results of Cases A and B.

1. Cases A and B: The obstacle moved directly towards the agent at different velocities respectively, as depicted in Fig. 15. For Case A, the obstacle moved at the same speed as the agent. The agent maintained at a maximum speed until the obstacle was within range. It responded appropriately as seen from its Velocity and Heading angle profiles. The agent responded with a gradual change in heading angle to avoid collision. It remained at the changed course for a while before converging to the destination. For Case B, as the obstacle

moved faster than the agent, the agent responded earlier with a larger change in velocity. As the CA event ended faster, the agent in Case B reached the destination earlier.

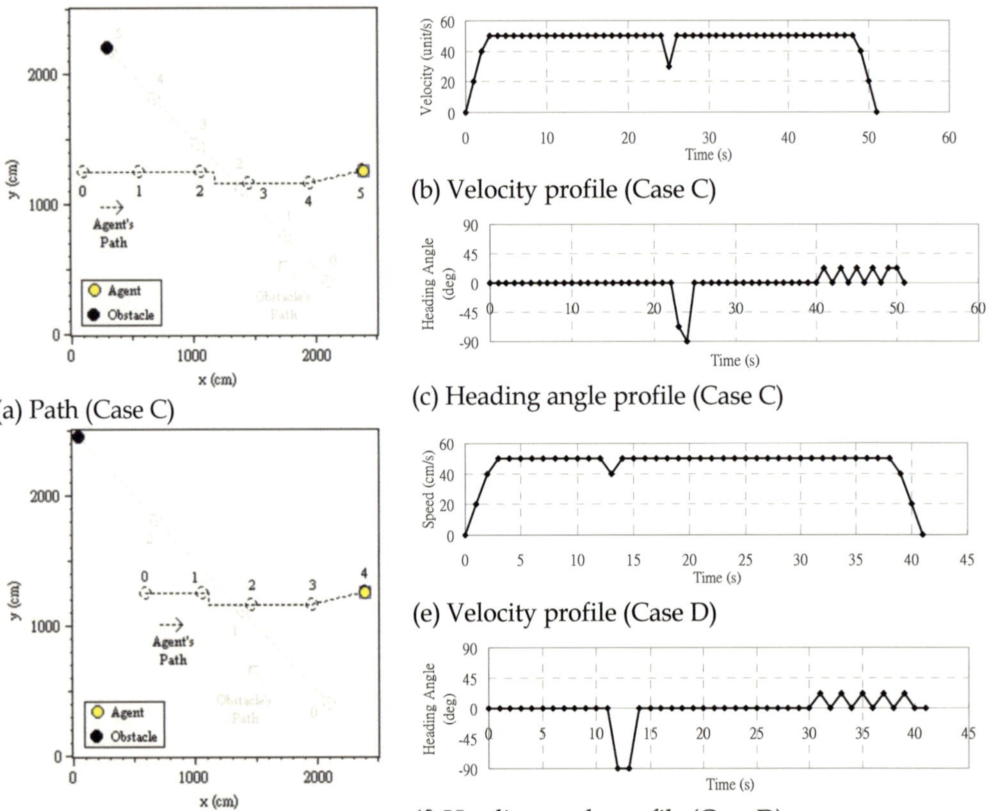

(a) Path (Case C)

(b) Velocity profile (Case C)

(c) Heading angle profile (Case C)

(d) Path (Case D)

(e) Velocity profile (Case D)

(f) Heading angle profile (Case D)

Fig. 16. Simulation results of cases C and D.

2. Cases C and D: The obstacle crossed path with the agent at an angle of $\frac{3}{4}\pi$, as depicted in Fig. 16. For Case C, when obstacle speed is the same as the agent, the agent moved to the right slightly to let the obstacle pass. For Case D, the agent responded earlier and also decided to let the obstacle passed first. As the obstacle moved faster in this case, the velocity and heading angle changes of the agent were larger.

Case		ψ (rad)	v_o (cm/s)	$\lvert\bar{v}_{r,i}\rvert$ (cm/s)
E	Obstacle 1	$3\pi/4$	50	92.39
	Obstacle 2	$3\pi/4$	50	92.39
F	Obstacle 1	$\pi/2$	50	70.71
	Obstacle 2	$\pi/2$	50	70.71

Table 2. Summary of simulation parameters with TWO obstacles.

3. Cases E and F: To deal with two obstacles simultaneously. The obstacles moved at speed v_o=50 cm/s in both cases, but at different heading angles. Case E, as depicted in Fig. 17(a-c),

consists of two obstacles moved at an intersecting angle of ¾π with respect to the agent. As can be seen from its V and H profiles, there are two responses: one at t=23s when Obstacle 1 approached the agent first, and one at t=29s when Obstacle 2 followed. The speed changes in both responses were minor, while the agent stepped backward in the first instance to avoid collision. For Case F, two obstacles moved perpendicularly to the agent as depicted in Fig. 17(d-f). There were two distinct responses (at t=9s and 22s), both of which required slowing down and change in heading angle to let the obstacle pass first.

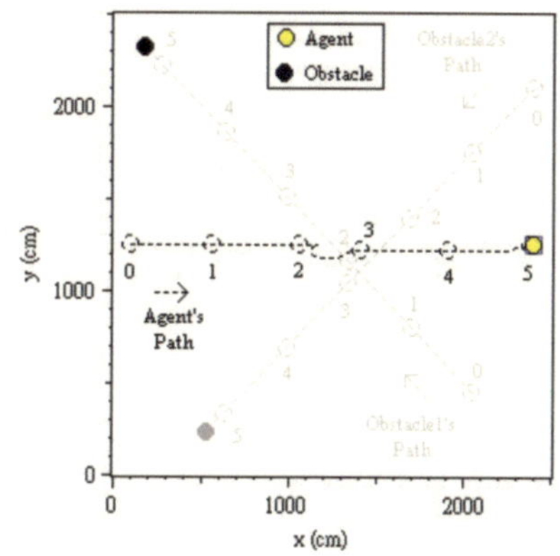

(a) Path (Case E)

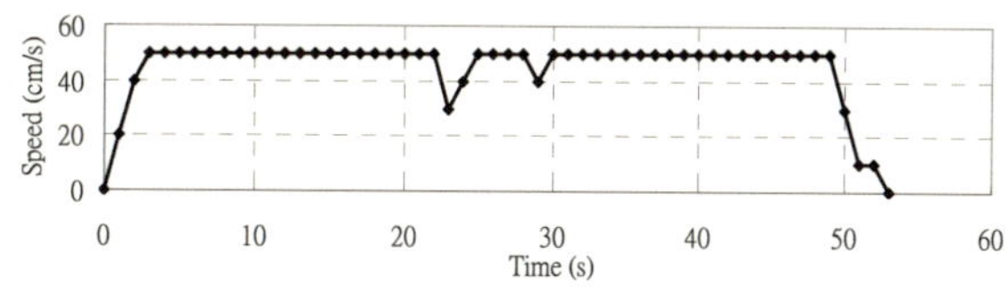

(b) Velocity profile (Case E)

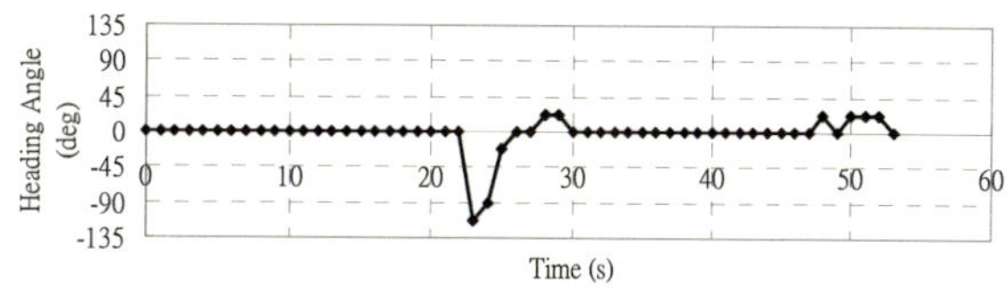

(c) Heading angle profile (Case E)

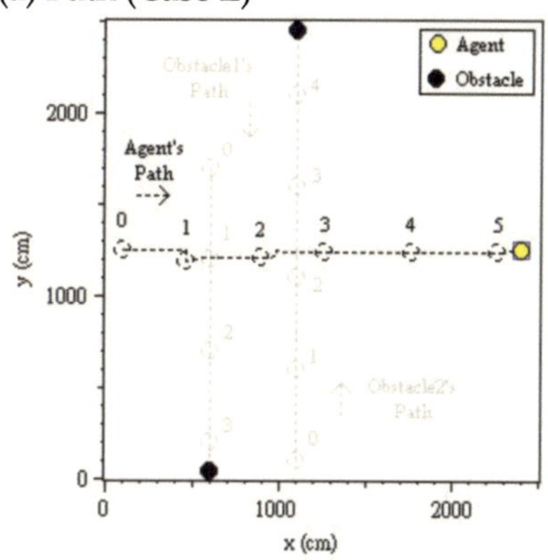

(d) Path (Case F)

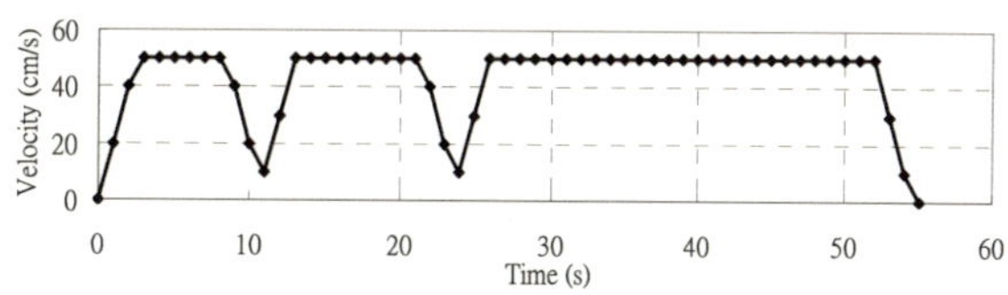

(e) Velocity profile (Case F)

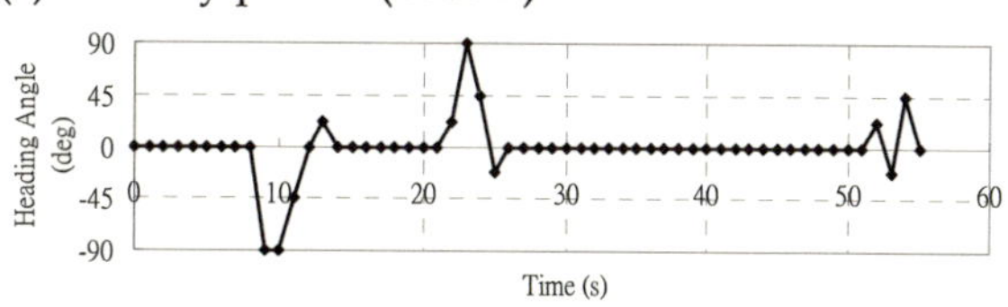

(f) Heading angle profile (Case F)

Fig. 17. Simulation results of cases E and F.

Case	ψ (rad)	v_o (cm/s)	$\lvert\bar{v}_{i,r}\rvert$ (cm/s)
G	π	50	100
H	$3\pi/4$	50	92.39

Table 3. Summary of simulation parameters with a GROUP of obstacles.

4. Cases G and H: To deal with a larger number of obstacles in the DE. In Case G, seven obstacles moved in a cluster towards the agent at v_o=50 cm/s. From the path diagram as depicted in Fig. 18(b), as the obstacles were well apart, the agent found no difficulty in navigating through them, as shown in its V and H profiles. For Case H, the cluster of seven

obstacles moved at an angle of ¾π with respect to the agent. Again, the agent navigated through the cluster appropriately, without collision.

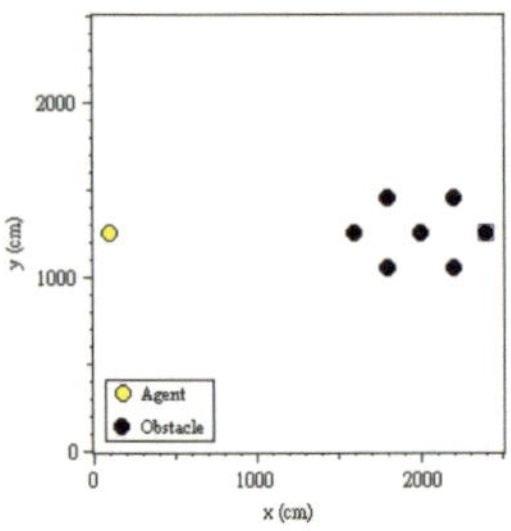

(a) Original Positions (Case G)

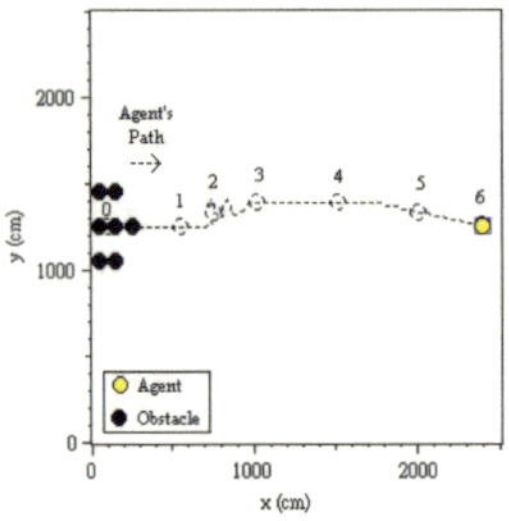

(b) Path (Case G)

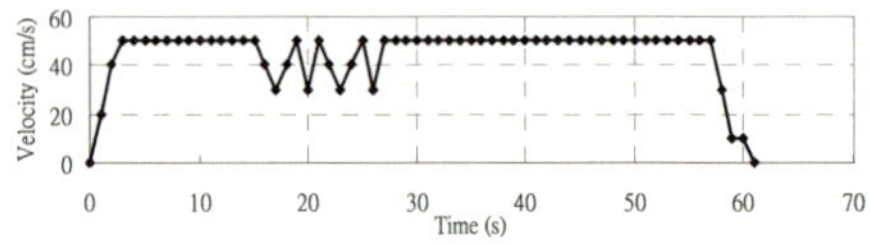

(c) Velocity profile (Case G)

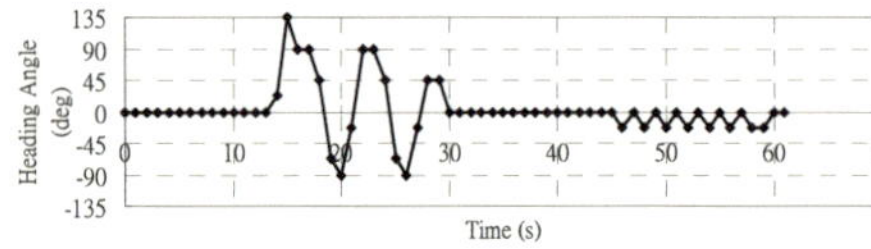

(d) Heading angle profile (Case G)

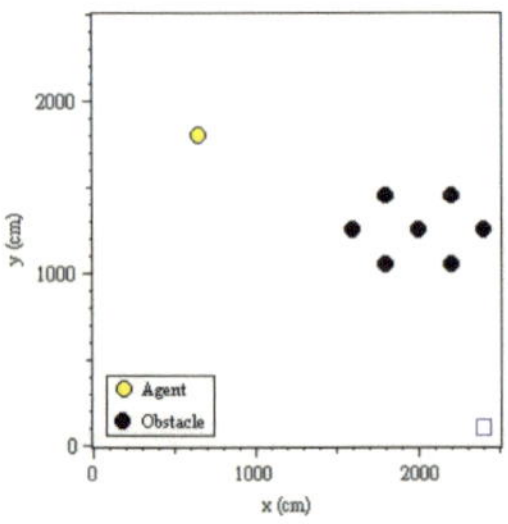

(e) Original Positions (Case H)

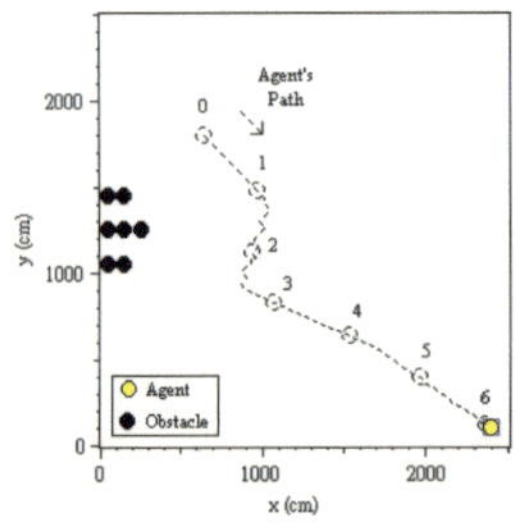

(f) Path (Case H)

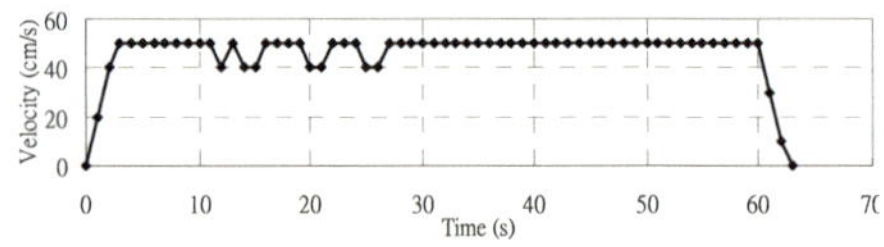

(g) Velocity profile (Case H)

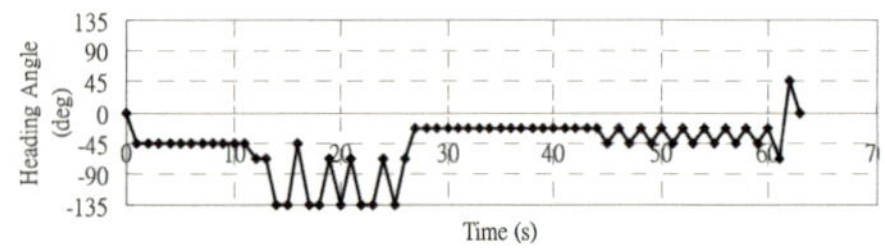

(h) Heading angle profile (Case H)

Fig. 18. Simulation results of cases G and H.

4.6 Obstacles at variable velocity

The objective of this simulation is to study agent behavior in handling a simple randomly changing environment. In Cases I and J, a single obstacle moved at varying velocity directly towards the agent ($\psi=\pi$). The obstacle's velocity ranges are 0-50 cm/s and 0-100 cm/s respectively, in step of 10 cm/s. The agent was evaluated over 1,000 episodes in the same environment in each case. A summary of the two cases is given in Table 4.

Case	ψ .rad)	v_o (cm/s)	$\lvert\bar{v}_{r,i}\rvert$.(cm/s)	Number of collision-free Episodes	Mean Path Time (s)
I		0-50	50-100	976	62.97
J		0-100	50-150	957	59.32

Table 4. Simulation parameters with ONE obstacle at random speed.

The results show that for Case I, the proportion of collision-free episodes is 97.6% and a mean path time of 62.97s. A collision-free episode is one that the agent travels to the destination without causing any collision. When compared with the shortest path time (50s), the agent used an extra of 12.97s more. For Case J, the obstacles moved faster in a wider range. As a result, the number of collision-free episodes was reduced to 95.7%, but the mean path time was also reduced to 59.32s. This can be explained as because of the faster moving obstacles, the agent experienced more collisions, but managed less convoluted paths.

4.7 Inaccurate sensor measurement

In this simulation, we investigate how the proposed method tolerates inaccuracy in sensor measurements. As in Cases A & B at three different speeds (v_o=10, 50 or 100 cm/s), the output of the sensor simulator was deliberately corrupted by a Gaussian noise function that has a mean (μ) of $\mu=d_i$ and standard deviation (σ) of $n\times\mu$ where n=0, 0.1, 0.2, 0.3, 0.4, 0.5, and 0.6 (Ye et al., 2003). For each set of n and v_o, Q-values for CA are set to zeros initially and the agent was trained for 10,000 episodes. After training, and the agent was evaluated in the same environment for 1,000 times with different n and v_o. Table 5 depicts the simulation summary.

n	v_o = 10 cm/s ($\lvert\bar{v}_{r,i}\rvert$ = 60 cm/s)		v_o = 50 cm/s ($\lvert\bar{v}_{r,i}\rvert$ = 100 cm/s)		v_o = 100 cm/s ($\lvert\bar{v}_{r,i}\rvert$ = 150 cm/s)	
	Collision-free Episodes	Mean Path Time (s)	Collision-free Episodes	Mean Path Time (s)	Collision-free Episodes	Mean Path Time (s)
0	1000	57	1000	57.00	1000	53.00
0.1	1000	56.79	1000	54.43	1000	54.71
0.2	999	55.40	987	56.05	957	59.89
0.3	979	62.37	996	58.45	987	61.49
0.4	997	65.55	979	58.33	725	80.45
0.5	991	57.52	989	59.04	816	71.31
0.6	995	61.93	954	65.58	576	92.01

Table 5. Robustness to sensor noise.

From Table 5, for n<0.2, none of the obstacle speed would cause collision. For $n\geq0.2$, collision began to appear. At low speed, the number of collisions can be kept small with a worst case of 2.1%. For $\lvert\bar{v}_o\rvert$ =50 cm/s, the number of collision-free episodes was reduced to 95.4% at n=0.6. For $\lvert\bar{v}_o\rvert$ =100 cm/s, it went down to 57.6%, or almost half of the episodes have collisions. This is logical as slow obstacles are easier to avoid compared with fast obstacles, and inaccurate sensor measurements make it harder to avoid collision.

For mean path time, it generally increases when n increases, although minima appear at n=0.2 for low speed, n=0.1 for medium speed and n=0 for high speed. As in Case A, the mean path time is longer when obstacle speed is low because of more convoluted paths. As n increases, the agent learnt to respond earlier to such inaccuracy and resulted in shorter paths. However, for larger n, the agent travels extra steps in order to cope with the large sensor error, which resulted in even longer path. The same applies when obstacle speed is relatively higher, except that the minima appear when n is smaller because the agent responded earlier in this case.

4.8 Randomly moving obstacles and performance comparison

The purpose of this simulation is to evaluate the proposed method in an environment with up to 50 moving obstacles, and compare it against another navigation method that is designed to work in such a complex environment. Obviously, those that work on static environment (Pimenta et al., 2006; Belkhouche et al. 2006; Jing et al. 2006), those that consider relatively simple cases with very low obstacle density (Soo et al. 2005; Kunwar & Benhabib, 2006), or those that assume perfect communication among agents, e.g. robot soccering (Bruce & Veloso, 2006), are unsuitable. A suitable candidate is the artificial potential field method proposed by Ratering & Gini (R&G) (Ratering & Gini, 1995), which was simulated in a relatively complex environment with high density of multiple moving obstacles. To enable the comparison, obstacles size was reduced to 20 cm in diameter, and the obstacles were placed and moved randomly in speed and direction, as in (Ratering & Gini, 1995). The origin and destination of the agent were located at the lower left hand corner and upper right corner of the environment, respectively. Since the obstacles moved randomly, the prediction was not used in the proposed method. Different obstacle density D and obstacle velocity v_o were studied, and results are tabulated in Table 6. Each result shown in the table was derived from 100 episodes after training. The R&G method used static potential filed and dynamic potential fields to handle static and moving obstacles respectively, and their results are also depicted in Table VI.

Obstacle speed v_o (cm/s)	No. of obstacles	Obstacle Density D	$\lvert\vec{v}_{r,i}\rvert$ (cm/s)	**Average path time (s)**	St. dev. path time	**No. of collision-free episodes**	Average no. of collisions	St. dev. No. of collisions
10	10	0.0005	40-60	**68.25 (79.07)**	16.16 (13.40)	**99 (99)**	0.01 (0.02)	0.1 (0.20)
10	20	0.001	40-60	**80.1 (93.92)**	50.27 (20.93)	**100 (95)**	0 (0.06)	0 (0.28)
10	30	0.0015	40-60	**92.71 (110.19)**	59.19 (27.35)	**97 (98)**	0.11 (0.02)	0.83 (0.14)
10	40	0.002	40-60	**99.24 (126.23)**	53.56 (34.25)	**95 (92)**	0.07 (0.09)	0.33 (0.32)
10	50	0.0025	40-60	**111.55 (135.06)**	58.39 (41.06)	**94 (82)**	0.15 (0.25)	0.63 (0.61)
30	10	0.0005	20-80	**68.58 (80.75)**	7.84 (11.98)	**99 (99)**	0.01 (0.01)	0.1 (0.10)
30	20	0.001	20-80	**75.03 (96.17)**	14.27 (23.43)	**99 (95)**	0.01 (0.05)	0.1 (0.22)
30	30	0.0015	20-80	**80.12 (110.95)**	16.29 (28.18)	**96 (89)**	0.07 (0.18)	0.43 (0.59)
30	40	0.002	20-80	**89.58 (116.94)**	28.13 (28.91)	**94 (80)**	0.08 (0.46)	0.34 (1.11)
30	50	0.0025	20-80	**91.93 (125.46)**	21.07 (32.30)	**92 (72)**	0.14 (0.59)	0.62 (1.18)
50	10	0.0005	0-100	**69.62 (85.10)**	8.60 (18.56)	**91 (92)**	0.25 (0.46)	1.53 (2.41)
50	20	0.001	0-100	**74.39 (97.56)**	10.68 (19.37)	**88 (75)**	0.2 (0.74)	0.64 (1.56)
50	30	0.0015	0-100	**84.19 (111.48)**	15.47 (23.09)	**85 (63)**	0.17 (1.44)	0.43 (3.16)
50	40	0.002	0-100	**93.67 (123.48)**	24.95 (29.11)	**77 (37)**	0.43 (2.66)	0.98 (3.60)
50	50	0.0025	0-100	**101.31 (127.72)**	29.13 (29.49)	**69 (32)**	0.68 (3.22)	1.64 (3.61)

Table 6. Cases of randomly moving obstacles in a fixed area. (Numbers in brackets show the results of R&G Method (Ratering & Gini, 1995))

In general, for the same $|\vec{v}_{r,i}|$, the no. of collision-free episodes decreases as D increases for the proposed method. Obviously, more obstacles in a fixed area increase the chance of collision. This is also true when $|\vec{v}_{r,i}|$ increases. In the extreme, only 69% of episodes are collision-free when $|\vec{v}_{r,i}|$=0-100 cm/s and D=0.0025 (max). When compared with the R&G method, when D is very low, differences in no. of collision-free episodes between the two methods are insignificant. However, when D is larger (>10 obstacles), the proposed method performed consistently better. This is also the case when $|\vec{v}_{r,i}|$ increases. On average, the improvement on the no. of collision-free episodes is 23.63%, whereas the best is slightly over 115% for the largest D.
For average path time, it increases as D increases. This is to be expected as there are more obstacles and more CA actions that resulted in longer path time. On the other hand, for small $|\vec{v}_{r,i}|$ and large D, clustering of obstacles becomes a real possibility that can block the agent's path. This is confirmed by the large standard deviation of path time when compared with other larger $|\vec{v}_{r,i}|$. Although the R&G method employed the adjustable hill extent method to deal with this issue, their average path times are in fact longer. When $|\vec{v}_{r,i}|$ is large, obstacle clustering is reduced, but their speed makes it necessary to make more convoluted path to avoid them, therefore the resultant path time is longer, with smaller standard deviation. Again, there is a minimum in average path time at medium $|\vec{v}_{r,i}|$ depending on D. When compared with R&G method, an average improvement of 20.6% is achieved.

5. Conclusion

In this chapter we have presented a multiple goal reinforcement learning framework and illustrated on a two-goal problem in autonomous vehicle navigation. In general, DAQL can be applied in any goals that environmental response is available, whereas QL would suffice if environmental response is not available or can be ignored. A proportional goal fusion function was used to maintain balance between the two goals in this case. Extensive simulations have been carried out to evaluate its performance under different obstacle behaivors and sensing accuracy. The results showed that the proposed method is characterized by its ability to (1) deal with single obstacles at any speed and from any directions; (2) deal with two obstacles approaching from different directions; (3) cope with large sensor noise; (4) navigate in high obstacle density and high relative velocity environment. Detailed comparison of the proposed method with the R&G method reveals that improvements by the proposed method in path time and the number of collision-free episodes are substantial.

6. Acknowledgement

The authors would like to thank the anonymous referees for their thorough review of the paper and many constructive comments. The work described in this paper was partially supported by a grant from the Research Grants Council of the Hong Kong Special Administration Region, China (Project No.HKU7194/06E), and was partially supported by a postgraduate studentship from the University of Hong Kong.

7. References

Belkhouche F., Belkhouche B., Rastgoufard P. (2006). Line of sight robot navigation toward a moving goal, *IEEE Transactions on Systems, Man and Cybernetics, Part B*, 36, 255-267

Boutilier C. (1996). Planning, learning and coordination in multi-agent decision processes, *Sixth conference on Theoretical Aspects of Rationality and Knowledge (TARK `96)*, pp. 195-201, The Netherlands

Boutilier C., Dearden R., Goldszmidt M. (2000).Stochastic dynamic programming with factored representations. *Artificial Intelligence*, 121, 49-107

Bruce J.R., Veloso M.M. (2006). Safe multirobot navigation within dynamics constraints, *Proceedings of the IEEE Special Issue on Multi-Robot Systems*, 94, 1398-1411

Claus C., Boutilier C. (1998). The Dynamics of Reinforcement Learning in Cooperative Multiagent Systems, *Fifteenth National Conference on Artificial Intelligence*, pp. 746-752

Doya K., Samejima K., Katagiri K., Kawato M. (2002). Multiple model-based reinforcement learning. *Neural Computation*, 14, 1347-1369

Er M.J., Deng C. (2005). Obstacle avoidance of a mobile robot using hybrid learning approach. IEEE Transactions on Industrial Electronics, 52, 898-905

Feng Z., Dalong T., Zhenwei W. (2004). Multiple obstacles avoidance for mobile robot in unstructured environments, *Proceedings of the 2004 IEEE International Conference on Robotics, Automation and Mechatronics*, vol.141, pp. 141-146, Singapore

Fiorini P., Shiller Z. (1998). Motion planning in dynamic environments using velocity obstacles. International Journal of Robotics Research, 17, 760-772

Ge S.S., Cui Y.J. (2000). New potential functions for mobile robot path planning. *IEEE Transactions on Robotics and Automation*, 16, 615-620

Guestrin C., Koller D., Parr R. (2001). Multiagent Planning with Factored MDPs, *Proceedings of the 14th Neural Information Processing Systems (NIPS-14)*, pp. 1523-1530

Kaelbling L.P. (1993). *Learning in embedded systems*, MIT Press, Cambridge, Mass.

Kaelbling L.P., Littman M.L., Moore A.W. (1996). Reinforcement learning: A survey. *Journal of Artificial Intelligence Research*, 4, 237-285

Hu J.L., Wellman M.P. (2004). Nash Q-learning for general-sum stochastic games. *Journal of Machine Learning Research*, 4, 1039-1069

Huang B.Q., Cao G.Y., Guo M (2005). Reinforcement Learning Neural Network to the Problem of Autonomous Mobile Robot Obstacle Avoidance, *Proceedings of the Fourth IEEE International Conference on Machine Learning & Cybernetics*, pp. 85-89, Guangzhou

Jacobs R.A., Jordan M.I., Nowlan S.J., Hinton G.E. (1991). Adaptive Mixtures of Local Experts. *Neural Computation*, 3, 79-87

Jing R., McIsaac K.A., Patel R.V. (2006). Modified Newton's method applied to potential field-based navigation for mobile robots. *IEEE Transactions on Robotics*, 22, 384-391

Kehtarnavaz N., Li S. (1988). A collision-free navigation scheme in the presence of moving obstacles, *Proceedings of IEEE International Conference on Computer Vision and Pattern Recognition*, pp. 808-813

Kunwar F., Benhabib B. (200).Rendezvous-Guidance Trajectory Planning for Robotic Dynamic Obstacle Avoidance and Interception. *IEEE Transactions on Systems, Man and Cybernetics, Part B*, 36, 1432-1441

Large F., Sekhavat S., Shiller Z., Laugier C. (2002). Towards real-time global motion planning in a dynamic environment using the NLVO concept, *Proceedings of the 2002 IEEE/RSJ International Conference on Intelligent Robots and Systems*, vol.601, pp. 607-612, Lausanne, Switzerland

Latombe J.-C. (1991). *Robot motion planning*, Kluwer Academic Publishers, Boston

Laurent G., Piat E. (2001).Parallel Q-learning for a block-pushing problem, *Proceedings of the IEEE/RSJ Int. Conf. on Intelligent Robots and Systems*, vol.281, pp. 286-291, USA

Laurent G.J., Piat E. (2002). Learning mixed behaviours with parallel Q-learning, *Proceedings of the 2002 IEEE/RSJ International Conference on Intelligent Robots and Systems*, vol.1001, pp. 1002-1007, Lausanne, Switzerland

Littman M.L. (2001). Value-function reinforcement learning in Markov games. *Cognitive Systems Research*, 2, 55-66

Minguez J., Montano L. (2004). Nearness diagram (ND) navigation: Collision avoidance in troublesome scenarios. *IEEE Transactions on Robotics and Automation*, 20, 45-59

Minguez J. (2005). The obstacle-restriction method for robot obstacle avoidance in difficult environments, *Proceedings of the 2005 IEEE/RSJ International Conference on Intelligent Robots and Systems*, pp. 2284-2290

Miura J., Uozumi H., Shirai Y. (1999). Mobile robot motion planning considering the motion uncertainty of moving obstacles, *Proceedings of the 1999 IEEE International Conference on Systems, Man, and Cybernetics*, vol.694, pp. 692-697, Tokyo, Japan

Mucientes M., Iglesias R., Regueiro C.V., Bugarin A., Carinena P., Barro S. (2001). Fuzzy temporal rules for mobile robot guidance in dynamic environments. *IEEE Transactions on Systems Man and Cybernetics Part C-Applications and Reviews*, 31, 391-398

Ngai D.C.K., Yung N.H.C. (2005a). Double action Q-learning for obstacle avoidance in a dynamically changing environment, *Proceedings of the 2005 IEEE Intelligent Vehicles Symposium*, pp. 211-216, Las Vegas, USA

Ngai D.C.K., Yung N.H.C. (2005b). Performance evaluation of double action Q-learning in moving obstacle avoidance problem, *Proceedings of the 2005 IEEE International Conference on Systems, Man, and Cybernetics*, vol. 861, pp. 865-870, Hawaii, USA

Oriolo G., Ulivi G., Vendittelli M. (1998). Real-time map building and navigation for autonomous robots in unknown environments. *IEEE Transactions on Systems Man and Cybernetics Part B-Cybernetics*, 28, 316-333

Pimenta L.C.A., Fonseca A.R., Pereira G.A.S., Mesquita R.C., Silva E.J., Caminhas W.M., Campos M.F.M. (2006). Robot navigation based on electrostatic field computation, *IEEE Transactions on Magnetics*, 42, 1459-1462

Puterman M.L. (1994). *Markov decision processes : discrete stochastic dynamic programming*. John Wiley & Sons, New York

Ratering S., Gini M. (1995). Robot Navigation in a Known Environment with Unknown Moving Obstacles. *Autonomous Robots*, 1, 149-165

Qu Z.H., Wang J., Plaisted C.E. (2004). A new analytical solution to mobile robot trajectory generation in the presence of moving obstacles. *IEEE Transactions on Robotics and Automation*, 20, 978-993

Shensa M. (1981). Recursive least squares lattice algorithms--A geometrical approach. *IEEE Transactions on Automatic Control*, 26, 695-702

Shiller Z., Large F., Sekhavat S. (2001). Motion planning in dynamic environments: obstacles moving along arbitrary trajectories, *Proceedings of the 2001 IEEE International Conference on Robotics and Automation*, vol.3714, pp. 3716-3721, Seoul

Soo J. E., Seul J., Hsia T.C. (2005). Collision avoidance of a mobile robot for moving obstacles based on impedance force control algorithm, *Proceedings of the IEEE/RSJ*

International Conference on Intelligent Robots and Systems 2005 (IROS 2005), pp. 382-387

Stentz A. (1994). Optimal and efficient path planning for partially-known environments, *Proceedings of the 1994 IEEE International Conference on Robotics and Automation*, vol. 3314, pp. 3310-3317, 1994

Stentz A. (1995). The focused D* algorithm for real-time replanning, *Proceedings of the 14th International Joint Conference on Artificial Intelligence*, IJCAI '95, Montreal, Canada, August 1995

Sutton R.S. (1992). *Reinforcement learning*, Kluwer Academic Publishers, Boston

Sutton R.S., Barto A.G. (1998). *Reinforcement learning : an introduction*, MIT Press, Cambridge, Mass.

Uchibe E., Asada M., Hosoda K. (1996). Behavior coordination for a mobile robot using modular reinforcement learning, *Proceedings of the 1996 IEEE/RSJ International Conference on Intelligent Robots and Systems '96*, vol.1323, pp. 1329-1336

Watkins C.J.C.H., Dayan P. (1992). Q-Learning. *Machine Learning*, 8, 279-292

Yamamoto M., Shimada M., Mohri A. (2001). Online navigation of mobile robot under the existence of dynamically moving multiple obstacles, *Proceedings of the 4th IEEE Int. Symposium on Assembly & Task Planning*, pp. 13-18, Soft Research Park, Japan

Yang S.X., Meng M.Q.H. (2003). Real-time collision-free motion planning of a mobile robot using a neural dynamics-based approach. *IEEE Transactions on Neural Networks*, 14, 1541-1552

Ye C. (1999). *Behavior-Based Fuzzy Navigation of Mobile Vehicle in Unknown and Dynamically Changing Environment*. Pd.D. Thesis, Department of Electrical and Electronic Engineering, The University of Hong Kong, Hong Kong

Ye C., Yung N.H.C., Wang D.W. (2003). A fuzzy controller with supervised learning assisted reinforcement learning algorithm for obstacle avoidance. *IEEE Transactions on Systems Man and Cybernetics Part B-Cybernetics*, 33, 17-27

Yoon H.U., Sim K.B. (2005). Hexagon-Based Q-Learning for Object Search with Multiple Robots, *Proceedings of Advances in Natural Computation: First International Conference*, ICNC 2005, pp. 55-66, Changsha, China

Zhu Q.M. (1991). Hidden Markov Model for Dynamic Obstacle Avoidance of Mobile Robot Navigation. *IEEE Transactions on Robotics and Automation*, 7, 390-397

22

An Intelligent Marshaling Based on Transfer Distance of Containers Using a New Reinforcement Learning for Logistics

Yoichi Hirashima
Osaka Institute of Technology
Japan

1. Introduction

Recent shipping amount in maritime transportation keeps growing, and efficient material handling operations at marine ports becomes important issue. In many cases, containers are used for transportation of cargos, and thus the growth of shipping amount leads to the growth of the number of containers. In a marine port, containers are shifted between seaborn and landside transportation at container yard terminal. Espesially, shifting containers from landside into a vessel is highly complex, including many constraints and sensitive parameters. In addition, the complexity grows at an exponential rate according to the linear growth of the number of containers. Thus, the material hadling operation occupy a large part of the total run time of shipping at container terminals.
This chapter addresses to improve throughput of the material handling operations for loading container into a vessel by using reinforcement learning. Commonly, each container in a vessel has its own position determined by the destination, weight, owner, and so on (Günther & Kim, 2005). Thus, the containers have to be loaded into a vessel in a certain desired order because they cannot be rearranged in the ship. Therefore, containers must be rearranged before loading if the initial layout is different from the desired layout. Containers carried into the terminal are stacked randomly in a certain area called bay and a set of bays are called yard. The rearrangement process conducted within a bay is called marshaling.
In the problem, the number of stacks in each bay is predetermined and the maximum number of containers in a stack is limited. Containers are moved by a transfer crane and the destination stack for the container in a bay is selected from the stacks being in the same bay. In this case, a long series of container movements is often required to achieve a desired layout, and results that are derived from similar initial layouts can be quite different. Problems of this type have been solved by using techniques of optimization, such as genetic algorithm (GA) and multi agent method (Koza, 1992; Minagawa & Kakazu, 1997). These methods can successfuly yield some solutions for block stacking problems. However, they adopt the environmental model different from the marshaling process, and cannot be applied directly to generate marshaling plan to obtain the desired layout of containers.
Another candidate for solving the problem is the reinforcement learning (Watkins & Dayan, 1992), which is known to be effective for learning under unknown environment that has the Markov Property. The Q-learning, one of the realization algorithm for the reinforcement learning, can be applied to generate marshaling plan, with evaluation-values for pairs of the

layout and movement of container. These values are called Q-value. The optimal series of container movements can be obtained by selecting the movement that has the best evaluation for each layout. However, conventional Q-learning has to store evaluation-values for all the layout-movement pairs. Therefore, the conventional Q-learning has great difficulties for solving the marshaling problem, due to its huge number of learning iterations required to obtain admissible plan. Recently, a Q-learning method that can generate marshaling plan has been proposed (Motoyama et al., 2001). Although these methods were effective for several cases, the desired layout was not achievable for every trial so that the early-phase performances of learning process can be spoiled. Modefied methods (Hirashima et al., 2005; 2006) has been proposed to improve marshaling plan, and the environmental model considering groups of containers is shown to be effective to reduce the total number of movements of containers.

This chapter introduces a new environmental model integrated in reinforcement learning method for marshaling plan in order to minimize the transfer distance of container-movements. A container transfer process consists of 4 elements: 1. holding a container by a crane, 2. removing the container, 3. placing the container, and 4. releasing it from the crane. In the proposed method, elements 1., 3. and 4. are evaluated by the number of container-movements, and the transfer distance of container-movements in the element 2. is considered by using a weighted cost of a container-movement. Then, evaluation values reflect the total transer-distance of containermovements, and the distance is minimized by using the reinforcement learningmethod. Consequently, selecting the best evaluation values leads the best series of container movements required to obtain a desired layout. Moreover, each rearranged container is placed into the desired position so that every trial can achieve one of desired layouts. In addition, in the proposed method, each container has several desired positions in the final layout, and the feature is considered in the learning algorithm. Thus, the early-phase performances of the learning process can be improved.

The remainder of the chapter is organized as follows. The marshaling process in container yard terminals is elaborated in section 2, followed by problem description. Also, in this section, desired positions and transfer distance of containers are newly explained. In section 3, a new Q-Learning algorithmbased on the transfer distance of containers is detailed. Computer simulations are conducted for several cases and proposed method is compared to conventional ones in section 4. Finally, concluding remarks are given in section 5.

2. Problem description

Figure 1 shows an example of container yard terminal. The terminal consists of containers, yard areas, yard transfer cranes, and port crane. Containers are carried by trucks and each container is stacked in a corresponding area called bay and a set of bays constitutes a yard area. k containers, $c_i\,(i=1,\cdots,k)$, are assumed to be exist in a bay, and each bay has n_Y stacks that m_Y containers can be laden. A position of each container is discriminated by using discrete position numbers, $1,\cdots,n_Y\cdot m_Y$. Then, the position of the container c_i is described by $x_i\,(1\le i\le k, 1\le x_i\le m_Y\cdot n_Y)$, and the state of a bay is determined by the vector, $x=[x_1,\cdots,x_k]$. Figure 2 shows an example of initial layout of container and the desired layout for $k=8, m_Y=n_Y=4$. In the figure, the state vector for the initial layout is $[13,10,9,11,14,15,16,12]$, and $[13,14,15,16,9,10,11,12]$ for the desired layout.

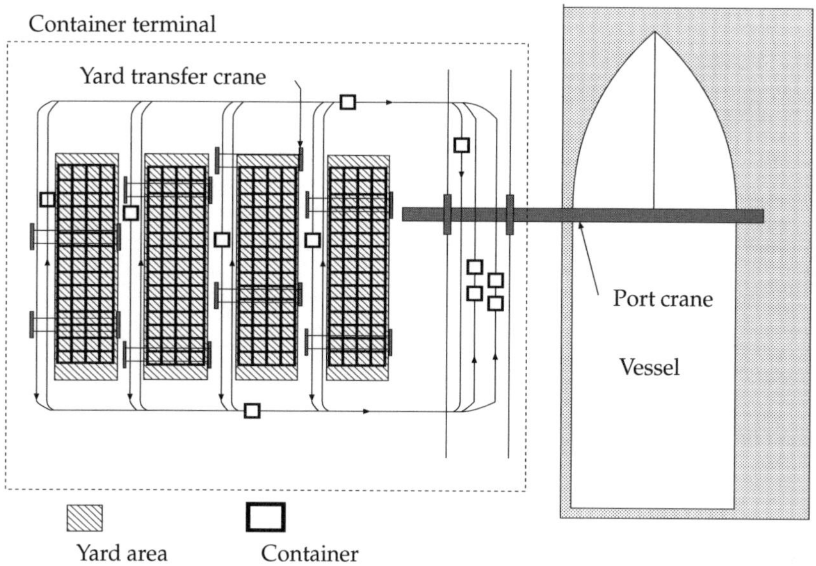

Fig. 1. Container terminal

2.1 Grouping

The desired layout in a bay is generated based on the loading order of containers that are moved from the bay to a vessel. The container to be loaded into the vessel can be located at any stack if it is on top of the stack. This feature yields several desired layouts for the bay.

2.1.1 Horizontal group

In the addressed problem, when containers on different stacks are placed at the same height in the desired layout of a bay, it is assumed that the positions of such containers can be exchanged. Figure 3 shows an example of desired layouts, where $m_y = n_y = 3, k = 9$. In the figure, containers are loaded into the vessel in the descendent order. Then, containers c_7, c_8, c_9 are in the same group (group$_1$), and their positions are exchanged because the loading order can be kept unchanged after the exchange of positions. In the same way, c_4, c_5, c_6 are in the group$_2$, and c_1, c_2, c_3 are in the group$_3$ where positions of containers can be exchanged. Consequently several candidates for desired layout of the bay are generated from the original

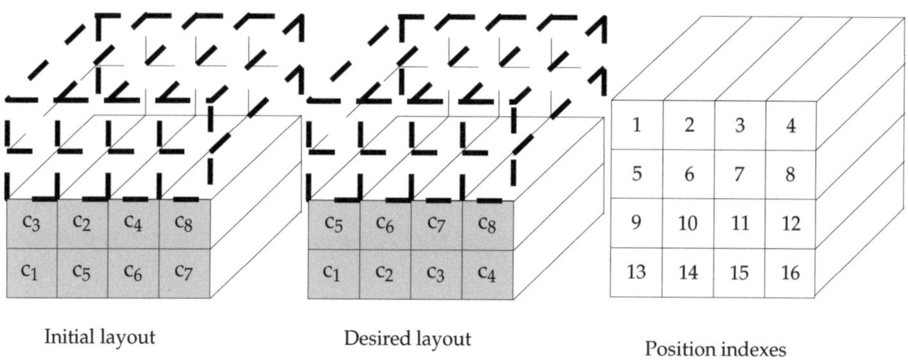

Fig. 2. Example of container layouts in a Bay

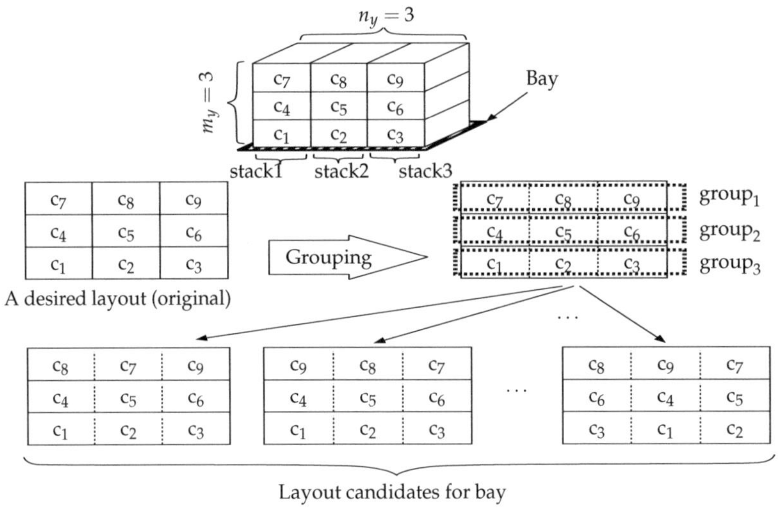

Fig. 3. Horizontal group

desired-layout.

2.1.2 Heap group

In addition to the horizontal grouping, a "heap group" for n_y containers at the top of stacks in the original desired-layout (group$_1$) is generated as follows:

1. n_y containers in group$_1$ can be placed at any stacks if their height is same as the original one.
2. Each of them can be stacked on other $n_\text{y} - 1$ containers when both of followings are satisfied:
   (a) They are placed at the top of each stack in the original disired-layout,
   (b) The container to be stacked is loaded into the ship before other containers being under the container.

Other groups are the same as ones in the horizontal group, so that the heap group contains all the desired layout in the horizontal group.
Figure 4 depicts an example of heap group for $k = 9, n_\text{y} = 3$. In the figure, containers are loaded into a vessel by the order $c_9, c_8, c_7, \cdots$. Then, c_9 can be placed on c_7 and c_8, c_8 can be placed on c_7, so that the number of desired layouts is incresed.

2.2 Marshaling process

The marshaling process consists of 2 stages: ① selection of a container to be rearranged, and ② removal of the containers on the selected container in ①. After these stages, rearrangement of the selected container is conducted. In the stage ②, the removed container is placed on the destination stack selected from stacks being in the same bay. When a container is rearranged, n_y positions that are at the same height in a bay can be candidates for the destination. In addition, n_y containers can be placed for each candidate of the destination. Then, defining t as the time step, $c_\text{a}(t)$ denotes the container to be rearranged at t in the stage ①. $c_\text{a}(t)$ is selected from candidates $c_{y_{i_1}}$ $(i_1 = 1, \cdots, n_\text{y}^2)$ that are at the same height in a desired layout.

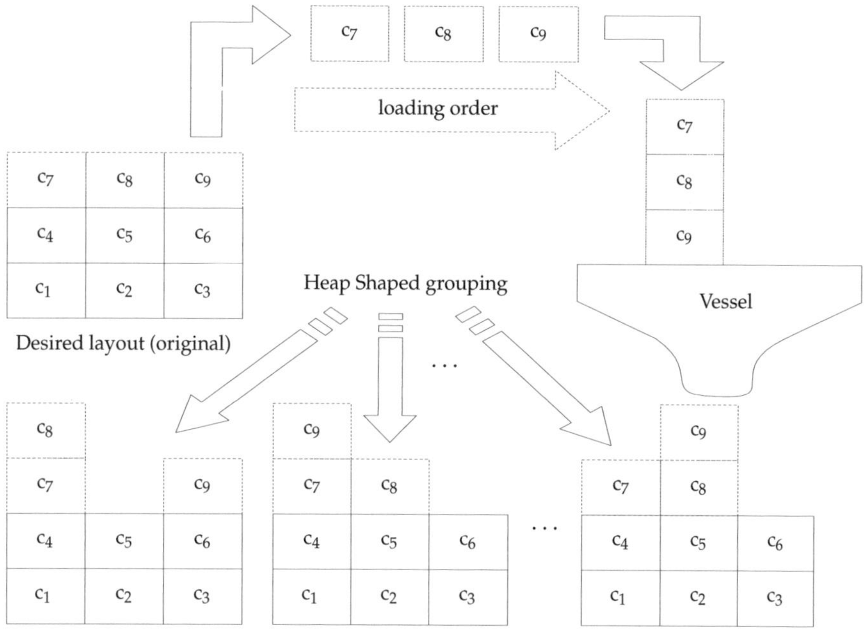

Fig. 4. Heap group

A candidate of destination exists at a bottom position that has undesired container in each corresponding stack. The maximum number of such stacks is n_Y, and they can have n_Y containers as candidates, since the proposed method considers groups in the desired position. The number of candidates of $c_a(t)$ is thus $n_Y \times n_Y$. In the stage ②, the container to be removed at t is $c_b(t)$ and is selected from two containers $c_{y_{i_2}}$ $(i_2 = 1,2)$ on the top of stacks. c_{y_1} is on the $c_a(t)$ and c_{y_2} is on the destination of $c_a(t)$. Then, in the stage ②, $c_b(t)$ is removed to one of the other stacks in the same bay, and the destination stack $u(t)$ at time t is selected from the candidates u_j $(j = 1, \cdots, n_Y - 2)$. $c_a(t)$ is rearranged to its desired position after all the $c_{y_{i_2}}$s are removed. Thus, a state transition of the bay is described as follows:

$$x_{t+1} = \begin{cases} f(x_t, c_a(t)) & \text{(stage ①)} \\ f(x_t, c_b(t), u(t)) & \text{(stage ②)} \end{cases} \quad (1)$$

where $f(\cdot)$ denotes that removal is processed and x_{t+1} is the state determined only by $c_a(t), c_b(t)$ and $u(t)$ at the previous state x_t. Therefore, the marshaling plan can be treated as the Markov Decision Process.

The objective of the problem is to find the best series of movements which transfers every container from an initial position to the goal position. The goal state is generated from the shipping order that is predetermined according to destinations of containers. A series of movements that leads a initial state into the goal state is defined as an episode. The best episode is the series of movements having the minimum transfer distance of contaners to achieve the goal state.

3. Reinforcement learning for marshaling plan

In the selection of c_a, the container to be rearranged, an evaluation value is used for each candidate $c_{y_{i_1}}$ $(i_1 = 1, \cdots, r)$, where r is the number of candidates. In the same way, evaluation values are used in the selection of the container to be removed c_b and its destination u_j ($j = 1,\cdots,n_y - 2$). Candidates of c_b is $c_{y_{i_2}}$ ($i_2 = 1,\cdots,n_y$). The evaluation value for the selection of $c_{y_{i_1}}$, $c_{y_{i_2}}$ and u_j at the state x are called Q-values, and a set of Q-values is called Q-table. At the lth episode, the Q-value for selecting $c_{y_{i_1}}$ is defined as $Q_1(l,x,c_{y_{i_1}})$, the Q-value for selecting $c_{y_{i_2}}$ is defined as $Q_2(l,x,c_{y_{i_1}},c_{y_{i_2}})$ and the Q-value for selecting u_j is defined as $Q_3(l,x,c_{y_{i_1}}, c_{y_{i_2}},u_j)$. The initial value for Q_1,Q_2,Q_3 is assumed to be 0. Then, Q_3 is updated by the following equation:

$$\begin{aligned} &Q_3(l,x_t,c_a(t),c_b(t),u(t)) = \\ &\quad (1-\alpha)Q_3(l-1,x_t,c_a(t),c_b(t),u(t)) + \alpha[R + V_{t+1}] \\ &V_t = \begin{cases} \gamma \max\limits_{y_{i_1}} Q_1(l,x_t,c_{y_{i_1}}) & (\text{stage } ①) \\ \gamma \max\limits_{y_{i_2}} Q_2(l,x_t,c_a(t),c_{y_{i_2}}) & (\text{stage } ②) \end{cases} \end{aligned} \tag{2}$$

where $\gamma, (0 < \gamma < 1)$ denotes the discount factor and α is the learning rate. Reward R is given only when the desired layout has been achieved.
In the selection of $c_b(t)$, the evaluation value $Q_3(l,x, c_a(t),c_b(t),u_j)$ can be referred for all the u_j ($j = 1\cdots n_y - 2$), and the state x does not change. Thus, the maximum value of $Q_3(l,x, c_a(t),c_b(t),u_j)$ is copied to $Q_2(l,x,c_a(t),c_b(t))$, that is,

$$Q_2(l,x,c_a(t),c_b(t)) = \max_j Q_3(l,x,c_a(t),c_b(t),u_j). \tag{3}$$

In the selection of $c_a(t)$, the evaluation value $Q_1(l,x, c_a(t))$ is updated by the following equations:

$$Q_1(l,x_t,c_a(t)) = (1-\alpha)Q_1(l-1,x_t,c_a(t)) + \alpha[R + V_{t+1}]. \tag{4}$$

In order to reflect the transfer distance of the removed container into the corresponding evaluation value, the discount factor γ is used. In the proposed method, γ has smaller value for larger transfer distance, so that smaller transfer distance has better evaluation. In the following, the calculation method of γ is explained.
Define D as the transfer distance of a removed container. For simplicity, D is set as 1 for a removal between neighboring positions in the horizontal or the vertical direction. Then, by assuming each container is moved either horizontal or vertical direction, the maximum value of D satisfies $\max D = 2m_y + n_y - 1 \stackrel{\text{def}}{=} D_{\max}$. Then, $1 \le D \le D_{\max}$. Figure 5 shows an examples of $D_{\max}$ for $m_y = n_y = 6$. Using D and $D_{\max}$, γ is calculated as follows:

$$\gamma = \frac{D_{\max} - (\beta D - 1)}{D_{\max}}. \tag{5}$$

The size of γ is determined by putting $0 < \beta < 1$, where larger transfer distance yealds larger discount so that the smaller transfer distance obtains the better evaluation value.
$c_a(t)$, $c_b(t)$, $u(j)$ is determined by the soft-max action selection method(Sutton & Barto, 1999). Probability P for selection of each candidate is calculated by

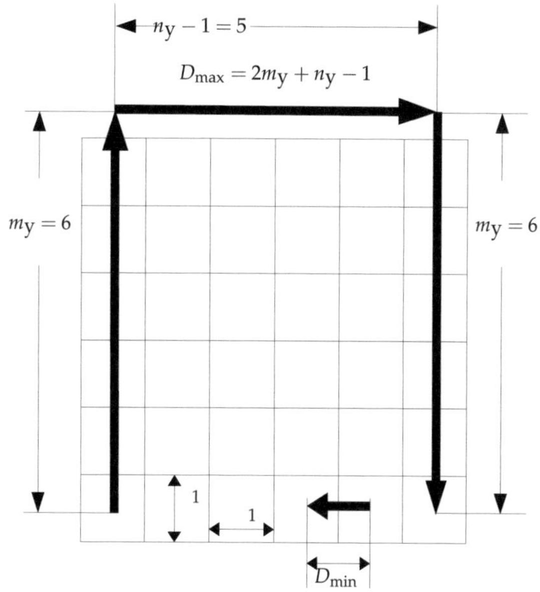

Fig. 5. Transfer distance of a container

$$\tilde{Q}(\tilde{x},u_L) = \frac{Q(l,\tilde{x},u_l) - \min_u Q(l,\tilde{x},u_L)}{\max_u Q(l,\tilde{x},u) - \min_u Q(l,\tilde{x},u)} \tag{6}$$

$$P(\tilde{x},u_L) = \frac{\exp(\tilde{Q}(\tilde{x},u_L)/\mathrm{T})}{\sum_u \exp(\tilde{Q}(\tilde{x},u_L)/\mathrm{T})}, \tag{7}$$

where $\tilde{x} = x_t, u_L = c_{y_{i_1}}$ for selecting $c_a(t)$, $\tilde{x} = (x_t, c_a(t)), u_L = c_{y_{i_2}}$ for selecting $c_b(t)$ and $\tilde{x} = (x_t, c_a(t), c_b(t)), u_L = u_j$ for selecting $u(t)$. Also, T is the thermo constant.
By using the update rule, restricted movements and goal states explained above, the learning process is described as follows:

[1]. Rearrange $c_a(t)$ if possible, and count the number of containers being in the goal positions and store it as n
[2]. If $n = k$, go to [10]
[3]. Select $c_a(t)$ to be rearranged
[4]. Store $(x, c_a(t))$
[5]. Select $c_b(t)$ to be removed
[6]. Store $(x, c_a(t), c_b(t))$
[7]. Select destination position u_j for $c_b(t)$
[8]. Store $(x, c_a(t), c_b(t), u_j)$
[9]. Remove $c_b(t)$ and go to [5] if another $c_b(t)$ exists, otherwise go to [1]
[10]. Update Q-values referred in [3],[5],[7].

4. Simulations

Computer simulations are conducted for $k = 18, m_y = n_y = 6$, and learning performances of following 3 methods are compared:

(A) proposed method using horizontal grouping and heap grouping,

(B) conventional method only using horizontal grouping (Hirashima et al., 2006),

(C) conventional method without grouping (Hirashima et al., 2005).

Figure 6 shows the initial state of the yard and an example of desired layout. The desired layout is fixed for method (C), and is exteded for methods (A),(B) by grouping. Parameters used in the proposed method are set as $\alpha = 0.8, \beta = 0.8, T = 0.1, R = 1.0$. A trial starts from a initial state and ends when all the containers are rearranged to the buffer. Containers, from c_1 to c_{18}, are loaded into a vessel by ascending order.

Initial layout Original desired layout

Fig. 6. Initial layout and original desired layout

Figure 7 shows the results, where the horizontal axis expresses the number of trials. The vertical axis expresses the minimum transfer-distance of removed containers to achive a desired layout found in the past trials. Each result is averaged over 20 independent simulations. Among these simulations, dispersions of averaged data are indicated by error bars on some tipical data points at 1000th, 5000th, 10000th, 50000th, 150000th, 20000th and 250000th trials. Method (A) could derive solutions with smaller transfer-distance of container as compared to methods (B),(C). Moreover, in early stages, learning performances of method (A) is much better than that of methods (B),(C), because method (A) has augmented desired layouts including the original ones in methods (B),(C), so that the method (A) has obtained the layout that can reduce the total transfer-distance of container. Figure 8 dipicts final layouts generated by methods (A),(B). The final layout of method (C) is identical to the one dipicted in Figure 6. In the figure, positions of conainers in the same height are exchanged. In the layout obtained by method (A), c_1, c_2, c_3 are located on other containers in the same group, whereas this layout does not regarded as desired layout in methods (B),(C), so that the total distance of movements of containers is reduced.

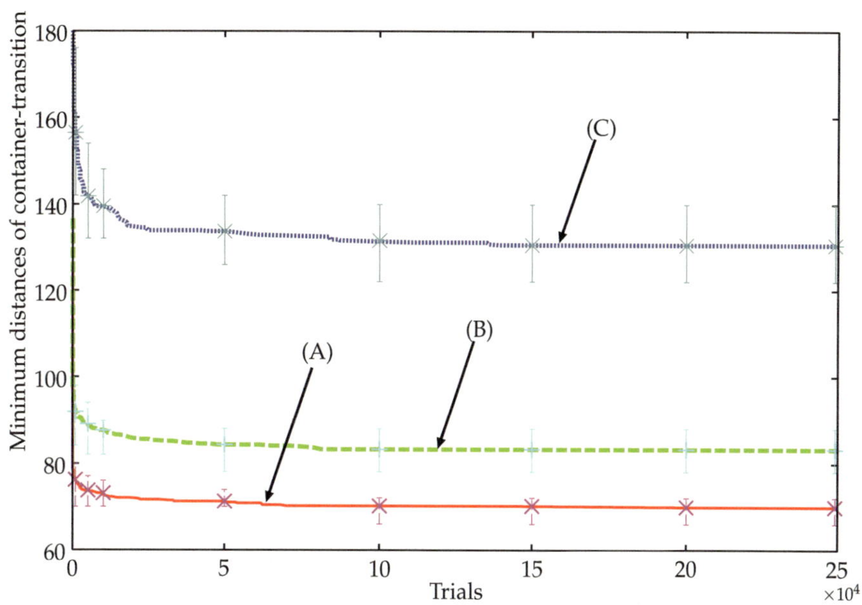

Fig. 7. Performance comparison

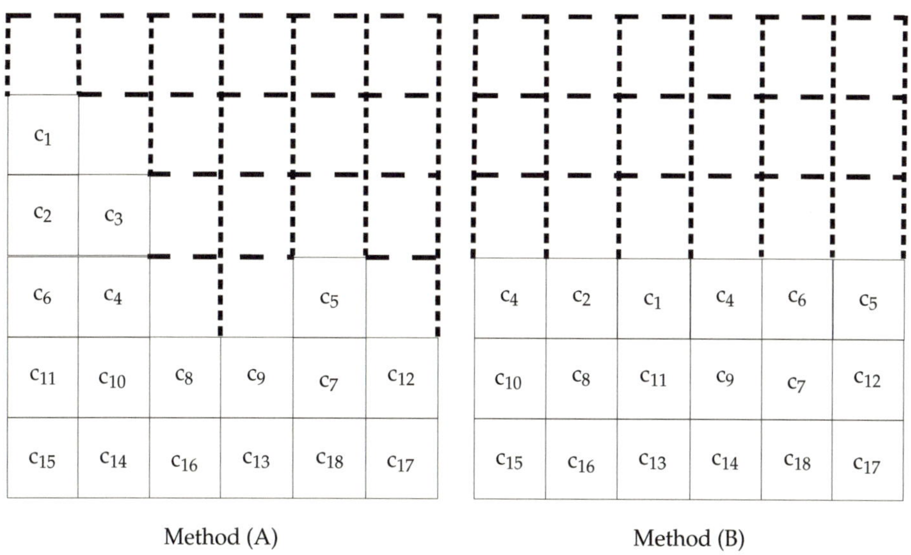

Fig. 8. Final layouts

5. Conclusions

A new marshling method for containers at marine terminals has been proposed. In the proposed method, Q-Learning is used to derive marshaling plan considering the transfer distance of container that is required to achieve desired layout of the bay. As a consequent, the layout of container, rearrange order of containers, destinations of removed containers are simultaneously optimized, so that the total transfer distance of containers is minimized. The proposed method applied for realistic scale problems, and showed much better performance for improving solutions as compared to conventional methods.

6. References

Günther, H. O. & Kim, K. H. (2005). *Container Terminals and Automated Transport Systems*, Springer.

Hirashima, Y., Ishikawa, N. & Takeda, K. (2006). A new reinforcement learning for group-based marshaling plan considering desired layout of containers in port terminals, *International Conference on Networking, Sensing, and Control* pp. 670–675.

Hirashima, Y., Takeda, K., Furuya, O., Inoue, A. & Deng, M. (2005). A new method for marshaling plan using a reinforcement learning considering desired layout of containers in terminals, *Preprint of 16th IFAC World Congress* We-E16-TO/2.

Koza, J. R. (1992). *Genetic Programming : On Programming Computers by means of Natural Selection and Genetics*, MIT Press.

Minagawa, M. & Kakazu, Y. (1997). An approach to the block stacking problem by multi agent cooperation, *Trans. Jpn. Soc. Mech. Eng. (in Japanese)* C-63(608): 231–240.

Motoyama, S., Hirashima, Y., Takeda, K. & Inoue, A. (2001). A marshaling plan for container terminals based on reinforce-ment learning, *Proc. of Inter. Sympo. on Advanced Control of Industrial Processes* pp. 631–636.

Sutton, R. & Barto, A. (1999). *Reinforcement Learning*, MIT Press, Cambridge.

Watkins, C. J. C. H. & Dayan, P. (1992). Q-learning, *Machine Learning* 8: 279–292.

23

Distributed Parameter Bioprocess Plant Identification and I-Term Control Using Decentralized Fuzzy-Neural Multi-Models

Ieroham Baruch, Rosalba Galvan-Guerra and Sergio-Miguel Hernandez M.
CINVESTAV-IPN, Mexico City, Department of Automatic Control, Mexico

1. Introduction

In the last decade, the Computational Intelligence tools (CI), including Artificial Neural Networks (ANN) and Fuzzy Systems (FS), applying soft computing, became universal means for many applications. Because of their approximation and learning capabilities, the ANNs have been widely employed to dynamic process modeling, identification, prediction and control, (Boskovic & Narendra, 1995; Haykin, 1999; Bulsari & Palosaari, 1993; Deng & Li, 2003; Deng et al., 2005; Gonzalez-Garcia et al., 1998; Padhi & Balakrishnan, 2003; Padhi et al., 2001; Ray,1989). Many applications have been done for identification and control of biotechnological plants too, (Padhi et al., 2001). Among several possible neural network architectures the ones most widely used are the Feedforward NN (FFNN) and the Recurrent NN (RNN), (Haykin, 1999). The main NN property namely the ability to approximate complex non-linear relationships without prior knowledge of the model structure makes them a very attractive alternative to the classical modeling and control techniques. Also, a great boost has been made in the applied NN-based adaptive control methodology incorporating integral plus state control action in the control law, (Baruch et al., 2004; Baruch & Garrido, 2005; Baruch et al., 2007). The FFNN and the RNN have been applied for Distributed Parameter Systems (DPS) identification and control too. In (Pietil & Koivo, 1996), a RNN is used for system identification and process prediction of a DPS dynamics - an adsorption column for wastewater treatment of water contaminated with toxic chemicals. In (Deng & Li, 2003; Deng et al., 2005) a spectral-approximation-based intelligent modeling approach, including NNs for state estimation and system identification, is proposed for the distributed thermal processing of the snap curing oven DPS that is used in semiconductor packaging industry. In (Bulsari & Palosaari, 1993), it is presented a new methodology for the identification of DPS, based on NN architectures, motivated by standard numerical discretization techniques used for the solution of Partial Differential Equation (PDE). In (Padhi & Balakrishnan, 2003), an attempt is made to use the philosophy of the NN adaptive-critic design to the optimal control of distributed parameter systems. In (Padhi et al., 2001) the concept of proper orthogonal decomposition is used for the model reduction of DPS to form a reduced order lumped parameter problem. The optimal control problem is then solved in the time domain, in a state feedback sense, following the philosophy of adaptive critic NNs. The control solution is then mapped back to the spatial domain using the same basis functions. In (Pietil & Koivo, 1996), measurement data of an industrial process are generated by solving the PDE numerically using the finite differences method. Both centralized and decentralized NN models are introduced and constructed based on this data. The models are implemented on FFNN using Backpropagation (BP) and Levenberg-Marquardt learning algorithms.

Similarly to the static ANNs, the fuzzy models could approximate static nonlinear plants where structural plant information is needed to extract the fuzzy rules, (Baruch et al., 2008a, Baruch et al., 2008b, Baruch et al., 2008c; Baruch & Galvan-Guerra, 2008; Baruch & Galvan-Guerra, 2009). The difference between them is that the ANN models are global models where training is performed on the entire pattern range and the FS models perform a fuzzy blending of local models space based on the partition of the input space. So, the aim of the neuro-fuzzy (fuzzy-neural) models is to merge both ANN and FS approaches so to obtain fast adaptive models possessing learning, (Baruch et al., 2008a). The fuzzy-neural networks are capable of incorporating both numerical data (quantitative information) and expert's knowledge (qualitative information), and describe them in the form of linguistic IF-THEN rules. During the last decade considerable research has been devoted towards developing recurrent neuro-fuzzy models, summarized in (Baruch et al., 2008a). To reduce the number of IF-THAN rules, the hierarchical approach could be used (Baruch et al., 2008a). A promising approach of recurrent neuro-fuzzy systems with internal dynamics is the application of the Takagi-Sugeno (T-S) fuzzy rules with a static premise and a dynamic function consequent part, (Baruch et al., 2008a). The paper of (Baruch et al., 2008a) proposed as a dynamic function in the consequent part of the T-S rules to use a Recurrent Neural Network Model (RNNM).

Some results of this RNNM approach for centralized and decentralized identification of dynamic plants with distributed parameters are given in (Baruch et al., 2008a; Baruch et al., 2008b; Baruch et al., 2008c; Baruch & Galvan-Guerra, 2008; Baruch & Galvan-Guerra, 2009). The difference between the used in the other papers fuzzy neural model and the approach used in (Baruch et al., 2008a) is that the other one used the Frasconi, Gori and Soda RNN model, which is sequential one, and in (Baruch et al., 2008a), it is used the RTNN model, which is completely parallel one. But it is not still enough because the neural nonlinear dynamic function ought to be learned, and the Backpropagation learning algorithm is not introduced in the T-S fuzzy rule. For this reason in (Baruch et al., 2008a) the RTNN BP learning algorithm (Baruch et al., 2008d) has been introduced in the antecedent part of the IF-THAN rule so to complete the learning procedure and a second hierarchical defuzzyfication BP learning level has been formed so to improve the adaptation and approximation ability of the fuzzy-neural system, (Baruch et al., 2008a). This system has been successfully applied for identification and control of complex nonlinear plants, (Baruch et al., 2008a).

The aim of this chapter is to describe the results obtained by this system for decentralized identification and control of wastewater treatment anaerobic digestion bioprocess representing a Distributed Parameter System (DPS), extending the used control laws with an integral term, so to form an integral plus state control action, capable to speed up the reaction of the control system and to augment its resistance to process and measurement noises. The analytical anaerobic bioprocess plant model (Aguilar-Garnica et al., 2006), used as an input/output plant data generator, is described by PDE/ODE, and simplified using the orthogonal collocation technique, (Bialecki & Fairwether, 2001), in four collocation points and a recirculation tank. This measurement points are used as centres of the membership functions of the fuzzyfied space variables of the plant.

2. Description of the direct decentralized fuzzy-neural control with I-term

The block-diagrams of the complete direct Fuzzy-Neural Multi-Model (FNMM) control system and its identification and control parts are schematically depicted in Fig.1, Fig. 2 and Fig. 3. The structure of the entire control system, (Baruch et al., 2008a; Baruch et al., 2008b; Baruch et al., 2008c) contained Fuzzyfier, Fuzzy Rule-Based Inference System (FRBIS), and defuzzyfier. The FRBIS contained five identification, five feedback control, five feedforward control, five I-term control, five total control T-S fuzzy rules (see Fig. 1, 2, 3 for more details).

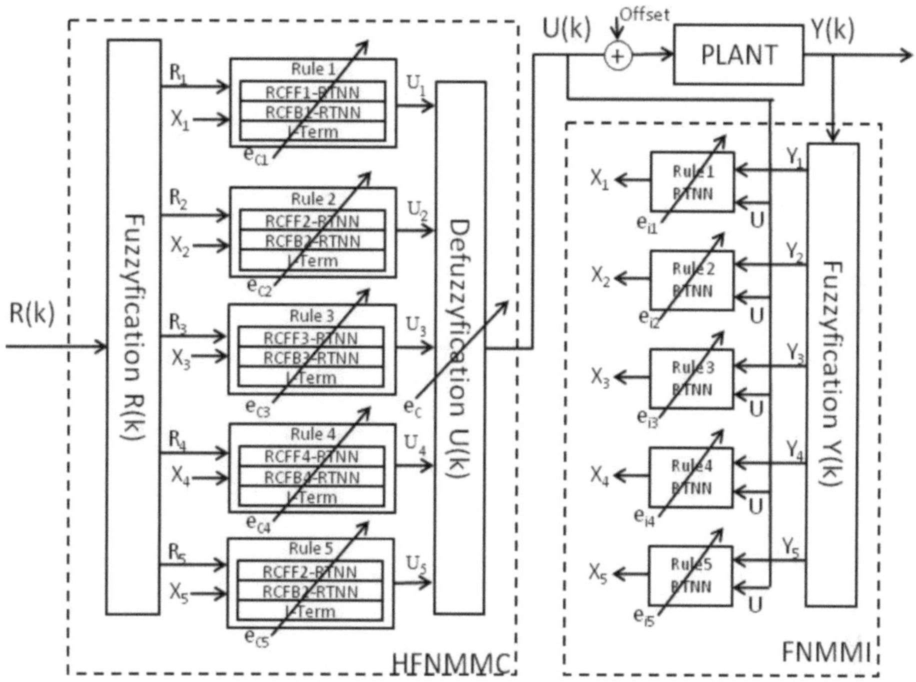

Fig. 1. Block-Diagram of the FNMM Control System

The plant output variables and its correspondent reference variables depended on space and time. They are fuzzyfied on space and represented by five membership functions which centers are the five collocation points of the plant (four points for the fixed bed and one point for the recirculation tank). The main objective of the Fuzzy-Neural Multi-Model Identifier (FNMMI), containing five rules, is to issue states and parameters for the direct adaptive Fuzzy-Neural Multi-Model Feedback Controller (FNMMFBC) when the FNMMI outputs follows the outputs of the plant in the five measurement (collocation) points with minimum error of approximation. The control part of the system is a direct adaptive Fuzzy-Neural Multi-Model Controller (FNMMC). The objective of the direct adaptive FNMM controller, containing five Feedback (FB), five Feedforward (FF) T-S control rules, five I-term control rules, and five total control rules is to speed up the reaction of the control system, and to augment the resistance of the control system to process and measurement noises, reducing the error of control, so that the plant outputs in the five measurement points tracked the corresponding reference variables with minimum error of tracking.
The upper hierarchical level of the FNMM control system is one- layer- perceptron which represented the defuzzyfier, (Baruch et al., 2008a). The hierarchical FNMM controller has

two levels - Lower Level of Control (LLC), and Upper Level of Control (ULC). It is composed of three parts (see Fig. 3): 1) Fuzzyfication, where the normalized reference vector signal contained reference components of five measurement points; 2) Lower Level Inference Engine, which contained twety five T-S fuzzy rules (five rules for identification and twenty rules for control- five in the feedback part, five in the feedforward part, five in the I-term part, and five total control rules), operating in the corresponding measurement points; 3) Upper Hierarchical Level of neural defuzzification.
The detailed block-diagram of the FNMMI (see Fig. 2), contained a space plant output fuzzyfier and five identification T-S fuzzy rules, labeled as RI_i, which consequent parts are RTNN learning procedures, (Baruch et al, 2008 a). The identification T-S fuzzy rules have the form:

$$RI_i\text{: } \textbf{\textit{If}}\ x(k)\ \textbf{\textit{is}}\ A_i\ \textbf{\textit{and}}\ u(k)\ \textbf{\textit{is}}\ B_i\ \textbf{\textit{then}}\ Y_i = \Pi_i\,(L,M,N_i,Y_{di},U,X_i,A_i,B_i,C_i,E_i),\ i=1\text{-}5. \quad (1)$$

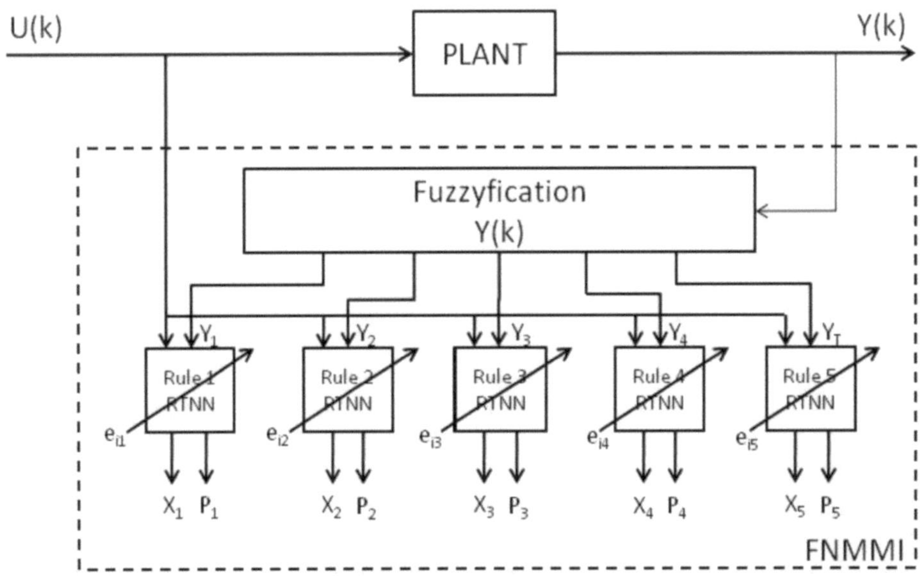

Fig. 2. Detailed block-diagram of the FNMM identifier

The detailed block-diagram of the FNMMC, given on Fig. 3, contained a spaced plant reference fuzzyfier and twenty control T-S fuzzy rules (five FB, five FF, five I-term, and five-total control), which consequent FB, and FF parts are also RTNN learning procedures, (Baruch et al., 2008a), using the state information, issued by the corresponding identification rules. The consequent part of each feedforward control rule (the consequent learning procedure) has the M, L, N_i RTNN model dimensions, R_i, Y_{di}, E_{ci} inputs and U_{ffi}, outputs used by the total control rule. The T-S fuzzy rule has the form:

$$RCFF_i\text{: } \textbf{\textit{If}}\ R(k)\ \textbf{\textit{is}}\ B_i\ \textbf{\textit{then}}\ Uff_i = \Pi_i\,(M, L, N_i, R_i, Y_{di}, X_i, J_i, B_i, C_i, E_{ci}),\ i=1\text{-}5. \quad (2)$$

The consequent part of each feedback control rule (the consequent learning procedure) has the M, L, N_i RTNN model dimensions, Y_{di}, X_i, E_{ci} inputs and U_{fbi}, outputs used by the total control rule. The T-S fuzzy rule has the form:

$$RCFB_i\text{: } \textbf{\textit{If}}\ Y_{di}\ \textbf{\textit{is}}\ A_i\ \textbf{\textit{then}}\ Ufb_i = \Pi_i\,(M, L, N_i, Y_{di}, X_i, X_{ci}, J_i, B_i, C_i, E_{ci}),\ i=1\text{-}5. \quad (3)$$

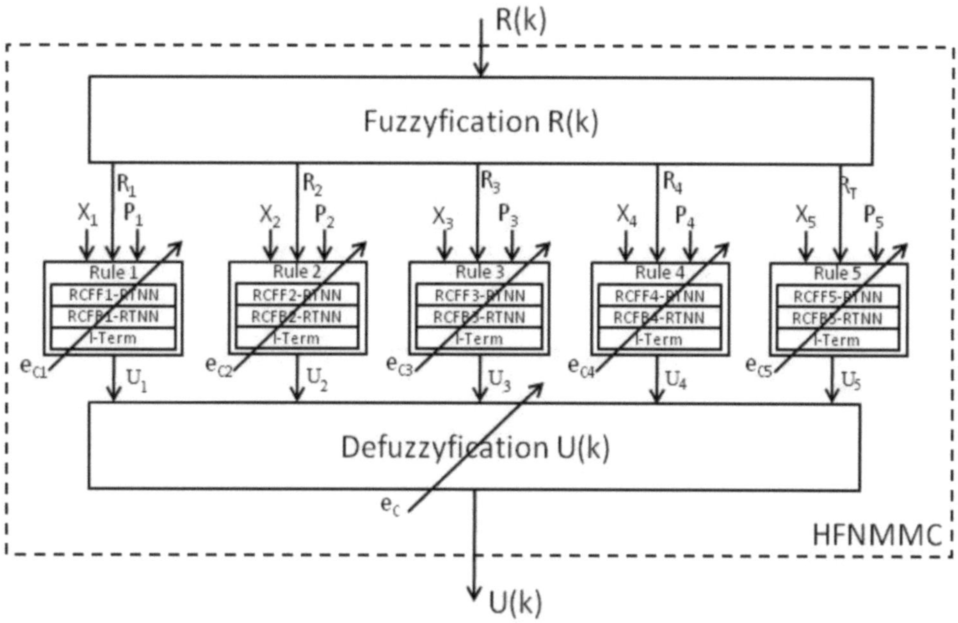

Fig. 3. Detailed block-diagram of the HFNMM controller

The I-term control algorithm is as follows:

$$UIt_i\,(k+1) = UIt_i\,(k) + To\,K_i\,(k)\,E_{ci}\,(k),\ i=1\text{-}5; \tag{4}$$

where To is the period of discretization and K_i is the I-term gain. An appropriate choice for the I-term gain K_i is a proportion of the inverse input/output plant gain, i.e.:

$$K_i\,(k) = \eta\,(C_i\,B_i)+. \tag{5}$$

The product of the pseudoinverse $(C_i\,B_i)+$ by the output error E_{ci} (k) transormed the output error in input error which equates the dimensions in the equation of the I-term control. The T-S rule, generating the I-term part of the control executed both equations (4), (5), representing a computational procedure, given by:

$$RCIt_i\text{: } \textbf{\textit{If}}\ Y_{di}\ \textbf{\textit{is}}\ A_i\ \textbf{\textit{then}}\ UIt_i = \Pi_i\,(M, L, B_i, C_i, E_{ci}, To, \eta),\ i=1\text{-}5. \tag{6}$$

The total control corresponding to each of the five measurement points is a sum of its corresponding feedforward, feedback, and I-term parts, as:

$$U_i\,(k) = -U_{ffi}\,(k) + U_{fbi}\,(k) + U_{Iti}\,(k),\ i=1\text{-}5. \tag{7}$$

The total control is generated by the procedure (7) incorporated in the T-S rule:

$$RC_i\text{: } \textbf{\textit{If}}\ Y_{di}\ \textbf{\textit{is}}\ A_i\ \textbf{\textit{then}}\ U_i = \Pi_i\,(M, U_{ffi},\,, U_{fbi}, U_{Iti}),\ i=1\text{-}5. \tag{8}$$

The defuzzyfication learning procedure, which correspond to the single layer perceptron learning is described by:

$$U = \Pi\,(M, L, N, Y_d, Uo, X, A, B, C, E). \tag{9}$$

The T-S rule and the defuzzification of the plant output of the fixed bed with respect to the space variable z ($\lambda i,z$ is the correspondent membership function), are given by:

$$RO_i\text{: } \textbf{\textit{If}}\ Y_{i,t}\ \textbf{\textit{is}}\ A_i\ \textbf{\textit{then}}\ Y_{i,t} = a_i^T Y_t + b_i,\ i=1,2,3,4; \qquad (10)$$

$$Y_z=[\Sigma_i\ \gamma_{i,z}\ a_i^T]\ Y_t + \Sigma_i\ \gamma_{i,z}\ b_i\ ;\ \gamma_{i,z} = \lambda_{i,z}\ /\ (\Sigma_j\ \lambda_{j,z}). \qquad (11)$$

The direct adaptive neural control algorithm, which appeared in the consequent part of the local fuzzy control rule RCFBi, (3) is a feedback control, using the states issued by the correspondent identification local fuzzy rule RIi (1).

3. Description of the indirect (sliding mode) decentralized fuzzy-neural control with I-term

The block-diagram of the FNMM control system is given on Fig.4. The structure of the entire control system, (Baruch et al., 2008a; Baruch et al., 2008b; Baruch et al., 2008c), contained Fuzzyfier, Fuzzy Rule-Based Inference System, containing twenty T-S fuzzy rules (five identification, five sliding mode control, five I-term control, five total control rules), and a defuzzyfier. Due to the learning abilities of the defuzzifier, the exact form of the control membership functions is not need to be known. The plant output variable and its correspondent reference variable depended on space and time, and they are fuzzyfied on space. The membership functions of the fixed-bed output variables are triangular or trapezoidal ones and that - belonging to the output variables of the recirculation tank are singletons. Centers of the membership functions are the respective collocation points of the plant. The main objective of the FNMM Identifier (FNMMI) (see Fig. 2), containing five T-S rules, is to issue states and parameters for the indirect adaptive FNMM Controller (FNMMC) when the FNMMI outputs follows the outputs of the plant in the five measurement (collocation) points with minimum MSE of approximation.
The objective of the indirect adaptive FNMM controller, containing five Sliding Mode Control (SMC) rules, five I-term rules, and five total control rules is to reduce the error of control, so that the plant outputs of the four measurement points tracked the corresponding reference variables with minimum MSE%. The hierarchical FNMM controller (see Fig. 5) has two levels - Lower Level of Control (LLC), and Upper Level of Control (ULC). It is composed of three parts: 1) Fuzzyfication, where the normalized reference vector signal contained reference components of five measurement points; 2) Lower Level Inference Engine, which contained twenty T-S fuzzy rules (five rules for identification, five rules for SM control, five rules for I-term control, and five rules for total control), operating in the corresponding measurement points; 3) Upper Hierarchical Level of neural defuzzification, represented by one layer perceptron, (Baruch et al., 2008a) . The detailed block-diagram of the FNMMI, given on Fig. 2, contained a space plant output fuzzyfier and five identification T-S fuzzy rules, labeled as RI_i, which consequent parts are learning procedures, (Baruch et al., 2008a), given by (1). The block-diagram of the FNMMC, given on Fig. 5, contained a spaced plant reference fuzzyfier, five SMC, five I-term control, and five total control T-S fuzzy rules. The consequent parts of the SMC T-S fuzzy rules are SMC procedures, (Baruch et al, 2008 a), using the state, and parameter information, issued by the corresponding identification rules. The SMC T-S fuzzy rules have the form:

$$RC_i\text{: } \textbf{\textit{If}}\ R(k)\ \textbf{\textit{is}}\ C_i\ \textbf{\textit{then}}\ U_i = \Pi_i\ (M, L, N_i, R_i, Y_{di}, X_i, A_i, B_i, C_i, E_{ci}),\ i=1\text{-}5. \qquad (12)$$

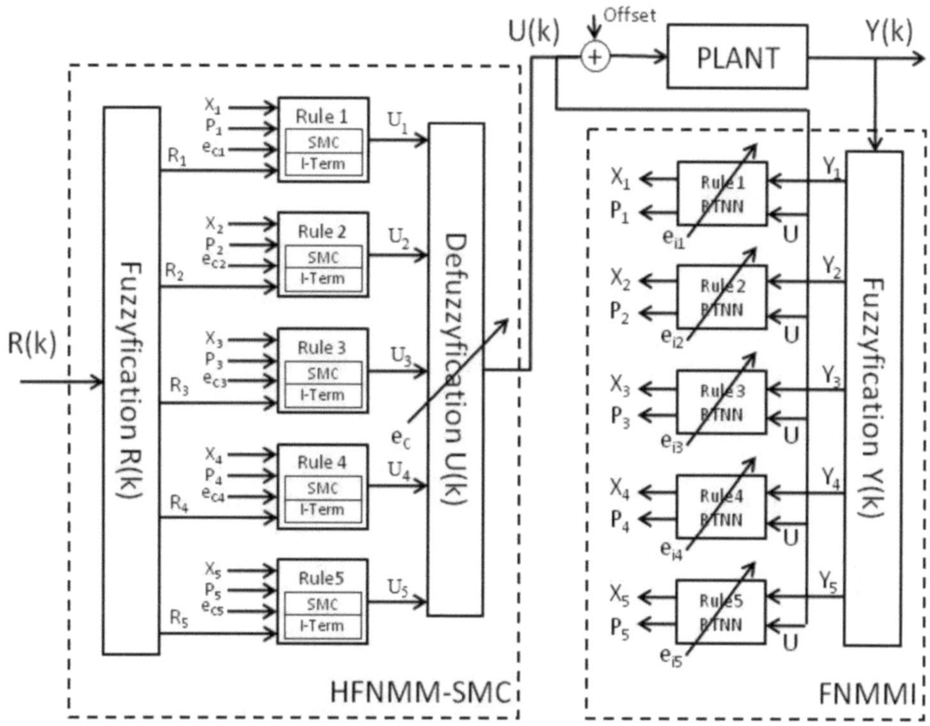

Fig. 4. Block-diagram of the FNMM control system

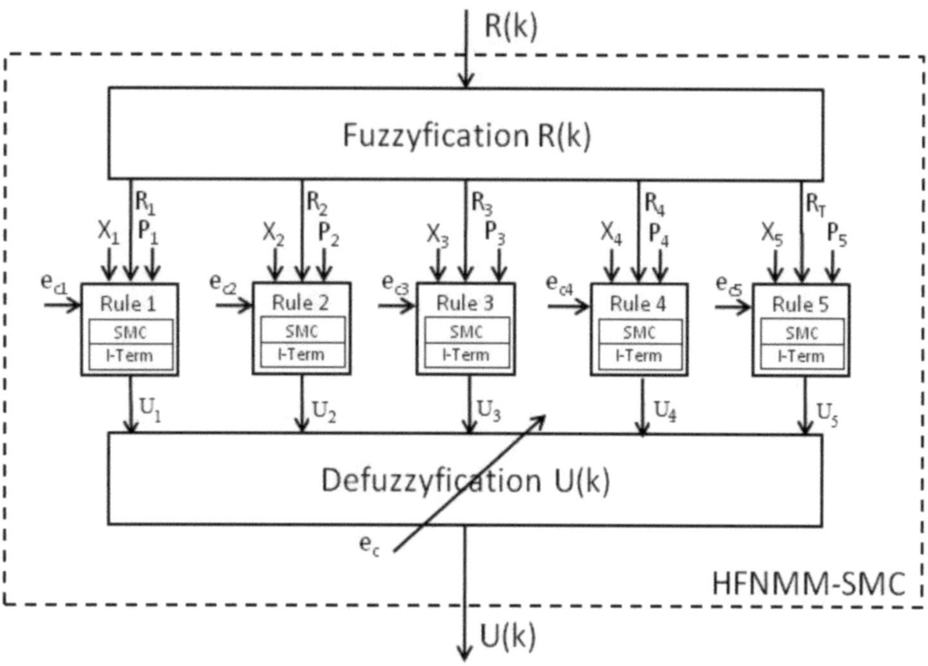

Fig. 5. Detailed block-diagram of the HFNMM controller

The I-term control algorithm and its corresponding T-S fuzzy rule are given by (4), (5), (6). The total control corresponding to each of the five measurement points is a sum of its corresponding SMC and I-term parts, as:

$$U_i\,(k) = U_{smci}\,(k) + U_{Iti}\,(k),\ i\text{=}1\text{-}5. \tag{13}$$

The total control is generated by the procedure (13) incorporated in the T-S rule:

$$RC_i\text{: } \textbf{\textit{If}}\ Y_{di}\ \textbf{\textit{is}}\ A_i\ \textbf{\textit{then}}\ U_i = \Pi_i\,(M, U_{smci}, U_{Iti}),\ i\text{=}1\text{-}5. \tag{14}$$

The defuzzyfication learning procedure, which correspond to the single layer perceptron learning is described by (9), (10), (11).
Next the indirect SMC procedure will be briefly described.

3.1 Sliding mode control system design

Here the indirect adaptive neural control algorithm, which appeared in the consequent part of the local fuzzy control rule RCi (12) is viewed as a Sliding Mode Control (SMC), (Baruch et al., 2008a; Baruch et al., 2008d), designed using the parameters and states issued by the correspondent identification local fuzzy rule RIi (1), approximating the plant in the corresponding collocation point.
Let us suppose that the studied local nonlinear plant model possess the following structure:

$$X_p(k+1)=F[X_p(k),-U_p(k)];\ Y_p(k)=G[X_p(k)]\,, \tag{15}$$

where: $X_p(k)$, $Y_p(k)$, $U(k)$ are plant state, output and input vector variables with dimensions Np, L and M, where L>M (rectangular system) is supposed; F and G are smooth, odd, bounded nonlinear functions. The linearization of the activation functions of the local learned identification RTNN model, which approximates the plant leads to the following linear local plant model:

$$X(k+1)=AX(k)+BU(k);\ Y(k)=CX(k); \tag{16}$$

where L > M (rectangular system), is supposed. Let us define the following sliding surface with respect to the output tracking error:

$$S(k+1) = E(k+1) + \sum_{i=1}^{P} \gamma_i E(k-i+1)\ ;\ \ |\gamma_i| < 1; \tag{17}$$

where: $S(\cdot)$ is the sliding surface error function; $E(\cdot)$ is the systems local output tracking error; γ_i are parameters of the local desired error function; P is the order of the error function. The additional inequality in (17) is a stability condition, required for the sliding surface error function. The local tracking error is defined as:

$$E(k) = R(k) - Y(k); \tag{18}$$

where R(k) is a L-dimensional local reference vector and Y(k) is an local output vector with the same dimension. The objective of the sliding mode control systems design is to find a control action which maintains the systems error on the sliding surface assuring that the output tracking error reached zero in P steps, where P<N, which is fulfilled if:

$$S(k+1)=0. \tag{19}$$

As the local approximation plant model (16), is controllable, observable and stable, (Baruch et al., 2004; Baruch et al., 2008d), the matrix A is block-diagonal, and L>M (rectangular system is supposed), the matrix product (CB) is nonsingular with rank M, and the plant states X(k) are smooth non- increasing functions. Now, from (16)-(19), it is easy to obtain the equivalent control capable to lead the system to the sliding surface which yields:

$$U_{eq}(k)=(CB)^{+}\left[-CAX(k)+R(k+1)+\sum_{i=1}^{P}\gamma_i E(k-i+1)\right]+Of, \tag{20}$$

$$(CB)^{+}=\left[(CB)^{T}(CB)\right]^{-1}(CB)^{T}. \tag{21}$$

Here the added offset Of is a learnable M-dimensional constant vector which is learnt using a simple delta rule (see Haykin, 1999, for more details), where the error of the plant input is obtained backpropagating the output error through the adjoint RTNN model. An easy way for learning the offset is using the following delta rule where the input error is obtaned from the output error multiplying it by the same pseudoinverse matrix, as it is:

$$Of(k+1)=Of(k+1)=Of(k)+\eta(CB)^{+}E(k). \tag{22}$$

If we compare the I-term expression (4), (5) with the Offset learning (22) we could see that they are equal which signifyed that the I-term generate a compensation offset capable to eliminate steady state errors caused by constant perturbations and discrepances in the reference tracking caused by non equal input/output variable dimensions (rectangular case systems). So introducing an I-term control it is not necessary to use an compensation offset in the SM control law (20).

The SMC avoiding chattering is taken using a saturation function inside a bounded control level Uo, taking into account plant uncertainties. So the SMC has the form:

$$U(k)=\begin{cases} U_{eq}(k), & \text{if } \|U_{eq}(k)\|<U_0 \\ \dfrac{-U_0U_{eq}(k)}{\|U_{eq}(k)\|}, & \text{if } \|U_{eq}(k)\|\geq U_0. \end{cases}; \tag{23}$$

The proposed SMC cope with the characteristics of the wide class of plant model reduction neural control with reference model, and represents an indirect adaptive neural control, given by (Baruch et al., 2004). Next we will give description of the used RTNN topology and learning.

4. Description of the RTNN topology and learning

4.1 RTNN topology and recursive BP learning

The block-diagrams of the RTNN topology and its adjoint, are given on Fig. 6, and Fig. 7. Following Fig. 6, and Fig. 7, we could derive the dynamic BP algorithm of its learning based on the RTNN topology using the diagrammatic method of (Wan & Beaufays, 1996). The RTNN topology and learning are described in vector-matrix form as:

$$X(k+1) = AX(k) + BU(k);\ B = [B_1 ; B_0];\ U^T = [U_1 ; U_2]; \tag{24}$$

$$Z_1(k) = G[X(k)]; \tag{25}$$

$$V(k) = CZ(k);\ C = [C_1 ; C_0];\ Z^T = [Z_1 ; Z_2]; \tag{26}$$

$$Y(k) = F[V(k)]; \tag{27}$$

$$A = \text{block-diag}(Ai),\ |Ai| < 1; \tag{28}$$

$$W(k+1) = W(k) + \eta\, \Delta W(k) + \alpha\, \Delta W_{ij}(k-1); \tag{29}$$

$$E(k) = T(k)-Y(k); \tag{30}$$

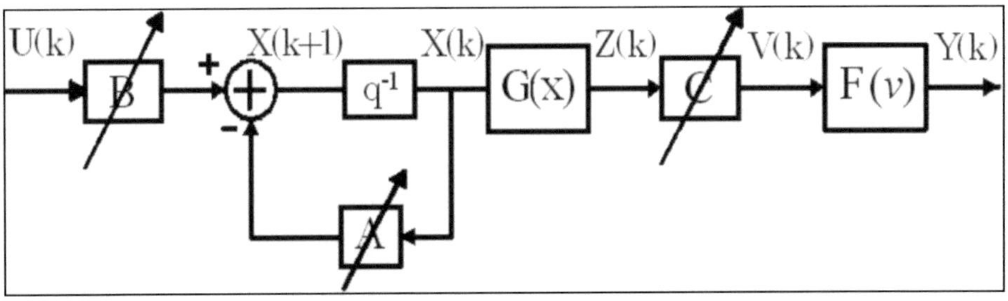

Fig. 6. Block diagram of the RTNN model

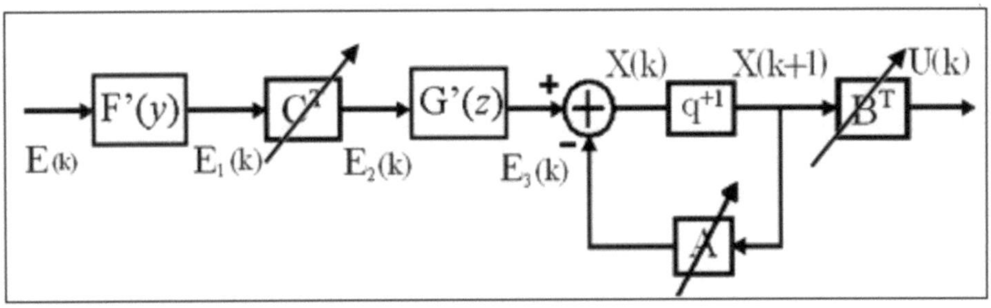

Fig. 7. Block diagram of the adjoint RTNN model

$$E_1(k) = F'[Y(k)]\, E(k);\ F'[Y(k)] = [1-Y^2(k)]; \tag{31}$$

$$\Delta C(k) = E_1(k)\, Z^T(k); \tag{32}$$

$$E_3(k) = G'[Z(k)]\, E_2(k);\ E_2(k) = C^T(k)\, E_1(k);\ G'[Z(k)] = [1-Z^2(k)]; \tag{33}$$

$$\Delta B(k) = E_3(k)\, U^T(k); \tag{34}$$

$$\Delta A(k) = E_3(k)\, X^T(k); \tag{35}$$

$$Vec(\Delta A(k)) = E_3(k) \square X(k); \tag{36}$$

where: X, Y, U are state, augmented output, and input vectors with dimensions N, (L+1), (M+1), respectively, where Z_1 and U_1 are the (Nx1) output and (Mx1) input of the hidden layer; the constant scalar threshold entries are $Z_2 = -1$, $U_2 = -1$, respectively; V is a (Lx1) pre-synaptic activity of the output layer; T is the (Lx1) plant output vector, considered as a RNN reference; A is (NxN) block-diagonal weight matrix; B and C are [Nx(M+1)] and [Lx(N+1)]-augmented weight matrices; B_0 and C_0 are (Nx1) and (Lx1) threshold weights of the hidden and output layers; F[·], G[·] are vector-valued tanh(·)-activation functions with corresponding dimensions; F'[·], G'[·] are the derivatives of these tanh(·) functions; W is a general weight, denoting each weight matrix (C, A, B) in the RTNN model, to be updated; ΔW (ΔC, ΔA, ΔB), is the weight correction of W; η, α are learning rate parameters; ΔC is an weight correction of the learned matrix C; ΔB is an weight correction of the learned matrix B; ΔA is an weight correction of the learned matrix A; the diagonal of the matrix A is denoted by Vec(·) and equation (34) represents its learning as an element-by-element vector products; E, E_1, E_2, E_3, are error vectors with appropriate dimensions, predicted by the adjoint RTNN model, given on Fig.7. The stability of the RTNN model is assured by the activation functions (-1, 1) bounds and by the local stability weight bound condition, given by (28). Below a theorem of RTNN stability which represented an extended version of Nava's theorem, (Baruch et al., 2008d) is given.

Theorem of stability of the BP RTNN used as system identifier (Baruch et al., 2008d). Let the RTNN with Jordan Canonical Structure is given by equations (24)-(28) (see Fig.6) and the nonlinear plant model, is as follows:

$$X_{p.}(k+1) = G[\, X_p(k), U(k)\,],$$

$$Y_p(k) = F[\, X_p(k)\,];$$

where: $\{Y_p(\cdot), X_p(\cdot), U(\cdot)\}$ are output, state and input variables with dimensions L, N_p, M, respectively; F(·), G(·) are vector valued nonlinear functions with respective dimensions. Under the assumption of RTNN identifiability made, the application of the BP learning algorithm for A(·), B(·), C(·), in general matricial form, described by equation (29)-(36), and the learning rates η (k), α (k) (here they are considered as time-dependent and normalized with respect to the error) are derived using the following Lyapunov function:

$$L(k) = L_1(k) + L_2(k);$$

Where: $L_1(k)$ and $L_2(k)$ are given by:

$$L_1(k) = \frac{1}{2} e^2(k),$$

$$L_2(k) = tr\left(\widetilde{W}_A(k)\widetilde{W}_A^T(k)\right) + tr\left(\widetilde{W}_B(k)\widetilde{W}_B^T(k)\right) + tr\left(\widetilde{W}_C(k)\widetilde{W}_C^T(k)\right);$$

where: $\widetilde{W}_A(k) = \hat{A}(k) - A^*$, $\widetilde{W}_B(k) = \hat{B}(k) - B^*$, $\widetilde{W}_C(k) = \hat{C}(k) - C^*$, are vectors of the estimation error and (A^*, B^*, C^*), $(\hat{A}(k), \hat{B}(k), \hat{C}(k))$ denote the ideal neural weight and the estimate of the neural weight at the k-th step, respectively, for each case.

Then the identification error is bounded, i.e.:

$$L(k+1) = L_1(k+1) + L_2(k+1) < 0,$$
$$\Delta L(k+1) = L(k+1) - (k);$$

where the condition for $L_1(k+1)<0$ is that:

$$\frac{\left(1-\frac{1}{\sqrt{2}}\right)}{\psi_{\max}} < \eta_{\max} < \frac{\left(1+\frac{1}{\sqrt{2}}\right)}{\psi_{\max}};$$

and for $L_2(k+1)<0$ we have:

$$\Delta L_2(k+1) < -\eta_{\max}\left|e(k+1)\right|^2 \alpha_{\max}\left|e(k)\right|^2 + d(k+1).$$

Note that η_{max} changes adaptively during the RTNN learning and:

$$\eta_{\max} = \max_{i=1}^{3}\{\eta_i\};$$

where all: the unmodelled dynamics, the approximation errors and the perturbations, are represented by the d-term. The Rate of Convergence Lemma used, , is given below. The complete proof of that Theorem of stability is given in (Baruch et al., 2008d).

Rate of Convergence Lemma (Baruch et al., 2008a). Let ΔL_k is defined. Then, applying the limit's definition, the identification error bound condition is obtained as:

$$\overline{\lim_{k\to\infty}}\frac{1}{k}\sum_{t=1}^{k}\left(\left|E(t)\right|^2 + \left|E(t-1)\right|^2\right) \le d.$$

Proof. Starting from the final result of the theorem of RTNN stability:

$$\Delta L(k) \le -\eta(k)\left|E(k)\right|^2 - \alpha(k)\left|E(k-1)\right|^2 + d$$

and iterating from k=0, we get:

$$L(k+1) - L(0) \le -\sum_{t=1}^{k}\left|E(t)\right|^2 - \sum_{t=1}^{k}\left|E(t-1)\right|^2 + dk,$$

$$\sum_{t=1}^{k}\left(\left|E(t)\right|^2 + \left|E(t-1)\right|^2\right) \le dk - L(k+1) + L(0) \le dk + L(0).$$

From here, we could see that d must be bounded by weight matrices and learning parameters, in order to obtain: $\Delta L(k) \in \mathbb{L}(\infty)$.

As a consequence:. $A(k) \in \mathbb{L}(\infty)$, $B(k) \in \mathbb{L}(\infty)$, $C(k) \in \mathbb{L}(\infty)$,

The stability of the HFNMMI could be proved via linearization of the activation functions of the RTNN models and application of the methodology using LMI.

Theorem of stability of the BP RTNN used as a direct system controller. Let the RTNN with Jordan Canonical Structure is given by equations (24)-(28) and the nonlinear plant model, is given above. Under the assumption of RTNN identifiability made, the application of the BP learning algorithm for A(·), B(·), C(·), in general matricial form, described by equations (29)-(36) without momentum term, and the learning rate η (k) (here it is considered as time-dependent and normalized with respect to the error) are derived using the following Lyapunov function:

$$L(k) = L_1(k) + L_2(k);$$

where: L1 (k) and L2 (k) are given by:

$$L_1(k) = \frac{1}{2}e^2(k),$$

$$L_2(k) = tr\left(\widetilde{W}_{A(k)}\widetilde{W}_{A(k)}^T\right) + tr\left(\widetilde{W}_{B(k)}\widetilde{W}_{B(k)}^T\right) + tr\left(\widetilde{W}_{C(k)}\widetilde{W}_{C(k)}^T\right);$$

where: $\widetilde{W}_{A(k)} = \widehat{A}(k) - A^*$, $\widetilde{W}_{B(k)} = \hat{B}(k) - B^*$, $\widetilde{W}_{C(k)} = \widehat{C}(k) - C^*$, are vectors of the estimation error and $\left(A^*, B^*, C^*\right)$ and $\left(\widehat{A}(k), \hat{B}(k), \widehat{C}(k)\right)$ denoted the ideal neural weight and the estimate of the neural weight at the k-th step, respectively, for each case.

Let us define: $\psi_{\max} = \max_k \left\|\psi(k)\right\|$, and $\vartheta_{\max} = \max_k \left\|\vartheta(k)\right\|$, where $\psi(k) = \frac{\partial o(k)}{\partial W(k)}$, and $\vartheta(k) = \frac{\partial y(k)}{\partial W(k)}$, where W is a vector composed by all weights of the RTNN, used as a system controller, and $\|\cdot\|$ is an Euclidean norm in $\Re^n$.

Then the identification error is bounded, i.e.:

$$L(k+1) = L1(k+1) + L2(k+1) < 0,$$

$$\Delta L(k+1) = L(k+1) - L(k);$$

where the condition for L1 (k+1) < 0 fulfillment is that the maximum rate of learning is inside the limits:

$$0 < \eta_{\max} < \frac{2}{\vartheta_{\max}^2 \psi_{\max}^2},$$

and for L2(k+1) < 0, we have:

$$\Delta L_2(k+1) < -\eta_{\max}\left|e(k+1)\right|^2 + \beta(k+1).$$

Note that $\eta_{\max}$ changes adaptively during the learning process of the network, where:

$$\eta_{\max} = \max_{i=1}^{3}\{\eta_i\}.$$

Here all: the unmodelled dynamics, the approximation errors and the perturbations, are represented by the β-term, and the complete proof of that theorem and the rate of convergence lemma, are given in (Baruch et al., 2008d).

4.2 Recursive Levenberg-Marquardt RTNN learning

The general recursive L-M algorithm of learning, (Baruch & Mariaca-Gaspar, 2009) is given by the following equations:

$$W(k+1)=W(k)+P(k)\nabla Y\left[W(k)\right]E\left[W(k)\right], \tag{37}$$

$$Y\left[W(k)\right]=g\left[W(k),U(k)\right], \tag{38}$$

$$E^2\left[W(k)\right]=\left\{Y_p(k)-g\left[W(k),U(k)\right]\right\}^2, \tag{39}$$

$$DY\left[W(k)\right]=\left.\frac{\partial g\left[W(k),U(k)\right]}{\partial W}\right|_{W=W(k)}; \tag{40}$$

where W is a general weight matrix (A, B, C) under modification; P is the covariance matrix of the estimated weights updated; DY[·] is an nw-dimensional gradient vector; Y is the RTNN output vector which depends of the updated weights and the input; E is an error vector; Yp is the plant output vector, which is in fact the target vector. Using the same RTNN adjoint block diagram (see Fig.7), it was possible to obtain the values of the gradients DY[·] for each updated weight, propagating the value D(k) = I through it. Applying equation (40) for each element of the weight matrices (A, B, C) in order to be updated, the corresponding gradient components are as follows:

$$DY\left[C_{ij}(k)\right]=D_{1,i}(k)Z_j(k), \tag{41}$$

$$D_{1,i}(k)=F_j'\left[Y_i(k)\right], \tag{42}$$

$$DY\left[A_{ij}(k)\right]=D_{2,i}(k)X_j(k), \tag{43}$$

$$DY\left[B_{ij}(k)\right]=D_{2,i}(k)U_j(k), \tag{44}$$

$$D_{2,i}(k)=G_i'\left[Z_j(k)\right]C_iD_{1,i}(k). \tag{45}$$

Therefore the Jacobean matrix could be formed as:

$$DY\left[W(k)\right]=\left[DY\left(C_{ij}(k)\right),DY\left(A_{ij}(k)\right),DY\left(B_{ij}(k)\right)\right] \tag{46}$$

The P(k) matrix was computed recursively by the equation:

$$P(k)=\alpha^{-1}(k)\left\{P(k-1)-P(k-1)\Omega\left[W(k)\right]S^{-1}\left[W(k)\right]\Omega^{T}\left[W(k)\right]P(k-1)\right\}; \qquad (47)$$

where the S(·), and Ω(·) matrices were given as follows:

$$S\left[W(k)\right]=\alpha(k)\Lambda(k)+\Omega^{T}\left[W(k)\right]P(k-1)\Omega\left[W(k)\right] \qquad (48)$$

$$\Omega^{T}\left[W(k)\right]=\begin{bmatrix} & & \nabla Y^{T}\left[W(k)\right] & & \\ 0 & \cdots & 1 & \cdots & 0\end{bmatrix};$$
$$\Lambda(k)^{-1}=\begin{bmatrix}1 & 0\\ 0 & \rho\end{bmatrix};\ \ 10^{-4}\le\rho\le10^{-6}; \qquad (49)$$
$$0.97\le\alpha(k)\le1;\ \ 10^{3}\le P(0)\le10^{6}.$$

The matrix Ω(·) had a dimension (nwx2), whereas the second row had only one unity element (the others were zero). The position of that element was computed by:

$$i=k\bmod(nw)+1;\ \ k>nw \qquad (50)$$

After this, the given up topology and learning are applied for an anaerobic wastewater distributed parameter decentralized system identification.

5. Analytical model of the anaerobic digestion bioprocess plant

The anaerobic digestion systems block diagram is depicted on Fig.8. It consists of a fixed bed reactor and a recirculation tank. The physical meaning of all variables and constants (also its values), are summarized in Table 1. The complete analytical model of wastewater treatment anaerobic bioprocess, taken from (Aguilar-Garnica et al., 2006), could be described by the following system of PDE:

$$\frac{\partial X_1}{\partial t}=(\mu_1-\varepsilon D)X_1,\ \ \mu_1=\mu_{1\max}\frac{S_1}{K_{S1}X_1+S_1}, \qquad (51)$$

$$\frac{\partial X_2}{\partial t}=(\mu_2-\varepsilon D)X_2,\ \ \mu_2=\mu_{2s}\frac{S_1}{K_{S2}X_2+\frac{S_2^2}{K_{I2}}}, \qquad (52)$$

$$\frac{\partial S_1}{\partial t}=\frac{E_z}{H^2}\frac{\partial^2 S_1}{\partial z^2}-D\frac{\partial S_1}{\partial t}-k_1\mu_1X_1, \qquad (53)$$

$$\frac{\partial S_2}{\partial t}=\frac{E_z}{H^2}\frac{\partial^2 S_2}{\partial z^2}-D\frac{\partial S_2}{\partial t}-k_2\mu_1X_1, \qquad (54)$$

$$S_1(0,t)=\frac{S_{1,in}(t)+RS_{1T}}{R+1},\ \ S_2(0,t)=\frac{S_{2,in}(t)+RS_{2T}}{R+1},\ \ R=\frac{Q_T}{DV_{eff}}, \qquad (55)$$

Variable	*Units*	*Name*	*Value*
z	$z\in[0,1]$	*Space variable*	
t	D	*Time variable*	
E_z	m^2/d	*Axial dispersion coefficient*	1
D	1/d	*Dilution rate*	0.55
H	m	*Fixed bed length*	3.5
X_1	g/L	*Concentration of acidogenic bacteria*	
X_2	g/L	*Concentration of methanogenic bacteria*	
S_1	g/L	*Chemical Oxygen Demand*	
S_2	mmol/L	*Volatile Fatty Acids*	
ε		*Bacteria fraction in the liquid phase*	0.5
k_1	g/g	*Yield coefficients*	42.14
k_2	mmol/g	*Yield coefficients*	250
k_3	mmol/g	*Yield coefficients*	134
μ_1	1/d	*Acidogenesis growth rate*	
μ_2	1/d	*Methanogenesis growth rate*	
μ_{1max}	1/d	*Maximum acidogenesis growth rate*	1.2
μ_{2s}	1/d	*Maximum methanogenesis growth rate*	0.74
K_{1s}'	g/g	*Kinetic parameter*	50.5
K_{2s}'	mmol/g	*Kinetic parameter*	16.6
K_{I2}'	mmol/g	*Kinetic parameter*	256
Q_T	m^3/d	*Recycle flow rate*	0.24
V_T	m^3	*Volume of the recirculation tank*	0.2
S_{1T}	g/L	*Concentration of Chemical Oxygen Demand in the recirculation tank*	
S_{2T}	mmol/L	*Concentration of Volatile Fatty Acids in the recirculation tank*	
Q_{in}	m^3/d	*Inlet flow rate*	0.31
V_B	m^3	*Volume of the fixed bed*	1
V_{eff}	m^3	*Effective volume tank*	0.95
$S_{1,in}$	g/L	*Inlet substr. Concentration*	
$S_{2,in}$	mmol/L	*Inlet substr. Concentration*	

Table 1. Summary of the variables in the plant model

$$\frac{\partial S_1}{\partial z}(1,t)=0, \quad \frac{\partial S_2}{\partial z}(1,t)=0, \tag{56}$$

$$\frac{dS_{1T}}{dt}=\frac{Q_T}{V_T}\left(S_1(1,t)-S_{1T}\right), \quad \frac{dS_{2T}}{dt}=\frac{Q_T}{V_T}\left(S_2(1,t)-S_{2T}\right). \tag{57}$$

For practical purpose, the full PDE anaerobic digestion process model (51)-(57), taken from (Aguilar-Garnica et al., 2006), could be reduced to an ODE system using an early lumping technique and the Orthogonal Collocation Method (OCM), (Bialecki & Fairwether, 2001), in four points (0.2H, 0.4H, 0.6H, 0.8H) obtaining the following system of OD equations:

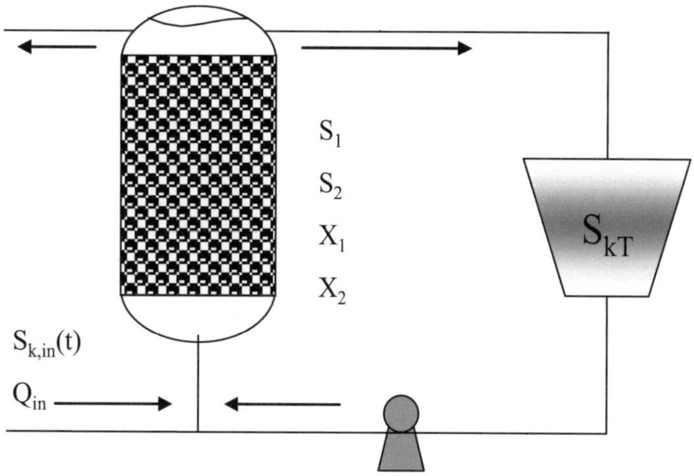

Fig. 8. Block-diagram of anaerobic digestion bioreactor

$$\frac{dX_{1,i}}{dt}=\left(\mu_{1,i}-\varepsilon D\right)X_{1,i},\quad \frac{dX_{2,i}}{dt}=\left(\mu_{2,i}-\varepsilon D\right)X_{2,i}, \tag{58}$$

$$\frac{dS_{1,i}}{dt}=\frac{E_z}{H^2}\sum_{j=1}^{N+2}B_{i,j}S_{1,j}-D\sum_{j=1}^{N+2}A_{i,j}S_{1,j}-k_1\mu_{1,i}X_{1,i}, \tag{59}$$

$$\frac{dS_{2,i}}{dt}=\frac{E_z}{H^2}\sum_{j=1}^{N+2}B_{i,j}S_{1,j}-D\sum_{j=1}^{N+2}A_{i,j}S_{2,j}-k_2\mu_{1,i}X_{2,i}-k_3\mu_{2,i}X_{2,i}, \tag{60}$$

$$\frac{dS_{1T}}{dt}=\frac{Q_T}{V_T}\left(S_{1,N+2}-S_{1T}\right),\quad \frac{dS_{2T}}{dt}=\frac{Q_T}{V_T}\left(S_{2,N+2}-S_{2T}\right), \tag{61}$$

$$S_{k,1}=\frac{1}{R+1}S_{k,in}(t)+\frac{R}{R+1}S_{kT},\quad S_{k,N+2}=\frac{K_1}{R+1}S_{k,in}(t)+\frac{K_1R}{R+1}S_{kT}+\sum_{i=1}^{N+1}K_iS_{k,i}, \tag{62}$$

$$K_1=\frac{A_{N+2,1}}{A_{N+2,N+2}},\quad K_i=\frac{A_{N+2,i}}{A_{N+2,N+2}}, \tag{63}$$

$$A=\Lambda\phi^{-1},\quad \Lambda=\left[\omega_{m,l}\right]=(l-1)z_m^{l-2}, \tag{64}$$

$$B=\Gamma\phi^{-1},\quad \Gamma=\left[\tau_{m,l}\right],\quad \tau_{m,l}=(l-1)(l-2)z_m^{l-3},\quad \phi_{m,l}=z_m^{l-1}, \tag{65}$$

$$i=2,\ldots N+2,\quad m,l=1,\ldots N+2. \tag{66}$$

The reduced plant model (58)-(66), could be used as unknown plant model which generate input/output process data for decentralized adaptive FNMM control system design, based on the concepts, given in (Baruch et al., 2008a; Baruch et al., 2008b; Baruch et al., 2008c; Baruch et al., 2008d). The mentioned concepts could be applied for this DPS fuzzyfying the space variable z, which represented the height of the fixed bed. Here the centers of the membership functions with respect to z corresponded to the collocation points of the simplified plant model which are in fact the four measurement points of the fixed bed, adding one more point for the recirculation tank.

6. Simulation results

In this paragraph, graphical and numerical simulation results of system identification, direct and indirect control, with and without I-term, will be given. For lack of space we will give graphical results only for the X1 variable. Furthermore the graphical results for the other variables possessed similar behavior.

6.1 Simulation results of the system identification using L-M RTNN learning

The decentralized FNMM identifier used a set of five T-S fuzzy rules containing in its consequent part RTNN learning procedures (1). The RTNN topology is given by the equations (24)-(28), the BP RTNN learning is given by (29)-(36), and the L-M RTNN learning is given by (37)-(50). The topology of the first four RTNNs is (2-6-4) (2 inputs, 6 neurons in the hidden layer, 4 outputs) and the last one has topology (2-4-2), corresponding to the fixed bed plant behavior in each collocation point and the recirculation tank. The RTNNs identified the following fixed bed variables: X_1 (acidogenic bacteria), X_2 (methanogenic bacteria), S_1 (chemical oxygen demand) and S_2 (volatile fatty acids), in the following four collocation points, z=0.2H, z=0.4H, z=0.6H, z=0.8H, and the following variables in the recirculation tank: S_{1T} (chemical oxygen demand) and S_{2T} (volatile fatty acids). The graphical simulation results of RTNNs L-M learning are obtained on-line during 600 iteration with a step of 0.1 sec. The learning rate parameters of RTNN have small values which are different for the different measurement point variables (ρ=0.1 and α=0). The Figs. 9-11 showed graphical simulation results of open loop decentralized plant identification. The MSE of the decentralized FNMM approximation of plant variables in the collocation points, using the L-M and BP RTNN learning are shown in Tables 2 and 3. The input signals applied are:

$$S_{1,in} = 0.55 + 0.15\cos\left(\frac{3\pi}{80}t\right) + 0.3\sin\left(\frac{\pi}{80}t\right), \quad (67)$$

$$S_{2,in} = 0.55 + 0.05\cos\left(\frac{3\pi}{40}t\right) + 0.3\sin\left(\frac{\pi}{40}t\right). \quad (68)$$

The graphical y numerical results of decentralized FNMM identification (see Fig. 9-11, and Tables 2, 3) showed a good HFNMMI convergence and precise plant output tracking (MSE 0.0083 for the L-M, and 0.0253 for the BP RTNN learning in the worse case).

Collocation point	X_1	X_2	S_1/S_{1T}	S_2/S_{2T}
z=0.2	0.0013	0.0012	0.0049	0.0058
z=0.4	0.0013	0.0013	0.0058	0.0049
z=0.6	0.0013	0.0013	0.0071	0.0055
z=0.8	0.0014	0.0013	0.0083	0.0070
Recirculation tank			0.0080	0.0058

Table 2. MSE of the decentralized FNMM approximation of the bioprocess output variables in the collocation points, using the L-M RTNN learning

Collocation point	X_1	X_2	S_1/S_{1T}	S_2/S_{2T}
z=0.2	0.0015	0.0023	0.0145	0.0192
z=0.4	0.0015	0.0044	0.0098	0.0164
z=0.6	0.0030	0.0009	0.0092	0.0133
z=0.8	0.0046	0.0048	0.0045	0.0086
Recirculation tank			0.0168	0.0253

Table 3. MSE of the decentralized FNMM approximation of the bioprocess output variables in the collocation points, using the BP RTNN learning

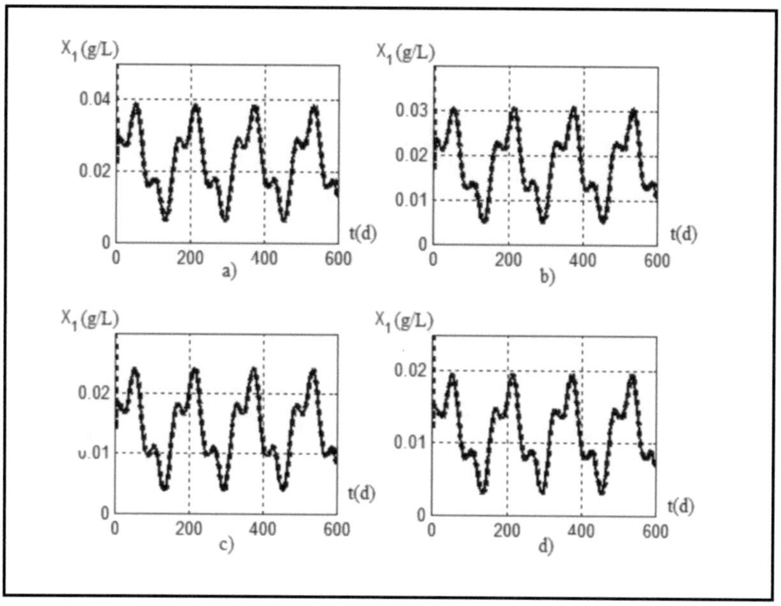

Fig. 9. Graphical simulation results of the FNMM identification of X1 in a) Z=0.2H; b) 0.4H; c) 0.6H; d) 0.8H (acidogenic bacteria in the corresponding fixed bed points) by four fuzzy rules RTNNs (dotted line-RTNN output, continuous line-plant output) for 600 iteration of L-M RTNN learning

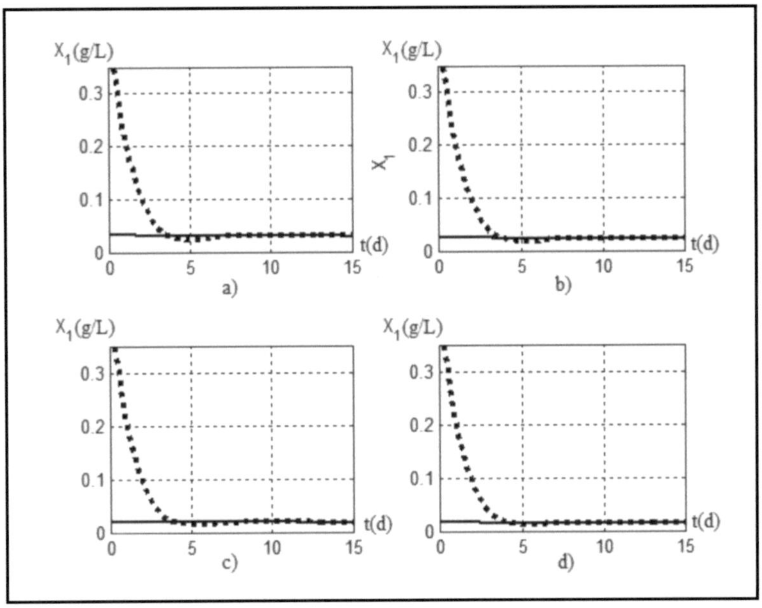

Fig. 10. Detailed graphical simulation results of the FNMM identification of X1 in a) Z=0.2H; b) 0.4H; c) 0.6H; d) 0.8H (acidogenic bacteria in the corresponding fixed bed points) by four fuzzy rules RTNNs (dotted line-RTNN output, continuous line-plant output) for the first 15 iterations of the L-M RTNN learning

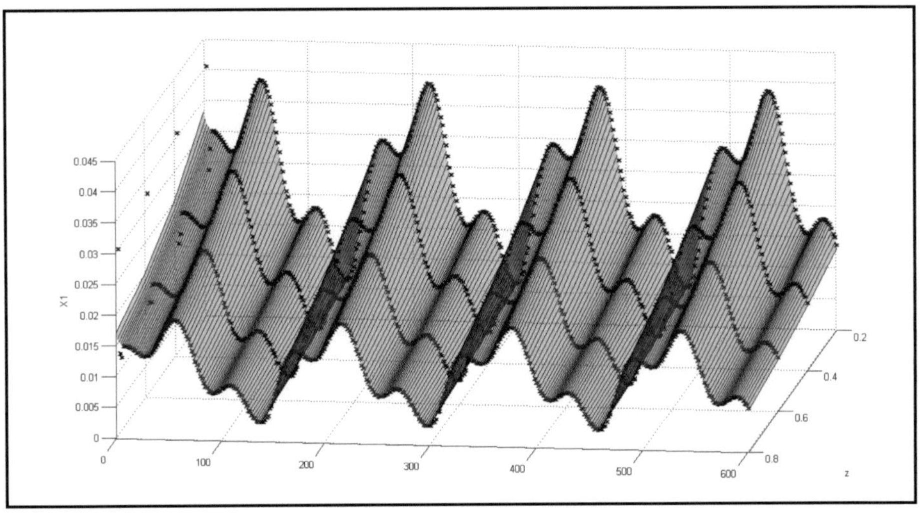

Fig. 11. Graphics of the 3d view of X1 space/time approximation during its L-M RTNN learning in four points

6.2 Simulation results of the direct HFNMM control with I-term and L-M RTNN learning

The topology of the first four RTNNs is (12-14-2) for the variables in the collocation points x=0.2H, z=0.4H, z=0.6H, z=0.8H and for the recirculation tank is (8-10-2). The graphical simulation results of RTNNs L-M learning are obtained on-line during 600 iterations (2.4

hours) with a step of 0.1 sec. The learning parameters of RTNN are ρ=0.2 and α=1; while the parameter of the I-term are η=0.01 and α=1e-8. Finally the topology of the defuzzifier neural network is (10-2) with parameters η=0.0035 and α=0.00001.
The Figs. 12-17 showed graphical simulation results of the direct decentralized HFNMM control with and without I-term, where the outputs of the plant are compared with the reference signals. The reference signals are train of pulses with uniform duration and random amplitude. The MSE of control for each output signal and each measurement point are given on Table 4 For sake of comparison the MSE of direct decentralized HFNMM proportional control (without I-term) for each output signal and each measurement point are given on Table 5.

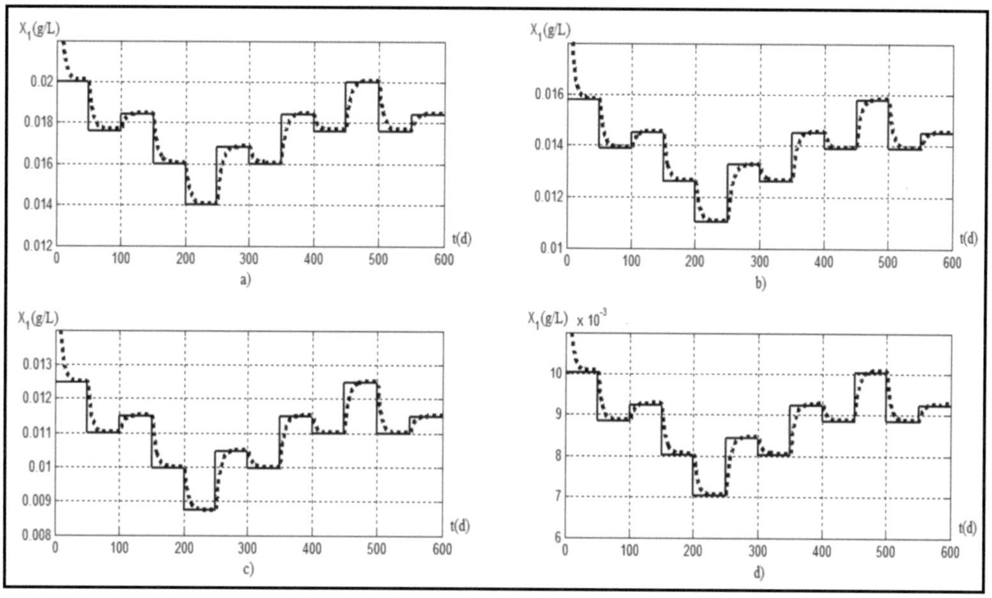

Fig. 12. Results of the direct decentralized HFNMM I-term control of X1 (acidogenic bacteria in the fixed bed) (dotted line-plant output, continuous-reference) in four collocation points (a) 0.2H,b) 0.4H, c) 0.6H, d) 0.8H) for 600 iterations

Also, for sake of comparison, graphical results of direct decentralized HFNMM proportional control (without I-term) only for the X1 variable will be presented. The results show that the proportional control could not eliminate the static error due to inexact approximation and constant process or measurement disturbances. The graphical and numerical results of direct decentralized HFNMM I-term control (see Fig. 12-13, and Tables 4, 5) showed a good reference tracking (MSE is of 0.0097 for the I-term control and 0.0119 for the control without I-term in the worse case). The results showed that the I-term control eliminated constant disturbances and approximation errors and the proportional control could not.

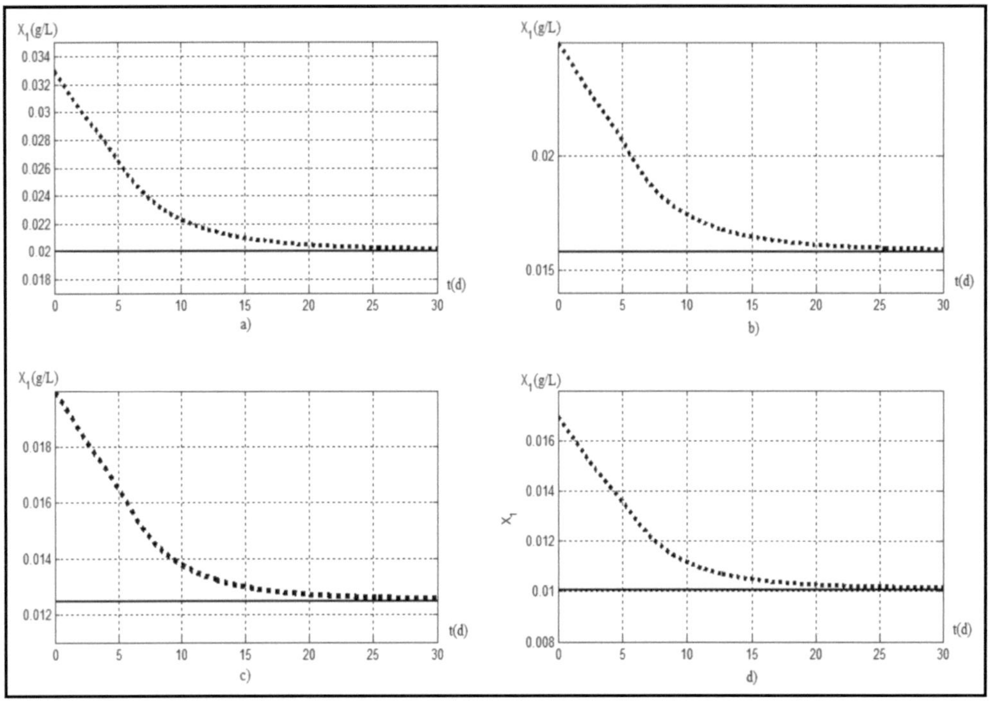

Fig. 13. Detailed graphical results of the direct decentralized HFNMM I-term control of X1 (acidogenic bacteria in the fixed bed) (dotted line-plant output, continuous-reference) in four collocation points (a) 0.2H, b) 0.4H, c) 0.6H, d) 0.8H) for the first 30 iterations

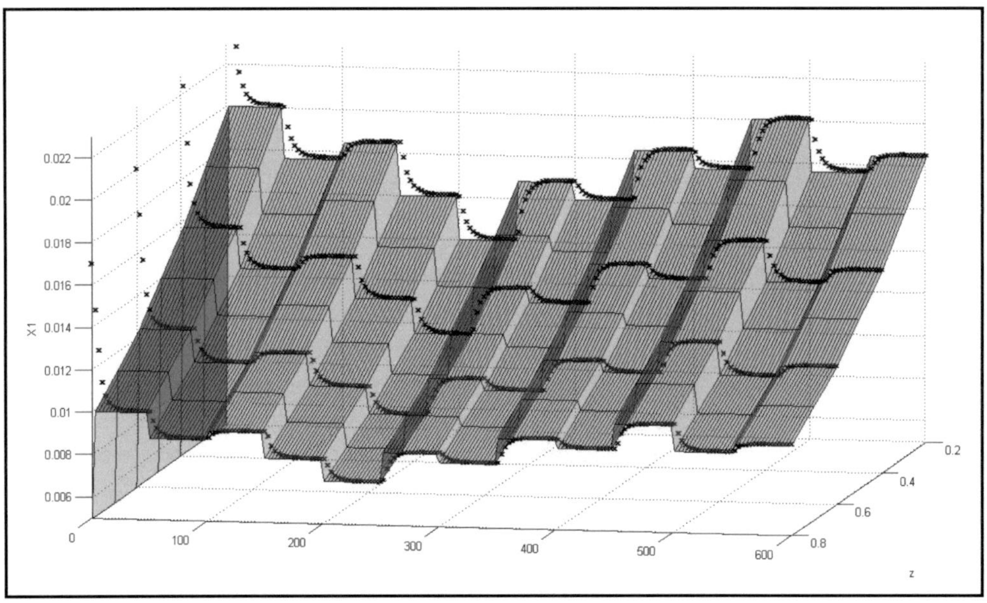

Fig. 14. Graphics of the 3d view of X1 space/time approximation and direct decentralized HFNMM I-term control in four collocation points of the fixed bed

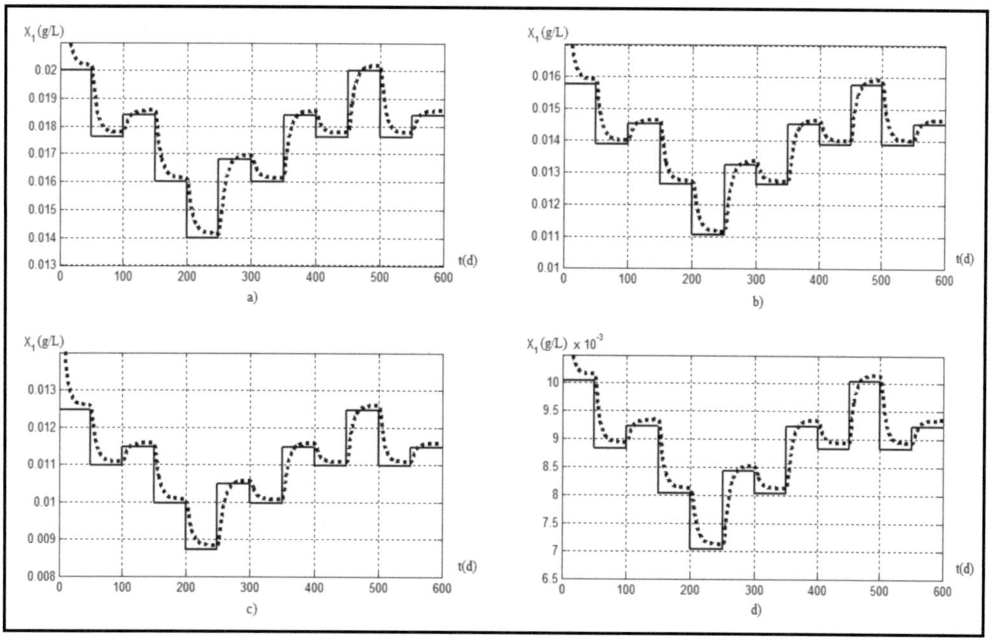

Fig. 15. Results of the direct decentralized HFNMM control without I-term of X1 (acidogenic bacteria in the fixed bed) (dotted line-plant output, continuous-reference) in four collocation points (a) 0.2H, b) 0.4H, c) 0.6H, d) 0.8H) for 600 iterations

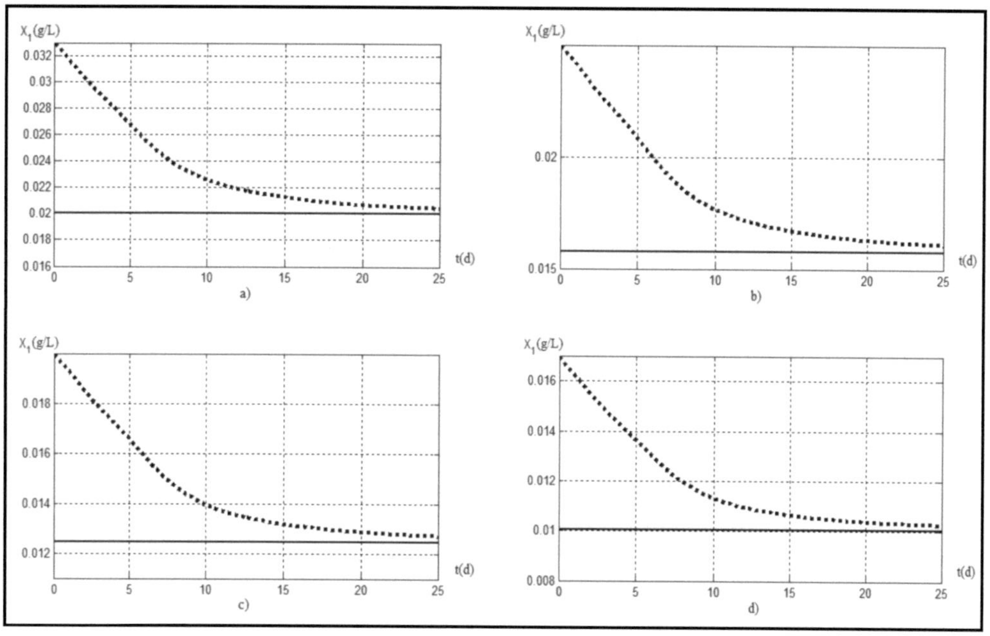

Fig. 16. Detailed graphical results of the direct decentralized HFNMM control without I-term of X1 (acidogenic bacteria in the fixed bed) (dotted line-plant output, continuous-reference) in four collocation points (a) 0.2H, b) 0.4H, c) 0.6H, d) 0.8H) for the first 30 iterations

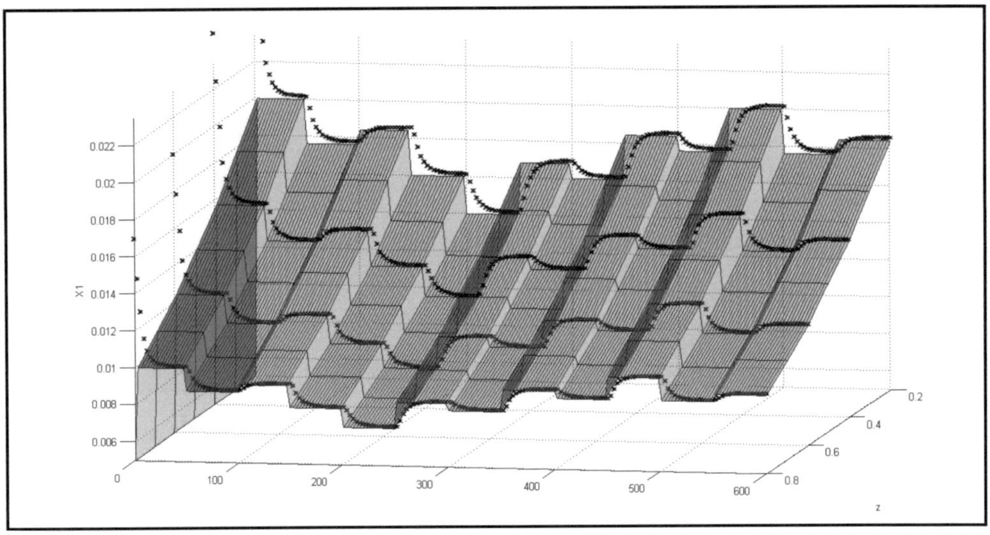

Fig. 17. Graphics of the 3d view of X1 space/time approximation and direct decentralized HFNMM proportional control (without I-term) in four collocation points of the fixed bed

Collocation point	X_1	X_2	S_1/S_{1T}	S_2/S_{2T}
z=0.2	0.0011	0.0013	0.0065	0.0097
z=0.4	0.0009	0.0011	0.0051	0.0090
z=0.6	0.0008	0.0011	0.0042	0.0074
z=0.8	0.0006	0.0010	0.0037	0.0063
Recirculation tank			0.0060	0.0086

Table 4. MSE of the direct decentralized HFNMM I-term control of the bioprocess plant

Collocation point	X_1	X_2	S_1/S_{1T}	S_2/S_{2T}
z=0.2	0.0012	0.0016	0.0084	0.0119
z=0.4	0.0009	0.0014	0.0068	0.0107
z=0.6	0.0007	0.0012	0.0055	0.0089
z=0.8	0.0006	0.0010	0.0045	0.0073
Recirculation tank			0.0068	0.0092

Table 5. MSE of the direct decentralized HFNMM proportional control (without I-term) of the bioprocess plant

6.3 Simulation results of the indirect HFNMM I-term SMC and L-M RTNN learning

The neural network used as defuzifier in the control with BP learning rule has the toplogy (10-2) with learning parameters η=0.005 and α=0.00006. For the simuulation with the L-M RTNN learning we use a saturation U_0=1 with γ=0.8. In the integral term we used the parameters for the offset (Of), η=0.01 and α=1e-8. The Figs. 18-23 showed graphical simulation results of the indirect (sliding mode) decentralized HFNMM with and without I-term control. The MSE of control for each output signal and each measurement point are given on Table 6. The reference signals are train of pulses with uniform duration and random amplitude and the outputs of the plant are compared with the reference signals.

Collocation point	X_1	X_2	S_1/S_{1T}	S_2/S_{2T}
z=0.2	0.0010	0.0011	0.0052	0.0089
z=0.4	0.0007	0.0009	0.0040	0.0084
z=0.6	0.0006	0.0009	0.0037	0.0063
z=0.8	0.0006	0.0008	0.0034	0.0061
Recirculation tank			0.0051	0.0074

Table 6. MSE of the indirect decentralized HFNMM I-term control of the bioprocess plant

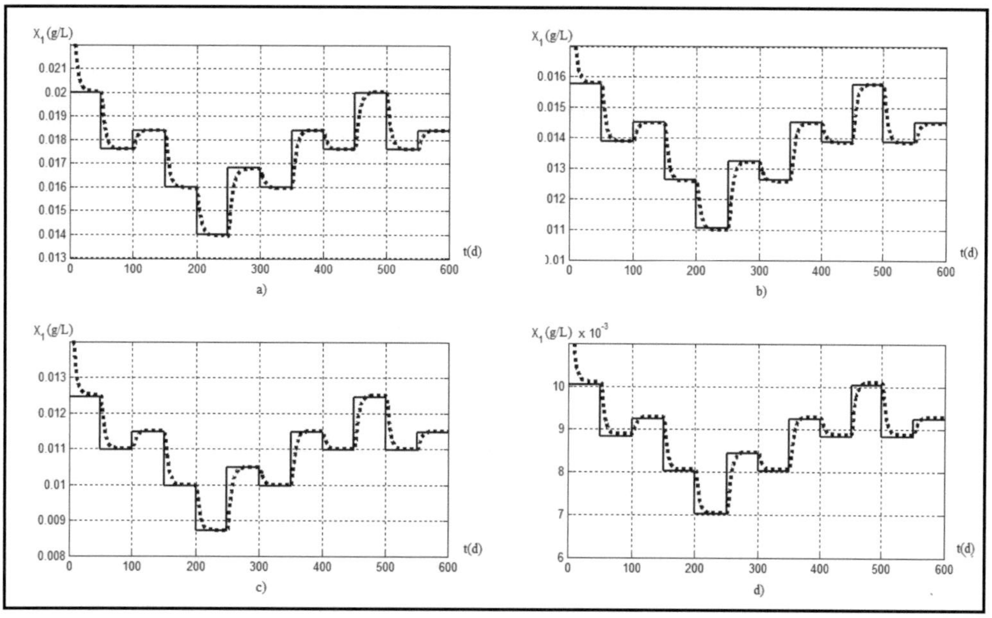

Fig. 18. Results of the indirect (SMC) decentralized HFNMM I-term control of X1 (acidogenic bacteria in the fixed bed) (dotted line-plant output, continuous-reference) in four collocation points (a) 0.2H, b) 0.4H, c) 0.6H, d) 0.8H) for 600 iterations

Collocation point	X_1	X_2	S_1/S_{1T}	S_2/S_{2T}
z=0.2	0.0013	0.0018	0.0101	0.0139
z=0.4	0.0010	0.0016	0.0083	0.0125
z=0.6	0.0008	0.0014	0.0068	0.0104
z=0.8	0.0007	0.0012	0.0057	0.0085
Recirculation tank			0.0070	0.0095

Table 7. MSE of the indirect decentralized HFNMM proportional control (without I-term) of the bioprocess plant

The graphical y numerical results (see Fig. 18-23, and Tables 6, 7) of the indirect (sliding mode) decentralized control showed a good identification and precise reference tracking (MSE is about 0.0089 in the worse case). The comparison of the indirect and direct decentralized control showed a good results for both control methods (see Table 3 and Table 4) with slight priority for the indirect control (9.8315e-5 vs. 1.184e-4) due to its better plant dynamics compensation ability and adaptation.

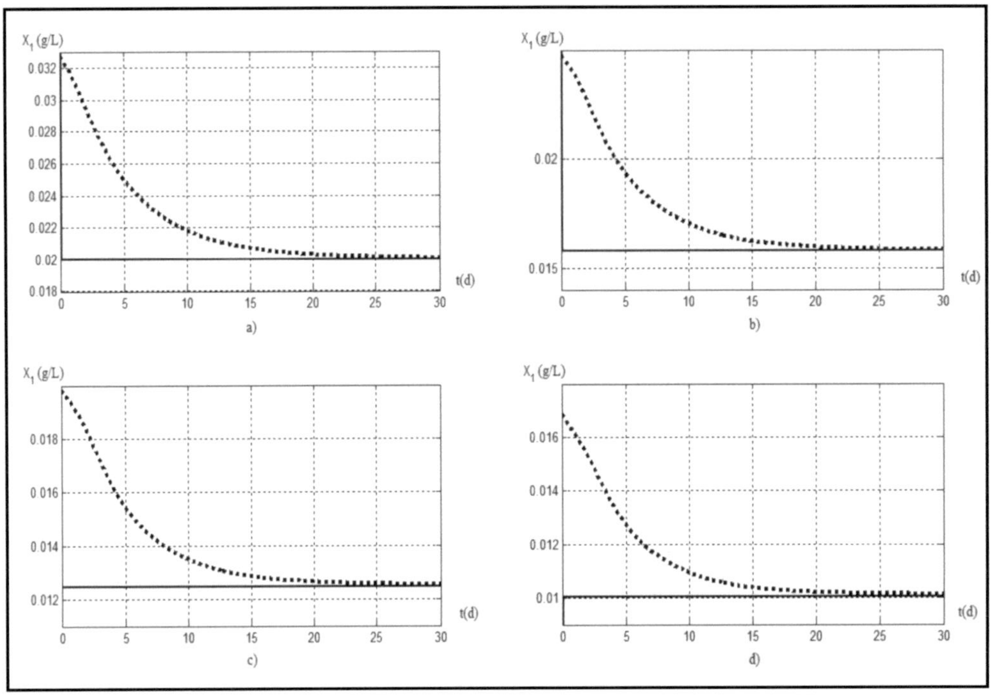

Fig. 19. Detailed graphical results of the indirect (SMC) decentralized HFNMM I-term control of X1 (acidogenic bacteria in the fixed bed) (dotted line-plant output, continuous-reference) in four collocation points (a) 0.2H, b) 0.4H, c) 0.6H, d) 0.8H) for the first 30 iterations

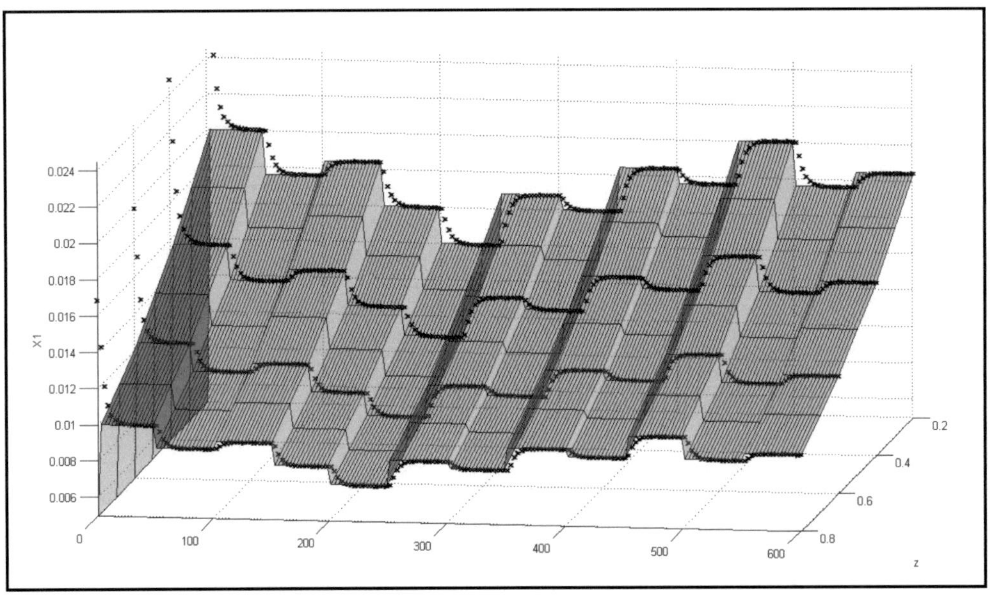

Fig. 20. Graphics of the 3d view of X1 space/time approximation and indirect decentralized HFNMM I-term control in four collocation points of the fixed bed

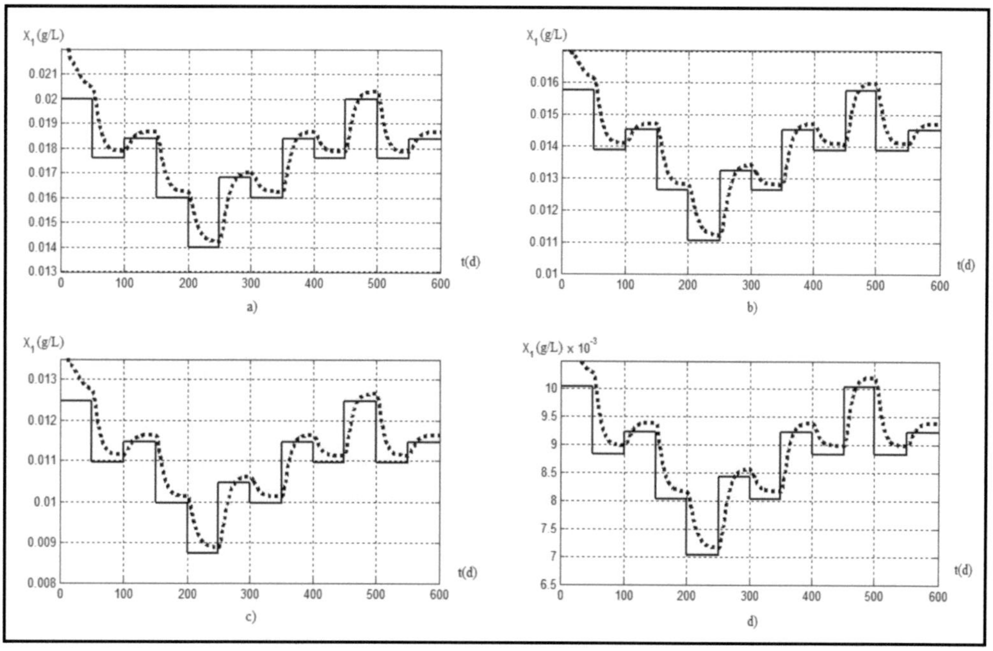

Fig. 21. Results of the indirect (SMC) decentralized HFNMM proportional control (without I-term) of X1 (acidogenic bacteria in the fixed bed) (dotted line-plant output, continuous-reference) in four collocation points (a) 0.2H, b) 0.4H, c) 0.6H, d) 0.8H) for 600 iterations

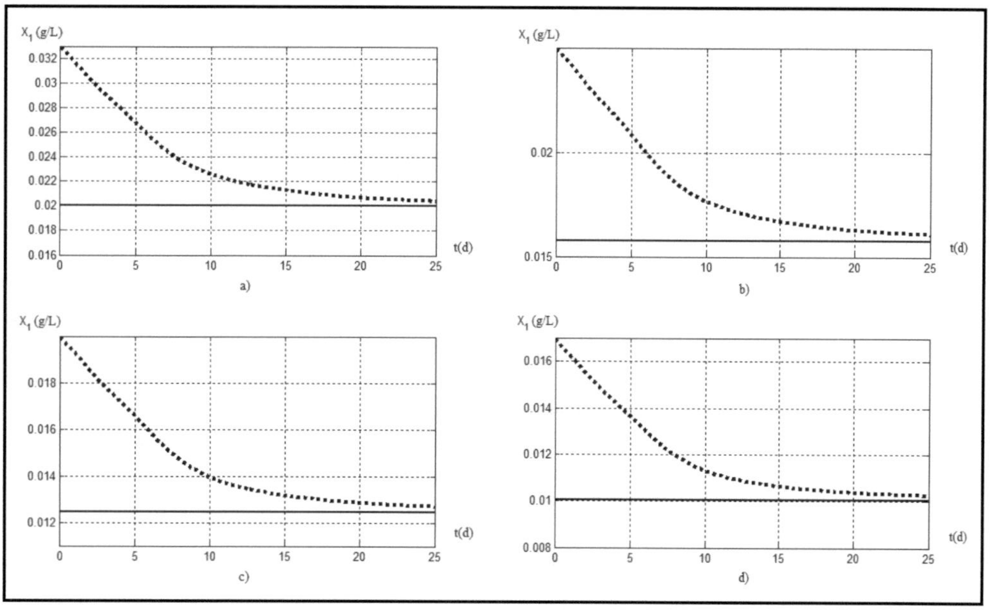

Fig. 22. Detailed graphical results of the indirect (SMC) decentralized HFNMM proportional control (without I-term) of X1 (acidogenic bacteria in the fixed bed) (dotted line-plant output, continuous-reference) in four collocation points (a) 0.2H, b) 0.4H, c) 0.6H, d) 0.8H) for the first 25 iterations

For sake of comparison, graphical results of indirect decentralized HFNMM proportional control (without I-term) only for the X1 variable are presented. The results show that the proportional control could not eliminate the static error due to inexact approximation and constant process or measurement disturbances.

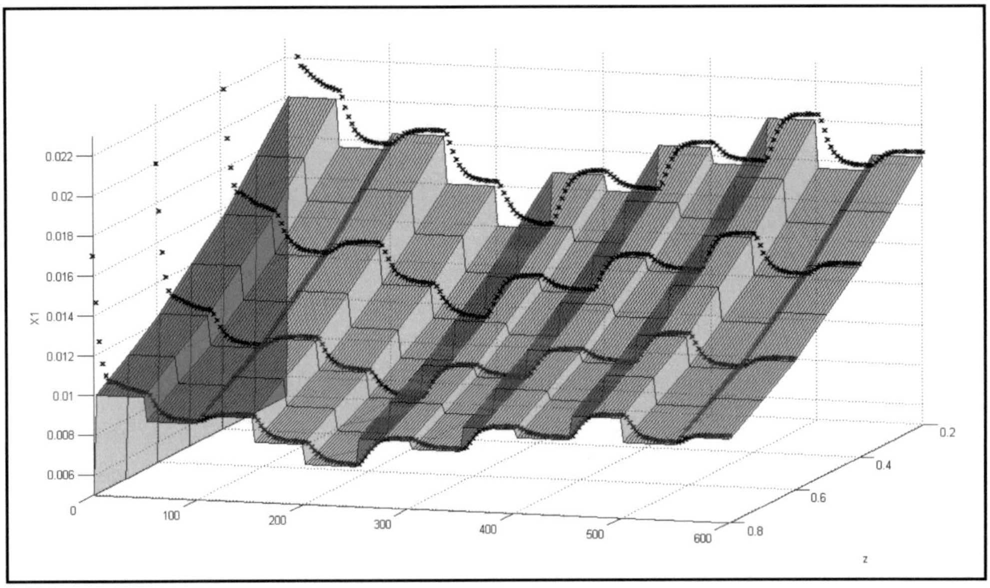

Fig. 23. Graphics of the 3d view of X1 space/time approximation and indirect decentralized HFNMM proportional control (without I-term) in four collocation points of the fixed bed

7. Conclusion

The chapter proposed decentralized recurrent fuzzy-neural identification, direct and indirect I-term control of an anaerobic digestion wastewater treatment bioprocess, composed by a fixed bed and a recirculation tank, represented a DPS. The simplification of the PDE process model by ODE is realized using the orthogonal collocation method in four collocation points (plus the recirculation tank) represented centers of membership functions of the space fuzzyfied output variables. The obtained from the FNMMI state and parameter information is used by a HFNMM direct and indirect (sliding mode) control with or without I-term. The applied fuzzy-neural approach to that DPS decentralized direct and indirect identification and I-term control exhibited a good convergence and precise reference tracking eliminating static errors, which could be observed in the MSE% numerical results given on Tables 4 and 6 (2.107e-5 vs. 1.184e-4 vs. 9.8315e-5 in the worse case).

8. References

Aguilar-Garnica F., Alcaraz-Gonzalez V. & V. Gonzalez-Alvarez (2006), Interval Observer Design for an Anaerobic Digestion Process Described by a Distributed Parameter Model, *Proceedings of the Second International Meeting on Environmental Biotechnology and Engineering: 2IMEBE*, pp. 1-16, ISBN 970-95106-0-6, Mexico City, Mexico, September 2006

Baruch, I.S.; Barrera-Cortes, J. & Hernandez, L.A. (2004). A fed-batch fermentation process identification and direct adaptive neural control with integral term. In: *MICAI 2004: Advances in Artificial Intelligence, LNAI 2972,* Monroy, R., Arroyo-Figueroa, G., Sucar, L.E., Sossa, H. (Eds.), page numbers (764-773), Springer-Verlag, ISBN 3-540-21459-3, Berlin Heidelberg New York

Baruch, I.S.; Beltran-Lopez, R.; Olivares-Guzman, J.L. & Flores, J.M. (2008a). A fuzzy-neural multi-model for nonlinear systems identification and control. *Fuzzy Sets and Systems,* Elsevier, Vol. 159, No 20, (October 2008) page numbers (2650-2667) ISSN 0165-0114

Baruch, I.S & Galvan-Guerra, R. (2008). Decentralized Direct Adaptive Fuzzy-Neural Control of an Anaerobic Digestion Bioprocess Plant, In: Yager, R.R., Sgurev, V.S., Jotsov, V. (eds), *Fourth International IEEE Conference on Intelligent Systems,* Sept. 6-8, Varna, Bulgaria, ISBN: 978-1-4244-1740-7, vol. I, Session 9, Neuro-Fuzzy Systems, IEEE (2008): pp. 9-2 to 9-7.

Baruch, I.S. & Galvan-Guerra, R. (2009). Decentralized Adaptive Fuzzy-Neural Control of an Anaerobic Digestion Bioprocess Plant. In: *Proc. of the 2009 International Fuzzy Systems Association World Congress, 2009 European Society for Fuzzy Logic and Technology Conference, IFSA/ EUSFLAT 2009,* 20.07-24.07.09, Lisbon, Portugal, ISBN 978-989-95079-6-8 (2009): pp. 460-465

Baruch, I.S.; Galvan-Guerra, R.; Mariaca-Gaspar, C.R. & Castillo, O. (2008b). Fuzzy-Neural Control of a Distributed Parameter Bioprocess Plant. *Proceedings of theIEEE International Conference on Fuzzy Systems, IEEE World Congress on Computational Intelligence, WCCI 2008,* June 1-6, 2008, Hong Kong, ISBN: 978-1-4244-1819-0, ISSN 1098-7584, IEEE (2008), pp. 2208-2215

Baruch, I.S.; Galvan-Guerra, R.; Mariaca-Gaspar, C.R. & Melin, P. (2008c). Decentralized Indirect Adaptive Fuzzy-Neural Multi-Model Control of a Distributed Parameter Bioprocess Plant. *Proceedings of International Joint Conference on Neural Networks, IEEE World Congress on Computational Intelligence, WCCI 2008,* June 1-6, 2008, Hong Kong, ISBN: 978-1-4244-1821-3, ISSN: 1098-7576, IEEE (2008) pp. 1658-1665

Baruch, I.S & Garrido, R. (2005). A direct adaptive neural control scheme with integral terms. *International Journal of Intelligent Systems, Special issue on Soft Computing for Modelling, Simulation and Control of Nonlinear Dynamical Systems, (O.Castillo, and P.Melin - guest editors),* Vol. 20, No 2, (February 2005) page numbers (213-224), ISSN 0884-8173

Baruch, I.S.; Georgieva P.; Barrera-Cortes, J. & Feyo de Azevedo, S. (2005). Adaptive recurrent neural network control of biological wastewater treatment. *International Journal of Intelligent Systems, Special issue on Soft Computing for Modelling, Simulation and Control of Nonlinear Dynamical Systems, (O.Castillo, and P.Melin - guest editors),* Vol. 20, No 2, (February 2005) page numbers (173-194), ISSN 0884-8173

Baruch, I.S.; Hernandez, L.A.; Mariaca-Gaspar, C.R. & Nenkova, B. (2007). An adaptive sliding mode control with I-term using recurrent neural identifier. *Cybernetics and Information Technologies, BAS, Sofia, Bulgaria,* Vol. 7, No 1, (January 2007) page numbers 21-32, ISSN 1311-9702

Baruch, I.S. & Mariaca-Gaspar, C.R. (2009). A Levenberg-Marquardt learning algorithm applied for recurrent neural identification and control of a wastewater treatment bioprocess. *International Journal of Intelligent Systems,* Vol. 24, No 11, (November 2009) page numbers (1094-1114), ISSN 0884-8173

Baruch, I. S., Mariaca-Gaspar, C.R., and Barrera-Cortes, J. (2008d). Recurrent Neural Network Identification and Adaptive Neural Control of Hydrocarbon Biodegradation Processes. In: Hu, Xiaolin, Balasubramaniam, P. (eds.): *Recurrent Neural Networks*, I-Tech Education and Publishing KG, Vienna, Austria, ISBN 978-953-7619-08-4, (2008) Chapter 4: pp. 61-88

Bialecki B. & Fairweather G. (2001), Orthogonal Spline Collocation Methods for Partial Differential Equations, *Journal of Computational and Applied Mathematics*, vol. 128, No 1-2, (March 2001) page numbers (55-82), ISSN 0377-0427

Boskovic, J.D. & Narendra, K. S. (1995). Comparison of linear, nonlinear and neural-network-based adaptive controllers for a class of fed-batch fermentation processes. *Automatica*, Vol. 31, No 6, (June1995), page numbers (817-840), ISSN 0005-1098

Bulsari, A. & Palosaari, S. (1993). Application of neural networks for system identification of an adsorption column. *Neural Computing and Applications*, Vol. 1, No 2, (Jun2 1993) page numbers (160-165), ISSN 0941-0643

Deng H. & Li H.X. (2003). Hybrid Intelligence Based Modeling for Nonlinear Distributed Parameter Process with Applications to the Curing Process. *IEEE Transactions on Systems, Man and Cybernetics*, Vol. 4, No. 4, (October 2003) page numbers (3506 - 3511), ISSN 1062-922X

Deng H., Li H.X. & Chen G. (2005). Spectral-Approximation-Based Intelligent Modeling for Distributed Thermal Processes. *IEEE Transactions on Control Systems Technology*, Vol. 13, No. 5, (September 2005) page numbers (686-700), ISSN 1063-6536

Gonzalez-Garcia R, Rico-Martinez R. & Kevrekidis I. (1998). Identification of Distributed Parameter Systems: A Neural Net Based Approach, *Computers and Chemical Engineering*, Vol. 22, No 1, (March 2003) page numbers (S965-S968), ISSN 0098-1354

Haykin, S. (1999). *Neural Networks, a Comprehensive Foundation*, Second Edition, Section 2.13, pp. 84-89; Section 4.13, pp. 208-213, Prentice-Hall, ISBN 0-13-273350-1, Upper Saddle River, New Jersey 07458

Padhi R. & Balakrishnan S. (2003). Proper Orthogonal Decomposition Based Optimal Neurocontrol Synthesis of a Chemical Reactor Process Using Approximate Dynamic Programming, *Neural Networks*, vol. 16, No 5-6, (June 2003) page numbers (719 - 728), ISSN 0893-6080

Padhi R., Balakrishnan S. & Randolph T. (2001). Adaptive Critic based Optimal Neuro Control Synthesis for Distributed Parameter Systems, *Automatica*, Vol. 37, No 8, (August 2001) page numbers (1223-1234), ISSN 0005-1098

Pietil S. & Koivo H.N. (1996). Centralized and Decentralized Neural Network Models for Distributed Parameter Systems, *Proceedings of CESA'96 IMACS Multiconference on Computational Engineering in Systems Applications*, pp. 1043-1048, ISBN 2-9502908-9-2, Lille, France, July 1996, Gerf EC Lille, Villeneuve d'Ascq, FRANCE

Ray, W.H. (1989). *Advanced Process Control*, pp.133-242, Butterworths Publishers, ISBN 0-409-90231-4, Boston, London, Singapore, Sydney, Toronto, Wellington

Wan E. & Beaufays F. (1996). Diagrammatic Method for Deriving and Relating Temporal Neural Networks Algorithms, *Neural Computations*, Vol. 8, No.1, (January 1996),) page numbers (182–201), ISSN 0899-7667

24

Optimal Cardiac Pacing with Q Learning

Rami Rom[1] and Renzo DalMolin[2]
SORIN CRM
[1]Israel
[2]France

1. Introduction

With Reinforcement Learning (RL), an agent learns optimal behavior through trial-and-error interactions with a dynamic environment. On each step of interaction, the RL agent receives as input some indication of the current state of the environment. The agent then chooses an action to generate as output. The action changes the state of the environment, and the value of this state transition is communicated to the agent through a scalar reinforcement signal. The agent behavior should choose actions that tend to increase the long run sum of values of the reinforcement signal[1].

Cardiac Resynchronizayion Therapy (CRT) is an established therapy for patients with congestive heart failure (CHF) and intraventricular electrical or mechanical conduction delays. It is based on synchronized pacing of the two ventricles [5-7] according to the sensed natural atrium signal that determines the heart rhythm. The resynchronization task demands exact timing of the heart chambers so that the overall stroke volume for example is maximized for any given heart rate (HR). Optimal timing of activation of the two ventricles is one of the key factors in determining cardiac output. The two major timing parameters which are programmable in a CRT device and determine the pacing intervals are the atrioventricular (AV) delay and interventricular (VV) interval.

The adaptive Cardiac Resynchronization Therapy (CRT) cardiac pacemaker control system [2-4], solves a reinforcement learning problem. Accordingly, an implanted cardiac pacemaker is an agent connected to its environment, the patient heart and body, through an implanted electric leads and a hemodynamic sensor. The agent chooses the actions to be delivered, which are the stimulation AV delay and VV interval parameters that are used to resynchronize the right and left ventricles contractions in each heart beat. The agent task is to learn the optimal AV delay and VV interval that maximize the long run cardiac performance in all heart rates.

In order to simulate the resynchronization RL problem a responsive electro-mechanical heart model is needed for generating the expected environment responses to the agent CRT pacemaker stimulations with different AV delays and VV intervals. The responsive electro-mechanical heart model needs to simulate both the heart electrical activity and the correlated heart and body mechanical activities responsive to electrical stimulation delivered in the right and left ventricles with different AV delay and VV interval.

P. Glassel et al [8], provided a system for simulating the electrical activity of the heart that included a computer controlled heart model for generating and displaying the simulated electrogram signals. The simulation system included various hardware components and software designed to realize the electrical activity of a responsive heart model. However, P. Glassel et al heart model did not simulate the mechanical activity of the heart such as the left ventricle stroke volume, the volumes and pressures of the heart chambers during the systole and diastole cardiac cycles and hence cannot be used for developing a CRT device agent.

A development system of adaptive CRT devices control systems that includes a simplified hemodynamic sensor model was presented by Rom [9]. The aim of the simplified hemodynamic sensor model was to allow a machine learning algorithm to be developed and tested in a simulation with no need to develop a full responsive electro-mechanical heart model. Developing a responsive electro-mechanical heart model is an immense task that needs a model of both the full cardiovascular system and the autonomous nerve system of a CRT patient.

The hemodynamic effects of changes in AV delays and VV intervals delivered to CRT patients were studied by Whinnett et al [10]. In this study, the authors applied non-invasive systolic blood pressure (SBP) monitoring, by continuous finger photoplethysmography (Finometer), to detect hemodynamic responses during adjustment of the AV delay of CRT, at different heart rates. The authors presented CRT response surfaces of systolic blood pressure measurement dependence on paced AV delay and VV intervals. The CRT response surface changed from patient to patient and depended also on the heart rate. The authors suggested that optimization of CRT devices is more important at higher heart rates where CRT patients are more symptomatic. The authors concluded that continuous non-invasive arterial pressure monitoring demonstrated that even small changes in AV delay from its hemodynamic peak value have a significant effect on blood pressure. This peak varied between individuals, was highly reproducible, and was more pronounced at higher heart rates than resting rates.

P. Bordachar et al [11] in a prospective echocardiographic study investigated the respective impacts of left ventricular (LV) pacing, simultaneous and sequential biventricular pacing on ventricular dyssynchrony during exercise in 23 patients with compensated heart failure and ventricular conduction delays. The authors concluded that the optimal interventricular delay was different in rest from exercise in 57% of the patients. In addition the authors showed that changes from rest to exercise in LV dyssynchrony were correlated with changes in stroke volume and changes in mitral regurgitation.

Odonnell et al [12] showed, in 43 CHF patients after CRT implantation in a follow-up study, that the optimal AV delay and VV interval found with echocardiography changed significantly over 9 months of follow-up period.

G. Rocchi et al [13] showed recently that exercise stress Echo is superior to rest echo in predicting LV reverse remodelling and functional improvement after CRT. The authors reported that exercise stress Echo enables identification of CRT responders with about 90% success rate comparing to the current methods that give only about 70% success rate which is still a major problem with CRT today.

According to the clinical studies recited above, the AV delay and VV interval need to be optimized for each CRT patient, may have different optimal values in exercise comparing to rest condition, and may change during 9 months follow up period.

Several optimization methods of control parameters of pacemaker devices in correlation with hemodynamic performance were published. D. Hettrick et al [14], proposed to use the real time left atrial pressure signal as a feedback control mechanism to adjust one or more device parameters. D. Hettrick et al proposed to identify specific characteristics and attributes of the left atrial pressure signal that correlate to hemodynamic performance and to adjust the AV delay parameter of implanted dual chamber pacemaker accordingly.

R. Turcott [15], provided a technique for rapid optimization of control parameters of pacemakers and implanted cardioverters and defibrillators. Turcott proposed to pace the heart with a sequence of consecutive short evaluation periods of equal duration. Turcott proposed to monitor the transient cardiac performance during each of the evaluation phases and to estimate the optimal parameter settings based on changes in the transient cardiac performance from one parameter settings to another.

Hettrick et al and Turcott proposed to use a gradient ascent scheme to adjust the AV delay and VV interval control parameters based on the left atrial pressure signal features (Hettrick et all), and changes in the transient cardiac performance from one parameter settings to another measured by any hemodynamic sensor (Turcott). Hettrick et al and Turcott did not propose to use advanced optimization algorithms for the adjustments of the AV delay and VV interval. Gradient ascent methods may converge slowly, especially in a biological noisy environment, such as the cardiac system. Furthermore, gradient ascent methods may converge to a sub optimal local maximum. Hence, a simple gradient ascent method may result in sub-optimal therapy delivered to CRT patients. The mentioned gradient ascent methods disadvantages together with the clear clinical need of CRT patients to receive optimal therapy may open the door to a more sophisticated machine learning methods that can guarantee convergence and delivery of tailored to the patient optimal therapy.

An adaptive CRT device control system based on reinforcement learning (RL) and using spiking neurons network architecture was presented in [2-4]. The adaptive CRT device control system architecture used a RL method combined with a Hebbian learning rules for the synaptic weights adjustments. The adaptive CRT device control system aim was to optimize online the AV delay and VV interval parameters according to the information provided by the implanted leads and a hemodynamic sensor.

The adaptive CRT device control system used several operational states with a built in priority to operate in an adaptive state aimed to achieve optimal hemodynamic performance. Other operational states were used to initialize the system and to operate as fallback states. The adaptive CRT device control system architecture and operation is described in section 2 herein below.

A Q Learning (QL) and a probabilistic replacement schemes were integrated with the adaptive CRT control system in [16] and are presented in section 3 herein below. QL guarantees convergence online to optimal policy [17], and implemented in a CRT device controller, QL achieves optimal performance by learning the optimal AV delay and VV interval in all heart rates.

With QL, an iterative equation that converges to the optimal policy is solved and a lookup table is calculated. A probabilistic replacement scheme is utilized that replaces an input from a hemodynamic sensor with an input from the lookup table when selecting the next applied AV delay and VV interval. The probability to replace the hemodynamic sensor input with the calculated lookup table value depends on the lookup table difference sign and magnitude that are used as confidence measure for the convergence of the QL scheme. QL combined with the probabilistic replacement scheme improve system performance over time that reach optimal performance even in the face of noisy hemodynamic sensor signal expected with the cardiac system, see Whinnett et al for example [10].

The major advantages of the adaptive CRT control system presented in this chapter are:

1. QL scheme guarantees convergence to optimal policy which in the adaptive CRT application translates to a guarantee to learn the optimal pacing timings (i.e. guarantee to learn online the optimal AV delays and VV intervals).

2. QL converges to the optimal AV and VV values in rest and in exercise where CRT patients are more symptomatic and the converged optimal values are stored in a lookup table that guides the controller operations.
3. Since the Adaptive CRT control system converges to the optimal AV and VV values online, a stress echo test proposed by P. Bordachar et al [11] and G. Rocchi et al [13] in a follow up procedure may not be needed.
4. AV delay and VV interval optimization methods that use a pre-defined sequence of control parameters in a scan test may fail to converge to the true optimal values. Different pre-defined sequences of varying control parameters may lead to different heart conditions and responses, resulting in different estimated values of AV delay and VV intervals since the cardiac system is regulated by the autonomous nerve system and has a delayed time response till it stabilize in a new heart condition.

In summary, an optimization method of the AV delay and VV interval that gradually converges to the optimal set of values is described in this chapter. The optimization method aim is to allow the cardiac system and the autonomous nerve system to stabilize gradually and reach optimum hemodynamic performance in correlation with a learned set of optimal control parameters delivered by the implanted pacemaker. Furthermore, the optimization method aim is to learn the optimal AV delay and VV interval in different heart conditions, and to identify and deliver the learned optimal values safely and efficiently.

This chapter is organized as follows: In section 2 the adaptive CRT device control system architecture and operation are presented and the integration of QL and a probabilistic replacement scheme with the adaptive CRT device control system is presented in section 3. In section 4 simulation results performed with CRT response surface models are presented and section 5 is a conclusion.

2. Adaptive CRT device control system architecture and operation

The adaptive CRT device control system learns to associate different optimal AV delay and VV interval in each heart condition for a CHF patient treated with an implanted CRT device. The adaptive CRT control system uses a deterministic master module to enforce safety limits and to switch between operational states online with a build-in priority to operate in an adaptive state (implemented with a build-in priority state machine). The adaptive CRT control system uses further a slave learning module that implements QL and a probabilistic replacement schemes. The learning module includes leaky I&F neural networks and sigmoid neural networks in order to learn to identify the heart state and to deliver optimal therapy. The adaptive control system uses both supervised learning and a model free reinforcement learning scheme. Supervised learning is used at initialization and fall back states of the priority state machine while QL is used in the higher priority adaptive atate. In the higher priority adaptive state, hemodynamic sensor signal and a QL lookup table calculted online are used. The control system architecture and operation is described herein below.

2.1 Adaptive CRT device control system architecture

The adaptive CRT device control system includes the following main modules:

5. Spiking neurons network.
6. Pattern recognition sigmoid neurons network.
7. Built-in priority state machine.
8. Configuration and register file.

2.1.1 Spiking neurons network architecture

Neural network architectures are inspired by the human brain [18]. Spiking neural networks [19] are closer to biological neural networks and have advantages over other neural networks architectures (such as sigmoid neurons based network) in real time control applications. The spiking neural network perform parallel computation locally and concurrently, in real time. A leaky integrate-and-fire neuron module and a dynamic synapse module are the building blocks of the spiking neurons architecture.

Leaky integrate-and-fire (I&F) neuron

The leaky I&F neuron module is a simplified model of a biological neuron and is naturally adapted for control tasks where the learning objective is a time interval as in the adaptive CRT device where the learned control parameters are the AV delay and VV interval. The leaky I&F neuron is implemented as a digital state machine and two leaky I&F neurons networks are used, one for learning the right AV delay and the second for learning the left AV delay. The interventricular (VV) interval is the time difference between the right and the left optimal AV delays learned by the two leaky I&F neurons. Each leaky I&F neuron is connected to a series of dynamic synapses, typically about 80 dynamic synapses are connected to each leaky I&F neuron. The dynamic synapses weights are adjusted online, in each synapse locally and concurrently (in a hardware version of the controller), according to a set of learning rules in the non-adaptive state and to a second set of learning rules in the adaptive state.

The leaky I&F neuron digital state machine is set initially to idle state waiting for an atrial sensed event. When an atrial sensed event occurs (sensed by an implanted lead in the right atria) the leaky I&F neuron state machine transits to a wait state where in each time step (typically a 1 milli second time step) the outputs of all dynamic synapses connected to the leaky I&F neuron are added to the value stored in a membrane potential register and compared with a threshold value. When the accumulated membrane potential value crosses the threshold value the state machine transits to a fire state, a spike is emitted through the leaky I&F neuron output, and the membrane potential register is reset to 0. The timing of the emitted spike measured relative to the sensed atrial event in milliseconds is the AV delay and the CRT device stimulates the right ventricles accordingly (the left ventricle is stimulated when the left leaky I&F neuron fires a spike similarly). Next the state machine transits to a refractory state for a predefined time period. The leaky I&F neuron state machine transits back to the initial idle state after the refractory period expired and it waits in the idle state to the next atrial sensed event.

A leakage function that reduces the membrane potential value gradually at a pre-defined rate is implemented as a constant value subtracted from the membrane potential register at a constant rate. The leakage function adds timing sensitivity to the leaky I&F neuron and is used to generate a coherent operation of the dynamic synapse. The I&F neuron membrane potential threshold is set to a value that can be crossed only when 3 to 5 dynamic synapses in a short time period emit a maximal post synaptic response (PSR). The dynamic synapses module is described below.

Dynamic synapse

Each dynamic synapse is implemented as a digital state machine. When an atrial event is sensed, a milli second timer starts to count and is used to trigger the dynamic synapses in a time sequence with a pre-defined time delay of 4 msec typically. After receiving the trigger from the timer, each synapse state machine is propagated using it's own local timer from state to state. The dynamic synapse states are: IDLE, WAIT, PRE-HEBB, HEBB, POST-HEBB,

REFRACTORY. Each dynamic synapse releases a post synaptic response in the HEBB state. The PSR magnitude is equal to the adjustable stored synaptic weight and is a time decaying function after the initial PSR is released. All the dynamic synapses PSR's are accumulated in the leaky I&F neuron membrane potential, and when the leaky I&F neuron emits a spike, the dynamic synapse state at the time of the spike in each synapse (may be WAIT, PRE-HEBB, HEBB, POST-HEBB or REFRACTORY state) is captured and stored. The adjustments of the synaptic weights occur at the next sensed atrial event according to the locally captured synapse state and to the learning scheme (supervised learning in the non adaptive state and reinforcement learning in the adaptive state). Typically the synaptic weight stored in each synapse has values between 0 and 31.

Dynamic synapse sub groups and time interleaving

The dynamic synapses are divided to 5 sub groups according to heart rate ranges, from low heart rate range, to high heart rate range and are interleaved according to their excitation time order and heart rate group. The excitation timer triggers the appropriate dynamic synapses sub group according to the time relative to the sensed atrial event in each heart beat and to the current heart rate. The division of the dynamic synapse to sub groups allows learning and adjusting the optimal AV delay and VV interval in each heart rate range in real time throughout the CRT device operation in a patient body which is typically 5 to 7 years. This architecture allows efficient delivery and adjustment of the learned optimal values with faster convergence to the current optimal values.

Supervised learning in the non adaptive state

In the initial and the fall-back non-adaptive CRT state, the adaptive CRT device stimulates the two ventricles using the AV delay and VV interval values programmed by a clinician. The supervised learning task is to train the leaky I&F neurons to fire (i.e. emit a spike) at the programmed values relative to the sensed atrial event in each heart beat. The learning task is to create significant and coherent post synaptic responses of 3 to 5 synapses at the proper times. The released PSR's are then accumulated in the leaky I&F neuron membrane potential that crosses the threshold and fire at the target time (the programmed AV delay and VV interval). Generally, the learning rule increases the synaptic weights in those dynamic synapses that release a PSR just before the target time and reduces synaptic weights values of other dynamic synapses.

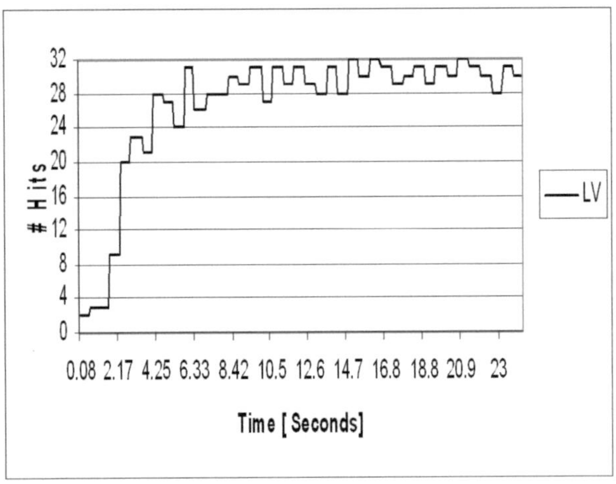

Fig. 1. Hit count rate convergence.

A hit count rate is defined as the number of hits of the leaky I&F neuron spikes at a time window overlapping the target time (the programmed AV delay and VV interval). The I&F neuron learns to fire at the target time window and the number of hits in a time frame of 32 cardiac cycles is used as a performance measure (shown in Fig. 1 above). When the leaky I&F neurons hit count rate achieves a high value (~30) in a time frame, the learning task is converged and a transition to the adaptive state is allowed. When the leaky I&F neurons hit count rate falls below a predefined value (~10) in a time frame, the learning task failed to and a transition to a lower priority state is forced by the build-in priority state machine.

Reinforcement learning in the adaptive state

In the adaptive CRT state a hemodynamic sensor signal responsive to pacing with different AV delay and VV interval is used as the reinforcement immediate reward [1]. Whinnett et al showed in a clinical study [10] that a CRT response surface with a global maximum as a function of the stimulation intervals AV delay and VV interval exist. The adaptive CRT device control system reinforcement learning scheme [2-4], assumes that a CRT response surface exists, and accordingly the synaptic weights reach a steady state values that causes the leaky I&F neurons to fire at the correct timings correlated with the CRT response surface maximum.

The synaptic weights adjustments in the RL scheme are performed in two adjacent cardiac cycles as described in details below. In the first cardiac cycle, a pacing register is increased or decreased by a pre programmed step, Δ. In the next cardiac cycle, the adaptive CRT controller stimulate the heart with the new value and the hemodynamic response is received. Using the current and the previous hemodynamic response and the stored HEBB states of each dynamic synapse, the synaptic weights adjustments are made in each synapse locally and concurrently.

A random stepping mechanism is utilized as follows. In the first cardiac cycle a pacing register value is increased or decreased according to the I&F neuron spike timing, initialized by the sensed atrial event, and compared with the current pacing register value:

$$T_{Spike} > P \qquad P = P + \Delta \tag{1a}$$

$$T_{Spike} < P \qquad P = P - \Delta \tag{1b}$$

4 possible states are defined according to the flow diagram shown in Fig. 2 below

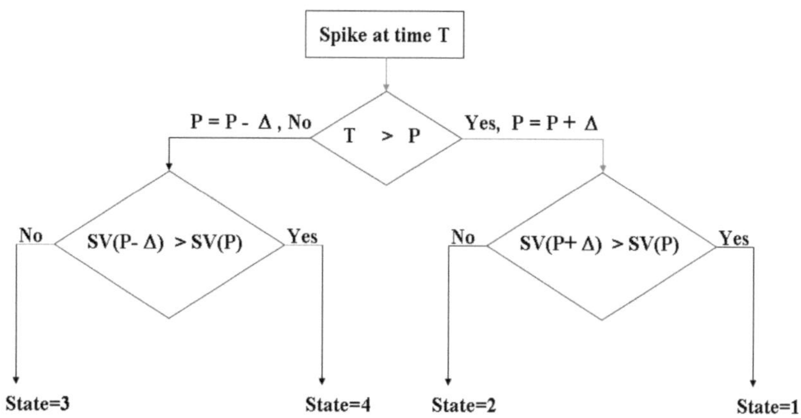

Fig. 2. Synaptic adjustments flow diagram.

Where SV(P) and SV(P+/- Δ) are the hemodynamic response immediate reward stored in the current and the previous cardiac cycles (SV is the stroke volume extracted from the hemodynamic sensor signal and is used as a CRT response surface). A hemodynamic sensor model [9] is used in the simulations presented in section 4 to extract the SV values with different AV delay, VV interval and heart rate.
Next, according to the 4 possible states shown in Fig. 2 and the stored HEBB state in each synapse (PRE_HEBB, HEBB and POST HEBB) , the synaptic adjustments are :

$$W_i=W_i+\lambda \text{ when \{PRE\_HEBB, 3 or 1\} or \{HEBB, 4 or 2\} or \{POSTHEBB, 4 or 2\}} \quad (2a)$$

$$W_i=W_i-\lambda \text{ when \{HEBB, 3 or 1\} or \{POST HEBB, 3 or 1\} or \{PRE HEBB, 4 or 2\}} \quad (2b)$$

The synaptic weights are typically limited to the values of 0 to 31, with a a step value λ, typically 0.125.

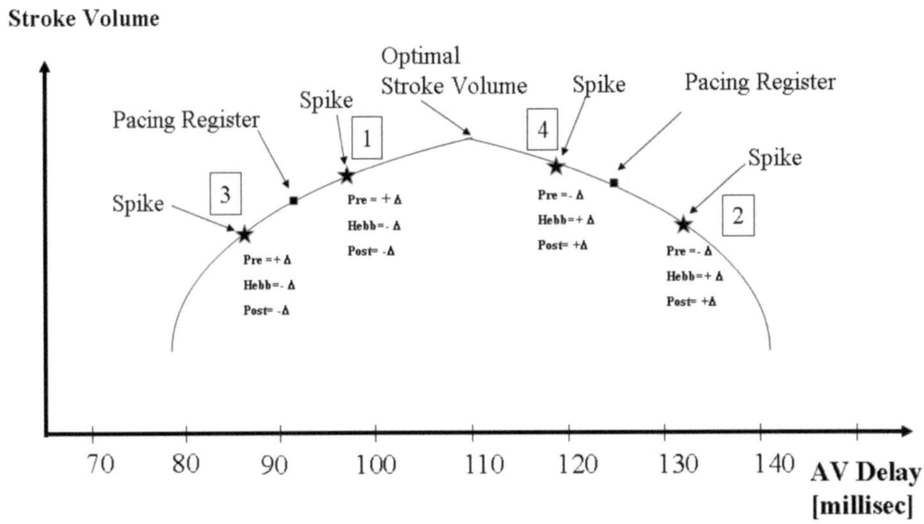

Fig. 3. Synaptic adjustments and the CRT response surface.

In summary, the synaptic adjustments learning rule uses the Hebbian states stored in each dynamic synapse and the hemodynamic responses in two adjacent cardiac cycles to train the leaky I&F neurons to fire at the optimal timing that correlates with the maximal value of the CRT response surface (as a result of coherent release of several dynamic synapse PSR's at the approperiate learned time). The adaptive CRT device control system learns to track the CRT response surface maximum online. When the heart rate changes, the CRT response surface shape changes too [10], and new optimal AV delay and VV interval values are learned and other steady state values of synaptic weights are obtained and stored at the dynamic synapses. Since these changes of the CRT response surface shape and the correlated optimal AV delay and VV interval are learned and stored at the dynamic synapses continuousuly in both the non adaptive and adaptive CRT states, the method maximizes the long term sum of the immediate rewards (i.e. the hemodynamic responses). In section 3 a QL scheme is presented that use Watkins and Dayan iterative equation and adds a probabilistic replacement scheme to QL [16].

2.1.2 Pattern recognition sigmoid network architecture

The pattern recognition sigmoid network includes two sigmoid neuron networks where each network has 16 sigmoid neurons in a layer, 16 synapses are connected to each sigmoid neuron, 3 hidden layers and one linear output neuron. The two sigmoid networks are trained by a standard supervised learning delta rule [18]. The inputs to the pattern recognition networks are temporal patterns of the last 16 hemodynamic sensor responses stored at the controller memory in each heart beat. The supervised training values that the sigmoid network recieves every heart beat is the firing time of the leaky I&F neurons relative to the sensed atrial signal, i.e. the right AV delay for one network and the left AV delay for the second network. The pattern recognition networks learns to associate the learned optimal AV delay and VV interval of the leaky I&F neurons network with a temporal patterns of hemodynamic responses, i.e. hemodynamic performance signals exteracted from the hemodynamic sensor. Hence, the pattern recognition network learns to associate optimal AV delay and VV interval with a heart condition characterized by the temporal patterns of hemodynamic sensor. The operation of the build-in priority state machine described below depends on the successes and failures of the pattern recognition network to output the correct AV delay and VV interval values comparing to the values obtained by the leaky I&F neutons.

2.1.3 Configuration and registers file

The configuration and register file unit stores programmable parameters, such as the initial AV delay and VV interval, and other parameters needed for the initialization of the adaptive CRT control system. The programmable values of the AV delay and VV interval are used in the initialization and fall back non adaptive CRT state while in the non adaptive state the adaptive CRT device controller deliver stimulations with the learned optimal AV delay and VV intervals that correlates with the maximal hemodynamic responses values of the CRT response surface.

2.1.4 Build-in priority state machine

Fig. 4 shows the adaptive CRT priority state machine that has a build in logic that continuously directs the state machine to prefer and to transit to the highest priority adaptive state [21]. Switching to higher priority states require meeting convergence criteria and failing to meet convergence criteria results in transitions back to lower priority states. The lower priority initial and fallback state, the non adaptive CRT state, is the starting state. In the non adaptive CRT lower priority state, the leaky I&F neurons networks adjust their synaptic weights until convergence conditions are met (hit count rate is high) and the build-in priority state machine can switch to a higher priority state, delivering optimal therapy with best hemodynamic performance. The build-in priority state machine in the higher priority adaptive state is guaranteed to deliver the optimal AV and VV Intervals using QL and a probabilistic replacement scheme. In the non adaptive CRT lower priority state the AV delay and VV interval programmed by a clinician are delivered as initialization and safety fallback values. The adaptive CRT build in priority state machine operation and switching conditions are described below.

Non-adaptive CRT state

In the non adaptive CRT state, the CRT device uses a programmed AV delay and VV interval delivering biventricular pacing with fixed AV delay and VV interval. In the non-adaptive CRT state, a leaky integrate and fire (I&F) neurons synaptic weights are trained using a supervised learning scheme and the synaptic weights reach a steady state values that bring the leaky I&F neurons to fire at the programmed AV delay and VV interval timings with high hit count rate as shown in Fig. 1 above, and after convergence is achieved switching to adaptive state is allowed.

Gradient ascent (GA) state

In the GA CRT state the AV delay and VV interval values are changed according to a random stepping mechanism (see equation 1a and 1b above), and the leaky I&F neurons synaptic weights are trained using a Hebbian and reinforcement learning scheme shown in Figs. 2 and 3 above. The leaky I&F neurons synaptic weights reach a steady state values that bring the leaky I&F neurons to fire at the optimal AV delay and VV interval correlated with the maximum of a CRT response surface extracted from a hemodynamic sensor that reflect for example the stroke volume dependence on the changing AV and VV delays. The GA scheme is designed to track continuously the maximum stroke volume on the CRT response surface as a function of pacing intervals in all heart condition. The leaky I&F neurons output the learned optimal pacing intervals with changing heart rates efficiently using a division of the dynamic synapses to sub groups according to the heart rate range.

QL state

In the QL state, the QL lookup table calculated according to Watkins and Dayan iterative equation [17], are used in addition to the hemodynamic sensor input according to a probabilistic replacements mechanism described in section 3. Q Learning combined with the probabilistic replacement mechanism enables the system to perform optimally also in a noisy biological environment and to improve the overall system performance online using its own predictions. The QL state brings the best hemodynamic performance, learned from the patient hemodynamic responses. The Adaptive CRT build-in priority state machine directs the control system to this highest priority QL state continuously [21].

Fail QL state

In the FAIL-QL state the pattern recognition sigmoid neurons networks re-adjust their synaptic weights in order to map the input temporal patterns of CRT response with the leaky I&F neurons networks outputs.

Switching criteria

Switching between the four states occurs automatically back and forth during operation according to the heart condition and system performance with a build in preference to operate in the QL state that brings the best hemodynamic performance.

Switching from the non-adaptive CRT state to the GA state occurs according to convergence of the leaky I&F neurons networks supervised learning scheme in the non-adaptive CRT state. The two leaky I&F neurons (one for the right AV delay and the second for the left AV delay) need to hit a target times with high rates in a time frame in order to enable a transition as shown in Fig. 1 above.

Switching from the GA state to the optimal QL state occur according to successful association of the temporal pattern recognition sigmoid neural networks predictions (predicted AV delay and VV interval) compared with the I&F neurons network predictions. A hit count rate is calculated for the pattern recognition sigmoid neural networks similar to the hit count rate calculated for the leaky I&F neurons and the hit count rate value of the sigmoid neural networks are used as a performance measure that allows transition to the QL state when it crosses a predefined threshold value.

Fallback from the GA state to the non-adaptive CRT state occurs according to pre-defined system failures that can be for example too low or too high AV delay and VV interval

(crossing pre-defined safety limits), too low or too high heart rate (or other arrhythmia detected) or a poor neural networks performance expressed as a too low hit count rate of the leaky I&F neuron due to sudden drifts of the networks outputs.
Fallback from the QL state to the FAIL QL state occurs if too low hit count rate of the temporal pattern recognition sigmoid neurons networks are obtained. Fallback from the QL state to the FAIL QL state occurs when a sudden change in the heart condition occurs resulting in unfamiliar to the pattern recognition neural networks temporal patterns of hemodynamic sensor values. In such case, the pattern recognition sigmoid neurons networks need to learn to associate the new temporal patterns with new learned optimal values achieved by the leaky I&F neurons network in the new heart condition in order to switch back to a higher priority state.

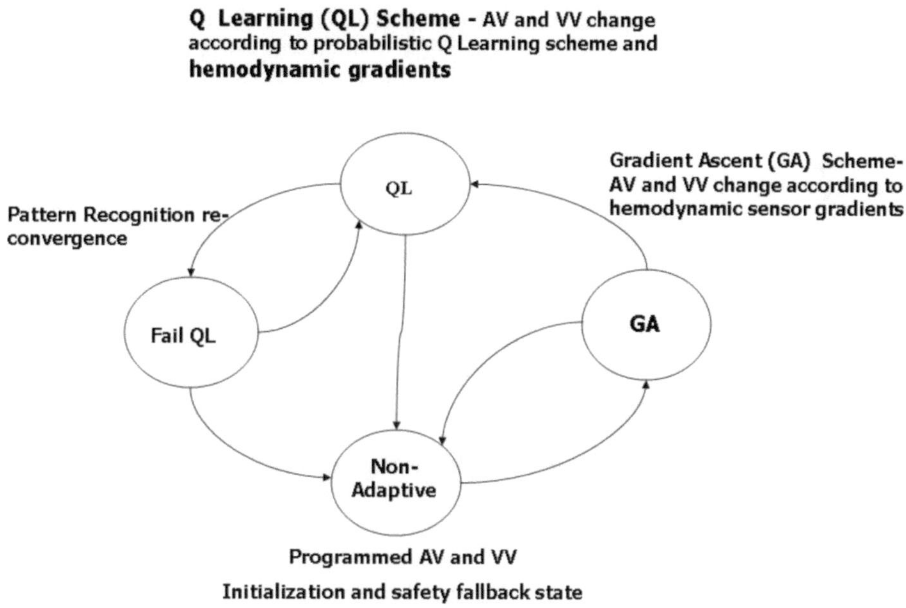

Fig. 4. Build-in priority state machine

2.2 Device optimization during Implantation

Due to the complexity and the cost of the follow up procedures using echocardiography, about 80% of CRT patients are not optimized in the US according to studies presented in Cardiostim conference, France 2006. It is known that more then 30% of CRT patients do not respond to CRT and that CRT non-responders are identified only after 3 to 6 months with quality of life (QOL) questioners or 6 minutes hall walk distance test.
The CLEAR study [22], with 156 pateints enrolled in 51 centers in 8 countries, demonstrated reduced mortality and heart failure related hospitalization in patients whose CRT device was optimized on a regular basis. Final results showed that regular optimization of CRT using Sorin Group's SonR sensor technology improved clinical response rate to 86% as compared to 62% in patients recieving standard medical treatment.
An adaptive CRT device, presented in this chapter, may be used to validate and identify responders to CRT in acute way[20]. The RL algorithm that changes automatically pacing

delays and converge gradually to maximal stroke volume of a CRT response surface will enable a clinician to identify a responder in 2-5 minutes during CRT implantation as simulated in Fig. 5 below. A clinician may monitor the device operation on a programmer screen and validate the hemodynamic improvement according to a CRT responder curve shown in Fig. 5. Optimal CRT and lead positioning during CRT device implantation may turn a non-responder to a responder and a responder to a better responder [6]. The adaptive CRT device implant may allow a clinician using a responder curve to change and validate lead position and achieve optimal lead positioning sites during the implantation procedure. Hence, in addition to the potential long term benefits of a machine learning based adaptive CRT device control system, aimed to manage an implanted CRT device continuously in a patient body for typically 5 to 7 years, the adaptive CRT device control system presented in this chapter may allow:

1. Acute Identification of CRT responders during implantation procedure.
2. Optimal lead positioning validation during implantation procedure.

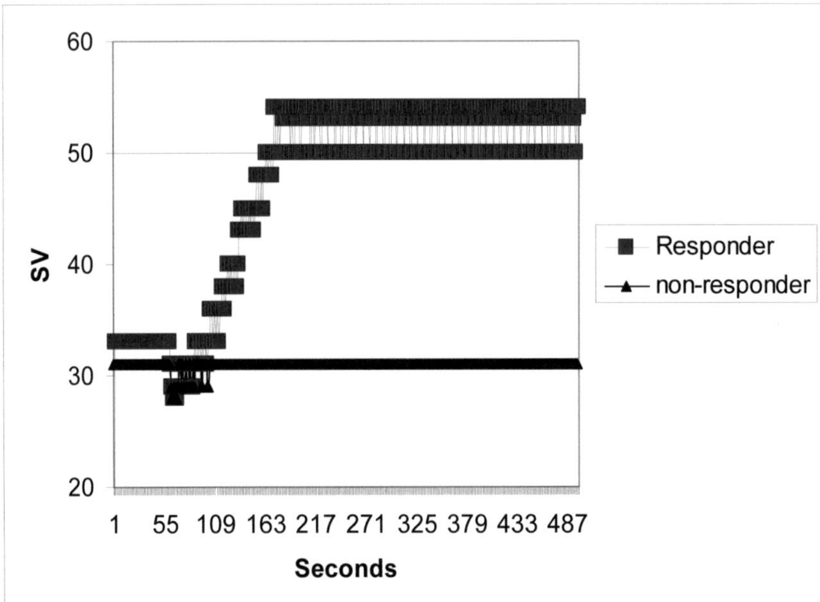

Fig. 5. CRT responder curve

3. Q Learning and cardiac resynchronization therapy

"Reinforcement learning differs from the more widely studied problem of supervised learning in several ways. The most important difference is that there is no presentation of input/output pairs. Instead, after choosing an action the agent is told the immediate reward and the subsequent state, but is not told which action would have been in its best long-term interests. It is necessary for the agent to gather useful experience about the possible system states, actions, transitions and reward actively to act optimally. Another difference from supervised learning is that on-line performance is important; the evaluation of the system is often concurrent with learning"[1].

Watkins and Dayan QL is a model free reinforcement learning scheme where the agent converge to the optimal policy online solving an iterative equation, shown below, and without apriori knowledge of the environment states transitions [17].

$$(S,A)= Q(S,A)+ \alpha(R(S,A)+ \gamma\, Q_{\max A} (S,A) -Q(S,A)) \tag{1}$$

A is the agent action, S is the environment state, Q(S,A) is the expected discounted reinforcement of taking action A in state S, R(S,A) is an immediate reward response of the environment, α is a small learning rate factor ($\alpha << 1$), γ is a discount factor (smaller then 1), $Q_{\max A}$ (S,A) is the learned optimal policy, i.e. the optimal action A that give maximum Q value at a given state, S, out of the possible set of actions A. The converged solution of Watkins and Dayan iterative equation is stored in a lookup table.
With a CRT device, the two parameters that need to be optimized are the AV delay and the VV interval. Watkins and Dayan QL lookup table is calculated for each configuration of AV and VV values and for each configuration the possible actions assumed are limited to an increase or a decrease by constant value ΔP at a time (typically 5 ms step size is used) applied in the next cardiac cycle.

$$(S,A) = Q(AV, VV, AV +/- \Delta P, VV +/- \Delta P) \tag{2}$$

A represents the pacemaker stimulation timings, AV delay and VV interval, S is the heart hemodynamic performance extracted from a hemodynamic sensor signal, Q(S,A) is the calculated lookup table using a specific AV delay and VV intervals parameters and action A, R(S,A) is the immediate reward (a stroke volume extracted from the hemodynamic sensor signal as an examples). $Q_{\max A}$ (S,A) is the converged Q value expected with the optimal AV delay and VV intervals and optimal action A.
Watkins and Dayan proved [17] that by solving the iterative equation, the agent learns the optimal policy in a model free reinforcement leaning problem with a probability of 1 when the action space is visited enough times such that exploration of the action space is sufficient. The importance of Watkins and Dayan proof, adopted here for CRT pacemakers, is that the stimulation timings obtained by solving the iterative equation are guaranteed to converge to the optimal AV delay and VV without making any assumptions regarding the CRT responses surface shape. The guarantee to converge to the optimal AV delay and VV interval is the valuable benefit of using a sophisticated machine learning method, such as QL, in a CRT pacemaker. Since the AV delay and VV interval parameters are crucial for the success of the therapy [10-13, 21], the guarantee to converge to the optimal AV delay and VV interval is an important advantage over other optimization methods that do not guarantee convergence to optimal values. Furthermore, this advantage should open the door to implementation of machine learning methods, such as QL, in implanted medical devices such as CRT pacemakers and defibrillators.
In the adaptive CRT control system presented here two control parameters, the AV delay and VV interval, were optimized at different heart rates. The QL scheme will be even more beneficial if more control parameters are needed to be optimized. In general, a QL scheme will be more beneficial when the action space is big and the agent needs to select its action from a bigger set of possible actions (i.e. control parameters).

3.1 Probabilistic replacement scheme

QL combined with a probabilistic replacement mechanism allows the adaptive CRT device to replace input gradients with its own predictions learned from the hemodynamic responses to pacing with different AV delay and VV interval. Q Learning combined with probabilistic replacement mechanism enables the system to perform optimally also in a noisy biological environment, such as the cardiac system, and to improve the overall system performance using its own predictions. The probabilistic replacement scheme selects between input from a hemodynamic sensor and a calculated value obtained from the QL lookup table with a probability that depends on the calculated lookup table. The magnitude of the difference of the optimal action Q value and a sub-optimal action Q value is used as a confidence measure in the probabilistic replacement scheme [16].

Fig. 6 is a flow chart diagram, explaining the leaky I&F spiking neurons synaptic weight adjustmants combined with the probabilistic replacement scheme. The modification shown in Fig. 6 comparing to the flow diagram of Fig. 2 is that the selection conditions depends now on the stroke volumes difference (calculated in the current and previous cardiac cycle) or the QL lookup table difference magnitude which is used as a confidence measure of the probabilistic replacement scheme. After a selection of one out of four possible states is performed, the synaptic weight adjustment are performed in the same manner as described in [2-4 and 16]. The probabilistic replacement mechanism affects the synaptic weight adjustments directly since it determines the selection of one of the four possible states shown in Fig. 6 , and it affects the random stepping mechanism indirectly since the spike timing , T, depends on the values of the adjusted synaptic weights and T value compared to the pacing register value, P, determines the step selection.

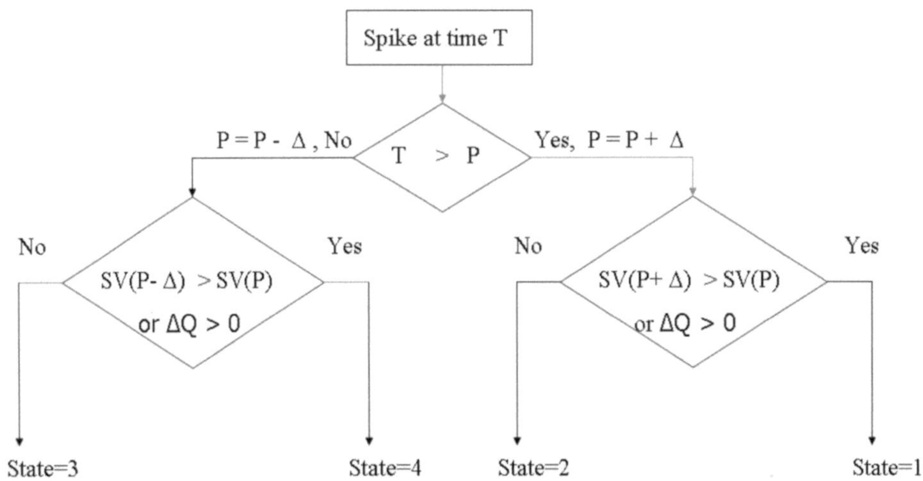

Fig. 6. Synaptic adjustments with the probabilistic replacements scheme

Regulation of α and threshold parameters

Watkins and Dayan iterative equation (Eq. 1) learning rate parameter α, determines the convergence rate of the solution of the iterative Q Learning lookup table. With a high value of α the QL iterative equation will converge faster. However, in noisy environment a too big α parameter may cause instability in the Q Learning scheme. Hence an automatic regulation of α is used to ensure proper performance. The regulation scheme is based on a replacements rate counter calculated online and a maximal steady replacement rate value is typically 80%. This high limit value determines the effectiveness of the probabilistic replacement scheme.

When a QL replacement is performed as shown in Fig. 6, a replacement counter is incremented and the replacement counter is reset to 0 every 2000 cardiac cycles typically.

The number of replacements performed in a time period depends on the α value and on 3 threshold values that are used in the replacement probabilistic mechanism. The α parameter is set initially to a low value (typically 0.02) and is incremented slowly if the replacement rate is below the programmed high limit (typically 80%) until it reach the maximal value allowed for α (typically 0.05). When the replacement rate is higher then the maximal value allowed α is decreased (lower limit for α is typically 0.002).
The 3 thresholds values regulation scheme depends on the value of α and on the calculated replacement rate. The initial thresholds values are set to low values (typically 10, 20 and 30). The values of the 3 thresholds determine three ranges for selecting the lookup table prediction replaceing the hemodynamic sensor input and determining 3 confidence ranges. The magnitude of the difference of the optimal action Q value and a sub-optimal action Q value is compared with the 3 threshold values and accordingly a replacement of the hemodynamic sensor input with the lookup table prediction is selected with a probability that depends on the 3 ranges. When the diffefence magnitude is high, a replacement is performed with a high probability and vice versa.
When α is maximal (0.05) and the replacement rate is still too low the thresholds will be lowered. When α is minimal (typically 0.002) and the replacement rate is still too high the 3 thresholds will be incremented gradually till the replacement rate will be lowered. The aim of both α and the 3 thresholds values regulation is to maintain a steady replacement rate close to the maximal value required (typically 80%). The replacement rate value defines the efficiency of the QL scheme to correct errors of noisy biological inputs using the learned environment responses acquired in the QL lookup table (the probabilistic replacement mechanism use the magnitudes of the diffefnce in addition to it's sign).

4. Simulation results

In the simulation results section we first show that the adaptive CRT control system learns to deliver the optimal pacing timings, i.e. the optimal AV delay and VV interval that maximize the CRT response with varying heart rate (Fig. 7). Next we show that with the combined QL and probabilistic replacement mechanism, the adaptive CRT control system reach the optimal performance in a noisy environment almost independent to the noise level (Fig. 8). We compare simulation results with and without the combined QL and probabilistic replacement mechanism to show that it out perform a simple gradient ascent scheme with varying noise levels (Fig. 9), and finally we show that QL scheme enables the system to escape from local maximum and to converge to the global maximum of a CRT response surface (Fig. 10).
Simulations of the adaptive CRT device control system and the CRT response surface were performed using Matlab-Simulink version 7.6. The adaptive CRT control system application was coded in C and compiled as a Simulink S-function. Simulink S-functions were also used for implementing timers (Atrial-Atrial timer that defines the simulated heart rate and for the AV and VV delays for example) in order to simulate a real time, interrpts based application.
Fig. 7 shows the AV delay and VV interval obtained in a simulation that starts at a heart rate of 60 beats per minute (BPM), then the heart rate changes to 100 BPM and to 120 BPM and relax back to 100 BPM and to 60 BPM periodically. Pre programmed optimal AV delay of the simulated CRT response surface were 160 ms at 60 BPM, 130 ms at 100 BPM and 90 ms at 120 BPM. Optimal pre programmed VV intervals were 0 at 60 BPM, -10 at 100 BPM and -30 at 120 BPM. The simulation results shown in Fig. 7 follow accurately the optimal values.

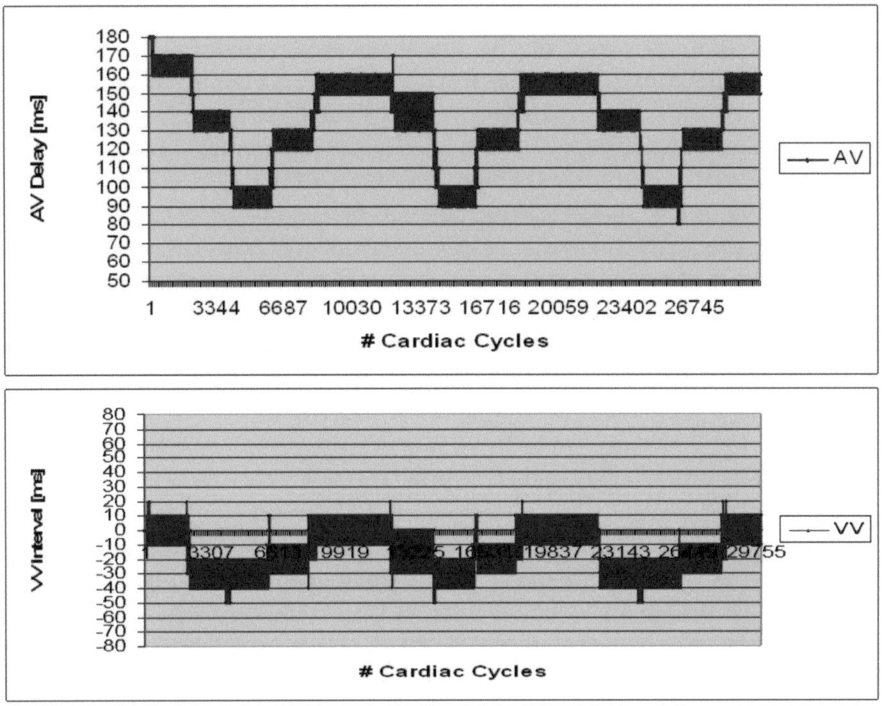

Fig. 7. Dynamic optimization of AV and VV intervals

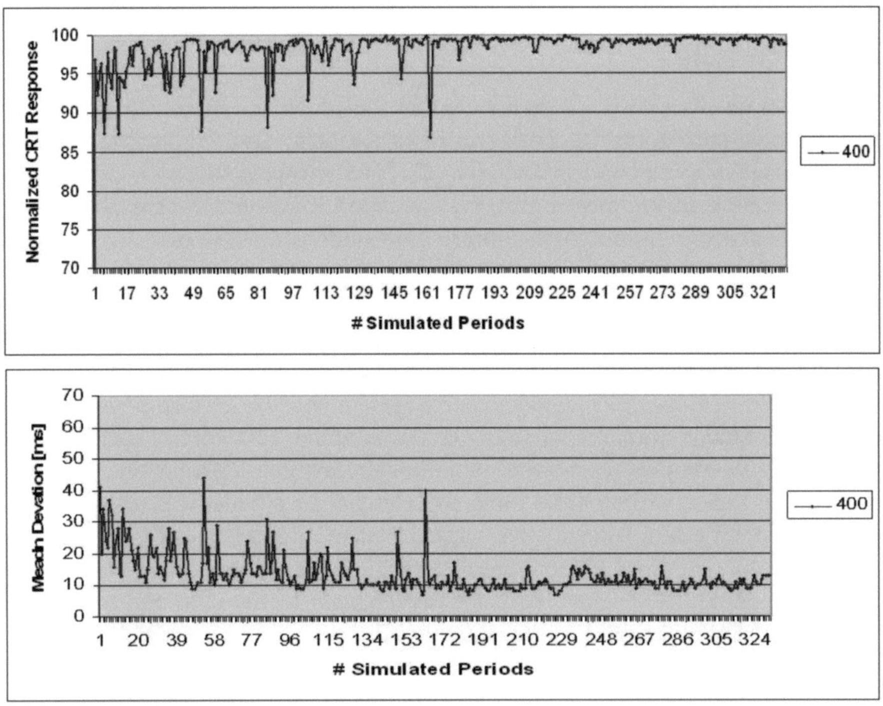

Fig. 8. RT responses convergence with QL in a noisy environment

Fig. 8 shows a normalized CRT response (defined further below) in its upper part and an average deviation from optimal values in its bottom part, calculated during a long simulations with varying heart rate. The normalized CRT response grows during the simulation and shows deeps at the first part of the simulation. After convergence of the combined QL and probabilistic replacement mechanism, the normalized CRT response reach the maximal value with almost no deeps and remain steady at the maximal value while the noise level added to the hemodynamic sensor signal is effetive during all the simulation. The average deviation from optimal AV delay and VV values shown in Fig 8 bottom part is high initially, shows some peaks during a convergence period with generally lower values and then reach a minimal steady value of 10 msec. Fig. 8 proves in a simulation that the adaptive control system learns to deliver pacing with optimal AV and VV intervals in rest and exercise conditions in a noisy environment and the overall system performance improves during the simulation and reach the optimal performance, i.e. the agent learns and acts according to the optimal policy in a noisy environment.

Since the CRT surface responses are proportional to the patient cardiac output, Fig. 8 shows that the combined QL and probabilistic replacement mechanism has the potential to increase the cardiac output of CRT patients which is a major goal of CRT. Hence machine learning methods may be clinically beneficial to CHF patients and this advantage may open the door for machine learning methods implemented in implanted medical devices [16, 23, 24].

Fig. 9 shows the adaptive CRT device system performance with and without learning with varying random noise levels added to the hemodynamic sensor input, i.e. to the CRT response surface. The system performance with a simple gradient ascent scheme (without learning) falls linearly with the growing random noise level to below 70% of the optimal performance while QL combined with the probabilistic replacement scheme is able to improve the system performance and keep it almost at the optimal system performance with no noise at all noise levels shown.

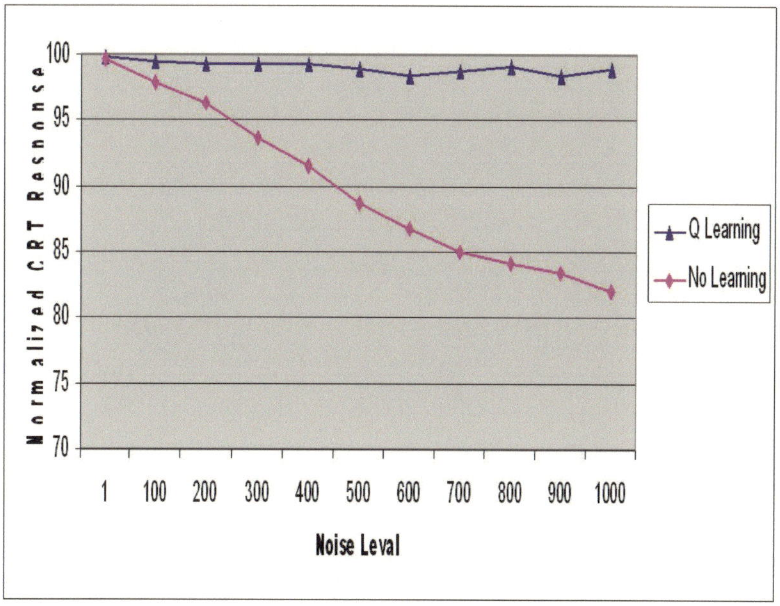

Fig. 9. System performance with QL in noisy environment

The normalized CRT response shown in Figs. 8 and 9 is defined as a normalizaed average of CRT responses calculated during each simulation period of 2000 cardiac cycles.

$$\text{Averaged CRT Response} = 1/2000 * \Sigma_1^{2000} \text{ CRT Response(i)} \quad (3)$$

A normalize CRT Response, that takes into account the surface global maximal value and the minimal value at a given heart rate is calculated according to Eq. 4 below:

$$\text{Normalized CRT Response} = [\text{Averaged CRT Response} - \text{CRT Response Min}]/[\text{CRT Response Max} - \text{CRT Response Min}] * 100 \quad (4)$$

Where at heat rate of 60 BPM :
CRT Response Min = CRT Response (worst values AV=60,VV=0)
CRT Response Max = CRT Response (optimal values AV=160,VV=0) .
An important aspect of the QL based adaptive CRT control system is its ability to converge to the global maximum of the CRT response surface when it includes also a local maximum. Fig. 10 shows the pacing histogram obtained with a long simulations of 1 million cardiac cycles with random noise and compares the results obtained with and without Q Learning. The simulation starts at low AV delay of 90 ms in vicinity of a local maximum in the simulated CRT response surface. The simulated pacing histograms shows that without QL the histogram has a stronger peak at the local maximum of 90 ms and a weaker peak at the global maxima of 160 ms. With Q Learning the histogram is peaked at the global maximum of 160 ms and only a small peak is seen at the local sub optimal maximum of 90 ms.

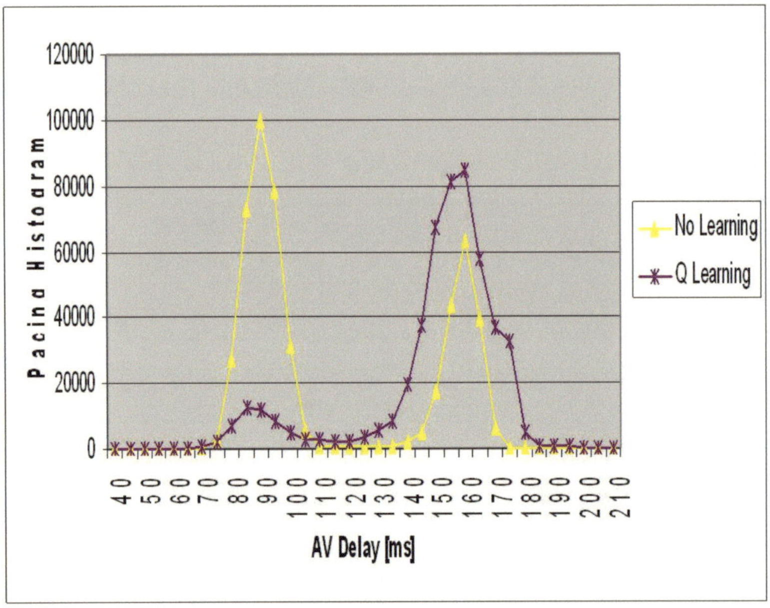

Fig. 10. Convergence to the global maxima with QL

7. Conclusions

In this chapter we present an adaptive control system for a CRT device based on QL and a probabilistic replacement mechanism aimed to achieve patient specific optimal pacing

therapy for CHF patients implanted with a CRT device. The learning target was to learn to deliver optimal AV delay and VV interval in all heart conditions and in a biological noisy environment. The adaptive control system uses a deterministic master module that enforce safety limits and switch between operational states online with a build-in priority to operate in the adaptive state, and a learning slave module that use QL and probabilistic replacement mechanism and includes leaky I&F neural networks and sigmoid neural networks in order to identify heart conditions and to learn to deliver optimal therapy.
A combined QL and probabilistic replacement mechanism may allow the adaptive CRT device to replace hemodynamic sensor inputs with its own calculated predictions learned from the environment responses to pacing. The combined QL and probabilistic replacement mechanism may enable the adaptive CRT control system to perform optimally in a biological noisy environment, such as the cardiac system.
The adaptive CRT device aim is to increase the patient hemodynamic performance (cardiac output for example) and to be clinically beneficial to CRT patients especially in high heart rates where CRT patients are more symptomatic [10]. Pre-clinical and clinical studies are needed to prove the clinical benefits of an adaptive CRT device bases on machine learning methods.
Adaptive control systems that learn to deliver optimal therapy were proposed for two other implanted medical devices: Vagal stimulation device that learns to regulate the patient heart rate combined in one can with a CRT device that improve cardiac efficiency by learning to optimize at the same time also the AV delay and VV interval [23], and a deep brain stimulation (DBS) device adaptive control system that learns the optimal control parameters that reduce uncontrolled movements of Parkinson's disease patients [24].

8. References

[1] Leslie P. Kaebling, Michael L. Littman and Anderw W. Moore, "Reinforcement Learning: A Survey", Journal of Artificial Intelligence Research 4 , 237-285, 1996.K.
[2] R. Rom, "Adaptive Resynchronization Therapy System", US Patent 7,657,313, July 2004.
[3] R. Rom, J. Erel, M. Glikson, K. Rosenblum, R. Ginosar, D. L. Hayes, "Adaptive Cardiac Resynchronization Therapy Device: A Simulation Report", Pacing and Clinical Electrophysiology. Vol. 28, pp. 1168-1173, November 2005.
[4] R. Rom, J. Erel, M. Glikson, K. Rosenblum, O. Binah, R. Ginosar, D. L. Hayes, "Adaptive Cardiac Resynchronization Therapy Device Based On Spiking Neurons Architecture", IEEE-TNN, Vol 18, Number 2, 542-550, March 2007.
[5] A. Ellenbogen,B. L. Wilkoff, and G. N. Kay , "Device Therapy for Congestive Heart Failure", Philadelphia, Pennsylvania, Elsevier Inc., 2004, pp 47-91.
[6] D. L. Hayes, P. J. Wang, K. Sackner-Bernstein, S. J. Avirsatham,"Resynchronization and Defibrillation for Heart Failure, A Practical Approach", *Oxford, UK,* Blackwell Publishing, 2004, pp 39-72.
[7] D. L. Hayes and S. Forman, "Cardiac Pacing. How it started, Where we are, where we are going", Pacing and Clinical Electrophysiology, vol. 27, pp. 693-704, May 2004.
[8] P. Glassel et al, in "Interactive Cardiac Rhythm Simulator", US Patent 5,692,907, August 1995.
[9] R. Rom, "Heart Simulator", US Patent application 2008/0103744, Oct 2006.
[10] Z. I. Whinnett, J. E.R. Davis, K. Wilson, C. H. Manisty, A. W Cohw, R. A Foale, D W. Davies, A. D Hughes, J. Mayet and D. P Francis, "Haemodynamic effects of

changes in AV and VV delay in cardiac Resynchronization Therapy show a consistent pattern: analysis of shape, magnitude and relative importance of AV and VV delay", Heart published online, 18 May 2006, doi:10.1136/hrt.2005.080721.
[11] P. Bordachar, S. Lafitte, S. Reuter, K. Serri, S. Garrigue, J. Laborderie, P. Reant, P. Jais, M. Haissaguerre, R. Roudaut, J. Clementy, "Echocardiography Assessment During Exercise of Heart Failure Patients with Cardiac Resynchronization Therapy", American Journal of Cardiology, Vol. 97 , June 2006 , pp. 1622-5.
[12] D. Odonnell, V. Nadurata, A. Hamer, P. Kertes and W. Mohammed, "Long Term Variations in Optimal Programming of Cardiac Resynchronization Therapy Devices", Pacing and Clinical Electrophysiology, vol. 28, January 2005, suppl. 1, pp. S24-S26.
[13] G. Rocchi et al, in "Exercise stress Echo is superior to rest echo in predicting LV reverse remodelling and functional improvement after CRT", European Heart Journal (2009), 30, 89-97.
[14] D. Hettrick et al, in "System and a Method for Controlling Implantable Medical Devices Parameters in Response to Atrial Pressure Attributes", US Patent Application 11,097,408, March 2005.
[15] R. Turcott, in "System and a Method for Rapid Optimization of Control Parameters of an Implantable Cardiac Stimulation Device", US Patent 7,558,627, Sep 2003.
[16] R. Rom, "Optimal Cardiac Pacing with Q Learning", WO 2010/049331, Oct 2008.
[17] Christopher Watkins and Peter Dayan, "Q Learning", Machine Learning 8, 279-292, 1992.
[18] Stamatios Kararalopoulos, "Understanding Neural Networks and Fuzzy Logic", IEEE Press, 1996.
[19] Wolfgang Maas and Christopher Bishop, "Pulsed Neural Networks", MIT Press, 2001.
[20] R. Rom, "Optimizing and Monitoring Adaptive Cardiac Resynchronization Therapy Devices", PCT WO 2006/061822, June 2006.
[21] R. Rom, "Intelligent Controll System for Adaptive Cardiac Resynachronization Therapy Device", US Patent application 2010/145402, July 17 2006.
[22] Sorin Group Press Release, "CLEAR Study Demonstrates Automatic Optimization of CRT with SONR Improves Heart Failure Patients Response Rates ",June 17th, 2010 , http://www.sorin-crm.com/uploads/Media/clear_study_pressrelease.pdf.
[23] R. Rom, "Adaptive Resynchronization Therapy and Vagal Stimulation System ", US Patent application 2008/0147130, Aug 2007.
[24] R. Rom, "Optimal Deep Brain Stmilation with Q Learning", WO 2010/049331, Oct 2008.